Romantic and Revolutionary theatre, 1789–1860

Taking as notional parameters the upheaval of the French Revolution and the events leading up to the unification of Italy, this volume charts a period of political and social turbulence in Europe and its reflection in theatrical life. Apart from considering external factors such as censorship and legal sanctions on theatrical activity, this collection of documents examines the effects of prevailing operational conditions on the internal organization of companies, their repertoire, acting, stage presentation, playhouse architecture and the relationship with audiences. Also covered are technical advances in stage machinery, scenography and lighting, the changing position of the playwright and the continuing importance of various street entertainments, particularly in Italy, where dramatic theatre remained the poor relation of operatic theatre and itinerant acting troupes still constituted the norm. The 460 documents, many of them illustrated, have been drawn from sources in Britain, France and Italy and have been annotated, and translated where appropriate.

The book will be of value to researchers and students of drama or theatre studies and will appeal to all those interested in the history of European theatre.

Theatre in Europe: a documentary history

General editors

Glynne Wickham
John Northam
W. D. Howarth

This series presents a comprehensive collection of primary source materials for teachers and students and serves as a major reference work for studies in theatrical and dramatic literature. The volumes focus individually on specific periods and geographical areas, encompassing English and European theatrical history. Each volume presents primary source documents in English, or in English translation, relating to actors and acting, dramatic theory and criticism, theatre architecture, stage censorship, settings, costumes and audiences. These sources include such documents as statutes, proclamations, inscriptions, contracts and playbills. Additional documentation from contemporary sources is provided through correspondence, reports and eye-witness accounts. The volumes also provide not only the exact source and location of the original documents, but also complementary lists of similar documents. Each volume contains an introduction, narrative linking passages, notes on the documents, a substantial bibliography and an index offering detailed access to the primary material.

Published

Restoration and Georgian England, 1669–1788, compiled and introduced by David Thomas and Arnold Hare, edited by David Thomas

National Theatre in Northern and Eastern Europe, 1746–1900, edited by Laurence Senelick

German and Dutch Theatre, 1600–1848, compiled by George W. Brandt and Wiebe Hogendoorn, edited by George W. Brandt

Naturalism and *Symbolism in European Theatre, 1850–1918*, edited by Claude Schumacher

French Theatre in the Neo-classical Era, 1550–1789, edited by William D. Howarth

English Professional Theatre, 1530–1660, edited by Glynne Wickham, Herbert Berry and William Ingram

The Medieval European Stage, 500–1500, edited by William Tydeman

Romantic and Revolutionary theatre, 1789–1860

Edited by

DONALD ROY

Compiled and introduced by

VICTOR EMELJANOW
Professor of Drama, University of Newcastle, New South Wales

DONALD ROY
Emeritus Professor of Drama, University of Hull

KENNETH RICHARDS
Emeritus Professor of Drama, University of Manchester

LAURA RICHARDS
Formerly Senior Lecturer in Italian, University of Salford

 CAMBRIDGE
UNIVERSITY PRESS

PUBLISHED BY THE PRESS SYNDICATE OF THE UNIVERSITY OF CAMBRIDGE
The Pitt Building, Trumpington Street, Cambridge CB2 IRP, United Kingdom

CAMBRIDGE UNIVERSITY PRESS
The Edinburgh Building, Cambridge, CB2 2RU, UK
40 West 20th Street, New York, NY 10011–4211, USA
477 Williamstown Road, Port Melbourne, VIC 3207, Australia
Ruiz de Alarcón 13, 28014 Madrid, Spain
Dock House, The Waterfront, Cape Town 8001, South Africa

http://www.cambridge.org

First published 2003

Printed in the United Kingdom at the University Press, Cambridge

Typeface Photina 10/12.5 pt   *System* LaTeX 2_ε [TB]

A catalogue record for this book is available from the British Library

ISBN 0 521 25080 3 hardback

Contents

List of documents

Asterisks before titles indicate illustrated documents

IV   Actors and Acting

Editor's preface

At the risk of appearing editorially 'Eurosceptic', it has been decided to group all documents in this volume discretely by country as well as by category. Whilst instructive parallels may certainly be drawn between the respective theatrical experiences of Britain, France and Italy during the period, so many discrepancies need to be taken into account, political and social no less than cultural in nature, that this arrangement seemed the most logical; one that may also afford inquisitive readers a pleasurable opportunity to trace common themes and national variations for themselves.

For similar reasons, the chronological parameters of the volume are intentionally somewhat elastic. Theatre practice has always evolved at different tempos in different societies and, within such domestic rhythms, does not necessarily subscribe to any broader sociopolitical calendar. Besides, organically theatrical factors may come into play, which are no respecters of timescales in the outside world. The year 1789 represents a meaningful landmark for France, as does 1860 for Italy, but neither date has a comparable resonance in the context of events on this English side of the Channel. Hence, although the bulk of the documents collected here fall within these titular limits, others have been included that illuminate the period from without.

The major difficulty shared by all the contributors to the volume has been to determine what to omit. Such was the expansion in publishing, notably in topical and journalistic publishing, over these years that there is a profuse abundance of documentation to select from, and many choice items have had to be excluded through sheer lack of space, often all the more painfully so for having already been lovingly translated. What remains will still, it is hoped, constitute an adequately rich and varied harvest.

General editors' preface

In appointing appropriately qualified editors for all the volumes in this documentary history it has been our aim to provide a comprehensive collection of primary source materials for teachers and students on which their own critical appraisal of theatrical history and dramatic literature may safely be grounded.

Each volume presents primary source documents in English, or in English translation, relating to actors and acting, dramatic theory and criticism, theatre architecture, stage censorship, settings, costumes and audiences. Editors have, in general, confined their selection to documentary material in the strict sense (statutes, proclamations, inscriptions, contracts, working drawings, playbills, prints, account books, etc.), but exceptions have been made in instances where prologues, epilogues, excerpts from play-texts and private correspondence provide additional contemporary documentation based on an author's authority or that of eye-witnesses to particular performances and significant theatrical events.

Unfamiliar documents have been preferred to familiar ones, short ones to long ones; and among long ones recourse has been taken to excerpting for inclusion all passages which either oblige quotation by right of their own intrinsic importance or lead directly to a clearer understanding of other documents. In every instance, however, we have aimed to provide readers not only with the exact source and location of the original document, but with complementary lists of similar documents and of secondary sources offering previously printed transcripts.

Each volume is equipped with an introductory essay, and in some cases introductory sections to each chapter, designed to provide readers with the appropriate social background – religious, political, economic and aesthetic – as context for the documents selected; it also contains briefer linking commentaries on particular groups of documents and concludes with an extensive bibliography.

Within this general presentational framework, individual volumes will vary considerably in their format – greater emphasis having to be placed, for example, on documents of control in one volume than in another, or with dramatic theory and criticism figuring less prominently in some volumes than in others – if each volume is to be an accurate reflection of the widely divergent interests and concerns of different European countries at different stages of their historical development, and the equally sharp differences in the nature and quality of the surviving documents volume by volume.

Glynne Wickham (Chairman)
Bristol University, 1997

Acknowledgements

A corporate debt of gratitude is owed to the international brigade of librarians, curators and archivists who have lent assistance in the preparation of this volume; in Britain, at the British Library, the Theatre Museum, the Public Record Office, the John Rylands University Library, Manchester, and the Brynmor Jones Library, University of Hull; in the United States, at the Henry Huntington Library; in France, at the Bibliothèque Nationale, the Bibliothèque de l'Arsenal, the Bibliothèque de la Comédie-Française, and the Archives Nationales; and in Italy, at the Biblioteca Burcardo and the Biblioteca Nazionale, Rome, the Biblioteca Nazionale, Florence, the Museo-Biblioteca dell'Attore, Genoa, and the Biblioteca Brera, Milan. Equally helpful has been the contribution made by a small group of research assistants: Jennifer Aylmer, OBE, Dr Karina Smith, Dr Margaret Leask and Sonya Langelaar.

The authors must also record their appreciation for the co-operation received from the following institutions in granting permission to reproduce pictorial documents, as indicated: the Huntington Library, San Marino, California (**66, 69, 76(a), 77(a), 78(a), 79, 139(b), 147, 155, 158, 159, 160, 169(b), 171**); the British Museum (**177**), the Victoria and Albert Museum (**111**) and the Theatre Museum, London (**72**); the Bibliothèque Nationale (**303, 366, 368(b)**) and the Maison de Victor Hugo Paris (**381(b)**); the Harvard Theatre Collection (**295**); the Biblioteca Burcardo, Rome (**399, 404, 409, 414, 420, 423, 427, 428, 429, 431, 432, 443, 451**: photographs by Oscar Savio).

During the lengthy period of the volume's gestation we have been perennially sustained by the patience and encouragement of the general editors of the Theatre in Europe series, particularly Professor W. D. Howarth, and by Sarah Stanton and Dr Victoria Cooper of Cambridge University Press.

Finally, we wish to thank the British Academy and the School of Arts Research Committee, University of Hull, for financial support towards the realization of this project.

Except where stated otherwise, all translations of documents written in French or Italian have been made by the authors of those sections. Punctuation has occasionally been modified in the interests of clarity.

Part One: Britain

Edited by VICTOR EMELJANOW

Introduction

The terms 'Romantic' and 'Revolutionary' suggest a clear-cut stylistic evolution informing British acting techniques, stage presentation and audience tastes in the period 1790 to 1850. In fact such a perspective is difficult to sustain in a period of social and aesthetic turbulence characterized by the clash between the old and the new and by determined efforts to retain the verities of the past on the part of performers and those managers who believed that the award of letters patent entitled them to a perpetual theatrical monopoly. On the other hand, there were equally determined attempts on the part of new audiences and new theatrical speculators to take control of an emerging entertainment industry.

A key factor that contributed to this aesthetic turbulence was the change in audience composition. Indeed, the term 'audience' itself becomes problematic in this period. Those who now gathered in the 'auditorium' were no longer principally occupied with 'listening' but with watching – each other, as well as the stage presentation. The size of the large patent theatres in London reflected an awareness on the part of managers that the population of the metropolis had hugely increased but no awareness at all that the new mix of spectators would bring with it the demise of the old, easy-going familiarity of eighteenth-century theatre-going, which had characterized relationships not only between the spectators themselves but also between spectators and performers. It became obvious that a limited number of officially sanctioned theatres in the rapidly expanding urban areas was insufficient, and so the period saw the struggle between those managers with vested interests and a new breed of theatrical entrepreneurs determined to take the financial risk involved in building new theatres and fully expecting to make money from a newly emerging urban proletariat. These struggles took place in cities like Edinburgh, Glasgow, Leeds, Sheffield, Manchester, Birmingham and Liverpool, as well as in London. By 1850 the speculators had won their various battles, though at the expense of the provincial theatrical circuits, which were unable to withstand the centralization of theatrical power in the larger cities and their magnetic influence on the increasing numbers of performers who were jostling for public recognition. Moreover, by 1850, with the attendance of a highly self-conscious middle class determined to see and hear its values embodied and expressed on stage, there is evidence to suggest the re-emergence of a theatre 'audience'.

The period 1790 to 1850 saw the development of the most influential dramatic genre to emerge in the last 200 years. To be sure, English melodrama had its roots in the Gothic Romanticism of the eighteenth century, itself highly influenced by German Romantic writers. Equally important, however, and more enduring, was the influence of French writers such as Pixérécourt and Scribe, who invested melodrama with the democratic values of 'entertaining and instructing' the post-Revolution French 'citizenry'. These influences coexisted, thus enabling English melodrama to become a site of conflict between aristocratic and bourgeois values, manifested in the economic struggles between landed gentry or urban capitalists and the cottagers or urban wage-earners that form the basis of much melo-dramatic playwriting. Because melodrama embodied the conflicts between rich and poor, country dweller and city dweller, it was eminently translatable. When it became possible by the improvements in transport for performers to travel easily, not only between towns but also between countries, melodrama became the *lingua franca* of the English-speaking dramatic world.

The effects melodrama, the size of the theatres and the change in audience composition ex-erted upon stage presentation and the nature of acting cannot be overestimated. Spectators wanted both fantasy and recognizable reality to be 'realized' on stage with the utmost au-thenticity, which further blurs the distinction between 'romanticism' and 'realism'. Theatre managers struggled to present in their performances the technical innovations as well as the fruits of geographical and archaeological discovery with which spectators were becoming familiar outside the theatre. Surrounded by rapid change, spectators became increasingly intolerant of a theatre practice that relied on inherited conventions or the recycling of exist-ing resources. This became a further site of conflict, as the new theatre speculators found themselves torn between, for example, cost-cutting on scenery and costuming, and the need to show that they were responsive to their patrons' demands for fresh experiences by investing in new, spectacular displays. Performers were caught in the middle of this con-flict. Overly reliant upon an actor–audience relationship of familiarity, and upon 'lines of business' that imposed constraints on performers' creative potentials, they struggled in the early part of the nineteenth century to reconcile the demands of spectators both for novel forms of expressiveness and immediately recognizable behaviour. In order to meet these demands performers clustered around the figures of Edmund Kean and William Charles Macready, and emulated them. This ensured that the traditions of romanticism and realism in performance would continue to exist side by side throughout the period.

I   *Theatre, the law and management practices*

THEATRES AND THE LAW

The period 1789–1843 was characterized by debates, often heated, over the rights enjoyed by patent theatres – Drury Lane and Covent Garden (and to a lesser extent, the Haymarket in London and the Theatres Royal in the provinces) – to monopolize the performances of legitimate plays and the limit placed on the number of theatres within the City of Westminster. Debates also took place over the question whether the state had the power to control the theatrical repertoire through the office of the Examiner of Plays, and over the prerogative of dramatists to exercise control over their own works through adequate copyright protection.[1]

The Enabling Act of 1788 had empowered magistrates to grant licences for the performance of certain kinds of entertainments within a twenty-mile radius of London and Westminster, and for the 'legitimate' drama in theatres situated outside that area, for a period not exceeding sixty days.[2] In addition, specific legislation could give letters patent to provincial cities,[3] while the Lord Chamberlain maintained absolute control over the City of Westminster. Not only was this administration cumbersome but it also privileged the holders of letters patent. Already proprietors of minor theatres had felt the pressure of the law in the eighteenth century: the Royalty Theatre had been forced to close, and an act to allow the Sadler's Wells Theatre to extend the terms of its licence was defeated. Both involved advocacy on behalf of patent rights by R. B. Sheridan, who was both a part-owner of Drury Lane and a Member of Parliament.[4]

As the populations of the major centres, especially London, began to increase, the monopoly of legitimate drama exercised by the patent theatres and their resolute opposition to enlarging the number of licensed theatres permitted to perform this drama became irksome to entrepreneurs less interested in the preservation of a 'national drama' than in making money. Such prerogatives also appeared to be out of touch with an audience increasingly assertive in its demands for the democratization of entertainment. The struggle to free the stage in London intensified in the period after 1808, which saw the destruction by fire of both the patent theatres in the first decade of the nineteenth century.

The period to 1830 was marked by prosecutions and memorials to the Lord Chamberlain launched by the patent theatres, with particular assaults on the Olympic and Sans Pareil Theatres [5]. At the same time, the period saw an erosion of patent authority, both through the success of the minors in catering for a neighbourhood clientèle by using the 'illegitimate' forms of entertainment and through the absorption of those same forms into the repertoire of the patent theatres themselves, thereby making their claims to dramatic exclusiveness irrelevant. The minutes of evidence of the Select Committee on Dramatic Literature and its final report [**9, 10**] demonstrated in 1832 that it was no longer in the best interests of the drama to make it the sole responsibility of a few theatre managers, who had in any case saddled themselves with huge financial liabilities.

The passing of the Theatre Regulation Act in 1843 [**17**], though it centralized the power of theatre licensing by placing it entirely within the jurisdiction of the Lord Chamberlain, did remove the legislative confusions that had been inherited from the eighteenth century and dissolved the separation between 'major' and 'minor', 'legitimate' and 'illegitimate'.

In 1832 the Select Committee had also discussed censorship and the position of the playwright within an emerging theatre industry. In the first half of the century the real irritation caused by the Lord Chamberlain's Examiner of Plays was not so much his interference in excising irreligious, immoral or unpatriotic references, but rather his insistence on examining the scripts well in advance and in charging what were regarded as extortionate fees [**6, 14**]. This was particularly trying when managers were jostling for patrons, and were often called upon to make rapid changes in programme in cases where entertainments had met with a hostile reception. As far as the playwrights were concerned, the decline in the fortunes of the patent theatres, particularly in the 1820s, the huge salaries paid to stars by managers in their desperate efforts to stave off bankruptcy by offering glittering attractions, and the growth in the number of theatres after 1812, all contributed to insecurity and exploitation.[5] Moreover, the absence of any protection from dramatic piracy or of any control over their own property made the profession of the playwright extremely difficult to justify [**12**].[6]

---

[1] For a brief summary of the situation bridging the eighteenth and nineteenth centuries, see *The Revels history of drama in English*, vol. VI (London: Methuen, 1975), pp. 40–4.

[2] See David Thomas and Arnold Hare, *Restoration and Georgian England, 1660–1788* (Cambridge: Cambridge University Press, 1989), no. 193.

[3] Newcastle had been granted one in 1787 and others would soon follow: Bath, 1797; Chester, 1798; Bristol, 1799; Kingston upon Hull and York, 1803; Liverpool, Birmingham and Margate, 1807; Edinburgh, 1809. See Watson Nicholson, *The struggle for a free stage in London* (London: Constable, 1906; reprinted New York: Blom, 1966), p. 139.

[4] See Thomas and Hare, *Restoration and Georgian England*, no. 191.

[5] See James Boaden, *Memoirs of the life of John Philip Kemble, Esq.* (London: Longman, 1825), vol. II, p. 74 and J. R. Stephens, *The censorship of English drama, 1824–1901* (Cambridge: Cambridge University Press, 1980) pp. 25–50.

[6] See Stephens, *Censorship*, pp. 84–96.

THE MONOPOLY QUESTION

After the destruction of Covent Garden in 1808 the argument for another theatre, which had been put forward at the time of the Royalty Theatre submission in 1788, surfaced again. It was raised in the Privy Council on 16 March 1810. The petition, however, was denied on 14 April.[1]

---

[1] See Nicholson, *Struggle for a free stage*, pp. 192–224 for a full account of these proceedings and Sheridan's implacable opposition.

I   The arguments for a third theatre, 1810

W. C. Oulton, *A history of the theatres of London* (London: Martin & Bain, 1818), vol. 1 (Drury Lane, 16 March 1810), p. 183

Sanguine expectations were still entertained of having a third winter theatre, calculated for *hearing* and *seeing*; the prices of admission to be the same as those of the summer theatre on the Haymarket. The application, however, before the *second* theatre was rebuilt, was certainly premature and injudicious [. . .]

[. . .] Mr Warren, as leading counsel for the petitioners, addressed their lordships (Master of the Rolls, the Attorney General and members of the Privy Council). He contended that the patents, granted to the present theatres, did not go to the exclusion of another; and allowing, for a moment, that they did, it was, in his opinion, doubtful whether the prerogative of the crown could be borne out in granting a monopoly. Monopolies in trade had been declared unlawful; and in amusements, according to the letters of the law, they were also void, the moment the places became the source of trade and profit. The petitions which had been laid before their lordships, from the patentees of the established theatres, denied the necessity of a third theatre, and stated that they had not made more than 6 per cent of their principal. That might be; but there was a question, whether misman-agement had not caused it? This was yet to be proved. It was also urged that his clients had taken advantage of the two unfortunate fires which had taken place; this he denied, and their lordships might be sensible of it, when they reflected on the great increase of the population in London. When those patents were granted, there were not half the inhabitants that are at present to fill them. At certain periods of the year, there was a great increase of strangers in the city, which Covent-garden theatre, as it now is, and Drury-lane theatre, rebuilt, in its great-est magnitude and pomp, could *not* contain. Their argument was, that they have *enlarged their theatres as the population had increased*. Be it so. But their lordships would recollect, while they widened the area of their theatres, they *prevented the public from being entertained*; they put them at such a distance from the stage, that the countenance of the performer could not be discerned, without he distorted the muscles of his face to that degree, that, to those nearer the stage, it appeared ludicrous; the same with the voice; it was so strained, that nature was forgotten. he wished their lordships not to consider the petition of his clients, as theirs alone, but *that of the public*. There were *one million* of persons, in and about this metropolis, who visited theatres; and could it be supposed, that two were sufficient to contain them? It was contended, in the petitions, that even those were not always filled: this was not the fact, for they were filled to more than an overflow, when the entertain-ments were worthy of the attendance of the public. The application of his clients was for a charter, which, in his opinion, would not give them an advantage over the other theatres, by their being an incorporated body. It was not a corporation for speculation; £200,000 had been subscribed, which would be laid out in the build-ing and decorations; this would always be a sufficient security. It was stated, that it would put the subscribers in a better situation than those of the existing theatres, as it relieved them from personal responsibility. This argument, in his opinion, was nugatory; for, by the charter, the incorporated body would be responsible, instead of a single personal security.

The failure to have a third theatre approved in London brought the monopoly situation into sharp focus. The article that follows concentrates on the evasions employed by minor theatres to circumvent the law, the exposure of audiences to inferior entertainments as a consequence, and the dangers that audiences incurred as a result of being forced to travel long distances.

2   An early attack against the patent theatres' monopoly, 1813

J. Lawrence (ed.), *Pamphleteer*, 2 (1813), pp. 382–5

In 1787, John Palmer was threatened by Messrs. Harris, Linley, and Colman, with a prosecution, should he act regular dramas on his newly erected Royalty theatre; and even when it was open for musical and pantomimical performances, an information was laid against Delpini for only crying out 'Roast Beef', while acting the part of clown [. . .]

It is an undecided point, whether theatres improve the morality of a nation; the legislator, however, may be content if they contribute not to deprave it: but it is decided, that good plays might improve the national taste. Why, therefore, when a number of minor theatres are opened, are they prevented from acting the legitimate productions of the best dramatists? Is the legislature afraid of improving the taste of the people? The Surry [*sic*] theatre has, in the opinion of many judges, just the dimensions that a theatre ought to have, and even that of Tottenham Court Road, and the Sans-souci must be magnificent edifices compared to those, on which Shakespeare's works were first performed. But in order to favor [*sic*] the monopolists, the minor theatres are confined to melo-dramas. All unjust regulations will be evaded. Even the lower classes of people have too much taste to relish the farrago of nonsense, to which the liberality of Mr Harris and colleagues would confine them. Some plays of a higher order have been brought forward at the minor theatres; but at the end of a few sentences the harpsichord is sounded, to the surprise of the stranger, who perhaps conceives that the instrument has been touched by accident; and this manoeuvre is practised, that the piece may come under the denomination of a melo-drama [. . .]

These little theatres are more adapted to the representation of many regular dramas, particularly of the *pieces bourgeoises*, than the cathedral theatre of Covent Garden; and as the manager there has shown such a predilection for the Brute Creation, the public would not lose, were he to exchange patents with Astley, whose rights, by the bye, he seems to have infringed. Let the works of Rowe and Otway, Farquhar and Goldsmith, be performed at the Royal Circus, and horses and elephants keep possession of Covent Garden:[1] the size of both theatres recommends the exchange [. . .]

The moralists, who judge that more theatres for the regular drama would be productive of vice, consent that the minor theatres should exhibit burlettas, rope-dancers, and dancing dogs; as if the young apprentice would be less affected by the allurements of a courtezan, during the feats of a tumbler, than during the performance of George Barnwell.

Beside, though the lobby of each of the great theatres is a focus of vice; youth and inexperience, who cannot have thrown aside a sense of decency, are less exposed to temptation there, than in their walk home to a distant quarter of the metropolis. Could every inhabitant here, as at Paris, find a theatre in his own district, the danger of seduction would be of shorter duration.

---

[1] This refers to the revival of Colman's *Blue Beard* at Covent Garden, chiefly noted for the employment of an equestrian troop of horses.

3 The effects of the patent monopoly on playwriting, 1812

'Theatrical correspondence', *Examiner* (December 1812), p. 602

If the stage were free, a Dramatist might follow the bent of his genius. He would introduce the characters that his judgment or fancy should prompt; and it would be the interest of the manager to procure performers qualified to do them justice. Whereas now the dramatist is reduced not only to consider the pretensions, the vanity, the abilities of the Actors and Actresses, but their age and corpulency. He must take their measure as well as the stage tailor.

If the Stage were free, every Manager would endeavour to induce an Author of talent to give him the preference; whereas now an Author must go cap in hand to solicit the favour of a Manager; and should he succeed in this, some Actor or Actress may think that the part destined for them would not exhibit them to advantage, and may refuse to co-operate. Few Authors of rank, of liberal sentiment or independent fortune, would enter a green-room cabal. Hence the degeneracy of our Drama. Scenes of high life have been pourtrayed [*sic*] by individuals, who have had little intercourse with good company, and genteel comedy has given place to buffoonery and brogue.

THE LEGAL POSITION OF A MINOR THEATRE

The Sans Pareil was built by John Scott and opened in 1806. In 1819 it would be renamed the Adelphi [**76a**].

4   Licence issued to the Sans Pareil, 1817

PRO LC7/10, fo. 60

I do hereby give Leave and Licence unto John Scott esquire to have performed for his benefit, Burlettas, Music and Dancing with Spectacles and Pantomime at his Theatre situated between Heathcock Court and Bullen Court in the Strand within the Liberties of Westminster from Michaelmas next to Easter 1818[.] Given under my Hand and Seal this 10th day of July 1817[.] In the 57th year of His Majesty's Reign.

(signed) Ingram Hereford
Chamberlain

5   Memorial to the Lord Chamberlain by the patent theatres, 1818

PRO LC7/4, part 1[1]

> The joint Memorial of the Proprietors of the two Theatres of Drury Lane and Covent Garden to His Majesty's Lord Chamberlain the Most Noble the Marquis of Hereford against the infringement and abuse of the Licenses [sic] of the Proprietors of the Olympic and Sans Pareil Theatres

My Lord,

Engaged as your memorialists are in the arduous duties of managing and supporting the interests of their large and immensely expensive Establishments, Your Lordship may be assured that they would not willingly, or without cause, take up your Lordship's time, by again urging their well founded complaints, against the Proprietors of the Olympic and Sans Pareil Theatres, acting under the Lord Chamberlain's License [sic] [. . .]

With [. . .] the Evidence they can produce that the regular Drama is now nightly performing at the above mentioned Theatres, your Lordship must excuse the alarm of the Proprietors of the two Patent Theatres, who, at once, see their long dreaded fears realized and who find their long established Patent rights destroyed, upon the faith of which, a million of money has been of late years embarked in their two Theatres [. . .]

The memorialists then complain about Lord Dartmouth,[2] the Lord Chamberlain's predecessor and his indiscriminate licensing.

[. . .] Your Lordship may, perhaps, feel averse to alter any act of your immediate Predecessor, but even Lord Dartmouth himself would have been the first to put a stop to such daring infringement of his Licenses [sic]. His Lordship never contemplated, that when he granted Mr Astley a License [sic] for the Olympic to keep his Horses from the time of the Closing to the Opening of his Amphitheatre that he was granting a License [*sic*] to play such a Trajedy [*sic*] as Fazio,[3] nor did he think, when he granted a License [*sic*] to Mr Scott, for his daughter Miss Scott, to perform in Burlettas, that he was granting him a power of engaging a regular Company of Comedians to perform whatever pieces they may chuse [*sic*]; for thus (as we find) the term, *Burletta*, is now construed at these Theatres. But it can easily be proved, that Burletta is distinguished from Tragedy, Comedy, Opera, Farce, etc. by its being *a piece in verse, accompanied by Music*; for example, the pieces of the Dragon of Wantley, Midas, The Golden Pippin, Poor Vulcan [. . .] are *Burlettas* and totally different from the Pieces acted at these Theatres, which are neither more or less than pieces of the Regular Drama [. . .] It can be proved by Evidence [. . .] that a sum upon average exceeding £130, is nightly taken at their doors, the whole, or the greatest part of which is taken from the doors of the two Patent Theatres [. . .] It may be thought a hard case that these Theatres should be suppressed, after their Proprietors have laid out money in enlarging them. *The Great increase in their size, since the Olympic and Sans Pareil Theatres were first Licensed, is one of the chief points complained of, and your Memorialists suffer in the exact ratio to that increase* [. . .]

[1] Accompanying this document are further statements in evidence as well as Elliston's correspondence beginning 12 April 1818. See also LC1/ letterbook B, fo. 93.

[2] Lord Dartmouth had been Lord Chamberlain from 1804 to 1810. See Nicholson, *Struggle for a free stage*, pp. 164–74.

[3] Though Henry Milman's tragedy had been performed at Covent Garden (5 February 1818), it had already appeared under the title *The Italian Wife* at the Surrey in 1816.

THE ROLE OF THE EXAMINER

George Colman succeeded John Larpent as Examiner in 1824. It was his venality and self-righteous puritanism that offended those opposed to censorship.[1]

[1] See Stephens, *Censorship*, pp. 22–5.

6   George Colman exercises his authority as Examiner

'The Drama', *British and Foreign Review*, 2 (1836), p. 381

(a) A circular to theatre managers on licensing irregularities, 1826

14th November 1826. Brompton Square

SIR, – I am directed by the Lord Chamberlain to remark to you, and other managers of all the theatres under his control, within the city and liberties of Westminster, that upon various occasions besides upon benefit nights, at most of the theatres above mentioned, certain songs, duets, and other productions, have been of late interpolated, and made part of the evening's entertainments, without the licences for such performances which is there required.

I am also directed to refer you to the Act of Parliament which declares, that such *unlicensed* performances render you liable to heavy fines, and to the forfeiture of the grant by which you open your theatre.

I am further instructed to apprize [*sic*] you, that, if the present intimation be disregarded in the aforesaid theatres, it will occasion a recourse to measures which the Lord Chamberlain has hitherto forborne to adopt.

Finally, I am desired to state, that all, or any part of, vocal music, recitations, and dialogues, which may have been sung, repeated, printed, or have obtained publicity, in other places,* are still new to the aforesaid theatres, on their first introduction there; and, when so introduced, must be previously licensed, like other such novelties, by the Lord Chamberlain.

> I have the honour to be,
> Sir,
> Your obedient servant,
> G. Colman.

* By 'other places' are meant places *out of* the Lord Chamberlain's jurisdiction;– and most licences granted by him, for performances in other places *within it* (as in Bath, York, etc.), are not sufficient for those theatres in Westminster, and its liberties, which are not empowered to act the *whole range of the Drama*. Theatres limited in the nature of their entertainments (as the English Opera House, and the Adelphi and Olympic Theatres) must of course abide by the restrictive specifications contained in their annual licence. G. C.

(b) The censor at work

[...] Please to omit the following underlined words in representing the Opera called, 'Not for me', etc.[1]

> —Damme if I do.'
> 'As you please; only don't swear; all holy and profane words are prohibited, even on the stage, now-a-days.'
> 'Vivid. The Heavens forbid!'
> 'Vivid.—damn it, if I ain't stammering.'

Mem. Miss Virulent exclaims occasionally, 'Merciful Powers!' which expression, if it do not mean something palpably different from the Powers of God and Heaven, ought to be omitted.

> G. Colman
> 20th June, 1828.

[1] Note to the manager of the Lyceum after examining the script of *Not for Me; or, the New Apple of Discord*, a ballad opera adapted from the French. The play opened on 23 August 1828.

The agreement between the three patent theatres and the Lord Chamberlain's office shows that there could be bad feeling and a sense of unjust competition even between those theatres that enjoyed a London monopoly. The Haymarket was particularly affected when extensions to the length of the winter theatre seasons encroached on its summer season, thereby preventing actors from working there.

7   An agreement on the dates of opening by the three major London theatres, 1826

Covent Garden Theatre Letterbook of H. Robertson 1823–49, BM Add. MSS 29643

Regulations relating to the Theatres Royal Drury Lane and Covent Garden and the Little Theatre in the Haymarket.

Lord Chamberlain's Office
June 19 1826

The little Theatre to open on the 15th of June and to close the 15th October 1827 and to have three months free of competition, the Winter Theatres being closed from the 1st of July to the 1st of October of the same year.

The Winter Theatres shall not restrain their Actors from Acting at the Haymarket Theatre between the 1st of July and the 1st of October 1827.

Montrose

We the undersigned do hereby agree to the above arrangement without prejudice to the Patent rights of the Theatres Royal Drury Lane and Covent Garden.

Stephen Price, Lessee of the T. R. Drury Lane
C. Kemble for self and the other Proprietors of
T. R. Covent Garden.

8   The monopoly retards cultural development in the greatly enlarged London, 1832

Covent Garden Theatre Letterbook of H. Robertson 1823–49, BM Add. MSS 29643

In the largest and most cultivated metropolis of Europe, where the population is calculated at a million and a quarter,– where, at least, there are an hundred thousand well educated adults whose pursuits are entirely those of pleasure, or literature and the arts,– where the elegant, the learned and the talented of the whole empire congregate,– where the mass of people are eagerly seeking knowledge, and daily progressing in intelligence,– where there are societies, institutions, and means of all kinds for the dissemination of knowledge, and the enlargement and elevation of the intellect, there are Two theatres, (which having no means,) are empowered to perform the regular and reasonable Drama – and 17 or 18 others,[1] (which are suitably constructed for it), where nothing but Tom foolery–Farce–Sing song–Dancing–and Dumb show, can be exhibited. This admirable contrivance for the degradation of society is further assisted by the two theatres, where the regular Drama may, but cannot be properly performed, being situated close together, at the farthest possible distance from the circle of respectable suburbs where the most intelligent and best educated portions of society reside,– the Regent's Park and the Clapham Road – Kensington and Stratford – are a tolerable two hours journey from either of these emporiums of the regular Sock and Buskin, whilst at the Minor Theatre, so conveniently constructed, and well situated for the performance of regular plays, nothing but pieces tending to degrade still more the minds of the people, may be performed. The anomaly is perfectly ridiculous [. . .]

[1] There were in fact twenty theatres operating throughout the greater London area in 1832, including the patent theatres. See H. Barton Baker, *History of the London stage, 1576–1903* (London: Allen, 1889), vol. I, pp. x–xiv.

THE SELECT COMMITTEE AND ITS REPORT

The Select Committee of the House of Commons was convened as a direct result of a petition to Parliament initiated by Bulwer-Lytton in May 1832. It sought to investigate not only the viability of the theatrical monopoly but also matters relating to authorship rights.[1]

[1] The vigorous debate can also be found in [Leigh Hunt], 'The play-goer', 'The question between the great and the minor theatres', *Tatler* (22 Dec. 1831), p. 595, and 'The minor theatres', *Examiner* (December 1822), pp. 9–10.

9   The Select Committee examines some of the monopoly issues, 1832

British parliamentary papers, stage and theatre 1, introduced by M. L. Norstedt (Dublin: Irish University Press, 1968), pp. 24, 155, 132

(a) J. Payne Collier describes the benefits of theatrical free trade

279. [. . .] The effect upon the public would be, that they would visit those theatres where they would hear the best plays acted in the best way, according to my opinion, in smaller theatres than those that are now erected. I am of the opinion also that the licensing of smaller theatres would not at all deteriorate the school of acting; for I do not think that we have at present any means of fairly judging of the manner in which the school of acting is affected by the minor theatres [. . .] There are no good actors at the minor theatres at present, inasmuch as they are always acting under the apprehension of a prosecution; and they have never acted with that degree of encouragement which they probably would receive from the public if they were allowed to act plays without control, except such control as they might be under from the licencer [*sic*] [. . .] I think the consequence of allowing plays to be acted at the minor theatres would, in the first instance, be the ruin of a number of speculators; but that would be the case in any branch of trade that was opened immediately [. . .] but that evil would ere long correct itself [. . .] It would afford great encouragement to authors to write plays, if the state of the law regarding authorship were also altered.

(b) Morris, lessee of the Haymarket, assesses the effects of the taste for German and French operas

2760. What do you conceive the damage to be to your theatre in consequence of these performances? [. . .] – The receipts at the Haymarket are experiencing very great depression at present from various causes; first of all, I think from the German and French operas. Under the old understanding between the patent theatres, Covent Garden and Drury Lane, and the Haymarket and the Italian Opera, it was settled by His Majesty and the Lord Chamberlain, that nothing more than an Italian opera on Tuesday and an Italian opera on Saturday should be permitted, with the exception of about four benefits, which generally came on Thursdays, given to their two leading singers and dancers; but now it is open every night. Monday night there is Robert le Diable; Tuesday night, the Italian opera; Wednesday night, the German opera, and so on every night in the week [. . .]

2764. Which would you prefer being put down, the minor theatres or the fine representations?– They are equally prejudicial; the German plays and the French plays certainly have been frequented by persons in a higher class of society; that affects the boxes, but I do not think it affects the pit and gallery so much as the representations at the minor theatres; the pit and gallery are most excessively affected by the minor theatres playing the regular drama.

(c) Macready comments on the effects of deregulation on the acting profession

2340. [. . .] I feel it is much easier to act in a small theatre than in a large one, and I should say that for merely domestic scenes and for simple dialogue, where there is nothing of pomp or circumstance attending it, I should prefer a small theatre; but for Shakspeare's plays, I should think very few of them can be found which can have due effect given to them in a small theatre.

2341. Should you consider that the Haymarket would be large enough to allow a fair acting of Shakspeare's plays?– I speak from having seen Kean act in the Haymarket. In scenes where only two persons have been upon the stage, I have lost myself to the size of the theatre, but when a great number have occupied the stage, I have felt the want of space, and too great proximity of the performers to me.

2342. Supposing the legitimate drama were to be allowed to the small theatres, would it not appear that, if the public generally shared in your opinion, the large theatres would not be much injured, because, as they would perform Shakspeare's plays better than the small theatres could do, they would not be injured by that competition?– [. . .] they would offer so many markets for talent, that they would take those as nightly auxiliaries that ought to be stationary actors in large theatres, in order to make an efficient regular company, which never could be the case if we had opportunities of going for large sums of money to the small theatres; it would be better for us, but I think it would be for the loss of the public, inasmuch as there would be a great many plays tolerably done, but it would be almost impossible to congregate an efficient company in any one theatre.

2350. Do you think that if the large theatres were able by large capital to get better companies, that the public would so encourage those theatres that the others would not be able to flourish?– I think that small theatres would proceed upon the plan of engaging the best actors as auxiliaries; they would be able to pay them for a fortnight or a month's engagement much more than a large theatre could pay them for the season, which is the way they now engage them [. . .]

The deliberations of the Select Committee resulted in the report that they presented on 2 August 1832. Bulwer-Lytton followed this by introducing a bill that would have implemented the committee's recommendations. Though it was passed by the House of Commons it was defeated in the House of Lords (2 August 1833).[1]

---

[1] The composition of the committee was twenty-four, including Edward Bulwer-Lytton as chairman, radical and liberal politicians such as Thomas Slingsby Duncombe, Henry Lytton and Richard Lalor Sheil, and conservative politicians such as Viscount Porchester and Lord John Russell. What many of them had in common was an interest in playwriting.

10   Report of the Select Committee, 1832

British parliamentary papers, pp. 3–6

In examining the state of the Laws affecting the interests and exhibition of the Drama, Your Committee find that a considerable decline, both in the Literature of the Stage, and the taste of the Public for Theatrical Performances, is generally conceded. Among the causes of this decline, in addition to those which have been alleged, and which are out of the province of the Legislature to control, such as the prevailing fashion of late dinner hours, the absence of Royal encouragement, and the supposed indisposition of some Religious Sects to countenance Theatrical Exhibitions, Your Committee are of opinion, that the uncertain administration of the Laws, the slender encouragement afforded to Literary Talent to devote its labours towards the Stage, and the want of a better legal regulation as regards the number and distribution of Theatres, are to be mainly considered.

2. In respect to the Licensing of Theatres, Your Committee are of opinion, that the Laws would be rendered more clear and effectual by confining the sole power and authority to license Theatres throughout the Metropolis (as well as in places of Royal Residence) to the Lord Chamberlain; and that his – the sole – jurisdiction, should be extended twenty miles round London (that being the point at which Magistrates now have the power of licensing Theatres for the legitimate Drama). And as Your Committee believe that the interests of the Drama will be considerably advanced by the natural consequences of a fair competition in its Representation, they recommend that the Lord Chamberlain should continue a Licence to all the Theatres licensed at present, whether by himself or by the Magistrates. Your Committee are also of opinion, partly from the difficulty of defining, by clear and legal

distinctions, 'the Legitimate Drama', and principally from the propriety of giving a full opening as well to the higher as to the more humble orders of Dramatic Talent, that the Proprietors and Managers of the said Theatres should be allowed to exhibit such plays as have received or shall receive the sanction of the Censor.

3. Your Committee believe that the number of Theatres thus licensed (although they might be more conveniently distributed) would suffice for the accommodation of the Public, in the present state of feeling towards Theatrical Performances, and also for the general advantages of competition; at the same time, as Theatres are intended for the amusement of the Public, so Your Committee are of opinion that the Public should have a voice in the number of Theatres to be allowed. And Your Committee would therefore respectfully submit to the House, that if a Requisition, signed by a majority of the Resident Householders in any large or populous Parish or District, be presented to the Chamberlain, praying for his Licence to a new Theatre in the said Parish or District, the Chamberlain should be bound to comply with the Public wish. Your Committee are of opinion, that all abuse in the exercise of the Licence thus granted, would be effectually prevented, by leaving to the Chamberlain the power of applying to the Home Department for the summary suppression of any Theatre which may notoriously have outraged the conditions of its License [sic], or the rules of Public decorum.

4. Your Committee would also recommend, that the Chamberlain should possess the same power for the summary suppression of any Theatre, exhibiting any sort of Dramatic Representation without the sanction of his Licence; considering, that as the Public can procure the Licence if it approve the Theatre, so any Theatre not licensed would probably not be less opposed to the desire of the Public than to the provisions of the Law.

5. With respect to the Licensing of Plays, Your Committee would advise, in order to give full weight to the responsibility of the situation, that it should be clearly understood that the office of the Censor is held at the discretion of the Lord Chamberlain, whose duty it would be to remove him, should there be any just ground for dissatisfaction as to the exercise of his functions. Your Committee would recommend some revision in the present system of Fees to the Censor, so (for instance) that the Licence of a Song and the Licence of a Play may not be indiscriminately subjected to the same charge; and this revision is yet more desirable, in order to ascertain whether, in consequence of the greater number of Plays which, by the alterations proposed by Your Committee, would be brought under the control of the Censor, some abatement in the Fees charged for each night might not be reasonably made, without lessening the present Income of the Licencer [sic].

6. In respect to the exclusive privileges claimed by the two Metropolitan Theatres of Drury Lane and Covent Garden, it appears manifest that such privileges have neither preserved the dignity of the Drama, nor, by the present Administration of the Laws, been of much advantage to the Proprietors of the Theatres themselves. And Your Committee, while bound to acknowledge that a very large sum has been invested in these Theatres, on a belief of the continuation of their legal monopoly of

exhibiting the Legitimate Drama, which sum, but for that belief, would probably not have been hazarded, are nevertheless of opinion, that the alterations they propose are not likely to place the Proprietors of the said Theatres in a worse pecuniary condition than the condition confessed to under the existing system.

7. In regard to Dramatic Literature, it appears manifest that an Author at present is subjected to indefensible hardship and injustice; and the disparity of protection afforded to the labours of the Dramatic Writer, when compared even with that granted to Authors in any other branch of Letters, seems alone sufficient to divert the ambition of eminent and successful Writers from that department of intellectual exertion. Your Committee, therefore, earnestly recommend that the Author of a Play should possess the same legal rights, and enjoy the same legal protection, as the Author of any other literary production; and that his Performance should not be legally exhibited at any Theatre, Metropolitan or Provincial, without his express and formal consent.

8. By the regulations and amendments thus proposed in the existing system, Your Committee are of opinion that the Drama will be freed from many present disadvantages, and left to the fair experiment of Public support. In regard to Actors, it is allowed, even by those Performers whose Evidence favours the existing Monopoly, that the more general exhibition of the regular Drama would afford new schools and opportunities for their art. In regard to Authors, it is probable that a greater variety of Theatres at which to present, or for which to adapt, their Plays, and a greater security in the profits derived from their success, will give new encouragement to their ambition, and, perhaps (if a play is never acted without producing some emolument to its Writer) may direct their attention to the more durable, as being also the more lucrative, classes of Dramatic Literature; while, as regards the Public, equally benefited by these advantages, it is probable that the ordinary consequences of Competition, freed from the possibility of licentiousness by the confirmed control and authority of the Chamberlain, will afford convenience in the number and situation of Theatres, and cheap and good Entertainment in the Performances usually exhibited.

July 1832.

PLAYWRIGHTS AND THE LAW

Planché[1] recounts how he was approached by a provincial manager for the rights to *Charles XII*, which he had written for Drury Lane and which had been performed there on 11 November 1828. The subsequent negotiations and the failure of the manager to pay for the rights led to agitation on behalf of dramatic authors at the Select Committee on Dramatic Literature.

---

[1] James Robinson Planché (1796–1880), a prolific writer of plays, also produced the first history of British costume and is credited with introducing the genre of extravaganza to the English stage. Much of his best work was done with Madame Vestris, notably at the Olympic Theatre from 1831 to 1839 [**51a, 51b, 184a, 184b, 188, 198**].

11   The need for copyright protection, 1828

J. R. Planché, *Recollections and reflections* (London: Tinsley, 1872), vol. 1, pp. 148–9

The piece not being printed and published, which, at that period, would have entitled any manager to perform it without the author's permission, Mr Murray, of the Theatre Royal, Edinburgh, wrote to inquire upon what terms I would allow him to produce it. I named the very moderate sum of ten pounds, which he admitted I was perfectly justified in asking, but declined paying, on the plea that since the introduction of half-price in the provinces, the expenses attendant on the production of afterpieces was barely covered by the receipt they brought. This was all very well; but Mr Murray had the dishonesty to obtain surreptitiously a MS copy of the piece, and the effrontery, in the face of the above excuse, to produce the piece, without my permission, at *whole price* leaving me to my remedy. I did not bring an action against him, but I asked Poole, Kenny [*sic*], Lunn, Peake, and some others of the working dramatists of the day to dine with me in Brompton Crescent and talk the matter over; and it was agreed that steps should be immediately taken to obtain the protection of an Act of Parliament.

The arguments in the Select Committee report addressing the position of dramatic authors did bear fruit. The Honourable George Lamb, who had been a member of the Select Committee, introduced a bill that was passionately supported by Bulwer-Lytton. Though the bill recognized the difference between published works and performance, those who benefited principally were publishers rather than authors.[1]

---

[1] See Stephens, *Censorship*, pp. 90–5. Stephens maintains that this was the first and only Copyright Act specifically to try to recognize the special problems of the playwright and the crucial difference between the publication of a literary work and a dramatic performance (p. 91).

12   The Dramatic Copyright Bill, 1833

3 William IV cap. XV, *Collection of the public general statutes passed in the third and fourth years of the reign of HM King William IV* (London: Eyre & Strahan, 1833). p. 138[1]

Whereas by an Act passed in the Fifty-fourth Year of the Reign of his late Majesty King George the Third, intituled *An Act to amend the several Acts for the Encouragement of Learning, by securing the Copies and Copyright of printed Books to the Authors of such Books, or their Assigns*, it was amongst other things provided and enacted, that from and after the passing of the said Act the Author of any Book or Books composed, and not printed or published, or which should thereafter be composed and printed and published, and his Assignee or Assigns, should have the sole Liberty of printing and reprinting such Book or Books for the full term of Twenty-eight Years, to commence from the Day of first publishing the same, and also, if the Author should be living at the End of that Period, for the Residue of his natural Life: And whereas it is expedient to extend the Provisions of the said Act; be it therefore enacted by the King's most Excellent Majesty, by and with the Advice and Consent of the Lords Spiritual and Temporal, and Commons, in this present

Parliament assembled, and by the Authority of the same, That from and after the passing of this Act the Author of any Tragedy, Comedy, Play, Opera, Farce, or any other Dramatic Piece or Entertainment, composed, and not printed and published by the Author thereof or his Assignee, or which hereafter shall be composed, and not printed or published by the Author thereof or his Assignee, or the Assignee of such Author, shall have as his own Property the sole Liberty of representing, or causing to be represented, at any Place or Places of Dramatic Entertainment whatsoever, in any part of the United Kingdom of *Great Britain* and *Ireland*, in the Isles of *Man*, *Jersey*, and *Guernsey*, or in any Part of the *British* Dominions, any such Production as aforesaid, not printed and published by the Author thereof or his Assignee, and shall be deemed and taken to be the Proprietor thereof; and that the Author of any such Production, printed and published within Ten Years before the passing of this Act by the Author thereof or his Assignee, or which shall hereafter be so printed and published, or the Assignee of such Author, shall, from the Time of passing this Act, or from the time of such Publication respectively, until the End of Twenty-eight Years from the Day of such first Publication of the same, and also, if the Author or Authors, or the Survivor of the Authors, shall be living at the End of that Period, during the Residue of his natural Life, have as his own Property the sole Liberty of representing, or causing to be represented, the same at any such Place of Dramatic Entertainment as aforesaid, and shall be deemed and taken to be the Proprietor thereof: Provided nevertheless, that nothing in this Act contained shall prejudice, alter, or affect the Right or Authority of any Person to represent or cause to be represented, at any Place or Places of Dramatic Entertainment whatsoever, any such Production as aforesaid, in all Cases in which the Author thereof or his Assignee shall, previously to the passing of this Act, have given his Consent to or authorized such Representation, but that such sole Liberty of the Author or his Assignee shall be subject to such Right or Authority.

II. And be it further enacted, That if any Person shall, during the Continuance of such sole Liberty as aforesaid, contrary to the Intent of this Act, or Right of the Author or his Assignee, represent, or cause to be represented, without the Consent in Writing of the Author or other Proprietor first had and obtained, at any Place of Dramatic Entertainment within the Limits aforesaid, any such Production as aforesaid, or any Part thereof, every such Offender shall be liable for each and every such Representation to the Payment of an Amount not less than Forty Shillings, or to the full Amount of the Benefit or Advantage arising from such Representa-tion, or the Injury or Loss sustained by the Plaintiff therefrom, whichever shall be the greater Damages, to the Author or other Proprietor of such Production so represented contrary to the true Intent and Meaning of this Act, to be recovered, together with Double Costs of Suit, by such Author or other Proprietors, in any Court having Jurisdiction in such Cases in that Part of the said United Kingdom or of the *British* Dominions in which the Offence shall be committed; and in every such Proceeding where the sole Liberty of such Author or his Assignee as aforesaid shall be subject to such Right or Authority as aforesaid, it shall be sufficient for the Plaintiff to state that he has such sole Liberty, without stating the same to be subject to such Right or Authority, or otherwise mentioning the same.

III. Provided nevertheless, and be it further enacted, That all Actions or Proceedings for any Offence or Injury that shall be committed against this Act shall be brought, sued, and commenced within Twelve Calendar Months next after such Offence committed, or else the same shall be void and of no effect.

IV. And be it further enacted, That whenever Authors, Persons, Offenders, or others are spoken of in this Act in the Singular Number or in the Masculine Gender, the same shall extend to any Number of Persons and to either Sex.

[1] Formally it was an act to amend the Laws Relating to Dramatic Literary Property.

13   The Lord Chamberlain considers the question of theatrical fees, 1836

A. Bunn, *The stage, both before and behind the curtain* (3 vols., London: Bentley, 1840), vol. II, p. 181[1]

FEE ON LICENSING THEATRICAL ENTERTAINMENTS

This is a fee of 2l 2s for every play, song, or other theatrical entertainment licensed under the provisions of the Act of the 10th George II, c. 28, by the Lord Chamberlain, previously to public representation. It is payable by the managers of the several theatres within the jurisdiction of the Lord Chamberlain, to the examiner of theatrical entertainments, and produced in the year 1835 the sum of 291l 18s.

The payment of this fee appears to have existed for nearly a century; and it was stated to us by the late Mr Colman, that although he considered himself clearly entitled to the fee of 2l 2s for every song or short piece licensed, as well as for every play however long, yet in practice he had sometimes only charged one fee upon several new songs licensed upon the occasion of a performer's benefit, and had relinquished his fee altogether in some special cases.

The fee is not charged for a song which is written in, and forms part of any play or opera; nor is it paid in cases where the license [*sic*] is refused by the Lord Chamberlain.

We are of the opinion that fees of this nature may with propriety be continued, provided their amount is commensurate with the labour and responsibility cast upon the examiner, and not, as at present, remaining an unvarying fee of 2l 2s upon every occasion, whether the new production be short or long – a system which, in its operation, presses unduly and heavily upon the managers of those theatres at which new pieces of one and two acts are frequently produced under the sanction of the Lord Chamberlain's license [*sic*]. In this view of the subject we are fully borne out by the opinion of the Select Committee of the House of Commons on dramatic literature, whose report to that House, in the month of July 1832, upon the subject of the fees on licenses [*sic*], was as follows: 'Your Committee would recommend some revision in the present system of fees to the censor, so (for instance) that the license of a song, and the license [*sic*] of a play, may not be indiscriminately subject to the same charge.'

Having fully considered this subject, we are induced to recommend to your Majesty's consideration, that the following would be a fair and proper scale of fees, to be in future payable to the examiner upon licensing all theatrical entertainments, namely –

For a License [*sic*] for every Dramatic piece of three of more acts   £2 0 0
For a License [*sic*] for every Dramatic piece of one or two acts, or for a   1 0 0
Pantomime containing prose or poetry
For a License [*sic*] for a Song, Address, Prologue or Epilogue   0 5 0

The death of Mr Colman having caused a vacancy in the appointment of examiner, the Lord Chamberlain has stated that his successor has been appointed, with a distinct understanding that the scale of fees would be subject to revision. We consider that the scale proposed by us will afford a fair and adequate remuneration for the office, provided the salary now payable under your Majesty's warrant is increased to the extent of about 50l per annum.

[1] Bunn quotes the report that the Lord Chamberlain issued on 28 December 1836.

LEGAL INCONSISTENCIES AND EVASIONS

Makeshift theatrical venues flourished, especially in more densely packed areas of London, in this case north of Oxford Street. Many were erected in the courtyards of inns or inside warehouses. The repertoire largely consisted of cut-down versions of popular melodramas, comic songs and dances.[1]

[1] See Henry Mayhew's description of a Smithfield penny gaff in the 1850s in *London labour and the London poor* (London: Griffon, 1864), vol. I, pp. 42–4.

14   The prosecution of an unlicensed penny gaff, 1838

Times (10 March 1838), p. 7[1]

HATTON-GARDEN.– For some time past numerous complaints have been made to the magistrates of this office of two penny theatres, the one in Mortimer-market, Tottenham-court-road, and the other in a field adjacent to Bagnigge-wells-road, where gangs of young thieves nightly assembled. On Wednesday last several of the inhabitants of Mortimer-market, attended at the office to complain of the former establishment [. . .] Inspector Jenkins, and a body of constables of E division, proceeded to the theatre, and captured the manager, performers, and musicians, and the whole of them were yesterday brought to the office and placed at the bar [. . .]

The prisoners gave their names, Edward Ewyn, manager, Ann Green, Eliza Cambell, Maria Lewis, Henry Woodford, John Jones, Joseph Burrows, John Smith,

John Dennis, James Pillar, John Golden, and James Brierly. The prisoners, some of whom were attired in their theatrical habiliments, with their countenances painted, made a very grotesque appearance.

Duke [from the District Office] being sworn stated, that in consequence of a warrant, on Thursday night last, about 9 o'clock, he proceeded with other officers to a penny theatre in Mortimer-market, St Pancras, where he found the whole of the prisoners, some of whom were engaged in performing their parts, whilst Ewyn, the manager, was employed taking money at the doors, and the woman Green was acting as check-taker. Cambell and Lewes [sic] were enacting their parts upon the stage, and Joseph Burrows was in his theatrical dress between them, with his face painted, and wearing a huge pair of mustachios. John Pillar was in a temporary orchestra with a large violoncello, scraping away most melo-dramatically, whilst the players were endeavouring to humour the sounds, and to suit their action to the word, and the word to the action; and just at that part of the performance where Burrows had to exclaim, 'The officers of justice are coming', witness and his brother officers rushed upon the stage and apprehended the whole of them.

Mr ROGERS.– What description of audience was there?

Duke.– A ragged dirty set, principally consisting of boys and girls; two of them were barefooted, and had scarce a rag to cover them, and did not seem to have been washed for a month. The theatre was of the most wretched description: there was a temporary stage, and bits of scenery. The boys said they were errand boys and servants. Brierly and Smith said, they were country actors out of engagements, and had visited the place out of curiosity.

Mr Mallett.– Had they an inscription, that they were 'Licensed pursuant to Act of Parliament?'

Duke.– They had not. On the gates was written up, 'for the evening's performance, the "Spectre of the Grave"; after which a comic song by Mr Ewyn; to conclude with "The Key of the Little Door"'. They found various theatrical dresses and other properties, with stars, swords, etc., now produced.

Bayliss proved having paid 1d for admission. He paid the money to the woman Green. Ewyn was at the door, and he confessed that he was the manager. He took him into custody, and subsequently he apprehended Lewis and Cambell, at the back of the stage, in their theatrical dresses.

Mr ROGERS.– Have you got 'the Spectre of the Grave' here?

Inspector Jenkins– No, your worship, he vanished. The other male performers were dressed in sandals and armour, with their helmets up.

Hall and the other officers corroborated the above evidence. Several inhabitants of Mortimer-market proved that they were every night alarmed by firing of guns, alarms of 'fire', clashing of swords, the most boisterous ranting and shrieks from the voices of the ladies of the *corps dramatique*, and the place was a perfect nuisance to the neighbourhood.

The owner of the place stated, that on the 24th of January he let the place to a person named Summers, for chair-making, when it was turned into a theatre.

Ewyn said, he had engaged with Summers to divide the profits of the theatrical speculation. Summers agreed to take the place, and he (Ewyn) to provide the scenery and wardrobe; 'and proud I am to say, that I have conducted the consarn [sic] respectably, which some of the neighbours can testify. "This is the head and front of my offending–no more."'

Inspector Jenkins said that about a month ago he called on Ewyns [sic], and cautioned him, but he said that the magistrates had nothing to do with the matter.

Mr ROGERS, addressing the prisoners, said that they had received a warning which they did not heed. He should not now order them to find bail, but would discharge them, and if they dared to repeat their performances after this admonition, he would grant a warrant for their apprehension, and every one of them should find bail or be committed. They had held out temptation to the children of poor persons, some of whom, it appeared, were without shoes and nearly naked, who robbed their parents or others for the purpose of procuring the penny for admission. He would order their paraphernalia to be restored to them, but on condition that they would remove their fittings up and desist from any future performances.

Ewyns.– You must give me time to take down the seats and decorations.

Mr ROGERS.– You must take them down this day.

Ewin [sic] (with a start).– What! This day! Impossible!

Mr ROGERS directed Inspector Jones to see the mandate obeyed, which he promised to do.

[1] See also *Era* (27 January 1839), p. 209, for a further arrest in the New Cut near Marsh-gate. Not all prosecutions were successful: see the minutes of evidence of the Select Committee in 1832, questions 3490–517.

The odd situation occasioned by the prohibition of all but sacred concerts on Wednesdays and Fridays in Lent, which applied to theatres within the City of Westminster, demonstrated yet again the irrelevance of the distinction between the major and the minor theatres.

15   The patent theatres suffer under the legal prohibition of Lenten performances

(a) Planché remembers the anomalous Lenten restrictions

Planché, *Recollections and reflections*, vol. II, p. 75

Lent arrived, and the theatres in the parish of St Paul, Covent Garden, were rigorously restricted from the performance of a moral or poetical play on Wednesdays or Fridays during that period; but a theatre that happened to be on the other side of Oxford Street or of Waterloo Bridge was unaffected by this prohibition, and though the manager of the Adelphi might not dream of playing the whole of one of the spectacular 'burlettas', which were at that period so popular there, no objection was made to his exhibiting tableaux from them, and adding any tomfoolery which was *not* dramatic, by way of keeping holy the said Wednesdays and Fridays. The performers at Drury Lane and Covent Garden lost two nights' salary every week, but then they could go to Greenwich or Richmond, and act what they pleased there. Lent was only a sacred season within the circle described by the wand of the Lord Chamberlain. Passion Week itself was unknown in the theatres two or three miles from St James's Palace [. . .][1]

(b) The House of Commons recommends the abolition of Lenten restrictions, 1839

Bunn, *The stage, both before and behind*, vol. III, pp. 138–9[2]

The Albany, March 2, 1839

Sir,

[. . .] I enclose a copy of the resolution agreed to by the House of Commons:

'That it is the opinion of this house, that during Lent no greater restrictions should be placed on theatrical establishments within the city of Westminster, than are placed upon the like amusements at the same period, in every other part of the metropolis.'

It seems to me impossible, after this deliberate proceeding of the House of Commons, that the Lord Chamberlain should any longer interpose his *veto* to the further injury of those who have already suffered so much by the course which the House of Commons has condemned. The words of the Act show that the subject is wholly in the discretion of the Lord Chamberlain: he may, if he pleases, and without any appeal from his decision, put a stop to all theatrical amusements in Westminster, AT ALL TIMES. The Act does not specify the Wednesdays and Fridays in Lent, nor any other days or day in the year, but places absolute powers of prohibition in the hands of the Lord Chamberlain.

It is, therefore, I repeat, a mere question of discretion, and I cannot for a moment imagine that this officer of the court will exercise his discretion in positive defiance of the recorded opinion of the House of Commons [. . .]

[1] The anomalous situation was also condemned in *Examiner* (23 February 1834), p. 123.
[2] A letter from T. S. Duncombe to Bunn concerning the decision by the House of Commons to recommend the allowance of performances during Lent within Westminster. Duncombe had introduced a motion on 27 February. See Nicholson, *Struggle for a free stage*, pp. 391–404.

16   The patent monopoly and its effect on actors

F. G. Tomlins, *A brief view of the English drama* (London: Mitchell, 1840), p. 109

The difficulties that beset the highest rank of acting, the hazards of its position, the uncertainties of its rewards, and the dubiousness of its station as regards polished society, are such as to deter men possessing the requisite attainments and abilities from attempting the pursuit. The ultimate object of candidates for the highest theatrical honours is to be permanently fixed at one of the national theatres. But to get there requires qualities rarely united in one being, and to maintain themselves when there, a combination of circumstances beyond their control. Owing to the vast size of the theatres, and the enormous rent and expenses, the managers play a desperate game, and make a stupendous outlay to command success. Variety and novelty are the chief objects they keep in view, in order to attract and secure the heterogeneous class that can alone fill their theatres. For this purpose they engage three, if not four, companies of actors: a set for tragedy and comedy – one for melodrama and pantomime – a large operatic company – and another for spectacle and ballets. To the regular actor and acting, this is fatal. If a *prima donna* become a favourite, there is a run on the piece, and the other three sets, or two of them at least, are what is technically termed, 'shelved'; that is, they are for forty, or fifty, or even a hundred nights, entirely withdrawn from the public notice, and from the practice of their art. In many instances they have been harassed by petty arts until they have thrown up their engagements in disgust, and if they do not suffer in this way, they rust in an idleness that is equally injurious to them. This would not be the case if there was not a monopoly, because then these four kind of companies would each find a theatre for itself, and the portion of the public who might still like to witness the species of drama it preferred, would have the advantage of doing so, and not be, as at present, debarred from it during the run of one particular piece [. . .]

[. . .] The situation of the intellectual actor seems to be worse than ever. He shifts from theatre to theatre, and is associated, at the will of his manager, with horses and wild beasts. He is made to partake of the risk of the loss at the theatre where he is, though he has no share in the gains beyond his stipulated salary. He is the first to suffer; and it now seems a common proceeding to declare half or almost no salaries at the end of the week, provided the houses have fallen off. The injustice of making him thus participate in the risk is so much the greater, as it is incurred for the most part upon a portion of the speculation in which he is no way concerned [. . .] He thus runs the risk of the three companies incorporated under one management, and the failure of the operatic, melodramatic, or pantomimic company involves him in ruin. Was he playing in a theatre specially devoted to his branch of the art, he would at all events incur only the risk of his own pursuit.

THE THEATRE REGULATION ACT

Though the Theatre Regulation Act's provisions abolished the patent monopoly, the act greatly extended the powers of the Lord Chamberlain in respect of censorship, which now affected all theatres both metropolitan and provincial throughout Great Britain.[1]

---

[1] An Act for Regulating Theatres passed on 22 August 1843.

17   The Theatre Regulation Act, 1843

6 & 7 Vict. cap 68, *Collection of the public general statutes passed in the sixth and seventh years of the reign of HM Queen Victoria* (London: Eyre & Strahan, 1843), p. 58

Whereas it is expedient that the Laws now in force for regulating Theatres and Theatrical Performances be repealed, and other Provisions be enacted in their Stead: Be it enacted by the Queen's most Excellent Majesty, by and with the Advice and Consent of the Lords Spiritual and Temporal, and Commons, in this present Parliament assembled, and by the Authority of the same, That an Act passed in the third Year of the Reign of King *James* the First, intituled *An Act to Restrain the Abuses of Players*; and so much of an Act passed in the Tenth Year of the Reign of King *George* the Second for the more effectual preventing of the unlawful playing of Interludes within the Precincts of the Two Universities in that Part of *Great Britain* called *England*, and the places adjacent, as is now in force; and another Act passed in the Tenth Year of King *George* the Second, intituled *An Act to explain and amend so much of an Act made in the Twelfth Year of the Reign of Queen* Anne, intituled '*An Act for reducing the Laws relating to Rogues, Vagabonds, Sturdy Beggars, and Vagrants into One Act of Parliament, and for the more effectual punishing such Rogues, Vagabonds, Sturdy Beggars, and Vagrants, and sending them whither they ought to be sent*', as relates to common *Players of Interludes*; and another Act passed in the Twenty-eighth Year of the Reign of King *George* the Third, intituled *An Act to enable Justices of the Peace to license Theatrical Representations occasionally, under the Restrictions therein contained*, shall be repealed: Provided always, any Licence now in force granted by the Lord Chamberlain, or granted by any Justices of the Peace under the Provisions of the last-recited Act, shall continue in force for the Times for which the same were severally granted, or until revoked by the Authority by which they were severally granted.

II. And be it enacted, That, except as aforesaid, it shall not be lawful for any Person to have or keep any House or other Place of public Resort in *Great Britain*, for the public Performance of Stage Plays, without Authority by virtue of Letters Patent from Her Majesty, her Heirs and Successors, or Predecessors, or without Licence from the Lord Chamberlain of Her Majesty's Household for the Time being, or from the Justices of the Peace as herein-after provided; and every Person who shall offend against this Enactment shall be liable to forfeit such Sum as shall be awarded by the Court in which or the Justices by whom he shall be convicted, not exceeding Twenty Pounds for every Day on which such House or Place shall have been so kept open by him for the Purpose aforesaid without legal Authority.

III. And be it enacted, That the Authority of the Lord Chamberlain for granting Licences shall extend to all Theatres (not being Patent Theatres) within the Parliamentary Boundaries of the Cities of *London* and *Westminster*, and of the Boroughs of *Finsbury* and *Marylebone*, the *Tower Hamlets*, *Lambeth*, and *Southwark*, and also within those Places where Her Majesty, Her Heirs and Successors, shall, in their

Royal Persons, occasionally reside: Provided always, that, except within the Cities and Boroughs aforesaid, and the Boroughs of *New Windsor*, in the County of *Berks*, and *Brighthelmstone* in the County of *Susses* [*sic*], Licences for Theatres may be granted by the Justices as herein-after provided, in those Places in which Her Majesty, Her Heirs and Successors, shall occasionally reside; but such Licences shall not be in force during the Residence there of her Majesty, Her Heirs and Successors; and during such Residence it shall not be lawful to open such Theatres as last aforesaid (not being Patent Theatres) without the Licence of the Lord Chamberlain.

IV. And be it enacted, That for every such Licence granted by the Lord Chamberlain a Fee, not exceeding Ten Shillings for each Calendar Month during which the Theatre is licensed to be kept open, according to such scale of fees as shall be fixed by the Lord Chamberlain, shall be paid to the Lord Chamberlain.

V. And be it enacted, That the Justices of the Peace within every County, Riding, Division, Liberty, Cinque Ports, City and Borough in *Great Britain* beyond the Limits of the Authority of the Lord Chamberlain, in which Application shall have been made to them for any such Licence as is herein-after mentioned, shall, within Twenty-one Days next after such licence shall have been made to them in Writing signed by the Party making the same, and countersigned by at least Two Justices acting in and for the Division within which the Property proposed to be licensed shall be situate, and delivered to the Clerk to the said Justices, hold a Special Session in the Division, District, or Place for which they usually act, for granting Licences to Houses for the Performance of Stage Plays, of the holding of which Session Seven Days Notice shall be given by their Clerk to each of the Justices acting within such Division, District or Place; and every such Licence shall be given under the Hands and Seals of Four or more of the Justices assembled at such Special Session, and shall be signed and sealed in open Court, and afterwards shall be publicly read by the Clerk, with the names of the Justices subscribing the same.

VI. And be it enacted, That for every such Licence granted by the Justices a Fee, not exceeding Five Shillings for each Calendar Month during which the Theatre is licensed to be kept open, according to such Scale of Fees as shall be fixed by the Justices, shall be paid to the Clerk of the said Justices.

VII. And be it enacted, That no such Licence for a Theatre shall be granted by the Lord Chamberlain or Justices to any Person except the actual and responsible Manager for the Time being of the Theatre in respect of which the Licence shall be granted; and the Name and Place of Abode of such Manager shall be printed on every Play Bill announcing any Representation at such Theatre; and such Manager shall become bound himself in such penal Sum as the Lord Chamberlain or Justices shall require, being in no Case more than Five Hundred Pounds, and Two sufficient Sureties, to be approved by the said Lord Chamberlain or Justices, each in such penal Sum as the Lord Chamberlain or Justices shall require, being in no Case more than One Hundred Pounds, for the due Observance of the Rules which shall be in force at any Times during the Currency of the Licence for the Regulation of such Theatre, and for securing Payment of the Penalties which such Manager may be adjudged to pay for Breach of the said Rules, or any of the Provisions of this Act.

VIII. And be it enacted, That in case it shall appear to the Lord Chamberlain that any Riot or Misbehaviour has taken place in any Theatre licensed by him, or in any Patent Theatre, it shall be lawful for him to suspend such Licence or to order such Patent Theatre to be closed for such Times as to him shall seem fit; and it shall also be lawful for the Lord Chamberlain to order that any Patent Theatre or any Theatre licensed by him shall be closed on such public Occasions as to the Lord Chamberlain shall seem fit; and when any such Licence shall be suspended, or any such Order shall be in force, the Theatre to which the same applies shall not be entitled to the Privilege for any Letters Patent or Licence, but shall be deemed an unlicensed House.

IX. And be it enacted, That the said Justices of the Peace at a Special Licensing Session, or at some Adjournment thereof, shall make suitable Rules for insuring Order and Decency at the several Theatres licensed by them within their Jurisdiction, and for regulating the Times during which they shall severally be allowed to be open, and from Time to Time, at another Special Session, of which Notice shall be given as aforesaid, may rescind or alter such Rules; and it shall be lawful for any One of Her Majesty's Principal Secretaries of State to rescind or alter any such Rules, and also to make such other Rules for the like Purpose, as to him shall seem fit; and a Copy of all Rules which shall be in force for the Time being shall be annexed to every such Licence; and in case any Riot or Breach of the said Rules in any such Theatres shall be proved on Oath before any Two Justices usually acting in the Jurisdiction where such Theatre is situated, it shall be lawful for them to order that the same be closed for such Time as to the said Justices shall seem fit; and while such Order shall be in force the Theatre so ordered to be closed shall be deemed an unlicensed House.

X. Provided always, and be it enacted, That no such Licence shall be in force within the Precincts of either of the Universities of *Oxford* or *Cambridge*, or within Fourteen Miles of the City of *Oxford* or Town of *Cambridge*, without the consent of the Chancellor or Vice Chancellor of each of the said Universities respectively; and that the Rules for the Management of any Theatre which shall be licensed with such Consent within the Limits aforesaid shall be subject to the Approval of the said Chancellor or Vice Chancellor respectively; and in case of the Breach of any of the said Rules, or any Condition on which the Consent of the Chancellor or Vice Chancellor to grant any such licence shall have been given, it shall be lawful for such Chancellor or Vice Chancellor respectively to annul the Licence, and thereupon such Licence shall become void.

XI. And be it enacted, That every Person who for Hire shall act or present, or cause, permit, or suffer to be acted or presented, any Part in any Stage Play, in any Place not being a Patent Theatre or duly licensed as a Theatre, shall forfeit such Sum as shall be awarded by the Court in which or the Justices by whom he shall be convicted, not exceeding Ten Pounds for every Day on which he shall so offend.

XII. And be it enacted, That One Copy of every new Stage Play, and of every new Act, Scene, or other Part added to any old Stage Play, and of every new Prologue or Epilogue, and of every new Part added to an old Prologue or Epilogue, intended to be produced and acted for Hire at any Theatre in *Great Britain*, shall be sent to the Lord Chamberlain of Her Majesty's Household for the Time being, Seven Days at least before the first acting or presenting thereof, with an Account of the Theatre where and the Time when the same is intended to be first acted or presented, signed by the Master or Manager, or one of the Masters or Managers, of such Theatre; and during the said Seven Days no Person shall for Hire act or present the same, or cause the same to be acted or presented; and in case the Lord Chamberlain, either before or after the Expiration of the said Period of Seven Days, shall disallow any Play, or any Act, Scene, or Part thereof, or any Prologue or Epilogue, or any Part thereof, it shall not be lawful for any Person to act or present the same, or cause the same to be acted or presented, contrary to such Disallowance.

XIII. And be it enacted, That it shall be lawful for the Lord Chamberlain to charge such Fees for the Examination of the Plays, Prologues and Epilogues, or Parts thereof, which shall be sent to him for Examination, as to him from Time to Time shall seem fit, according to a Scale which shall be fixed by him, such Fee not being in any Case more than Two Guineas, and such Fee shall be paid at the Time when such Plays, Prologues and Epilogues, or Parts thereof, shall be sent to the Lord Chamberlain; and the said Period of Seven Days shall not begin to run in any Case until the said Fee shall have been paid to the Lord Chamberlain, or to some Officer deputed by him to receive the same.

XIV. And be it enacted, That it shall be lawful for the Lord Chamberlain for the Time being, whenever he shall be of opinion that it is fitting for the Preservation of good Manners, Decorum, or of the public Peace so to do, to forbid the acting or presenting of any Stage Play, or any Act, Scene, or Part thereof, or any Prologue or Epilogue, or any Part thereof, anywhere in *Great Britain*, or in such Theatres as he shall specify, and either absolutely or for such Time as he shall think fit.

XV. And be it enacted, That every Person who for Hire shall act or present, or cause to be acted or presented, any new Stage Play, or any Act, Scene, or Part thereof, or any new Prologue or Epilogue, or any Part thereof, until the same shall have been allowed by the Lord Chamberlain, or which shall have been disallowed by him, and also any Person who for Hire shall act or present, or cause to be acted or presented, any Stage Play, or any Act, Scene, or Part thereof, or any Prologue or Epilogue, or any Part thereof, contrary to such Prohibition as aforesaid, shall for every such Offence forfeit such Sum as shall be awarded by the Court in which or the Justices by whom he shall be convicted, not exceeding the sum of Fifty Pounds;

and every Licence (in case there be any such) by or under which the Theatre was opened, in which such Offence shall have been committed, shall become absolutely void.

XVI. And be it enacted, That in every case in which any Money or other Reward shall be taken or charged, directly or indirectly, or in which the Purchase of any Article is made a Condition for the Admission of any Person into any Theatre to see any Stage Play, and also in every Case in which any Stage Play shall be acted or presented in any House, Room, or place in which distilled or fermented Exciseable Liquor shall be sold, every Actor therein shall be deemed to be acting for Hire.

XVII. And be it enacted, That in any Proceedings to be instituted against any Person for having or keeping an unlicensed Theatre, or for acting for Hire in an unlicensed Theatre, if it shall be proved that such Theatre is used for the public Performance of Stage Plays, the Burden of Proof that such Theatre is duly licensed or authorized shall lie on the Party accused, and until the contrary shall be proved such Theatre shall be taken to be unlicensed.

XVIII. And be it enacted, That after the passing of this Act it shall be lawful for any Person against whom any Action or Information shall have been commenced, for the Recovery of any Forfeiture or pecuniary Penalty incurred under the said Act of the Tenth Year of the Reign of King *George* the Second, to apply to the Court in which such Action or Information shall have been commenced, if such Court shall be sitting, or if such Court shall not be sitting to any Judge of either of the Superior Courts at *Westminster*, for an Order that such Action or Information shall be discontinued, upon Payment of the Costs thereof incurred to the Time of such Application being made, such Costs to be taxed according to the Practice of such Court; and every such Court or Judge (as the Case may be), upon such Application, and Proof that sufficient Notice has been given to the Plaintiff or Informer, or to his Attorney, of the Application, shall make such Order as aforesaid; and upon the making of such Order, and Payment or Tender of such Costs as aforesaid, such Action or Information shall be forthwith discontinued.

XIX. And be it enacted, That all the pecuniary Penalties imposed by this Act for Offences committed in *England* may be recovered in any of Her Majesty's Courts or Record at *Westminster*, and for Offences committed in *Scotland* by Action or Summary Complaint before the Court of Session or Judiciary there, or for Offences committed in any Part of *Great Britain* in a summary Way before Two Justices of the Peace for any County, Riding, Division, Liberty, City, or Borough where any such Offence shall be committed, by the Oath or Oaths of One or more credible Witness or Witnesses, or by the Confession of the Offender, and in default of Payment of such Penalty together with the Costs, the same may be levied by Distress and Sale of the Offender's Goods and Chattels, rendering the Overplus to such Offender, if any there be above the Penalty, Costs and Charge of Distress; and for Want of sufficient Distress the Offender may be imprisoned in the Common Gaol or House of Correction for any such County, Riding, Division, Liberty, City, or Borough for any Time not exceeding Six Calendar Months.

XX. And be it enacted, That it shall be lawful for any Person who shall think himself aggrieved by any Order of such Justices of the Peace to appeal therefrom to the next General or Quarter Session of the Peace to be holden for the said County, Riding, Division, Liberty, City, or Borough, whose Order therein shall be final.

XXI. And be it enacted, That the said Penalties for any Offence against this Act shall be paid and applied in the first Instance towards defraying the Expences incurred by the Prosecutor, and the Residue thereof (if any) shall be paid to the Use of Her Majesty, Her Heirs and Successors.

XXII. Provided always, and be it enacted, That no Person shall be liable to be prosecuted for any Offence against this Act unless such Prosecution shall be commenced within Six Calendar Months after the Offence is committed.

XXIII. And be it enacted, That in this Act the Word 'Stage Play' shall be taken to include every Tragedy, Comedy, Farce, Opera, Burletta, Interlude, Melodrama, Pantomime, or other Entertainment of the Stage, or any Part thereof: Provided always, that nothing herein contained shall be construed to apply to any Theatrical Representation in any Booth or Show which by the Justices of the Peace, or other Persons having Authority in that Behalf, shall be allowed in any lawful Fair, Feast, or customary Meeting of the like Kind.

XXIV. And be it enacted, That this Act shall extend only to *Great Britain*.

XXV. And be it enacted, That this Act may be amended or repealed by any Act to be passed in this Session of Parliament.

THE EFFECTS OF DEREGULATION

The former minor theatres were quick to take advantage of the new provisions, although the Surrey, among others, had been evading the law for some time. To the Lord Chamberlain's request for information about a theatre newly under his jurisdiction, Frances Davidge, the Surrey's proprietor since the death of her husband, wrote a detailed response, accompanied by an application for a new licence.

18   The Surrey Theatre solicits a licence under the new regulations, 1843

PRO LC7/5, fo. 14 (5 September 1843)

In reply to your Lordship's letter of yesterday requiring to know the dates of the commencement and termination of each season during which the Surrey Theatre has been open for the Entertainment of the Public in the course of the last five years and also a general description of the class of Pieces that have been performed there during the same period, I have the honor to state for your Lordship's information that the Surrey Theatre has been licensed by the magistrates for the County of

Surrey hitherto in October of each year and that the Theatre has been open for Public Entertainment for the last ten years on every night during the year, save the nights of Ash Wednesday, Good Friday, Christmas Eve, the Passion Week and occasions of Public Mourning – The Class of Entertainment given at the Surrey Theatre consists of that enumerated in the 23rd Sectn. of the Act recited in your Lordship's Letter and which has been divided so as to give a varied entertainment every evening.– For the last three years I have found it advantageous to give after the close of the Patent Theatres a round of Operas which have been sustained by the Principal Singers from those Theatres – In addition to the foregoing and in answer to your Lordship's enquiry I have to state that immediately on the Burning down of Astleys Theatre an arrangement was entered into with the late Mr Ducrow and the Surrey Theatre was converted for some months into an amphitheatre and Equestrian performances took place under his direction.–

The character of the Theatre is vouched by the fact that during the whole period of my management not the slightest complaint has been made either as to the class of Entertainment or otherwise.–

In conclusion I beg to state that I am the Sole Lessee of the Surrey Theatre holding under a lease granted by Admiral Sir John West for a Term of nearly seven years yet unexpired at a rental of Seventeen hundred pounds per annum – That I have usually upwards of two hundred persons employed in the Theatre during the whole year.–

The Theatre is called 'Davidge's Royal Surrey Theatre' – Is situate in the Blackfriars Road in the Parish of Saint George the Martyr in the Borough of Southwark in the County of Surrey – Is capable of accommodating about 7 or 800 persons in the Boxes – from 12 to 1400 in the Pit and from 12 to 1400 in the Gallery. The Theatre has just been put into perfect repair at an outlay of upwards of Fifteen hundred pounds[.]

The foregoing particulars I trust will be sufficient for your Lordship and to entitle me to the Licence to be granted by your Lordship of which I am most anxious to avail myself and which your Lordship directing to be made out to me with as little delay as practicable will confer an obligation on–

> Your Lordship's –
> Most obedt. Humble Servant
> F. Davidge.

19   Samuel Lane of the Britannia Saloon, Hoxton, responds to police complaints, 1844

PRO LC7/6

My Lord,

It having been communicated to me that complaint has been made to your Lordship by the Superintendent of Police as to my management of the Britania [*sic*] Saloon under your Lordship's Licence – In reply to such Charge I can only say I am totally ignorant of any cause existing for such complaint and deny most emphatically that the price of Admission to such Saloon is now or ever has been two pence, or that I am in the habit of admitting to the audience part of the Theatre either Water Cress Girls or persons that vend Hearth Stones.

The prices of Admission are the same as other Places of the like kind under your Lordship's Licence – And not a complaint has been made to the Police Court in the district arising from any disturbance in the Saloon or management thereof – Having only heard of this complaint to day and my Licence expiring on the 29th instant I have not the time necessary to rebut the charge as fully as I otherwise could or if your Lordship would hear evidence[.] I have not the slightest hesitation in stating that the greatest injustice would be done in withholding my licence on the mere assertion of an individual and without giving me an opportunity of personally meeting the charge – I am now under engagement with nearly 100 persons who are in my employ – I have but one day given me to meet an accusation which is not only to deprive myself but so large a number of persons of their bread – The only reason I can assign for the complaint is that about a week since about 40 or 50 boys congregated outside the Saloon and I was compelled to seek the assistance of the Police to remove them but my impression is that such boys were sent there for the purpose of creating a disturbance and to bring me into disrepute – The Saloon is constantly attended by two Police Constables one sworn by Her Majesty's Commissioners of Police and one appointed by myself – I need hardly mention to your Lordship that as a Director of a place of Public Amusement I cannot refuse admission to any person conducting themselves with propriety and respectably attired and as to morals of persons visiting such place being contaminated the answer is that the performance is under the surveillance of your Lordship's reader, every entertainment given there being first licensed by your Lordship – I again most respectfully beg to impress and urge on your Lordship the utter ruin that surrounds me If your Lordship at so short a notice take from me your Lordship's Licence, should your Lordship not feel satisfied with this explanation[.] I hope and trust your Lordship will extend the Licence for a fortnight until I can get such evidence as will fully convince your Lordship of my entire innocence and the groundlessness of the accusation.[1]

> I am my Lord,
> Your Lordships Obedt St.
> Samuel Lane
> Britannia Saloon
> 27 Sept. 1844.

---

[1] Despite police objections on 3 October 1844, corroborating the presence of prostitutes and juvenile thieves at the saloon and listing the charges brought before the magistrates (PRO LC7/6, report of Superintendant J. Johnston of N. Division), the Britannia was granted a provisional licence on 10 October for two months (PRO LC7/6, copy of the letter of Sir William Martins, 10 October 1844).

20   The price war between theatres and saloons, 1846

PRO LC7/6, 'Reduction of Prices at the Theatres', ffos. 1–24

4th Decr. 1846 Mr John Johnson and Mr Nelson Lee, Managers of the *New Standard Theatre* called.[1]

Competition with the Saloons the sole and lamentable cause for the reduction of their Prices.

It is impossible for a Theatre to compete on equal terms with a Saloon.

A Saloon opened for no charge whatever would even compete unfairly with a Theatre.

As an instance of the great advantage the Saloons possess, they mention the fact that Mr Brading,[2] when his son came of age, gave about 2000 free admissions, and he has boasted that on that night he made more profit than he ever had done before. Mr Lee has personal knowledge that the various Saloons in his neighbourhood issue [. . .] free admissions to those parties who expose their Bills, on Thursdays and Fridays – vizt. Grecian – Albert – Britannia – Effingham.

They mention that when Managers of the Pavilion they paid £1000 a year Rent and £500 a year Gas and about £120 a week for the Company and other Expences [*sic*] – and just opposite to the Pavilion was the Effingham Saloon, where the prices were 6d and 3d.

Messrs Johnson and Lee entered the present Standard Theatre about 2 years ago – it cost £5000 in Building. They pay Rent £650 a year which they consider as £1000 a year the Money they had advanced for the Building reckoning the difference. Gas £350 a year – weekly Expences about £90 or £95.– At Christmas time about £110 a week.

Within 5 minutes walk are the Grecian, Albert and Britannia Saloons – about 10 minutes walk – the Effingham Saloon.

They would be very conscious if it were possible for the Lord Chamberlain to regulate the Prices of the Theatres and Saloons but they see that, were the Prices of the Saloons fixed, they could easily evade the Regulations by giving, in return for the 1/- ticket of admission, 2 sixpenny tickets for Refreshments.

[. . .] Ruin was staring in their faces by the advances the Saloons have of late made – There was no regular System with the Saloons until the New Act of Parliament came into operation. Most of them did certainly exist, but they did not generally venture upon Dramatic Entertainments – The Magistrates who granted Licences for Music and Dancing never winked at dramatic entertainments at these Saloons.

It was anticipated by the Theatrical Profession that the New Act, that gave them liberty to Act Stage Plays, would benefit the Theatres generally, but the encouragement the Saloons have received under the Act, far counterbalances any good they derive from it [. . .]

Messrs Johnson and Lee allude to the Britannia Saloon – Parties are admitted at the stated Price, or by Order, as the case may be – but they are not allowed to go out of the Premises without paying again should they return to the Saloon, which compels them to take what refreshment they require, upon the Premises.–

Mr Cabell, Publican of the Red Cross Tavern, Bethnal Green, informed Mr Lee, about a month ago, that the Publicans in the neighbourhood of these Saloons were about addressing a Memorial to the Lord Chamberlain against the Saloons, in consequence of their Trade being interfered with.

The Grecian Saloon (Mr Rouse's) is the only respectable Saloon – His is as good and well managed as any Theatre [. . .]

---

[1] Minutes of an interview of Nelson Lee and John Johnson at the Lord Chamberlain's Office concerning their prices of admission. The *Sunday Times* had an article entitled 'The Threepenny Theatres' which appeared on 22 November 1846 (p. 6), in which it drew attention to the lowering of prices at the Standard, Victoria, City of London and Pavilion theatres, whereby now it was possible to attend in the galleries for the sum of 3d. The article listed earlier attempts to attract audiences by lowering prices – Stephen Kemble at Drury Lane and Osbaldiston at Covent Garden – which proved unsuccessful. Lee and Johnson responded on 29 November, calling attention to the advantages that the tavern theatres enjoyed, and the paper wrote a public appeal to the Lord Chamberlain to regulate matters (6 December 1846, p. 5).

[2] Brading was proprietor of the Albert Saloon and contradicted the statement in his interview.

MANAGEMENT AND COMPANY PRACTICES

Many of the old eighteenth-century practices persisted into the nineteenth century, particularly in the provinces. Nevertheless, what differentiates the two periods is the growth of a theatre industry in the early nineteenth century in which speculators played a large part and which saw the commodification of drama. The history of the theatre becomes in part a history of economic investment, of managerial defalcations, cost-cutting and economic strategies, which saw both performers and playwrights suffer. London 'stars' began regular tours of the provinces, often demanding salaries that highlighted the discrepancies between them and those of the resident stock company [**33, 38, 39, 41**]. At the same time provincial managers found themselves coping with an audience demand to see the latest London repertoire, which their physical resources could not sustain [**40**]. The advent of railways in the 1830s, which enabled theatre-goers to travel to London, actors to move easily between centres and entire companies from London to tour the provinces, heralded the demise of the provincial stock companies, beginning in the 1830s [**43**].

In London the changing composition of the audiences and their volatility, often reflective of the political volatility outside of the theatre, brought considerable problems. This is best represented by the OP Riots, which punctuated the opening of the new Covent Garden Theatre in 1809 [**109a–d**]. The growing number of minor theatres in competition with each other as well as with the patent theatres accentuated the search for new dramatic forms that would appeal to audiences whose tastes were fickle and whose sense of their own powers increased markedly during the first thirty years of the nineteenth century.

Managerial cost-cutting measures could most easily be imposed on performers, especially in areas they regarded as their traditional privileges. Performers at the patent theatres had grown accustomed to lengthy periods of regular employment and saw their attachment to the theatres as a secure lifetime career. In 1800 actors at Covent Garden tried to bring pressure on its management to guarantee their rights concerning benefits,[1] access to free tickets,[2] a continuous salary regardless of whether they were actually performing, and assistance with the provision of costuming.[3] Whilst the Lord Chamberlain's response urged a conciliatory process between the parties, it was weighted towards the interests of the proprietors.[4]

[1] Benefit nights formed a significant supplement to a performer's salary. After the theatre's deductions, and dependent on the status of the individual performer, it was customary to pocket either half or all of a night's takings. They became a strategy whereby managements could negotiate a lower salary, holding out the benefit night as a lucrative carrot.

[2] Orders or free ticket entitlement was a system of reward much exploited by managements as well. It enabled them to secure free advertising and to curry favour with influential people. It could, however, be financially disastrous. For the significant numbers of orders on any given night see **22**, **25**, **26**, **28** and E. B. Watson, *From Sheridan to Robertson* (New York: Blom, 1963), pp. 104–5.

[3] Performers maintained a repertoire of character roles and lines of business [**129**] and could legitimately decline to perform outside these parameters.

[4] See also *Dramatic Censor or Weekly Theatrical Report* (10 May 1800), pp. 143–4.

21   The Lord Chamberlain replies to a petition by actors about managerial practices at Covent Garden, 1800

Times (20 February 1800), p. 3

I have read the several Papers submitted to my perusal by the PROPRIETORS of Covent Garden Theatre, and JOHN JOHNSTONE, JOSEPH GEORGE HOLMAN, ALEXANDER POPE, CHARLES INCLEDON, JOSEPH S. MUNDEN, JOHN FAWCETT, THOMAS KNIGHT, and HENRY E. JOHNSTON, Eight of the Performers, and at their request I have taken into consideration the matters in difference between them, upon which my opinion is as follows:

One of the principal matters of complaint, on the part of the Performers, appears to arise from the charge on their Benefits. This, I observe, has been usually settled by particular agreement between them and the Proprietors; and by articles under which many of the Performers are now engaged, such charge is fixed at £140.– But it appears that before the commencement of the present season, notice was given that the charge in future would be £160. Without doubt, therefore, the additional charge cannot vary any prior agreement; but with respect to subsequent engagements, I do not think it unreasonable, on the part of the Proprietors, to stipulate with Performers for the payment of £160, as a fixed charge on their Benefits.

The other objections made to the regulations and conduct of the Proprietors, on the subject of Benefits, do not seem to me to be well founded; but I do recommend to the Proprietors to give a month's notice of Benefit Nights, if that shall be considered by the Performers as more for their advantage than a notice of three weeks.

With respect to Orders, which the Performers claim for admission of their friends to the Theatre, I think it unquestionably must be left to the Proprietors to issue them at such times, and to such extent, and on such terms as they shall think proper.

The Fine for Refusal of a Character, and the Forfeiture of Salary during the illness of a Performer, are very proper subjects of agreement between the parties; and I think the Proprietors act prudently in requiring that what is called the Sick Clause in the Article shall be continued, and in raising the Fine to £30.–But such increased Fine cannot affect prior engagements.

As to the right claimed by the Performers of keeping a cast of characters, and their objection to the Proprietor's right of dismissing them, it appears to me to be absolutely necessary for the good management of the Theatre, that the Proprietors should have the power of dismissing Performers at the expiration of particular engagements; and of employing them, while engaged, in such characters as the Proprietors shall think proper. And I find that the Proprietors disclaim all compact* with Drury-Lane Theatre, for the purpose of precluding a Performer dismissed from one Theatre, from being employed at the other.

The claim of Gloves, Ribbons, etc. ought to be stipulated for by the Performers in their agreements, if they think it material to require a supply of these articles; but they cannot otherwise be expected from the Proprietors.

It is not to be supposed, that the Proprietors will seek unnecessary occasions of closing the Theatre on any nights during the season; but no doubt can be entertained of their right to close the Theatre at such times as they shall think necessary for their own advantage; and such part of the Performer's salary as is made payable each night on which a Theatrical performance shall be exhibited, must, of course, cease when the Theatre is closed.

These are my sentiments on the several subjects of complaint brought forward by the above-named Performers against the Proprietors, from which it appears that in my opinion they are by no means well-founded; but I cannot omit this opportunity of recommending to all parties an oblivion of what has passed in the course of these disputes, being desirous of restoring peace and harmony to a Theatre, which so largely contributes to the amusement of the public.

SALISBURY (L.S.)

Abington-street, May 3, 1800

---

* The PATENT insists, that no Performer belonging to one Theatre, shall be engaged by the other, without the express leave of the *Governor* of the Theatre, from which such Performer secedes.

The large patent theatres were hampered by the need to maintain standing companies for music, drama and ballet. What the figures show is the financial significance of the boxes in relationship to the size of both theatres. When fashionable audiences declined and the boxes emptied, the income from the pit and gallery could not offset this loss. The figures also show the disparity between the salaries of the actor-manager, the group of principal performers and the remainder of the acting company.

22   The costs of running the patent theatres, 1805

Dramatic Censor (12 January 1811), p. 100

The following is said to be a correct statement of what the two Metropolitan theatres would hold, in money and people, in July, 1805.

COVENT GARDEN

	Persons
Boxes, four tiers	1230
Pit	632
Two Shilling Gallery	822
One Shilling Gallery	360
Total Persons when full	3044
In Money, when full, about	600l

When Master BETTY performed *Romeo* at this Theatre, the Receipts in Money were 634l exclusive of Renters' Shares, and Persons on the Free List.

The Nightly Expences [*sic*] were	160l
Average Nightly Receipts during the Season	300l

DRURY LANE

	Persons		l	s	d
Boxes	1828	at 6s	548	8	0
Pit	800	3s 6d	140	0	0
First Gallery	670	2s	67	0	0
Upper Gallery	308	1s	15	8	0
When full	3611	Money	770	16	0

The Boxes were known, on some few particular occasions, to have holden 1,960 persons;– the Pit 930;– the First Gallery 682;– and the Upper Gallery 426.

The expences, including Performers, Lights, Ground-rent, Taxes, and every contingent, were upwards of 200l per night.

THE SALARIES WERE AS UNDER:

	£	s	d
One at	31	10	0
Four at	17	17	0
Four at	15	15	0
Twenty at	10	10	0
Ten at	8	8	0
Ten at	7	7	0
Six at	6	6	0

Six at	5	5	0
Ten at	3	3	0
Ten at	2	2	0
Fifty at	1	11	6
Ten at	1	10	0

Total 740l per week, or about 124l per night.

The Season, in both Theatres, consisted of 35 weeks, or 200 nights.

Even the Haymarket Theatre, which had retained its eighteenth-century tradition that patrons would all attend at first price, was forced to make concessions.[1]

[1] Foote had received his patent in 1766. See Thomas and Hare, *Restoration and Georgian England*, no. 187.

23   The Haymarket introduces a second price, 1811

John Genest, *Some account of the English stage from the Restoration in 1660 to 1830* (10 vols., Bath: Carrington, 1832), vol. VIII, p. 251

Sept 16, 1811 Haymarket. The Public is, with the greatest deference, informed that the Annual License [*sic*] of this theatre is extended to five months, being one month longer than the original grant – in consequence therefore of this protraction, the Proprietors have agreed to venture on receiving *second price*[1] – to establish this without a certainty of loss, those prices are now adopted, which were taken on former and similar occasions – namely, when the house was hired by the DL and CG Managers, and when the chief Proprietor here carried on the performances, on his own account, for the greatest part of the Winter, during the rebuilding of the late DL theatre – the only departure from these precedents will be that the second price to the pit will be sixpence *less* – First price – boxes 6s – pit 3s – first Gallery 2s – upper Gallery 1s – Second price – boxes 3s – pit 1s 6d – first Gallery 1s – upper Gallery 6d.

With the above exceptions second price had never been taken at the Hay. from the time of Foote's Patent.

[1] 'First price' designated the amount payable at the commencement of the evening's entertainment. 'Second price' was intended to attract those who were either unable to pay the full price or whose work or dining habits prevented them from attending earlier.

24   The costs of hiring an equestrian troop, 1811

Dramatic Censor (19 February 1811), p. 156

The Equestrian Commandant is to share equally with the Histrionic Chiefs, after 250l each night: which, as the theatre now holds between seven and 800l will probably leave a nightly profit to the gentlemen of the stable of 250 guineas; who are likewise to have 50l per night, provided the Managers should think fit to play any other after-piece than *Blue Beard*[1] [. . .]

[1] George Colman's *Blue Beard; or, Female Curiosity* had first appeared at Drury Lane in 1798. The introduction of Astley's horses in 1811, by which the patent theatre was seen to be emulating the example of the minor theatres, caused a furore but contributed to Covent Garden's most profitable season. Frederick Reynolds refers to the 1810/11 season as the Theatre's 'largest annual receipt', with £21,000 taken in 'the first forty-one nights of *Blue Beard*' (*The life and times of Frederick Reynolds* (London: Colburn, 1827; 2 vols., reprinted New York: Blom, 1969, pp. 403–4). See also Clifford Leech and T. W. Craik, *The Revels history of drama in English* (London: Methuen, 1975), vol. VI, p. 31.

Samuel Whitbread, whose efforts had largely been responsible for Drury Lane's reconstruction nearly three years after its destruction by fire, made a public statement on the contentious issue of free admissions on 9 December 1812.[1]

[1] Oulton commented that the theatre kept a register of those entitled to free admissions and this had to be personally signed 'previous to their entrance into the theatre'.

25   The policy of free admissions to the theatre, 1812

Oulton, *History of the theatres*, vol. I, p. 249

'On the subject of free-admissions: in departing from customs which had grown into great abuse, they trust it will be found they have acted with propriety – They have it not in their power to admit any claim of right to free-admission, without proof of its legality; and they have granted as much indulgence as they thought their duty permitted.

To the proprietors of other theatres, and to authors, as their performances are acted, or may be brought out at Drury Lane; to the higher classes of the members of the present theatrical company; and to the eminent survivors of former companies, retired from the stage, they have thought themselves justified in offering free admissions, and doubt not the approbation of the subscribers. Nor do they think any objection can be taken to the facility they have been desirous of affording to fair and open criticism, by the tender of free-admissions to the London journals, to the extent proffered, of two free-admissions to each newspaper. The persons availing themselves of such proffer, of course, conforming to the regulations established for the government of free-admissions whatever.

These offers of free-admissions to the gentlemen connected with the daily and weekly press, have in some instances been accepted; in other cases refused, with expressions of good-will, on the grounds of that mutual and amicable independence on which it so desirable the national theatres and the press should stand; in a few cases they have been rejected, with marks of dissatisfaction [. . .]'

COVENT GARDEN AND DRURY LANE: COMPARATIVE
INCOME FIGURES

Comparative figures show that Drury Lane was doing very badly in relation to Covent
Garden. The equestrian troop that accompanied Colman's *Blue Beard* easily outshone the
appearance of Edmund Kean at Drury Lane.[1] The figures again show the importance of
the boxes in terms of receipts and the large number of free seats given to actors and to
shareholders.

[1] According to the General Account (Ledgers of Covent Garden Theatre, BL Add. MSS 29637) this was
only the fourth occasion in a month when receipts had been as high. Nevertheless, the situation at
Drury Lane was far worse. Its smallest receipt during the entire 1816 season was on 10 December,
when the house takings amounted to £64.3.6. It would average £151.3.6 per night, with a nightly
free list of 567 (see receipts of performances at Drury Lane Theatre, BL Add. MSS 29711).

26 Tally sheets for Covent Garden and Drury Lane, 16 December 1816

Enthoven Collection, Theatre Museum, Covent Garden and Drury Lane boxes

(a) Covent Garden, 1816

1816	*Monday 16th December*								*71st Night*	
	Guy Mannering with Blue Beard[1]									
Total No.	FIRST ACCOUNT	£	s	d	Total No.	Latter Account		£	s	d
	Boxes	No. Paid				Boxes	No. Paid			
207	Haselar	176			86	Haselar	78	13	13	
148	Maynard	148			208	Maynard	208	36	8	
454	Glew	156			163	Glew	139	24	6	6
809		480	150	10	457		425			
	Pit					Pit				
216	Roberts	215			12	Roberts	12	1	4	
185	Cole	182								
182	Few	182			23	Cole	23	2	6	
583		579	101	6	6	35		35			
	Gal.					Gal.				
139	Tapsel	132			38	Tapsel	38	1	18	
149	Strahan	142			59	Strahan	59	2	19	
288		274	27	8	97		97			

	Up. Gal.						Up. Gal.				
184	Little	184	9	4		60	Little	60	1	10	
1864		1467	288	8	6	649		617	84	4	6
	1st Acct.										
649	2d Acct.	617	84	4	6						
2513	Total	2084	372	13							

Renters, Tontine, Liberty & Cards					Orders					
		Number	Value				Number	Value		
			£	s				£	s	d
Boxes	1st Acct.	283	99	1	Boxes	1st Acct.	96	33	12	
	2d Do.	32	5	12		2d Do.				
Pit	1st Acct.	4		14	Pit	1st Acct.				
	2d Do.				Pit	2d Do.				
Gal.	1st Acct				Gal.	1st Acct.	14	1	8	
	2d Do.					2d Do.				
Up. Gall.					Up. Gal.	1st Acct.				
			£105	7				£35		
	Receipt		£372	13	Paid					
					Duke of			12	9	6
					Cambridge. Half a yrs					
					Dividend to					
					Michaelmas					
	After Money]		4	9						
	14th Inst]									
					Mr Coutts			12	9	6
					Do. to Do.					
					Mr Millar			12	9	6
					Do. to Do.					
	Private Box		3	3						
			£380	5						
			3	3						
			£383	8						

(b) Drury Lane, 1816

16th. Decr. 1816   ***71st Night***

Iron Chest & Robin Hood[2]

	First Account						Second Account					
	Free	Paid	Passes	£	s	d	Free	Paid	Passes	£	s	d
Paid in Boxes		192		67	4			135		23	12	6
New Renter's Nominee	33						55					
Subscription Nominee	10						5					
Free Privilege	10						17					
In Boxes	53	192		67	4		77	135		23	12	6
Passed to Boxes			1		3	6			30	2	5	
Paid in Pit		452		79	2			134		13	8	
New Renter's Nominee	16						8					
Subscription Nominee	3						1					
In Pit	19	452		79	5	6	9	134		15	13	
Passed to Pit			7		10	6			1		1	
Passed to Boxes												
Paid in Gallery		105		10		6		75		3	15	
In 2s. Gallery		105		11		6		75		3	16	
Passed to Boxes												
Passed to Pit									1		1	6
Passed to 2s. Gallery			4		4				9		4	6
Paid Upper Gallery		151		7	11			122		3	1	
In Upper Gallery		151		7	15			122		3	7	
	72	900		165	5		86	466		46	8	6

	£	s	d
Nights Receipt	211	13	6
Brought forward	12992	12	6
Total	13104	12	6

Orders:

Rae	137
W [Winston]	96
	233

Tickets:

Kean	38	Kelly	2
Cooke	4	G. Wood	2
Dowton	2	Spring	6
Munden	2	Ward	7
Johnstone	1	Bartley	2
Oxberry	2	Bland	2
Knight	2	Richardson	2

	Holland	2		Davison	2
	Horn	2		F. M. Kelly	2
	Pyne	1		Palmer	2
					86
				N Papers	61
					380
Pit Orders					
	Rae	2			
	N Papers	10			
		12			
Gallery Orders				(Sgd) E. Warren	
	Rae	48			
	Tickets	20			
		68			

---

[1] See **152** and **159**. Daniel Terry had adapted Walter Scott's *Guy Mannering; or, the Gipsey's Prophecy* for Covent Garden (12 March 1816).

[2] George Colman's *The Iron Chest* had first been performed at Drury Lane on 12 March 1796. Edmund Kean played the part of Mortimer on this occasion. It was also the first night of MacNally's *Robin Hood; or, Sherwood Forest*.

In order to make more money managements also adopted a number of strategies to accommodate changes in dining habits by more fashionable members of the audience.

27   An attempt to run two performance sessions at the Lyceum, 1817

Times (22 September 1817), p. 3[1]

Ladies and gentlemen,

The depressed state of all theatrical property, and the obvious decline of public interest in the once favourite amusements of the drama, are increasing evils, which have been ascribed by various conjectures to various causes. To comment generally on these would in this place be impertinent; but, amongst others a large portion of the public have advanced that the early hour of commencing the performances, renders it impossible to attend an amusement which interferes with the late hours of dinner, or the protracted hours of business; and a no less considerable body of the community have complained, that the late hours to which the representations of the stage are extended, materially derange the ordinary habits of life to which they are accustomed. All parties, however, have agreed in condemning, as with one voice, the length of theatrical performances, in which the attention of the auditors can rarely be kept alive during a period of at least five hours; and never without fatigue both of body and mind.

In some degree, to remedy the evil complained of by those whose habits of life or avocations would not permit their early attendance at theatres, the custom of taking half-price was introduced. But it must be obvious to every one, that this plan has been found incompetent to its object. Many persons who would be desirous to witness the early part of a performance, are indisposed to pay the price of a whole evening's entertainment for that portion of it only which they can enjoy; and it may reasonably be supposed, that thousands who might wish to enter the theatre at a later hour (as at the usual time of second price) are wholly excluded by the certainty of finding the best seats occupied. Thus, numberless persons, from the one or the other cause, are deterred from frequenting the amusements of the stage.

Long experience and much reflection on these contending difficulties, have suggested to the proprietor of this theatre a mode of reconciling them. It is obvious, that to accommodate one principal class of the patrons of theatres, the performances must commence at an early hour; and to gratify another no less important class, they must be continued to a late one: and as the man of leisure cannot be induced to forego his present habits of dining at the old English supper time; and as the man of business, and other persons of early and domestic pursuits, cannot be prevailed upon to abridge their hours of *sleep*, in order to compliment with their company the performance of a midnight melo-drama, it is become necessary, to the interests (if not the very existence) of theatres, that some measure should be adopted to meet the wishes and tastes of both classes, on whom their prosperity so immediately depends.

With this view, it is proposed, as an experiment, for the few remaining nights of this season, to try the plan (so novel to a regular theatre) of dividing every evening's entertainment into two distinct parts or performances. Each performance to consist of a full three-act opera; or of a short opera, with a ballet, or a musical entertainment.

The first performance (the doors to open at half-past five) to begin at six o'clock precisely, and to last till about nine.

The second performance to begin at half-past nine, and to conclude at twelve.

Although, as the entertainments of theatres have increased in length, it has never been proposed, on that account, to increase the price of admission; yet now that it is intended to limit their duration, it is respectfully and cheerfully proposed that the following reductions shall take place: the price of admission to either performance will be, Boxes 3s – Pit 2s – Gal. 1s – Up. Gal. 6d.

The boxes and places will be taken for either performance; and the grand saloon, with its admired decorations, will be appropriated, by a new arrangement, to the use of the company visiting the boxes at the second performance, and as a promenade for the company to wait for their carriages, on leaving the boxes at the conclusion of the early entertainments [. . .]

---

[1]   The Haymarket company was performing at the Lyceum. Bartley, the acting manager [**48b**] addresses the audience after the performance on Saturday 20 Sept.

THE HAYMARKET THEATRE'S ACCOUNTS

The 1820 season was the last under the management of George Colman the Younger of the old Haymarket theatre, which was originally built in 1766. The new theatre would reopen in July 1821 [69].

28   Haymarket Theatre accounts

Enthoven Collection, Theatre Museum Haymarket box

(a) Tally sheet, 31 July 1820[1]

The Beggars Opera, The Actor of All Work, with The Travellers Benighted[2]

Theatre-Royal, Hay-Market

1820			31st July			nineteenth Night	
Total No.		No. Paid		£	s	Orders	
403	Boxes	315	Mr Pearce	78	15	Mr Morris order	52
			Odd Money		10	Mr O'Keefes do	2
						Mr Terrys do	6
						Liberty list	2
						Debentures	8
						News Cards	14
						Mr Morris's do	1
						Performers	2
							88
264	Pit	239	Mr Slyth	35	17	Mr Morris' orders	11
			Odd money		6	News cards	2
						from the boxes	3
						Do. 1st Gallery	6
							22
145	Gallery	93	Mr Owers	9	6	Mr Morris's orders	45
			Odd money		7	from the Up. Gally	7
							52
177	Upper G.	165	Mr Stabler	8	5	Mr Morris's orders	12
						ORDERS	
						Boxes 88	22
						Pit 25	3	15
						Gallery 52	5	4
						Upper Gally. 12	12
989		812		133	6		

		£	s	£	s
Receiv'd after	the account was Clos'd		10	31	11
	After Money	3	9		
	Receipt	£137	5	137	5
		Total Receipts		£168	16

(b) Receipts for July 1820[3]

Account of Receipts and Disbursements of the Treasurer of the Hay Market Theatre from 10th to 31st of July 1820 both inclusive

Receipts				Disbursements				
1820				1820				
July	10	Receipt	76	5	July	10	The Annual Dinner	£13	13	
	11	do	40	17		15	Weekly Bills	38	13	9
	12	do	80	18			Nightly and Weekly}			
	13	do	71	8			Salaries of Performers}	188	18	4
	14	do	67	10			Servants & Band}			
	15	do	68	18		22	Weekly Bills	29	0	11
	17	do	110	12			Nightly and Weekly}			
	18	do	130	3			Salaries of Performers}	265	3	4
	19	do	139	—			Servants & Band}			
	20	do	123	16		29	Weekly Bills	39	15	10
		6 Debentures sold at}					Weekly salaries of}			
		£4..4.. each Nr 1,2,3,4,5,6}	25	4			Performers Servants}	268	18	6
	21	Receipt	103	13			and Band}			
	22	do	243	9						
	24	do	210	6				£844	3	8
	25	do	177	3						
	26	do	165	11			*A Copy of this sent to Mr Winston*			
	27	do	171	6			1st August 1820			
	28	do	161	3						
	29	do	47	15						
		3 Debentures sold at}						E. Pritchard		
		£4..4..each No.7,8,9}	12	12						
	31	do	137	5						
		£	2434	14						
			Errors				Excepted			

---

[1] It should be noted that although it was a large house on Monday 31 July, the free orders amounted in value to nearly a quarter of the entire box office income. The monies received show that only 812 out of 989 patrons actually paid.

[2] George Colman the Younger's *The Actor of All Work* had first been licensed at the Haymarket in August 1817, while *The Travellers Benighted* (an anonymous adaptation of M. G. Lewis's *Raymond and Agnes*) had first appeared there in September 1811.

[3] Despite the orders, the management made a profit of £1590 during the month of July.

Given the success of the minor theatres, especially those such as the Olympic in the heartland of the West End, in attracting audiences, and their relative impunity from prosecution, managers of patent theatres were at their wits' end in their attempts to find ways to reduce their operating costs. In a memorial to Sir Robert Peel, dated 17 March 1833, Alfred Bunn pleaded for government funding as the only means to help the patent theatres out of their financial difficulties.[1]

¹ Peel declined to support Bunn's request in a letter of 18 March 1835 quoted in the same volume, (p. 233).

29   Alfred Bunn petitions the Secretary of State, 1833

A. Bunn, *Stage, both before and behind*, vol. 1, p. 231

The Humble Memorial of Alfred Bunn, Lessee of the Theatres Royal Drury Lane and Covent Garden, to the Right Honourable Sir Robert Peel, His Majesty's Secretary of State, etc., etc., etc.

Sheweth,

That every effort which the knowledge and enterprise of the most experienced and celebrated professors of the dramatic art have used to support the national theatres, with a taste and splendour required by this vast metropolis, have for a series of years totally failed, involving the respective parties in irretrievable ruin.

That the humble exertions of your memorialist in uniting the two patent theatres, though they have been highly approved of by the public, and have tended in a great degree to reduce the probability of those frightful losses sustained by his predecessors, have nevertheless been frustrated by the general want of patronage; and as such undertaking was considered the only means of saving the two properties, these expectations have been defeated, your memorialist is reduced to the necessity of finally closing these national establishments.

That not only is the general spirit of the country essentially undramatic, but that these theatres are still further unprotected by the thorough discountenance of the wealthy nobility and gentry, who in other European Kingdoms have annual private boxes in all their principal theatres.

That in addition to such patronage, the leading theatres of France, Italy, and Germany, receive permanent support from their respective governments, and one theatre in Paris alone is given rent free to the lessee, together with an annual grant of 30,000l.

That as the only possible means of preventing the immediate closing of these buildings, and the probable ruin of hundreds, your memorialist humbly prays that some grant from the Treasury may be extended to their support, and to prevent such aid being cavilled at, your memorialist is prepared to point out those plans by which the public might participate in the amusements to the extent to which they thereby would thus contribute.

In 1834 Francis Place examined the income and expenditure of the patent theatres, especially Covent Garden since its rebuilding in 1809, and demonstrated that audiences were no longer capable of sustaining the large patent theatres. He took particular issue with the Covent Garden proprietors' evidence at the Select Committee hearings in 1832, which sought to preserve their special prerogatives.

30   Large patent theatres are no longer viable, 1834

F. P. [Francis Place], *Monthly Magazine* (March 1834), p. 364 f.

Mr Harris [. . .] says that, when he gave up the theatre to Messrs [Charles] Kemble, Willett, and Forbes in 1821, the floating debt was 60,000l. Captain Forbes, in his evidence before the House of Commons' Committee, shows that it is now 84,000l, and, consequently, that 24,000l have been added to it. Mr Kemble in his evidence says, 'within the last few years we ourselves have advanced 30,000l; three of the proprietors alone have done it within the last ten years.'

Here, then, are the sums of 24,000l and 30,000l, to which must be added the voluntary subscription in 1829, not less probably than 3000l; and thus the money sunk, lost, and gone cannot be less than 57,000l, which is equal on an average of 5,700l for each of the ten seasons [1821–31].

Mr Harris shows that during the first twelve seasons there was an annual income beyond expenses, exclusive of interest, etc. of	£13,500
Captain Forbes and Mr Kemble show that there was no such income during the last ten seasons, but there was an annual defalcation of	5,700
Making an average difference against the last ten seasons of	£19,200

Captain Forbes [. . .] says, 'I merely state facts. The loss has been 20,000l a year since 1820.' This the captain attributes to the minors intercepting the money on its way to the majors [. . .] The captain says the minors take 40,000l a year from the majors, and he puts down a loss of 40,000l a year to that one cause. The captain indiscreetly proves too much, if he proves anything; for, were his statement correct, it would be conclusive evidence that the public have countenanced the smaller theatres, and abandoned the two large ones to their fate.

Captain Forbes says that the average loss of the last ten seasons is	£20,000
Mr Robertson [treasurer of Covent Garden under Harris] shows that the average net income of the first twelve seasons was	66,289
Captain Forbes shows that the average income of the last three seasons was	44,666
Annual difference	£21,623

It has been shown, from Mr Harris's statements, that during the twelve first seasons [1809–1821] the house was not on average much more than half filled with spectators. Applying the same rule to the three last seasons alluded to by Captain Forbes, it appears that the sum received on each night averaged 240l, which is 116l less than was received on an average during the first twelve seasons; but the house will hold 650l, and consequently it was not quite two-fifths, and considerably less than half filled [. . .]

31   Bunn tries to run the two patent theatres simultaneously, 1834

G. Raymond, *The life and enterprises of Robert William Elliston, comedian* (London: Routledge, 1857), p. 233

The managerial scheme was to work the two theatres with a company and a half. The actors who had performed in the play at one house, were usually required to bear a part in the farce at the other. Broad Court and Martlett Buildings, from about half past nine at night, to a quarter from ten, exhibited a most extraordinary scene!

Actors half attired, with enamelled faces, and loaded with the paraphernalia of their art, were passing and repassing [. . .] whilst the hurried interchange of quaint words – 'stage waits' – 'music on' – 'rung up', etc., would have perplexed the stranger with a thousand surmises. Double-basses, trombones, long drums, books, and wearing apparel carried on the heads of figure-dancers, apparently just started from their beds [. . .]

At the season of Christmas, when the state of alterations was at its height, the female figure-dancers pattered from one house to another six times during the evening, and underwent the operation of dressing and undressing no less than eight.

THE PERFORMER: OBLIGATIONS AND REWARDS

Conditions for actors were little different from those that existed in the late eighteenth century,[1] although the movement of London actors seeking provincial employment, especially during the summer, threatened to swamp local acting companies and could create considerable misunderstandings.

The following conditions of employment were attached to all agreements between Elliston and his performers in the early nineteenth century. Elliston had taken over the ailing Olympic Theatre from Astley, opening it under his management on 19 April 1813, and relinquishing it when he became manager of Drury Lane in 1819.[2]

[1] See Thomas and Hare, *Restoration and Georgian England*, nos. 198, 199, 200.
[2] See C. Murray, *Robert William Elliston, Manager* (London: STR, 1975), chapter 3 [**35**].

32   Conditions of employment at the Olympic Theatre, 1813–18

BL, Theatre Cuttings 47–48 Olympic Theatre

I. EVERY Lady and Gentleman to attend rehearsals punctually. One Quarter of an Hour will be allowed for the difference of Clocks. If absent after that time to be fined One Shilling. For Non-attendance during rehearsal Five Shillings. If through wilful neglect, One Night's Salary. Inattention or neglect during such Rehearsal or Rehearsals, for each offence One Shilling.

II. Any Performer performing imperfectly, after a sufficient time allowed, shall forfeit Five Shillings.

III. Any Performer introducing improper jokes; neglecting or omitting any part of the Evening's performance (without the Manager's consent); or for inattention or improper behaviour on the Stage, during any part of the Entertainments, to forfeit One Guinea.

IV. Any Performer refusing to play any Part or Parts, Character or Characters, which are appointed them by the Manager, or the Deputy-Manager, to fine One Week's Salary. If the Performer refuses to play the Part a second time, the forfeit or discharge of the party to be at the option of the Manager.

V. Making Stage business stand, or not coming on at the proper entrance, Five Shillings.

VI. Any Performer standing between the wings, in sight of the Audience, or talking so loud as to interrupt the business of the Stage, to fine Half-a-Crown. If any Performer brings any friend or relation, or suffers their servant to stand behind the Scenes, they will be fined a Week's Salary.

VII. Should any of the Performers absent themselves at Night from their duty in the Theatre, or refuse doing the business or Parts allotted them, on any pretence whatever (real illness excepted), such Performer so neglecting to be fined, or discharged, at the option of the Manager.

VIII. Any Performer doing the business of another, or any Part thereof, without the consent of the Manager, each party to be fined a Week's Salary.

IX. All Dresses will be regulated and approved by the Acting manager. Any Performer making any alteration to such dresses, or refusing to wear them, shall forfeit One Guinea.

X. No excuse can be taken from any Person appearing in Liquor on the Stage; but should any Performer be capable of the crime, they shall forfeit One Week's Salary; or if such conduct is repeated, to be at the option of the Manager to discharge such Performer.

XI. Quarrelling in any part of the Theatre, if to the interruption of a Rehearsal or Business on the Stage, the offending parties shall forfeit One Guinea each; but if a blow be given, the striker shall forfeit his Week's Salary.

XII. Any Person playing tricks with the Properties, Dresses, or any other Article belonging to the Evening's Exhibition, shall forfeit Five Shillings; and if any of the Properties, Dresses, or any Thing appertaining to the Theatre, be wilfully or negligently destroyed, the full value of the same shall be paid for by the Person found guilty of the offence.

XIII. Any one neglecting to deliver up the Properties he or she may have occasion to use, in the course of the Evening's Performances, to the Property-man, shall forfeit Five Shillings, except he or she be a principal Performer, and their attention to the Stage Business prevents them; in that case, the Dressers to be answerable, and subject to the same penalty.

XIV. Every Performer must attend Half an Hour before the time specified for the commencement of the Evening's Entertainments, except in case of illness, or other casualty, or fine from Half-a-Crown to One Guinea. If he or she occasions the Stage to wait for them, the same fine.

XV. Any Person advertising, or causing to be advertised, or printing, or causing to be printed, any Bill of Entertainment for this Theatre, without the consent of the Manager previously obtained in writing, shall forfeit the sum of Five Guineas.

XVI. Any Performer or Person belonging to the Company, disposing of his or their Benefit, or Benefits, or any Part or Parts thereof, or permitting Tickets to be issued in any name or names, but his or theirs, or allowing any part of the Receipts or Emoluments arising from such Benefit or benefits, or any Part or Parts thereof, to be for the use of any public or private measure, or any Person or Persons whatever, without the consent of the Manager, in writing, first had and obtained, shall forfeit Fifty Pounds Sterling.

XVII. If the prompter shall be guilty of any neglect in his office, or does not return such Performers as are subject to forfeits for non-observance of any Rules or Regulations of this Theatre, he shall forfeit from One Shilling to One Guinea.

XVIII. Performers are expected, in the Articles they themselves provide, such as Stockings, Dancing Pumps, Stage Jewels, Feather, etc., to be correspondently neat and clean, under the forfeiture of from One Shilling to One Guinea; and to adhere strictly to dressing their Characters, through the run of a Piece, in exact conformity to the original Dress determined on by the Acting Manager.

XIX. Any Performer or Person belonging to the Company, who shall, on any pretence whatever, tear or make holes in the Green Curtain, shall forfeit from Half-a-Crown to One Guinea; and any one climbing up to the Balcony Box, or disfiguring the Stage Doors, or any part thereof, either during the Performance, or at any other period, to forfeit from Half-a-Crown to One Guinea.

XX. Any Performer wearing a part of their Dress under their own Clothes, or the Dress appertaining to another Character, they may have to perform in the course of the Night, or in any Piece they do not belong, to forfeit from One Shilling to One Guinea.

Relations between actors and managers were often strained, not only by the desire on both parts to make money but also by an ignorance about local conditions on the part of metropolitan actors. In 1818 Junius Brutus Booth brought an action against T. Wilson

Manley, the manager of a circuit that included Stamford, for breach of contract. Manley had suggested a visit of two nights; in the event Booth performed on neither and sued for compensation and expenses.[1]

[1] On Manley, see **43** and Sybil Rosenfeld, 'The theatrical notebooks of T. H. Wilson Manley', *Theatre Notebook*, 7 (1952), pp. 2–12. Booth (1796–1860) had made his Covent Garden début in 1816 and had played opposite Edmund Kean in 1817. He would leave for the United States in 1821. He was known for his inveterate ability to disappoint audiences by not appearing at his scheduled performances.

33   Misunderstandings between a provincial manager and a London performer: T. Wilson Manley and Junius Brutus Booth, 1818

Theatrical Inquisitor and Monthly Mirror (January–June 1818), p. 414

Theatrical Law Report, Court of King's Bench, June 17.

Mr Adolphus, for the plaintiff, represented to the Court and Jury, that in consequence of the celebrity obtained by his client on the London boards, Mr Manley, desirous to increase the popularity of his Theatre, and treat his auditory with a *dish* of novelty from the metropolis, wrote a friendly letter to Mr Booth, for the purpose of inducing him to come down and perform two nights, if practicable, consistently with his engagements at Covent Garden. This letter, dated the 7th March, was as follows:

'My dear Sir, – This is our fair-time – we fill good houses without stars – better with them. Come and play Tuesday 10th, and Wednesday 11th, and share half after 10l each night. It may be 25l or 30l; nay more – just as they bite! And there ends our bargain. If you say *aye*, wrap it up in a letter – if *no* – adieu! "And for my love, I pray you wrong me not." – *Shaksp.* – Iago, Sir Giles, or Richard III.

Yours,   T. W. MANLEY

To J. B. Booth, Esq.'

This letter was received by the Plaintiff on Saturday; and on Monday he answered, closing with the offer, and requesting the defendant to secure him a lodging. He went to Stamford accordingly, and arrived in time to play one of the parts above mentioned on Tuesday 10th March; but to his great surprise, he found that he had not been announced in the bills: on the contrary, *Rugantino*, and *The Wedding Day*, had been fixed as the entertainments of the evening. He made his appearance at the theatre, but he was told that he could not play, but might go home to his lodgings. He inquired if he were to perform tomorrow night; but it was answered, that it did not suit the manager that he should. The plaintiff, however, remained for two days in Stamford, doing nothing, but ready if called upon; and when the time for which he could be absent had expired, he paid for his lodging, and returned to his engagement at Covent Garden. The cause of this disapprobation was soon apparent: – the Marquis of Exeter, a greater *star* [. . .] than Mr Booth, had commanded the pieces on the night in question, and the manager and proprietor, the defendant, was quite satisfied that the house would be well filled: he became, therefore, quite indifferent to, and independent of, the plaintiff, who, if he had remained in Stamford, would probably have attracted but a comparatively small company, for the play-going disposition of the town would be nearly satisfied by the two nights when the Marquis was there [. . .]

Lord Ellenborough, however, was of opinion, that as Mr Manley had stipulated in his proposal that Mr Booth should come down in time for all arrangements necessary to his performance of the parts mentioned, Iago, Sir Giles Overreach, and Richard, on the two nights mentioned, namely the 9th and 10th of March; and as Mr Booth had so arranged matters as not to be there until seven in the evening of the first night, and as he agreed only to the performance of the two first-mentioned characters, and referred the part of Richard for subsequent consideration, he had not closed with the precise terms of the bargain proposed by Mr Manley; he could not, therefore, hold the defendant to those precise terms. Had he been a man of the world, he would have waited Mr Manley's answer by return of post to his own modification of the bargain; but having objected to the precise terms of Mr Manley's letter, he could not hold the latter to the engagement [. . .]

Nellie Tree, a dancer performing at Sadler's Wells during the summer recess of the patent theatres, wrote to the Drury Lane treasurer James Winston, seeking re-employment at Drury Lane for the 1819/20 season at a higher salary, but was forced to settle for her former terms of employment.

34   A performer negotiates, 1819

BL, Percival Collection, vol. 4, ffos. 104, 106

(a) Nellie Tree writes to James Winston

Sir,

For the last four seasons I have been the Columbine of Drury Lane Theatre, and I have also filled the situation of principal serious dancer with the privilege of orders and the first green room for three pounds per week, the terms I received on my *first* becoming a member of the Establishment.

I was last year aprised [*sic*] that my salary was considered inadequate to my exertions in the Theatre, and that my new engagement should be more advantageous –

My salary at Sadler's Wells is *six* pounds per week; I do not name this as a guide to any proposal I may be honour'd with, as I should prefer leaving to you the naming the terms upon which Mr Elliston would be pleased to receive me as the Columbine and principal serious dancer of Drury Lane Theatre –

May I Sir request the favor of an early reply, as my winter arrangements will, of course, be shaped by the communication you may do me the honor to make –

I remain Sir

Your obliged and obedient sevt.

N. Tree
Sadler's Wells Theatre
Aug. 10, 1819

To J. Winston Esq. T.R.D.L.

(b) Nellie Tree accepts her terms of employment

Miss Tree begs to acknowledge with her best thanks the receipt of Mr Winston's polite note; she will be happy to accept the same salary and privileges she has hitherto received *as Principal Dancer* and *Columbine*, and will hold herself engaged *upon such* terms at Drury Lane Theatre for the ensuing season –

Sadler's Wells Theatre
August 21 1819
To Mr Winston, Esq.
T.R.D.L.

After serious mismanagement, which had left Drury Lane with a debt of £90,922, the proprietors agreed to confirm Elliston as lessee in 1819. He had enjoyed a successful term as manager of the Olympic Theatre and was determined to impose a policy of cost-efficiency, especially as it affected the performers.[1]

[1] See Murray, *Elliston*, pp. 84–116.

35   Elliston takes over Drury Lane, 1819

J. Cowell, *Thirty years passed among the players in England and America* (New York: Harper, 1845), p. 71

Elliston took the reins under very different auspices. He was the lessee, and literally uncontrolled, and a long and distinguished favourite with the public; his nature too, admirably fitting him not to allow old friendships, humanity, or kindness of heart to interfere with his interests. His theatre, to use his own expression, was not 'intended as an hospital for invalids'; all the old servants of the public were, therefore, discharged, or those only retained on salaries graded to the extreme of what their abject necessities obliged them to accept. For years the manager of the Surrey and the Olympic, he brought with him the experience purchased in that school to add to his admitted knowledge of the legitimate drama, and followed by crowds of the *utile*, who, for the honour of belonging to Drury Lane, would act for little salary, or none at all; always ready, and possessed, in an unequalled degree, of the fascinating power of persuading the public to anything he wished, he took the direction of the theatre with the best possible chance of success – for a time, at any rate [. . .]

At the same time, in order to outbid his rivals, Elliston offered large salaries to starring actors, a practice that only served to emphasize the discrepancies between leading performers and the rest of the company.

36   Competition for stars, 1821

Bunn, *Stage, both before and behind*, vol. i, pp. 21–2

Mr Elliston, in one respect, laid the foundations of a system which has conduced to the destruction of the patent theatres [. . .] to a greater extent than the act of any other individual has been able to achieve. In the season of 1821/2, Mr Liston was engaged at Covent Garden theatre, on a weekly salary of 17l, with an additional 7l for his wife, and in a fit of discontent he sought from the proprietors a slight addition. Mr Elliston having ascertained there was some hesitation in their according this addition, stepped forward, and offered him 50l per week, which the comedian instantly accepted. Up to this period there had been an understanding between the two theatres, that no performer, engaged at one house, should be qualified to engage at the other, without undergoing a year's absence from the metropolis, and that the dramatic pieces produced at the one should not be represented at the other establishment. Mr Elliston broke through both these understandings; first, by employing Mr Liston, and then by bringing him forward in *Guy Mannering, Rob Roy*, etc., etc., dramas considered, by purchase and general outlay on their original production, to belong to the rival theatre.

At the other end of the spectrum from the stars, some of the worst treated performers were the chorus and *corps de ballet* at the Opera or at the patent theatres, though their work formed an integral part of the repertoire. It was rare for a class action to be taken.

37   Female chorus singers win a financial discrimination case, 1826

Times (18 July 1826), p. 3

Signor Baptista Velluti was proceeded against by the female chorus singers of the King's Theatre, to recover the sum of 1l. each, for work and labour done, by singing for him on the night of his benefit [. . .]

[. . .] They were engaged by Mr Ebers [the manager] to sing during the season, but they had concluded their engagements before the benefit of Signor Velluti arrived. About a month before this time, Mr Rubbi, the master of the chorus singers, having assembled them all, male and female, in the Green-room, read a letter to them from Mr Velluti, promising them one guinea each if they performed their parts well [. . .] The night arrived, and it was acknowledged that they performed their parts well. The gentlemen chorus singers had been paid, but the ladies had been refused [. . .]

Mr DUBOIS [the magistrate] [. . .] considered that the terms of the letter might be taken to mean the choristers generally; and, though the masculine gender was particularly referred to [. . .] the others [. . .] were included in the term [. . .]

The learned JUDGE decided, that the ladies having performed the labour, were entitled to the reward.

[. . .] It appears that, according to the system of the large theatres, of screwing down the salaries of the minor performers, in order to give enormous sums to the principals, the choristers had been paid during the first part of the season at 5s 2^1/$_2$d per night, or 11s 7d per week, out of which they had to buy shoes, gloves, and flowers, adapted to the costume of the various characters; they had for some months to attend the rehearsals every day, half-past nine to five; on some days dress was to be found them, but was often neglected, and they were seen performing the characters of Grecian virgins in the dresses of Spanish peasants, etc.; and petticoats of such extraordinary brevity, that they might have been mistaken for kilts, were sent to them from the wardrobe. In the course of the season Signor Velluti interceded for the gentlemen, and obtained an advance of their salary to 15s per night. The ladies struck – Madame Pasta interceded for them – and obtained the enormous advance of 1s 2^1/$_2$d, making altogether 7s per night [. . .]

Speculation was as common in the provinces as in London. It was all too easy for a manager to lease an ailing theatre, and to gather a group of people together on the promise of a share in box office receipts. As the document below points out, there were hidden costs that allowed the manager to appropriate monies for his own use.

38   Unscrupulous managers and provincial sharing companies in the 1820s

R. Dyer, *Nine years of an actor's life* (London: Longman, Rees, 1833), pp. 127–8

The number of petty managers who infest all parts of this country are incalculable, and of course the number of persons employed by them is proportionately great; but they only increase the eleemosynary population, and do no service to society either by their industry or by example. For such persons the treadmill has no terrors, because they boldly enter towns where the cautionary notice is displayed, that 'All vagrants found begging in this borough will be apprehended.' I never encountered but one manager of the speculative class, and he had engaged an expensive company without the means to pay his first week's salaries; and finally left his tradesmen and performers to regret their connexion with a swindler. The miseries of a sharing scheme, the lowest of all theatrical speculations, never fell to my lot; but they have been described to me in most lively colours. A person who is in possession of sundry scenes and dresses calls himself a manager, and fits up a theatre. He then collects his adventurers, and the probable receipts are agreed to be shared amongst them. Out of each night's receipts the expense of rent, printing, and lighting, is first taken; and the remainder is divided in equal shares, SIX of *which* go to the liquidation of the stock debt – FOUR to the manager – and one each to the company. This *stock debt*, incurred for the original outlay, is never acknowledged to be paid by the manager, as in fact it constitutes his authority; for a contumacious actor is made obedient when the stock debt is advanced as a justifiable reason for withholding the supplies. Every thing is shared after the performance; the very candle-ends are objects of competition; and many a luckless wight has gone 'in darkness' to bed, when a long exhibition has burnt the candles to a wick, and the share of profits has not given a sufficiency to buy a 'farthing rush-light'. Under such managers actors are thrown on the public commiseration, and if one spark of pride or good feeling is previously entertained, the sense of humiliating dependance extinguishes it, and they become adepts in solicitation.

The state of the Theatre Royal, Liverpool, after the death of its manager, Knight, was not a happy one. The theatre had been run down but there seemed to be no good reason for its penury, despite its manager's claim that the running of a theatre with a large company and a succession of London stars was proving prohibitively expensive.

39   The costs of running a theatre in Liverpool, 1821

Liverpool Theatrical Investigator (17 July 1821), pp. 157–8, reprinted in R. J. Broadbent, *Annals of the Liverpool stage* (Liverpool: E. Howell, 1908), p. 137

[. . .] the theatre pays no government taxes; nor is it assessed at more than two-thirds of the rack-rent for the poor rates; admitting therefore that it pays all parish taxes, the amount will scarcely reach £400 per annum. The length of the season is generally more, but never less, than six months; the theatre must therefore be open twenty-six weeks at least; consequently, the rent and taxes (£2,100) which is stated at 'about £100 per week' amounts to no more than £80 and a fraction per week [. . .] There are, we believe, sixteen male performers, who are paid from twenty shillings to fifty shillings per week (fifty shillings is the very highest salary!), their salaries, therefore, taken at the utmost, cannot amount to more than £28 per week. Ten female performers, say £15 per week. Musicians, or rather mostly apologies for musicians, £19 10s, per week [. . .] Twelve door keepers, money takers, etc., whose salaries (box bookkeeper into the bargain) will not average more than 16s per week, 9l 12s. Scene shifters and scene *daubers*, 6l per week. Lighting, 8l per week. Printing and advertising, 8l per week [. . .] Now, allowing 25l 18s per week for the supernumeraries, and incidental expenses, the weekly expense will amount to 200l, or 40l per night.

The London performers [. . .] are generally engaged for a fortnight; and, to use a managerial expression, 'share after the expenses'; we will suppose, therefore [. . .] that, at one of these benefits, there shall be 170l in the house:– 60 guineas, in the first place, will be deducted for what are called the *expences* [*sic*], to which may be added a number of items, for extra *properties*, etc., which will, on an average, increase the amount to 70l – there still remains 100l which is divided between the Managers and the *Star*, the latter paying for the extra printing, advertising, etc., out of his fifty; while the managers pocket altogether 120l. Now, if only one benefit took place each week, and the receipts of the other four nights amounted, in the whole, to only 80l (20l per night) it is clear the management could not lose. But, judging from former seasons, more than one Star-Benefit occurs weekly, the stock houses have also averaged much more than 20l per night: take, then, into consideration the *native* performers' benefits for the last five weeks of the season, which average to the management more than 60l per night, and some tolerable idea may be formed of the manner in which ample fortunes have been made [. . .]

The decline in the fortunes of the provincial circuits, as well as the Theatres Royal in towns outside London, could be directly attributed to the existence of a stylistic hegemony on the part of London theatres. Provincial audiences, however, wanted to see starring actors and plays that reflected the spectacular staging only the large patent theatres could adequately display. These conditions relegated stock company actors to serving as supernumeraries to a visiting celebrity, and audiences were exposed to pale, though expensive, imitations of London originals.

40   London practices and their effect on provincial theatres, 1821

The Thespian (Liverpool) (13 and 17 August 1821), pp. 41–3, 89–92

The monopoly of the two London houses, contracts the eminent stations of the profession into an extremely narrow compass [. . .] The trick and extravagance also, which have become necessary to produce effect in such enormous theatres not only render those prizes more precarious, but throw no little dishonour on the attainment of them [. . .]

Nor is this contraction and perversion of the hopes and efforts of the performer, the only evils resulting from the monopoly of the London playhouses. The London performers participate in that monopoly; and exact from the provincial managers such enormous terms for their aid, during their summer months, that these managers are unable to afford anything more than a bare subsistence to the regular members of their own companies. Hence it is that a provincial actor has little encouragement for exertion. Whatever may be his talents, his industry or his study, the chances of his attaining eminence and profit on the London boards, are a little less than a hundred to one against him; and it is nearly impossible for him to secure anything out of his salary for the comfort of his age [. . .]

Is it impossible for the provincial theatres to shake off some portion of their dependence upon the theatricals of the Metropolis? Is it impossible to establish an independent theatre in Liverpool, the second town in the kingdom, such as the inhabitants might encourage as their own: in which they might be proud of the talents of a superior company and look to the occasional visits of some of the most distinguished ornaments of the London theatres, rather for a variety of excellence, than as the objects for whom alone the theatre, under the present system, seems to be opened and maintained?

[. . .]

[. . .] if the provincial theatres, instead of imitating and servilely repeating the ostentatious absurdities of the London stages, were to restrain their efforts to the exhibition of sterling pieces, by well-encouraged companies of their own, they would merit the thanks, and undoubtedly obtain the patronage, of the respective communities to which they belong.

It is, indeed, truly ridiculous to see pieces, which have been planned for the scenic effect of enormous stages, attempted to be given on the boards of provincial theatres; where one-tenth of the expense necessary to give the only effect for which such pieces were contrived, would consume the receipts of a month. Such pieces are also brought forward in provincial towns generally for the accommodation of a London performer, who demands an extravagant remuneration for exhibiting contortions, which, however judicious they may be in extensive theatres, where little else than contortions can be visible, are truly ridiculous on a more moderate stage, and serve only to pervert the judgment of hundreds, who, too willingly, sacrifice their better taste, rather than be thought to be wanting in the taste of the metropolis [. . .]

Though the provincial circuits were in decline, there were still forty-four in existence, some operating for only a few weeks or months during the year to accommodate summer visitors or to complement race meetings or fairs. The salaries were low, except at well-established centres such as Bath, Bristol, Liverpool, Manchester and Edinburgh, where living expenses were proportionately higher as well.[1]

[1] See Allardyce Nicoll, *A history of English drama, 1660–1900* (Cambridge: Cambridge University Press, 1959), vol. IV, pp. 233–9 for further details about specific circuits.

41   Provincial circuits: managers and salaries, 1827

Leman Rede, *The road to the stage* (London: Smith, 1827), pp. 9 ff.

Manager's Names	Towns or Circuits	Salary, etc.
BARNETT	Reading, Newbury, Gosport, Guildford, Ryde (Isle of Wight), open the whole year round	Average per week 1 pound
BENNETT, S.	Exeter (for six months of the year, beginning at Christmas)	Aver. 1 10s
BENNETT, J.	Worcester, Wolverhampton, Loughborough, Ashby-de-la-Zouch	18s to 1 5s
BLAND	Durham, Sunderland, North and South Shields, Stockton-on-Tees, Scarborough[i]	1 1s to 1 11s 6d[ii]
BROOKE	Hastings, Faversham, Eastbourne, Rye, Folkstone, Tenterden	1 1s[iii]
BRUNTON, R.	Plymouth and Birmingham	At Birmingham, 1 10s to 3 10s At Plymouth, 1 5s to 2 10s

Manager's Names	Towns or Circuits	Salary, etc.
BURTON	Arundel and Little Hampton. The Arundel Theatre is open in the Winter seasons, and the Hampton until the Worthing Theatre opens	Aver. 1 1s
COOKE	Liverpool New Circus	Aver. from 2 to 5[iv]
CRISP, CHAS	Warwick, Hereford, Bridgnorth Stourbridge, Carmarthen	1 1s to 1 5s
CHARLTON	Bath	1 5s to 3 10s
DOWTON, Wm	Rochester, Tonbridge Wells, Maidstone and Canterbury	1 1s[v]
DAWSON	Penzance, Bodmin, Truro, Redruth, Penryn, Falmouth, Devonport, and Halestone	1
DECAMP	Sheffield, Chester and Shrewsbury	1 1s to 1 15
DOWNE	York, Leeds, Hull, Doncaster and Wakefield	1 1s to 3
EVANS and BURTON	Worthing (four months' season), summer	1 to 1 10s
FISHER, D.	Beccles, Bungay, Eye, Sudbury, Swaffham, North Walsam, Downham, Halesworth, East Dereham, Woodbridge, and Newmarket	Average 1
HARVEY	Weymouth, Jersey and Guernsey[vi]	Aver. 1 10s
HANNAM	Chelmsford and Andover (for two months, about August)	18s to 1 5s
HOWARD	Lancaster, Preston, Blackburn, Stockdale and Rochdale	1 to 1 5s
HUGGINS and CLARKE	Worksop, Pontefract, Horncastle, Gainsborough, Mansfield, Rotheram, Louth and Brigg	18s to 1 1s
HARRIS	Dublin[vii] (for six months' season, commencing in December)	2 to 6
JACKMAN	Buckingham, Aylesbury, Bedford, Woburn, Wallingford, Woodstock	1
KLANERT	Richmond (*Surrey*) (season commences latter end of July and closes in November, four months)	1 1s
LEWIS and BANKS	Liverpool and Manchester	1 5s to 4

Manager's Names	Towns or Circuits	Salary, etc.
LEE	Torrington, Taunton, Wells, Bridge-water, Bridport and Barnstaple[viii]	18s
MACARTHY[ix]	Cork, Limerick, and Waterford (will open on the 16th of next April, at Cork)	1 10s to 2 10s
MACREADY[x]	Bristol and Swansea	1 5s to 2 10s
MAXFIELD, KELLY and COLLINS	Portsmouth, Southampton and Winchester	1 1s to 1 10s
MORGAN	Twickenham, Cobham, Mitcham, Wimbledon, Henley-upon-Thames	15s
MARSHALL	Greenwich (from Christmas to Easter)	1 1s
MASTERS	Lynn (open six weeks in the year, commencing 14th February)	1 5s to 3 10s
MURRAY, W[xi]	Edinburgh (two seasons in the year, winter and summer, open altogether about nine months)	1 5s to 6 or 7
MANLEY	Halifax, Derby, Retford, Nottingham, Chesterfield, Bolton (*Lancashire*), Newark, and Stamford	1 1s to 1 5s
NICHOLSON	Newcastle-upon-Tyne, Harrowgate, Richmond (*Yorks.*) and North Allerton	1 1s to 1 11s 6d[xii]
PENSON	Newport (*Isle of Wight*), Lymington and Salisbury	1 1s
RYDER	Caledonian Theatre, Edinburgh, Aberdeen, Perth, Dundee, and Belfast in Ireland	1 5s to 2 2s[xiii]
ROBERTSON	Huntingdon, Lincoln, Boston, Spalding, Grantham, Wisbech, Newark, and Peterborough	1 1s
RUSSELL	Brighton and Lewes (open 10 months in the year)	1 5s to 2
SCOTT	Old Circus and the Pavilion, Liverpool[xiv]	1 10s to 3
SMITH	Norwich, Yarmouth, Cambridge, Colchester, Bury St Edmonds and Ipswich	1 5s to 3

Manager's Names	Towns or Circuits	Salary, etc.
STANTON, Ch.	Stafford, Newcastle-under-Lyne, Drayton, Newport, Oswestry, Wrexham, Ashborne, Burton-upon-Trent	I IS
SAVILLE[1]	Margate, Ramsgate, Gravesend, Sandwich, Deal, and Dover	I 5s
SAUNDERS	Cardigan, Aberystwith and Bishop Castle[xv]	18s
THORNHILL	(Derbyshire), Buxton, Matlock, Bath and Bakewell	I
WILLIAMS	Merthyr Tydfil, Tenby, Cardiff, Abergavenny and Monmouth[xvi]	I IS

i. This company usually consists of twelve men and eight women.

ii. Benefits to share the receipts with the manager after the first 10 pounds, which sum is exclusively his.

iii. Hastings salaries rather better.

iv. On some occasions, Mr Cooke has given 10 pounds per week to one performer.

v. With the exception of about two performers.

vi. In these towns it must be remarked provisions, lodgings, etc. are peculiarly cheap.

vii. About forty performers are generally engaged on this establishment.

viii. Mr Lee has other towns that he visits, once in two or three years, at his discretion.

ix. Formerly of the East London and Dublin theatres.

x. Father of the celebrated tragedian.[2]

xi. Manager for Mrs H. Siddons.[3]

xii. Gives much larger salaries at Newcastle than anywhere else.

xiii. Much larger salaries and company at Edinburgh than any of his other towns.

xiv. The salaries both here and at Mr Cooke's establishments are uncertain, for in the production of extraordinary novelty, or the procuration of particular talent, they have extended their terms to ten guineas per week or even more.

xv. Some other towns in the neighbourhood; which he gives preference to is uncertain.

xvi. Mr W also occasionally visits other towns.

[1] On the Saville managements, see Carol J. Carlisle, 'The Faucit Saville brothers; or, theatre and family', in R. Foulkes (ed.), *Scenes from provincial stages* (London: STR, 1994), pp. 114–26.

[2] On Macready, see K. Barker, *The Theatre Royal, Bristol, 1766–1966*, (London: STR, 1974).

[3] On Murray, see J. C. Dibdin, *The annals of the Edinburgh stage* (Edinburgh: Cameron, 1888).

Contractual arrangements between managers and leading actors could be generous. Such actors could be guaranteed employment regardless of whether the theatre was open and could even be exempt from the fines and deductions that managers were entitled to impose. Moreover, they could insist on the performance of roles within their repertoire.

42   Contract between Macready and Bunn, 1835

Reprinted in J. C. Trewin, *Mr Macready: a nineteenth-century tragedian* (London: Harrap, 1955), p. 110

It is agreed this 21st day of September, 1835, between Alfred Bunn and William Charles Macready,

That the said Alfred Bunn shall engage the said William Charles Macready as the Principal Tragedian at the Theatre Royal, Drury Lane, on a salary of thirty pounds per week, play or no play, for thirty weeks and a half; the payment of the said full salary of £30 to commence from Thursday, October 1, 1835, and to be continued, without any interruption or deduction, on any pretence whatsoever, until Saturday, March 5, 1836, being a period of twenty-two weeks and a half (from which date, March 5, to Monday, April 4, 1836, the said Alfred Bunn and William Charles Macready have no claim whatever on each other): the payment of said salary of £30, free of all deduction, to be recommenced by Alfred Bunn to W. C. Macready, from April 4, and paid to May 27, being a period of eight weeks, making altogether thirty weeks and a half (in gross amount £915 for thirty weeks and a half, in weekly payments of £30), for which Alfred Bunn has the power of requiring the services of W. C. Macready four nights in each week of this engagement.

That W. C. Macready is to have the clear half of the total receipts of a night appropriated for a benefit, which shall be the first, without exception, in the season, and on a Monday night.

That Alfred Bunn shall produce immediately after Christmas the Tragedy called *The Bridal*, altered from Beaumont and Fletcher's *The Maid's Tragedy*, on the usual terms of £33 6s 8d per night to the ninth night, and £100 for the twentieth.

That W. C. Macready is to be subject to no forfeit or fine by Alfred Bunn, under any pretence whatsoever, and that he is to have the same privilege of orders as during his last season at Drury Lane Theatre.

That W. C. Macready may be required to perform any parts in the list, given in by him, and such others as are classed in the leading tragedy, but not such as he, W. C. Macready, may deem as partaking of a melo-dramatic character, and that he is to have the choice of characters on all occasions, with sufficient notice for the proper study of new parts.

That W. C. Macready shall not be required or asked to act the characters of *Sir Giles Overreach, Joseph Surface*, or *Rob Roy*, and that he is to have a dressing-room to himself, secure from removal or intrusion.

That in the event of W. C. Macready being deterred by illness, or any other calamity, from appearing before the public, his salary is to be discontinued, until he shall report himself capable of resuming his duties.

That upon the infringement, at any time or times, of any of the above-named conditions, W. C. Macready shall have the power of giving notice that his engagement is null and void, and that the same shall be null and void upon the delivery of such notice.

The death knell of the provincial stock company was sounded when entire London companies started to tour, using railways to convey not only the performers but sets and costumes as well.

43   The first London touring company, 1847

James Rodgers, 'Reminiscences of an old actor, II', *Birmingham Daily Mail* (22 January 1886), p. 2, reprinted in Broadbent, *Annals of the Liverpool stage*, p. 158.[1]

When the lease of that [the Liver Theatre, Liverpool] expired I arranged with Mr Simpson to open the old Theatre Royal there with him for a fortnight. Mr Simpson's object was to introduce Buckstone and Mrs Fitzwilliam in the new farce *Box and Cox*[2] which had just made a great sensation in London, and in which Buckstone had been specially commanded to perform at Windsor. The two had previously been playing with Charles Mathews at the Lyceum. *Box and Cox* was a very great success in Liverpool, and this circumstance is interesting for the reason that its success caused the very first introduction of the travelling company system which has since revolutionized the English theatre. I took the company *en bloc* to the old Queen's Theatre in Manchester, and we played there with the greatest success, and then we began an extensive tour with *Box and Cox* and *The Green Bushes*. This, as far as I know, was the very first occasion in England of a complete company travelling from town to town with the same piece.

[1] Rodgers managed the Liver Theatre and other country theatres, including the Isle of Man, Shrewsbury, Coventry and Worcester, ending his days in Birmingham as the owner of the Prince of Wales.
[2] J. M. Morton's farce had opened at the Lyceum, London, on 1 November 1847.

PLAYWRIGHTS: OBLIGATIONS AND REWARDS

Managers were quick to reward playwrights whose work guaranteed success, especially writers of comedy. Among popular playwrights were George Colman the Younger at Covent Garden and Richard Cumberland at Drury Lane, both of whom could earn large sums of money but were unprotected from acts of managerial piracy. Colman, moreover, was the manager of the Haymarket Theatre and wielded considerable influence. Cumberland had established his reputation under Garrick and wrote prolifically until his death in 1811.[1]

[1] Colman's reputation for comic writing was best represented in his plays *The Heir at Law* (1797) and *John Bull* (1803).

44   The earnings of a successful playwright, 1801–2

R. B. Peake, *Memoirs of the Colman family* (London: Bentley, 1841), vol. II, p. 413

Colman received very considerable sums for his plays. For 'The Poor Gentleman', and 'Who Wants a Guinea?' he was paid 550l each, then the customary price for a five-act comedy; that is to say, 300l on the first nine nights, 100l on the twentieth night, and 150l for the copyright.* For 'John Bull'[1] (the most attractive comedy ever produced, having averaged 470l per night for forty-seven nights), Mr Harris paid 1000l and Colman afterwards received twice an additional 100l, making 1200l. Mr Harris was accustomed to pay an author one or two hundred pounds above the 550l, when the drama was very successful, which was the case with most of Colman's plays.

* That is to say, 33l 6s 8d per *night* for the first nine nights – 100l on the twentieth night – and 100l, on the fortieth night. This was the plan settled by Cumberland with Sheridan, at Drury Lane, and Harris, at Covent Garden, for remunerating authors, instead of their (generally losing) benefits. The copyright was usually understood to be a distinct bargain – the proprietor of the theatre was to have the refusal, at any *bona fide* price offered by a bookseller.

[1] *The Poor Gentleman* opened at Covent Garden on 11 February 1801; *Who Wants A Guinea?* on 18 April 1805; *John Bull* on 5 March 1803.

Despite the success of Colman or Cumberland, the dramatist's position was a precarious one. Often he performed the functions of an actor or stage manager as well. As a house dramatist, his contract would stipulate the number of plays to be written and the copyright of them would be retained by the theatre's management for possible later sale to publishers. In Thomas Dibdin's case, he was able to negotiate a regular salary with minimal requirements while employed in the Kent circuit. When at Covent Garden his salary almost doubled.[1]

[1] Dibdin was engaged by Covent Garden in 1800, after spending time with Sarah Baker of the Kent and Canterbury circuit as a house dramatist and occasional actor for the year 1798/9.

45   A house dramatist's earnings in the early 1800s

T. Dibdin, *Reminiscences* (London: Colburn, 1827): (a) vol. 1, p. 241; (b) pp. 325–7

(a) Thomas Dibdin in the provinces

I now begged to decline acting altogether, as my time seemed likely to be completely occupied in a pleasanter way. My five pounds per week were to be continued the year round, for the yearly production of a pantomime and a one-act piece upon any local or temporary subject, arising, like 'the Mouth of the Nile', from circumstances of public interest: but the pieces I had already produced were to be included in said five pounds per week, with an additional two hundred pounds for copyright of the 'Birthday' and 'Jew and Doctor': the profits therefore, of my first season's engagement stood thus:–

Salary from October till the close of the theatre, about	£170 0s
For the two above-named copyrights retained by the theatre	£200 0s
Copyright of 'Horse and Widow' sold to Mr Barker	20 0
Ditto of 'Five Thousand a Year' sold to Messrs. Robinson & Co.	60 0
Ditto songs in pantomime, to Barker	6 6s
Ditto 'Mouth of the Nile', to Barker	10 0
	466 6s

(b) Dibdin's fourth season at Covent Garden[1]

A Musical farce, called 'the Escapes', was put in preparation, certain duetts [sic], songs, etc. in which wanted nothing but the words to complete them; and I was applied to [. . .]

I also wrote the songs, etc. for Mr Fawcett's melo-drame of the 'Brazen Mask', and those in a *petite piece* called the 'Definitive Treaty', the prologue to Sir Lumley Skeffington's comedy called the 'Word of Honour', etc., etc. These little matters, and the successful pantomime of 'Harlequin's Almanack', added to the 'Cabinet', constituted the whole of my productions for this season. I received £400 for the 3rd, 6th, 9th, and 20th nights of the 'Cabinet'; £150 for the copy-right, reserving the privilege of selling the words of the songs in the theatre, which netted about £150. I gave great offence to the retail venders [sic] of the song-books in the theatre, by publishing them at ten-pence each book. The songs of a first opera always had been printed at one shilling; but the fruit-women, who scorn to take less than silver, expect an advance; so that a gentleman would be compelled to give eighteen-pence, which I always considered a shameful imposition, and which I was the first to remedy; as by printing them at ten-pence they were sold at a shilling, which could not be refused. This douceur was, however, thought too trifling, although I received but seven-pence halfpenny for each book, out of which I had to pay all expenses of printing and publication: my profit was, consequently, much less than that of the retailers in the theatre, who cleared four-pence halfpenny by every book, unaccompanied with any risk or expense whatever, as they returned all unsold copies in my hands. When I therefore gained £150 by the sale, they could have little cause to complain on the receipt of a much larger profit; and yet, for many nights, they refused to sell the songs at all, because they were not allowed to tax the public in their usual way. My plan has been ever since adopted in all theatres [. . .]

[1] *The Escapes; or, The Water Carrier* was performed on 14 October 1801; *The Brazen Mask; or, Alberto and Rosabella* on 5 April 1802; *The Cabinet* on 9 February 1802.

Adaptations of the story of Don Giovanni became enormously popular, especially after the success of Moncrieff's *Giovanni in London*, which was performed at the Olympic in 1817. As an author, Dibdin was well aware of the unscrupulous theft of playwrights' property, but as the manager of the Surrey Theatre he was prepared to participate in this practice, especially since the original in this case was not English.

46   Managerial piracy at the Surrey, 1817

Dibdin, *Reminiscences*, vol. ii, p. 135

[. . .] but the great hit of the season [1817] was 'Don Giovanni', which bur-lesque laid the ground-work for innumerable Giovannis in London, Dublin, and every-where else. I saw Mozart's opera on a Tuesday – (one of the band of the King's Theatre whispered me from the orchestra, as I sat in the pit, 'You come here to take something away with you!') I went home, set my scene-painters and myself to work, and called a rehearsal for the following Monday. I had finished the first act late on the Saturday night, when Raymond came in and supped with me, and we read it together at five in the morning. As I did not write on Sunday, I had to compose the second act on Monday morning, so as to meet the performers at one p.m.; and for the first time, not being quite ready for the appointed moment, I requested another hour; at the expiration of which, I read them the piece complete; and on Monday, May 12th, it commenced a run of more than one hundred nights [. . .] I next altered Miss Joanna Baillie's tragedy of 'Constantine Palaeologus', and produced it as a melo-drama, with the title of 'Constantine and Valeria'. Sanderson's music, and the style in which the choruses were got up, rendered great assistance to this piece, during the run of which, I had the pleasure of a visit from the celebrated Monsieur Talma, who expressed his astonishment at so much effect being produced in a minor theatre: the correctness of the costume, both as to scenery and dresses, he much admired [. . .][1]

---

[1] *Constantine and Valeria; or, The Last of the Caesars* was performed at the Surrey on 23 June 1817. On literary piracy and its methods see J. R. Stephens, *The censorship of English drama, 1824–1901* (Cambridge: Cambridge University Press, 1980), pp. 84–6. On Talma's concern for 'correct' costume, see **357** and **358**.

47   Manoeuvrings between Covent Garden and Drury Lane, 1822–3

John Genest, *Some account of the English stage*, vol. IX, p. 198

Jan 28, 1823 CG Never acted, Nigel, or the Crown Jewels [. . .] the celebrated novel called the Fortunes of Nigel did not seem well calculated to be turned into a play, but such was the rage for dramatizing the novels attributed to Walter Scott, that 2 plays were formed from it, and a 3rd was intended for DL.

Elliston finding that the Two Galley Slaves[1] was to be brought out at CG with a considerable expectation of success, procured a copy of the French piece, and had it translated in the greatest hurry possible – by this manoeuvre he was able to bring it out at DL on the same night as the other piece at CG – Elliston having commenced hostilities in this unhandsome manner, C. Kemble thought himself authorized to retaliate – it was well known that Terry had dramatized the Fortunes of Nigel with a view of bringing it out at DL, where Liston was to play the King, and Miss Stephens, Margaret – C. Kemble employed some other person to turn the novel into a play, and produced it at CG – not so much with an expectation of doing himself good as of doing Elliston harm, by forestalling the representation at DL, which could not take place until the engagement of Liston and Miss Stephens should commence – the play acted on this evening is in 5 acts – it is a very poor piece – it was much disapproved of, and merely tolerated for some few nights, on account of some appropriate views of London, which were beautifully painted – the author of Nigel, or the Crown Jewels has very injudiciously written it in blank verse – in consequence of the ill success of this play, the one intended for DL never made its appearance.

[1] On Scott's popularity see **89** and **93**. *Two Galley Slaves*, a melodrama by J. H. Payne, was produced on 6 November 1822.

THE BACKSTAGE INDUSTRY

The proliferation of responsibilities within a developing theatre industry meant that the number of people employed on a permanent basis increased enormously and added to the costs of large theatres. Probably the most important functionary on whom managers relied was the stage manager, sometimes identified with the acting manager, although the two functions could be separated. The stage manager was responsible for handling all stage business and, as Bartley points out, for insuring that the plays had received a licence from the Examiner of Plays.[1]

[1] Bartley had a long and distinguished career, both as an actor and as a stage manager. Elliston used him as his acting manager at the Birmingham Theatre Royal in 1813 and he replaced Raymond as acting manager at the English Opera House in 1816. He remained with the Covent Garden company from the 1820s and served under Macready. He was a member of Charles Kean's original company at the Princess's in 1850 and died in 1858.

48   The functions of a stage manager

(a) The duties of the stage or acting manager as explained by William Lewis[1]

James Boaden, *Memoirs of the life of John Philip Kemble Esq.* (2 vols., London: Longman, 1825), vol. ii, pp. 369–70.

As the stage manager, his duties were the almost daily attendance upon rehearsals; and that often uncomfortable intervention between the manager, Mr Harris, and his authors or his actors [. . .] One part of the duty of a stage manager is to cast and arrange the plays which are brought out. This, in course, requires a just estimate of the talents and steadiness of the company [. . .] In new plays to be sure, the stage manager may be supposed to get the assistance of their authors. But it is only the veteran bard, who can be of the least use on such occasions [. . .] a young writer is cruelly startled when he is asked, in a particular scene, 'how many attendants he will have on?' Or, 'what parts of the stage' his characters are to occupy? The same unforeseen puzzle falls upon him, when he is desired 'to move' his performers during the dialogue, so as that their positions at last may be convenient for their *exit*. In the getting up of old plays, or such as have lain aside even for a few years, the first question asked upon a stage is, 'How is the *business* done; who knows it?' The acting manager should, therefore, be a person of long experience, and have served himself under able generals. The drill is the principle of order – If you seldom rehearse, your acting will be intolerable. Where a part is written out with the mere accompaniment of the cues, a perception must be very quick indeed to be reasonably sure of the meaning. Questions, therefore, continually occur, *how* such a passage should be spoken? Your acting manager should be as ready in his reply, as the bow or courtesy which always follows the information. Again, in well regulated theatres, the pronunciation should be uniform. If he should chance to catch, during the rehearsal, a little barn-door syllable or false accent, he will take the proper opportunity, *aside*, to refine the utterance, with neither tart derision nor growling severity. As to the cadence of the speakers, it is almost impossible to meddle with it – perhaps the performer may be allowed his own tune, provided he sings it agreeably. About *emphasis* the manager may be as learned as he will.

[1] Lewis was stage manager at Covent Garden for twenty-one years as well as being one of its leading comedians. He retired in 1809 and died in 1813.

(b) George Bartley describes his function as stage manager at Covent Garden

Select Committee on Dramatic Literature, minutes of evidence, 1832

3220. What are the duties of stage-managers? – Very extensive.

3221. Do they extend over all the new pieces that are produced? – Over the production of them all.

3222. Is it you who directs what pieces shall be performed? – No, they are given into my hands by the proprietors; they have been [. . .] given into my hands by Mr Laporte, who is the lessee.

3223. Then you look at them, and see which of them you will recommend? – No; they have been in the habit sometimes of asking my opinion whether such a piece should or should not be acted, but I do not know that they have ever gone on my individual opinion in any one instance.

3224. They have been given you to cast? – No, the proprietors will always take a part in the casting of a piece, they generally cast it themselves; Mr Kemble was the person who generally cast the pieces; my duty was to bring them on the stage; [. . .] and the general arrangement of what we technically call the business of the stage, is my department.

3225. It does not come under your province to send them to the licencer [*sic*]? – Yes, they are never sent to the licencer till they are given into my hands to produce, and that is the first step I have to take.

49   Practices and personnel at the opera, King's Theatre, 1820s

John Ebers, *Seven years of the King's Theatre* (London: Ainsworth, 1828; reprinted New York: Blom, 1969), pp. 360–4, 370–2

To take care of the House, and to attend to the doors of the Theatre, to the boxes and the stage, a great number of servants are employed. The housekeeper's situation is one of some trust, and usually filled by a person of corresponding character. The housekeeper superintends the state of the Theatre, as to cleanliness and neatness, has apartments in the House, and a box appropriated to her own use. The box-keepers number about twenty, and receive salaries amounting aggregately to about three hundred pounds. The expense of the military guard employed at the door amounts annually to upwards of one hundred and fifty pounds.

The company of performers are naturally to be considered under two distinct classes as attached to the opera or to the ballet. The opera is under the guidance of the director of the music, if any is employed. The director assists the manager in the selection of the performances; and when fixed upon, he distributes the parts to the singers, and directs the general routine of representation, the effecting of which, in the minuter details, devolves on the stage-manager, and the conductor of the music. By these, according to their several departments, the due execution of the parts is attended to, the training of the chorus-singers and inferior performers, the management of the scenery, and the performance of the orchestra. The engagements for the orchestra are in general made by the director; those of the performers, and other persons employed, by the manager [. . .]

[. . .] Should [a composer] be retained, his duties are regulated by the terms of his engagement, and consist primarily in composing of operas for the Theatre, and attending to the mounting of them, when ready to be put in rehearsal.

The composer [. . .] moulds the first rough score of his music on the scale of the piano-forte, and this, when completed, forms the ground-work, or skeleton of the entire piece. The music having been applied to the words which are supplied by the poet of the Theatre, the next step is to adapt the different parts of the music to the capabilities of the performers, to whom the characters of the opera, when cast, are to be allotted [. . .] This adaptation being made, the scene of operations having been hitherto confined to the composer's apartment, the concert-room of the Theatre, or some room of similar dimensions, is resorted to, and an embryo rehearsal of the whole vocal part of the opera gone through, the accompaniment being as yet limited to the composer's piano-forte.

Before proceeding to the stage, the orchestral parts require to be set, and these are now added, according to the nature of the expression to be conveyed, and the strength of the instrumental music of the Theatre [. . .]

The opera having by these gradations received its form, and the composer's finishing touches being bestowed upon it, it is committed to rehearsal in the regular manner, the getting up, or mounting, being performed under the superintendance of the composer, with the director, conductor, and stage-manager, though two of these latter characters frequently unite in the same person [. . .]

> [. . .] Connected with the business of the stage are the
> Scene Painter and his Assistants.
> Property Man
> Head Tailor
> Head Mantua-maker
> Wardrobe Keeper
> Draper for the Men
> Do. for the Ladies.

The dresses are, at least in the estimation of foreigners, whether in the opera or ballet, a subject of great moment, and of frequent disagreement, as every singer or dancer has an almost invincible abhorrence of sparing the treasury, by making use of any dresses already in the wardrobe, however excellent, every one choosing to exercise his own taste in the adaptation of his garb.

The dresses naturally introduce the dressing rooms, the regulations of which, as established by the usage of the theatre, are amusingly adapted to the rank of the performers. A prima donna is entitled to a separate dressing-room, with a sofa, and two wax-candles. The same principle obtains with the chief male performers, and with the first and second dancers of both sexes. Ludicrous as it may seem, these marks of precedency are insisted upon with the greatest exactness. Madame Vestris went beyond all others, and furnished herself with two additional candles; and one night, there not being, by some inadvertency, candles enough in the house, she stood on the stage behind the curtain, and refused to dress for her part until the required number of lights was obtained.

The performers inferior in station to those I have mentioned, dress in two general rooms, appropriated respectively to the ladies and gentlemen of the company. There is, however, a universal desire for the distinction of separate rooms, and sometimes an express article of the engagement provides for this question.

50   Backstage company at Drury Lane in the 1820s

H. Foote, *Companion to the theatres* (London: Marsh & Miller, 1829), pp. 39–40

Stage – Stage-manager, pantomime director, chorus and ballet masters, prompter, his deputy, copyist (with several assistants), property-man and call-boy.

Orchestra – Director of the musical department, leader of the band, six or eight first violins, ditto second, two tenors, two violincellos, three or four double basses, oboe and flageolet, first and second flutes, first and second clarionets, first and second horns, first and second bassoons, trombone, trumpet and bugle, piano-forte, bells, carillons, or small bells, and kettle-drums, other instruments being occasionally introduced; music copyist (with several assistants), and an attendant upon the orchestra to lay out the music.

Painting-room – Four principal painters constantly employed, exclusive of accessory principals, subordinates, colour-grinders, etc.

Decorative Machinery, etc., – The property-maker, machinist, master carpenter, six or eight carpenters, and from 24 to 30 scene men. The property-maker and master carpenter, generally are the joint machinists.

Wardrobe – Master tailor, and keeper of the gentlemen's wardrobe, etc. Mistress of the ladies' wardrobe, with numerous assistants. Each principal performer has a separate dresser.

House Department – Treasurer, under ditto, house-keeper, his assistant, about ten money-takers, as many check-takers, box-keeper (with numerous attendants), lamplighters, firemen, porters, and watchmen: the latter are on duty in the theatre during the whole of the night.

On special occasions, for grand spectacles, etc., supernumeraries are engaged by the night, the aggregate salaries of whom frequently amounts to 50l per week.

THE VESTRIS±MATHEWS MANAGEMENTS

Eliza Vestris was the first female theatre manager in London and in the period to 1839 was responsible for reforms which signalled a determined attempt to improve the status particularly of the minor theatres and to win over a respectable clientèle of middle-class audiences. Together with Planché, she is credited with introducing the form of extravaganza to the English stage and initiating the use of a box set.[1]

[1] See *Theatrical Observer*, 3791 (10 February 1834) and John H. McDowell, 'The historical development of the box set', *Theatre Annual* (1945), pp. 65–83. Other noted female managers to follow included Sarah Macready at Bristol, Sarah Baker at Kent, Mary Warner at Sadler's Wells, Frances Davidge at the Surrey, as well as Marie Wilton at the Prince of Wales and Sara Lane at the Britannia in the second half of the century.

51   Madame Vestris opens her management of the Olympic, 1831

(a) (London: Wilkes, 1834), pp. i–ii; (b) J. R. Planché, *The two Figaros*, in B. Webster (ed.), *The acting national drama* (6 vols., London: Chapman & Hall, 1837), vol. 1.

(a) Prologue to *Olympic Revels; or, Prometheus and Pandora*

Noble and Gentle! – Matrons! – Patrons! – Friends!
Before you here a venturous woman bends!
A warrior woman – that in strife embarks,
The first of all dramatic Joan of Arcs.

Cheer on the enterprize, thus dared by me!
The first that ever led a company!
What though, until this very hour and age,
A lessee-lady never owned a stage!
I'm that *Belle Sauvage* – only rather quieter,
Like Mrs Nelson, turned a stage proprietor!
Welcome each early and each late arriver –
This is my omnibus, and I'm the driver!
Sure is my venture, for all honest folk,
Who love a tune, or can enjoy a joke,
Will know, whene'er they have an hour of leisure,
Wych-street is best to come to for their pleasure.
The laughter and the lamps, with equal share,
Shall make this house a *light*-house against care.
This is our home! 'Tis yours, as well as mine;
Here Joy may pay her homage at Mirth's shrine;
Song, Whim, and Fancy jocund rounds shall dance,
And lure for you the light Vaudeville from France.
Humour and Wit encourage my intent,
And Music means to help to pay my rent.
'Tis not mere promise – I appeal to facts;
Henceforward judge me only by my *acts*!
In this, my purpose, stand I not alone –
All women sigh for houses of their own;
And I was weary of perpetual dodging
From house to house, in search of board and lodging!
Faint was my heart, but with Pandora's scope,
I find in every *box* a lurking hope;
My dancing spirits know of no decline,
Here's the first *tier* you've ever seen of mine.
Oh, my kind friends! befriend me still, as you
Have in the bygone times been wont to do;
Make me your ward against each ill designer,
And prove Lord Chancellor to a female *Minor*.
Cheer on my comrades, too, in their career;
Some of your favourites are around me here.
Give them – give me – the smiles of approbation,
In this Olympic game of speculation;
Still aid the petticoat on old, kind principles,
And make me yet a Captain of *Invincibles*![1]

---

[1] Vestris began her management on 3 January 1831. The address was written by J. D. Reynolds. The reference to the *Invincibles* is to her success in Thomas Morton's play of the same name, in which she had appeared at Covent Garden in 1828.

(b) Planché comments on Madame Vestris's achievements, 1836

In a time of unexampled peril to the best interests of the Drama – whilst Theatrical property was at the lowest ebb – the larger Theatres changing hands continually, and the ruin of their lessees involving that of hundreds of their unfortunate dependents, – the little Olympic, the most despised nook in the dramatic world, became not only one of the most Popular and Fashionable Theatres London ever saw, – but served as a life-boat to the respectability of the stage, which was fast sinking in the general wreck. Your *success* is a matter of notoriety – not so however, the principal *causes* of your success [. . .]

In the first place, you have never suffered a temporary decline of attraction to scare you into the destructive system of filling your Boxes with orders.

Secondly – You have never suffered your Play-bill to be disgraced by a puff;[1] but rigidly restricted it to the simple announcement of the Performances.

Thirdly – In the production of *every* Drama, without regard to its comparative importance – the most scrupulous attention has been paid to all those accessories which form the peculiar charm of Theatrical Representation, by perfecting the illusion of the scene, and consequently at the same time every possible chance of success has been afforded to the author.

Fourthly – That if notwithstanding such aid, a Drama has occasionally failed, it has been as soon as possible withdrawn in deference to the opinion of the public.

Fifthly – That the advantage of early hours was first perceived, by the audiences of the Olympic. The performances having been generally so regulated as to enable families to reach their homes before midnight.

---

[1] The puff was a grossly inflated piece of advertising that suggested that patrons would receive more than the theatre could in fact give.

Vestris and her husband, Charles Mathews, opened their management of Covent Garden in 1839 immediately following that of Macready, who had enjoyed an artistically successful period of management between 1837 and 1839. They hoped that their reputation for stylish productions at the Olympic would follow them to the larger theatre, and opened there with *Love's Labour's Lost*, an elaborately artificial play of literary conceit. At the same time, they attempted to recoup their expenses of refurbishment by economizing on set and costume and raising prices. Both proved to be misjudgements.

52   Vestris and Mathews assume the management of Covent Garden, 1839

Era (6 October 1839), p. 15

The dramatic season has commenced, though only one of the national theatres has as yet entered the field, and most heartily do we [. . .] wish that the enthusiasm of Monday night would last through the season. But we fear those times are gone by when a comedy of Holcroft's, or Morton's or Reynolds's, would draw forty-four hundred-pound houses with no other expense to the manager than two or three chamber scenes, and three or four new coats and breeches. Yet it was gratifying to witness the return of that theatrical enthusiasm and excitement even for one night, and it was certainly exhibited at Covent Garden Theatre on its opening for the first time under the management of Madame Vestris [. . .]

We were sorry to see the experiment announced of the eighteenpenny gallery, and still more sorry to see that our contemporary, *John Bull*, pointed it out to the reprobation of the public. The consequence was, that the first efforts of the fullest house that Covent-garden has witnessed for many a day, were directed to the reform of what the audience considered an infringement on their rights. When Madame Vestris, therefore, came forward to speak the address which had been advertised, scarcely a word could be understood, and Mr C. Mathews accordingly came on and led her off. A council having been held of the powers behind the scenes, Mr C. Mathews again came forward, and announced that both galleries should for the future be open at one shilling [. . .] What could have induced the commencement of the season with one of the earliest, and certainly one of the worst, of Shakspeare's plays, we are at a loss to conceive [. . .] It shows no respect for Shakspeare to perform those plays which are so decidedly un-dramatic [. . .] and as a proof that 'Love's Labours Lost' has so been considered, is that it has never been played since the days of Charles the First. It is a series of brilliant conceits, showing the genius of Shakspeare in all its luxuriance without the tact which characterised his after productions. It is a play that scarcely forms a fair criterion by which to judge Madame Vestris's management or company [. . .]

The Vestris–Mathews management of Covent Garden was burdened with the huge number of employees needed to run a large theatre. Together with some repertorial miscalculations, their management would render them bankrupt and they abandoned the theatre in 1842, a year before the passing of the Theatre Regulation Act.

53   Company numbers employed at Covent Garden, 1840

Charles Dickens, *The life of Charles James Mathews* (London: Macmillan, 1879), vol. II, pp. 92–3

THEATRE ROYAL, COVENT GARDEN
*A Return of all Persons engaged in this Establishment during the
Week ending 26th December, 1840*

Company		
	Gentlemen	38
	Chorus singers	8
	Ladies	34
Band		32
Officers		9
Box-keepers		2

Check and Money takers		15
Bradwell's Department:		
Workers	60	
Supers	22 = 82	82
Scenery Department (Painting-room)		10
Sloman's Department:		
Carpenters	26	
For working Pantomime	80	
Cassidy	1 = 107	107
Gentlemen's Wardrobe:		
Workers	24	
Dressers	14	
Extras	18 = 56	56
Ladies' Wardrobe:		
Workers	42	
Dressers	14	
Attendants	2	
Mrs Thomas and Mrs Lewis	2 = 60	60
Supers (per Hormer):		
'Midsummer Night's Dream'	52	
Pantomime	37 = 89	89
Extra Chorus and Band		13
Property Department		4
Printers, Billstickers, Upholsterers, Housekeeper, etc.		57
Watch and Fire men		5
Police		4
Attendants at Bar, etc., in Drysdale's employment:		
Boxes	16	
Pit	18	
Gallery	8 = 42	42
Place-keepers		7
Box-keepers (Deputies)		10
Total		684

Managers had been aware since the early years of the century that financial failure could be avoided if fashionable audiences could be attracted to the boxes. After his unsuccessful attempts to run Drury Lane and Covent Garden, Bunn leased the St James's Theatre for a short period and introduced a later starting time to accommodate the dining habits of fashionable audiences, which would become the norm at West End houses.

54   A new starting time for fashionable audiences, 1839

Era (27 October 1839), p. 51

The St James's Theatre, under Mr Bunn's management, and patronised by our principal leaders of *ton*, will open on the 2nd November with a powerful operatic company [. . .] The curtain is not to rise until eight o'clock, the first time of such a regulation in an English theatre. The private boxes, we are told, are nearly all taken for the season by the nobility.

Neighbourhood theatres were quick to use the new opportunities for legitimacy conferred by the passing of the 1843 Act. In the case of Sadler's Wells, the theatre was situated in the middle of the fast-growing commercial district of Islington. Its lessee, Thomas Greenwood, a respected apothecary, persuaded Phelps and Warner, both established performers, to undertake the theatre's artistic management. Given the financial failures of both former patent theatres and the opportunity to perform a range of legitimate plays, Phelps and Warner embarked on what was considered a hazardous venture.

55   Samuel Phelps and Mrs Warner announce their intentions at Sadler's Wells, May 1844[1]

BL, Percival Collection, 1844 (Crach 1. Tab.4.b.4)

MRS WARNER and MR PHELPS, of the Theatres Royal, Drury Lane, Covent Garden, and Haymarket, present their respectful compliments, and request attention to the following outlines of a plan which they trust will not be without interest for the respectable inhabitants of this neighbourhood.

Mrs Warner and Mr Phelps, have embarked in the management and performances of SADLER'S WELLS THEATRE, in the hope of constantly rendering it what a theatre ought to be; a place for justly representing the works of our great dramatic poets. This undertaking is commenced at a time when the Theatres which have been exclusively called 'Patent', are closed, or devoted to very different objects from that of presenting the real drama of England, and when the Law has placed all theatres upon an equal footing of security and respectability, leaving no difference, except in the objects and conduct of the managements.

These circumstances justify the notion that each separate division of our immense metropolis with its 2,000,000 of inhabitants, may have its own well-conducted theatre within a reasonable distance of the houses of its patrons.

For the North of London, they offer an entertainment selected from the first stock drama in the world, reinforced by such novelties as can be produced by diligence and liberality, intending that the quality of their novelties shall constantly improve as time will be given to procure and prepare them; and a Company of acknowledged talent, playing such characters as they must be called upon to sustain at Drury Lane and Covent Garden, were these houses now devoted to the drama. These attractions are placed in a theatre where all can see and hear, and at a price fairly within the habitual means of all.

They commence under the disadvantage of a very short preparation, and they are aware that some errors and deficiencies are quite inseparable from such a circumstance. They trust that their names are a sufficient guarantee for the honest endeavour to deserve public patronage, and they promise that the trust of the Public and its encouragement shall be met by continued zeal and liberality, increasing constantly with the means of shewing it. They will endeavour to confirm what may be found satisfactory, supply what may be at first deficient, and above all, exalt the entertainments, to meet the good tastes of their audiences.

They feel assured that such an endeavour is not unworthy of the kind encouragement of the more highly educated and influential classes. There may be differences of opinion as to the existence of Theatres altogether; there can be none as to the truth that if theatres are to exist, they should aim at the highest possible refinement and produce the most intellectual class of enjoyment which their audiences can receive.

They intend to continue their attempt as long as they can feel reasonable hope of making Sadler's Wells Theatre the resort of the respectable inhabitants of its neighbourhood for the highest purpose of theatrical entertainments.

Any Patron with whom this Circular is left, will, on sending an address card to the Box Office, have an admission for One forwarded, as it is the wish of the management (and their motive for this departure from their otherwise strict system of giving no Orders), to afford to those who may take an interest in their plan, an opportunity of judging for themselves, and to speak of the undertaking as they may think it deserves.

[1] Circular distributed by Phelps and Mrs Warner to the neighbourhood of Sadler's Wells in 1844.

The Phelps–Warner venture proved remarkably successful in winning to the theatre a respectable middle-class audience. Under the sole management of Phelps after 1846, its policy would identify Sadler's Wells as the home of a literary drama until 1862.

56   Phelps brings a new feeling to Sadler's Wells, 1844

Theatre Journal (3 August 1844), p. 244

Nothing can be a more convincing proof as to the public feeling on the subject of what is understood by the legitimate drama, than by the play-going public finding their way in such numbers to this *now* very ably conducted theatre. The manager has been progressing for the last two months in a manner most creditable to himself, and to the benefit of the public, finding his exertions are patronised to an extent which he could not expect from the fallen state of the drama. He has not failed to bring forward the choicest plays of Shakespear [sic], and to avail himself of the best actors that were within his reach, but at the same time to make every improvement in and out of the theatre, that could be put in practice for the comfort and convenience of the audience.

On entering the theatre on Monday evening, we found that in a few short hours the whole of the saloon had been carpeted, and the public accommodated with backs fitted up to every box, making the seats in this theatre as easy and as comfortable as at any house in the metropolis.

Mr Notter, the most experienced box-keeper, who has filled this situation for as many years with credit to himself, at Drury Lane and Covent Garden, is engaged, and the box department is now under his superintendance. His politeness and urbanity of manners are such that we feel assured the establishment will be greatly benefitted by his exertions.

The performance commenced with the tragedy of Hamlet which has been long in preparation. The splendour of the scenery is beyond our reach to give an adequate idea of; but we cannot refrain from noticing the scene – *the exterior of the castle by moonlight*, – and the manner in which the *ghost* disappears. This is quite novel and cleverly managed. The dresses are of the most costly description, and the play in the getting up cannot be surpassed. The principal parts were cast as follows:– *Hamlet*, Mr Phelps; *Laertes*, Mr J. Webster; *Polonius*, Mr A. Young; the *King*, Mr G. Bennett; the *Ghost*, Mr H. Marston:– *Queen*, Mrs Warner, and *Ophelia*, Miss Lebatt. Of the performance we shall avail ourselves of another opportunity [...] Suffice it to say, the play was altogether most ably performed, and each actor received their due reward from as respectable an audience as any theatre in the metropolis can boast of.

We cannot close our remarks without observing, that whoever has the arrangement of the music between the acts, they ought to pay a little more attention as to the subject of the play – to give all the light and flimsy airs that were played on this occasion between the acts of a tragedy, shows not only a want of taste, but in great measure destroys the impression made by the actors and the author.

II Playhouses

INTRODUCTION

Until the building of the Royalty Theatre, Wellclose Square, in 1787, eighteenth-century theatre-going in London was confined to the three patent theatres, Drury Lane, Covent Garden and the Little Theatre, Haymarket, plus the King's Theatre for opera, Sadler's Wells located in Islington for summer entertainments, and Astley's Amphitheatre and the Royal Circus in south London for acrobatic shows and equestrian performances, with occasional visits to booth shows such as Richardson's at the Smithfield or Bartholomew Fairs. Theatre building in the provinces, on the other hand, complemented the proliferation of provincial circuits from the middle of the eighteenth century.[1] From 1794, however, the focus of attention switched to London and the history of the period to 1850 is marked by extensive theatre building by speculators, which saw seventeen new theatres constructed between 1830 and 1843 and the consequent collision between the interests of the 'major' patent theatres and managements of new 'minor' theatres, the latter catering to the desire for diverse theatrical entertainment on the part of a rapidly expanding metropolitan audience.

The taste of the new London audiences for spectacular, romantic, as well as realistic environments on stage imposed itself also on the architecture of theatrical interiors. The principal effects can be seen in the ways in which the acting space became less important than the scenic space, exemplified by the retreat of the forestage and the removal of the proscenium doors used by actors to enter or exit, in order to incorporate performers within a scenic environment. Just as important were the constant remodelling and adaptation of the auditoria in order to improve sightlines and to focus attention on the stage (assisted by the introduction of gas as a means of illumination from 1817). Increasing competition between theatres saw continuing attempts to refurbish interiors in order to flatter the audience's sense of occasion by emphasizing ostentatious decoration, comfort and accessibility. This affected the policies of all the theatres, as they jostled for the patronage of fashionable audiences or those with a disposable income sufficient to fill the boxes, the most expensive parts of the house. In this they were by and large unsuccessful. The expense involved in refurbishment of the theatres, to say nothing of the initial building costs, could not be recouped at the box office. The period to 1850 saw the collapse of patent monopoly, with which the managements of Drury Lane and Covent Garden were unable to come to terms. Indeed, there is little evidence to suggest a managerial vision capable of administering huge theatres intended to monopolize the theatre-going of a London population, which, by the 1830s, no longer lived in their vicinity. At the same time the proprietors of the newly built theatres came to realize that their existence depended on the numbers who could be attracted continuously to the pit and the galleries, the cheaper parts of the house.

1   See David Thomas and Arnold Hare, *Restoration and Georgian England, 1660–1788* (Cambridge: Cambridge University Press, 1989), pp. 284–301 and James Winston, *The theatric tourist* (London: T. Woodfall, 1805), which reproduces drawings of twenty-four provincial theatres and a manuscript index that lists a further 273. (See also I. Mackintosh and G. Ashton, *The Georgian playhouse*, Arts Council exhibition catalogue, 1975, nos. 356–79, and Eric Irvin, 'More drawings from Winston's *Theatric Tourist*', *Theatre Notebook*, 19 (1964–5), pp. 64–6.)

THE LONDON PATENT THEATRES

Both Covent Garden and Drury Lane were rebuilt between 1792 and 1794 to the designs of Henry Holland, who introduced the continental horse-shoe shaped auditorium in both theatres. The redesigned Covent Garden opened on 17 September 1792. In order to improve sight-lines, especially from the boxes, Holland provided for raised benches with the fronts bowed to allow leg room. The boxes were all cantilevered, thus eliminating the need for supporting columns, which interfered with visibility. Further alterations were carried out in 1794 and 1796. Finally, in 1803, when John Philip Kemble became manager and part-owner of the theatre, the entire interior was changed. Holland had intended the proscenium doors to be built obliquely to the front of the stage, but by 1803 these doors were once again placed at right angles to it. The stage was raised by 10 feet to allow for better pit visibility. In addition, the various alterations increased the audience capacity from 2,797 to 3,013. This is the theatre depicted in the Rowlandson picture.[1]

1   R. Leacroft, *The development of the English playhouse* (London: Methuen, 1973), pp. 134–9.

57   Covent Garden Theatre, 1808

The microcosm of London (London: Ackermann, 1808), vol. 1, p. 212, Rowlandson aquatint

The theatre burned down on 20 September 1808 and reopened on 18 September 1809 to the designs of Robert Smirke.[1] In order to defray the costs, Kemble raised the price of admission to the boxes from 6s to 7s, to the pit from 3s 6d to 4s, and erected a third tier of boxes intended to be let for £12,000 per year.[2] The third row of boxes had private antechambers and full-length partitions. Above this tier was the 2s gallery, which had side boxes, the backs of which were painted to resemble drapery, and above these were the so-called pigeonholes, which housed the 1s gallery. The devotion of a third tier of boxes to a privileged section of society, together with the impossible conditions of the upper gallery, prompted the OP Riots [**109a–d**].[3] The illustration of the interior clearly shows the supporting pillars of the boxes and the lighting by glass chandeliers.[4] It also shows the proscenium stage, with the two doors 42 feet apart.

---

[1] The costs of rebuilding the theatre amounted to £150,000. Insurance covered only £44,500 (Britton and Pugin, *Public buildings of London*, vol. 1, p. 214). Private donations and a public subscription of shares at £500 each raised the remainder of the money. Barton Baker, *History of the London stage*, vol. 1, p. 147 and Sheppard, *Survey of London*, vol. xxxv, p. 78.

[2] *Ibid.*

[3] For the conditions of the 1s gallery, see Rowlandson's satirical engravings, for example BM Satires no. 1811:11797, reproduced in Mackintosh and Ashton, *Georgian playhouse*, no. 265. These pigeon-holes were not to be removed until 1812. The illustration shows the sides that were closed off in 1812.

4 James Boaden estimated that 270 wax candles needed to be supplied for the auditorium, together with 300 Argand lamps for stage lighting (*Memoirs of the life of John Philip Kemble* (London: Longman, Hurst, 1825), vol. II, p. 490, quoted in Leacroft, *Development of the English playhouse*, p. 179.

58   Interior of the rebuilt Covent Garden, 1809

The microcosm of London (London: Ackermann, 1809), vol. III, p. 263, Rowlandson and Pugin aquatint

As a result of the OP Riots further modifications to Covent Garden were made in the period up to 1824. Principal amongst these were the introduction of gas lighting in the auditorium in 1817, the raising of the low proscenium arch by 5 feet to allow better visibility for the galleries, the opening up of some of the private boxes, and the removal of the proscenium doors and most of the chandeliers from the front of the tiers. The latter were replaced by a large central chandelier with supplementary ones at the front of the lower circle of boxes.[1] By 1824 gas was also used for stage lighting [**67c**, **172**, **175**].[2] The seating capacity was thus: public or open boxes, about 1,200; the pit, 750; second gallery, 500; first gallery, 350; total, 2,800.

1 Leacroft, *Development of the English playhouse*, pp. 184–7, and the isometric reconstruction fig. 112, p. 183. Sheppard, *Survey of London*, vol. XXXV, pp. 93–7.
2 Though by 1826 gas was used both in the auditorium and on stage, the argument about the smell of gas and the theatre's poor ventilation continued. There were also aesthetic considerations that favoured the softer candle lighting.

59   Backstage in the new theatre, 1824

J. Britton and A. Pugin, *Illustration of the public buildings of London* (London: Weale, 1825–8), vol. II, pp. 222–3

The Stage is large and commodious. On the right of the Auditory, or left of the Stage, are the passages which lead to the superior and inferior green-rooms; the former of which is handsomely fitted up: at one end is a stove, and opposed to it a large looking-glass for the performers to adjust their dresses by, previously to going on the stage. The seats for the performers are covered with crimson, and the windows are decorated by crimson curtains; the room is handsomely carpeted, and there is a large chimney-glass over the stove, with a portrait of the late T. Harris, Esq., so many years proprietor of the Theatre. Performers receiving under a certain salary are not allowed to enter this room but on particular occasions. The inferior green-room is up a flight of stairs, and is neatly fitted up; and here is a piano-forte for the singers to try their songs, and for the choristers to learn their music. Beyond the best green-room is the manager's room, and the passage leads on to the coffee-room, property-room, and others appropriated to the business of the Theatre. The scene-rooms, carpenter's shop, etc., are in this part of the building. The stage is principally lighted by gas [. . .][1]

The Flies, or that part of the Theatre surmounting the stage [. . .] consist of two storeys. These are filled with the machinery used in lowering the curtain, drops, wheels, borders, clouds, etc. etc.; and adjoining them is the painting-room, which is furnished with sky-lights, and measures in length 72 feet, and in width 32 feet [. . .]

[1] Stage measurements quoted are: depth of stage from the front lighting to the back of the stage wall, 68 feet; width, 82 feet 6 inches; height of the flats, 21 feet; width of each flat, 14 feet; height of wings, 21 feet by about 4 feet.

60   The auditorium of the new Covent Garden, 1824

Britton and Pugin, *Public buildings of London*, vol. II, pp. 219–22[1]

The Auditory.– The form of the Auditory is that of the horse-shoe: the width at the extremities is 51 feet 2 inches; and the depth, from the front lights to the front of the boxes, 52 feet 9 inches. There are three tiers of boxes, each containing twenty-six, including those in the proscenium; and there are seven boxes on each side above them and parallel with the lower gallery. The number of private boxes are [*sic*] twenty-six [. . .] To the principal private boxes are attached private rooms, with fire-places. The width of the lower gallery is 55 feet, the depth 40. The width of the upper gallery is 55 feet, the depth 25.

The appearance of the house is very imposing: the colour is a subdued yellow, relieved by white, and superbly enriched with gilding. Around the dress circle are wreaths inclosing [*sic*] the Rose of England, in burnished gold; the first circle displays the Thistle of Scotland, and the second circle the Shamrock of Ireland: and these three emblems are alternately placed, with fancy devices, in rich borderings, etc., in every part of the Auditory; which, from the reflection of the lights, gratifies the prevalent taste for splendour with one blaze of refulgence. The back and sides of the pit are decorated by the representation of dark crimson drapery, as are the interiors of all the boxes [. . .] The boxes are supported by small iron columns, fluted, and gilt. The ceiling, over what is called the slip boxes, exhibits panels of blue, relieved by white, and enriched with gold. The middle part of the ceiling is circular; in the centre of which [. . .] is suspended a chandelier of glass, [. . .] illumined by two circles of gas lights [. . .] The proscenium is supported by four pilasters, painted to imitate Sienna marble. Stage doors are wholly dispensed with. The top of the proscenium, from whence the curtain descends, is an arch of about 38 feet wide and 3 feet deep; surmounting a superb drapery border of crimson, white and gold, elegantly disposed upon a transverse bar of gold, terminated on each side with a lion's head: in the centre of this drapery is the King's Arms. For the green curtain is substituted a drop, representing a luxuriant profusion of drapery; crimson, white, and gold (to match the borders), drawn up by cords and tassels [. . .]

The number of superbly brilliant cut-glass chandeliers, which are hung round the Auditory, is fourteen; with three gas-lights in each. In the two extreme dress boxes are large looking-glasses.

The King's box is always fitted up on the left of the audience, in the dress circle, and occupies the extent of three or four of the boxes.

[1] Quoted in part in Sheppard, *Survey of London*, vol. xxxv, pp. 96–7.

61   Gas lighting removed from the Covent Garden auditorium, 1828

Theatre (22 November 1828), p. 114

The Managers of Covent Garden Theatre have deemed it necessary to close their house for a week, in order that all the gas pipes may be removed from the interior, and that wax lights may be substituted. Mr FAWCETT, the Stage Manager, has published the following address to the public:–

'When the brilliancy of gas illuminations attracted the public admiration, the Proprietors of this Theatre, anxious to adopt every improvement which would give brilliancy to the scenery, and the appearance of the Theatre, introduced it; and, to prevent the accidents which the best street illumination is liable to, they, at great expense, constructed gasometers. Finding, however, that, with the utmost care and skill, the introduction of gas, in the audience part of the Theatre, produced an offensive odour; and the public having suffered inconvenience and disappointment in their amusement [. . .] the Proprietors have determined to remove the gas, not only from the Box Circles, but from all internal avenues leading to them, as well as to the Pit and Galleries [. . .] The Public is in consequence, respectfully informed that, as the proposed improvements cannot be executed in less than a week, the Theatre will remain closed till Monday, the 24th instant [. . .]'

Covent Garden received its new name, the Royal Italian Opera House, in 1847. Two additional tiers of boxes were built and the size of the pit was increased to provide an overall capacity of 2,255. The central glass gas chandelier was supplemented by branches for candles. Heating was installed, together with an improved ventilation system.[1]

[1] Leacroft, *Development of the English playhouse*, pp. 187–90 (the illustration is also reproduced as fig. 115).

62   Interior of the new Opera House, Covent Garden, 1847

Builder (10 April 1847), p. 170

DRURY LANE

More spectacular than Holland's achievement at Covent Garden in 1792 was the realization of a completely new Drury Lane, which opened on 12 March 1794 with a seating capacity of 3,611 (although reputedly it could hold 3,919). It was self-consciously intended to be one of the great playhouses of Europe, with a stage and machinery more elaborate than at any other European theatre.[1] Like Foulston's plans for the Theatre Royal, Plymouth, in 1811, the new Drury Lane was intended to be part of a leisure complex, with coffeehouses and shops, all surrounded by a colonnade of Ionic columns. This part was never realized. The theatre building itself was lavishly decorated in a colour scheme of light blue, white, silver and beige, with mirrors and cut-glass chandeliers.[2] The proscenium doors were eliminated. Considerable attention was paid to reducing the risk of fire by including large water tanks intended to service both stage and auditorium. In addition, an iron safety curtain was installed to cut off the stage from the auditorium.

---

[1] The machinery was designed and executed by Rudolph Cabanel for a stage 83 feet wide, 92 feet long and 108 feet high. (Holland's description of his intentions, quoted in Sheppard, *Survey of London*, vol. xxxv, p. 49.)
[2] *Ibid*, pp. 49–51.

63   Suggestions for the refurbishment of Drury Lane, 1791

Drury Lane Memoranda, BL, C.120.h. 1, unidentified clipping, 5 July 1791

In the rebuilding of this Theatre, a correspondent suggests, that it would be a great improvement, to have the floor of the pit, and the seats of it on a level, and not sloping, and one above another as at present. If the stage be raised to a proper height, so as to be on a line with the average height of the foreheads of the persons seated, all would see well, and not intercept each others views, as may be observed when crowds stand round a scaffold on which any shew is exhibited; all see equally; those at a distance as well as those near.[1]

If the floor of the stage was made to slant more, and three or four rows of lamps in the front rising a very little one above the other, it would not be necessary to have the screen-boards so high, as at present, which has the inconvenience of hiding the legs of the Performers, and is disagreeable.

Our Correspondent suggests also, the propriety of having the boxes, and the audience part of the house as plain as possible, to *keep it down*, in the Painter's language, that the decorations and scenery of the stage may not suffer by contrast. In the late Opera-House, in the Haymarket, the pit and galleries were so elegant and showy, that the painting of the scenes looked poor and flat; and one was perpetually tempted to turn from the stage, and please the eye with a view of the audience.

---

[1] In fact, the stepped pit was to be retained in 1794 with a rise of 10 degrees (Sheppard, *Survey of London*, vol. xxxv, p. 52).

64   The opening of the new Drury Lane Theatre, 1794

Drury Lane Memoranda, BL, C.120.h. 1, unidentified clipping, 22 April 1794

This commodious and magnificent Theatre opened yesterday evening with the Tragedy of MACBETH. The crowd, as might well be imagined, was immense;– not a place was to be had in any part, long before the curtain drew up; and, barring a few interruptions from the hurry and anxiety naturally attending a night of bustle such as this, the audience seemed in general like the gracious *Duncan*, shut up in 'measureless content'.

The late hour at which the Play concluded (for the Epilogue was not finished till 20 minutes past 11), precludes us from entering at large upon the performances. With the merits of the Performers the Public is well acquainted. KEMBLE and Mrs SIDDONS, feeling the inspiration of the evening, were never more themselves.– PALMER, as a *Stranger*, found himself perfectly at home; the reception sufficiently evinced how well his best friends were delighted with the banishment of *Macduff* 'from Stotland' [*sic*].

C. KEMBLE, the younger brother of the Manager, is an actor of much promise – his speeches were given with good emphasis and discretion; his tones frequently reminded us of STEPHEN KEMBLE and Mrs SIDDONS.

The scenery of *Macbeth* is extremely beautiful, and the scenes, departing from the custom of the Old School, ascend instead of sliding on grooves. The various views of the blasted heath are happily contrasted with those of the Castle of Macbeth; the wings were not so well worked as may be expected when practice shall have made the Machinists perfect.

In getting up this tragedy, great attention has evidently been bestowed to the notes of the several commentators; among the boldest alterations is that of laying BANQUO's Ghost, and making the troubled spirit only visible to the 'mind's eye' of the guilty and distracted tyrant. The aerial car of *Hecate* has a happy effect. The Witches 'hover though fog and filthy air', no longer on switch or broom, but perform their magic incantations with rods – though, by the bye, the furbishing of Hecate fares the worse for the exchange. The Armed Spirit was not quite so potent as he ought to have been, for the spring of the trap threw him on his knees.– The dance about the cauldron from its fantastic round, we should suggest was suggested by *Fuzeli*.– The black spirits passed muster tolerably well, but the white ones wore greatly the resemblance of the dancing dogs of old.– Those barren spectators who regarded not the text, indulged a hearty laugh at their expence [*sic*]!

In the course of the evening, the Gods made a violent remonstrance against the chandeliers, which obstructed their view of the stage – they were soon appeased by a promise from Mr Kemble that the evil should be rectified against this evening: this was an inconvenience generally complained of in the back from Boxes – *verbum sat*.

The prologue, delivered with great spirit and feeling by Mr KEMBLE, touched on the excellence of our Constitution; the beauties of our Poets, and concluded with a well turned compliment to SHAKESPEARE, the acknowledged genius of the House.

The Epilogue, which might truly be termed occasional, introduced Miss FARREN as the *Housekeeper*, shewing off all the beauties and conveniences of the new building,– her description was illustrated by scenery, and a boy was introduced rowing a boat on a canal of REAL water. The iron curtain is also alluded to, and the Epilogue, which has full matter enough to serve for a farce, terminates with a view of SHAKESPEARE and his mulberry tree, with the favourite song of 'Behold this fair goblet', from the Jubilee.[1]

---

[1] See Leacroft's isometric reconstruction in *Development of the English playhouse*, pp. 142–3 and the Edward Dayes watercolour of 1795, reproduced as the frontispiece of Sheppard, *Survey of London*, vol. XXXV.

65   Alterations to Drury Lane, 1797

Drury Lane Memoranda, BL, C.120.h. 1, unidentified clipping, 1797

DRURY-LANE

Opened on Tuesday, the 19th of September, with *The School for Scandal* and *The Children in the Wood* [. . .]

The alterations that have taken place in the interior of the theatre, in conformity to a plan of Mr Holland, the original architect of the house, are as follow. The pit is considerably lowered, and rendered more sloping, so that the audience in that part of the theatre have a much better view of the stage, and the view is wholly unobstructed. There are two additional boxes on each side, to those nearly on a level with the pit.

There is a stage door on each side, forming a segment of a circle, and over these doors are two tiers of boxes. The effect of this addition is a contraction of the width of the stage, and an additional space behind the scenes, which gives more facility to the movement of the scenery.

That part of the ceiling which is immediately over the *proscenium*, or stage, is made to slope off towards the back of the stage; an alteration that gives more distinctiveness to the voice, and prevents all reverberation. These are the most material alterations. The boxes, which were before lined with blue, now have a crimson lining; and all the ornamental parts which were of silver gilding, such as the front of the boxes, and the pillars, are now of gold.

There is a saloon at the back of the pit, belonging to the boxes, in which are compartments for the sale of refreshments, plays, books of songs, etc.

The additional boxes are not open to the public in general, but engaged by subscription.

These alterations, though extensive, do not break the unity of the *coup d'œil*, which is as chaste and elegant as before, though with more warmth and relief.

The view from the stage of 1804, which masks the stage doors, shows a cut sky cloth and the movable screen that could narrow the width of the proscenium.

66   Interior of Drury Lane, 1804

Pugin illustration. Henry Huntington Library

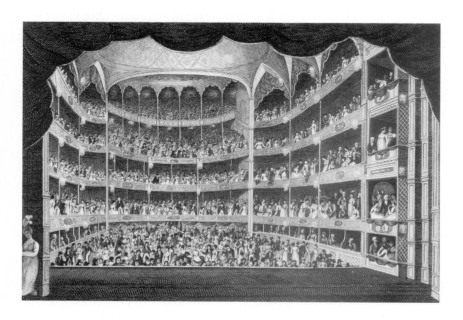

Despite the fire precautions, Holland's theatre was destroyed on 24 February 1809 and would not reopen until 10 October 1812. Benjamin Wyatt, the theatre's architect, tried to address the specific issues of visibility and audibility, the ease with which spectators could enter and exit from the theatre, the size of the auditorium, and the opportunity for 'the more rational and respectable class of Spectators' to avoid contact with prostitutes and disreputable people generally.[1] Though he did not succeed in overcoming the difficulties of audibility, Wyatt's determination to define the 'spectatory' and the stage as areas of discrete activity marks the beginning of the picture-frame stage. The resistance of the actors can be judged from the occasions when the proscenium arch doors were replaced. In 1822 Elliston spent £22,000 on completely renovating the theatre and this was carried out to the designs of Samuel Beazley.[2]

[1] Benjamin Wyatt, *Observations on the Design of the Theatre Royal, Drury Lane*, 1813, quoted in Leacroft, *Development of the English playhouse*, p. 166 and Sheppard, *Survey of London*, vol. xxxv, p. 60 and plate 32a.
[2] G. Raymond, *Memoirs of Robert William Elliston*, vol. II, p. 315 and Sheppard, *Survey of London*, vol. xxxv, pp. 64–5. For the isometric reconstruction of Drury Lane after 1822, see Leacroft, *Development of the English playhouse*, p. 192, fig. 116.

67   Drury Lane as modified in 1822

Britton and Pugin; *Public buildings of London*, vol. 1, pp. 252–8

(a) Description from the stage

The general tone of the colouring is a light warm drab, profusely decorated with ornaments in gold, and in some parts blended with a light red colour. In its original state, as constructed by Mr Wyatt, the auditory included three-fourths of a circle, the diameter of which, across the pit to the line of the breastwork of the dress boxes, was 58 feet; and the extreme distance, from the front of the stage to the back-wall of the boxes facing it, was 53 feet 9 inches. The present form, as designed by Mr Beazley, is nearly that of the horse-shoe; [. . .] from the front [of the stage] [. . .] to the dress boxes, the extreme distance is 48 feet.

The fronts of the dress boxes are tastefully embellished by a series of representations [. . .] from the most popular of Shakspeare's dramas; and in the two extreme boxes are large looking-glasses [. . .] Grecian ornaments, of varied design, in running patterns, with rosettes, wreaths, etc., adorn the fasciæ of the different tiers; the whole presenting a blaze of golden enrichments. Brass guards are continued round the fronts of the upper boxes and slips, and of the upper and lower galleries. From plain gold-like brackets rich cut-glass lustres are suspended: each of four lights, having bell-glasses inverted over the burners. The seats of the pit are covered with crimson cloth, and a rail-work back has been recently attached to every alternate row[1] [. . .]

[. . .] From an opening in the centre [of the ceiling], a very large cut-glass lustre descends, which is lit by gas [. . .]

(b) The stage from the auditorium

The *Proscenium*, as now arranged, is exceedingly different from its original state, as designed by Mr Wyatt, and from which it has been several times altered. On each side, elevated on a lofty pedestal, forming a parallelogram, are two demi-columns, of the Corinthian order, fluted,* and superbly gilt, supporting an entablature, above which, in semicircular niches, are allegorical statues of Tragedy and Comedy [. . .] On each side, between the columns, are three private boxes, the fronts of which are crimson, plaited; the plaits of each middle box centering [*sic*] in a radiant head of Apollo, gilt: there is, also, another private box, nearly level with the stage, in the pedestal or basement, on each side, masked by a pierced ornamental (movable) panel, exhibiting a lyre amidst foliage, in dead and burnished gold. The King's box is that between the columns, on the left of the auditory, which ranges from the dress circle: [. . .]

---

* These columns are of wood; they are hollow, and the apparent flutings are real apertures, through which the performances can be seen from the private boxes: the capitals are of plaster.

Between the acts, during a performance, a rich drop scene is substituted for the curtain: it was executed by Marinari and Station (the figures being by the latter), at an expense of about 700l. It is a fine composition of Grecian ruins and figures, within a highly wrought fancy bordering, or frame, heightened with gold. Another elegant drop scene, by Station, which is used between the play and the afterpiece, includes the Coliseum, and other remains of classic architecture, with figures, landscapes, etc. The weight of each of these drops, with the roller and necessary adjuncts, is about 800 lb [. . .]

(c) Description of the new stage and backstage facilities

The *Stage*, although of great extent, and longer than that of Covent Garden, is sometimes insufficient for the convenient representation of the spectacles introduced here; notwithstanding that a large archway has been cut through the main wall, eastward, into an adjoining building originally intended for a scene-room. There is, likewise, a deficiency of depth in the cellar below the mexxonine [*sic*] floor, which occasionally prevents the machinery, in pantomimes, from being worked so readily as the business requires [. . .] In the principal *Green Room* is a large looking-glass, in panels, measuring 8 feet 3 inches by 4 feet 6 inches, for the performers to adjust their dresses by, previously to appearing before the audience; [. . .] The inferior Green Room, which contains a piano-forte, for the use of the performers and choristers, is part of a separate building, attached to the outer wall of the theatre. There are also ranges of stabling for twenty horses [. . .] The stage is, principally, enlightened by gas, the pipes being arranged below the flooring, and having their extremities partially inserted in grooves, so as to admit of their being moved in accordance with the play of the machinery.[2]

[. . .] Among the recent alterations was a complete removal of the stage doors; and all entries before the curtain were made through a tent-like opening in a superb drop-scene, but the latter was disused after the first season.

Over the stage are the *Flies*, etc., [. . .] [which] contain the windlasses, machinery, etc. employed in lowering the curtain, drops, borders, clouds, cars, and other appendages to the scene. In the line with the upper flies, over the auditory, are carpenters' shops, property-rooms, store-rooms, etc. The *Painting Room*, which is over the eastern extremity of the stage, is 79 feet in length, and nearly 31 feet in height and width.

The *Scene Room* is a detached building at the north-east angle of the theatre, but having a communication with the stage, and also with Drury Lane. Its length is 73 feet 3 inches, and its medium width about 30 feet [. . .]

Among the many alterations which have been made in this theatre, since its construction by Mr Wyatt, has been the piercing the main walls by numerous internal doorways; the original communications between the different parts of the house having been so few and so extremely inconvenient, that the business could not be properly carried on.

---

[1] The capacity of the house is quoted as: dress circle boxes (26, holding 9 people), 234; first circle (14 boxes, holding 14 people), 196; the second circle, 480; 20 private boxes holding 8 people, 160; 16 family boxes holding 6 people, 96; 8 proscenium boxes with 8 people each, 64; slips, 130; pit, 800; lower gallery, 550; upper gallery, 350, making a total of 3,060.

[2] The dimensions of the stage are quoted as: the width of the proscenium, 46 feet 6 inches; from the front of the stage to the curtain, 12 feet 9 inches (p. 255); from the orchestra to the back wall, 96 feet 3 inches; the width of the stage, 77 feet 5 inches; the height of the flats, 21 feet with each flat 14 feet in width; the height of the wings, 21 feet with a width of between 5 and 8 feet (p. 257).

THE KING'S THEATRE

This theatre, variously know as the Queen's, the King's, Her Majesty's, His Majesty's, or more popularly, the Opera House, had been extensively remodelled in 1796. Its auditorium was extensively redecorated in 1807.[1] The illustration shows the extremely large stage, which forced a number of box patrons to see the backs of performers, the curtained box divisions and the false marble fronts of the first tier. The capacity was about 2,500, comprising a pit (800), boxes (900) and a gallery (800), with prices of 10s 6d for box and pit seats and 5s for a gallery seat. Between 1816 and 1818 further changes were made to the exterior of the building and a central gas chandelier replaced those attached to the front of the boxes.

[1]   See Thomas and Hare, *Restoration and Georgian England*, nos. 231–5 and Sheppard, *Survey of London*, vol. XXIX, part I, pp. 239–41.

68   The King's Theatre, 1809

Rowlandson and Pugin aquatint, in Ackermann's *Microcosm of London*, vol. I, p. 26

THE HAYMARKET THEATRE

The Haymarket Theatre had remained almost unaltered since the eighteenth century, having been refurbished in 1777 by George Colman the Elder.[1] In 1821, at a cost of £18,000, it was entirely rebuilt but still remained an intimate theatre, seating no more than 1,000. Unlike other theatres, which had horseshoe interiors, the boxes were arranged as a rectangle with straight sides, and candle and oil lighting continued in use until gas was introduced in 1843. The stage was also modified at that time to eliminate the forestage.[2] The illustration shows the palm-tree pillars and an auditorium lit by cut-glass chandeliers arranged round the boxes, rather than by a central ceiling source.[3]

[1] For the shape of the old eighteenth-century theatre, see Thomas and Hare, *Restoration and Georgian England*, no. 230.
[2] Leacroft, *Development of the English playhouse*, p. 170.
[3] Britton and Pugin, *Public buildings of London*, vol. I, pp. 270–2.

69   Opening night of the new Haymarket Theatre, 1821

Schnebbelie engraving from Wilkinson's *Londina illustrata* (1823). Henry Huntington Library

70   Nash's Haymarket Theatre, 1821
Britton and Pugin, *Public buildings of London*, vol. 1, pp. 270–2

(a) The exterior of the theatre

The three middle doors lead to the boxes; the outer, on the right, to the box-office, and that on the left to the pit. In the intermediate spaces are four large lamps or lanterns for gas. The gallery entrances are on each side, without the portico; [. . .] The exterior width of the theatre is 61 feet; its height to the top of the parapet 47 feet 9 inches; and its length 134 feet 6 inches.

(b) Description of the interior from the stage

The Auditory differs from those of the other theatres in form; the sides being straight, and the centre a small segment of a large circle; but the fronts of the side boxes project semi-circularly.

The arch of the proscenium, and that part of the auditory where the side and front boxes connect, are supported by richly gilt palm-trees, instead of pillars [. . .]

The fronts of the boxes are decorated with raised chequered or net-work ornaments of gold, on a reddish purple ground. The seats and curtains are crimson, and the insides of the boxes morone [*sic*]. The ceiling is neat and fanciful, but it has not the usual characteristic of a modern theatre, a pendant central lustre and gas-lights. Indeed, this is the only patent theatre in which gas is not used, it being wholly lighted with oil, and spermaceti candles; the latter exhibited in a very handsome circle of cut-glass chandeliers, holding some five and others six lights. There are two circles or tiers of boxes, besides half-tiers, parallel with the lower gallery. In the first circle are five private boxes, and on the second tier, eight. The Saloon, which fronts Charles Street, is elegantly fitted up, and contains conveniences for refreshments.

The dramas peculiar to this theatre are light comedy, comic opera, and broad farce [. . .] The house holds upwards of 300l.[†]

[†] The company engaged at this theatre (which is discriminatively termed the 'Summer House'), is composed of the best provincial performers that can be collected; with three or four of the most popular actors from the winter houses, who join the Haymarket when their respective theatres close.

PROVINCIAL THEATRES ROYAL

Provincial theatre managers soon tried to emulate the metropolis, and by the early nineteenth century, to seek the award of letters patent. Some of the more significant were the Ipswich Theatre Royal (1803), the Birmingham Theatre Royal (1807), the Theatre Royal, Plymouth (1813), the Liverpool Royal Amphitheatre (1821), the New Theatre, Leicester (1836) and the Theatre Royal, Newcastle-upon-Tyne (1837).[1]

[1] See Richard Southern, *The Georgian playhouse* (London: Pleiades Books, 1948), pp. 54–62; Leacroft, *Development of the English playhouse*, pp. 197–206, and, on Plymouth specifically, Harvey Crane, *Playbill: a history of theatre in the West Country* (Plymouth: MacDonald & Evans, 1980), pp. 71–6.

71   Theatre Royal, Birmingham, 1825

Engraving reproduced in John E. Cunningham, *Theatre Royal: the history of the Theatre Royal, Birmingham* (Oxford: G. Ronald, 1950), p. 49

The building was reopened after a fire in 1794 and became a Theatre Royal in 1807. It burned down again in 1820, but was rebuilt under the management of Alfred Bunn almost immediately, with an auditorium lit by gas.

72   Theatre Royal, Newcastle-upon-Tyne, 1837, exterior

Collard and Carmichael coloured etching, H. R. Beard Collection, F152–19, Theatre Museum

Built in 1837 to the designs of Benjamin Green, the theatre's impressive façade reflects the theatre building as a cultural artefact. According to Richard Southern, the interior already possessed a proscenium arch with a defined scenic stage.[1]

[1] Southern, *Georgian playhouse*, plates 50–4 illustrate the building plans and the interior.

LONDON MINOR THEATRES

A number of playhouses that began operations in the eighteenth century continued to exert a substantial influence, notably Sadler's Wells, the Lyceum, the Royal Circus and Astley's. Both their opening times and the range of their repertoire were severely curtailed – to summer seasons, when the patent theatres were closed, and to music, dancing and non-textual entertainments. Nevertheless, as the exclusive rights of the patent theatres began to erode, and as their constant rebuilding after fires attests, these theatres sought to extend their seasons and their repertoire.

The most distinctive minor theatre was Astley's, which retained its identification with horsemanship and spectacular recreations of famous battles throughout the nineteenth century. Astley began his equestrian entertainments in a partially covered venue on the south bank of the Thames, near Westminster Bridge, in 1775. His second, covered theatre opened in 1784, but was burned down in 1794, and a third building opened in 1795 as the Royal Amphitheatre. This also burned down in 1803 and was rebuilt to open in 1804. The theatre was specially noted for its equestrian spectacles under the management of Andrew Ducrow, 1830–41. The illustration shows the 44-foot ring, which was covered with earth and sawdust, the 4-foot curved enclosure and the exits for horses and riders on each side. Although by 1825 the illumination was by gas, it would appear that at this earlier stage both the central chandelier and the other lighting clusters were candlelit. This building survived until it too burned down in 1841.[1]

[1] Britton and Pugin, *Public buildings of London*, vol. I, pp. 284–6. Barton Baker (*History of the London stage*) comments that 'Every great battle, from Waterloo to Kassassin, has probably been at some time depicted upon that stage' (vol. II, p. 227). See E. Sherson, *London's lost theatres of the nineteenth century* (London: 1925; reprinted New York: Blom, 1969), pp. 52–76 and A. H. Saxon, *Enter foot and horse* (New Haven: Yale University Press, 1968), pp. 12–15 and plates 2 and 8.

73   Interior of Astley's Amphitheatre, 1808

Rowlandson aquatint in Ackermann's *Microcosm of London*, vol. i, p. 23

Opened in 1771 as a riding school and a place for the exhibition of horsemanship in competition with Astley's, the first designated theatre building calling itself the Royal Circus was
erected in 1782 under the management of Charles Hughes and Charles Dibdin the Elder.
After the destruction by fire in 1799 and again in 1804,[1] it was rebuilt in 1805 with a circus
ring not dissimilar to that of Astley's. Under Elliston's management in 1809 this was dismantled and replaced by a conventional pit, and the theatre was renamed the Surrey. Apart
from interior redecoration in 1852, this building remained in continuous operation until its
destruction by fire in 1865.

---

[1] There is some imprecision about the actual date of the theatre's destruction. Barton Baker gives
1803 (*History of London stage*, vol. ii, p. 230), while Diana Howard, *London theatres and music halls,
1850–1950* (London: Library Association, 1970) situates it precisely as 12 August 1805 (p. 233).

74   Royal Circus interior prior to 1809

Rowlandson and Pugin aquatint, in Ackermann's *Microcosm of London*, vol. III, p. 13

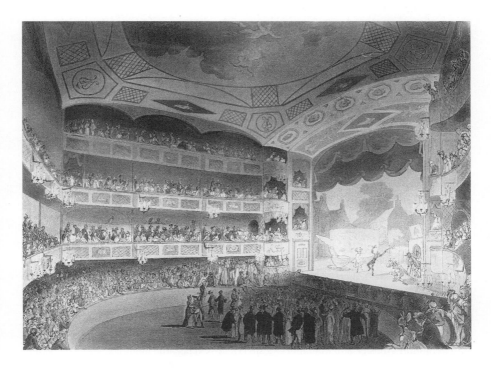

The Coburg Theatre was built as a speculative venture to profit from the construction of Waterloo Bridge. It was hoped that the opening up of Lambeth would attract a fashionable clientèle. In 1833 it was renamed the Royal Victoria. Its capacity varied from 3,835, including standing room, to a more conservative 2,700.[1]

[1] These estimates are based on William Davidge's 1832 account to the Select Committee on Dramatic Literature and the Lord Chamberlain's total in 1843 (PRO LC7/5 1843–4). The exterior of the Coburg and the looking-glass curtain reflecting the interior of the theatre in 1822 are reproduced in Sheppard, *Survey of London*, vol. XXIII, part 1, plates 19 and 20.

75   The opening of the Coburg Theatre, 1818

European Magazine (May 1818), p. 434

This elegant little Theatre opened on Monday, May 11, with a melo-dramatic spectacle, entitled '*Trial by Battle*'. The incidents were numerous and well arranged; the scenery was diversified and painted with considerable skill. Allowing for their first appearances, the performers all acquitted themselves in a satisfactory manner, and the piece was loudly applauded. The ballet of *Alzora and Nerine* followed, and the entertainments concluded, at a late hour, with a pantomime called *Midnight Revelry*.– The accommodations for the audience at this theatre are very well arranged. The three tiers of boxes are disposed in the amphitheatrical form: the two lower are painted of a fawn colour, with crimson octagonal compartments, enclosing imitations of white bas-reliefs, and varied by the alternate mixture of gilded wreaths. The frontispiece of the proscenium, with the appropriate heraldic arms, is neatly executed. The upper boxes and gallery front are adorned with a tolerable chaste imitation of a Grecian sculptured frieze. The ceiling, in its compartments, harmonizes agreeably with the rest of the house. From the centre, a large and magnificent cut-glass light is suspended, with a number of lamps of a bulbous form, of ground glass, not of gas, but sufficient to exhibit the transparency and prismatic colouring of the pendant crystals. The way from town to this new place of amusement is direct enough; but, as the Waterloo-bridge Company have taken an interest in completing this Theatre, they should also take care that the road from their bridge be lighted; and, still more, that the footpath, for a part of the way, be better fenced against the accidents of persons in the dark falling into the marshes.

Built by a merchant, John Scott, the Sans Pareil Theatre was one of the earliest speculative ventures. It opened on 27 November 1806 with a repertoire of music, recitations and fireworks, later supplemented by acrobats, animal shows and burlettas. The building itself was noteworthy for the abolition of boxes and the establishment of a dress circle above the widened pit – a new configuration that would become the norm.[1] In 1819 the theatre was renamed the Adelphi, and particularly under the managements of Terry and Yates (1825–42) and Benjamin Webster and Madame Celeste (1844–58) became identified with the performance of sensational melodrama. The theatre was extensively redecorated in 1848, but by 1858 its condition was so poor that it was pulled down and rebuilt.[2]

[1] *Revels history of drama in English*, vol. VI, 1750–1880, p. 82.
[2] *Illustrated London News* (7 October 1848), p. 224 and Barton Baker, *History of the London stage*, vol. II, pp. 73–97.

76   The Sans Pareil and the Adelphi

(a) Interior of Sans Pareil Theatre, *c.* 1816

G. Jones engraving, Henry Huntington Library

(b) Theatre Royal, Adelphi, 1858[1]

Builder (25 December 1858), p. 871

[1] The illustration shows T. H. Wyatt's design, with the adoption of the widened pit, dress circle stalls and orchestra stalls (now standard practice) and the new act curtain designed by Clarkson Stanfield. The stage protruded beyond the proscenium arch by 4 feet. Wyatt increased the width of each seat to 1 foot 10 inches in order to make them more comfortable. The building was regarded as remarkable, especially in its use of wrought and riveted iron (Builder, 11 December 1858, pp. 833–4 and 25 December 1858, p. 870).

The Lyceum opened as a place for entertainment in 1765. It was partially rebuilt in 1794 and completed in 1809 when it was renamed the English Opera House to reflect the managerial policy of performing English ballad opera, cut-down versions of German and Italian operas and musical farces. It was again rebuilt to the designs of Samuel Beazley and reopened on 15 June 1816. Barton Baker refers to the distinctive feature of the building as a 72×40 foot saloon fitted up as a wintergarden.[1] In 1817 gas was introduced for stage lighting. This enabled magic lantern shows modelled on de Loutherbourg's Eidophysikon to be shown.[2] After its destruction by fire in 1830, Beazley again provided the design for the new theatre, which opened on 12 July 1834. In 1844 its name was changed to the Theatre Royal, Lyceum.[3]

[1] Barton Baker, History of the London stage, vol. II, p. 38.
[2] R. Altick, The shows of London (Cambridge, MA: Harvard University Press, 1978), pp. 121–7.
[3] Barton Baker, History of the London stage, vol. II, pp. 35–53; Howard, London theatres, pp. 144–5.

77   The English Opera House and the Royal Lyceum

(a) English Opera House (Lyceum), 1817

Burney engraving, Henry Huntington Library

(b) Interior of the Royal Lyceum Theatre, 1847[1]

Builder (23 October 1847), p. 507

[1] The illustration shows the 1834 building as redecorated by Vestris and Mathews, when they became the lessees in October 1847 (*Builder*, 16 October 1847, pp. 489–94).

Philip Astley built the Olympic Theatre in order to extend his activities into a winter season. It opened on 18 September 1806 with a programme of 'horsemanship, vaulting and pantomime'.[1] In 1813 it was bought by Elliston, who remodelled the theatre in an effort to attract a more fashionable audience, and who retained it until 1819. The theatre was subsequently redecorated on a number of occasions, and gas was installed in 1826.[2] The last major refurbishment occurred in 1831 on the commencement of Vestris's very successful management. The theatre burned down in March 1849, but was rebuilt to the designs of F. W. Bushill to open again in December of the same year.

[1] *Monthly Mirror* (September 1806), quoted in R. Mander and J. Mitchenson, *The lost theatres of London* (London: New English Library, 1975), p. 256. The journal describes the theatre as small and capable of holding no more than £80. It had a raised orchestra and the auditorium was lit by twelve Argand-type lamps.
[2] Barton Baker (*History of the London stage*) maintains that gas may have been used to light the saloons and exterior of the theatre as early as 1815 (vol. II, p. 12).

78   The Olympic Theatre, old and new

(a) The Olympic Theatre, 1816

Schnebbelie engraving for Wilkinson, *Londina illustrata*. Henry Huntington Library[1]

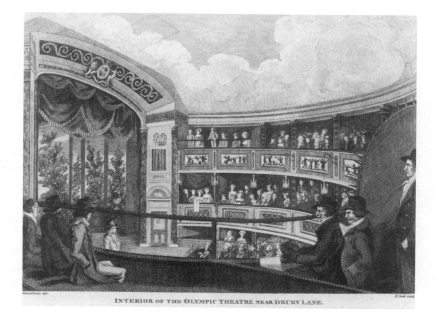

INTERIOR OF THE OLYMPIC THEATRE NEAR DRURY LANE.

[1] The illustration shows the theatre before Elliston further redecorated it in 1818 and installed a central glass chandelier.

(b) Description of the new Olympic Theatre, 1849

Builder (22 December 1849), pp. 601–2

On the *Ground Floor* (and shown on the plan), are the principal entrances [. . .] also the pit and pit-stalls, with separate entrances to stalls; two proscenium boxes, a refreshment-room, water closet, etc.; the orchestra, proscenium and stage, green-room, porters' room, and entrance to the stage, with separate way for horses and scenery.

On the *Box Floor* are six private boxes, three on each side; four tiers of dress and two tiers of back seats, in the centre of the house; a corridor at back of boxes, with separate staircases to slips and private boxes; a small *salon*, ladies' cloak-room, separate water-closets, urinal, etc.

On the *Gallery Level* are two private (proscenium) boxes and four slip boxes, a spacious gallery, with refreshment place, carpenters' store-rooms, etc. Over the sides and back of the stage are the flies and painting-room; and there are two best dressing-rooms, closet, etc., over the green-room and stage entrance.

In the roof, over pit and gallery, is the carpenter's workshop, 40 feet long by 45 feet wide, communicating with the flies and painting-room [. . .]

The stage, 55 feet wide and 45 deep, is so arranged that any portion can be removed singly or altogether, as occasion may require. These movements are effected by means of multiplying windlass barrels placed on each side of the basement-floor, adjusted by a new species of machinery, by which the level of the stage is depressed into inclined grooves, wrought in the sides of the principal timbers of the stage, and thereby drawn off to any distance required: in point of fact, the whole of the practical surface of the stage may be cleared, leaving nothing but the skeleton, in two minutes; so that, if required to show a gulf or chasm in scenic arrangement, the means of effect are very great. The stage is an inclined plane, of $^1/_2$ inch to the foot, and is arranged with four entrances, with working grooves for wings and flats, the whole made practicable. The traps are worked by graduated balance-weights, so that any degree of velocity can be obtained by setting them accordingly. The gas battens are the whole length of the proscenium, and are also hung with balance-weights. The borders are hung in a similar manner. The painting-room is at the back of the stage, above the 'flies', and there is a frame working down on to the stage, on which the scenes can be placed, and taken up and painted with the least possible trouble. The scene repository, at the north-west angle [. . .] will hold sixty pairs of flats.

The form of the theatre is an elongated horseshoe, with but few projections, so as not to present any interruption to sight or sound [. . .] The height from the pit floor to the highest part of the ceiling is about 36 feet. The stalls contain 38 sittings, the pit will hold from 800 to 850 persons, the boxes about 200, and the gallery 700 to 750.

The Royalty Theatre, Wellclose Square, had opened in 1787 and was renamed the East London in 1810. The illustration shows the exterior just prior to its destruction by fire in 1826. It was rebuilt as the Brunswick and opened on 25 February 1828, but as a result of inadequate safety precautions the building collapsed three days later, killing sixteen people.[1]

---

[1] For views of the interior, see Thomas and Hare, *Restoration and Georgian England*, nos. 237–8; Sherson, *London's lost theatres*, plate facing p. 44; and Southern, *Georgian playhouse*, plates 6–13.

79   Exterior of East London Theatre (formerly the Royalty), 1826

Daniel Havell engraving, published by Taylor. Henry Huntington Library

EAST LONDON THEATRE.

III Repertoire, taste and audiences

INTRODUCTION

The rebuilding of Drury Lane Theatre in 1794 signalled the end of an old era characterized by a comfortable Georgian intimacy between actors and spectators, well-ordered social divisions within the auditorium, and a dramatic repertoire based on the acknowledged canon of legitimate plays: Shakespeare, sentimental tragedies and text-based comedies of character. The size of the new Drury Lane suggested a response to an increased demand for theatre-going in London, a demand that could be satisfied only by enlarging the dimensions of the legitimate playhouses. The size also reflected and catered to a significant change in theatrical taste: the spectacular representations of fantasy, which the new technology, already suggested by de Loutherbourg, would be able to realize.

Although the term *melodrama* would not formally appear on the English stage until Thomas Holcroft's *A Tale of Mystery* in 1802, the taste for melodrama had already been anticipated, particularly in Gothic manifestations of which Monk Lewis's *The Castle Spectre* (1797) was the most celebrated example, but which also included such adaptations of popular novels as Jephson's *The Castle of Narbonne* (1781) and James Boaden's *Fontainville Forest* (1794). The influence of the Gothic could also be felt in such tragedies as Joanna Baillie's *De Montfort* (1800), as well as pervasively in the work of Coleridge and Byron. The new technology would be harnessed to the depictions of Gothic castles, dungeons and supernatural phenomena. This pseudo-medievalism could just as easily embrace the exoticism of eastern locations, the world of supernatural horror within a Turkish caliphate, for example. While the settings might be strange and the characters aristocratic, Gothic melodrama was unashamedly populist, with many of its sentiments democratic and anti-authoritarian. Although in the first instance English Gothic was much affected by German models, especially the plays of Kotzebue, French influences would prove to be more enduring through adaptations of Pixérécourt and, later, Scribe.

The taste for melodrama was universal, and demands for its performance could not be satisfied merely by the patent theatres, either in London or in the provinces. The new workforce who continued to flood into London and the main provincial manufacturing centres from the end of the eighteenth century provided a battleground for the struggle between the patent 'major' theatres and entrepreneurs who sought to appeal to the new urban proletariat by building additional theatres in areas of population growth and by catering to the taste for melodrama. The first half of the nineteenth century was dominated by efforts to solicit the patronage of new audiences and to identify their leisure habits in the context of an emerging industrial economy. This led in turn to a need to redefine the role of the theatre itself. The many articles in middle-class journals of the period that deplore 'the degeneracy of the stage' reflect a nostalgia for eighteenth-century values, a profound distrust of the new audiences and of the ascendancy of their non-literary tastes, which had usurped the received tradition of the stage as exemplary educator and cultural mirror. Above all, control of dramatic taste had been wrested from literary authors and placed in the hands of speculators in dramatic property: egoistic actor-managers and a growing technical lobby represented by scene decorators, costumiers and special effects machinists. Much of this discussion centred on the dependence of the English stage on appropriated French models and the failure of English playwrights to provide literary leadership, a challenge which the Romantics had conspicuously declined to accept.

At the same time it was obvious that melodrama was unlikely to go out of fashion. It was a form that responded quickly to societal moods and changes. British naval successes against the French during the Napoleonic Wars, the increasing domination of world trade by Britain and the huge expansion of her merchant fleet were reflected in the celebratory nautical melodramas about the British tar, which proliferated from 1795 onwards. The importance of the family unit and its impregnability in a climate of economic insecurity and industrial change became the basis of the domestic melodramas, which all theatres embraced from the late 1820s. These forms, however, should not be considered diachronically. Gothic, nautical and domestic elements often coexisted in plays, although each became more or less prevalent as anxieties and social priorities changed. Moreover, each of these elements continued to exist throughout the nineteenth century. Melodrama as a mode of discourse influenced and intersected with a variety of other expressive modes, from the novel and poetry to the staging of political demonstrations.

Though literary critics denigrated melodrama as unworthy of serious attention, the theatre in the period up to 1850 was unabashedly a visual rather than a text-based one. Although writers like Sheridan Knowles, Bulwer-Lytton and Talfourd were capable of producing plays that successfully gave melodrama a literary patina, their stage success depended upon the dramatist's ability to attract the attentions of a significant performer or theatre company prepared to take the necessary financial risk. Such plays were immeasurably enhanced if they included opportunities for lavish spectacle and costuming (which explains the relative success of plays like Byron's *Sardanapalus*, Talfourd's *Ion* or Knowles's *Virginius*). The non-textual appeal of much theatre in the period can also be seen in the demand for spectacular recreations of historical events, in mythological extravaganzas and in the elaborate stage directions of play-texts that described stage 'business'. This emphasis on the visual aspects of performance was a response both to an audience demand for visual stimulus and to the conditions of viewing.

The building of large theatres after 1794 in response to consumer pressure effectively destroyed the old social divisions of boxes, pit and galleries and replaced these with economic divisions, although these were by no means watertight. The new problems thus created were those of audibility and visibility. At the same time, the conditions of viewing continued to reflect the sense of social occasion of eighteenth-century theatre, which facilitated social intercourse and insured that spectators remained more conscious of each other than of the actions on stage. This not only affected the nature of the performances, but also reinforced the importance of the control over the stage exerted by the auditorium. The Old Price and Monte Cristo riots at Covent Garden and Drury Lane in 1809 and 1848 respectively demonstrated some of the ways in which the auditorium itself could be a site of melodramatic spectacle. The disappearance of clear social demarcations and the invasion by a new audience from the beginning of the nineteenth century go some way towards explaining the absence of fashionable theatre-goers, about which many critics complained, and the desperate attempts by theatre managers to offer a programme of constant novelty to audiences about whose identity and tastes they were uncertain. If the fashionable and more expensive boxes were empty, the pit and the galleries needed to be filled and this could best be achieved by, on the one hand, constant changes in repertoire, and, on the other, by the variety of differing attractions within any given performance, which matched the mobility and heterogeneous nature of the spectators (in which equation the addition of a new audience component at 'half price' was a significant complication).

The volatility of the spectators remained a constant challenge to actors and managers throughout the period. The political and social circumstances outside the theatre – the libertarianism popularized by the French Revolution, the war effort, which created a huge industrial and trading boom up to 1815, the anti-Royalist demonstrations against George IV, the agitation over the 1832 Reform Bill, the upheavals associated with the Chartists from the late 1830s to 1848, the economic hardships of the 1840s – all affected audience behaviour as much as the lit auditoria and the provision of food and drink conspired to perpetuate a sense of continuing social engagement, and, on occasions, afforded an opportunity in the theatre to voice grievances and to take issue with social and economic inequities.

From the 1840s the demography of theatre audiences began to change. Theatres began to define themselves and their repertoire and were able to attract a middle class that desired to see its values reflected on the stage. The Theatre Regulation Act of 1843 brought all theatres under the control of the Lord Chamberlain, gave them equal legitimacy and enabled local audiences to enjoy a range of performances hitherto confined to the Theatres Royal. Nowhere in London was the influence of an increasingly dominant middle class more directly felt than at Sadler's Wells, where in 1844 Samuel Phelps instituted a managerial policy of Shakespearean and literary revivals. His success over the ensuing eighteen years seemed to corroborate the existence of an audience prepared to rediscover a literary drama uncluttered by spectacular upholstery. Queen Victoria's inauguration of the Windsor Theatricals at the end of 1848, in which individual performers and companies were invited to appear at the castle on a regular basis, seemed to validate a renewed middle-class interest in the theatre as an appropriate manifestation of rational amusement. The Phelps experiment, however, was a unique one and mirrored the socioeconomic composition of his theatre's Islington neighbourhood rather more than any general change in the nature of theatre-going itself. Theatres in London such as the Surrey, the Victoria, the Standard and the City of London continued their practices of appealing to a local constituency by utilizing the methods of novelty and variety and of showing, long after 1850, melodramas that documented the trials of the underprivileged and the triumph of virtue within a nautical, Gothic or domestic context.

80   The enlarged patent theatres and their effects on tastes and perceptions, 1795

G. Colman, *Sylvester Daggerwood; or, New Hay at the Old Market* (London, 1808), pp. 31–2[1]

Since the preference, we know,
Is for pageantry and shew,
'Twere a pity the public to balk–
And when people appear
Quite unable to hear,

'Tis undoubtedly needless to talk.
Let your Shakespeares and Jonsons go hang, go hang!
Let your Otways and Drydens go drown!
Give us but Elephants, and white Bulls enough,
And we'll take in all the town.

Brave boys!

II

Or if, tardily, the sound
Travels all the house round,
'Twixt the action and words there's a breach;
And it seems as if Macbeth,
Half a minute after death,
On his back, made his last dying speech.
Let your Shakespeares, etc.

III

When on matters of State,
Stage Heroes debate,
Intelligence so slowly is got,
'Twere better they began
On the new-invented plan,
And with Telegraphs transmitted you the plot.
Let your Shakespeares, etc.

IV

But our House here's too small
That there's no need to bawl,
And the summer will rapidly pass;
So we hope you'll think fit
To hear the Actors a bit,
Till the Elephants and Bulls come from grass.
Then let Shakespeare and Jonson go hang, go hang!
Let your Otways and Drydens go drown!
Give 'em but Elephants and white Bulls enough,
And they'll take in all the town–

Brave Boys!

---

[1] The concluding song of Colman's satirical play, written for the opening of the Haymarket theatre, 9 June 1795.

81   Spectacle and the distortion of the stage's function, 1799

Scots Magazine (June 1799), pp. 378–80[1]

Happy were it for us, Sir, if the dramatic writers of the present day, were formed on this great pattern, if they studied to 'hold the mirror up to nature, to shew virtue her own feature and scorn her own image', to paint in glowing colours the happiness resulting from a rigid observance of the principles of rectitude, and the torment and misery which are engendered by guilt. But alas, the stage has degenerated from its original purpose. The visitor of the Theatre now no longer sees a rational entertainment, or receives lessons of morality, but is doomed to sit all the night long beholding what is hardly a suitable amusement for the nursery; camels and elephants moving with solemn steps across the stage, noise and pageantry substituted in the place of a regular plot, the house ringing with balderdash and declamation, and superb scenery presented for the pleasure of the eye, instead of a rational amusement to the understanding, and a useful lesson to the heart.

[1] From a letter to the editor.

THE ROMANTICS AND MELODRAMA

Though most of the Romantic writers wanted to write for the stage, they were ultimately defeated by its demands, especially the physicalization of action, and their unwillingness to entrust their work to the judgement of a popular audience. The exception was Matthew Gregory Lewis ('Monk' Lewis), whose *Castle Spectre* was the most successful manifestation of Gothic romanticism on the stage. The play was first performed at Drury Lane on 12 December 1797, and its subsequent popularity established the importance of supernaturalism and pseudo-medievalism.

82   The characteristics of Gothic Romanticism on stage, 1797

Prologue to M. G. Lewis, *The Castle Spectre* (London: Bell, 1798), partly reprinted in Allardyce Nicoll, *A history of English drama* (Cambridge: Cambridge University Press, 1959), vol. III, p. 51

Far from the haunts of men, of vice the foe,
The moon-struck child of genius and of woe,
Versed in each magic spell, and dear to fame,
A fair enchantress dwells, Romance her name,
She loathes the sun, or blazing taper's light:
The moon-beamed landscape and tempestuous night
Alone she loves; and oft, with glimmering lamp,
Near graves new-open'd, or 'midst dungeons damp,
Drear forests, ruined aisles, and haunted towers,
Forlorn she roves, and raves away the hours!
Anon, when storms howl and lash the deep,
Desperate she climbs the sea-rocks beetling steep;
There wildly strikes her harp's fantastic strings,
Tells to the moon how grief her bosom wrings,

And while her strange song chaunts fictitious ills,
In wounded hearts Oblivion's balm distills.

[She beckons the dramatic author to follow her to the River Conway and its ruined castle]

Soon as near Conway's walls her footsteps drew,
She bade the youth their ancient state renew:
Eager she sped the fallen towers to rear:
'Twas done, and fancy bore the fabric here.
Next choosing from great Shakespeare's comic school,
The gossip crone, gross friar, and gibing fool–
These, with a virgin fair, and lover brave,
To our young author's care the enchantress gave;
But charg'd him, ere he bless'd the brave and fair,
To lay the exulting villain's bosom bare,
And by the torments of his conscience show,
That prosperous vice is but triumphant woe!

83   Coleridge addresses Wordsworth about the challenges of writing melodrama, 1798

Letter to William Wordsworth, LXXVIII, January 1798, in E. H. Coleridge (ed.), *Letters of Samuel Taylor Coleridge* (London: Heinemann, 1895), vol. I, pp. 236–8

Coleridge has read *The Castle Spectre* and condemns its language, its characterization, its superheated emotionalism and its derivative sentiments, and finally addresses what he calls 'Conduct'.

[. . .] the Conduct of the Piece is, I think, *good*; except that the first act is *wholly* taken up with explanation and narration. This play proves how accurately you conjectured concerning *theatric* merit. The merit of the 'Castle Spectre' consists wholly in its *situations*. These are all borrowed and all absolutely *pantomimical*; but they are admirably managed for stage effect. There is not much bustle, but *situations* for ever. The whole plot, machinery, and incident are borrowed. The play is a mere patchwork of plagiarisms; but they are very well worked up, and for stage effect make an excellent *whole* [. . .] This play struck me with utter hopelessness. It would [be easy] to produce these situations, but not in a play so [constructed] as to admit the permanent and closest beauties of style, passion, and character. To admit pantomimic tricks, the plot itself must be pantomimic [. . .]

Though the works of Goethe and Schiller heavily influenced early Romanticism, they were outweighed by the popular versions of plays by August von Kotzebue (1761–1819). The character of Mrs Haller in *The Stranger* provided Sarah Siddons with one of her most successful roles.

84   The corrupting influence of German drama, 1799

Hannah More, *Strictures on the modern system of female education* (London: Cadell & Davies, 1799), vol. 1, pp. 45 ff.

We have hitherto spoken only of the German *writings*; but as there are multitudes who seldom read, equal pains have been taken to promote the same object through the medium of the stage: and this weapon is, of all others, that against which it is, at the present moment, the most important to warn the more inconsiderate of my countrywomen.

As a specimen of the German drama, it may not be unreasonable to offer a few remarks on the admired play of the *Stranger*.[1] In this piece the character of an *adultress*, which, in all periods of the world, ancient as well as modern, in all countries heathen as well as Christian, has hitherto been held in detestation, and has never been introduced but to be reprobated, is for the first time presented to our view in the most pleasing and fascinating colours. The heroine is a woman who forsook her husband, the most affectionate and the most amiable, and lived for some time in the most criminal commerce with her seducer. Repenting at length of her crime, she buries herself in retirement. The talents of the poet during the whole piece are exerted in attempting to render this woman the object, not only of the compassion and forgiveness, but of the esteem and affection, of the audience. The injured husband, convinced of his wife's repentance, forms a resolution, which every man of true feeling and Christian piety will probably approve. He forgives her offence, and promises her through life his advice, protection, and fortune, together with every thing which can alleviate the misery of her situation, but refuses to replace her in the situation of his wife. But this is not sufficient for the *German* author. His efforts are employed, and it is to be feared but too successfully, in making the audience consider the husband as an unrelenting savage, while they are led by the art of the poet anxiously to wish to see an adultress restored to that rank of women who have not violated the most solemn covenant that can be made with man, nor disobeyed one of the most positive laws which has been enjoined by God [. . .]

[1] Benjamin Thompson's translation of Kotzebue's *Menschenhass und Reue* (Misanthropy and repentance) was first performed at Drury Lane on 24 March 1798.

85   Critical and literary responses to Gothic melodrama, 1802

W. R. Spencer, *Urania; or, The Illuminé* (London: Ridgeway, 1802)[1]

> Though rigid Truth, in narrow bounds, confine
> The tame Historian's limited design;
> Though hence the cold Philosopher may draw
> Sage maxims, founded upon Reason's law;
> Not so the Poet checks his bolder fires;

Dull is the Bard whom sober sense inspires!
The unshackled Muse disdains such vulgar rule,
And claims prescriptive right – to play the fool.

Shall then fastidious spleen with critic spite
Presume to censure what it *fears* to write?
Shall captious wits, to *modern* Genius foes,
The rich improvements of the stage oppose?
The public palate, saucily 'tis said,
Glutted with offal, is on garbage fed;
And soon, cry these Alarmists of the stage,
(who hope the mischiefs that these fears presage,)
Soon, one and all, Box, Gallery and Pit,
The Stage itself, will loath the name of wit;
Day after day, our Spectre Drama's cramm'd
With heavenly spirits, or with goblins damn'd,–
of tame extravagance a cumbrous mass,
That barren brains on patient fashion pass,–
By low Phantasmagoria-Farce debased,
The dull Lyceum of degenerate taste!

With these, a flimsy, flippant tribe combine,–
Authors,– who blush to throw their pearls to swine;
Vain of the triumphs of *rejected* plays,
And talents, never mortified by praise;
Who humbly vaunt, who haughtily confess
Their tasteful toils uninjur'd by success,–
Seldom insulted by a *three-days run*,
And complimented often with – *not one*:
Glow worms of wit, exposed to light, they fade;
But shine and sparkle in their native shade!
Their boast, their proud distinction, *not* to please,
Hooted and hiss'd they calmly sit at ease;
While conscious genius happily supplies
The laurel wreaths a niggard world denies.

[1] Prologue written by the Rt. Hon. Lord John Townshend.

The first play designated a melodrama was Thomas Holcroft's *A Tale of Mystery*, adapted from Guilbert de Pixérécourt's *Coelina, ou, l'Enfant du mystère*, produced in Paris in 1800.[1] Though still under the influence of the Gothic in its Italianate setting, the play's main innovations lay in the use of music to heighten emotional effectiveness and of a major character, Francisco, who was dumb and whose expressiveness was confined entirely to the use of what Coleridge described as 'pantomime'.

¹ Thomas Holcroft (1745–1809) had written *The Road to Ruin* (1792) and a successful adaptation of Beaumarchais's *The Marriage of Figaro* as *The Follies of a Day* (1784). Pixérécourt (1773–1844), together with Eugène Scribe (1791–1861), would provide a fertile source of English adaptations for the first half of the nineteenth century.

86   Describing the first melodrama and its effectiveness, 1802

(a) Genest, *Account of the English stage*, vol. VII, pp. 578–9; (b) *Morning Chronicle* (Monday 15 November 1802)

(a)   Nov. 13, 1802, CG Never acted, Tale of Mystery. Count Romaldi = H. Johnston: Francisco (his brother) = Farley: Bonamo = Murray: Stephano (his son – in love with Selina) = Brunton: Michelli (a miller) = Blanchard: Malvoglio (Romaldi's confederate) = Cory: Montano = Claremont: Fiametta (servant to Bonamo) = Mrs Mattocks: Selina (supposed niece to Bonamo – in love with Stephano) = Mrs Gibbs: acted about 37 times – the scene lies in Savoy – about 7 or 8 years before this Melo-drame begins, Fiametta had found Francisco dangerously wounded by some assassins – her cries had brought Michelli to her assistance – and Francisco's life was saved – at the opening of the piece, Francisco had been lately received into the family of Bonamo – Bonamo asks him who he is – Francisco, who is dumb, writes his answers – he acknowledges that he is a noble Roman, but will not tell the name of his family – Romaldi and Francisco start back on seeing each other – Montano enters, expresses his surprise at the sight of Romaldi, and makes a hasty exit – Romaldi and Malvoglio intend to kill Francisco, but are prevented – Romaldi leaves Bonamo's house with threats – joyful preparations are made for the intended wedding of Stephano and Selina – Malvoglio brings Bonamo a certificate, from which it appears that Selina is the daughter of Francisco – Montano had denounced Romaldi and Malvoglio as the assassins who had nearly killed Francisco 7 or 8 years ago – Malvoglio is taken by the Archers – Romaldi attempts to make his escape in disguise – at the conclusion, the Archers prepare to shoot him – Francisco places himself before his brother – and the curtain falls – this is a very interesting piece, in 2 acts by Holcroft – professedly borrowed from the French – it was the first of those Melo-drames, with which the stage was afterwards inundated – tho' this mixture of dialogue and dumb-show, accompanied by music, be an unjustifiable species of the drama, yet it must be acknowledged, that some of the Melo-drames have considerable merit – the Tale of Mystery was the first and best.

(b)   THEATRE-ROYAL, COVENT-GARDEN.– On Saturday night the *Melo-drama* made its appearance. There is certainly no affectation in giving it this name, as it is quite unlike any thing that has hitherto been brought out upon the English stage. It contains a mixture of every different species of theatrical representation. We have by turns tragedy, comedy, and farce, pantomime, dancing, and music. It may be thought that to blend things in their nature so different and so contrary in the effects they produce, must only be to create confusion and to excite disgust.

An uncommon share of ingenuity and address is no doubt requisite; but by the exercise of these the author has prepared one of the most interesting and delightful spectacles that ever was exhibited. He has known to manage the transitions so skilfully, that we are never presented with a scene of pathos, of gaiety, or of show, for which we had not been previously prepared. The sudden change, instead of occasioning an unpleasant shock to the feelings, only serves to heighten the effect of each particular part of the entertainment, from the contrast between what goes before, and what follows [. . .]

Monk Lewis was able to transfer Gothic values to the equally exotic East (much as Colman had done in *Blue Beard* in 1798). This time he incorporated a taste for live animals on stage, much to the chagrin of critics, who regarded it as demeaning, especially at a patent theatre like Covent Garden.

87   Gothic melodrama absorbs an eastern setting, 1811

Genest, *Account of the English stage*, vol. VIII, pp. 235–7

April 29, 1811 C.G. Timour the Tartar. Timour (Khan of the Tartars) = Farley: Oglou (his father) = Fawcett: Agib (Prince of Mingrelia) = Master Chapman: Zorilda = Mrs H. Johnston: Selima = Miss Bolton: Liska = Mrs Liston:– acted 44 times [. . .] – in the 1st act there is a combat on horseback between two of the Tartars – in this and in the other scenes the horses acted wonderfully well – this grand romantic Melo-drama was written by Lewis – he says in his advertisement – 'this trifle was written merely to oblige Mr Harris, who prest me very earnestly to give him a *Spectacle*, in which Horses might be introduced – but having myself great doubts of the success of these new performers, I constructed the Drama in such a manner, that by substituting a combat on foot for one on horseback, the Cavalry might be omitted without injury to the plot' – from this account it should seem that Lewis began to write Timour the Tartar before the horses had appeared with so much success in Blue Beard– [. . .] on this evening between the play and entertainment a considerable degree of hissing took place, and placards were exhibited against the horses – however the advocates for rational performers and rational amusements were in a decided minority, and the Melo-drama was received with great applause.

88   The deficiencies of Coleridge's *Remorse* at Drury Lane, 1813

Times (25 January 1813), [p. 3][1]

We speak with constraint and unwillingly of the defects of a work which must have cost its author so much labour [. . .] But to conceal truth is only to do final injury: and it must be acknowledged that this drama has sins [. . .] Its first fault, and the most easily avoided, is its unwieldy length: it is almost five hours long. Its next, is its passion for laying hold of everything that would allow an apology for a description. Murderers stop short with the dagger in their hands, to talk of 'roses on mountain sides': fathers start back from their children to moralize: and a lover, in all the outrage of disappointed love, lingers to tell at what hour of the day he parted from his mistress,– how she smiled, and how the sun smiled,– how its light fell upon the vallies [*sic*], and the sheep, and the vineyards, and the lady [. . .] This may be poetical, but it has no connexion with the plain, rapid, and living truth of the Drama. There is an essential difference in those two branches of the art. With the mere poet, time is nothing [. . .] To the dramatist, time is everything [. . .] We are slow to speak of faults as applied to this writer: but he has not yet learned this value of time. His plot is intolerably curved and circuitous, indistinct beyond all power of pleasurable apprehension, and broken beyond all reach of continued interest [. . .]

[1] A review of Coleridge's *Remorse*, which opened on January 23 with Elliston, Mrs Glover and Miss De Camp. Coleridge adapted it from his earlier *Osorio* (1798). See also Henry Crabb Robinson's diary for 23 January, 1813, in Eluned Brown (ed.), *The London theatre 1811–1866* (London: STR, 1965).

Walter Scott had translated Goethe's *Goetz von Berlichingen* in 1799, and although he did attempt to write plays as late as 1830, his influence was most felt through adaptations of his works, notably Daniel Terry's versions of *Guy Mannering, or, The Gypsey's Prophecy* (Covent Garden, 1816) and *The Heart of Midlothian* (Covent Garden, 1819) and Thomas Dibdin's *Ivanhoe* (Surrey, 1820). In common with the other Romantics, he felt unable to address the practical demands of stage performance.

89   Scott declines to write a play for Elliston, 1819[1]

Raymond, *Life and enterprises of Elliston*, p. 270

Dear Sir – I am favoured with your letter, and am obliged by your opinion of my supposed dramatic talents. But the time is long gone by that I could, or dared, have attempted anything for the stage, and I by no means feel disposed to risk any reputation I have acquired, upon so slippery and uncertain an adventure. It is not so much the power of conceiving dramatic character, and putting its expressions into the language of passion, which ensures success in the present day, as the art of constructing a fable, and interesting the spectators in a series of events, which proceed gradually to a striking conclusion. Now, if I had in my better days any talent of the former description, it is much impaired by a course of bad health; and of the last and most material requisite to success, I never possessed a shadow; for I never yet began a poem upon a preconcerted story, and have often been well-advanced in composition before I had any idea how I was to end the work.

I wish you, my dear sir, every success in your new and difficult situation, and have the honour to be,

Very much your faithful servant,
Walter Scott.

Abbotsford, 3rd August, 1819.

[1] For Scott's views about the theatre, see his *Essay on drama* (1819), in *Prose works* (Edinburgh, 1834), vol. VI, p. 392. Robert William Elliston (1774–1831), one of the most distinguished actor-managers of the early nineteenth century, had taken on the management of Drury Lane in 1819 and wrote to Walter Scott soliciting a new play from him [**32, 35, 36, 47, 145, 163, 164**].

In 1819 Shelley wrote to Thomas Love Peacock informing him that he had finished a new play, *The Cenci*. He hoped that Peacock would use his political influence at Covent Garden to get it produced.[1] Shelley's extreme reticence to have his name associated with *The Cenci* until it was a success, and his delusion that such a play would be acceptable, indicate how little the Romantics knew of the business of the theatre and the realities of stage censorship, which precluded the play from public performance until 1922.

[1] See Allardyce Nicoll, *A history of English drama, 1660–1900* (Cambridge: Cambridge University Press, 1959), vol. IV, pp. 196–7.

90   Shelley wants *The Cenci* produced, 1819

Reprinted in F. L. Jones (ed.), *P. B. Shelley: letters* (Oxford: Oxford University Press, 1964), vol. II, pp. 504–5

Livorno July 1819.

My dear Peacock,

[. . .] The object of the present letter is to ask a favour of you – I have written a tragedy on the subject of a story well known in Italy, & in my conception eminently dramatic – I have taken some pains to make my play fit for representation, & those who have already seen it judge favourably [. . .] I send you a translation of the Italian Mss. on which my play is founded; the chief circumstance of which I have touched very delicately; for my principal doubt as to whether it would succeed as an acting play hangs entirely on the question as to whether any such a thing as incest in this shape however treated wd. be admitted on the stage – I think however it will form no objection, considering first that the facts are matter of history, & secondly the peculiar delicacy with which I have treated it –

I am exceedingly interested in the question of whether this attempt of mine will succeed or no – I am strongly inclined to the affirmative at present, founding my hopes on this, that as a composition it is certainly not inferior to any of the modern plays that have been acted, with the exception of Remorse, that the interest of its plot is incredibly greater & more real, & that there is nothing beyond what the multitude are contented to believe that they can understand, either in imagery opinion or sentiment.– I wish to preserve a complete incognito, & can trust to you, that whatever else you do, you will at least favour me on this point [. . .] After it had been acted & successfully [. . .] I would own it if I pleased, & use the celebrity it might acquire to my own purposes.–

What I want you to do is to procure for me its presentation at Covent Garden. The principal character Beatrice is precisely fitted for Miss O'Neil [*sic*], & it might even seem to have been written for her – (God forbid that I shd. see her play it – it wd.

tear my nerves to pieces) and in all respects it is fitted only for Covent Garden. The chief male character I confess I should be very unwilling that any one but Kean[1] shd. play – that is impossible, & I must be contented with an inferior actor.– I think you know some of the people of that theatre, or at least someone who knows them, & when you have read the play, you may say enough perhaps to induce them not to reject it without consideration [. . .]

Ever yours most faithfully,
P. B. S.

[1] Eliza O'Neill and Edmund Kean were regarded by the Romantics as the prime exponents of extreme passion. Eliza O'Neill (1791–1872) had begun her association with Covent Garden in 1814 and would retire from the stage in 1819. Macready was much impressed by her Italianate passion as Juliet. See also H. Barton Baker, *Our old actors* (London: Bentley, 1878), pp. 429–32. For Kean see docs. **140–3**.

91   Romantic objections to theatre audiences, 1821

Preface to Byron's *Marino Faliero*, quoted in *British Stage and Literary Cabinet* (5 May 1821), p. 38[1]

I have had no view to the stage. In its present state it is, perhaps, not a very exalted object of ambition; besides, I have been too much behind the scenes, to have thought it so at any time. And, I cannot conceive any man of irritable feeling putting himself at the mercies of an audience. The sneering reader, and the loud critic, and the tart review, are scattered and distant calamities; but, the trampling of an intelligent or an ignorant audience on a production which, be it good or bad, has been a mental labour to the writer, is a palpable and immediate grievance, heightened by a man's doubt of their competency to judge, and the certainty of his own imprudence in electing them his judges. Were I capable of writing a play which could be deemed stage-worthy, success would give me no pleasure, and failure great pain. It is for this reason that, even during the time of being one of the Committee of one of the Theatres, I never made the attempt, and never will.

[1] Subsequently reprinted in *The works of Lord Byron* (London, 1832–3), vol. XII. In spite of his objections the opening of the play took place at Drury Lane on 25 April 1821. See John Genest, *Some account of the English stage*, vol. IX, sv 25 April 1821.

Regardless of the hesitations of the Romantics and the opprobrium of literary critics, the taste for melodrama was a pervasive one. It was perhaps time for critics to examine the merits of melodrama and the reasons for its popularity.

92   An evaluation of the appeal of early melodrama, 1818

E. H. 'On melo-drama', *Theatrical Inquisitor and Monthly Mirror* (May 1818), pp. 158–62

The imagination of the multitude, has, for a long time, been so completely under the fascination of this species of drama, [. . .] that one is at a loss what portion of merit to assign to it; and as the arguments which are advanced in opposition to it seem decidedly to divest it of the slightest degree of literary value, so is it hazardous to pronounce against that, which evidently possesses so extensive an influence over the imagination of the public [. . .] [the writer then discusses the nature of tragedy and comedy] [. . .] So far from being a mixture of tragedy and comedy, it is widely remote from either; and except its dialogue and scenic aid, has nothing in common with them. It affects neither the intellect nor the feelings [. . .] it is addressed to the imagination only. In short it is merely a romance, dramatized; [. . .] it is to be judged by the same rules, and is admired by the same class of persons – And who are these? They are persons to whom any exertion of the intellect is absolute toil, and carefully to be avoided, who like to have their other faculties lulled into slumber, whilst the imagination is excited and amused: [. . .] Such are romance readers, such are the admirers of melo-drama. A world which is different from our own, characters claiming little affinity with humanity, striking, marvellous, and improbable incidents, and combinations, these are the leading features common to both [. . .]

[. . .] Whether the minds of our theatrical audiences are kept in a state of so painful tension during the day, that they can relish only this soothing sort of charm, instead of any more lively relaxation, is a question I will not attempt to answer[1] [. . .] [b]ut it is a branch of public amusement, and therefore should be noticed; and it must be judged by those rules which will apply to it [. . .] A melo-drama may be dull, or interesting; a work of imagination, as it is, it may be brilliant and lively, or tedious and insipid; the incidents may be striking or insignificant; the fable well or ill constructed; the effect pleasing or otherwise; the dialogue elegant or energetic, coarse or puerile, character, that is, a natural delineation of character, is almost out of the question; for a natural character placed among the fantastic creatures of imagination, would be like a civilized European in the midst of a band of savages. But the monsters of melo-drama may be amusing or otherwise. As far as these points extend, melo-drama may be criticised [. . .]

[1] See **82** and **85**. A recurring complaint about melodrama was its escapist qualities.

By the 1820s nautical and domestic versions of melodrama had displaced the Gothic, both at the patent theatres and in the neighbourhood theatres. Yet as the following playbill demonstrates, melodrama's eclecticism allowed all three strands to coexist. The scenic elements clearly illustrate this. The playbill also testifies to a continuing taste for the spectacular and for animals on stage, albeit on this occasion impersonated by a man.

93   A spectacular naval melodrama at a 'Minor' theatre, 1822

Surrey Playbill, author's collection

SURREY THEATRE

This present Thursday, Jan. 24th, 1822

Will be acted for the 16th time, with New Music, Scenes, Dresses, and appropriate Decorations, THE

PIRATE,

or the

WILD WOMAN OF ZETLAND.[1]

The Overture and new Music composed by Mr Sanderson. The Scenery designed and executed by Mr Wilson (who has kindly afforded the Assistance of his Talents on this occasion) Mr H. Wilson, Mr Pitt and Assistants. The Dresses by Miss Freelove, Miss Lucas, and Assistants. The Machinery by Mr Johnson. The Decorations and Properties by Mr Morris, Miss C. Lucas, and Assistants. The Dances and Melodramatic Action by Mr Ridgway.

CHARACTERS

Mertoun [. . .] Mr Bengough Mordaunt Mertoun, his Son [. . .] Mr S. H. Chapman

Magnus Troil (Udaller, or Chief of the Island of Zetland) Mr Clifford

Clement Cleveland (the Pirate) Mr Finn   Captain Goffe, his Associate,

Mr Boyle

Lieutenant Bunce	)		Mr Gomery
Lieutenant Fletcher	)Pirates		Mr Ridgway
Hawkins (Boatswain)	)		Mr Brunton
Barlow (Coxwain)	)		Mr Ellis

Captain Weatherport (Commander of the Halcyon frigate) Mr Belgrave

Provost of Kirkwall, Mr Jackson   Claud Halcro (a superannuated Poet of Zetland)

Mr Salter

Brice Snailsfoot (a travelling Jogger or Pedlar) Mr Wyatt

Triptolemus Yellowley (a scholastic Yorkshire Farmer) Mr Herring

Who will introduce Mr T. Dibdin's Song from 'Family Quarrels' of 'I was Yorkshire

Too.'

Eric Scambister (Punchmaker of Burgh Westra) Mr Brindle   Nicolas,

Mr Honer.

Officers, islanders, and Pirates, Messers Pitt, Leslie, Drewell, Byrne, Shaw, Walker,

Jameson, Granby, Burnet, Emery, etc.

NORNA (the Wild Woman of Zetland, a supposed Prophetess and Sorceress),

MRS GLOVER

Minna (Daughter of Magnus Troil) Miss R. Adcock Brinda (Sister of Minna)

Miss Jonas Miss Barbara Yellowley, Mrs Brooke

Lady Gloweroram, Mrs Salter   Clara and Maddie (her Nieces) Miss Pitt and Miss
Jonas
Swertha (Domestic of Mertoun), Miss Spence   Tronda (Servant of Triptolemus),
Miss Hudson
Zetland Ladies and Lasses, Mesdames Myers, Bartlett, Rigby. Misses Ellis,
Shepherd, Merrit, Ponder, etc.
In Act I
A STORM AND SHIPWRECK
In Act II
A ZETLAND SWORD DANCE.
With a Northern Flag – a Pas Seul by Miss Adcock – and a Dance by the
Characters.
In Act III
A SEA FIGHT
BETWEEN THE HALCYON FRIGATE AND THE FORTUNE'S FAVORITE
with the
EXPLOSION AND DESTRUCTION OF THE PIRATE'S VESSEL.[2]
In the Course of the Piece will be introduced the following
Entire New Scenery
Castellated entrance of the House of the Udaller Magnus Troil
Picturesque Interior of the Udaller's residence
Wild and Stormy Pass in the Isle of Zetland
Characteristic Kitchen at Hafra the Farm-House of Triptolemus Yellowley
Desolate and Savage View near Jarlshoff the residence of Mertoun
Distant Ocean–Storm and Shipwreck
Sea View and the Ranzelman of Zetland's Cottage
Interior of the Ranzelman's Hut
Eccentric Ball Room of Magnus Troil–the Decorations formed from the Heads of
Vessels, Pieces of Wreck, etc
Moonlight Garden Exterior of Troil's House
Open Sea View–the Fortune's Favorite at Anchor
Romantic arched Marine Rock and distant Ocean
Distant View of the Orkney Islands
Interior of a Ship Cabin, Etc.
Dilapidated Cloisters in Kirkwall Abbey, used as the Pirate's Prison
Norna's Magic Asylum
TO CONCLUDE WITH THE
Man and the Monkey
in which
The Wonderful Ape will go through his astonishing Performances on the
CORDE VOLANTE
on FRIDAY, to conclude with
Leonora; or the Apparition on the White Horse

And on SATURDAY, with
TEKELI.
[. . .]
Doors open at Half-past Five and begin at Half-past Six. Boxes 4s. Pit 2s. Gallery 1s.
Half-price at Half-past Eight.
Stage Manager, Mr Bengough. Leader of the Band, Mr Sanderson. Ballet master
and Director of the Melodramatic Action, Mr Ridgway.
[. . .]

¹ The play, by the prolific T. J. Dibdin (who was also the Surrey's manager), was adapted from Scott's
   novel and had opened on 7 January 1822.
² Audience members entering at half-price would have been in time to see the third act, together with
   the performance of the French pantomimist Gouffé as a monkey.

PLAYS AND PLAYWRITING

Despite the popular demand for melodrama from the end of the eighteenth century, the new
theatres had to be careful in the face of opposition from the patent theatres to any attempt
to perform a spoken text. This particularly affected performances of Shakespeare.

94   Macbeth as dumb-show, 1809¹

Reprinted in A. C. Sprague, 'A Macbeth of few words', in *All these to teach* (Gainesville:
University of Florida Press, 1965), p. 35

[. . .]
Faithful to nature and the drama's law,
From this great source [Shakespeare] our promis'd scenes we draw
MACBETH, the regicide MACBETH, portray–
His ruthless consort and her direful sway.
Though not indulg'd with fullest pow'rs of speech
The poet's object we aspire to reach:
The emphatic gesture, eloquence of eye,
Scenes, music, every energy we try,
To make your hearts for murder'd Banquo melt;
And feel for Duncan as brave Malcolm felt;
To prove we keep our duties full in view,
And what we must not *say*, resolve to *do*;
Convinc'd that you will deem our zeal sincere,
Since more by *deeds* than *words* it will appear.

¹ In an attempt to circumvent the laws regarding the performance of the 'legitimate drama' Elliston
   produced *Macbeth* as 'a Ballet of Music and Action', in a version by J. C. Cross with music by Thomas
   Busby. It was performed at the Royal Circus on 31 August 1809. The prologue assures the audience
   that they will see an authentic *Macbeth*.

Just as important was the invention of the new 'burletta' form, under whose umbrella non-
patent theatres attempted to perform comedies. Inevitably the form blurred any distinctions

between serious dramas with music and comic dramas with music, which made burlettas at times indistinguishable from melodrama.

95   What is a burletta?

George Colman the Younger, *Random records* (London: Colburn & Bentley, 1830), vol. I, pp. 51, 52[1]

For my own part,– the rooted notions of an old theatrical Stager make it difficult for me to consider a burletta otherwise than as a *drama in rhyme*, and which is *entirely musical*;– a short comick piece, consisting of *recitative* and *singing*, wholly accompanied, more or less by the orchestra [. . .]

[. . .] That the Minor Theatres supposed a Burletta to be what I conceive it, is pretty evident from their practice, since they were allow'd to exhibit this kind of entertainment:–

They first performed it according to the definition I have just given;– they then made their Recitative appear like Prose, by the actor running one line into another, and slurring over the rhyme;– soon after, a harpsichord was touch'd *now and then*, as an accompaniment to the actor;– sometimes once in a minute;– then once in five minutes;– at last – not at all;– till, in the process of time, musical and rhyming dialogue has been abandon'd; and a Burletta now, if it *be* one, is certainly an old friend with quite a new face.

[1] Also in R. B. Peake, *Memoirs of the Colman family*, vol. II, p. 397. George Colman the Younger, after a successful career as a dramatist, became Examiner of Plays from 1824 to 1836.

By the 1830s the writing of melodrama had turned into an industry, and few playwrights could ignore its attractiveness. Many were earning their living by quickly adapting French melodramas for immediate consumption by English audiences. The Romantics had failed to set a theatrically viable example. Probably the most influential figure in advancing the cause of the dramatic repertoire was Edward Bulwer-Lytton, who not only chaired the 1832 Select Committee on Dramatic Literature but who was also responsible for the Dramatic Copyright Act (1833), which gave playwrights some control over their property [12]. It was time to suggest guidelines for dramatists that would offer a new approach to serious playwriting and utilize the advantages of spectacular staging.

96   The need for a 'modern' English drama reflecting contemporary issues, 1833

E. Bulwer-Lytton, *England and the English* (London: Bentley, 1833; ed. Standish Meacham, Chicago: University of Chicago Press, 1970), pp. 311–12[1]

The SIMPLE, [. . .] is one legitimate (and I hold the *principal*) source of the modern tragedy – its materials being woven from the woes – the passions – the various and multiform characters – that are to be found in the different grades of an educated and highly civilized people;– materials a thousand times more rich, subtle, and complex, than those sought only in the region of royal existence, the paucity of which we may perceive by the monotonous sameness of the characters into which, in the regal tragedy, they are moulded [. . .]

Another and totally distinct source of modern tragedy may be sought in the MAGNIFICENT [. . .] Instead of abusing and carping at the public for liking the more gorgeous attractions, be it the task of our dramatists to elevate the attractions themselves [. . .] The astonishing richness and copiousness of modern stage illusion opens to the poet a mighty field, which his predecessors could not enter [. . .] Not then by pondering upon inapplicable rules,– nor by recurring to past models,– not by recasting hacknied [sic] images, but by a bold and masterly adaptation of modern materials to modern taste, will an author revive the glories of the drama.

[1] Bulwer-Lytton (1803–73) takes issue with the sources of inspiration used by English dramatists – slavishly plagiarizing the French and relying on Elizabethan models for verse drama. Now that English playwrights have the protection of the Dramatic Copyright Act and can look forward to the abandonment of the monopoly system (in fact not to eventuate until ten years later), he urges them to harness modern preoccupations and theatrical tastes in order to provide English drama with a new pedigree. Bulwer-Lytton would himself become a successful writer of plays, notably *The Lady of Lyons* (1838), *Richelieu* (1839) and *Money* (1840). See Nicoll, *History of English drama*, vol. IV, pp. 173–5.

The aesthetic guidelines of Bulwer-Lytton are given a further practical dimension in Mayhew's sound advice to would-be authors about staging.

97   How to succeed as a playwright, 1840

E. Mayhew, *Stage effect* (London: Mitchell, 1840), pp. 58 ff.

Properties should always be quiescent. It argues a want of perception to make them actors, or entrust them with the action; for, if this is done with an appearance of success, such things invariably distract the attention, by claiming applause separate from the real interest of the scene; besides which, they are apt to be ludicrously unreal, or so much the contrary as to stand away from the general truth.

To make this more clear, let us imagine some incident in a piece depends upon the appearance of an eagle. To heighten the effect, the author describes the terrible aspect of the bird and kindles the fancy of the audience; immediately on which the property-man lowers his stuffed effigy of the creature; which, though it shall be an admirable resemblance, and shall move its head and flap its wings, must obviously have so little the appearance of life, that the actors shall stand apart from it. On the other hand, living animals have too strong a sense of reality to blend in with the scene. The actor's art consists chiefly in forgetting his personality, and assuming a character and feelings foreign to his real one,– a delusion these simple creatures are incapable of abetting him in. The player may take on, but the horse is an honest, bona fide horse, without any love for hypocrisy; he will snort when the prince is talking, will make the canvas trees give way to his curvetings, and though a whole army may be perishing in a desert, he will look sleek and comfortable, and persist with his hoofs that the ground is made of wood. Animals, however well trained, perform their parts with so much composure, that it has the appearance of ludicrous condescension, and places the performers in a miserable contrast. All the vanity and frivolity of the stage is made apparent by the test of reality, and the reason is provoked into criticism upon the meanness of, as it were, so gross an attempt at actual deception.

Next in practical importance to the properties, are the scenes of the theatre. An author will best please the painter, and certainly consult his own interest, by studying variety in his directions; not confining his incidents to chambers, but occasionally introducing streets and landscapes.

There are but three different kinds of scenery; known by the terms, *drops* or *cloths*, *flats* and *set-scenes*. The rest, as wings and side pieces, (houses, bowers, rocks, etc., which, when a change takes place, are pushed on and joined to the wings,) being adjuncts. Formerly, the chief part of all stock scenery consisted of *drops*, as is still the case in most country theatres; but these are now seldom used in London, flats having superseded them; except close to the proscenium, where they are lowered, when any extraordinary space is required to display the scene which is to follow.

Further from the foot-lights than the middle of the stage, *flats* are seldom used, the remaining half being devoted to *set-scenes*, which, in the painter's and manager's estimation, are the first kind; and a piece is generally cared for by the theatre in proportion to the number of set-scenes bestowed on its production. Any scene, however, written 'A Palace', 'A Cottage,' can be made a set-scene; but there are some which cannot be well represented in any other form – those wherein any part is required to be practicable; as staircases down which the characters have to descend; bridges, across which the actors have to pass, etc.; or where machinery is necessary to aid the effect, as torrents, waves, etc.; and in general all, which are other than a picture on a flat surface, may be reckoned *set-scenes*.

It was once desirable an author should so construct his plot, that *flats* and *set-scenes* might alternate one the other; and this, for authors not intimate with the theatre, is still a good plain rule, though the improvement of machinery now enables the carpenter to work several *set-scenes* consecutively; but it needs some acquaintance with the capabilities of the theatre to do this with effect, and the accidents and delays, common on the first nights of pantomimes, are cautions not to be disregarded.

There are two terms frequently occurring in stage directions, '*discovered*' and '*closed-in*', – the importance of which it may be necessary to explain.

'*A Discovery*' is where the act-drop ascends and shews a party at tea, etc., or a front scene is drawn aside, and a council, etc., seen behind it. Some depth of stage is usually given to scenes in which these occurrences take place; because, unless the footmen are seen to clear the stage (a practice now disapproved of), the chairs and tables must be 'closed in', or shut from view, by the scene which follows; therefore in no instance ought a set-scene to follow one in which there is discovery requiring these properties. Neither should a death take place in a front scene, unless it be the ending of an act or the action is directed so as to remove the body – for the footmen would not look well walking away with the corpse.

Concerning *traps*, etc., no directions can be of any value, the carpenter of the theatre being the only person who need study these mysteries. Let the author give his imagination free scope, and he can hardly write directions which cannot be fulfilled.

It may be well, before leaving this part of the subject, to endeavour to ascertain the value of scenes and properties to an author. Actors and managers regard these aids very proudly; and for 'the getting up of a piece', often assume the merit of its success; forgetting the many yearly brought out, with lavish expenditure, which are condemned on the night of their production. Though a weak piece, especially of the melo-dramatic cast, may gain support from the splendour of the accessories, the fact proves, that no help an author can obtain from the theatre will render a *bad* drama successful. He should never sacrifice his feeling to suggestions from the management, by cutting for this effect, or elongating for that. Above all, he should never write what are called *carpenter-scenes* – little scenes of dialogue introduced to give time for mechanical arrangements. To have his piece performed, is but a means – the end is its success. His interests are those of a theatre. But vanity is more powerful than interest; and nothing is more common than to sacrifice the author rather than inconvenience the carpenter. Actors are too apt to look on authors as people who need their instruction, and to resent, as obstinacy, any resistance to the theatrical laws which regulate the scenes and properties. The worth of their suggestions will be easily ascertained, by considering the effect such aids to a drama have on the minds of the audience. No art can give reality to *the scenes*. Reality is only acknowledged when the reason is convinced; and in the theatre, the instant the reason questions, illusion ceases. Spectacle is a toy to amuse the senses, and, through them, lull the reason. Scenes, also, have other uses; they spare long passages of mere description, and may be rendered suggestive. This is their highest merit. It seems 'as gross as ignorance made drunk', to talk of their giving *reality*. Illusion can only be perfected through the feelings. All *really feel* with *Lear*; but who ever felt for scenes and properties? Stanfield's art[1] excites admiration; Bradbury's ingenuity claims applause; each in his province pleases our sensations,– but it is in *the passion only, the drama is a reality*; and it has justly fallen into contempt, in proportion as it has lowered its power for the exaltation of its inferiors.

[1] Clarkson Stanfield (1793–1867), a distinguished painter in his own right, had worked in the theatre since 1815. At the time Mayhew was writing, Stanfield was working as a scene painter for Macready at Covent Garden.

Despite Bulwer-Lytton's advice and the occasional success of such plays as Dion Boucicault's *London Assurance* in 1839 and Bulwer-Lytton's own *Money* in 1840, which seemed to presage a resurgence of English comic writing, playwrights continued to borrow from French sources. A literary drama seemed as remote as ever.

98   The failings of contemporary playwriting, 1843

Spectator, 16 (1843), p. 1113

What with Anglo-Italian operas, Anglo-French vaudevilles, and ballets that need no Anglicizing, the British stage is almost denationalized. Beyond an absurd farce or a trashy melodrama, not a single new piece written by an English author has been produced at any theatre for months passed; with the exception of Mr BOURCICAULT's [*sic*] *Woman*,[1] the failure of which was the first of a succession of disasters that caused the closing of Covent Garden [. . .]

Novelty is essential to the prosperity of a theatre; and it must be excellent of its kind, or it will not last long enough to repay the expense of producing it: the less excellence there is the more novelty is required. Repeated failures make managers afraid of untried ventures; and they fall back on the living French and the dead English dramatists – authors that neither require remuneration nor remonstrate against ill-usage.

[. . .] Modern dramatists, instead of seeking out the principles of their art, as exemplified in SHAKSPERE and other great masters, are content to parody the phraseology and caricature the characters of a past age; and find it easier to disguise and pass off as their own the stolen children of the French, than to rear the offspring of their own brain [. . .] We have dramatic poems in abundance, but no dramas: poets speak eloquently *of* and *for* their characters, but not *in* and *through* them: they talk when they should be doing, and *describe* in stead of *presenting* scenes [. . .]

[1] Dion Boucicault's *Woman* had opened at Covent Garden on 2 October 1843. Effectively, Covent Garden ceased to operate as a venue for straight dramatic performances after the collapse of the Vestris and Mathews management in 1842. It would reopen in 1847 as an opera house.

Most critical complaints about melodrama had revolved around its explicit appeal to visceral emotions, which ran counter to the critical perception that the proper role of the theatre was as a forum for social and personal improvement. This was an élitist and aristocratic viewpoint, which, in the 1840s, seemed at odds with social upheavals in England and on the Continent. The debate about dramatic 'legitimacy' had become irrelevant since the passing of the Theatre Regulation Act of 1843 [**17**], and it was perhaps a good time to make melodrama itself a legitimate form. The following document addresses melodrama's own pedigree.

99   A spirited defence of melodrama, 1844

A. B. R., 'What can be done for the drama?', *Cicerone* (2 March 1844), pp. 209–10

There is, it is not too much to say, more dramatic talent in England at this moment than there has existed since the time of Shakspere. And what keeps it under?

[. . .] The rules of legitimacy [. . .] The legitimate drama of the present day is very bad – it was never otherwise. But the people think that the fault lies in the dramatist or the actor, while it in reality lies in the system under which the legitimist delusion compels both dramatist and actor to work. It is impossible to serve both God and mammon, and it is just as hard a task to please an enlightened audience by adhering to the legitimate drama. Shakspere never was a legitimate dramatic writer. His mighty genius overleaped the paltry bounds of old conventionality. Shakespere was the greatest melodramatist who ever lived. The term is not one of reproach, but of the highest praise. His dramas are essentially melodramatic, and they are not the less splendid on that account. Then why are they called tragedies? Because it is the cant of the day to call old melodramas tragedies. If *George Barnwell* had been produced in our time, it would not have been a tragedy but a domestic drama, and Lillo's *Fatal Curiosity*, or Forde's *Duchess of Malfy* [*sic*], would have both been dubbed blood and murder melodramas. Nay, more, were *Macbeth* to be played for the first time tomorrow, how our legitimist critics would sneer it down! [. . .]

The writer then refers to *Hamlet, Othello* and *The Merchant of Venice* as examples of Shakespeare's facility for founding 'passion' upon 'incident', the stock-in-trade of melodrama.

We cannot love, or dread, or hate, without persons and circumstances to love, dread, or hate. Now, the pervading fault of the legitimate drama is that it rejects as beneath it that upon which all dramatic interest must be founded. The drama ought to be a reflex of life, allowing, of course, for those exaggerations necessary for the production of scenic effect; but the legitimate drama continually aspires to soar above life – to reject those sources of emotion and passion which the romance-writer so freely makes use of, and to depict and analyse extreme fear, thrilling anxiety, deep despair, without admitting those hair-breadth escapes, imminent dangers and rapidly-succeeding and varying incident and adventure from which all these emotions ought naturally to spring [. . .]

The writer concludes, after surveying the insipid quality of much modern writing, that melodrama has much to offer, especially through adaptations from the French.

Let us shiver old conventionalities and thread-bare rules of composition. Let the dramatist follow the Romancist [*sic*]. Let him dismount from his stilts. Let him throw more incident and less speech-making into his plays. Let him not despise the aid of the painter and the musician. Finally, let him look for a verdict to the audience, and not to the professed critic; and let him be assured that the breathless pause of excitement, the loud full-mouthed burst of applause, or the involuntary tear which may dim gentle eyes, are all prouder tributes to his success than the cant of a thousand 'legitimate' critics.

AUDIENCES: CONDITIONS OF VIEWING

Throughout most of the nineteenth century theatre-going was regarded fundamentally as a social activity, as though the performance was merely an excuse for a party. The auditoria remained lit throughout the evening, even after the introduction of controllable gas lighting from 1817, and performers continually competed with spectators for their attention. After 1763 the practice of admitting spectators at half-price became almost universal, which had the effect of bringing in a new audience who expected to be fully entertained. Playwrights and managers ignored this at their peril.

100   The significance of the half-price audience, 1800

Dibdin, *Reminiscences*, vol. i, p. 275[1]

'My dear Tom!' said Lewis,[2] 'this will be your first five-act production; and don't be offended, if an old practitioner ventures to offer [...] the fruits of his long experience. Half-price is a very proper privilege for those whose time or pockets do not afford them an opportunity of visiting the theatre earlier; but it is often the bane of an author, on the first night of a five-act play. The newcomers know nothing of the foregone part of the drama; and having no context with which to connect allusions in the fourth and fifth acts, are apt to damn, without consideration, that which they are no judges of; [...] To be forewarned against this contingency, contrive to make some character (either in the heat of passion, or in any way you please) briefly run over all the foregoing part of the story, so as to put everyone in possession of what they otherwise would have lost by absence; and, take my word, you will reap the benefit of it.'

[1] See Dutton Cook, 'Half-price at nine o'clock', in *The book of the play* (London: Sampson, Low, 1881), pp. 195–202.
[2] William Lewis's personal advice to Dibdin, which the latter includes for the benefit of young dramatists. Dibdin had been asked by Harris, the manager of Covent Garden, to modify his play *Liberal Opinion*, which had been performed there in 1800, into a five-act play. He took Lewis's advice and rewrote it as *The School for Prejudice*, which premièred on 3 January 1801.

Though there were complaints that the dimensions of the new theatres hampered visibility and audibility, both playwrights and audiences stood to benefit: successful playwrights could negotiate more money and spectators seemed to respond to the greater opportunities for sociability.

101   Playwrights and audiences prefer larger theatres, 1808

F. Reynolds, *The life and times of Frederick Reynolds* (London, 1827), vol. ii, pp. 377–8[1]

The *Exile* was performed in November [10], 1808 [at Covent Garden]: my profits amounted to six hundred pounds, and the receipts for twenty-two nights averaged on each, upwards of four hundred pounds. But when Mr Harris [...] was compelled to leave the Opera House,– where the public could scarcely either *hear or see*,– and perform at the little theatre in the Haymarket,– where the public could enjoy *both these faculties*, in their perfection,– the receipt on the first night *The Exile* was performed there, barely amounted to one hundred and sixty pounds.

[. . .] I must add, that, on the nights, Mrs Siddons, Kemble, and Cooke, performed in *The Gamester*, and in *Venice Preserved*, the receipts were frequently *less*; a convincing proof, I imagine, that, though the public usually censure and abuse large theatres, yet, in *their hearts*, they infinitely prefer them to those of a less size: involuntarily feeling that in addition to their superior cheerfulness, accommodation, and magnificence, they afford far more scope for the effects of those lasting theatrical *stars*,– scenery, pageantry, and music.

[1]   Frederick Reynolds (1764–1841) was, together with Cumberland and Colman, one of the most successful playwrights to bridge the eighteenth and early nineteenth centuries.

Even so, the spectators' gratification at spectacular theatre could be impaired by the length of time needed to set up the elaborate staging. This also protracted the evening, and returning home late through unlit streets could be hazardous.

102   Distance and duration as impediments to London theatre-going, 1814

Theatrical Inquisitor, 4 (1814), p. 5

SIR,

I have often heard it wondered at, why there were so few frequenters of the Theatre in this metropolis compared with cities on the continent, or even our large towns in England [. . .]

The great distances from the play-houses, and the frequent disappointments that persons coming from a distance meet with, added to the great lengths of the entertainments, make it a business, attended with labour and care, for the greatest part of the inhabitants of London to view a play, so that, on the following day, instead of being delighted with the past evening, they are fatigued and resolve not soon to return; the consequence is, that they do not return till a new actor, or a new piece, or some friend from the country, brings them back again [. . .]

Another thing I have observed that greatly injures theatrical effect, is, the length of time taken between the scenes, during which the audience loses that warmth of feeling, that interest, that is and ought to be excited, and on which the pleasure of dramatic representation chiefly depends [. . .]

When the interval between the acts is long, the thread is broken, and the effect greatly diminished, besides, the time being lengthened, is one great cause of the fatigue of the evening [. . .]

A Traveller.

The social occasion could also bring out the worst in terms of social self-consciousness.

103   Behaviour in the boxes, 1816

W. Hazlitt, *A view of the English stage* (London: Robert Stodart, 1818), p. 243

It is unpleasant to see a play from the boxes. There is no part of the house which is so thoroughly wrapped up in itself, and fortified against any impression from what is passing on the stage; which seems so completely weaned from all superstitious belief in dramatic illusion; which takes so little interest in all that is interesting. Not a cravat nor a muscle was discomposed, except now and then by some gesticulation of Mr Kean, which violated the decorum of fashionable indifference [. . .]

104   The discomfort of the galleries at Covent Garden, 1819

British Stage and Literary Cabinet (July 1819), p. 218

[Of the Two Shilling Galleries] I began to ascend a dark, and apparently endless, flight of stairs.[1] By-and-by, I reached a turning, where my progress was delayed by a kind of wicket, behind which stood a man, who demanded of me [. . .] coins of silver. I complied with his request, and continued my journey [. . .] At length, the well-known hum of a theatrical audience saluted my ears; a faint ray of light met my eyes; and, after mounting exactly one hundred steps, I arrived at my destination [. . .] The heat was intolerable; and, moreover, as to seeing and hearing what was passing upon the Stage, the occupants of this hell in miniature might nearly as well have been on the very house-top. Figure to yourself [. . .] about two or three hundred human beings 'cabinn'd, cribb'd, confin'd' in a wretched cock-loft; their view, bad as it is, rendered worse by sundry massy pillars supporting the ceiling, which is as black as pitch, and extremely low [. . .]

[Of the One Shilling Gallery] The road upwards, I found very similar to the one I have just described; and after paying the toll, and ascending one hundred and nineteen steps [. . .] I reached the top [. . .] The Two Shilling retreat, I had thought bad enough; but *this* was [. . .] *worse and worse.* Four rows of narrow benches are all the accommodation afforded; and so abrupt is the descent, that it seems as if a false step would inevitably procure for a man the freedom of the theatre, by precipitating him into the pit. The situation of the spectators exactly resembles that of a set of people on the roof of a house, peeping over the parapet to discover what is passing in the area. As to seeing and hearing with any comfort, it is quite out of the question. They who have been in the back rows of the third tier of boxes, may form some faint notion of the state of their fellow-sufferers in the galleries [. . .]

[1] The letter writer describes a visit towards the end of the season, in June.

Complaints about the late hours were still being voiced in 1831. The concern, however, was now tied to an increasing middle-class tendency to dine later than the traditional dinner hour of 2 p.m., which made getting to the theatre for a performance commencing at 6.30 p.m. more difficult.

105   Changing social habits and the late hours of performances, 1831

[Leigh Hunt], *Tatler*, 3 (1831), pp. 22–3

Everyone complains of the late hours to which theatrical performances are protracted [. . .]

This dire advantage, or supposed advantage, taken of the English propensity to have enough for their money, originated, there is reason to believe, in the practice that came up at the Haymarket, of giving us three of their small farces for the old stock play and afterpiece [. . .]

Madame VESTRIS[1] [. . .] was the first to innovate on this custom. She knew, that three or four hours of good sprightly entertainment, with the eyes open, was better than pretending to pleasure, half asleep. She announced that her theatre would close at a reasonable hour. It did so; and it is understood that she had a remarkably successful season. We are persuaded that if the other theatres would do as much, the result would be the same. The young and old alike, both of whom were play-goers twenty years ago, are almost equally shut out from the theatres, when they are so late. The late hours frighten mothers and grandmothers. It is not pleasant to take children away before the entertainments are over, and it is impossible to keep them up till one or two o'clock.

There is a notion perhaps with managers, that because hours in general are thrust forward, and people dine so much later than formerly, they like to find as much for their money when they arrive at the theatres, as they used when they dined sooner. But if you look around at theatre audiences now-a-days, it will be pretty evident that they do not consist of very fashionable people.

[1] Madame Vestris (1797–1856) had taken over the Olympic Theatre as lessee in 1830, and had announced innovations both in staging and in spectator comfort [see **51a, 51b, 53, 184a, 184b**].

By the 1830s some critics were challenging the traditional social emphasis of theatre-going and were suggesting that the proper focus of interest should be the stage rather than other spectators. Improvements made at the opening of the Covent Garden season in 1832 drew attention to the significant contribution of auditorium lighting.

106   Auditorium lighting and audience viewing habits, 1832

New Monthly Magazine (1 November 1832), p. 485

The other two improvements [to Covent Garden] that we have alluded to are, the arrangement of eight or ten centre boxes of the lower circle into stalls, and the introduction of a splendid chandelier. This latter [. . .] is a half measure only, and therefore, of little value. What was wanted was, to get rid of the numerous *small* chandeliers, which distract the eye, and thus greatly injure the *coup d'œil*; and, what is of much more importance, make the audience part of the house much *too* light, and thus remove or break up the attention from the stage-performances, and in so doing fritter away the habitual interest that would otherwise be excited by them. At present, the English people go to the theatre quite as much to see and be seen by the *audience*, as to witness the performances which are the ostensible cause of their coming; and where this is conspicuously the case there can be none of that real taste and earnest love for the drama on which the actual condition of that drama mainly depends.

AUDIENCES: COMPOSITION AND BEHAVIOUR

There are many instances in the eighteenth and nineteenth centuries of disturbances in the theatre. Sometimes spectators took the opportunity to demonstrate their financial whip hand over managers. Frequently they took exception to changes in programme or to the substitution of actors. Descriptions of these disturbances give an insight not only into behaviour but also into the make-up of the audience.

107   A fracas at Drury Lane, 1790

BM, Drury Lane Memoranda, unidentified clipping, 10 May 1790

LOVE FOR LOVE, and the SPOILED CHILD, which were to have been performed at the above Theatre on Saturday last, were deferred, on account of the indisposition of MRS JORDAN, the WEST INDIAN, and the ISLAND OF ST MARGUERITE, were substituted in their place.– This the audience were made acquainted with by hand-bills delivered to them on their entering the house.

Previous to the drawing up of the curtain, an apology was made, stating that, in consequence of the sudden alteration, Messers AICKIN and PACKER, who were not in either of the pieces originally intended for representation that evening, could not be met with, and no other means of presenting the WEST INDIAN remained, than Messers *Williams* and *Maddocks* being permitted to *read* the parts of *Stockwell* and *Captain Dudley*. This the audience refused to comply with, and insisted on having their money returned, which was at last done.

The Pit was cleared, not even *one* person remaining; but during the second act, four people came in, and no more till the half-price. About thirty staid [*sic*] in the boxes, and not a sufficient number to fill the front rows of the galleries!

The WEST INDIAN with *two parts* in it read, and a house thus uncomfortably thin, dragged dismally through the three first acts.– The half-price produced considerable amendment in the appearance of the house; and the performers, profiting from the indulgence of the audience, exerted themselves with some success to enliven the scene.

We cannot close this account without lamenting the awkward situation in which the Manager is frequently placed, by the *sudden indisposition of principal performers*;– it was near four o'clock before Mr KEMBLE was aware of the necessity for altering the play [. . .]

An enduring cause of disturbance and complaint on the part of audiences was the presence of prostitutes, especially in the saloons and in the boxes. It was often seen as a principal reason for the absence of 'respectable' spectators.

108   A disturbance over a prostitute at Drury Lane, 1808

Examiner (14 February 1808), p. 43

BOX-LOUNGING BLACKGUARDS.– The audience at Drury-lane Theatre were on Tuesday evening, disturbed by a pugilistic contest between Capt. B. of the Navy, and Mr C. a city merchant. The cause of quarrel was a STRUMPET! Those GENTLEMEN fought several rounds before the arrival of the constables put an end to the disgraceful scene. They retired from the theatre; but in a short time Mr C. returned to seek for the woman, whom he found in company with another GENTLEMAN. A second quarrel took place, and the audience were again distracted and alarmed. The parties, however, at length retired to a coffee-house, where another blackguard conflict ensued.– Such scenes are a disgrace to the Police of the Theatre.[1] Constables are in constant attendance, and it is much to be wished that whenever such disturbances occur, they were compelled to do their duty, and see the offending persons taken into custody. The Managers would find their interest in such arrangement, for then the virtuous and amiable part of the community would no longer be afraid of visiting our theatres, where at present a riot is as much to be expected as the rising of the curtain.

[1] These were employees of the theatre rather than members of any regular police force, which did not appear until after 1829.

The most celebrated audience disturbance in the nineteenth century took place in 1809 on the reopening of Covent Garden after its destruction by fire in 1808. The huge cost of rebuilding had led John Philip Kemble to raise the prices and to reserve more of the auditorium for private boxes in order to augment his income. The result was a protest that began in September and was not resolved until December 1809. Although the events suggested a purely theatrical dissatisfaction with managerial policy – hence the name OP or Old Price Riots – the protest was a well-organized political occasion, which challenged Tory authoritarianism, represented by the figure of the theatre manager, and asserted the spectators' inalienable right to free assembly in a 'national' theatre.[1]

[1] See further Marc Baer, *Theatre and disorder in Georgian London*, (Oxford: Clarendon Press, 1992) and Elaine Hadley, *Melodramatic tactics: theatricalized dissent in the English marketplace, 1800–1865* (Stanford, CA: Stanford University Press, 1993).

109   The reopening of Covent Garden and the commencement of the OP Riots, 1809

(a) [Leigh Hunt], *Examiner* (24 September 1809), pp. 608–10, reprinted in L. H. Houtcheons (ed.), *Leigh Hunt's dramatic criticism* (Oxford: Oxford University Press, 1950), pp. 26–7; (b) *Times* (10 November 1809), p. 3; (c) [Leigh Hunt], *Examiner* (19 November 1809), pp. 744–6, in Houtcheons, *Hunt's dramatic criticism*, pp. 32 ff; (d) William Cobbett, *Register* (16 December 1809), reprinted in *Covent Garden Journal*, 2, appendix no. 137

(a) An account of events

It was ardently hoped by all the lovers of the Theatre, that the Managers of Covent Garden, in shewing their taste for the fine arts, would have shewn also a liberality worthy of the taste, and thus increased the respectability and the true interest of the stage: but people, it seems, are destined to be disappointed, who expect from these men any thing but the merest feelings of tradesmen. The new theatre opened on Monday night with the increased prices of 4s to the Pit, and 7s to the Boxes, and if the town at least expected an increase of comfort on the occasion, it was to be disappointed even in that respect [. . .]

In the audience part of the theatre, *appearances* are still as magnificent, but there is a sad abridgment of comfort. Those who had obtained seats in the *lower boxes* or *pit* might certainly feel themselves comfortable enough to look about and admire the aspect of the place [. . .]

But the Managers, in all this display of taste, seem to have had no eye to the improvement of the public taste, but to have obeyed a certain aristocratic impulse of their pride, and consulted little but the accommodation of the higher orders. The people felt this immediately. It is certainly monstrous to pay seven shillings for admission to the garrets at the top of the house, where you can neither see nor hear, and still more monstrous, when you see a whole circle taken from the public by way of private boxes with ante-chambers, to make room for which the places and comforts of the lower orders have been so circumscribed: that old nuisance, the basket, as it is called, has been preserved to give the usual effect to the noise and interruption of the lobbies, and thus if the accommodations are confined in some respects, the theatre is altogether as large in others, as the avarice of the Managers and their contempt for a real taste in the drama could make it. In no such theatre can a true taste be excited, because a true drama, which requires nicety of expression in the voice and countenance, cannot be felt in it: SHAKESPEARE may be played to the pit and side boxes, but he will be little better than dumb and blind shew to the people in the basket, who pay seven shillings to hear nothing but noise, or to those in the upper boxes, who pay seven shillings to see nothing but indecency. Naturally therefore the rise of the old prices entirely disgusted the public, and their disgust was increased by various attempts on the part of the Managers and their friends to plead the excuse of necessity [. . .]

On MR KEMBLE'S appearance in the dress of *Macbeth*, the character he was about to play, he was received with a partial applause, which was instantly drowned in a torrent of execration, and after plaintively bowing, and looking as tenderly disconsolate as he could, for a minute or two, he was compelled to retire. The curtain then drew up, and the noise and outcry that followed were continued with an energy truly terrific the whole evening [. . .] Every species of vocal power was exercised on the occasion, and some persons seemed to pride themselves in shewing their invention at making a noise: in one corner of the pit you had a heap of groans, in another a combination of hisses, in a third a choir of yells, in a fourth a doleful undulating moaning, which, mingling with the other sounds, reminded you of the infernal regions, when in an instant the whole house seemed about to be rent asunder with a yah! of execration, whenever MR KEMBLE presented himself from the side-scenes. When MRS SIDDONS appeared, and seemed to petition for a little compassion, there was a general groan of disgust; but the death of her brother in the last act was followed by triumphant shouts of exultation, as if the spectators congratulated themselves on this temporary demise. After the farce, some persons, said to be magistrates, appeared on the stage, but soon vanished before the general indignation; and it was not till two o'clock that the audience retired [. . .]

[. . .] Each succeeding evening increased in noise: to catcalls were added horns and trumpets; and to a placard of two, banners all over the house covered with proverbs, lampoons, and encouragements to unanimity. An attempt on Tuesday night to fasten one of these placards on the stage curtain at the end of the perfor-mances, which closed at half past nine, produced a whole regiment of Bow-street officers, constables, and bruisers on the stage, the trap-doors were opened to guard against approach, and when all this was found to be no intimidation, a noise of pumping was heard by way of inuendo [sic], and one or two engine pipes were insinuated through the stage door, a threat that served no purpose but to make the indignation of the audience ten times hotter. A respectable gentleman of the name of LEIGH then addressed them, and exhorted them to a proper perseverance, a les-son which they put in practice the next night, Wednesday, with unabated energy. The actors by this time had become the audience, and the audience the actors, and Mr KEMBLE seeing no probable termination of the tragedy, again presented himself and begged to know, in the usual frigid way which he mistakes for dignity, '*of what the House had to complain?*' This ludicrous piece of affectation produced the usual burst of impatience and execration, but after another very temperate and strenuous exhortation from Mr LEIGH, the Manager again made his appearance; he stated that 'for the last ten years the Proprietors have not received for their capital more than *six per cent.*', and talked of 'the exigencies of dress and scenery', having 'doubled, trebled and quadrupled', besides other expences 'too numerous to mention', and 'with which he was in fact *unacquainted*'. This egregious trifling produced nothing but laughter: the same indignant vociferation was kept up all Thursday evening, and on Friday Mr KEMBLE once more presented himself 'to submit a proposal'. This proposal was to submit the decision of the question to a few great men, such as the 'Governor of the Bank of England', the '*Attorney-General* of *England*', etc. etc., but it said nothing about lowering the prices till the question *should be* decided. Of course, the speaker met with his usual reception. The audience, less molested than before with the interference of the peace-officers, were left to amuse their lungs to their hearts' content, and so they were doing last night when this paper went to press [. . .]

(b) A disparaging account of the composition of the audience

SIR,

Desirous of judging, from our own observation, of the conduct of the managers of Covent Garden Theatre, and that of the oppositionists, I was of a party on Tuesday night, which went at an early hour (about a quarter of an hour before the overture to the Exile began) the better to view the sort of persons who gained admission. We found about a hundred in the pit. A phalanx was formed, two deep, in front next the orchestra, and scouting parties were stationed in the centre and back, composed of the very outcasts of society, aided by some *respectable* police officers and pugilists.

Taking our station near the centre, we found a party of four or five miscreants, one a sweeper of a tennis-court, a rascal of the vilest description; another of the gang in brown striped breeches, black stockings and a black neckcloth, apparently a thief; two others, stout men, with unwashed and unbarbed faces, *tatsmen*, or hustlers, and a secondary officer of police, formed this groupe [*sic*] [. . .]

Another set consisted of a stable-boy, in a fustian jacket and trowsers, covered with filth, two blackguards in loose drab coats, a negro, with an oil-skin hat and silver-band, and a fellow who seemed to be a waterman to hackney-coachmen, or a link-boy. Here also, at hand, were two police-officers, who, with some skulking scoundrels, serving as spies, presently surrounded us.

In the boxes were a most motley group. The *ladies* seemed to have *got up their duds* for the occasion. The *gemmen* had on their best attire, with here and there a turned cravat. One fellow sported a scarlet uniform of some *wollunteer corpse*, and in an elegant manner quizzed the audience through a pair of old woman's tortoise-shell spectacles. His party was composed of two ladies, with delicate *ruby* arms, and a respectable looking barber, near St Martin's Lane, who shaves at the *new* price – three half-pence.

Mr Lazarus too occupied, with two young ladies, a front row in the front boxes. Similar parties continued arriving until half-price, most of whom seemed to be *tried* men, when many of these scoundrels decamped; the OPs being too strong for them [. . .]

In GARRICK's days not such wretches would have been suffered in the pit as those who nightly infest the theatre before the curtain draws up. The managers injure their cause by such an insult to the public. If they must have *paper-men*,[1] to countenance their pertinacity, they ought at least to admit none but persons who can afford to maintain some decency of appearance.

MERCATOR

Queenhithe, Nov. 9. 1809

¹ Kemble had tried to 'paper' the house by distributing free passes to those who might support the management. The implication here is that he had distributed the passes indiscriminately.

(c) Kemble employs pugilists to maintain order

The impolitic and brutal conduct of the Managers of this Theatre has reached its climax. It is impossible that the public should ever forget the time, when to go to a play was to endanger one's liberty and very life. To seizures and skirmishes has now succeeded an unmixed brutality on the part of the retainers. These men, consisting of the lowest ruffians collected from every pot house about the place, enter the pit with avowed purposes of malice, some of them with their sticks furnished with spikes; the company are wounded in the face, have their hands run through, and are trodden down beneath the feet of the wretches; and finally, one gentleman of the name of COWLAM, who neither hissed nor wore a placard, but had brought an action against one of the Manager's friends, was assaulted on Wednesday last by a particular gang, and malignantly thrown down and trampled upon in such a manner, that he has been confined to an excruciating bed in danger of his life [. . .] With regard to the prices of admission, there are certainly many persons, who upon their own calculations, and out of regard for the Theatre, are willing to allow the rise; but nobody who converses on the subject, whether for or against the managers in this respect, looks upon the theatrical statement as anything but a list of mere *assertions*, which, in stating only a vague expenditure, and not its *causes* or *items*, have no pretence whatever to determine the question. With regard to the private boxes, [. . .] and with respect to the policy and brutality of the Managers, every body unites in laughing at the one and execrating the other. The private boxes are certainly the most obnoxious part of the whole managerial alterations: the lovers of the Theatre are not, generally speaking, of a temper to begrudge the advance of sixpence or a shilling, abstracted from any imposition [. . .] but a whole circle of the Theatre taken from them to make privacies for the luxurious great, is a novelty so offensive to the national habits, both on account of its contemptuous exclusions, and the ideas of accommodation it so naturally excites, that the Managers, granting that they suffer a great loss, deserve to suffer still more for their mercenary and obsequious encouragement of pride and profligacy [. . .]

(d) Proposals for resolving the dispute

1. Then the circle of *private boxes* should be done away, and the whole of the space open to the whole of the public, as in the old theatre.
2. The '*pigeonholes*', as they are called should be done away, and the shilling gallery thrown open.¹
3. All the *actions and prosecutions*, arising out of the row, should be dropped instantly.
4. A declaration from Mr Kemble, in person, on the part of the whole of the managers, that they recognize, in the fullest sense of the words, an absolute

right in the audience, or in any part of the audience, assembled at the theatre, to express, either by signs or noises of any sort their disapprobation of any person, or of anything within the theatre.

[1] These refer to the enclosure of the upper gallery into self-contained units, which resembled a series of pigeon coops [**58**].

Whereas managers at the large patent theatres may have had difficulty in identifying the precise composition of their audiences, both on account of sheer numbers and the fact that neither Covent Garden nor Drury Lane had a catchment of population on which they could rely, neighbourhood theatres had to contend with the socioeconomic circumstances of those who lived in their vicinity.

110   The audience at the Surrey, 1819

Dibdin, *Reminiscences*, vol. II, p. 110

[These successes[1]] [. . .] conjointly induced me to take the said Surrey theatre [. . .] without knowing or reflecting that the immediate neighbouring population surrounding the Obelisk in St George's-fields,[2] may be divided into three parts; of which one-third are living within certain rules, which proscribe their admission to the theatre; one-third are living in the odour of sanctity, which proscribes their entering the tents of the wicked ones, unless they can do it with a free admission; and then they must study how to go, without danger of being discovered, and impeached by the godly; the third-third may be subdivided into three more; one of which one-third go to a theatre, but never pay for their admission, and will wait weeks and months for the chance of an order; a second-third of the above-named third-third are in a state of poverty, which will not permit them to pay, or they would; and who, not knowing any mode of obtaining free admission, or not being able to dress decently if they had one, never go at all: the third-third of the above-named last third, if they happen to be play-going people, are to be divided between the three transpontine minor theatres, amounting to a twenty-seventh part of the neighbourhood, who perhaps go once a year.

[1] Dibdin's decision to take over the theatre was based on the profits he had made from his writings for the Surrey and Astley's.
[2] The Surrey was situated at the junction of Westminster Bridge Road and Waterloo Bridge Road in Southwark [**74**]. It lay in a large working-class area but was also able to attract a clientèle from the west of London, thanks to direct transport links across Westminster Bridge. For the sake of argument, however, Dibdin characterizes it as dependent upon local patronage: he refers to his clients' poverty, the fact that many reside within 'the rules' of the King's Bench debtors' prison, that others nurse a religious objection to theatre-going, while the remainder (usually traders and shopkeepers who had placed playbills in their windows) go when they are given a free seat or 'order' in recognition of their help in promoting the theatre.

Three prints illustrate clearly some conditions and difficulties experienced by spectators at a popular performance, possibly at Drury Lane. The subjects are probably drawn from two separate occasions: certainly (b) and (c) could both relate to the performance on the same pantomime night in December 1814.

III   'Theatrical pleasures', 1821

Theodore Lane prints, Victoria & Albert Museum[1]

(a) 'Crowding to the pit'[2]

(b) 'Snug in the gallery'[3]

(c) 'Taken places occupied'[4]

[1] In their catalogue for The Georgian Playhouse exhibition (London: Arts Council, 1975), sv 276, Iain Mackintosh and Geoffrey Ashton identify these as three of a set of six prints reissued in 1835, from a series that was first published in 1821. Mackintosh and Ashton suggest that the theatre depicted is Drury Lane.

[2] Although caricatured slightly, this shows both men and women struggling to get to the narrow passageway to the pit, while a pickpocket profits from the confusion. The absence of any queuing system meant that such scuffles as the one depicted could easily break out.

[3] A predominantly lower middle-class clientèle is depicted, although it includes at least one old-fashioned gentleman wearing a wig. A complaint at a woman wearing an obscuring bonnet is also shown.

[4] The plate portrays an expensively vulgar family arriving at a public box for the start of the pantomime at 10 p.m., only to find that their places have already been taken by a much more elegant group, who have occupied the box at full price. The suave box-keeper points out that it is too late. The studied elegance of the box-keeper reflects the sense of self-importance assumed by such 'servants of the theatre', against whom much criticism was levelled.

The writer of the following article argues that the size of Covent Garden actively encourages the inattentiveness of an audience. Moreover, theatre-going itself has become so uncomfortable that 'respectable' spectators stay away and managers are forced to fill up the house with free admissions. It is even suggested that the managers admit prostitutes deliberately.

112 The faults of Covent Garden and their effects upon audience composition and reception, 1823

Literary Guardian, 1 (1823), pp. 126–7

The first [. . .] is without doubt, the immense, unwieldy dimensions of the house itself. A rough statement will suffice.– The distance from the front of the dress boxes to the curtain, at Covent Garden Theatre, is, say about 65 feet, and the height of the third tier, about 40 feet from the pit; on this calculation the distance from the curtain at this part of the house is fully 75 feet. The back of the two-shilling gallery, we suppose, about 25 feet behind this, and that of the one-shilling gallery, some 6 or 8 feet more; making in all, at this furthest point, an interval of upwards of 100 feet between the spectator and the performer. We all know, from experience, that in many parts, even of the dress circle, the words are caught with great difficulty and by dint of constant straining, while the expression of the countenance is but very imperfectly discriminated. What must be their case then, who are seated at double our distance from the stage, and are continually surrounded by a buz [*sic*] and ferment which 'ears polite' can form but a feeble notion of? [. . .]

If anyone would be at pains to examine the nightly box list, and generally to survey the audiences [. . .] they will find, on the average, that the best seats of the dress boxes are occupied by, what are significantly called, 'country cousins', and their lion-showing London friends; the pit, by dull old bachelors, attorneys' and bankers' clerks, together with a few wives and daughters of respectable tradesmen; [. . .] The third and great part of the second circle are filled by orders and free tickets, with, after nine o'clock, a few half-tipsy gentlemen from the coffee-houses and taverns.

The present system of free admissions is wilfully and radically bad. Authors and actors are admitted of course, 'tis their legitimate right; editors of newspapers and their deputies must also be invited, this is a necessary evil of too long standing to be suddenly left off; but what justification, what excuse, can the managers offer for the present systematic arrangement by which a horde of prostitutes and street-walkers are nightly suffered to obtrude themselves upon, what would fain be considered, the precincts of respectable society? How can these managers feel surprise at the deserted state of their boxes, when they know that they have admitted, nay, courted the attendance of wretches whose very presence should be sufficient to banish everything respectable from their doors? Yet these very managers complain that the play-houses are no longer the fashionable resorts they used to be; that fathers prefer sitting at home, round their fires, with their wives and daughters, to bringing them ever and anon amid the noise and riot of a theatre; and, finally, that they no longer receive that encouragement from men of *taste* and patrons of art, which used formerly to fall to their lot [. . .]

113   A foreign visitor castigates the behaviour of English audiences, 1826

H. L. Pueckler-Muskau, *A tour in England, Ireland and France* (reprinted Zurich: Massie, 1940[1]), pp. 49–50

The most striking thing to a foreigner in English theatres is the unheard-of coarseness and brutality of the audiences. The consequence of this is that the higher and most civilized classes go only to the Italian Opera and very rarely visit their national theatre. Whether this be unfavourable or otherwise to the stage, I leave others to determine.

English freedom here degenerates into the rudest licence, and it is not uncommon, in the midst of the most affecting part of the tragedy or the most charming 'cadenza' of a singer, to hear some coarse expression shouted from the galleries in stentor voice. This is followed, according to the taste of the bystanders, either by loud laughter and approbation or by the castigation and the expulsion of the offender.

Whichever turn the thing takes, you can hear no more of what is passing on the stage, where actors and singers, according to ancient usage, do not suffer themselves to be interrupted by such occurrences, but declaim or warble away, 'comme si rien n'était'. And such things happen not once, but sometimes twenty times in the course of a performance and amuse many of the audience more than it does. It is also no rarity for someone to throw the fragments of his 'goûté', which do not always consist of orange-peels alone, without the smallest ceremony on the heads of the people in the pit or to shoot them with singular dexterity into the boxes, while others hang their coats and waistcoats over the railing of the gallery and sit in shirt-sleeves.

Another cause of the absence of respectable families is the resort of the hundreds of those unhappy women with whom London swarms. They are to be seen of every degree, from the lady who spends a splendid income and has her own box, to the wretched beings who wander houseless in the streets. Between the acts they fill the large and handsome foyers and exhibit their boundless effrontery in the most revolting manner.

It is most strange that in no country on earth is this afflicting and humiliating spectacle so openly exhibited as in the religious and decorous England. The evil goes to such an extent, that in the theatres it is often difficult to keep off these repulsive beings, especially when they are drunk, which is not seldom the case.

---

[1] Letter 5, 20 November 1826. See also E. M. Butler (ed.), *A Regency visitor* (London: Collins, 1957).

114   James Grant goes to the theatre in London, 1836

J. Grant, *The great metropolis* (London: Saunders & Otley, 1837): (a) p. 24; (b) pp. 89–91; (c) pp. 35–7

(a) The popularity of theatre-going, especially among the working class

The people of London are a theatre-going people [. . .] It is so powerful with a very numerous class, both in the higher and lower ranks of life, that it must be gratified at any sacrifice, and under any circumstances [. . .] They would be perfectly miserable were they to suffer eight or ten days to elapse without witnessing the representation of any new piece which chances to be brought out at any of the leading houses; and as new pieces are almost nightly coming out at one or other of the larger establishments, it will be readily perceived that the amount of expense incurred in the course of the year, by a theatre-going family, must be very great. The passion for theatricals is, if possible, still greater among the lower orders in the metropolis. To want meals during the whole of the day would be no privation at all to the persons to whom I refer, provided they could only by such privation provide themselves with the means of visiting the theatre at night. Many a hungry belly and ragged back is there among the host of the unwashed in the upper or one shilling galleries of Drury Lane and Covent Garden, and in the sixpenny elevations of the Surrey, Victoria, and other theatres. I believe that more of the youths among the lower orders in London, begin their careers as thieves in order that they may have the means of gratifying their *penchant* for theatricals, than from any other cause that could be named. I may mention as a singular illustration of the strength of this passion [. . .] that when any of the houses are expected to be unusually full, they will besiege the doors in great numbers, two or three hours before the time of opening them, in their anxiety to get a good seat. Though the doors of Drury Lane do not open till half-past six, I have repeatedly seen the passage leading to the one shilling gallery crowded with boys and young men of the class I have mentioned, as early as three o'clock.

(b) Popularity of pantomimes among young people

The pantomimes are a great source of attraction to young people; and as they are always brought out on 'Box-night', when there is something in the pockets of the lower classes, the galleries of the various theatres are, on these occasions, crowded to suffocation; and a more motley appearance was never assuredly presented than that which then graces the various galleries. The railing on the front seat exhibits a goodly array of all sorts of second-hand apparel [. . .] It has the appearance of a pawnbroker's shop: bonnets broken in the crown, or without any crown at all; caps 'all tattered and torn'; shawls which were once of various hues, but which are now [. . .] all pretty much of one colour; hats, coats, waistcoats, etc. etc., are all fastened to the railing along the whole front of the upper gallery. Then there are the 'gods' themselves [. . .] A very large proportion of 'the deities' on such occasions consists of chimney-sweep apprentices, who are by far, considering their limited means, the most liberal patronisers of the drama [. . .] There is also a fair sprinkling of bakers' apprentices on box-night [. . .] A large number of those who people the upper regions of the house appear in their shirt-sleeves; their coats are doffed because the heat of the place has become intolerable. Others are swearing and fighting; while cries of 'turn him out!' 'turn him out!' 'order, order!' 'silence there!' assail your ears from all quarters [. . .] The truth is, that they claim a prescriptive right to be as noisy as they please on box-night, and all efforts to preserve order would be perfectly useless.

(c) Going to the opera

The King's Theatre is the great place, among the metropolitan theatres, of fashionable resort. It is also very largely attended by merchants and others, who do not know a word of Italian. The reason is obvious: there is always a disposition among persons of wealth, however limited their education, and humble their origin, to follow, in such matters, in the wake of the aristocratic portion of society [. . .]

The persons who visit the King's Theatre must all go in full dress. Any disregard of this regulation will be inevitably attended by the exclusion of the party, no matter what his rank. Some years ago, it was necessary for gentlemen to have three-corner hats, but that regulation has been departed from, and gentlemen wearing hats of the usual shape are now admitted. It was customary a short time since for ladies and gentlemen to go on levee and drawing-room days to the Opera in full court dress [. . .] It was absolutely dazzling to behold.

Between the stalls and the stage of the King's Theatre, is the orchestra. A more effective band than that which is usually to be found at this theatre, is scarcely ever to be met with. Their performances do really afford a rich treat to the lovers of music [. . .]

Notwithstanding the disapproving tone of those who sought to dampen the sense of social occasion, the following account captures much of the excitement and immediacy that characterized going to the theatre.

115   An evening at the theatre, 1837

'Going to the theatre', *Fraser's Magazine* (March 1837), p. 382[1]

Oh, the glory of first breathing in the open pit – of hopping, skipping, jumping, from seat to seat, and of settling at length in the middle of the fourth row, with friend Jack on one side, and a fair stranger on the other; then to look up, and see the gods and goddesses tumbling into the galleries, amidst the din of catcalls, finger-whistling, shrill exclaims, and hoarse replies. Where rows of empty benches were to be seen a few minutes back, hats and bonnets and excited faces are now in parallels of busy motion; [. . .]

And now the pit and galleries are full. Boisterousness is subdued into a sort of murmuring undulation, with only occasional gusts of riot from above. The second circle is gradually filling, with men of positive, and ladies of middling, gentility. The third circle receives those who cannot have their wish in obtaining front seats elsewhere; and both circles are subsequently occupied by young professional men, who, on this occasion, patronise the player rather than the play [. . .]

The turnkeys begin to rattle at the doors of the dress circle. 'No. 5, first company!' Enter a paternal superintendant, his turbaned wife, and two dandy gallants. Down they come; the seats slam after them, and slap goes the door into its rebate. Thus it continues all around: 'Second company, No. 9!' 'First company, No. 4, and second, No. 6!' [. . .] The gods cry for 'Music!' One by one, the denizens of the o[r]chestra appear [. . .] eyeing the fulness of the house with indifferent, if not discontented, grimace [. . .] Oh, the delightful discord of the tuning, and the delicious smell of gas and orange peel. The stage lamps are rising: flash goes the flood of light over the blinking multitude [. . .] A bell is heard: the pit partially arranges itself. The orchestral leader takes his seat [. . .] A little more tuning yet: the leader looks around: three taps with his fiddlestick portends the coming crash. His head is down; his bow is up; across the strings; and – CRASH! – away they go.

The dress circle continues to fill. As the overture proceeds, anxieties come over us. We *hope* the gods will be graciously silent. Our palms itch to greet the hero of the night. The final chords are being played; and at length, one mighty volume of sound announces chord the last. 'Down!' 'hats off!' and down we sit, dragging our coat-tails around, and snugly depositing our hats between our knees.

The bell rings, and up goes the curtain, yielding a grateful body of cool air, and developing the 'three weird sisters'. The cunning of the scene is, however, at first provokingly disturbed, by the noise of latecomers into the dress circle. And now opens scene the second, with king Duncan and the 'bloody soldiers'. And now, the witches again – and now,

'A drum!– a Drum!– *Macbeth* doth come!'

The intervals between the acts are by no means deficient in interest; the fair splendours of the dress circle proving most attractive. Perhaps, the interregnum becomes enlivened by a squabble [. . .] The murmurings of incipient altercation gradually swell into breezes of hostility. All eyes are directed towards the scene of the action. Anon, we observe the numbers around, mounting the benches to get a peep into the cock-pit. The ladies in the boxes near are alarmed. The men become eagerly interested: the voices of the engaged swell louder; and louder still the voices of the backers. An oath is heard – a blow evidently given; then a struggle, and then a confused hubbub of 'Turn him out!' 'Give it him!' 'That's it!' 'There he goes [. . .] The men return to their seats; the ladies resume their tranquillity; the bell rings; and up goes the curtain for the next act.

Thus the play proceeds, till a brief disturbance possibly occurs during the entrance of the half-pricers, which [. . .] is always ingeniously contrived to take place at the wrong time.

The play concludes: the hero is prostrate, panting in death; and, on the fall of the curtain, he is called to life again, by the magic power of his own proper name

[. . .] Again, as at the beginning, we employ every possible means of deafening our quieter neighbours [. . .]

Freshly, as the shower after dusty heat, comes the farce, which is less wearing than tragedy, in being more sparing of the *intellectual* man; otherwise as regards the man physical, it is sufficently fatiguing: so that, by the conclusion of the performance, we are willing to depart, under the comforting anticipation of oysters and porter. A modified wish to be gone is evinced by the audience at large, during the progress of the last scene; while many are on their legs, employed in shawling, cloaking, buttoning up their greatcoats, and half throttling with worsted comforters their little children [. . .] Then follows the bustle of departure, in which the conditions of entrance are curiously reversed; for the pit avenue is quiet compared to the box portico. In the latter, all is riot and confusion. Loveliness remains impatiently shivering on the threshold, while gallantry runs to and fro in search of her ladyship's carriage. Then we have the call for hackney-coaches [. . .] the hoarse responses of the coachmen; the vociferations of footmen; the fiery zeal of link-boys; the trampling of vexed horses; the one, two, three of the carriage-steps, as they are let down; the four, five, six, and the closing slap of the door, as they are put up [. . .] Such are among the principal features of box company departure.

From the pit, on the contrary, moves a mass, dense, slow, and silent. Some linger behind to take a survey of the interior of the theatre; watching [. . .] the dying lights of the great central chandelier, and scenting the flavour of unconsumed gas [. . .] the servants of the theatre appear in various parts of the box-tiers; and the noise of falling seats reverberates in restored space. The gilded fronts of the boxes are veiled with their canvass [*sic*] coverings. The vast hall of excitement and multitude, becomes the tomblike abode of silence and desertion [. . .]

[1] The writer goes with his friend Jack R. to Covent Garden. The occasion is a benefit and part of the performance consists of *Macbeth*.

Although many of the assessments of theatres outside the West End exhibit a condescending attitude towards the nature of their audiences, manifestly theatres like the Surrey tried to retain their patrons by suggesting that their offerings were as good and as comprehensive as any to be found elsewhere, but at a fraction of the cost of admission. The repertoire presented also reveals that the legal differentiation between 'major' and 'minor' theatres was already all but dead.

116   The popularity of a neighbourhood theatre, 1841

'The Theatres', *Spectator*, 14 (1841) p. 638

A full house is a phenomenon on this side of the water [Westminster side]; it is a nightly occurrence on the other [the south bank of the Thames]: the Surrey Theatre is crammed to the ceiling as a matter of course; and while his brother managers think themselves lucky if they escape ruin, Mr DAVIDGE is making a rapid fortune. The secret of this success is cheapness: it dates from the time when the manager lowered the prices of admission one-half. The audiences are of a more miscellaneous character than at the high-priced theatres, but they are well-behaved; a little uproarious in their expressions of impatience, perhaps, and not nicely discriminating in their applause, but making up for deficiency of judgment in heartiness of delight at what pleases them. Nor is their taste so very low: 'Jim along Josey', being a novelty, is preferred to 'Othello', which is none; but the admirers of 'My Poll and Partner Joe', can also relish the *Sonnambula*. The entertainments must be good of their kind; and the humbler sort, being easily provided in perfection, and better appreciated, necessarily predominate: effective representation, however, is essential to make cheapness profitable. Since the failure of BALFE's attempts to revive English Opera, WILSON, Miss ROMER, LEFFLER, and other vocalists, have been singing at the Surrey, in *The Castle of Andalusia* and *Guy Mannering*, followed by *The Quaker*, and other musical afterpieces[1] [. . .] The moan about the 'decline of the drama' is cant: people like to go to the play, but they cannot afford to pay so much, and do not like to go so far from home for amusement; moreover, they like to see something that will give them the stimulus they require [. . .]

---

[1] The pieces alluded to are: a song by 'Jim Crow' Rice, the American blackface entertainer who had made his English début at the Surrey in 1836; J. T. Haines's *My Poll and My Partner Joe*, a nautical melodrama first presented at the Surrey in 1835; the enormously popular Henry Bishop version of Bellini's opera *La Sonnambula*, which had first appeared at Drury Lane in 1833; O'Keeffe's comic opera *The Castle of Andalusia*, first performed at Covent Garden in 1782; Terry's adaptation of Scott's *Guy Mannering*, given at Covent Garden in 1816; and Charles Dibdin's comic opera *The Quaker*, which had its first performance at Drury Lane in 1775.

On the passing of the Theatre Regulation Act in 1843, the Lord Chamberlain requested the police to provide him with an account of all London theatres now under his jurisdiction. The account clearly displays the range of entertainments, the predominance of melodrama and the relationship between repertoire and neighbourhood.

117   The relationship between audiences and repertoire at the former minor theatres, 1843

PRO LC7/5 1843–4 scrapbooks[1]

Description of Performances

The Surrey–	Operas, Nautical Melo Dramas, Pantomimes and occasionally the Regular Drama, the latter not more than a Month throughout the Year
Victoria–	Melo Dramas, Domestic Dramas of 3 acts, Burlettas, comic Interludes Pantomimes. The Regular Drama at Intervals of Six Weeks continued for Two or Three Weeks
City–	Melo Dramas, Burlettas, Ballets and Comedy for Benefits

Queens–	Melo Dramas, Ballets, very seldom Regular Drama not more than Eighteen Times during the Year and then only for Benefits for the Actors and Charitable Societies
Royal Pavilion–	Melo Dramas, Nautical Pieces, Burlettas, Pantomimes, and Shakspear [sic] occasionally for Benefits or a Week for the Theatre
Garrick–	Melo Dramas, Burlettas, Ballets, Pantomimes, Shakspear and Sheridan Knowles Plays occasionally, perhaps Thirty times during the Year
Sadlers Wells–	Melo Dramas, Burlettas, Ballets, Pantomimes; Shakspear and Sheridan Knowles Plays perhaps Twelve weeks during the Year, Horsemanship
Astleys–	Melo Dramas, Burlettas, Spectacles, Pantomimes and every description of Equestrianism
Princesses–	Operas, Burlettas, Melo Dramas, Ballets, Italian Operas and Regular Drama
Marylebone–	Burlettas, Melo Dramas, Ballets, Pantomimes, and Regular Drama incidentally [sic] for Benefits
Royal Standard–	Burlettas w. rarely Shakspear

The Audience

The Surrey–	sometimes Nobility and Gentry, Tradespeople, Mechanics in the Gallery. 4 Women to 1 Man in the Pit, the Husbands, Brothers being in the Gallery to save Expence
Victoria–	principally Mechanics in the Neighbourhood
City–	Persons in the Neighbourhood, many weavers
Queens–	Persons in the Neighbourhood, of an inferior class to the audience at the City
Royal Pavilion–	Persons in the Neighbourhood and many from the Docks, many sailors
The Garrick–	Principally the Neighbourhood, tradespeople and Mechanics
Sadlers Wells–	Tradespeople in the Neighbourhood, Brickmakers, Mechanics, Watchmakers
Astleys–	Ass [sic] classes from every part of the Town
Princesses	Fashionable, better Class of Tradespeople, Housekeepers etc. not confined to the neighbourhood
Marylebone–	Families from [illegible] and Montagu Sqr [sic] Schools in Winter, respectable Tradesmen, Mechanics etc. all from the Locality
Royal Standard–	Tradesmen, Mechanics, their Children, Silk weavers from Spitalfields etc.

---

[1] 'Theatres for the first time brought under the Lord Chamberlain's jurisdiction by the 6th & 7th of Victoria cap 68.' Notes put together, based on police reports and the evidence of proprietors,

concerning the Surrey, Victoria, City of London, Queen's, Royal Pavilion, Garrick, Sadler's Wells, Astley's, the Princess's, the Marylebone and Royal Standard theatres. The notes list the duration of the theatres' seasons, prices of admission and total numbers of audiences, hours of opening and closure, number of performers and their terms of contract.

The formal liberation from legal restrictions persuaded managers to improve the comfort and the tone of their establishments.

118   An East End theatre expands its repertoire, 1845

'Britannia Saloon, Hoxton', *Theatrical Journal* (13 September 1845), pp. 291–2

This place of amusement, since the spirited proprietor, Mr Lane, has recently expended upwards of a thousand pounds, towards embellishing, adding private side-boxes to render the visit pleasant to the public, and convenient to all classes of society, the Britannia Saloon, may now be pronounced a handsome theatre, and highly deserving the support it obtains – crowded houses nightly. The company altogether is above *par*; and Shakspeare, no longer monopolised at what used to be termed the 'legitimate theatres', can now be represented here without any libel on his language or fame [. . .]

The review describes a benefit performance of Rowe's *Jane Shore* as 'reflecting credit on any theatre'.

[. . .] The Britannia Saloon must be distinguished for CHEAP and intellectual entertainment, and must be considered one of the theatrical novelties of the present age – for an audience to be amused for upwards of four hours with tragedy, comedy, farce, dances, and songs, and all at the small charge of THREE PENCE.

In 1844 the actors Samuel Phelps and Mary Amelia Warner, together with the latter's husband Robert, took over the management of Sadler's Wells and proceeded with a unique experiment, a repertoire consisting almost entirely of 'literary drama'. By 1846 they had clearly succeeded in identifying their theatre with the serious, middle-class, cultural aspirations that seem to have prevailed in the north London suburb of Islington [55].

119   The behaviour of the audience at Sadler's Wells, 1846

'Sadler's Wells', *Theatrical Journal* (18 April 1846), p. 123

This phoenix-like establishment re-opened on Monday for the holiday folk, previous to the close of the season. The able managers adopted their usual legitimate course and produced the tragedy of 'Brutus',[1] in their usual style; the scenery, dresses, and decorations, all in perfect harmony of the time and people represented, and was well appreciated by the refined intellectuals of this part of London. But a short time ago we often heard remarked that the inhabitants of this locality could not appreciate the works of the Immortal Bard, but Messrs Phelps and Warner have proved the contrary, for we never witnessed an audience so quiet and attentive on a holiday night as on Monday last.

[1] *Brutus, or, The Fall of Tarquin* was a five-act tragedy by John Howard Payne, first produced at Drury Lane in 1818.

Though theatres like Sadler's Wells and the Britannia appear to have answered the Lord Chamberlain's desire for greater respectability, there were others which continued to exploit a fascination with criminal activities. This was regarded by the police as unhealthy and conducive to criminality on the part of the spectators.

120   The police report on visits to the theatres, 1845
PRO LC7/6 scrapbook 1844–5

(a) G or Finsbury Division Report
22nd July 1845

Agreeable to the Commissioners' Order of the 22nd instant I visited the undermentioned Theatres between the hours of 9 & 11 p.m. viz: the City of London, Sadler's Wells, Standard, Garrick & Pavilion.– I found the four last-mentioned Houses orderly, and the Company in each of them respectable.– There were a few Prostitutes in each of the Galleries, but the rest of the audience was composed of grown up persons, apparently labourers and mechanics.– The Pit & Boxes in each of the Houses appeared occupied by persons of a superior class to those in the Galleries, from what I could judge from their dress and demeanour.

The City of London Theatre I visited about a quarter past 9, in company with 2 other officers. Four hundred & sixty six persons had been admitted to the Gallery, which was crammed almost to suffocation. At the moment of my arrival a female with an infant in her arms begged I would allow her to pass as she feared something had happened to the infant from the intense heat.– Jack Sheppard was the piece performing,[1] and the uproar was tremendous.– The audience in this part of the house was composed of the youth of both sexes, whose ages varied from 11 to 18, and chiefly of the very lowest class of society, the majority of the males being without coats or jackets.– I, and the officers who were with me, saw several males the associates of thieves.– There were also between 40 & 50 young prostitutes, some apparently not more than 14 or 15 years old, and the language going forward among them was bad in the extreme.– Among those described above there were (on a rough calculation) from 70 to 100 children of both sexes apparently of a superior class from their manners and dress.– I saw more than 20 little girls decently dressed intermixed with the Prostitutes, some of whom from their gestures and manners towards the Boys they were with, were apparently making use of rude observations,– but it was almost impossible to get near them to ascertain.

This Theatre has for some time been very unprosperous, and it has only been within the last two or three weeks that it has improved, and this has been in consequence of the means adopted by the proprietor in issuing the Bills attached, and performing the popular piece of 'Jack Sheppard', which is quite a favourite with the lower classes, more especially of youth.–

There is no comparison between this and the other Theatres I visited. Every thing appeared there, considering the localities, to be conducted with propriety, but in this quite the contrary.– The staircase leading to the gallery is one mass of filth, and the smell intolerable,– and on several of the stairs the contents of the stomach had been cast,– and apparently the stairs had not been cleaned for many months.–

The prices of admission to the abovementioned Theatres are as follows,–

	Private Box	Public Box	Pit	Gallery
Sadler's Wells	4..6	2..0	1..0	0..6
Standard	4..6	2..0	1..0	0..6
Pavilion	4..0	2..0	1..0	0..6
Garrick	2..0	1..0	0..6	0..6
City of London, at present		0..8	0..6	0..3

(b) Police letter to the Lord Chamberlain

23rd July 1845.–

I again visited the City of London Theatre last night in company with P. Sgt Brannon and P. Constable Tate, and found the same description of company occupying the Gallery as on the previous evening.– The number admitted was about 500, being rather more than before.

'Jack Sheppard' was again performed with two other pieces.– Several convicted thieves were pointed out the Proprietor by the Officers.–

Agreeable to the Commissioner's order, I have made every possible enquiry to find the writer of the letter attached[2] who gives his address, 'Aldgate' – but hitherto without success.– I think it is likely the person occupies apartments only, as no one in Aldgate is acquainted with him.–

(Signed) G. Maisey
Superintendent

[1] Harrison Ainsworth's novel *Jack Sheppard* had appeared in 1839. By the end of the year more than eight dramatized versions of the life of the eighteenth-century thief and gaol escapee had appeared in London theatres. (See J. Russell Stephens, *The censorship of English drama, 1824–1901* (Cambridge: Cambridge University Press, 1980), pp. 61–77.)

[2] Though there is no attached letter in the Public Records Office, this must refer to an anonymous informant complaining about the effect of such plays upon conduct in the neighbourhood.

121   Comparing audiences at some London theatres, 1850

'Garrick Funnybone', *Theatrical Journal*, 11 (1850), p. 67

We have often noticed, on looking around us, a vast difference in the audiences who attend the various theatres. Price of admission will suggest itself to our readers as the primary cause of quiet, noisy, tolerably respectable, and fashionable audiences, but in many cases it is very certain that price is not the guage [sic] to determine the character of an audience. Treating the subject in a broad manner, we, like every body else, could of course testify to the wide difference in the position of those who visit the Haymarket and those who support the Victoria, but this is not our object; we wish to [. . .] prove that at two theatres where it is the same amount of admission, audiences of different degrees assemble. For instance, take the Adelphi and Lyceum. The prices are the same. The Lyceum boxes are much patronized by the nobility; the pit is in every respect highly respectable; the gallery extremely quiet, while the Adelphi has the most common audience of any establishment at the price this side of the water. What is the character of the performances at each place? At the Lyceum polite farces, extravaganzas, and other twaddle dressed with the greatest taste. At the Adelphi melo-dramas well put upon the stage, and broad inconsistent farces, in which the actors are allowed latitudes never even dreamed of any where else. Neither of them can be considered intellectual places of amusement, fine clothes being the standard of one house and improbabilities the other. At Drury Lane there is a mixed audience, for the majority of playgoers will pay more to see a performance there than at a smaller establishment, not because the entertainments are better, but chiefly because it is Drury Lane. No one would think of opening Drury Lane with a shilling pit, and why? Because the larger house commands the higher price, hence the immense talent required (as in the case of the Olympic) to make a small house profitable at best prices. Take for instance the galleries at the two last mentioned houses, Drury Lane and the Olympic. Both are shilling admission. The Drury Lane gallery fills better than any part of the house, the Olympic worse than any part of the house. The Olympic audience is about the quietest in London, they very rarely suffer themselves to be called into extravagance, the applause comes from the pit and the boxes, who are too powerful for the gallery, and an actor must be something extraordinary to get a call before the curtain. How different is the case at Sadler's Wells, where there is a good pit, a large gallery, and very thin boxes; once bring a man to the footlights, and set the gallery going, and stop them who can [. . .] the gods at whatever amount of extravagance must have their sixpence worth. The Surrey audience is a trifle lower than the Wells, and though the proprietors use every exertion to improve the taste, the melo-dramatic love still peeps forth, and to make things thoroughly palateable [sic] they are obliged to serve up a dish of 'nautical', or 'domestic' about ten in the evening.[1]

---

[1] Changing work patterns and longer hours ensured the continuing importance of a half-price audience, especially for theatres situated in a predominantly working-class neighbourhood. Such spectators were not prepared to be satisfied by the third act of a play and an insignificant afterpiece, but wanted a full-length domestic or nautical melodrama for their price of admission.

THE ATTENDANCE OF ROYALTY: ITS EFFECT ON AUDIENCES
AND REPERTOIRE

Though royalty had patronized the patent theatres and members of the royal household had attended performances at the minor theatres, the absence of regular royal patronage, especially at performances of legitimate drama, together with a prevailing preference for imported opera and animal displays, irritated English theatre managers. They were able to attribute the absence of 'fashionable' audiences, who would have paid for the more expensive private boxes, directly to a lack of leadership on the part of the royal family. Benjamin Webster used the presence of the Queen at one of his performances very astutely to advance his cause of extending the Haymarket's limited season.

122   The need for and significance of royal patronage, 1839

(a) *Actors by daylight* (1839), vol. II, pp. 64–5; (b) *Era* (20 January 1839), p. 19

(a) Her Majesty has reigned over England nearly two years, and in that period has visited its two principal theatres *seven times*, and the Italian Opera House – or the Queen's Theatre, as it is now more *properly* termed – nearly *fifty times*. This glaring neglect of the interests of native artists has had the effect [. . .] of inducing the public to neglect them too, and causing, as it were, the Italian Theatre, in the Haymarket, to rise and flourish upon the ruins of our own.

(b) Mr Webster has closed a most prosperous season at the Haymarket, being the only manager who has yet been able to keep open his theatre with profit to the extent of time lately granted to the houses not dignified with the title of patent. The Queen honoured the performance with her presence, and Mr Webster [. . .] most dexterously alluded to the circumstance of his being obliged by his licence to close this theatre just at the commencement of the most profitable part of the season. This was indeed getting the Queen's ear, and amused as her Majesty appeared to be – staying to the very end of the performances – might naturally make her turn round to the Lord Chamberlain, and say, 'Is this so?' [. . .] The following is the speech to which we allude:– 'Ladies and Gentlemen,– I have again to offer you my grateful acknowledgements for a most prosperous season, and that, too, in despite of the unprecedented attraction of the larger legitimates. The theatre has now been open 243 successive nights, and believe me, ladies and gentlemen, it is with no small degree of pride I find that the taste of the public for pure tragedy, comedy, and farce, unaided by grand scenic effects, has enabled the little theatre in the Haymarket to successfully hold the open tenor of its way unscathed, though with a veritable tempest on the one side, and real roaring lions on the other;[1] and it could still progress with increasing popularity, if the licence permitted it; and, had I not reason to be satisfied as it is, it might be deemed somewhat hard to be obliged to close the doors in the midst of the most festive season of the year, and when all the theatres look forward to a certainty of profit [. . .]'

The Queen seemed very attentive to this speech, and seemed highly delighted at the performances. In compliance with the enthusiastic calls of the audience, she came forward to acknowledge their plaudits; and at the conclusion of Strauss's '*Homage* [sic] *à la reine de la Grande Bretagne*' which finished with 'God save the Queen,' the whole house rose.

[1]   A few nights earlier, on Thursday 17 January, the Queen had gone privately to Drury Lane at 10 p.m. for a second time to view Van Amburgh and his lions. See George Rowell, *Queen Victoria goes to the Theatre* (London: Elek, 1978).

The pressure on Queen Victoria to show partisan favour towards English theatre culminated in the so-called 'Monte Cristo Riots', which took place at Drury Lane on 12 and 14 June 1848. A visit to London by the French theatre company, Théâtre Historique, with its adaptation of Dumas's *The Count of Monte Cristo*, occasioned a protest against what was described as a foreign artistic invasion. As with the earlier OP Riots, these disturbances could easily be dismissed as a merely xenophobic theatrical storm in a teacup. However, Chartist demonstrations had taken place throughout early 1848, and there is circumstantial evidence to suggest that theatre managers such as Webster used the volatile political climate to promote their efforts to solicit direct royal patronage.

123   The 'Monte Cristo' riots, 1848

Spectator (17 June 1848), p. 584

Drury Lane Theatre has been the scene of a disgraceful riot, got up by certain members of the theatrical profession, who are indignant at the occupation of (save the mark!) the 'national' establishment, by the French company of the Théâtre Historique. The policy of these very silly persons consists in occupying the pit of the theatre, making a continuous howling, so that not a word uttered by the actors is audible, and pointing out with marks of execration any person whom they may happen to detect in the act of applauding the foreign 'invaders'. Many of them provide themselves with huge tin whistles – on purpose, it would seem, to avoid the chance of pleading the right to a spontaneous utterance of opinion when brought before a Magistrate. They have determined that their attack shall look premeditated, and therefore illegal; and they have succeeded in disgusting every partial person except – the pick-pockets. The insults offered to foreigners and ladies, not only in the theatre but on their way to its door, gave a sad stamp of blackguardism to the proceeding. This indicates a want of education, which perhaps is one secret of the non-success of so many English actors.

The uproar of Monday having been renewed on Wednesday with increased acrimony and system, bills were issued by the management on Friday morning, stating that the house would be closed for that evening, and two farewell performances would take place next week, at much higher prices.

Queen Victoria yielded and began a series of regular invitations to Windsor Castle, which undoubtedly helped to persuade middle-class families of the respectability of theatre-going.

124   The Windsor theatricals, 1849

(a) H. Bolitho (ed.), *Further letters of Queen Victoria* (London: Thornton Butterworth, 1938), p. 15; (b) *Times* (26 January 1849), p. 8[1]

(a) Queen Victoria writes to the King of Prussia from Windsor Castle, 6 January 1849

Sire, my most honoured Brother,

Chevalier Bunsen has been helping us in an attempt to revive and elevate the English drama which has greatly deteriorated through lack of support by Society. We are having a number of performances of classical plays in a small, specially constructed theatre in the castle, and are collecting what still remains of the older art. The stage has been erected in the room which you occupied, the Rubens room [. . .]

(b) The *Times* reports

For the last month the plays acted in the Rubens Room at Windsor Castle, have afforded a fertile topic of conversation to those who take interest in the proceedings of the Court, and those who discuss the fluctuating fortunes of the British drama. The fact that the Sovereign bespoke a series of English theatrical performances as a recreation in her own palace, has at least the charm of novelty to recommend it to the attention of the curious. Fancy has wandered back to the days of Elizabeth and the first James, when such means of amusement were not uncommon; and perhaps, wandering forward, has augured that a new stock of dramatists worthy to compete with those of the Elizabethan era may spring into existence from the effect of the Windsor Theatricals [. . .]

The courtly assembly seems to have laid aside that frigidity which is usually the characteristic of private theatricals, and to have applauded with the zeal of a money-paying public, thoroughly pleased for the return of its outlay [. . .]

With the large public – the public outside the Castle – the question *àpropos* of these theatricals is, whether or not they confer a benefit on the English drama. That the benefit will not be of that immediately palpable nature which would result from half-a-dozen royal visits in state, and the crowds consequent thereupon, must, we think, be conceded by any impartial person. But at the same time we are inclined to decide that an indirect benefit to the English theatres is far from improbable.

When the highest personage in the land considers that an English dramatic performance is such an entertainment as to merit the construction of a stage in her own drawing-room, with all the appurtenances of a regular theatre, the opinion that the native drama is unfashionable receives an authoritative rebuke. The plays acted at Windsor Castle are the same that may be seen at the Haymarket and the

Lyceum; the actors in the Rubens Room are precisely the same individuals who appear on the public boards; and it would be absurd to say that an entertainment which occupies a high rank at Windsor, loses that rank when it comes to the metropolis.

The very circumstances that theatricals are now generally talked about, is in itself likely to be of advantage to the English drama. A certain elevated class of the public, by shunning English theatres and skipping English critiques, might soon lose sight of the native drama altogether. But now, the plays and the actors are forced upon the attention of the higher orders from another point. He who studies the proceedings of the Court, has an English theatrical programme thrust into his view; and the same course of reading which tells him that her Majesty took an airing, also informs him that Mr and Mrs C. Kean play *Hamlet* and *Ophelia*. The crowded state of the principal theatres would seem to indicate that an awakened interest for theatricals is already taking effect.

[1] Charles Kean had been asked to put together a programme to be held at Windsor during Christmas 1848. The article was probably written by Michael Nugent, the paper's theatrical reviewer at the time.

IV   Actors and acting

INTRODUCTION

There is little to suggest fundamental changes in acting traditions from the 1780s to the retirement of John Philip Kemble in 1817, or indeed in the conditions governing the actor's exercise of his or her art. Many of those who had contributed new insights were to continue their influence into the nineteenth century: Mrs Siddons did not retire until 1812; George Frederick Cooke died in the same year in the United States; the comic actors William Lewis and Joseph Munden retired in 1809 and 1824 respectively and Dorothy Jordan in 1815.[1] Nor did the new genre of melodrama precipitate acting in a new direction. There is much to suggest the continuation of eighteenth-century traditions of tragic technique and rhetorical gesture modified for use in melodrama.[2] The increase in the numbers of letters patent issued to provincial theatres also ensured the continuance of these regional centres as training grounds for the London stage.

Nevertheless, some changes were inevitable, even if acting styles were slowest in responding to changes in technology, the conditions of viewing and the composition of theatre audiences from the end of the eighteenth century. The elements that did contribute most to change were the expansion in the size of the patent theatres in London and the stress in melodrama upon non-verbal, physical modes of communication with an audience – what critics would call 'the pantomimic'. The size of the theatres and the response of managements to a growing taste for spectacular entertainment from the 1790s forced the performer to meet the challenge of the new developments through a search for fresh interpretations characterized not so much by internal consistency, but rather by the surprise of novelty. The relentless drive of melodramatic plotting necessitated the discovery of a physical language that built upon the eighteenth-century language of rhetorical displays of passion, but invested it with new, more precise gradations as well as emotional extremes. These, moreover, needed to be conveyed accurately and immediately to audiences unfamiliar with the established principles of rhetoric or the canon of English dramatic literature.

As the forestage retreated and the stage doors disappeared, so the 'status' of the actor as the privileged interpreter changed. It is within this context that the significance of Edmund Kean needs to be placed. Not only did he satisfy the craving for novelty of interpretation, but he was able to demonstrate the liberating effects of non-verbal, melodramatic expression upon the text-based genre of tragedy. The jagged emotional lines of melodrama and Romanticism generally were complemented by Kean's physicality and oscillating moods. His success spurred on many actors, who responded to the appeal of his techniques and the volatile moods of audiences for most of the period to 1850. Few, however, became truly successful; most appeared as mere imitators. Yet it was Kean and his admirers who were to determine the language of melodramatic acting that would persist until almost the end of the century.[3]

Just as significant for the development of a serious English acting style in the period was the influence of Macready. Undoubtedly inspired by Kean in his early days, he was equally impressed by French acting technique, especially that of Talma. Though less able by temperament to impose his authority upon the classic repertoire, Macready was unrivalled in his ability to suggest inner turbulence and domestic incongruities in a potentially tragic situation, thereby making it recognizable and accessible to the audience. In this he was ably partnered by Helen Faucit, who was similarly adept at reconciling formality with realistic character motivation.

Comic acting was also affected by the change in audience composition and the size of the theatres themselves. The eighteenth-century comedy of manners depended to a great extent on social stability and the acceptance of social verities. The blurring of class differences, the increasing disparities based on economic difference, together with the greater mobility of audiences, demanded a change in the comic repertoire. In a volatile society the only ascertainable common denominators were food, money, pretension and eccentricity, and these were to be seen through the distorting mirror of farce. The agricultural labourers flocking to the metropolitan centres, especially London, from the north or from Ireland, brought with them the stereotypes of behaviour lampooned by performers for an audience determinedly urban and streetwise, if not urbane. Urbanity would begin to surface in the 1830s, epitomized by the performances of Charles J. Mathews and his wife, Madame Vestris.[4]

[1]   See David Thomas and Arnold Hare, *Restoration and Georgian England*, nos. 299, 300, 301, 309–10, 327 and 337–9.
[2]   Alan Downer, 'Players and painted stage – nineteenth-century acting,' *PMLA*, 61 (June 1946), pp. 522–76.
[3]   'Melodramatic acting,' in Michael Booth, *English melodrama* (London: Jenkins, 1965), pp. 190–210.
[4]   See Michael Booth, *English plays of the nineteenth century* (Oxford: Oxford University Press, 1973–6), vol. III, pp. 145–53; vol. IV, pp. 145–53.

GETTING ON STAGE

The rise of the circuits from the 1770s marked the beginning of the evolution of the theatre into an industry. Theatres in York, Bath, Bristol, Dublin, Norwich and Edinburgh had become proving grounds for actors hoping eventually to attract the attention of London managers, and this practice continued throughout most of the period up to 1850. Although opportunities were limited, given the existence of only two patent theatres in London, with the Haymarket as the summer equivalent, and the tendency of actors to retain their positions in the Covent Garden and Drury Lane companies, the proliferation in the number of 'minor' theatres offered aspiring actors some alternatives. Nevertheless, although the business side of theatres became more formalized at the end of the eighteenth century – the move from profit sharing to a salary base, the establishment of contractual rules – many of the old practices endured.[1]

[1]   See Thomas and Hare, *Restoration and Georgian England*, nos. 199, 202, 215–16.

125   Negotiations with a provincial actor, 1802

Mrs A. Mathews, *Memoirs of Charles Mathews* (London: Bentley, 1838), vol. 1, pp. 344 ff.

(a) Letter from George Colman to Charles Mathews[1]

TO MR MATHEWS

Theatre Royal, Haymarket, 14th Sept. 1802

SIR,

Your merits as an actor having been mentioned to me, give me leave to propose an engagement to you, for next year, in my theatre. It is my intention to commence the season positively on the 15th of next May; and to continue it to the 15th of the following September. Should you think it eligible to embrace the opportunity which I now offer you, of performing for four months before a London audience, I beg you will be kind enough to inform me on what terms you will give me your assistance. At all events, I shall thank you for a speedy answer, directed to me, at Mr Jewell's, 26, Suffolk Street, Charing Cross. I am, Sir, your obedient servant,

G. COLMAN.

(b) Mathews's response

TO GEORGE COLMAN, ESQ.

Wakefield, September 23rd, 1802

SIR,

I feel much flattered by the offer of an engagement in your theatre, but cannot come to any determination on the subject, till I understand more particularly what situation you propose to me. I must beg leave to decline mentioning terms, as I am entirely ignorant of the salaries you usually give. I am so fortunate as to be in great fame on this circuit, in possession of the first cast of characters, and on the best of terms with my manager. It is indeed in every respect a most valuable situation, and it is only on very advantageous terms that I shall be induced to quit it. I most undoubtedly wish to perform in London, but must look for an ample compensation for resigning a lucrative situation, for an engagement of only four months.

I shall be obliged to you, sir, to let me know what salaries you can afford to give, and if I accede to your wishes, what business will be allotted me. This is a very material consideration, and I entreat that you will be as explicit as possible. I have performed in the York theatre the entire range of principal low comedy, and am well studied.

Have the goodness to inform me, if at any part of the season any of the established London performers are to be engaged. I shall thank you for an answer as soon as possible: we leave this place on Tuesday the 28th, after which time, be kind enough to direct – Theatre, Doncaster.

I am, Sir, your obedient servant,

CHARLES MATHEWS.

(c) Colman's response to Mathews's request for a salary of £10 a week

TO MR MATHEWS.

Suffolk-street, Oct. 8, 1802.

SIR,

The terms which you propose are certainly high, and perhaps unprecedented, for a performer who has not yet felt the pulse of a London audience; but the reasons stated for thus fixing your *ultimatum* appear to be founded on justice, to put vanity out of the question. I wave [*sic*], therefore, all mention of any risk incurred on my part in my new speculation, and embrace your offer. But to prevent all mistakes, permit me to state precisely what I conceive to be the engagement. Ten pounds a week and a benefit, of which benefit you pay the usual charges. You will perform from the 15th May to the 15th September inclusive. If you engage in London after your appearance with me, you give me the preference in a re-engagement. If you think any short memorandum requisite between us, I am willing to enter into it. If you conceive the letters that pass between us as sufficient, I am quite content that it should remain an agreement *upon honour.* Pray send me two lines speedily, which will be conclusive. I will (when we meet in the summer) do everything in my power to contribute to your reputation with the public, and your comfort in my theatre.

I am, Sir, your obedient humble servant,

G. COLMAN.

P.S.– Of course, your attendance will be expected in town a week or ten days (as I begin with novelties) previously to the opening of the theatre.

(d) Colman describes, at Mathews's request, the repertoire and range of characters envisaged

TO MR MATHEWS

October 23, 1802

DEAR SIR,

I am happy to find by your last letter of the 13th, that our agreement is completed [. . .] To give you this information (which I will as well as I now can, for you must naturally be anxious) I send you a parcel of crude hints and disjointed sentences, rather than a perfect system; but from these you will be able to make out a sketch of my general intentions. I will endeavour to be more particular in what most immediately regards yourself. Recollect, however, that there are secrets in the most petty theatrical states, and that I send you the outline of my scheme in confidence.

New matter, as fast as possible, after the commencement of the season. Certainly an occasional prelude on the first night. A new grand ballet of action almost immediately on the opening. A new light drama (of dialogue) to add to it, after a few nights of its run. New matter to follow the above sooner or later, in proportion as the preceding novelties may hit or miss. The prelude I shall write myself, and shall endeavour to cast in it, or leave out of it, such new performers whose reputations might be served or hurt, by appearing thus abruptly (for the first time) before a London audience. New actors, of whatever merit, cannot expect to be nursed so much, by giving intervals in their appearances, when they come into an established London company. The scheme is new; almost all the actors are new. If we wait for niceties the stage will stand still; off we must go at once! ding dong! helter skelter! and the new troops must commence regular action like the veterans. Now, let us see how this plan will militate against you, premising that I wish to do the best for you which such an undertaking will permit, and that I wish you to suggest anything to me which you think will contribute to your fame. The prelude you may be in, or out of, as you please. I think certainly better out; for as I wish to make you a great gun, it would be a pity to let you off like a squib, in a prelude, at first. When I say this, you need not fear having original characters enough (just as they may turn out, for that rests with the town), in the course of the season. The ballet on the opening, if it succeed, will be a favourable circumstance for you, for it will supply the place of many a light speaking drama (into which you will naturally afterwards be thrown), and give you breathing time. You will not thus be hurried from one character to another night after night, as if the arrangement were otherwise [. . .]

Let me now consider your first appearance. It must be immediately on the opening; but it shall be in whatever character you please. This is a subject which requires deliberation, and we have no time to deliberate. You tell me that you have performed in the 'York theatre the entire range of low comedy'. This is a very wide range indeed! But tell me also, in which part of that range you feel yourself to have succeeded most with the audience. Old men, country boys, dapper servants, mingled characters, like those of Munden, of sentiment and fun, etc. In short, make out a list of what you like, and send it to me. I would advise you to avoid, if possible, in your first appearance, the difficulty (it is a great one to avoid) of encountering comparison.

First impressions often make or mar. I remember, soon after Munden's first appearance in London, he ate, with uncommon success, a hundred pounds weight of plum-pudding in 'Two Strings to your Bow'.[2] The feat was new to a London audience. He had a good character in it, in which nobody had been seen before. Do you recollect anything in which you might make your appearance, under the same favourable circumstances? When you have recovered from the fatigue of reading this ('tis worse than a part of twenty lengths[3]) send me a line. Be assured that, from the reports I have heard of your merits, and from the candid, clear, manly style of your letters to me, I have your interests, abstracted from my own, fully at heart.

I am, dear Sir, most sincerely,

G. COLMAN

[1] Charles Mathews (1776–1835), the father of Charles James Mathews, was to gain a particular reputation for low comedy impersonations and one-man 'At Homes'. George Colman the Younger took over the management of the Haymarket Theatre from his father and retained it until 1820.

2 R. Jephson's one-act farce was first performed at Covent Garden on 16 February 1791. Joseph Munden
   had appeared in London in 1790 and was to retain his position at Covent Garden until his retirement
   in 1824 [**161**].
3 Traditionally a length consisted of forty-two lines.

The negotiations between Colman and Mathews were dignified and courteous. Mathews had already established himself as a comedian with the York circuit, and Colman was careful to make sure that his first appearance in London would not humiliate either of them. The transition from provincial to metropolitan success could be a hazardous one.

126   The perils of a provincial actor on the London stage, 1822

John Genest, *Some account of the English stage*, vol. IX, p. 191

Oct. 2, 1822 C.G. Speed the Plough.[1] Sir Philip Blandford = Egerton: Sir Abel Handy = W. Farren: Bob Handy = Jones: Henry = Abbott: Susan Ashfield = Miss Foote: Farmer Ashfield = Evans from Bath, 1st app.:– Evans had been Clerk to an Ironmonger with a good salary – having acted two or three times with some success, he gave up his situation and took to the stage – he had been engaged one season – he was a young man of some promise, but wanted practice extremely – his forte lay in such parts as Zekiel Homespun, but he had a very good voice, and *spoke* even Tragedy with propriety – C. Kemble, having lost Liston,[2] requested the Bath Manager to set Evans at liberty – Evans was probably much delighted with the offer of an engagement at C.G., not considering that all that glitters is not gold – he had not been long in his new situation, before the manager, with a strange want of judgment, cast him for Squire Tally-ho – he totally failed, and from that time to the end of the season, he seldom had a part given to him, which it must not have been a mortification to him to act – whereas if he had continued at Bath 4 or 5 years, he would probably have been fit for a London situation, when a vacancy might occur – Evans' fate should be a warning to others not to be too eager for a London engagement – improvement ought to be the first object with every young performer – improvement can only be obtained by practice – and a performer of any talent is sure to have a much greater variety of parts at Bath or York, than he can possibly expect at D.L. or C.G.

1 Thomas Morton's popular comedy was first produced at Covent Garden in 1800.
2 Charles Kemble (1775–1854) started his career as Malcolm in J. P. Kemble's *Macbeth* at Drury Lane in
   1794. He managed Covent Garden from 1823 to 1833, and was appointed Examiner of Plays in 1836.
   He was the father of Fanny Kemble [see **155**].

The performer's conditions of service during engagements at some of the smaller circuits could be primitive, even when the theatre buildings themselves were dignified with the name of Theatre Royal. The Theatre Royal, Bodmin, was one such example.[1]

¹ Compare Thomas and Hare, *Restoration and Georgian England*, nos. 213–15. Dawson was the manager of a Cornwall circuit that included Penzance and Truro. His payments to actors averaged £1 per week [see **41**].

127   Conditions for performing on the provincial circuits in the 1820s

R. Dyer, *Nine years of an actor's life* (London: Longman, Rees, 1833), p. 33

The Theatre-*Rural*, Bodmin stood in Back-lane, and when the players were gone was converted to a stable. The dressing-rooms *were* in the hay-loft. On the second season we had better accommodations in a pig-stye [*sic*], but of which I did not avail, as a chandler-friend allowed me to dress in his *melting-shop* [. . .] Our stage had little depth, and less breadth, while the room behind the scenes was proportionably less; and I remember that in Falstaff, Manager Dawson was obliged to unpad, as, with his artificial corpulence, he could not pass between the wings and the wall;– and that subsequently, on a fat lady's joining the company, she had certainly received her discharge had she been one hair's breadth stouter, for moving the wings nearer each other would have 'cabined, cribbed, confined' us, beyond endurance – and to knock down the walls was thought too expensive [. . .]

[. . .] The second probationary year began in the stable of the King's Arms, Launceston, which, having undergone sundry alterations, was yclept a theatre, and surely such a theatre never before had existence; its breadth (the stage) might have been *eight* feet, its depth the same – its height not more than six feet five inches; for on our opening night, the nodding plumes I wore in Aranza, absolutely were hid in the *flies*. The entrance behind the scenes passed over a large granite water-trough, and through a window about one yard square. The gentlemen had access to their dressing-room by a common ladder, which offered such insurmountable difficulties to Manager Dawson, that he invariably made his toilette on the stage [. . .] Every thing was conducted with the strictest regard to economy, and the duties of the prompter, scene-shifter, property-man, and candle snuffer, were alternately performed by Mr Dawson, senior, and Mr James Dawson. I have seen the former speak the tag of the piece, in the corner of the stage, whilst with one hand off the stage he rang the bell, and lowered the curtain, when the play had ended. James rang the bell, and raised the curtain, before going on for a song, and if he did not obey an encore, the trouble of raising the curtain again alone prevented him.

THE THEATRE AS INDUSTRY

The most obvious manifestations of a developing theatre industry could be seen in the huge increase in backstage personnel to accommodate the taste for spectacular staging. The presence of large numbers of performers employed for the season at patent theatres such as Covent Garden and Drury Lane also had its effect on the structure of the theatre's repertoire and the role of playwrights. Managers wanted dramatic vehicles that would actively employ both their actors and their companies of singers and dancers.

128   The significance of the performer, 1825

Pierce Egan, *The life of an actor* (London: Arnold, 1825; reprinted Pickering & Chatto, 1892), p. 87[1]

My dear boy, you are completely in error: you *must write* for the actors, and for the *actors* ALONE, if you wish to succeed with the public: you must take *measure* of them with accuracy, and *fit* them as nicely as the best tailor in the kingdom. Study their *capabilities*, and turn them to a good account. For instance, you recollect in Mr *Give-up-everything's* piece what he did for *me* and Miss *Consequence*: two great parts which told immensely. Our reputation as actors was thus increased; and his fame as an author was also extended.– The old-fashioned mode is now entirely exploded; and *authors* leave nothing to chance: it is true formerly they might write plays without thinking of any particular actor or actresses to personify the characters created in their closets; but modern authors are, or must be, men of business: they first make themselves master of the peculiar talents of every performer; ascertain the extent of their abilities in the scale of merit, and then write accordingly. Figure's of vast importance; a fine voice is also valuable; a strong voice, in some instances, very essential; the gait and manners of the actor highly necessary to be ascertained; and his *mind* (if he possesses any), or to what extent, is peculiarly requisite for the information of the author, in order that the actor may not be at variance with the character he has to represent before the critical eyes of the audience. My dear *Horatio*, connect the whole of the performers of this theatre together, like the keys of a musical instrument; play upon them all, but let not a note be out of tune. One more hint, by way of example; and I shall then leave you to follow your own judgment. Revise your Comedy; or, I should rather say, rewrite it: look round the theatre, and take *measure* of those performers who are most capable of giving effect to your *dramatis personae*. I think an *Irishman* might be introduced with considerable effect: in doing this you will be also serving the Treasury; as the performer I allude to receives his salary, and is but seldom employed. A *Yorkshire* servant, or a bumpkin with that dialect, would not at all injure, but rather add strength to your Comedy: that actor likewise is seldom before the public; therefore, in taking him off the *shelf*, the Management will be indebted to your exertions. If you can introduce a dance at the end of one of the acts, it will be an improvement to the Piece; and it will give exercise to our too much neglected *corps de ballet*. The rest I shall entirely leave to your taste and discretion.

[1] Egan's account is the fictional life of an actor but is drawn accurately and satirically. The actor-manager Peregrine Proteus gives the young would-be playwright some advice.

William Leman Rede was a successful actor and playwright whose career was associated particularly with provincial theatres and the minor theatres in London. It is his first-hand experience of the profession that underlies the comprehensive manual published by his brother and inseparable companion, Thomas. *The Road to the Stage* constitutes the most informative practical document of the period to 1850, and clearly demonstrates the expenses that would-be actors were obliged to incur.[1]

[1] See Michael Booth, *Theatre in the Victorian age* (Cambridge: Cambridge University Press, 1991), pp. 125–9.

129   Advice to would-be actors, 1827

Leman Rede, *The road to the stage* (London: Smith, 1827), pp. 7–34

(a) How to locate an agent

At the Harp (a public-house in Russell-street, immediately opposite the pit door of Drury), resides Mr Sims, the theatrical agent, and his hours of business are from eleven o'clock until three. On the payment of an introductory fee of seven shillings, he enters the name of the applicant in his books, together with the line of the drama he may wish to fill – and, on the procuration of a situation, he proportions his demand to the amount of the salary obtained; but it seldom exceeds the total of one week's stipend.

(b) On lines of business

On a rough calculation there are supposed to be about six thousand individuals who are known to possess claims to the titles of actor and actress – or, in more plain terms, who thoroughly know their business; the number of persons claiming those honours are perhaps barely seven times that number.

As music is decidedly becoming daily more popular in this country, first singers are proportionably in request. At Liverpool the leading vocalist has a salary of five pounds per week; and such is the dearth of male singers, that that is now considered the most profitable and safe line, and one for which an engagement can always be obtained.

Tragedy is, it has been justly observed, going out of fashion [. . .] but as improvements generally originate in the metropolis, so also do innovations, and tragedy, though inattractive in London, is not yet scouted in the provinces. As nearly all aspirants commence as tragedians, this line has always numerous professors; it is now, from the arrangements of modern managers, become imperative that a leading man should provide his own wardrobe [. . .] A tragedian always commands the best salary in the theatre, and in large establishments his situation is easy and profitable; in small ones he is expected to blend the light comedy with the serious business, and thus his labour, though not his profit, is marvellously increased.

Genteel comedy has been long called the most profitable line upon the stage – it requires a good modern wardrobe. In small theatres the light comedian must play the seconds in tragedy (Macduff, Richmond, etc.) – the salary is generally first-rate – at all events next to that of the leading man.

Low Comedy is supposed to be the best line, with reference to the benefit it insures, but this trusting to a very precarious chance – the salary is generally on a par with the light comedian.

First Old Men obtain somewhat similar terms. Walking Gentlemen (Charles Stanley, Henry Moreland, Harry Thunder, etc.) is a line that also requires an extensive wardrobe; this business is usually assigned to persons learning the rudiments of the profession – the salary is generally low; in Dublin even, not exceeding two guineas per week, and in many respectable companies not more than one.

The observations already made, apply to the other sex equally, with regard to the First Tragedy – Fine Ladies – Singing Chambermaids – Old Women – and Walking Ladies.

First Singing Ladies are much more numerous than male vocalists, a circumstance which the system of modern education accounts for – and, perhaps, for a lady the Old Woman may be considered the most profitable and safe line. Any young lady embracing this line, and possessed of even a moderate share of talent, could seldom lack a provincial engagement, and would stand an excellent chance of metropolitan distinction.

(c) A performer's costume requirements

TRAGEDY

A first tragedian, as theatres are now stocked, should possess:

Complete dresses for Hamlet, Richard, Macbeth and Rolla; and with them, and the stock, he may manage to dress a variety of characters.

He should have a wig for Octavian; ditto for Othello; ditto for Richard; and ditto for Lear; ringlets, etc.

An Old English sword; a Roman sword; a dress and regulation sword.

Stage hats of several descriptions [. . .]; these are most essential, as he will find no hats of any sort in country wardrobes; an opera and military hat are both indispensable.

Tight pantaloons, black and white, cannot be done without; and red, blue and green, will be found highly useful.

Russet boots and shoes; gauntlets, handsome and plain.

Lace collars and ruffs.

Sword belts, both of leather and chains.

Feathers, white and black, and heron's feathers for Rob Roy, etc.

The ornaments are innumerable. A star and hat ornaments, and a blue garter, wanted in all our historical plays, are amongst those of primary consideration.

LIGHT COMEDY

Everything that constitutes a fashionable modern wardrobe will be absolutely necessary.

Dress coats with steel buttons, trimmed as the court dresses are worn; an old coat with good buttons looks as well as a new one, as almost all theatrical things depend upon the ornaments upon them.

A military infantry uniform; sword ditto.

Ditto cavalry.

A dress sword; sword loop or white silk belt.

An opera hat, buckles and latchets.

A naval coat is also useful, though, even in the metropolis, I have seen a common blue coat with the epaulettes worn.

Epaulettes, both of silver and gold, the performer will do well to provide, for stock epaulettes are never peculiar for their brilliancy.

Wigs are less essential here, as most comedians wear their own hair, but for such parts as Rochester, they will be found indispensable.

GENERAL UTILITY

This is what young actors are generally engaged for, though to perform the duties of general utility requires an old actor; it is, in fact, to play the inferior parts in every line – to have the most to do – the least notice of doing it – and receive the lowest salary; it is (next to the situation of prompter) the Pandemonium of the profession.

For general utility a man should have almost everything [...] except the complete dresses.

I know it will be said that a performer can embark in the profession without the properties I have mentioned. I can myself adduce instances. A gentleman, now a member of the Drury Lane Theatre, started in Brunton's company with a pair of stage boots only, and they were a partnership concern between himself and another; but it is unnecessary to mention the misery and privation that individual suffered, or to name the number of parts that were taken from him, not because he could not play, but because he could not dress them.

LADIES' WARDROBE

Female aspirants for the pleasure of the scenic art are perhaps seldom aware that our provincial theatres have no wardrobe at all for the ladies, and that every thing they wear must be provided by themselves.

TRAGEDY

Black velvet dress with long and short sleeves.
White satin dress with long and short sleeves.
Scarlet robe; sandals.

Point lace drapery; black and whitepoints.
Gold spangled trimming.
Silver spangled trimming.
Plain and spangled drapery.
Dagger; coronet, stomacher.
Ornamented cestus for the waist.
Beads of all descriptions.
Ornaments of every kind for ear-rings, bracelets, and armlets.

COMEDY

Pink, blue, and white satin dresses.
Leno dresses with spangled trimming.
Leno dresses with satin trimming.
Feathers; fan; reticule.
Fashionable hat.
Shoes, silk stockings and gloves.
Black and white lace veils.
Flowers; beads; scarf.
Points for Spanish dresses.

MELO-DRAME

Scarlet stuff dress, with blue ribbons, pocket made in dress; French cap;
    white muslin apron trimmed.
Buff dress with blue or green ribbons.
Black velvet body made with stomacher.
Black ribbon and cross.
Gipsy hat; black mits; white mits.
Black shoes with buckles or clasps.
French head-dress.
Black velvet body with long and short sleeves.
Boy's dress.

GENERAL UTILITY

Silk fleshings.
Frock coat and trousers; white waistcoat.
Gentleman's shirt; false wristbands.
Black stock for neck.
Wellington boots.

These are essential for such characters as the 'Young Widow', Harriette, in 'Is he Jealous?' the 'Irish Widow' and numerous other parts in the drama.

Tunic; white silk pantaloons; russet boots.

Worked collar or frill for neck.

Hat and feathers; – for the 'Blind Boy', Myrtillo in the 'Broken Sword', the 'Wandering Boys', etc.

A complete Indian dress, with head-dress formed of feathers; bracelets and beads of all descriptions; – for Umba, in 'Perouse' and Yarico, in 'Incle and Yarico'.

A white satin or coloured fly; white satin loose Turkish trousers; slippers turned up at the toes; vest and turban with birds of Paradise plume; – for Artaxerxes, Aladdin, Zorayda, in the 'Mountaineers', and numerous other parts.[1]

Peasant's dress, Swiss, French, Spanish, Old English, etc. – for Savoyards of all nations [. . .]

Old woman's head-dress.

High heeled shoes.

A large and old-fashioned fan.

Mittens – long, short, plain, and ornamented with lace; muslin neckerchief for neck.

Old-fashioned earrings, and other ornaments.

Hooped petticoat; and open wrapper.

Old-fashioned bedgown and nightcap.

Various coloured things of the descriptions named will be requisite; – for Old Women.

(d) Conduct on entering the theatre

The first person you should inquire for is the prompter, to whom you make yourself known, and give your address; the prompter will introduce you to the stage-manager, who conducts you to the green-room, and introduces you to the rest of the company. The part assigned you, and a notice as to the rehearsal, will be sent you by the prompter, according to the address given, or delivered to you at the theatre by the call-boy, or prompter's assistant. As you read your character you will ascertain what properties are wanted in the different scenes you have to act, such as a purse, book, keys, bottle, etc., etc.; these you will make memorandums of, and on the night of performance hand the list to the property man, who will provide what you want, which, as you conclude each scene, you return to him. It is essential that these things should be returned *instanter*, as they may be wanted in the next scene; but if you have to deliver them to any party on the scene, the onus of returning them rests on him or her. After the rehearsal, your next care is to find the wardrobe-keeper, and ask to look at your dress; try it on, and show the dresser what alterations (if any) are necessary. It is the rule of every well-regulated theatre that you should wear no dress that has not been approved of by the manager; but in light comedy, where you provide everything, it is left to your own discretion. In such pieces it will be wise to consult your brother performers as to what costume they intend assuming; from a neglect of this precaution, I beheld at one of our first provincial theatres, Sir Benjamin Backbite, and Charles and Joseph Surface, habited exactly alike, a thing displeasing to the eye of the auditor, and destructive of scenic effect.

In the dressing-room, to which the prompter's boy will conduct you, you will find your name written at that part of it assigned for you to dress in; there the things provided by the theatre for you to wear will be sent by the wardrobe-keeper. It is no part of the duty of the dresser of a provincial theatre to clean the shoes or boots which you wear upon the stage; but this is usually done by him, for which he expects some little remuneration. Some few years since it was an understood thing that the things worn in the play should be washed for you by the establishment, but this custom is growing into disuse in the provinces – neither is it now general for a hairdresser to attend at the manager's expense; the performer will therefore be prepared to attend to himself in this particular; and it may be well to remark, that one of our greatest actors has said – 'Wear your own locks whenever it is not absolutely improper – the best wig is not so good as the worst head of hair' [. . .]

For leaving any portion of your dress, or completing the adjustment of it, in the green-room, there are established fines, but the necessities of the stage occasion these rules to be frequently departed from [. . .]

When dressed the performer should proceed instantly to the green-room, as no notice, but of the music having been rung in, is given in the dressing-room; the call-boy enters the green-room to call each actor and actress as they are wanted in each scene, who should then refer to their parts, to ascertain whether the scene is a hall, chamber, or garden, and not present the impropriety so often seen, even in London, of persons traversing the open air without chapeaus, bonnets, shawls, or gloves, or the vulgarity of entering drawing-rooms with hats upon their heads; indeed, it is highly improper to enter in a room scene with a hat at all.[2]

---

[1] Rodwell's one-act farce, *The Young Widow*, first performed at the Adelphi in 1824; Samuel Beazley's one-act operetta, *Is He Jealous?*, at the Lyceum in 1816; Garrick's comedy, *The Irish Widow*, which had been part of the Drury Lane repertoire since 1787; James Kenney's melodrama, *The Blind Boy*, was first seen at Covent Garden in 1807; William Dimond's melodrama, *The Broken Sword*, at Covent Garden in 1816; Kerr's adaptation, with Henry Bishop's music, *The Wandering Boys; or, The Castle of Olival*, at Covent Garden in 1814; *Perouse; or, The Desolate Island* had first appeared as a pantomime at Covent Garden in 1801 and was adapted as an 'historical ballet' for the Lyceum in 1818; George Colman's popular opera *Incle and Yarico* was produced at the Haymarket in 1787, and his *The Mountaineers* in 1795.

[2] Booth, *Victorian age*, pp. 104–9.

Though the passing of the Theatre Regulation Act in 1843 gave speculators the incentive to build more theatres, and thus provide more opportunities for employment, the period until the 1860s saw no new theatres erected in London. Moreover, the collapse of the provincial circuits brought unemployment to innumerable actors. Many were compelled to hawk their wares as travelling showmen. Conditions at the lower end of the industrial spectrum were as difficult as they had been in the early part of the century.

130   Conditions of travelling performers at mid-century

(a) H. Mayhew, *London labour and the London poor* (London: Griffon, 1864), vol. III, p. 154[1];
(b) *ibid.*, p. 150

(a) 'The pay of an actor in private business [i.e. performing in towns or in situations divorced from a fair] varies from two shillings and sixpence to three shillings, and each man is also supposed to sing two songs in each performance, which makes three performances a night besides performing a sketch. Your engagement lasts as long as you suit the audience; for if you're a favourite you may have such a thing as nine months at a time. Whenever we have a benefit it's a ticket one, which amounts to two hundred tickets and your night's salary, which generally brings you in a pound, with your pay included. There's one in the company generally has a benefit every Thursday, so that your turn comes once in about six months, for the musicians, and the checktakers, and all has their turn.

The expense of putting a new piece on the stage is not more than a pound, and that includes new scenery. They never do such a thing as buy new dresses. Perhaps they pay such a thing as six shillings a week for their wardrobe to hire the dresses. Some give as much as ten shillings; but then, naturally, the costume is more showy. All that we are supposed to find is russet boots, a set of fleshings, a ballet shirt, and a wig.

Town work is the more quiet and more general-business like. There's no casualty in it, for you're not in shares, but on salaries, and after your work there's your money, for we are paid nightly. I have known as much as thirty-five shillings a week given at one of these theatres, when the admission is only a penny or twopence. Where I was at it would hold from six to seven hundred people, and there was three performances a night; and, indeed, on Saturdays and Mondays generally four. We have no extra pay for extra performances. The time allowed for each representation is from one hour to an hour and three-quarters. If we find there is a likelihood of a fourth house, we leave out a song each singer, and that saves half an hour [. . .] We begin at six and are over a few minutes before twelve. When we do speaking pieces we have to do it on the sly, as we should be stopped and get into trouble.

(b) Mumming at fairs is harder than private business, because you have to perform so many times. You only wear one dress, and all the actor is expected to do is to stand up to the dances outside and act in. He'll have to dance perhaps sixteen quadrilles in the course of the day, and act about as often inside. The company generally work in shares, or if they pay by the day, it's about four or five shillings a day. When you go to get engaged, the first question is, 'What can you do?' and the next, 'Do you find your own properties, such as russet boots, your dress, hat and feathers, etc.?' Of course they like your dress the better if it's a showy one; and it doesn't much matter about its corresponding with the piece. For instance, Henry the Second, in 'Fair Rosamond', always comes on with a cavalier's dress, and nobody notices the difference of costume. In fact, the same dresses are used over and over again for the same pieces. The general dress for the ladies is a velvet skirt with a satin stomacher, with a gold band round the waist and a pearl band on the forehead. They, too, wear the same dresses for all pieces. A regular fair show has only a small compass of dresses, for they only goes to the same place once in a year, and of course their costumes ain't remembered.

The principal fair pieces are 'Blue Beard', 'Robert, Duke of Normandy', and 'Fair Rosamond, or the Bowers of Woodstock'. I recollect they once played 'Maria Marten',[2] at a fair, in a company I was with, and we played that in cavalier costume [...]

An actor's share will average for a fair at five shillings a day, if the fair is anything at all. When we don't work, we don't get paid, so that if we only do one fair a week, that's fifteen shillings, unless we stop to do a day or two private business after the fair.

[1] The original interviews by Mayhew had taken place between 1851 and 1852.

[2] George Colman's *Blue Beard* was first performed in 1798; *Fair Rosamond* probably refers to a version of C. Z. Barnett's play, which had appeared at Drury Lane in 1837. *Maria Marten or, The Murder in the Red Barn* became a favourite melodrama; the first London performance of the play appears to have taken place at the Pavilion Theatre. (H. G. Hibbert, *A playgoer's memories* (London: Grant Richards, 1920), pp. 83–6.)

THE ART OF THE ACTOR

There was little specific interest in acting theory in the early nineteenth century. Henry Siddons's book *Practical Illustrations of Rhetorical Gesture and Action*, published in 1822, merely perpetuated eighteenth-century models relating to the depiction of the passions.[1] The major sources of information about the principles of acting are to be found in the responses to particular performers by the new breed of theatre critic – Leigh Hunt, Charles Lamb, William Hazlitt, John Forster and George Henry Lewes. In their writings we can trace the on-going argument about rhetorically conventional acting as opposed to 'the natural'. Certainly, from the performer's perspective, the size of the theatres and the social character of theatre-going militated against anything other than presentational acting. It was very difficult not to take the audience into consideration.

[1] See Thomas and Hare, *Restoration and Georgian England*, nos. 293 and 296.

131   A German visitor comments on English acting, 1807

C. A. G. Goede, *The stranger in England; or, travels in Great Britain* (London: Mathew & Leigh, 1807), vol. II, pp. 208–10, 226

(a) The techniques of English performance

At first sight a belief might be entertained, that the English actors have fundamentally studied exterior propriety and decorum. Their action, upon the whole, is much more circumscribed than that of the Germans; and they do not so often violate certain rules of deportment. They never turn their backs on the public, and seldom shew their faces in profile, or hide them behind a pocket handkerchief, or their hands; they never approach too rapidly; nor do they unnecessarily touch each other; nor do they fight with their arms against the public, as if it were a ghost; they never cross their legs in an affected manner, nor stretch them out as a fencing master; and such like improprieties, of which many of our German actors cannot wean themselves. An English actor is free from the embarrassment which a German actor frequently suffers when he has nothing to say, and therefore knows not what to do with his dear person [. . .]

Nevertheless, I do not hesitate to affirm, that the general rules of decorum are less glaringly transgressed on the German stage, and still less so on the French stage of eminence, than on the boards of Drury Lane and Covent Garden. Indeed what the French term 'Convenances du Théâtre' which imports the correct association of age, character, situation and costume, are so shockingly violated by English performers, as to border on the ridiculous.

My German readers will scarcely credit me if I assure them, that Mrs Jordan, a lady upward of forty, with prodigious *embonpoint*, undertakes, in the wretched farce of 'The Virgin Unmasked', the part of Miss Lucy, a raw country girl of sixteen; so puerile, as to appear playing with her doll [. . .] But the audience at London, accustomed to such abominable distortions of character, not only suffer this marvellous representation, which is one of the most grotesque I ever witnessed on the stage, but reward the actress with the loudest, most rapturous and undivided applause.

(b) Emotional strengths and weaknesses of English actors

The English actors are peculiarly expressive in those tragical tones, which picture the commotion of the soul when agitated by passion, the force of decision and expanded energy. Wrath, wild grief, despair, glowing hatred, and thirsting revenge, are expressed with unrivalled effect by the eminent English actors. They are truly great in most situations where man, with obstinate audacity, dares to contest his will with Fate. They also succeed very happily in the tone of immoderate passion, which, stifled and suppressed, afterwards bursts forth with increased fury. They are matchless in that hollow language of the mind, which is peculiar to man in the moment he shudders at his own image; and perhaps on no other stage those convulsive tones, in which the bursting soul sighs forth its torments, are uttered with so much effect. But an attentive observer cannot fail to remark, that the English do not usually succeed in expressing soft and inward emotions. They seem wholly unacquainted with the tender tones of love, the warm effusions of friendship, and those modulated expressions by which man endeavours to open his heart, and harmoniously to associate with a congenial soul.[1] Even Kemble and Cooke, in these respects, display neither nature nor truth; and the warmest language of love, friendship, and confidence, as given by the poet, freezes

on their lips. The English actresses, with the exception of Mrs Powell, totally ab-
jure nature; their coldness and affectation, where they should be all emotion,
are insupportable.

It may, therefore, be easily concluded, how wretchedly many parts in comedy
must be sustained on the English stage; some representations, indeed, are beneath
all criticism: and English actors, in general, do not possess a natural easy tone of
conversation; they offend more in this than any other respect against the rules of
good declamation.

[1] This would be Macready's contribution to English acting technique [see **150**].

One of the most significant pieces of evidence for the early nineteenth century is Leigh Hunt's
evaluation of notable London performers. Critics were beginning to experience the discomfort of reconciling, on the one hand, the overt identification between actors and audiences
within a theatrical occasion that was confessedly an opportunity for social intercourse,
and, on the other, the demands for consistent and internalized characterization within
a role.

132   Leigh Hunt on faulty acting and its manifestations, 1808

Leigh Hunt, *Critical essays on the performers of the London theatres* (London: John Hunt,
1807), appendix, pp. 1–3

One of the first studies of an actor should be to divest himself of his audience,
to be occupied not with the persons he is amusing, but with the persons he is
assisting in the representation. But of all simple requisites to the mimetic art,
this public abstraction seems to be the least attained. Our good performers are
too fond of knowing they are good ones, and of acknowledging the admiration of
the spectators by glances of important expression: our bad performers are vainer
still [. . .] because not being able to enter into the interest of the scene they must
look for interest elsewhere. These men in reality never speak to one another, but
to the pit and to the boxes: they are thinking, not what the person spoken to
will reply, but what the audience think of their own speeches: they never speak a
soliloquy, because soliloquies are addressed to one's self, and they always address
their solitary meditations to the house: they adjust their neck-cloths; they display
their pocket-handkerchiefs and their attitudes; they cast aside long glances, and
say to themselves, 'There's a lady in the stage-box contemplating my shape! My
character sits well on me, and so do my small-clothes!' But let us imagine the
scene, in which this extravagance is performed, to be a real room enclosed in four
walls, for such a room the actor himself ought to imagine it. What then is he
looking at all this time? He is casting side-glances at a wainscot, or ogling a corner
cup-board.

The principal errors on local propriety may be divided into

Glancing at the boxes,
Ajusting [*sic*] the dress,
Telling the audience their soliloquies,
Wearing their hats in rooms, and
Not wearing them in the open air.

This last fault is almost as general as the first, and twice as ridiculous [. . .] It is evident, that when an actor comes into a field or into the street with his hat in his hand, he thinks nothing of the scene in which he is engaged, but of the audience before him [. . .] Were he to carry these mistakes into real life, how ridiculous would be the effects! What would be thought of a man who should stalk into a drawing-room with his hat on, or walk the public streets with it under his arm?

'NATURAL' ACTING

Although performance conditions tended to favour broad strokes of characterization, debate about the need for the actor to be involved in the role emotionally stretched back to the previous century. Both Garrick and Mrs Siddons had emphasized the importance of feeling. Nevertheless, from the end of the eighteenth century considerable discussion centred on the notion of appropriateness of behaviour and, increasingly, the need for internalization. Already by 1840 differences between 'realistic' and 'melodramatic' acting were being identified.

133   Helen Faucit explains the need to internalize painful emotion, 1836

Helen Faucit, *On some of Shakespeare's female characters* (London: Blackwood, 1885), p. 371

One thing which he impressed upon me I never forgot.[1] It was, on no account to give prominence to the merely physical aspect of any painful emotion. Let the expression be genuine, earnest, but not ugly. He pointed out to me how easy it was to simulate distortions – to writhe, for example, from the supposed effect of poison, to gasp, to roll the eyes, etc. These were melodramatic effects. But if pain or death had to be simulated, or any sudden or violent shock, let them be shown in their mental rather in their physical signs. The picture presented might be as sombre as the darkest Rembrandt, but it must be noble in its outlines; truthful, picturesque, but never repulsive, mean, or commonplace. It must suggest the heroic, the divine in human nature, and not the mere everyday struggles or tortures of this life, whether in joy or sorrow, despair or hopeless grief. Under every circumstance the ideal, the noble, the beautiful, should be given side by side with the real.

134   An actor prepares: Macready in the wings, 1839

James E. Murdoch, *The stage, or recollections of actors and acting* (Philadelphia: Stoddart, 1880), p. 121

In addition to the thorough discipline to which his vocal effects were submitted, Mr Macready's minutiae of details in what is termed stage-business were always premeditated and carefully and repeatedly practised before they were trusted to a public trial. The rehearsals of his plays (where the companies were of the standard order) afforded to those who could appreciate their artistic excellence a study of the histrionic art unique and invaluable to the profession.[1]

One night, just before making his entrance on the first scene of *Richelieu*,[2] the tragedian stopped and took hold of the protruding edge of a scene and began to practise his stage cough – in a dry, husky way at first, but gradually inceasing until it reached a suffocating kind of guttural spasm resembling somewhat a fit of whooping-cough in a child. Just as the climax of this cough was reached a stage-carpenter, who never had been present at a rehearsal, thinking, as he said, that Mr Macready was choking, unexpectedly exclaimed, 'Mr Macready, sir! sir!' accompanying the words with two or three sharp slaps of the back. With a scream the tragedian, now choking with anger, turned on the man, but before he could speak or the carpenter could offer an explanation the call-boy, pulling the sleeve of the cardinal's dress, cried out, 'Stage waiting, Mr Macready – stage waiting, sir.' Then, slowly putting one hand behind his back and the other on the shoulders of the monk Joseph, Richelieu began his measured walk towards the stage-entrance, uttering all the while, in half-coughing and half-growling tones, denunciations on the carpenter in return for the compliment he had paid him in taking his professional cough for a real one. Some time, of course, elapsed before he reached the side-door. The audience were waiting, but the artist could not hurry on that account; he coughed and tottered so well, however, when he got on the stage, that more than usual applause greeted his appearance.

[1] Macready's meticulous attention to detail was often at odds with the superficiality and shoddy preparation of many actors, to his intense disgust.
[2] Bulwer-Lytton's play, premièred at Covent Garden on 7 March 1839.

135   Helen Faucit records her reactions to Lady Macbeth and Macready's comments, 1842

Theodore Martin, *Helena Faucit, Lady Martin* (London: Blackwood, 1900), pp. 89–90

I am reminded how little the public knew of the disadvantages under which, in those days, one used sometimes to be called upon to play important parts. To an artist with a conscience, and a reputation to lose, this was a serious affair. In much the same hurried way I was originally required to act Lady Macbeth, and this before the Dublin audience, which, I had been told, was then in some respects more critical than that of London. After the close of the Drury Lane season, in June, I acted a few nights in Dublin with Mr Macready. Macbeth was one of his favourite parts, and to oblige the manager, Mr Calcraft, I had promised to attempt Lady Macbeth; but in the busy work of each day, up to the close of the London season, I had had no time to give the character any real thought or preparation. Indeed the alarm I felt at the idea of presuming to go upon the stage in such a character, made me put off grappling with it to the last possible moment. The mere learning of the words took no time. Shakespeare's seem to fasten, without an effort, upon the mind, and to live there for ever. Mr Macready at our one rehearsal taught me the business of the scene, and I confided to him the absolute terror I was in as the time of the performance drew near. He kindly encouraged me, and said, from what he had seen during the rehearsal, he was sure I would get on very well [. . .]

I have no remembrance of what the critics said. But Mr Macready told me that my banquet and sleep-walking scenes were the best. In the latter, he said, I gave the idea of sleep, disturbed by fearful dreams, but still sleep. It was to be seen even in my walk, which was heavy and unelastic, marking the distinction – too often overlooked – between the muffled voice and seeming-mechanical motion of the somnabulist, and the wandering mind and quick fitful gestures of a maniac, whose very violence would wake her from the deepest sleep,– a criticism I never forgot, always endeavouring afterwards to work upon the same principle, which had come to me then by instinct. Another remark of his about the sleep-walking scene I remember. He said: 'Oh, my child, where did you get that sigh? What can you know of such misery as that sigh speaks of?' He told me that my first scene was very promising, especially the soliloquy, also my reception of Duncan, but that my after-scenes with him were very tame. I had altogether failed in 'chastising with the valour of my tongue.'

The only criticism I remember on this my first attempt, besides Mr Macready's, was that of a most highly-cultivated and dear lady-friend, who said to me a day or two afterwards: 'My dear, I will never see you again in that character. I felt horror-stricken. Lear says of Cordelia, "So young and so untrue!" I should say of your Lady Macbeth, "So young and yet so wicked!"'

Her antipathy was equalled by my own. To the last night of my performing the character I retained my dread of it [. . .][1]

---

[1] See Thomas and Hare, *Restoration and Georgian England*, no. 315, for Sarah Siddons's notes on Lady Macbeth.

136   Differences between reality and pretence in performance

Spectator, 12 (1839), p. 1088

'Natural acting' we define to be the depicting of character and emotion by gesture and expression – the result of an impulse of the feelings controlled by the judgment and directed into the right channel by previous study: 'conventional acting' is an artificial substitution of stage mannerism for the spontaneous prompting of momentary feeling. To exemplify this distinction in the instance of living actors, would be difficult: all the examples are on the artificial side, the exceptions being accidental [. . .] All alike appear to proceed on a wrong system – that of minute attention to executive details, in preference if not to the entire exclusion of the essence of the character and the passion of the scene [. . .] Instead of trying an attitude for this speech, an expression for that line, and an action for the other situation, if the actor were to make himself thoroughly master of the psychological principles of the character, so as to put on a new set of feelings and ideas with the costume, he would be at no loss for the appropriate comments of face or movement – Nature would prompt him [. . .] The histrionic art, like every other, must have its rules; but such as tend to defeat its end may fairly be condemned as bad, the end of acting being to give to the assumption of an imaginary character the force of reality [. . .] Not that actual tears are required to be shed [. . .] it is enough to feign emotion: but most of our modern performers are content to *seem to be feigning*.

English dramatists had unscrupulously pirated the French repertoire since the end of the eighteenth century in order to satisfy their audience's demands for dramatic novelty. Nevertheless, English acting techniques generally lagged behind the French, especially in the depiction of realistic behaviour within a domestic environment. This deficiency became particularly noticeable as the development of theatrical technology enabled the stage to create authentic settings and immediately recognizable contexts.

137   The difference between French and English acting techniques, 1840

Spectator, 13 (1840), p. 804

By way of variety, and to renew old impressions, we looked in at the French Plays last night[1] [. . .] The common-place of the French stage is better than the choicest of the English, in respect of its being more true to real life – that is, French life. It is a microcosm of society. We see the actual people, walking and talking as they do among themselves: the verisimilitude is complete. The actors appear to think of themselves only in their assumed character, and to be wholly occupied with the business of the scene, not minding the audience: when they do take the spectators into their confidence, it is only as if they called the attention of an invisible acquaintance who was lying perdue. How different the unconstrained ease and freedom of their gestures and movements, from the stiff, formal, stage manner of our players – who, instead of wearing the assumed character like a well-fitting glove, as the French do, strut or shuffle about it as if it were a buckram suit they had never worn before, and that made them uncomfortably conscious of looking ridiculous or very fine. All their efforts are addressed pointedly to the audience – and very laboured and ostentatious the efforts are; and they seem to regard the scene only as an opportunity for the display of *their art* – such as it is. The fault is not so much that of individuals, as of the English school; which is based on a false principle – namely, that to appear natural in a play the actor must be very artificial.

[1] The critic had gone to the St James's Theatre on Friday 21 August. French plays had been performed regularly there since 1836.

THE ACTORS

Kemble was the most important actor to have bridged the eighteenth and nineteenth centuries. Since his début at Drury Lane in 1783, he, together with his sister Mrs Siddons, had dominated the tragic stage. Arguably, however, Kemble had reached the apogee of his career at the end of the eighteenth century. After taking over the management of Covent Garden in 1802 he was faced with problems that proved ultimately insurmountable. Not only did asthma make performances increasingly difficult, but his management of the theatre confronted him with the new audience's appetite for spectacular novelty and 'star' attractions, to which he succumbed despite all his own personal objections. Cumulatively, the Master Betty phenomenon of 1804–5, the destruction of Covent Garden in 1808, the turmoil of the OP Riots in 1809, the retirement of Mrs Siddons in 1812 and the competition with Edmund Kean after 1814 drained him physically and emotionally. After his retirement he left England and died in Switzerland in 1823.

138   John Philip Kemble's last performances, 1817

(a) [W. Hazlitt], *Times* (25 June 1817), p. 3[1]; (b) T. Martin, 'An eye-witness of John Kemble', *Nineteenth Century* (February 1880), pp. 276 ff.[2]

(a) Kemble as Coriolanus

Mr KEMBLE took his leave of the stage on Monday night in the character of *Coriolanus* [. . .]

It has always appeared to us that the range of characters in which Mr Kemble more particularly shone, and was superior to every other actor, were those which consisted in the development of some one solitary sentiment or exclusive passion. From a want of rapidity, of scope, and variety, he was often deficient in expressing the bustle and complication of different interests; nor did he possess the faculty of overpowering the mind by sudden and irresistible bursts of passion; but in giving the habitual workings of a predominant feeling, as in Penruddock, or The Stranger, in Coriolanus, Cato,[3] and some others, where all the passions move round a central point, and are governed by one master-key, he stood unrivalled. Penruddock in *The Wheel of Fortune*,[4] was one of his most correct and interesting performances, and one of the most perfect on the modern stage. The deeply-rooted, mild, pensive melancholy of the character, its embittered recollections and dignified benevolence, were conveyed by Mr Kemble with equal truth, elegance, and feeling. In The Stranger,[5] again, which is in fact the same character, he brooded over the recollection of disappointed hope till it became part of himself; [. . .] His person was moulded to the character. The weight of sentiment which oppressed him was never suspended; the spring at his heart was never lightened – it seemed as if his whole life had been a suppressed sigh! So in Coriolanus, he exhibited the ruling passion with the same unshaken firmness, he preserved the same haughty dignity of demeanour, the same energy of will, and unbending sternness of will throughout. He was swayed by a single impulse. His tenaciousness of purpose was only irritated by opposition; he turned neither to the right nor to the left; the vehemence with which he moved forward increasing every instant, till it hurried him on to the catastrophe [. . .] In such characters, Mr Kemble had no occasion to call to his aid either the resources of invention or the tricks of the art; his success depended on the increasing intensity with which he dwelt on a given feeling, or enforced a passion that resisted all interference or control.

In Hamlet,[6] on the contrary, Mr Kemble in our judgment unavoidably failed from a want of flexibility, of that quick sensibility which yields to every motive, and is borne away with every breath of fancy; which is distracted in the multiplicity of its reflections, and lost in the uncertainty of its resolutions [. . .] [Mr Kemble] played it like a man in armour, with a determined inveteracy of purpose [. . .] which is as remote from the natural grace and indolent susceptibility of the character, as the sharp angles and abrupt starts to produce an effect which Mr Kean throws into it.

In King John, which was one of Mr Kemble's most admired parts, the transitions of feeling, though just and powerful, were prepared too long beforehand, and were too long in executing, to produce their full effect. The actor seemed waiting for some complicated machinery to enable him to make his next movement, instead of trusting to the true impulses of passion [. . .]

[. . .] His Richard III wanted that tempest and whirlwind of the soul, that life and spirit, and dazzling rapidity of motion, which fills the stage, and burns in every part of it, when Mr Kean performs this character [. . .] Mr Kemble's manner, on the contrary, had always something dry, hard, and pedantic in it [. . .] but his monotony did not fatigue, his formality did not displease, because there was always sense and meaning in what he did. The fineness of Mr Kemble's figure may be supposed to have led to that statue-like appearance which his acting was sometimes too apt to assume; as the diminutiveness of Mr Kean's person has probably compelled him to bustle about too much, and to attempt to make up for the want of dignity of form, by the violence and contrast of his attitudes. If Mr Kemble were to remain in the same posture for half an hour, his figure would only excite admiration; if Mr Kean were to stand still only for a moment, the contrary effect would be apparent [. . .] Cato was another of those parts for which Mr Kemble was peculiarly fitted by his physical advantages. There was nothing for him to do in this character, but to *appear* in it. It had all the dignity of *still-life*. It was a studied piece of classical costume – a conscious exhibition of elegantly disposed drapery, that was all; yet, as a mere display of personal and artificial grace, it was inimitable [. . .]

   In short, we think the distinguishing excellence of his acting may be summed up in one word – *intensity*; in the seizing upon some one feeling or idea, in insisting upon it, in never letting it go, and in working it up, with a certain graceful consistency, and conscious grandeur of conception, to a very high degree of pathos or sublimity. If he had not the unexpected bursts of nature and genius he had all the regularity of art; if he did not display the tumult and conflict of opposite passions in the soul, he gave the deepest and most permanent interest to the uninterrupted progress of individual feeling; and in embodying a high idea of certain characters, which belong rather to sentiment than passion, to energy of will, than to loftiness or to originality of imagination, he was the most excellent actor of his time [. . .]

(b) Ludwig Tieck evaluates Kemble as Wolsey in *Henry VIII*

In the performance on this occasion, there was far more to praise than to blame, and John Kemble as Wolsey was admirable. My ear had at last become somewhat habituated to his inordinately slow, wailing mode of speaking, and as most of the performers spoke more rapidly than usual, especially the king, one grew more readily reconciled to the solemn tones of the old cardinal; and thus the play made the right impression as a whole. Kemble showed himself to be a truly great artist, especially after his fall, when the nobles, gathering round him, rejoice at his misfortune, and he, in the pride of his grief, but stately to the last, gives full vent to his emotions. The majesty in profound sorrow, the heart which is already broken, but gathers itself together once again in all its power to confront its malignant adversaries, the trembling of the voice, which, after a severe struggle, regains its firm, manly tone, all this was incomparably fine, and of the most consummate excellence.

[1] Hazlitt takes the opportunity to evaluate Kemble's career and achievements. Much of the article had already appeared in a slightly different form in the *Champion* of 20 November 1814. On this occasion Kemble appeared as Coriolanus, his most distinguished role.
[2] Theodore Martin translated sections from Ludwig Tieck's evaluations of English actors, which first appeared in *Dramaturgische Blätter* in 1826 but which reflected his visit in 1817. Tieck was generally unimpressed by Kemble and particularly offended by untoward and arbitrary alterations to Shakespeare's texts. Kemble performed the part on 17 June.
[3] Addison's tragedy had first appeared in 1713 and had retained its place in the repertoire.
[4] Cumberland's play had first been performed at Drury Lane in 1795.

[5] Benjamin Thompson's adaptation of Kotzebue, first performed at Drury Lane in 1798.
[6] See Thomas and Hare, *Restoration and Georgian England*, nos. 309 and 310.

The search for theatrical novelty embraced not only new staging techniques but also new kinds of performers. Live animals had been seen on stage since the end of the eighteenth century, but the appearance in London of Master Betty resulted in an almost hysterical passion to see a 13-year-old boy perform adult roles. It encouraged many imitators.

William Henry Betty, born in Shrewsbury in 1791, owed his success largely to the astute promotion of his father, who carefully cultivated his image in the provinces – Ireland, Scotland and subsequently Birmingham, Liverpool, Manchester – before selling his services to both Covent Garden and Drury Lane. His celebrity was short-lived. By 1805 metropolitan audiences no longer flocked to his performances, but he continued to act in the provinces until 1824. He died in Shropshire in 1872.[1]

[1] See Giles Playfair, *The prodigy: a study of the strange life of Master Betty* (London: Secker & Warburg, 1967).

139   The Master Betty phenomenon

(a) Genest, *Account of the English stage*, vol. VII, pp. 659–61; (b) Hellyer engraving published by Chatham in 1805. Henry Huntington Library

(a) His first performance on the London stage, 1804

Dec. 1, 1804 C.G. Barbarossa. Achmet = Master Betty, 1st app. in London Barbarossa = Hargrave: Zaphira = Mrs Litchfield: Irene = Mrs H. Siddons: before the play an occasional address, by C. Kemble.

The most extraordinary circumstance, which occurs in the whole history of the stage, took place at this time – a boy of the name of Betty, born in 1791, displayed a genius for acting, which, considering his age, was really astonishing, but his partisans, not content with saying he was a boy of great promise, insisted that he actually was at this moment a first rate performer, or that at least he would soon eclipse all competitors – Master Betty had played with great applause in Ireland and Scotland, at Birmingham, etc. – on this evening the audience was all impatience till the 1st act was over, as Master Betty was not to appear till the 2d – when he did appear, his success was complete [. . .]

Some little addition to Master Betty's height was made by art, but his figure was still such as to disqualify him from playing with men and women without a manifest breach of propriety – he represented filial affection, and such passions as he could feel, with considerable energy–he had little or no expression in his countenance – his action was remarkably good – his voice was very bad, and his mode of managing it peculiarly exceptionable – it seems to have been exactly a revival of that unnatural way of speaking, that musical cadence approaching towards recitative, which had prevailed on the stage (more or less) from about 1710 to 1740 [. . .]

(b) Master Betty as Young Norval in John Home's *Douglas*, 1805

MASTER BETTY,
in the Character of Young Norval.

THE ADVENT OF EDMUND KEAN AND ROMANTIC ACTING

No other actor embodied Romanticism's tortured emotionality so completely as Kean. Born probably in 1787, he had started his career as a child supernumerary, playing Cupid in Michael Kelly's adaptation of Garrick's *Cymon* in 1791, and after years as a stroller made his formal début as an adult in London in 1814. He died in 1833.

140   Hazlitt reviews Kean's début on the London stage as Shylock, 26 January 1814

Morning Chronicle (27 January 1814), reprinted in William Archer and R. W. Lowe (eds.), *Dramatic essays* (London: Walter Scott, 1895), pp. 2–38

Mr Kean (of whom report had spoken highly) last night made his appearance at Drury Lane Theatre, in the character of Shylock. For voice, eye, action, and expression, no actor has come out for many years at all equal to him. The applause, from the first scene to the last, was general, loud, and uninterrupted [. . .] Notwithstanding the complete success of Mr Kean in the part of Shylock, we question whether he will not become a greater favourite in other parts. There was a lightness and vigour in his tread, a buoyancy and elasticity of spirit, a fire and animation, which would accord better with almost any other character than with the morose, sullen, inward, inveterate, inflexible malignity of Shylock [. . .] In conveying a profound impression of this feeling, or in embodying the general conception of rigid and uncontrollable self-will [. . .] we have seen actors more successful than Mr Kean; but in giving effect to the conflict of passions arising out of the contrasts of situation, in varied vehemence of declamation, in keenness of sarcasm, in the rapidity of his transitions from one tone and feeling to another, in propriety and novelty of action, presenting a succession of striking pictures, and giving perpetually fresh shocks of delight and surprise, it would be difficult to single out a competitor. The fault of his acting was [. . .] an over-display of the resources of the art, which gave too much relief to the hard, impenetrable, dark groundwork of the character of Shylock. It would be endless to point out individual beauties, where almost every passage was received with equal and deserved applause. We thought, in one or two instances, the pauses in the voice were too long, and too great a reliance placed on the expression of the countenance, which is a language intelligible only to a part of the house.

141   Kean as Shylock, 1814

Annan and Swan engraving from a painting by W. H. Watt of 1814, in Doran's
(extra-illustrated) *Annals of the English stage* (London: Nimmo, 1888), vol. III, p. 374

142   Hazlitt on Kean's Sir Giles Overreach in Massinger's *A New Way to Pay Old Debts*, 1816

Examiner (18 February 1816), p. 107[1]

We saw Mr Kean's Sir Giles Overreach on Friday night from the boxes at Drury
Lane Theatre, and are not surprised at the incredulity as to this great actor's powers,
entertained by those persons who have only seen him from that elevated sphere.
We do not hesitate to say, that those who have only seen him at that distance,
have not seen him at all. The expression of his face is quite lost, and only the
harsh and grating tones of his voice produce their full effect on the ear. The same
recurring sounds, by dint of repetition, fasten on the attention, while the varieties
and finer modulations are lost in their passage over the pit. All you discover is
an abstraction of his defects, both of person, voice, and manner. He appears to

be a little man in a great passion. The accompaniment of expression is absolutely necessary to explain his tones and gestures: and the outline which he gives of the character, in proportion as it is bold and decided, requires to be filled up and modified by all the details of execution. Without seeing the workings of his face, through which you read the movements of his soul, and anticipate their violent effects on his utterance and action, it is impossible to understand or feel pleasure in the part. All strong expression, deprived of its gradations and connecting motives, unavoidably degenerates into caricature. This was the effect uniformly produced on those about us, who kept exclaiming, 'How extravagant, how odd', till the last scene, where the extreme and admirable contrasts both of voice and gesture in which Mr Kean's genius shows itself, and which are in their nature more obviously intelligible, produced a change of opinion in his favour.

[1] Hazlitt had seen the performance before, but on this occasion emphasizes the importance of Kean's facial mobility.

143   Kean's studied spontaneity

J. C. Young, *A memoir of Charles Mayne Young, tragedian* (London: Macmillan, 1871), p. 210

Poor Kean! I was but a boy when I saw him in his *decadence*,– worn out in constitution, not by years,– but I shall never forget him [. . .] His style was impulsive, fitful, flashing, abounding in quick transitions; scarcely giving you time to think, but ravishing your wonder, and carrying you along with his impetuous rush and change of expression. But this seeming spontaneity was not *chance-work*; much of it, most of it, was carefully premeditated and prepared. You might hear the same flutelike tones, the same waves of melody, the same cadence, night after night, in his delivery of the lines in Richard,–

> But soft, my love appears: look where she shines,
> Darting pale lustre like the silver moon
> Through her dark veil of rainy sorrow!

So, his delivery of Othello's 'Farewell' ran on the same tones and semitones, had the same rests and breaks, the same *forte* and *piano*, the same *crescendo* and *diminuendo*, night after night, as if he spoke it from a musical score [. . .]

So, all his most striking attitudes,– and he was the most picturesque of players,– all his most effective *points*, and abrupt transitions of voice and manner, were reproduced in oft-repeated performances of any particular character; so that his admirers were ready with their applause almost by anticipation, before the well-known *coup* was made [. . .] What then was Kean's peculiar merit? in what did his genius especially assert itself? In intensity, in the power of abstraction, and of identifying himself with a passion. In the words of John Kemble's involuntary praise,– 'he was *terribly in earnest*'. This was his master-quality; his next – which, indeed, followed from, if it was not included in the former – was his natural, and unforced, yet striking delivery of simple phrases, or passages of a familiar, conversational style. In these he threw away the tragic stilts entirely, and was easy, conversational, *un-stagey*. Thus, in Othello, his

> Were it my cue to fight, I should have known it
> Without a prompter,

always brought down the house, from the natural, yet pointed expression, conversational, yet full of meaning, with which he gave it [. . .]

144   Lucius Junius Brutus Booth's début as Richard III, 1817

[William Hazlitt], *Examiner* (16 February 1817), p. 108, reprinted in Archer and Lowe, *Dramatic essays*, p. 129

A gentleman of the name of Booth,[1] who, we understand, has been acting with considerable applause at Worthing and Brighton, came out in Richard, Duke of Gloucester, at Covent Garden on Wednesday [. . .] His face is adapted to tragic characters, and his voice wants neither strength nor musical expression. But almost the whole of his performance was an exact copy or parody of Mr Kean's manner of doing the same part. It was a complete, at the same time a successful, piece of plagiarism. We do not think this kind of second-hand reputation can last upon the London boards for more than a character or two. In the country these *doubles* of the best London performers go down very well, but they are the best they can get, and they have not the originals to make invidious comparisons with [. . .] We do not blame Mr Booth for borrowing Mr Kean's coat and feathers to appear in upon a first and trying occasion, but if he wishes to get a permanent reputation he must come forward in his own person [. . .] because, as far as we could judge, Mr Booth, in point of execution, did those passages the best in which he now and then took leave of Mr Kean's decided and extreme manner, and became more mild and tractable [. . .] In these he seemed to yield to the impulse of his own feelings, and to follow the natural tones and cadence of his voice. They were the best parts of his performance. The worst were those where he imitated, or rather caricatured, Mr Kean's hoarseness of delivery and violence of action, and affected an energy without seeming to feel it [. . .] The greatest drawback to Mr Booth's acting is a perpetual strut, and unwieldy swagger in his ordinary gait and manner, which, though it may pass at Brighton for *grand, gracious, and magnificent*, even the lowest of the mob will laugh at in London. This is the third imitation of Mr Kean we have seen attempted, and the only one that has not been a complete failure. The imitation of original genius is the *forlorn hope* of the candidates for fortune: its faults are so easily overdone, its graces are so hard to catch. A Kemble school we can understand; a Kean school is, we suspect, a contradiction in terms.

[1] Booth (1796–1852) made his career largely in America. See also **148** for a comparison between Kean and Forrest.

Though more noted as a theatre manager and comic actor, Elliston was influenced by both Kemble and Kean as a performer. He was a personality actor, who relied as much on his personal raffishness as on any technical expertise.[1]

[1] See Christopher Murray, *Robert William Elliston, manager* (London: STR, 1975).

145   Robert William Elliston as a tragic actor

Raymond, *Life and enterprises of Elliston*, p. 88

Elliston was an actor of what might be termed the Romantic School. Unlike in style, either of his great contemporaries, Kemble or Cooke, he was yet distinguished in some delineations of tragedy, by which the names of those two actors have become so justly memorable.

Of the commanding presence – the stoicism – which characterized so much the style of Mr Kemble, and of the classic bearing which, on the Roman scene, rendered him incomparably greater than any English actor history may have handed to us since the days of Betterton, Elliston had no perception. The metaphysical ponderings of *Brutus*, the inspelled imaginings of *Macbeth*, were seen in the very form and aspect of Kemble; but the fire of *Hotspur* and chivalry of *Henry V*, bright as they were in his beautiful portraiture, did not extinguish his fellow in art, who suffered but little by a propinquity to that great master.

Elliston was distinguished for flexibility and variableness of voice, which produced powerful effects; now the 'silver-toned Barry', and now again the manly intonations of Booth.

The mental abstraction which belongs to the character of *Hamlet*, met with a happy delineation in Elliston's efforts;– his tremulous awe, his impressive accents, when in the presence of his father's spirit, produced on his auditory a cleaving sympathy; like Betterton, 'he made the ghost equally terrible to the spectator as to himself'.

Mr Kemble was here too much the 'Prince of Denmark', – his awe too much at court, as though he might have uttered, '*Angels and ministers of state, defend us!*' And though Elliston by no means retained for any length of time, this ability in the part in question, yet in its brief possession, he was popularly considered to have had no superior. In the chastening interview with the players, Mr Kemble's style of instruction and manner rose far above the attempts of his young rival; and in the closet scene, Mr Kemble was equally his master [. . .]

The mixed character of *Orestes* was one of Elliston's most successful delineations. His depressed state of mind at disappointed passion, in the commencement of the play [. . .] The manner in which he related the death of Pyrrhus, and that wilderness of idea which precedes confirmed madness, exhibited a masterpiece of the Romantic School.

In *Romeo*, Elliston was always attractive;– a success multiplying his triumphs without greatly adding to his fame; as *Romeo* is perhaps the least intellectual character of Shakespeare's heroes. But the wild, romantic passion of the youthful Veronese, and that frightful despair, the last of mortal suffering, were powerfully portrayed by him:– the scene with *Friar Lawrence*, wherein he hears his sentence, 'banishment', and particularly the speech, concluding,–

> They may seize
> On the white wonder of dear Juliet's hand,
> And steal immortal blessings from her lips,

were also most effectively sustained [. . .]

Though far short of a *great tragedian*, Elliston was an impressive player of tragic parts. If not *Cato, Lear, Macbeth* or *Melantius*, he was *Juba, Edgar, Macduff,* and *Amintor*, without a superior. In the character of *Amintor* full of those inconsistencies and weaknesses, which, as in that of *Jaffier*, not infrequently gave a peculiar interest to the scene, Elliston won the praise of his auditors [. . .]

MACREADY AND THE MOVE TOWARDS REALISTIC ACTING

William Charles Macready (1793–1873) began his London career in 1816, after acting in his father's company in Bristol. Following his performance as Richard III at Covent Garden in 1819, he was acclaimed as a tragic actor and the successor to Edmund Kean. In fact his greatest successes came as a performer in the plays of Sheridan Knowles, Talfourd and Bulwer-Lytton, where he was able to combine his capacity for intense feeling with domestic sentiment. In many ways his style of performance anticipated the development of realistic acting, with its attention to the minutiae of everyday behaviour.

146   Macready begins his London career, 1816

[W. Hazlitt], *Examiner* (6 October 1816), p. 634[1]

Mr Macready's Mentevole, in the *Italian Lover*, is very highly spoken of. We only saw the last act of it, but it appeared to us to be very fine in its kind. It was natural, easy, and forcible. Indeed, we suspect some parts of it were too natural, that is, Mr Macready thought too much of what his feelings might dictate in such circumstances, rather than of what the circumstances must have dictated to him to do. We allude particularly to the half-significant, half-hysterical laugh, and distorted jocular leer, with his eyes towards the persons accusing him of the murder, when the evidence of his guilt comes out [. . .] His resumption of a spirit of defiance was not sufficiently dignified, and was more like the self-sufficient swaggering airs of comedy, than the real grandeur of tragedy, which should always proceed from passion. Mr Macready sometimes, to express uneasiness and agitation, composes his cravat, as he would in a drawing-room. This, we think, neither graceful nor natural in extraordinary situations. His tones are equally powerful and flexible, varying with the greatest facility from the lowest to the highest pitch of the human voice.

¹ Hazlitt had seen Macready's début at Covent Garden as Orestes in Ambrose Philips's *The Distressed Mother* on 16 September 1816. Macready's second Covent Garden play was Jephson's *Julia or, The Italian Lover*. In reviewing it, Hazlitt identified some of the characteristic elements of Macready's performance, which were to remain throughout his career.

Macready would come to rely on female performers responsive to his particular style. His most noted collaborators were Ellen Tree and Helen Faucit. It was during a rehearsal of *Ion* that they met.[1]

¹ Helen Faucit took over the part of Clemanthe in June 1836. See *Times* (18 January 1848) and C. E. Pascoe, *The dramatic list* (London: David Bogue, 1880), sv Mrs Charles Kean, pp. 217–25.

147   Ellen Tree as Clemanthe in Talfourd's *Ion*, 1836

Engraving published by J. Mitchell, 1839. Henry Huntington Library

Ellen Tree (1805–1880) was a distinguished performer before her marriage to Charles Kean in 1842. She played Clemanthe to Macready's Ion at the first performance of Talfourd's play at Covent Garden in May 1836. She was especially noted for her ability to make her characters 'exquisitely gentle and feminine'.

Edwin Forrest (1806–72) performed with both Edmund Kean and Junius Brutus Booth during their tours of the United States, and was much influenced by their style. He first visited England in 1836 and was immediately compared with Macready. He was an immensely physical actor, and such was his dominance of the American stage that it ensured a continuance of the Romantic acting tradition on the other side of the Atlantic until after 1850.

148   Edwin Forrest as Othello, 1836[1]

[John Forster], *Examiner* (30 October 1836), pp. 694–5

Every passage in his third and fourth acts was broken up into little fierce bursts of passion, contrasted with heavy drawlings of tenderness. Whenever a word occurred for what appeared to be 'a point', the word was wrenched from its place in the passion to suffer the point to have way. Whatever the immediate colour of the language might happen to be, that was given without regard to the general harmony and toning of the sentiment. An equal stress was laid, as it were, on every visible impression. One sense was never suffered to be interpreted by another and different sense [. . .] In a word, for this is the only conclusion we can come to, Mr Forrest had no intellectual comprehension of what he was about. All he showed was, that he had very closely watched the celebrated performance of Mr Kean, that he had brought away from it only the more vulgar and obvious points, and that, with certain physical requisites, his notion of the stage appeared to have been formed on the supposition that the intellectual part of an audience was to be reached [. . .] through the physical alone. Sound was substituted for sense through every portion of these great scenes. Where a tender word occurred it was spoken tenderly; where a fierce word, fiercely [. . .] The most ordinary temptation to a pause or a point was seized. 'For she had – eyes – and chose me!' When he spoke of his decline into years – 'Yet, that's not much' – he whined;– then he gave the 'She's gone! I am abused!' etc., in the rigid and compressed style of Kean;– then at the thought of 'these delicate creatures', we had tones that were meant to be tenderly sweet;– and finally, by way of winding up with a striking effect at the close of the tremendous 'I'd rather be a toad', etc., Mr Forrest literally sprang back with the demivolte of a fencer up the stage, and, catching his glimpse of the coming Desdemona, threw himself into a sort of tenderly gladiatorial position, and waited for the applause that broke from the stalls and the galleries [. . .]

Some time since we recollect expressing ourselves strongly on the mode in which Mr Kean, during the later years of his life, used to play the last act of *Othello*. It was no fault in the conception of that great actor; it was simply the result of his physical infirmities. He had always so much exhausted himself in the previous acts

that he was obliged to rest on a sofa during his fearful dialogue with Desdemona,
to gather strength for the murder [. . .] Now Mr Forrest improved on Mr Kean's
infirmity. The drawing up of the scene discovered him sitting quietly near the bed,
soliloquising with deliberate calmness! As he uttered the dreadful word, 'Have you
pray'd to-night, Desdemona?' – he coolly retreated from the bed and sat down upon
a sofa. The murder was a downright Old Bailey affair.

[1] Forster was a fervent supporter of Macready and a great friend. He was unashamedly partisan, and
had no time for the visiting American actor, Edwin Forrest. He had reviewed Macready as Othello a
year before, when he had played it at Drury Lane on 21 October 1835.

Charles Kean's significance rests not so much on his skills as an actor, but rather on his
pioneering work as a proto-director in the period from 1850, specifically during his tenure
of the Princess's Theatre, and also as the organizer of Queen Victoria's Windsor Castle
theatricals [**124a–b**] from 1848. After the death of his father in 1833, Charles Kean spent
the period to 1838 in the provinces, vowing to stay out of London until a manager was
prepared to give him his terms of £50 per night. Bunn engaged him on these terms as a rival
attraction to Macready at Covent Garden, and Kean opened at Drury Lane as Hamlet on
January 8, 1838.[1]

[1] See also J. G. Lockhart's letter to Lord Meadowbank (quoted in J. W. Cole, *The life and theatrical times of
Charles Kean, FSA* (London: Bentley, 1859), vol. I, p. 269, which identifies Kean's 'ordinary demeanour'
and 'quiet tones'.

149   Charles Kean's début and his new readings as Hamlet, 1838

[John Forster], *Examiner* (14 January 1838), p. 20, reprinted in Archer and Lowe, *Dramatic
essays*, p. 41

What we felt to be the pervading mistake of this performance of Hamlet we will at
once describe. It was too uniformly slow and elaborate; the same pitch-key of sad
sound prevailed too much throughout; when any change or relief was introduced it
was strained at too hard; and the general effect conveyed was something extremely
unlike the feeble and variable purpose, the quick sensibility, the thoughtful melancholy, the indolent philosophy of the real Hamlet. We know the temptations which
every actor has in such a character as this to exaggerate its subtle and delicate
shading for the purposes of the stage; but Mr Kean, as it appeared to us, attempted
these exaggerations in the wrong places [. . .]

Mr Kean is always graceful, but never sufficiently familiar in speech or bearing:
and he underacts the friendship and overacts the love. When he converses with
Horatio on his first entrance from Wittenberg, he stands in the centre of the stage
and Horatio in one corner of it – when he instructs the player (which he does
extremely well) he holds him at a still greater distance, though we fancy Hamlet at
that instant more than ever familiar with his old player friend – when Rosenkrantz
and Guildenstern visit him, he makes a violent and abrupt 'set' at them, whereas
it is one of the very nicest points of Hamlet to keep up, throughout that scene,

the quiet demeanour of conscious detection and cool observance, yet of friendly familiarity [. . .]

It is not difficult to trace to their source the majority of Mr Kean's mistakes in this arduous performance. It will be found, we think, that his chief power with an audience lies in effect of emotion and of sudden gusts of passion, and his own consciousness of this is betrayed in a habit of emphasising his level passages too much, of throwing them into startling contrast by long pauses, and of laying forceful and pathetic stress on lines that need no such aid [. . .] The speech after the disappearance of the Ghost, for instance – the words he then addresses to his friends, which in their tearful slowness could never have passed for 'wild and whirling' – the formal and melancholy precision with which he specially addresses Horatio – the entire misapprehension of the charming scene at Ophelia's grave, where he seems inclined to shed tears for the clay of 'Imperial Caesar', and addresses his remonstrance to Laertes in sad and solemn slowness – his most laborious and elaborate trifling with Osrick [sic] – are all illustrations of our objection.

In the scene of Hamlet's reappearance at the palace after meeting his dead father, Mr Kean entered without any disorder of dress, and the 'new reading' has been applauded. It is a very silly reading notwithstanding. We do not care if the disorder is intimated by an ungartered stocking, the usual mode, or any other and better; but intimated, or rather distinctly expressed, it most certainly should be. It is not only essential to the general conduct of the scene, but specially alluded to by almost everyone on the stage [. . .] Another 'new reading', really admirable, has been objected to – where in the fine soliloquy that closes the second act he changes his tone upon the epithet 'kindless'–

> Bloody, bawdy villain!
> Remorseless, treacherous, lecherous, kindless villain!

and by some tears of anguish at the word, expresses at once both Hamlet's pure and refined nature, and the weakness and sensibility of his temper. But this was not a new reading, though admirably rendered by Mr Kean. Mr Macready first gave it fame on the modern stage, and Garrick had startled an audience with it in older times [. . .] We have said that Mr Kean overacted Hamlet's love. He wept and sank with his face upon Ophelia's arm when he told her that 'he did love her once', and his voice prolonged itself into tremulous softness when he rushed back to give her 'a plague for her dowry'. We are aware that the elder Mr Kean infused the same affectionate tenderness into his worst upbraidings, and was much and most undeservedly praised for it. The scene, as Shakespeare designed it, needs no such refining to give it sense and the deepest sorrow [. . .] The first thing said by the King after leaving the concealment from which he has heard and seen the interview is decisive as to his impression –

> Love! his affections do not that way tend!
> Nor what he spake, though it lack'd form a little,
> Was not like madness –

which the King could not have said, if he had seen Mr Charles Kean instead of Hamlet [. . .]

150   'Was Macready a great actor?': an evaluation on his retirement, 1851

[G. H. Lewes], *Leader* (8 February 1851), reprinted in Archer and Lowe, *Dramatic essays*, p. 314[1]

It is a question often mooted in private, whether Macready was a *great* actor, or only an intelligent actor, or [. . .] an intrinsically bad actor. The last opinion is uttered by some staunch admirers of Kemble and Young, and by those critics who, looking at the drama as an *imitation of Nature*, dwell upon the exaggerations and other false colours wherewith Macready paints, and proclaim him, consequently, a bad artist. Now, in discussing a subject like the present, it is imperative that we understand the *point of view* from which we both look at it.

I am impressed with the conviction that the majority mistakes Art for an *imitation* of Nature. It is no such thing. Art is *representation*. This is why too close an approach to Reality in Art is shocking [. . .]

[. . .] Taking Art as a Representative rather than as an Imitative process, I say that the test of an actor's genius is not 'fidelity to Nature', but simply and purely his power of exciting emotions in you respondent to the situation – ideal when that is ideal, passionate when that is passionate, familiar when that is familiar, prosaic when that is prosaic. A bad actor mouths familiar prose as if it were the loftiest verse; but a good actor [. . .] if he were to play ideal characters with the same familiarity and close adherence to Nature as that which makes his performance of familiar parts charming, would equally sin against the laws of Art [. . .]

To compose a mask, or, if you like, to personate a character, there are three fundamental requisite conditions, which I will call – 1. *Conceptual Intelligence*; 2. *Representative Intelligence*; 3. *Physical Advantages*. The first condition is requisite to *understand* the character; the two last are requisite in different degrees to *represent* the character [. . .]

Having thus briefly indicated what I conceive to be the leading principles in the philosophy of acting, I proceed to apply them to Macready; and first say that, inasmuch as he possesses in an unusual degree the three requisites laid down, he must be classed among the *great* actors. His conceptual intelligence everyone will acknowledge. Even those to whom his peculiarities are offensive admit that he is a man of intellect, of culture [. . .] His conception always betrays care and thought, and never betrays foolishness. On the other hand, I never received any light from him to clear up an obscurity; my knowledge of Shakespeare is little increased by his performances. I cannot point to any one single trace of illumination – such as Edmund Kean used to flash out. This may be my fault; but [. . .] I say that Macready's knowledge of Shakespeare and his art [. . .] does not prove to me the greatness of intellect which his ardent admirers assume for him. The intelligence most shown by Macready is that which I have named representative intelligence, and which he possesses in a remarkable degree. Certain peculiarities and defects prevent his representing the high, heroic, passionate characters; but nothing can surpass his representation of some others; and connecting this representative intelligence with his physical advantages, we see how he can execute what he conceives, and thus become an actor. His voice – one primary requisite of an actor – is a fine one, powerful, extensive in compass, and containing tones that thrill, and tones that weep. His person is good, and his face very expressive [. . .]

[. . .] The anguish of a weak, timid, prostrate mind he can represent with a sorrowing pathos, as great as Kean in the heroic agony of Othello; and in all the touching *domesticities* of tragedy he is unrivalled. But he fails in the characters which demand impassioned grandeur, and a certain *largo* of execution. His Macbeth and Othello have fine touches, but they are essentially unheroic – their passion is fretful and irritable, instead of being broad, vehement, overwhelming. His Hamlet is too morbid, irritable, and lachrymose. Lear is his finest Shakespearian character – because the fretfulness and impatience of the old man come within the range of Macready's representative powers, of which the terrible curse may be regarded as the climax. King John, Richard II, Iago, and Cassius are also splendid performances; in each of them we trace the same characteristic appeal to the actor's peculiar powers. Although you can see him in no part without feeling that an artist is before you, yet if you think of him as a great actor, it is as Werner, Lear, Virginius, Richelieu, King John, Richard II, Iago – not as Othello, Macbeth, Hamlet, Coriolanus [. . .] I believe Macready to be radically unfitted for ideal characters – for the display of broad elemental passions [. . .] and peculiarly fitted for the irritable, the tender, and the domestic; he can depict rage better than passion, anguish better than mental agony, misery better than despair, tenderness better than the abandonment of love. But the things he can do he does surpassingly well; and for this, also, I must call him a great actor [. . .]

[1] Lewes asked the question rhetorically after Macready's final farewell performance on 3 February. See also the evaluation in the *Athenaeum* (1 March 1851), p. 251, which discusses Macready's identification with original roles and his less than successful performances in Shakespeare.

Much of the movement of actors between England and North America was dominated by English actors seeking to recoup their financial losses or to revive their flagging personal reputations abroad. Nevertheless a significant number of American actors appeared on the English stage [**148**] in the first half of the century. One of the most notable was Ira Aldridge (1807–67), the first Afro-American serious actor to perform in Britain, who made his initial appearance under the pseudonym of Keene at the Coburg (Victoria) Theatre in 1825. He first played Aaron in the provinces in 1849, and the play was subsequently revived at the Britannia in 1852.[1]

[1] For his performance in a version of Southerne's *Oroonoko*, called *The Revolt of Surinam; or, The Slave's Revenge*, at the Coburg, see *Times* (11 October 1825), and for an evaluation of his performance as

Aaron, see *Era* (26 April 1857), quoted in H. Marshall and M. Stock, *Ira Aldridge* (Washington, DC: Howard University Press, 1993), pp. 171–3.

151   Ira Aldridge as Aaron in *Titus Andronicus*, 1849–52
Engraving. Private collection

MELODRAMATIC ACTING

Melodramatic acting developed from the conventions of tragic acting. The pictorialization of passion, the musical use of vocal cadences, often unrelated to verbal meaning but complementing and augmenting the instrumental accompaniment to the plays, and the stylization and stereotyping encouraged by lines of business were all inherited from the eighteenth century and lasted until the silent cinema. Actors within a stock company were often required to move fluidly between the playing of tragedy and that of melodrama.[1] In the early part of the century Gothic and nautical melodrama were equally popular [**82, 85, 87, 93**].

[1]   See Booth, *English melodrama*, pp. 190 ff. and Booth, *Victorian age*, pp. 120–35.

152   **Mrs Egerton as Meg Merrilies in *Guy Mannering*, 1817**

De Wilde engraving, *Theatrical Inquisitor*, 10 (March 1817)

Mr.ˢ Egerton as Meg Merrilies.

"if ever the dead come back among the living.
I'll be seen in that glen many a night."
Guy Mannering Act 3 Scene 1.

Engraved for the Theatrical Inquisitor

London. Published April 1. 1817, by C. Chapple, Pall Mall.

Mrs Egerton, who was equally respected in tragedy and melodrama, began her stage career in Bath in 1803 and joined the permanent Covent Garden company in 1811. The part of Meg Merrilies was originally intended to be played by John Emery.[1]

[1] *Theatrical Inquisitor*, 10 (March 1817), pp. 163–5.

153   James Wallack in *The Brigand Chief*, 1829

Dramatic Magazine (1 January 1830), p. 342[1]

Mᴿ WALLACK,

as Alessandro Massaroni, in the Brigand.

London Published Jan.ʸ 1 1830. by Whittaker Treacher & Cᵒ , Ave Maria Lane.
and at the Artists Repository and Public Library, 37 Charlotte Street, Rathbone Place.

---

[1] See also 'Theatrical Portraits no. XVIII', *Theatrical Inquisitor*, 9 (March 1816), pp. 186–9.

James Wallack (1791–1864), noted particularly for his dashing flamboyance, was also a strong tragic actor and played opposite Macready. Planché's translation from the French opened at Drury Lane on 18 November 1829. *The Dramatic Magazine* (1 December 1829), p. 293 commented: 'The drama was eminently successful . . . and abounds with romantic incidents, effective situations, and excellent acting. Mr Wallack as the brigand chief, gave a splendid specimen of melo-dramatic acting; his attitudes were very striking and picturesque; he sung [*sic*] a national air with a considerable degree of taste'.

154   T. P. Cooke and Miss Scott in Jerrold's *Black Eyed Susan*, 1829

Sawyer engraving after Cruikshank, *Dramatic Magazine* (8 December 1829), p. 540

Drawn by Rob.t Cruikshanks and Engraved by Rich.d Sawyer.

M.R T.P. COOKE & MISS SCOTT,
as William and Susan,
in Black Eyed Susan.

London, Published Sept.r 1.st 1829. by Whittaker, Treacher & Co. - Ave Maria Lane.
and at the Artists Repository & Public Library, 37, Charlotte Street, Rathbone Place.

Thomas Potter Cooke (1786–1864) was chiefly identified with his performance of sailors – Long Tom Coffin in Edward Fitzball's *The Pilot* and William in Douglas Jerrold's *Black Eyed Susan*, which opened on 8 June 1829 at the Surrey Theatre. Miss Scott was a member of the Surrey company and had played the Dumb Boy in Fitzball's *The Inchcape Bell* in 1828.

155   Fanny Kemble as Julia in Sheridan Knowles's *The Hunchback*, 1832

W. Alais engraving, published by Payne in 1832. Henry Huntington Library

Frances Ann Kemble (1809–93), the daughter of Charles Kemble and niece of Sarah Siddons, began her stage career in 1829. She joined her father's company at Covent Garden, where she remained until 1832. She went with him to the United States, playing the character of Julia amongst others, and resided there until 1847. Reputedly, her performances at Covent Garden enabled Charles Kemble to make a profit for the first time.[1]

[1] See Pascoe, *Dramatic list*, sv Frances Ann Kemble, pp. 231–5.

156   Charles Kean's contribution to the acting of melodrama, 1852

G. H. Lewes on Charles Kean, 1852, reprinted in Archer and Lowe, *Dramatic essays*, pp. 185–8

What our actors want, and what they might learn from the French, is the drawing-room quietness of well-bred acting – the subordination of 'points' to character – the reliance upon nature. It is in these things that Charles Mathews surpasses all English actors, and has gradually earned for himself his peculiar reputation; it is by the absence of these that Charles Kean, out of melodrame, has acquired *his* peculiar reputation. Charles Kean, after vainly battling with fate so many years, seems now, consciously or unconsciously, settling down into the conviction that his talent does not lie in any Shakespearian sphere whatever, but in melodrames, such as *Pauline*,[1] or his last venture,

THE CORSICAN BROTHERS,[2]

where, as high intellect is not *de rigueur*, he is not restricted by its fastidious exigencies. It is certainly worth a passing remark, to note how bad an actor he is in any part requiring the expression of intellect or emotion,– in any part demanding some sympathy with things poetical,– in any part calling for *representative* power; and how impressive, and, I may say, *unrivalled*, he is in gentlemanly melodrama. The successful portions of his tragic characters are all melodramatic; and in *Pauline* and *The Corsican Brothers* he satisfies all the exigencies of criticism [. . .] and with this preface, let me say that *The Corsican Brothers* is the most daring, ingenious, and exciting melodrama I remember to have seen; and is mounted with an elegance, an accuracy, an ingenuity in the mingling of the supernatural with the real, and an artistic disposition of effects, such as perhaps no theatre could equal, certainly not surpass.

[. . .] Charles Kean plays the two brothers; and you must see him before you will believe how well and how *quietly* he plays them; preserving a gentlemanly demeanour, a drawing-room manner very difficult to assume on the stage [. . .] which intensifies the passion of the part, and gives it terrible reality.

[1] Adapted from the French by John Oxenford and first performed at the Princess's Theatre in March 1851.
[2] Adapted by Dion Boucicault and first performed at the Princess's Theatre in February 1852.

THE FACES OF COMIC ACTING

In London, comic acting was dominated by the Covent Garden company from 1792 until the early 1820s, thus ensuring the continuance of a genteel style of performance and repertoire into the first part of the nineteenth century. This tradition would be taken over by the Haymarket Theatre, especially under the management of Benjamin Webster (1837–53). However, changes reflecting the new, more bourgeois and less literary audiences were inevitable. Plays were tailored to specific actors with particular personalities, and comic playing became identified with specialist performers: Munden as the elderly eccentric; Emery and Liston as low comedy provincials; Johnstone or Power as the Irishman; Mrs Keeley as the pert lady's maid. This tendency to write plays for idiosyncratic 'personality' actors was regarded by critics, particularly Leigh Hunt, as the principal reason for the decline in the quality of comic writing in the early part of the century. Nevertheless, although extravagant farcical performances continued to be popular throughout the nineteenth century, audiences came to appreciate suavity and sophistication as exemplified by the mannered behaviour of actors such as Charles J. Mathews.

157   Mrs Jordan at the end of her career

Hunt, *Critical essays*, p. 163

In characters that require this expression, MRS JORDAN seems to speak with all her soul; her voice, pregnant with melody, delights the ear with a peculiar and exquisite fulness and with an emphasis that appears the result of perfect conviction; yet this conviction is the effect of a sensibility willing to be convinced rather than of a judgment weighing its reasons; her heart always precedes her speech, which follows with the readiest and happiest acquiescence.[1]

This subjection of the manner to the feelings has rendered MRS JORDAN in her younger days the most natural actress of childhood, of its outbursts of disposition, and its fitful happiness; and as her fancy has not diminished, and her knowledge of human nature must have increased, with her years, it would render her the most natural actress still, were it not for the increase of her person. To be very fat and to look forty years old is certainly not the happiest combination for a girlish appearance, and MRS JORDAN, with much good sense, seems to have almost laid aside her *Romps* and her *Little Pickles* for younger performers. So delightful however are the feelings and tones of nature, that there is still no actress who pleases so much in the performance of frank and lively youth, in SHAKSPEARE'S *Rosalind* for instance, and the broad sensibilities of the *Country Girl*.[2] With this frankness too she unites a power of raillery, seldom found in a performer of her honest cast [. . .] MRS JORDAN utters her more serious ridicule with the same simplicity and strength of feeling that always pervades her seriousness when it does not amount to the tragic, and she gives it a very peculiar energy by pronouncing the latter part of her sentences in a louder, a deeper, and more hurried tone, as if her good nature should not be betrayed into too great a softness and yet as if it wished to get rid of feelings too harsh for her disposition. Her lighter raillery still carries with it the same feeling, and her laughter is the happiest and most natural on the stage; if she is to laugh in the middle of a speech, it does not separate itself so abruptly from her words as with most of our performers; she does not force herself into those yawning, and side-aching peals, which are laboured on every trifling occasion [. . .] her laughter intermingles itself with her words, as fresh ideas afford her fresh merriment; she does not so much indulge as she seems unable to help it; it increases, it lessens with her fancy, and when you expect it no longer according to the usual habit of the stage, it sparkles forth at little intervals, as recollection revives it, like flame from half-smothered embers.

---

[1] Genest, *Account of the English stage*, vol. VIII echoed these sentiments at the time of Mrs Jordan's death on 5 July 1816. See also Thomas and Hare, *Restoration and Georgian England*, nos. 337–339b.

2 Garrick's adaptation of *The Country Wife*, first performed at Drury Lane in 1766.

158   Grimaldi as Clown in the pantomime *Mother Goose*, 1807

De Wilde engraving, 1807. Henry Huntington Library

Joseph Grimaldi (1778–1837), the most distinguished clown of the nineteenth century, began his career at Sadler's Wells in 1800 and joined the Covent Garden company in 1806. He was a multitalented performer, equally adept at serious roles and comic, but was identified principally with the role which made him famous, that of the exuberant, resourceful Clown in Thomas Dibdin's pantomime *Harlequin and Mother Goose; or, The Golden Egg*, first performed at Covent Garden on 29 December 1806. It played continuously until 23 June 1807 and was often revived thereafter. Many of the conventions of circus-clowning owe their origins to Grimaldi.[1]

[1] See the unsatisfactory biography that Charles Dickens edited shortly after Grimaldi's death. 'Boz', *Memoirs of Joseph Grimaldi* (London: Bentley, 1838), and R. Findlater, *Joe Grimaldi: his life and theatre* (Cambridge: Cambridge University Press, 1978), pp. 113–21.

159   John Emery as Dandie Dinmont in *Guy Mannering*, 1816

'T. J. C.' engraving. Henry Huntington Library

Mʳ EMERY,

As DANDIE DINMONT, in GUY MANNERING.

After a provincial apprenticeship with Tate Wilkinson, John Emery (1777–1822) joined the Covent Garden company in 1797, where he specialized in rustic countryman roles. He was often compared with Liston.[1]

1   See Leigh Hunt, *Critical essays on the performers of the London theatres*; Michael Booth, 'The acting of early nineteenth-century comedy', in *English plays of the nineteenth century*, vol. III, pp. 149–51; and *Theatrical Inquisitor*, 4 (April 1814), pp. 195–7.

160   Eliza Vestris as Captain Macheath in *The Beggar's Opera*, 1820

Henry Huntington Library

MADAME VESTRIS,
as
CAPTAIN MACHEATH

Published by W. Harrison Innes, 3, Charles St. Soho Square.

Though Eliza Vestris made her name as a singer, dancer and performer, especially in travesty roles, her most signal contribution to the theatre in the period lay in the area of management [**49, 51a–b, 105**]. Her performance as Macheath at the Haymarket opened on 22 July 1820.[1]

See Charles Pearce, *Madame Vestris and her times* (New York: Blom, 1969), pp. 52–4, and on her Olympic Theatre performances, William Appleton, *Madame Vestris and the London stage* (New York: Columbia University Press, 1974), pp. 51–80.

161   Talfourd evaluates Joseph Munden on his retirement in 1824

Quoted in T. Munden, *Memoirs of Joseph Shepherd Munden, by his son* (London: Bentley, 1844), p. 294

Mr Munden was by far the greatest comedian we ever saw;[1] – his vein of humour was the richest and most peculiar; his range of characters the most extensive; his discrimination the most exact and happy, and his finishing the most elaborate and complete. He received great advantages from nature, and improved them to the utmost by vigilant observation and laborious study. His power of face was the most extraordinary; for he had no singularity of feature – no lucky squint or mechanical grin; but the features which, when at rest, befitted well the sedate merchant or baronet of the old school, assumed, at his will, the strangest and most fantastic forms. This almost creative faculty was associated with another power of an opposite kind – the capability of imparting to every variety of form a substance and apparent durability as if it were carved out of rock. His action had no less body than flavour. In the wildest parts of farce he every minute put forth some living fantasy of his own, some new arrangement of features, creations among which Momus would have hesitated long which he should choose for his own proper use, as embodying most general traits of comic feeling [. . .]

Although Mr Munden's humour and his flexibility of countenance were the gifts which chiefly distinguished him from others, he shared largely in that pathos which belongs in a greater or lesser degree to all good comedians. It is natural that a strong relish for the ludicrous should be accompanied by a genuine pathos, as both arise from quick sensibility to the pecularities of our fellow-men, and the joys and sorrows by which they are affected. Those who are endowed with such qualities, too often presume upon their strength, and rely on the individual effects which they can produce in their happiest moods. But Mr Munden had a higher sense of the value of his art than to leave his success to accident, or to rest contented with doing something to make an audience laugh or weep without reference to the precise nature of the conception which he professed to embody. He studied his parts, in the best sense of the term, and with as careful and minute attention as though he were the driest and most mechanical of actors. When he had fully mastered the outlines of a part, he cast into it just so much of his resources of humour or of feeling as was necessary to give it genial life, and to discriminate its finest shades, and never enough to destroy its individuality, or melt down its distinctive features [. . .] Thus in his Old Dornton,[2] the pleasantries scattered through the part always served to heighten the images of paternal love with which it was fraught,– as in the fond return to bid the profligate son 'Good night'; the interview with the Widow Warren;

and the expression of pleasure on hearing the story of the tradesman, 'and so Harry has been your friend?', a little touch of familiar nature never exceeded on the stage [. . .] Great as his capacities were, he held them always in subservience to the requisitions of his author; and hence arose the uncommon variety and freshness of his characters. Hence also, it happened, that instead of falling off in age, as all actors must do who play merely from impulse, he grew more perfect and mellow in time, and identified himself more closely with the persons whom he represented, the oftener he played them. He did not merely give a certain quantity of passion or humour, and think he had done enough; but he considered the exact kind of passion or humour to be displayed, colouring but not hiding the emotions of the heart by the habits of the life, and softening the oddities he pourtrayed [sic] by associating them with those common feelings to which they were most nearly allied [. . .] We have seen him play three drunken parts in a night, and come out fresh in them all: and such was his practical discrimination, that we could not have transferred a tone or a stagger without injury to the inebriate sarcasms of Crack, the maudlin philanthropy of Nipperkin, or the sublime stupidity of Dozey![3] [. . .] In his sailors – a class generally represented under very broad characteristics – there was the same discrimination exhibited; [. . .] His Dozey, which was the last part he ever played, was perhaps the most extraordinary of all his personifications. This old tar – ignorant, stupefied with age and grog – seemed absolutely grand in the robustness of his frame and the rolling self-satisfaction of his gait, as one who had out-braved 'a thousand storms, a thousand thunders'. It was indeed a triumph of art, when the old enthusiasm of this stout-hearted and thick-headed veteran was kindled up, and he gave his animated description of a battle, ending with a wave of his handkerchief for the English flag, and cheering with all the energy of youth: a more characteristic picture was never exhibited in the drollest farce; nor was ever a truer or a nobler outburst of feeling called forth in the stateliest tragedy.

[1] Joseph Munden (1758–1832) was regarded as the finest, all-round low comedian on the London stage. He had acted successfully in the provinces before joining the Covent Garden company in 1790. He transferred to the Drury Lane company in 1813, where he remained until his retirement in May 1824. See W. Clark Russell, *Representative Actors* (London: Frederick Warne, 1883), pp. 256–61.

[2] In Thomas Holcroft's *Road to Ruin*, first performed at Covent Garden in 1792 and frequently revived.

[3] The characters referred to appear in Thomas Knight's *Turnpike Gate*, first performed at Covent Garden in 1799; O'Keeffe's *Sprigs of Laurel*, first performed at Covent Garden in 1793, and Thomas Dibdin's *Past Ten O'Clock and a Rainy Night*, first performed at Drury Lane in 1815, respectively.

162   John Liston as Paul Pry, 1825

Coloured engraving published by Webster, 1825. Private collection

M.ᴿ LISTON, as PAUL PRY.
"I hope I don't intrude."

Liston (1776–1846) joined the Haymarket company in 1805 after being recommended by Charles Kemble, with whom he had worked in Newcastle. Not as much of an all-round actor as Munden, his success largely depended on his extraordinary face, his characterization of 'vulgarity, folly and conceit' and his ability to extemporize on stage.[1]

[1] See J. Davis, *John Liston, comedian* (London: STR, 1985), and the contemporary evaluation in *The Drama; or, Theatrical Magazine* (January 1824), pp. 261–70.

163   Elliston's strengths as a comic performer

Leigh Hunt, *Tatler* (10 July 1831), pp. 35–6, reprinted in Archer and Lowe, *Dramatic essays*, p. 214

Mr Elliston was the best comedian, in the highest sense of the word, that we have seen.[1] Others equalled him in some particular points; Lewis[2] surpassed him in

airiness; but there was no gentleman comedian who comprised so many qualities of his art as he did, or who could diverge so well into those parts of tragedy
which find a connecting link with the graver powers of the comedian in their
gracefulness and humanity. He was the best Wildair, the best Archer [*The Beaux'
Strategem*], the best Aranza [Tobin's *The Honeymoon*]; and carrying the seriousness
of Aranza a little further, or making him a *tragic gentleman* instead of a comic,
he became the best Mortimer, and even the best Macbeth, of any performer who
excelled in comedy. When Charles Kemble acts comedy, he gives you the idea of
an actor who has come out of the chivalrous part of tragedy [. . .] Elliston being naturally a comedian, and comedy of the highest class demanding a greater
sympathy with actual flesh and blood, his tragedy, though less graceful than
Charles Kemble's, was more natural and cordial. He suffered and was shaken more
[. . .]

The tragedy of this accomplished actor was, however, only an elongation, or
drawing out, of the graver and more sensitive part of his comedy [. . .] When Kean
appeared and extinguished Kemble, Elliston seems prudently to have put out his
tragic lamp. In comedy, after the death of Lewis, he remained without a rival. He
had three distinguished excellencies – dry humour, gentlemanly mirth, and fervid
gallantry. His features were a little too round, and his person latterly bacame a great
deal too much so. But we speak of him in his best days. His face, in one respect,
was of that rare order which is peculiarly fitted for the expression of enjoyment: it
laughed with the eyes as well as the mouth. His eyes, which were not large, grew
smaller when he was merry, and twinkled with glee and archness; his smile was full
of enjoyment, and yet the moment he shook his head with a satirical deprecation,
or dropped the expression of his face with an inuendo [*sic*], nothing could be drier or
more angular than his mouth [. . .] He understood all the little pretended or avowed
arts of a gentleman, when he was conversing or complimenting, or making love –
everything which implied the necessity of attention to the other person, and a
just, and as it were, mutual consciousness of the graces of life. His manners were
the true *minuet dance* spirit of gentility [. . .] And then his voice was remarkable
for its union of the manly with the melodious; and as a lover nobody approached
him. Certainly nobody approached a woman as he did. It was the reverse of that
preposterous style of *touch and avoid* – that embracing at arm's length, and hinting
of a mutual touch on the shoulders – by which the ladies and gentlemen of the
stage think fit to distinguish themselves from the characters they perform [. . .]
Elliston made out that it was no shame to love a woman, and no shame in her
to return his passion. He took her hand, he cherished it against his bosom, he
watched the moving of her countenance, he made the space less and less between
them, and as he at length burst out into some exclamation of 'Charming!' or
'Lovely!' his voice trembled, not with the weakness, but with the strength and
fervour of its emotion. All the love on the stage, since this, (with the exception
of Macready's domestic tenderness) is not worth two pence, and fit only to beget
waiters.

[1] Hunt catalogued the excellences of Elliston in 1808 in his *Critical Essays*. At the time it was Elliston's versatility, especially in comedy, that had attracted Hunt, who had compared him to Charles Kemble. The comparison was still valid when Hunt offered this tribute on Elliston's death in 1831.

[2] William Lewis (1746–1813) joined the Covent Garden company in 1773 and retired in 1809. He was one of the principal comedians in the company, as well as its acting manager, for twenty-one years. He was particularly remembered for his combination of whimsy and elegance. See J. Doran, *Annals of the English stage from Thomas Betterton to Edmund Kean* (London: Nimmo, 1888), vol. III, pp. 303–4.

164   Elliston as Walter in Thomas Morton's *The Children in the Wood*

From an engraving by Woolnoth in *Cumberland's British Theatre*, vol. XVII (London: Cumberland, 1828)

Charles James Mathews (1803–78), the son of Charles Mathews [125a–d], introduced a style of comic performance which would influence English actors for the remainder of the century. Unlike earlier comedians, who maintained strong farcical connections in their styles of performance, Mathews concentrated on a persona of smooth urbanity. He inherited his father's facility for quick changes, and, as an author, wrote short plays like *The Humpbacked Lover* and *Patter Versus Clatter* to demonstrate his skills.

165   John Liston introduces Charles Mathews to the English public, 1835

BL, Olympic Theatre Cuttings 47–48: unidentified clipping, 30 October 1835

We have rarely seen public curiosity more excited, than on Monday night, on the occasion of Mr C. Mathews appearing for the first time on the English stage. It was not a rude vulgar desire to witness a new actor's demeanour in first passing through the ordeal of public opinion, but an eager wish to receive with kindness, and, if necessary, with indulgence, the son of an old and highly gifted actor. Mr C. Mathews, however, required only that justice should be awarded him, to obtain a most flattering reception. His own merits are such as to constrain applause on any stage in England. His task last night was no easy one. He had to appear before that many-headed monster-thing, 'the public', in two new pieces, and of one of these he was himself the author. This would be sufficient to keep down any rising spirit of ordinary character, but Mr Mathews seems to have collected together as many untoward circumstances as he could, for the purpose of showing how effectually he could triumph over them. After the first piece, when the curtain was drawn, Liston was seen standing near a chair in the centre of the stage, with handkerchief in hand, ready to deliver the introductory address. The two opening lines, imploring seriousness,

> Oh! let me beg this night with you there
> One moment to be serious and sincere.

had the very contrary effect. It was impossible to refrain from laughter at Liston trying to look serious; it was a moral impossibility; each effort to compose his grotesque features only rendered them the more truly comic. The address was highly applauded, however, and the *Hunchbacked Lover* [*sic*] commenced. This is a light trifle, in which a gay, dashing young fellow, *George Rattleton* (Mr C. Mathews) disguises himself in the great coat of his rival, *Mr Grimshaw*, in order to deceive *Sir Simon Snipe* (Mr F. Mathews), and obtain his daughter, *Louisa* (Miss Malcolm) to be his lawful wife. *Jenny* (Mrs Orger) is lamenting that the lovers have lost all chance of being united, when in bounds young Mathews, as *Rattleton*. He is slight in figure, easy in his movements, and extremely lively in his manner. He possesses wonderful volubility of utterance when he pleases, and though at present a little deficient in stage tact, he makes amends by the spirit which he infuses into every scene of his part. He recalled his father to our mind frequently during the night, and in the upper part of the face decidedly resembles him. He possesses in a marked manner the air of a gentleman, and will be an extremely valuable acquisition to the stage as the 'young lover' and the 'walking gentleman'. In the second piece, *Old and Young Stagers*, he and Liston kept the house in roars of laughter by their excellent enactment of a Coachman and a Tiger. Liston is the father, and has lived in *Sir Pompadour Puffendale's* family for forty years. He thinks the situation of coachman the noblest on earth, and is a staunch stickler for the dignity of his office. He despises the modern innovations, and is outrageous at his son's falling off from the good old manners of former times. The scene in which he gives the son an account of his rising to his present situation was admirable. He makes some excellent hits at the present state of the 'stage', and calls to mind, with a tender sorrow, which Liston renders extremely ludicrous, some of the old drivers [. . .] The plot of this piece turns on the scrapes which the 'Tiger' and his master, *Clement Puffendale* (Mr J. Vining) get into, and which, in some instances, are fathered on the coachman. In the last act they are just returned from Paris, and young Mathews gave, with good discrimination, the easy impudence of the travelled domestic. He was loudly applauded throughout, and most deservedly. His self-possession was much greater in the second piece than in the first, and we can safely predict that a single week will make a marked improvement. During the whole evening there was an evident feeling of pleasure throughout the house, at Mr Mathews' success, and the interest which Liston took in the fate of his old friend's son, was almost paternal. There was a touch of tenderness, a break in the voice, now and again which showed that Liston was thinking of 'gone-by days'. Altogether we have seldom passed a more pleasant evening; for what can afford more pleasure than to see merit rewarded, and above all in the son of one who so often afforded us heartfelt enjoyment.

166   Charles Mathews as George Rattleton in *The Humpbacked Lover*, 1835

Dickens, *Life of Mathews*, vol. II, p. 76

167   Mathews and the new comic style

Dickens, *Life of Mathews*, vol. II, pp. 74–5

The theatre for my *début* as an actor was chosen without a moment's hesitation. I had no passion for what was called the 'regular drama'. I had no respect for traditional acting, and had no notion of taking a 'line of business', as it is called – that is, undertaking for so much per week all the characters in comedy and tragedy, whether fitting or not, played by Mr Charles Kemble, or Mr Jones, or Mr Elliston, whose every movement was registered in the prompt-book, and from whose 'business', [. . .] no deviation was allowed. The lighter phase of comedy, representing the more natural and less laboured school of modern life, and holding the mirror up to nature without regard to the conventionalities of the theatre, was the aim I had in view. The Olympic was then the only house where this could be achieved, and to the Olympic I at once attached myself. There was introduced for the first time in England that reform in all theatrical matters which has since been adopted in every theatre in the kingdom. Drawing-rooms were fitted up like drawing-rooms, and furnished with care and taste. Two chairs no longer indicated that two persons were to be seated, the two chairs being removed indicating that the two persons were not to be seated. A claret-coloured coat, salmon-coloured trowsers with a broad black stripe, a sky-blue neckcloth with large paste brooch, and a cut steel eye-glass with a pink ribbon no longer marked the 'light comedy gentleman', and the public at once recognised and appreciated the change.

V   *Stage presentation*

INTRODUCTION

The nineteenth century saw the triumph of the scenic stage, with rapid advances in technology and the almost universal desire for pictorial realism, which affected equally the staging of Shakespeare, melodrama, pantomime and comedy. Indeed, scenic innovation soon outstripped the actor's ability to meet the challenge of increasingly realistic stage effects by offering a congruent realistic performance. Romanticism brought with it a desire to see spectacular realizations of exotic foreign environments and distant historical periods, as well as evocations of the supernatural, best seen in the work of the most successful Romantic dramatist, Matthew Gregory (Monk) Lewis, in the period 1797 to 1812. It became clear that stock scenery, which could be recycled over a number of plays, would no longer do. Audiences wanted to be assured of novelty and surprise. At the same time, they needed to be assured of the stage's authenticity, and this affected their reception of all aspects of staging, including the concealment of the mechanics required for stage effects, as well as costuming and lighting. The stage's transformations needed to be magical and sumptuous, or meticulously detailed, to gratify the wish for immediate recognition. This need was fuelled by the visual experiences and contacts with technology which audiences brought with them to the theatre. The use of gas for street lighting had already been demonstrated in 1807; exotic animals could be viewed at the Exeter 'Change; trade brought with it the artefacts of imperial expansion; Barker's and Burford's panoramas made authentic views of distant lands familiar and proximate, while machinery made things happen in the workplace with less obvious human intervention. Theatrical presentation could not afford to ignore these experiences.

The desire for novelty and authenticity was felt most acutely by the London theatres, although provincial theatres, increasingly affected by the need to employ London 'stars', tried unsuccessfully to keep up and had often to make do with the performance of new plays in the trappings of old scenery. Economics played a major part in this, especially as the London performers demanded large salaries. Nevertheless, the theatres in provincial centres such as Bristol, Manchester, Liverpool, Norwich and Plymouth did spend large sums of money on scenic refurbishment as an increasingly mobile audience demanded the genuine replica of a London experience.

As stage presentation became more sophisticated, the clash between the new realism and the conventions of theatre-going, inherited from the eighteenth century, became more obvious and incongruous. Complaints about inappropriate costuming had already surfaced at the end of the eighteenth century. Knowledge of what had been actually worn at various historical periods was disseminated by antiquarians and appropriated by actor-managers such as J. P. Kemble, to lend authority particularly to their productions of plays by Shakespeare. It was not, however, until 1823 that any concerted attempt was made, even by a patent theatre,

to be entirely consistent in terms of historical verisimilitude. The most significant development, after Garrick's use of directional lighting from concealed points behind the flats and of
footlights, was the introduction of gas, which allowed controlled lighting intensity and variety after 1817. But this was not universally admired and its extensive use in the auditoria made
for uncomfortably stuffy theatre-going. After 1837, with the introduction of limelight, textur-
ing of directional light became a reality to assist in providing a chiaroscuro effect for painted
backdrops, particularly when executed by a master such as Clarkson Stanfield. Special
lighting effects, however, brought the changing relationship between stage and auditorium
sharply into focus. If lighting and machinery were intended to draw the attention from the
auditorium to the stage picture, the traditional role of the theatrical experience as essentially
a social one would break down. Stage presentation emphasized the reason for the occasion,
but despite arguments which sought to reduce the importance of theatrical socializing, the
custom of a fully lit auditorium remained unchallenged throughout the period.

The convention of shutters and grooves, augmented by the 'rise and sink' method of
changing scenery, remained the norm until well into the nineteenth century, despite efforts
by managers such as Madame Vestris to create authentic interiors by the use of a box set
during the 1830s or occasional experiments with multiple settings. Numerous sets of grooves
allowed for a multiplication of scenes, and most effort was expended on elaborately painted
act drops and backcloths. On the other hand, theatres such as Astley's, Sadler's Wells and,
after 1845, the Standard could modify the stage by the use of machinery to produce an
environment for aquatic drama, or extend it into the auditorium to allow for circus events.

STAGE MACHINERY, LIGHTING AND EFFECTS

168   The installation of new machinery at Drury Lane, 1794

Unidentified clipping, February 1794 (BL, Drury Lane memoranda, c. 120. h.1)

The scenery of the new theatre, Drury-Lane, is chiefly constructed upon a principle
different from that of the other houses – there will be few scenes, which divide in
the middle – a rapid change, however, will be effected when necessary, by a part of
them rising from the stage, and a part dropping from the roof; also the furniture
of the stage will be brought on by machinery, without the aid of the livery servants
of the theatre, whose appearance at present frequently offends propriety.

The effect of real water was achieved by inserting a tank of water between rollers, which
rotated to give the effect of waves [173c].

169   The introduction of a dog and real water on stage, 1803

(a) F. Reynolds, *The life and times of Frederick Reynolds* (London: Colburn, 1827), vol. II,
pp. 350–1; (b) Laurie and Whittle engraving, published 25 January 1804. Henry
Huntington Library

(a) The introduction of real water on the stage, and of a dog to jump into it, from a
high rock, for the purpose of saving a child,[1] were both incidents, at that time, so

entirely unknown in theatrical exhibitions, that their very novelty rendered every body, during the production of the piece, most sanguine as to its success; [. . .] the water was hired from old father Thames, and the dog, of the proprietor of an *a-là-mode* beef shop.

The water we found tractable and accommodating; but during the first, and second rehearsals, *Carlo* (for such was the name of our hero), sulked [. . .] After several other successive trials he would not jump; but at last, owing to the platform on which he stood, being enclosed by two projecting scenes, and his attention being thus removed from the distractions of stage lights, boards, *et cetera*, he immediately made the desired leap, and repeated it at least a dozen times, as much to his own, as to our satisfaction. On the first representation of *The Caravan*, after his performance of this extraordinary feat, and after his triumphant *exit* with the supposed drowning child, the effect far exceeded our most sanguine expectations. [. . .]

Thanks to my friend *Carlo* [. . .] I cleared three hundred, and fifty pounds simply by a dog jumping into a small tank of water!

(b) 'The Roscius of Drury Lane', 1804

Publish'd Jany 25.1804 by LAURIE & WHITTLE, 53,Fleet Street,London.

C A R L O,
THE ROSCIUS OF DRURY-LANE THEATRE.

---

[1] John Genest's *Account of the English stage* refers to the fact that Reynolds's play *The Caravan, or The Driver and his Dog* opened on 5 December 1803 at Drury Lane and was performed 'between 30 and 40 times'.

170   Gothic spectacle on stage, 1807
General Evening Post (2 April 1807)

Mr Lewis[1] has given such a loose [*sic*] to his imagination, and introduced so many spectres of various descriptions, that a Jury of Ghosts should be impannelled to decide upon the merits of his performance [. . .] Observing how impatiently the audience endured the puerile attempts at wit in the first act, which was almost all dialogue, and how gladly they welcomed the second, where scarcely any thing but action was to be found, we could not help wishing that the dialogue were altogether omitted, and the piece performed with merely the action, the scenery, and a little explanatory recitative [. . .]

The scenery and machinery do infinite credit to the genius of Mr Johnston, the Mechanist, and called forth universal applause. The first scene, in which *Una* appears sleeping on a bank near the Castle, while the whole story of the piece is unfolded to her as in a dream, is exceedingly ingenius [*sic*] and beautiful. There is also much merit in the picturesque variety of the third scene, which exhibits a splendid Gothic Hall, with a gallery crowded with spectators, and an emblematic representation of the Four Seasons, who, as they move in a superb pageant, make offerings, peculiar to each, to the *Count*. At the close of the last scene, when the *Count* and the altar sink into the earth,[2] that opens to devour them, there was a general cry of *bravo!* which was redoubled when the piece was announced for a second representation. Indeed, while the passion for the marvellous prevails, this piece is likely to procure many crowded houses, and amply to repay the vast expense that must have attended the getting up of a spectacle of such splendour [. . .]

[1] From a review of the opening of 'Monk' Lewis's *The Wood Daemon; or, The Clock has Struck* (1 April) at Drury Lane.
[2] For the operation of the traps, see **173a**.

In 1816 Sadler's Wells was experiencing a disastrous financial season. Charles Dibdin tried every possible means to attract an audience. These included dogs as well as a 10-year-old French tightrope walker, Hyacinthe Longuemare, and a clown, Paulo, to replace the intermittently ill Grimaldi.[1]

[1] See D. Arundell, *The story of Sadler's Wells* (London: Hamish Hamilton, 1965), pp. 91–2.

171   Fireworks and acrobatics at Sadler's Wells, 1816

Henry Huntington Library

ŚADLERŚ WELLŚ.
Performances of PAULO *and the* INFANT PRODIGY. — 1816.

The Lyceum, or English Opera House, had seen a demonstration of the feasibility of using gas in 1805, and on 7 August 1817 a playbill announced that 'Gas lights will this evening be introduced over the whole stage', thereby anticipating its introduction at Drury Lane in September by a month. Covent Garden had lit its exterior and audience circulation areas in September 1815, and by 1829 most of the significant theatres in London were lit by gas.[1]

[1] See T. Rees, *Theatre lighting in the age of gas* (London: STR, 1976), pp. 9–11.

172   The use of gas for stage and auditorium lighting at Drury Lane, 1817

Examiner (7 September 1817), p. 570

DRURY-LANE THEATRE was to open last night, and Covent-Garden opens tomorrow. The improvements or alterations which the former has been making, we saw on Friday night, and can promise our Readers much satisfaction with the gas-lights, which are introduced not only in front of the stage, but at the various compartments on each side. Their effect, as they appear suddenly from the gloom, is like the striking of daylight; and indeed, it is in resemblance to day, that this beautiful light surpasses all others. It is as mild as it is splendid,– white, regular, and pervading. If the Italian Ambassador, as he entered London in the evening, took the ordinary lamps in the street for an illumination and an elegant compliment, what would he have thought had he passed through the lustre which is shed at present from so many of our shops? [. . .] The Theatre [. . .] lights are enclosed in glasses, and blinded from the audience by side-scenes and reflectors; but the result [. . .] is excellent, and a very great improvement; and if it is managed as well as we saw it on Friday, will enable the spectator to see every part of the stage with equal clearness. If the front light could be thrown, as day-light is, from above instead of below [. . .] the effect would be perfect [. . .]

The most significant document concerning early nineteenth-century staging is that contained in Rees's *Cyclopaedia*, compiled between 1803 and 1819. The lengthy article explains the use of traps, wings and grooves, flying machinery and lighting.

173   The mechanics of staging, 1803–19

A. Rees, *Cyclopaedia, or universal dictionary of arts, sciences and literature* (London: Longman, 1819), vol. XII, s.v. dramatic machinery[1]

(a) 'Apertures of the stage'

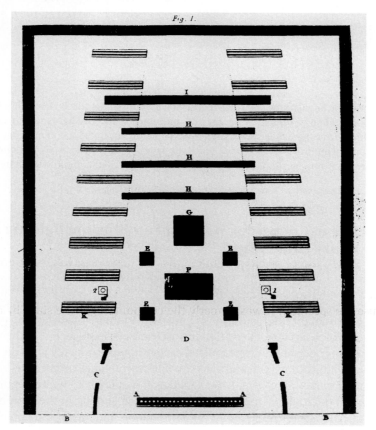

Fig. 1.

The first aperture in the stage immediately behind the orchestra, and in front of the proscenium and curtain, is that for raising and lowering the foot lights, both for the purpose of trimming the lamps, and of darkening the stage when required. It is marked by the letters A,A, fig. 1^2 [. . .] which is a horizontal plan of a stage 60 feet in length and 25 feet in breadth at the curtain line. In this plan, the lines which represent the side walls of the theatre are too much contracted, for it is necessary to give at least eight or ten feet of additional room for the performers and scene-shifters, behind each wing. The letters B,B, denote the line which forms the front of the stage behind the orchestra.

The next apertures are the side traps, of which any convenient number may be constructed. Four of these are exhibited in the plan, and are distinguished by the letters E,E,E,E. In the middle are two larger traps. The first, at F, is of an oblong form from six to seven feet in length, and from three to four feet in breadth. It is most frequently used for the grave scene in Shakspeare's tragedy of Hamlet.

The trap marked by the letter G is generally square, and is chiefly used for the sinking of the cauldron in the tragedy of Macbeth. Behind these, in larger theatres, where many changes of the scenery are frequently required, there are a number of longitudinal apertures across the stage, which are covered by planks movable upon hinges, so that by throwing them back, the stage may be opened in a moment. The use of these is to allow the flat scenes to sink through the stage when required. Three of these will be found in the plan, at the letters H,H,H, and are known by the name of *flaps*.

In the late Theatre Royal of Covent Garden,[3] much of the scenery, not in immediate use, was kept in a cellar under the stage. For the purpose of raising and lowering these scenes with facility, other apertures were made, and closed with square or rectangular pieces of wood, and could be placed or displaced in a few minutes: these were called sliders, and a plan of one is given at the letter I [. . .]

'Disposition of the Stage Lights'
There is, perhaps, no department of a theatre where so much pains ought to be taken, as in the disposition of the lights, for upon this, in a very great degree, depends the effect of the scenery, however nicely the perspective may have been executed by the painter, and every optical illusion calculated to astonish or amuse the spectator. It was formerly the custom to light the stage by a large chandelier, or frame of lamps, suspended in the middle of the proscenium, and elevated or depressed at pleasure. This still prevails in many parts of the continent, and even in Britain, is very generally used to illuminate the ring, or area of those theatres, where feats of horsemanship, and other athletic exercises, are exhibited.

It seems obvious, that the suspension of a chandelier directly in front of the spectator, must materially deteriorate the effect of an exhibition, which can only be considered as excellent in the degree in which it is a faithful copy of nature. When suspended over the proscenium of a large theatre, it must also greatly impede the vision of all spectators seated in the upper parts of the house. These inconveniences induced the late Mr Garrick, when patentee of the old Theatre Royal of Drury-lane, to remove the chandelier and substitute the frame of lamps now distinguished by the appellation of *foot lights*, and this improvement has been adopted in all other regular theatres in the British islands.

But although the adoption of foot lights removes the objections to the chandelier, they are still very far from producing the disposition of light and shade, which would be very desireable [*sic*] to increase the effect both of the scenery and of the countenances of the performers. The glare of light in the front, and parallel to the stage, besides the smoke which the lamps, however clean and nicely trimmed, always produce, inverts every shadow, and throws the shade upwards instead of downwards upon the performer's face. The most experienced professional men assign this as the reason, that the face of a performer must be so highly coloured to produce an effect in the front of the house, as to appear absolutely ridiculous to a stranger unconversant with the business [. . .]

To give a sufficient light to the stage side lights are used, as well as foot lights: these are generally placed between the wings, to turn upon a hinge, for the purpose of darkening the stage when necessary. A plan of these, which is very simple, will be found in fig. 1. The apparatus consists merely of an upright post, to which is attached a piece of tinned iron, forming two sides of a square, and movable upon joints or hinges, and furnished with shelves to receive the lamps or candles. That which gives light to the stage is represented by 1, and the position in which the side lights are placed, when the stage is partially darkened, by 2. Side lights are placed between every set of wings, on both sides of the stage.

Beside the foot and side lights, which are permanent, a number of occasional lights are disposed at times on different parts of the stage, to give effect to transparencies, and for other causes, of which, as they must be varied according to circumstances, no particular account can be given [. . .]

'Disposition of the Scenery'
The scenery of a theatre consists of the flat scenes which form the termination of the perspective across the stage, and the side scenes, or wings, which are disposed upon each side of the stage so as to be shifted as often as may be necessary, and to afford opportunities for the actors to come upon the stage, or quit it, at any of the intervals between the respective sets. Besides these, there are scenes which may be occasionally placed or displaced, such as the fronts of cottages, cascades, rocks, bridges, and other appendages, requisite in the representation of particular dramas. These are generally called pieces.

The flat scenes are of three kinds: the first of these are drops, or curtains, where the canvas is furled, or unfurled upon a roller, placed either at the top or bottom of the scene [. . .] The rollers, in either case, are made to revolve by means of cords tightened or slackened as may be necessary; and when the scenes are large it is usual to wind them up by means of a cylinder and a winch, as in the trap machinery.

Although the drop scenes are the most simple, it is necessary sometimes to have recourse to those scenes which are called flats. In these the canvas is stretched upon wooden frames, which are generally constructed in two pieces, so as to meet in the middle of the stage, the junction being in a perpendicular direction. The side frames are moved in grooves, composed of parallel pieces of wood fixed upon the stage, and so constructed that they may be removed with facility from one place to another. The upper part of the framing is also confined by a groove, to retain the perpendicular position of the flat scene. These are sometimes constructed, to save room, upon joints, by which they may either be lowered to the horizontal position, or drawn up to the side walls. In this respect their construction is pretty similar to that of a common draw-bridge. This plan was used in the late Theatre Royal, Covent Garden, where they were called flys [sic]. The principal use of the flats is where apertures, such as doors, windows, chimney pieces, etc. are wanted in the scene, which may be opened and shut as required; these are called [. . .] *practicable doors*, etc., because, when not to be used, they may be painted upon a drop scene. A third kind of scene is the profiled or open *flat*. This is used for woods, gateways of castles, and such purposes: it is framed exactly like the other, and the only difference consists in parts of the scene being left open to shew another behind, which terminates the view.

A very important part of the scenery of a theatre is the wings. These also are stretched upon wooden frames, and slide in grooves fixed to the stage. In some large theatres they are moved by machinery, in others by manual labour. The disposition of the grooves will be seen at the letters K,K, in fig. 1. In this figure are nine sets of wings, the front only of which are marked by the reference letter. The wings, like the flats, whether moved by the hand or by the aid of machinery, usually stand upon the stage.

(b) Wings and frames

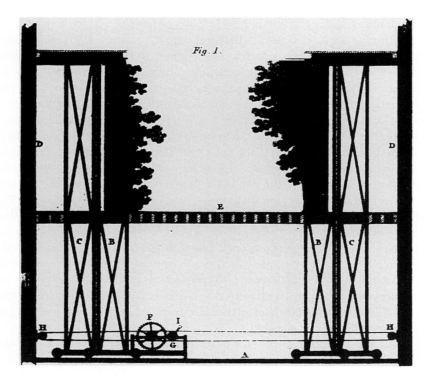

Fig. 1.

[This] [...] is a transverse elevated section of the stage cellar, and stage of a theatre, where the wings are moved by a cylinder, or barrel under the stage, as was done at Covent Garden. D,D, are the side walls of a house; at A is a strong horizontal beam of wood, such as builders generally call *sleepers*, laid upon the floor of the cellar under the stage. Of these there must be a sufficient number to serve as railways for the frames of all the wings to run upon: four of these frames are represented and distinguished by the letters BB, CC. The frames B,B, are in front of those marked C,C. Each frame runs upon two small wheels, to diminish the friction, and all passing through longitudinal apertures in the stage, which serve as guides, rise to a sufficient height above the stage to support the wings which are attached to them in front, so as to be quickly removed, and others substituted. The line of the stage is represented at E. Two frames at each side of the stage only are used for each set of wings. At F is a long cylinder, or barrel of wood, revolving upon iron axles, and extending from the front to nearly the back of the stage, so as to move all the wings at once. It will appear, by inspecting the plate, that the cords, or endless lines, passing from each frame round the barrel F, and over the directing pulley H, back to the same frame, are so disposed that when the upper part of the barrel is moved towards the right, the front frames B,B, will move forward upon the stage, and the back frames C,C, will be withdrawn. In this state they are represented in the figure. When the motion of the barrel is reversed, that of the frames will also be inverted; the back frames will advance, and the front ones will recede. When a change of scenery is requisite, the wings are taken off the frames which are out of the view of the spectators, and those fixed on which are to be next displayed. Upon the barrel F, is a wheel, moved by a pinion G, by means of the handle I, to give motion to the barrel, and increase the power. A horizontal fly wheel, like that of a jack, was also added, but in so short a motion it is not probable that it could be of great advantage [. . .]

(c) Sea machinery

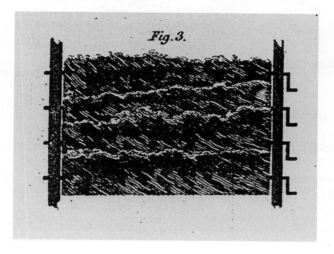

[This] [. . .] represents the common method of executing a sea scene. A certain number of horizontal axes being placed across the stage, with cross boards properly painted and cut or profiled, when turned upon their respective centres, produce the appearance of water, which may be represented either as tranquil or stormy as the occasion requires.

(d) The operation of a boat

To give the appearance of ships or boats, a very simple apparatus will suffice [. . .]

A frame of wood, moving upon friction wheels, is represented by the letters A,A, upon this the boat is placed upon an axis at B. From the aftermost part of the boat, a cord, passing over the pulley C, is conducted behind the scenes. The bow or fore part of the boat being made heavier than the after-part or stern, the cord, by being lightened or slackened alternately, will move the boat upon the axle B, and give it a motion very similar to that produced by the natural undulation of the waves. If the friction wheels are covered with cloth [. . .] and the axles smoothly turned and well oiled, the noise from friction will be avoided, which often destroys the illusion when boards without wheels are pushed across the stage. The frame A is drawn across the axles in [fig. 5], and all that is under the surface of the water (represented at D,) is concealed by a painted board. Two stops may be placed upon the carriage to regulate the vibration of the boat, as represented in the figure.

(e) The mechanics of flying

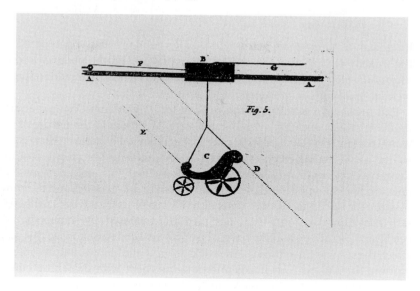

[This] [. . .] is a plan of a machine to produce the oblique ascent or descent of a car, horse, or any other body, above the stage. Upon a cross bar of wood A,A, passing between the platforms, and sufficiently high to be concealed from the spectators, is a box or frame B, moving upon rollers. A cord F, attached to this frame, is wound upon a barrel upon the platform. Another cord G, attached to any fixture upon the opposite side, and passing over a pulley in the box B, suspends the car C. When the cord F, is wound upon the barrel, the car will ascend in the direction of the dotted line D, and when unwound will descend in the same line by its own gravity. The cord E, will keep the car or other body steady [. . .] The cords are very slender and painted black, to elude the eye of the spectator. The lights are also strong in front and dim behind, to assist the optical deception [. . .]

[1] The significance of this document was first explored in R. Southern's *Changeable scenery* (London: Faber, 1952), which reproduces it in part, pp. 219–24, 272 ff. Southern also refers extensively to the stage machinery incorporated in Foulston's Theatre Royal, Plymouth, built in 1811–12, which is described and illustrated in J. Foulston, *The public buildings erected in the West of England* (London: Williams, 1838). See also Harvey Crane, *Playbill: a history of theatre in the West Country* (Plymouth: MacDonald and Evans, 1980), pp. 71–5.
[2] The diagrams were engraved by William Lowery.
[3] This refers to the Covent Garden theatre that was destroyed in 1808.

174   Special effects for *King Lear*, 1820

J. Cowell, *Thirty years passed among the players in England and America* (New York: Harper, 1845), p. 143

King Lear, as threatened, was produced after loud proclaim of preparation,[1] and the tragedy published as revised by the manager, and the poor '*nice-fruit-and-a-book-of-the-play*' women were obliged, on pain of dismissal, to add to their *ancient melody*, '*as adapted to the stage by R. W. Elliston, Esquire!*'

Full measure was taken of the taste of the Surrey and Olympic audience, in rendering the beautiful play as much like a melodrama as the nature of its action would permit. I wish I had a bill to refer to; but I remember great credit *was advertised* as due to the management in correcting the hitherto inaccurate costume, and Kean was clad in a *crimson velvet gown*, bedizened with gold buttons and loops down to his feet! and Russell, as Oswald, in white *silk stockings* and the same dress he wore for Roderigo! But the chief dependence of success was placed on a bran-new [*sic*] hurricane on shore, 'designed and invented' by somebody, 'after the celebrated picture by Loutherburg, of a *Storm on Land*'; but, to give this additional effect, the sea was introduced in the back-ground, the billows, painted after nature, 'curling their monstrous heads and hanging them with deafening clamours' – trees were made to see-saw back and forth, accompanied with the natural creak! creak! attending the operation; Winston had hunted up, *without any expense to the management*, every infernal machine that was ever able to spit fire, spout rain, or make thunder, and together were brought into full play behind the entrances. Over head were revolving prismatic coloured transparencies, to emit a continual-changing supernatural tint, and add to the unearthly character of the scene. King Lear would one instant appear a beautiful pea-green, and the next sky-blue, and, in the event of a momentary cessation of the rotary motion of the magic lantern, his head would be purple and his legs Dutch-pink. The common fault of all mankind is vaulting ambition, and, in the true spirit of that feeling, every carpenter, who was intrusted to shake a sheet of thunder, or in turn a rain-box, was determined that his element should be the most conspicuous of the party, and, together, they raised a hurly-burly [. . .] and not a word was heard through the whole of the scene. Kean requested that it might 'be let off easy' the next night. 'I don't care how many flashes of lightning you give me,' said he, 'but, for Heaven's sake, Winston, expel your wind and cut out your thunder.'

[1] The play opened in Nahum Tate's version on 24 April 1820 at Drury Lane. Elliston was to restore the original ending in 1823 – 'In obedience to the suggestions of men of literary eminence', – John Genest, *Some account of the English stage from the Restoration in 1660 to 1830* (Bath: Carrington, 1832) vol. IX, 10 February 1823, DL.

Critical self-consciousness about discrepancies between the social nature of theatre-going and the ostensible dramatic purpose of the theatrical event began early. This document is an early manifestation of the complaint that an overly lit auditorium detracted from the focus of attention on the stage. In addition, the letter contrasts the conventions of stage lighting with the desire to witness a realistic performance.

175   Deficiencies in lighting both the stage and the auditorium, 1825

'An Enemy of the Footlamps', *Monthly Magazine* (1 July 1825), p. 510

Notwithstanding the splendid improvements that have been made, of late years, in the embellishment of our theatres, everything has not yet been accomplished which a refined taste for the *luxuries* of theatrical entertainment might conceive and desire [. . .] The mode, for example, of lighting up the audience part of the house, and the front of the stage, is liable to sufficient objections. If the audience, indeed, are to be regarded as the spectacle, and the actors as the spectators, all is as it should be; for, certainly, the prospect from the stage, when the boxes are well filled with beauty and fashion, and the pit tolerably genteel, is splendid in the extreme [. . .] But all this light – this galaxy of wax and gas, to the vision of a part of the spectators at least, is rather an obstruction than an accommodation: a distraction to all.

'Dark through excess of bright *the stage* appears': and the effect upon the scene is often so preternatural, as to give no small offence to the picturesque eye [. . .]

Lighting the whole house from one central point above, if it can be fully effected, must, undoubtedly, be a very great improvement – especially if that light can be thrown on the front of the stage, with such vividness as to remove the necessity of those preternatural abominations, the footlights; which, especially when an actor or actress comes very forward upon the audience [. . .] exhibits the features, by means of the inverted shadows, in most ridiculous, and sometimes even frightful caricature. I could mention one actress, in particular [. . .] who looks, upon such occasions, as if, instead of a nose and eye-brows (to say nothing of the ascending shadows from the cheek-bones), she had three conical patches of court sticking-plaster stuck at triangles upon her face [. . .] Nor is the scenery, in some cases, without its share in the incongruous phenomena of up-ascending beams, whence walls and turrets shed their inverted shadows on the sky [. . .]

176   A plea for realistic lighting, 1847

Builder (12 June 1847), p. 281

I have often been struck with the classical or picturesque expression thrown over the features of even a very plain and inelegant countenance by the elevation of the artificial light, when alone reflected on it, from a point *exclusively above its level* [. . .] Of course, I do not mean that the light be elevated directly above the head, but immediately in front of it, at an angle, probably of forty-five degrees, *so that the expression of no feature be lost.*

Then, again, I had also often admired the purity and serenity, as well as brilliancy of effect produced on colours and on scenery under the like circumstances [. . .] in the windows of jewellers, drapers, etc.; and,– so far as regards perspective or scenery,– in picture galleries, where, I need scarcely add, the light in general is also made to descend exclusively from above [. . .]

STAGE SETTINGS

177   Scenic artist at work, 1790[1]

Michaelangelo Rooker aquatint. British Museum

---

[1] Also reproduced in Iain Mackintosh and Geoffrey Ashton, *The Georgian playhouse* (London: Arts Council, 1975), no. 293. Mackintosh and Ashton point out the significance of this illustration as the only representation of an English paint frame or scene room until 1874.

Sadler's Wells was able to use its access to the New River to create a water tank which effectively covered the entire stage. Charles Dibdin launched the 'aquatic theatre' on 2 April 1804. He tore up the stage of the theatre and built in a tank of water 90 feet long by 24 feet wide at its widest, narrowing to 10 feet, and 3 feet in depth. A further tank was built into the roof of the theatre to facilitate real waterfalls. Water was pumped up from the river, following an arrangement with the New River Company to provide mains supply at a cost of £30 per annum.

178   Sadler's Wells introduces an 'Aquatic Theatre', 1804

George Speaight (ed.), *Memoirs of Charles Dibdin the Younger* (London: STR, 1956), pp. 59–61

Having fixed upon exhibiting the *Siege of Gibraltar*, we procured from the dockyards at Woolwich, several Shipwrights and Riggers; and immediately set them at work to construct a large number of ships [. . .] upon a scale of one inch to a foot of those in the Navy; in exact imitation of which they were made, even to the slightest minutiae; they had their regular tiers and number of brass Cannon, cast on purpose for them, which were regularly fired, recharged, etc. in action. The same precision was observed in regard to their rigging [. . .]

Mr Andrews painted a very beautiful Drop Scene, that completely filled up all the Area of the proscenium (which by mechanism was enlarged in width 7 or 8 feet), representing the English grand fleet drawn up in battle line, against the combined fleets of France and Spain; which was let down to gratify the audience, while the preparations were making behind it, to set the Scene [. . .]

I engaged, for the express purpose of *performing in the water, swimming,* etc., a number of Boys and young Men [. . .]

[. . .] such was the impression which [*The Siege of Gibraltar*] made, that the feelings of the audience entered with such a lively interest into the gallant benevolence of the british [*sic*] Tars, rescuing their enemies from a watery grave, they never for an instant saw the glaring abandonment of perspective, proportion and scenic propriety, exhibited by Man of War's Boats, bigger than the largest ship of the line, and sailors compared with the 5 or 6 inch high mariners aboard the vessels, still more out of proportion. It is to be observed, however, that the Boats were contrived so to fill all the front of the water, and screen the ships – the topmasts excepted – from distant observation; also, that the ships were purposely enveloped in smoke, during the action of this feature of the scene; and therefore, owing to which, they appeared the only feature upon the scene [. . .] and – having saved the sailors – they disappeared as rapidly as they first came on [. . .]

Though Buckstone is often credited with introducing a multiple set to the English stage, this had been anticipated as early as 1809 in a performance of 'Monk' Lewis's *Venoni; or, the Novice of St Mark's*, which opened at Drury Lane on 2 December. The reactions to this experiment demonstrate the clash between the older conventions of direct audience address and a new attempt to suggest a 'fourth wall'.

179   An experiment with multiple staging, 1809

General Evening Post (3 December 1809)

The Drama seems to have been taken from a French Piece, called *Les Victimes Cloîtrées*, which was acted with great effect in Paris a few years ago, but its fate in the English Metropolis has not been so happy; for though the plot is simple, the incidents natural, and some of the situations interesting, yet from certain mechanical causes, the conclusion of the third act was interrupted with many marks of disapprobation.– It will hardly be understood, unless we explain it, how the dungeons both of the convent and monastery can be seen at the same time [. . .] The side next the audience of both these dungeons is represented to be removed, so that the audience see at the same time what *Josepha* is about in the convent dungeon, and what *Venoni* is doing in that of the monastery. But the worst of it is, that these dungeons do not come quite to the front of the stage, and are raised on platforms, so that they look like two dens for wild beasts, an appearance to which certain spikes, placed to prevent their contents from leaping on the stage, very much contribute. When Mr Elliston and Mrs H. Siddons appeared in these dens, without seeing each other, and soliloquized alternately [. . .] the scenery reminded us of 'that useful toy', a weather-house, in which now the woman pops out, and now the man. The ridiculousness of this, and of Mr Elliston's breaking away the stones of the wall that parted his dungeon from Mrs H. Siddons's, when the audience saw he might have overleaped the spikes in front of his dungeon, and entered hers in a moment, brought on a volley of disapprobation; in the midst of which, and some applauses [*sic*], the curtain dropped [. . .]

180   From presentational to representational staging

H. Foote, *Companion to the theatres* (London: Marsh & Miller, 1829), pp. 122–3

The mode of indicating locality in a scene, formerly, was by introducing such properties as were consistent with it. Thus, a table and a chair conveyed the idea of a chamber; a walking-staff of a street; and a balcony, or raised platform, at the upper end of the stage (which was a fixture) served for battlements, or any other elevated position.

It would seem that some machinists imagine themselves almost omnipotent; for Johnston, the machinist at Drury Lane, in 1798 (when *Blue Beard* was produced), on being asked whether he had better go to Pidcock's, at Exeter 'Change, and hire an elephant – replied, 'Not I; if I cannot make a better elephant than that at Exeter 'Change, I deserve to be hang'd.' His pasteboard horses in the same piece were admirably made.

The following inventory of scenery reflects the Olympic repertoire of pantomime – *The House that Jack Built*, Moncrieff's *Bamfyde Moore Carew; or, Harlequin King of the Beggars*, Elliston's burlesque of Pocock's *The Maid and the Magpie*, called *Another Maid and Another Magpie*, and

Moncrieff's *Giovanni in London*. The list also suggests that Elliston may have removed pieces of scenery used in Thomas Dibdin's *America; or, the Colonists* and Lawler's *Robinson Crusoe*, which he had mounted while manager of the Surrey.

181   A list of scenery at the Olympic Theatre, March 1817

BL, Olympic Theatre Cuttings 47–48[1]

Flats
 1–Landscape backed with an Indian place of festival
 2–American Wood with additional half flat OP of Cottage with door in it
 3–Cut Wood
 4–Sea View with Lighthouse
 5–Church and Village for Magpie door PS
 6–Norwood the Horns (?) change to shops
 7–Pantaloons Villa new sc. Leap door and sliding windows in OP
 8–Justice Dedimuss's House door in centre. Window in PS
 9–Outside Barn and Theatre door PS
 10–Jacks House
 11–Bath with Gothic Exterior
 12–Bath
 13–Booksellers Shop folding doors in centre
 14–India House, back. Gothic with Altar
 15–Albion bridge Street, Prison at Back
 16–Merlins Cave backd with prison
 17–Apothecaries and Fishmongers Shops
 18–Dairy and Butchers shop
 19–Garden
 20–Dance Garden
 21–Gothic
 22–Gothic
 23–Gothic arches (cut)
 24–Best Chamber folding doors in the centre and two other doors. Back-a Barn (inside)
 25–Managers Room–door and window OP. Leap in PS
 26–New Chamber was Cabin
 27–Inside Magpie Cottage–Door and Window in PS and centrepiece with door for Man and Monkey
 28–Inside Cottage–door OP. Back–Snow Scene
 29–A Dial-hand to move
 30–Inside Crusoe's Hut–Back–Grotto
 31–My Uncle's House–eight pieces
 32–Poultry Compton–open arches in centre Cloths
 1–Frontispiece
 2–New Interior

3–Library
4–Horizon
Three Arch Borders
Four Sky Borders
Wings

1 Pair	Old Frontispiece
1 do	New Frontispiece
2 do	Chamber to match frontispiece
2 do	Common Chamber (1 Magpie, 1 Managers House)
5 do	Gothic
4 Pair	Woods
3 do	Street
3 do	Garden
3 do	Rocks
2 do	Dance Garden (Bamf Moore Carew)
3 do	Pantomime last scene

1 Crane Wing PS
1 Mill Wing OP
1 Odd Chamber Wing OP
Fishermans Hut PS
Magpie Cottage OP
? Arrow house PS
Cottage for centre
Grocers Shop
Prison door PS
Lodging House half flat to match Bath flats
Setting pieces
Blackfriars bridge
London Bridge
Blackfriars Bridge with London on fire. Transparent. A side piece of the entrance
    to the Bridge
Country Bridge and Town
Rustic bridge (cut) and Water
Cut last scene of Pant. 3 pieces hinged together; 1 piece for centre
Norwood heath 1 row 2 pieces
Dedimuss House 1 row 2 pieces
Algiers 2 pieces
Garden door and set hedge 2 pieces
open white railings for do with Gate
Set Village 2 rows 4 pieces
Set Garden for Hourglass, 3 rows, 5 pieces
        front row Balustrade
        Secd row Garden
        third row Gents House

Set Garden for Bamf Moore C 3 rows 6 pieces
2 Bowers and backs OP and PS 4 pieces
Garden piece 7 by 7
Still Water 3 row rough at the back
Ground and Water
Castle piece abt 6 by 8
  do whole width of stage ab 10 ft high
  do 2 pieces
  do with aperture for Dog
  do with Tower flags etc. Robinson Crusoes outside of hut 3 pieces hinged
Foreign landscape and hills 11 feet high hinged together
2 Foreign huts with transp back
Cave foreign OP
Cave 11 ft high
Snow piece PS
Rock 11 by 11 PS
Rock 11 by 14 PS
do
Cross
Library Counter
2 pictures in frames painted
2 staircase pieces
Elephant
Windmill complete
Sea pieces various
Sphinx Head and Pedestal
Horse Don Juan
Hyde Park lamp post
Wood Demon figure
set ground piece OP
2 upright bushes
5 pieces for Horses head
a change piece (ship)
Lord Mayor's coach body
One piece open arch Lodoiska
one change piece 6ft high
Ship hull lying in water
4 Black backs

---

[1] Compare the inventories of scenery during the eighteenth century, especially David Thomas and Arnold Hare, *Restoration and Georgian England, 1660–1788* (Cambridge: Cambridge University Press, 1989), nos. 272, 273. For Elliston's management of the Olympic at this time, see Christopher Murray, *Robert William Elliston, manager* (London: STR, 1975), pp. 53–60.

182   The deficiencies of spectacular staging, 1827

James Boaden, *Memoirs of Mrs Siddons* (London: Gibbings, 1893), p. 403

But neither tragedy nor comedy ever seemed with me to derive a benefit propor-
tioned to the pains that have been taken in the scenic department of our stages.
When the scenes are first drawn on, or the roller descends, the work exhibited is
considered a few moments as a work of art; the persons who move before it then
engross the attention; at their exit it is raised or drawn off and is speedily forgotten,
or seen with indifference the second time. If the perspective as to the actor standing
in front of the scene was so accurate that the whole effect should be delusive, and
the impression be of actual sky and land and building (though an objection will
always remain to the abrupt junction of the borders with the tops of the scenes, the
wings, and the scoring line where the flats meet each other, the grooves in which
they move, the boarded stage, and other difficulties hitherto insurmountable), I
could understand the object of those who expend so much money on their elaboration; but I confess I am of opinion that they should never do more than suggest to
the imagination; and that it would not be desirable that the spectator should lose
his senses to the point of forgetting that he is in a regular theatre, and enjoying a
work of art invented for his amusement and his instruction by a poet, and acted by
another artist of corresponding talent called a player.

Whilst the requirements of realism may have been compromised by staging deficiencies,
audiences still demanded to see the realization of authentic stage pictures. Detailed stage
directions suggest this desire for pictorial accuracy, which may be compared to that of
contemporary narrative genre paintings.

183   The demands of realistic staging, 1829

W. T. Moncrieff, *The pestilence of Marseilles*, in *Cumberland's Minor Theatre*, vol. XI (London:
Cumberland, 1836), p. 28

The theatre[1] represents the interior, or grand parade of the town of Marseilles – a
large cathedral on the right with flight of steps, covered with inhabitants plague
struck – on the left the house of Monval – a bench near the door – all the windows
are closed – behind this, at the back, a large magazine or warehouse which has
been converted into a hospital – a black flag marks the various houses the plague
has visited – in the distance the sea, with the Fort of Saint John, and a cordon of
boats, with their cannons pointed towards the town – It is night – during the whole
of this act, the scene only being lighted with the dim croissets which hang at the
different corners of the streets, and the uncertain glimmering of the moon, which
has a dull blood tint.– At the rising of the curtain, the death carts conducted by
the city officers bearing torches, cross the stage – they are filled with the dead –
litters on which are inhabitants in various stages of the disorder, are also borne
past in different directions.– The heavy melancholy gloom, which is cast over the
whole, announces the agony of the population.– An old man, who seems a very

walking spectre, enveloped in a sort of winding sheet, and bearing a small casket under his arm, totters slowly across the stage, and at length sinks on the steps of the cathedral.– A mother bearing her infant in her arms, struck by the contagion, seeks to cross the square, but sinks at the foot of one of the boundary stones.– A young female, who is sitting on the bench at Monval's house, tries in vain to summon strength sufficient to regain her habitation – she makes an effort – rises – staggers a few paces, and falls.– An unfortunate wife who has been vainly seeking to soothe and succour her husband, who is lying on the ground and near expiring, stops an inhabitant, who passes, and implores his assistance – he flies in terror, and the wife sinks in despair on the body of her husband – faithful even to death – (death knell tolls solemnly at intervals) tableau of desolation.

[1] The stage directions for the beginning of Act 2. The play, based on a Pixérécourt original, *La Peste de Marseille*, opened at the Surrey on 20 October 1829.

Madame Vestris's management of the Olympic Theatre (1831–9) was noted not only for her managerial innovations but also for her insistence upon staging accuracy. These are best seen in her approach to interior settings and the use of authentic properties and costumes. There is much debate about the precise date when the box-set was introduced. Vestris is certainly credited with this innovation, which challenged the traditional wings and grooves, although ceiling cloths had been in use since 1829.[1]

[1] See J. H. McDowell, 'Historical development of the box set', *Theatre Annual* (1945), pp. 65–83; O. K. Larsen, 'A commentary on the "historical development of the box set"', *Theatre Annual* (1946), pp. 28–36; and J. H. Butler, 'Early nineteenth-century stage settings in the British theatre', *Theatre Survey*, 6 (1965), pp. 54–64.

184   Madame Vestris's theatrical innovations

(a) *Examiner* (24 February 1833), pp. 117–18; (b) 'An Old Stager' [Matthew Mackintosh], *Stage reminiscences* (Glasgow: Hedderwick, 1866), pp. 80–3[1]

(a) A box set in 1833

The little piece[2] [. . .] is evidently a translation from the French [. . .] We like the manner in which the stage is arranged; its more perfect enclosure gives the appearance of a private chamber, infinitely better than the old contrivance of wings.

(b) Authentic period recreations, 1835

Next morning, the scene-painter, machinist, costumier, and property-man of the Theatre were despatched to Hampton Court to take notes of everything necessary from the original paintings, deposited in the picture-gallery there [. . .] With the material thus obtained we set to work, and in a wonderfully short time the piece was ready for production [. . .] The first scene was the Mall, in St James's Park, beautifully reproduced from a print of the period of the play. The effect of this scene was much heightened by our making use of a passage, fully one hundred feet in length, which led from the back of the stage to Craven buildings, and by means of which the Mall was represented going away into perspective, with wonderful appearance of reality. On wires hung between the trees were suspended numerous cages with various kinds of singing birds – whose St Giles's owners managed to make them sing, too, to perfection. On the rising of the curtain this scene used to call forth the most enthusiastic applause, and the demonstration certainly did not diminish when Mr Hooper, looking the Merry Monarch to the life, came on, followed by his attendants, all in gorgeous and scrupulously correct costumes of the reign of Charles II. True to the life, the King was accompanied, moreover, by a number of genuine King Charles' spaniels. There were twelve in all of these little brutes and one couple of them alone [. . .] cost no less a sum than *seventy pounds sterling*! [. . .] Further in the animal department, were a magnificent pair of buck-hounds, specially procured from the Royal kennel at Windsor, led on by Madame herself in the character of the King's favourite page [. . .] Everything, in short, that taste and art could suggest and accomplish was done to make the scene as life-like as possible, and the result was certainly a great success. The second scene showed the fruit of our labours at Hampton Court. It was a correct model of the room in the Palace there, called the 'King Charles' Beauty Room', the back of it representing the wall, with the eight life-size pictures by Lely, each in its massive frame. The sides were hung with beautiful tapestry, which, though now used for the purposes of stage illusion merely, was the *bona fide* article, the real handiwork of ladies at King Charles the Second's Court [. . .] The ceiling of the scene was a painted representation of the twelve signs of the zodiac, and from the centre there hung a massive old crystal chandelier, with no less than fifty wax tapers burning in it. For the miscellaneous furniture and properties, we had searched the chief curiosity shops in London, until the smallest item required was procured in keeping with all the rest [. . .]

[1] Mackintosh, a carpenter in the Vestris management of the Olympic, describes the attention to detail in mounting a production of Planché's extravaganza *The Court Beauties* (12 March 1835). Vestris used her influence with Lord Adolphus Fitzclarence to allow copying of the material at Hampton Court.

[2] A review of J. R. Planché's *Promotion, or, A Morning at Versailles in 1750*, which opened at the Olympic Theatre on 18 February 1833. The review suggests that this is a very recent innovation, if not the first instance of a different form of staging.

Clarkson Stanfield (1793–1867) was particularly noted for his marine pictures and had worked as a theatrical painter from 1816. Though he was much admired for his panoramas, the theatrical use of these appears to date from the Covent Garden pantomime of 1821, *Friar Bacon and his Brazen Head*.

185   The first use of a theatrical panorama, 1821

'Theatrical journal', *European Magazine* (January 1821), p. 68; The review describes the events of the pantomime and the pursuit of the lovers on board 'a Dublin packet'

The conception of this scene was novel, both in design and execution. While the vessel proceeds, the scene rolls in the contrary direction; twilight darkens, and still the packet sweeps along, and still remote vessels pass her; the *steam-boat* is seen smoking on its way; the moon rises, throws its rays upon the water, and with it midnight is gone; the sky brightens, and morning shews the mountains round the bay of Dublin. The representation is accurate in outline of those picturesque hills, and this whole scene received great applause [. . .]

186   Clarkson Stanfield's panorama in *Henry V*, 1839

Times (11 June 1839), p. 5

The most novel and ingenious idea is the accompanying of the chorus by a succession of painted illustrations by Stanfield.[1] At first the curtain is removed, and discovers another curtain appropriate to the place, adorned with the arms of England and France, and with a border formed of the escutcheons of the principal characters of the piece. When this is withdrawn, Time is discovered upon a circular orifice occupied by clouds, which dissolve away, and present an allegorical scene representing 'the warlike Harry', with famine, sword, and fire at his heels, 'leashed in like hounds'. The scene vanishing, the play begins. The picture that in the same way preceded the second act exhibited Cambridge, Scroop [. . .] receiving bribes from France. The third act was ushered in by a moving diorama, by far the most splendid piece of scenery presented on the occasion. The English fleet is seen leaving Southampton, its course is traced across the sea, and the audience are gradually brought to the siege of Harfleur. By an ingenious arrangement the business of the act begins before the diorama has quite passed, and the picture, as it were, melts away into the actual siege by the characters [. . .] Another moving diorama, representing the French and English camps prior to the battle of Agincourt, introduced the fourth act, and another, of the King's triumphal entrance into London, brought in the fifth. Here, and indeed the whole of the scenery, was beautifully painted; but the siege of Harfleur was the grand point. The battle of Agincourt produced no effect; a little smoke was made to obscure the stage, and by a pantomime-trick process, the troops painted, as if in the distance, were converted into the same troops engaging. The fault was that the transformation took place immediately, before the audience.

[1] Despite general reservations about the equation of spectacle with the elevation of popular taste, the review praises the use of spectacular elements. The *Times* had already noticed Stanfield's panoramas in 1828, when he had been praised for his elaborate panorama in the Drury Lane pantomime *The Queen Bee; or, Harlequin and the Fairy Hive* (27 Dec. 1828). See also W. M. Merchant, *Shakespeare and the artist* (Oxford: Oxford University Press, 1959), p. 99.

187   Scenery and its painting, 1839

Penny Cyclopaedia (London: Charles Knight, 1841), vol. XXI, p. 19

Beginning with what is technically the *drop-scene*, as being the simplest of all, we have merely to remark that it is no more than a picture or single painted surface let down by way of blind or curtain between the acts, so as to close up the opening of the proscenium. As it generally continues to be used for an indefinite time – the one at Covent Garden has been there ever since the theatre was rebuilt (1809) – the drop is more carefully executed than back scenes, which, showy as they may be in effect, are required only for a season, and are at much greater distance from the spectators. As far too as pictorial effect and truth of perspective are concerned, a drop shows itself to far greater advantage than other scenery, which is composed of different pieces constituting what is called a set of scenes. These consist of the narrow upright pieces called *side-scenes or wings*, of the narrow horizontal ones (*hanging scenes or soffits*, painted to imitate a sky or ceiling, but chiefly intended to screen the space over the stage), and of the *back scene*. Backs again are of two kinds, viz. *rolling* scenes, which are let down from above, and *flats*, which are formed of two sliding scenes strained upon framing, like the wings, and meeting each other and uniting in the centre. These are employed when what are termed *practicable* scenes are required, that is, with doors, windows, etc., which admit of being used as real doors, etc.; or else when there is occasion that the 'flat' should suddenly open and discover another scene behind it. In addition to these, there are what are termed *open* flats, which are scenes cut out in places so that both the background is seen and the actors can pass through them. They are commonly used for the representation of groves or forests, but sometimes for interiors with open arches. There are besides what are technically known as *pieces*, narrow scenes placed obliquely on one side of the stage when it is wanted to show a cottage or corner of a house, with a *practicable* door in it. Lastly, there is *set scenery*, as it is termed, a species of stage decoration very recently introduced, where, instead of the usual wings ranged one behind the other, there is a single scene on each side extending from front to back, so that the stage is completely enclosed. By this means a more perfect representation of a room can be obtained than where wings are employed.

In fact, side-scenes or wings can be regarded as little better than so many de-tached screens absolutely necessary to shut out from view the space on each side of the stage, since in themselves they rather detract from than at all aid illusion and effect; more especially in interiors, where what should represent a continu-ous wall or surface on either side is broken into several pieces, which are besides placed parallel to the back scene or flat, instead of being at right angles to it. If the scenery be viewed exactly from the centre and from the true perspective distance, the defect thus occasioned is not very striking or offensive; but if the spectator be near to the stage, or placed on one side of the house, the whole becomes more or less distorted, and the wings only so many disjointed fragments, so that all scenic illusion is destroyed, and should the back scene be at a considerable distance, no part of it will be visible to those in the boxes next the proscenium, but merely the range of wings on one side and the gaps between them.

Scene-painting is executed in *distemper*, that is, with colours mixed up with size, the design being first made in a sketch, which is accurately laid down to

scale, and from which the perspective outlines are transferred to the larger surface. Instead of beginning with dead colouring, and then gradually working up
his picture, the artist puts in all his effects at once (as in fresco-painting) – the
full tone of the lights and shadows, finishing as he proceeds, and merely retouch-
ing those parts afterwards which require additional depth or brilliancy. In this
kind of painting, *bravura* of execution and strikingness of effect are indispensable, and nature must be rather exaggerated than the contrary; at the same time
care must be taken lest mere gaudiness be substituted for brilliancy and richness.
Further, as much of the costume of the piece depends upon him, it is important that the scene-painter should not only be well skilled in architectural delineation, but also well informed as to the styles of different countries and periods,
so as to avoid those errors and anachronisms which are frequently committed,
and which are sometimes so glaring that no beauty of execution can atone for
them.

Much of the effect of scenery depends upon a skilful mode of lighting it; in which
respect considerable improvements have taken place of late years, and the light is
now occasionally thrown from above, as well as from the sides and the foot-lights.
A variety of mechanical contrivances have also been brought to great perfection
so as to imitate particular effects in the most deceptive manner, such as those of
moonlight, where the moon breaks through the clouds and gleams upon water,
etc., changes of the sky from clear to stormy, or the contrary, the sudden glare of
fire, etc.

Though Planché was more noted for his historically accurate costuming and his meticulous
attention to spectacular detail, which complemented the productions of Madame Vestris,
his search for precision led him to experiment with 'authentic' Shakespearean staging. The
engagement of Mrs Nisbett, a celebrated comic performer, at the Haymarket for the season
suggested to Planché the idea of reviving *The Taming of the Shrew* in an authentic version,
including the Christopher Sly induction scene, instead of the Garrick version, *Katherine and
Petruchio*, which had been used for many years. In the event, the experiment was unique
and at odds with the prevailing taste for theatrical opulence.

188   Shakespeare without decor, 1844

J. R. Planché, *Recollections and reflections* (London: Tinsley, 1872), vol. II, p. 82

It also occurred to me to try the experiment of producing the piece with only two
scenes – 1. The outside of the little ale-house on a heath, from which the drunken
tinker is ejected by the hostess, and where he is found asleep in front of the door by
the nobleman and his huntsmen; and, 2. The nobleman's bedchamber, in which the
strolling players should act the comedy, as they would have done in Shakespeare's
own time under similar circumstances – viz., without scenery, and merely affixing
written placards to the wall of the apartment to inform the audience that the
action is passing 'in a public place in Padua',– 'a room in Baptista's house',– 'a
public road', etc.

[. . .] One difficulty was to be surmounted. How was the play to be finished [. . .] I hit upon the following expedient:– Sly was seated in a great chair in the first entrance, OP, to witness the performance of the comedy. At the end of each act no drop scene came down, but music was played while the servants brought the bewildered tinker wine and refreshments, which he partook of freely. During the fifth act he appeared to fall gradually into a heavy drunken stupor, and when the last line of the play was spoken, the actors made their usual bow, and the nobleman, advancing and making a sign to his domestics, they lifted Sly out of his chair, and as they bore him to the door, the curtain descends slowly upon the picture. Not a word was uttered [. . .]

The revival was eminently successful, incontestably proving that a good play, well acted, will carry the audience along with it, unassisted by scenery; and in this case also, remember, it was a comedy in *five* acts, without the curtain once falling during its performance.

189   Suggestions for improving realistic stage design, 1847

Builder (8 May, 1847) p. 210

The subject was resumed[1] with an examination of the advantages derivable from placing the scenery obliquely on the stage, referring of course to the wings and set-scenes, the flats or back-scenes being in the usual position. Some difficulties in perspective having been alluded to, it was stated that for drawing-rooms and apartments, the scenery ought to be arranged with due regard to the ground-plan of what is to be represented. This would enable actors to enter or take leave in a complete manner; they would not be observable by those in the side-boxes when approaching or lingering for that purpose, and their voices would reverberate and be carried into the body of the theatre [. . .]

Perspective [. . .] constitutes one of the greatest obstacles to perfection in scenic effects, and [the speaker] alluded to the defects which ordinarily appear in set-scenes, from their being made up of various parts, placed at intervals along the stage, each part drawn, probably, at a different perspective angle. The peculiar manner of treating perspective for theatrical purposes was explained. While the situation of spectators varies greatly, the treatment must necessarily be imperfect. It is, therefore, usual to set out scenery with two points of sight, but he preferred, in architectural subjects, to have *three*, and to have them placed near the centre, so as to counteract the effect of opposition in the horizontal features of the wings, whereby the scenes frequently are made to appear hoisted. Scenes shewing ground in perspective, are frequently spoiled by the visible junction of the wings and the floor, thus disturbing the illusion of distance attempted by the artist; and he would tint the lower portions of the scene with colour similar to that of the stage. Architectural drop-scenes were frequently objectionable from the same cause, and he maintained that they should never be thus applied, but only as pictures within frames, if at all.

The effect of linear and aerial perspective was adverted to, and the softening influences of colour in aerial perspectives were described as pertaining to the highest order of artistic talent. Scenes of this kind are composed of a number of parts, the flats representing sky and extreme distance, while the middle distance and foreground are broken into perspective forms. Float-lights being placed behind these parts, impart brilliant effects [. . .] resembling the sunny spots of a landscape.

Linear perspective required [. . .] very great consideration [. . .] The artist, however, has to contend with serious disadvantages from not being permitted to set out this class of scenes upon the stage instead of in the painting-room [. . .] Street architecture offers a peculiar difficulty from the actors influencing the scale by their comparative size; this illustrates the absurdity of placing a façade of the National Gallery or other well-known building within the area of a theatrical scene, without a proper regard to distance [. . .]

Mr Dwyer next alluded to the taste and refinement Madame Vestris had first presented to the public in her drawing-room scenes, elegantly and completely furnished [. . .] He admired this perfect kind of representation, and was pleased with the manner in which it had been extended to exteriors, garden scenes, etc., and he referred to the garden scene in the 'Lady of Lyons', at Sadler's Wells, in which the stage is covered with a painted cloth imitative of gravel walks, grass plots, shrubberies, etc. [. . .] In a snow scene in the 'Battle of Life', at the Lyceum, the stage was covered with painted canvas very successfully, and in the 'Flowers of the Forest',[2] the scene of a village church, with well-worn paths, etc., similarly treated, was equally skilful and pleasing [. . .]

He then noticed the machinery pertaining to theatres, and recommended the use of painted canvas placed on rollers sufficiently lofty so as to dispense with the series of curved, scolloped and straight fly borders, ordinarily representing sky, etc. He next reviewed the inconsistencies which occur in scenery, and properties, being of a different period in character and style to that of historical dramas, mentioning a scene in 'Lucia de Lammermoor', at the Italian Opera House, Covent Garden. It represents a Norman interior furnished with one chair of modern French style, and one table of doubtful period, the story of the opera being in 1669. He contended that those adjuncts are important, and that if costumes, manners, and customs are rendered faithfully, properties should receive equal attention [. . .]

---

[1] A report of a paper, 'Scenery and decorations of theatres', read by Mr John Dwyer to the Decorative Arts Society on 14 April 1847. Dwyer was opposed to the system of wings and flats and said so in the first part of his paper, which *The Builder* reported in its previous issue (vol. 5, p. 191).

[2] Bulwer-Lytton's *The Lady of Lyons; or, Love and Pride*, originally staged at Covent Garden in 1838, had been mounted by Phelps at Sadler's Wells in 1844; Albert Smith's stage adaptation of Dickens's story, *The Battle of Life*, opened at the Lyceum on 21 December 1846; J. B. Buckstone's *Flowers of the Forest* opened at the Adelphi on 11 March 1847.

Planché remembered the form of the traditional pantomime before its domination by spectacle and contrasted it with the new taste for spectacular extravagance. The remarks refer to his Christmas extravaganza, *The Island of Jewels*, which opened at the Lyceum on 26 December 1849.

190   Pantomime as lavish extravaganza, 1849

Planché, *Recollections and reflections*, vol. II, pp. 135–7

[. . .] I produced 'The Island of Jewels', and the novel and yet exceedingly simple falling of the leaves of a palm tree which discovered six fairies supporting a coronet of jewels, produced such an effect as I scarcely remember having witnessed on any similar occasion up to that period. But alas! 'this effect defective came by cause'. Year after year Mr Beverley's powers were tasked to outdo his former outdoings. The *last* scene became the *first* in the estimation of the management. The most complicated machinery, the most costly materials, were annually put into requisition [. . .] As to me, I was positively painted out. Nothing was considered *brilliant* but the last scene. Dutch metal was in the ascendant. It was no longer even painting; it was upholstery [. . .] The epidemic, however, spread in all directions, and attacked several other establishments and forms of entertainment with extreme violence. Where harlequinades were indispensable at Christmas, the ingenious method was hit upon of dovetailing extravaganza and pantomime. Instead of the two or three simple scenes which previously formed the opening of the pantomime, a long burlesque, the characters in which have nothing to do with those in the harlequinade, occupies an hour – sometimes much more – of the evening, and terminates with one of those elaborate and gorgeous displays which have acquired the name of 'transformation scenes', are made the great feature of the evening; and, consequently, after which the best part of the audience quit the theatre, and what is by courtesy called the 'comic business' is run through by the pantomimists in three or four ordinary street or chamber scenes. The usual number of curiously dressed people stream in and out of exhibitions or cross the stage; the usual number of policemen are bonneted; the steps are buttered; the red-hot poker is exhibited; the real live pig let out of the basket; and then [. . .] a portion of the transformation scene is suddenly discovered, sufficiently shorn of its beams to escape recognition by the two or three score of persons who have courageously sat out the performance [. . .]

William Bodham Donne (1807–82), who became Examiner of Plays in 1857, was a regular theatre-goer. He took particular exception to the taste for spectacle, which he identified with the productions of Charles Kean at the Princess's Theatre. Although he does not mention Planché by name, his comments relate directly to the antiquarianism with which Planché was associated.

191 A protest against 'upholstered' theatre, 1853

W. B. Donne, *Fraser's Magazine* (September 1853), p. 345

The passion, the poetry, the plot of *King John* and *Macbeth* will not now fill the pit or boxes, unless the manager lavishes a fortune on pictures of high Dunsinane, or on coats of mail and kilts such as were actually worn by the Earls and Thanes of the English and Scottish courts. We write this with all honour to the enterprising manager who has set these dramas on the stage so gorgeously and accurately accoutred. Yet we take leave to doubt whether, by this excess of decoration, they have not imposed new difficulties on the actor, whether, indeed, they have not made the substance of the drama less important than its accessories [. . .] We do not echo the objection which we have frequently heard that the upholsterer is called in to veil the defects of the actor, but we would submit that theatrical decoration has its limits, and that recently there has been a tendency to overstep them [. . .] We do not think that exact copies of the swords, helmets, and mantles of any given period are required for proper dramatic effects. We do not attach much importance to scenes representing the real localities of the dramatic action. It is enough that time and place be not confounded by anachronisms [. . .] We would not, were it possible, return to a green-baize curtain, labelled 'This is a street in Padua', or 'this is the wood of Ardennes'; neither would we insist upon a representation of the actual street or the actual wood [. . .] Above all things, an artistic sense of the beautiful should preside and predominate over scenical representations. The verse of Shakespeare should not be married to grotesque pictures of semi-barbarism. We confess that Mr Kean's arrangement of the banquet scene in *Macbeth* was unpleasing to us. It was too much like a booth at an agricultural meeting, with the banners of the county militia, hoisted over the Lord-Lieutenant's chair. It was doubtless correct, and as undoubtedly ugly.

STAGE BUSINESS

192 The influence of the Gothic on staging Shakespeare, 1794

W. C. Oulton, *A history of the theatres of London* (London: Martin & Bain, 1818), vol. I, Drury Lane, pp. 92–4

Banquo's Ghost in 'Macbeth' was rendered again visible to the audience. On the opening of the new Theatre in 1794, this spectre, like the air-drawn dagger, was only imagined by *Macbeth*, as the ghosts of *Pierre* and *Jaffier* (which originally ascended) are by *Belvidera*. *The Ghost of Banquo* has nothing to say, and is consequently no character: it is visible *only* to *Macbeth* who appears to 'look upon a *stool*'. The advocates for his visibility should recollect that the author has made it by its silence

'A false creation
Proceeding from a heat-oppressed brain.'

It is the ghost 'of the mind', and the appearance of it to the audience absolutely destroys the visionary effects of a guilty conscience. We may thank the spectres of Lewis and Boaden for the reappearance of *Banquo's* ghost at his Majesty's theatre after its abolition for nearly ten years. A distinction, however, should be made between the spectres of the romantic drama, and those of the legitimate. It is to be regretted that the ghost in 'Hamlet' has anything to say in the chamber scene between the mother and son, being then not generally visible, for the best actor is sometimes liable to start too soon or too late. In 1794, a great impropriety in this scene was removed at Covent Garden Theatre by a half length figure of the poisoned King of Denmark being discovered in the scene over the chimney piece, and the queen having a picture of her present husband on her arm as a bracelet. This amendment, however, perished with the scene and *Hamlet* sometimes brings in both pictures in his pocket. Except they be hung up as family ornaments, it is not likely that the existing King of Denmark would have suffered the likeness of the late one to remain in his chamber. It is natural for *Hamlet* to wear the picture of his beloved father, but he should snatch the portrait of his detested uncle and new father from the queen which she might wear suspended by a chain. This simple alteration requires no scene, and is adopted by Mr Kean.

The removal of the proscenium doors, which had privileged the performer, altered the whole nature of the actor/audience relationship as well as of stage business itself. Although this change was resisted, and many provincial theatres retained the traditional relationship into the middle of the nineteenth century, it signalled the progressive absorption of the actor within the scenic stage. Performers were now forced to acknowledge the reality of their physical surroundings.

193   Removal of the proscenium doors at Drury Lane, 1822[1]

Theatrical Observer (17 October 1822), n.p.

[. . .] our Manager, who scouts the fears
Of pulling an old house about his ears,
Has spared, of our late edifice's pride,
The outward walls, and little else beside;
Anxious has been *that* labour to complete
Which makes magnificence and *comfort* meet.
Anxious that multitudes may *sit* at ease,
And scantier numbers in no desert freeze;
That ample space may mark the liberal plan,
But never strain the eyes or ears of man:
Look round and judge; his efforts all are waste
Unless you stamp them as a work of taste;
Nor blame him for transporting from his floors

instead of all illusion being destroyed by the introduction of modern uniforms or plain clothes. The rage for melodrama and spectacle, which gradually obtained from this period, was productive at any rate of a still greater spirit of inquiry into ancient manners and habits. Print-shops and private portfolios were ransacked for the getting up of every new Easter piece [. . .] But alas! while the crusader donned his glittering hauberk of mail, to astonish the galleries on an Easter Monday, the bastard Faulconbridge, and the barons of King John, were dressed all the year round in the robes and armour of at best the seventeenth century. On Mr Kean's appearance, and consequent success, the most popular plays underwent considerable alterations and improvements in point of scenery and dresses at Drury Lane. Several gentlemen of acknowledged taste and information supplied the new Roscius with designs for his own wardrobe, and the proprietors of the theatre were not behindhand in their endeavours to assist the illusion of the scene. The stage-dress of Richard, which had been but little altered from the days of Garrick and Macklin, underwent various changes, particularly in the latter scenes; but his cloak still bore the *star* of the garter, as altered by Charles the First. The trunks were of the time of James the First, and the plumed hat, in the throne scene, of the reign of Charles the Second. Shylock assumed a red hat, lined with black [. . .] Othello's dress was wholly changed; but the correct costume was sacrificed to what the actor considered effect. The habits of King Lear and Richard the Second were certainly improved; and in a new but unsuccessful play, called 'Ina', the Anglo-Saxon costume was fairly enough represented.

In 1823 Mr Charles Kemble set about the reformation of the costume of Shakspeare's plays in good earnest. King John, the First Part of Henry the Fourth, As You Like It, Othello, Cymbeline, and Julius Caesar, were successively, and, as the public generally acknowledged, successfully revived. The actors, dreadfully alarmed in the outset lest they should be made to look ridiculous, were agreeably surprised by the impression produced upon the audience, and have now become as anxious to procure authorities to dress from, as they were previously annoyed at the idea of the innovation, and distrustful of the effect.

200   Dressing classical burlesque, 1831

Planché, *Recollections and reflections*, vol. i, pp. 179, 180

[. . .] we brushed up together the oft-rejected burlesque, founded on George Colman the Younger's story 'The Sun Poker', and named by me 'Prometheus and Pandora'; and, under the additional locally allusive title of 'Olympic Revels', it was produced on the 3rd of January, 1831[1] [. . .] Madame Vestris sustaining the part of Pandora. The extraordinary success of this experiment [. . .] was due not only to the admirable singing and piquante performance of that gifted lady, but also to the charm of novelty imparted to it by the elegance and accuracy of the costume; it having been previously the practice to dress a burlesque in the most *outré* and ridiculous fashion. My suggestion to try the effect of persons picturesquely attired speaking absurd doggrel [*sic*] fortunately took the fancy of the fair lessee, and the alteration was highly appreciated by the public; but many old actors could never get over their early impressions. Liston thought to the last that Prometheus, instead of the Phrygian cap, tunic, and trousers, should have been dressed like a great lubberly boy in a red jacket and nankeens, with a pinafore all besmeared with lollipop! [. . .] It would be superfluous to say more on this subject than simply that 'Olympic Revels' was the first of a series which enjoyed the favour of the public upwards of thirty years.

[1] Planché claimed that he, with the assistance of Charles Dance, had introduced the genre of classical burlesque into English theatre to inaugurate the Vestris management of the Olympic.

Part Two: France

Edited by DONALD ROY

Introduction

On 19 January 1791, when Louis XVI signed a bill abolishing all formal sanctions on the establishment and exploitation of theatrical enterprises, the symbolic aptness of his deed could scarcely have been more pronounced. Before the Revolution, professional theatre in France had been not unlike a microcosm of the monarchy itself, an institution founded on privilege and inherited authority. The two 'legitimate' theatres of Paris, the Théâtre-Français and the Académie Royale de Musique, normally referred to more simply as the Opéra, had been brought into existence by royal will, in the form of letters patent from Louis XIV, and could trace their practices, and much of their repertoire, back to the seventeenth century. Between them, and in their respective genres, they enjoyed a legal monopoly of spoken and sung drama. Another protégé of the Crown, the Comédie-Italienne, had over the years acquired a measure of admissibility along with its royal pension, but still had to pay a regular fee to the Opéra for the right to make use of musical accompaniment in its performances.

Alongside these, other theatrical undertakings alternately flourished and struggled for survival, notably those which had grown out of the annual fairs of Saint-Germain and Saint-Laurent (where the additional income they brought to parish funds earned them limited ecclesiastical protection), but which from the mid-eighteenth century had increasingly gravitated towards the new recreational territory centred on the boulevards to the north of the city. By definition, they were all 'illegitimate' and were tolerated by the Opéra only by virtue of the tributary payments they were required to make for infringing its musical monopoly. Nicolet, for example, the most celebrated fairground showman turned theatre proprietor, negotiated terms for a regular *abonnement*, which on the eve of the Revolution swelled the Opéra's coffers by 24,000 francs a year, while his closest rival, Audinot, was reported at the same time as being charged 30,000 francs. To encroach on the preserve of the Théâtre-Français was even more hazardous, and the show-booth theatres of the fairs and boulevards had been forced to resort to all manner of impostures and subterfuges, ranging from avowed parodies of dramatic texts to performances given behind a scrim curtain, or with some of the dialogue written on placards and mimed to the accompaniment of off-stage voices, if they hoped to avoid prosecution and the threat of closure.[1]

All this was changed by a stroke of the royal pen, which had the effect of delivering the French theatre from its past. The document to which Louis set his hand not only subsumed his authority within that of the National Assembly, but also abrogated all the theatrical privileges instituted by his ancestor, and did so in the name of one of the philosophical premises of the revolution, liberty.

It proved a short-lived liberty. The fear of royalist counter-revolution that sustained the Terror also served to polarize the theatrical community, provoking from certain minor theatres displays of pro-republican fervour and scurrilous anti-clericalism while exposing the erstwhile Crown theatres, the Théâtre-Français in particular, to hostile treatment as suspected rallying points for monarchist sympathy. It also fostered internal dissension within the national theatre itself, which caused the company to split into two, the more conservative half being subsequently thrown into prison on a charge of spreading seditious propaganda. With the arrival of Napoleon, the pendulum of political favour swung in the opposite direction. Not only did he, as First Consul, give official blessing to the reconstituted Théâtre-Français of 1799, but by an imperial edict of 1807 he made a sweeping cull of theatrical activity, effectively restoring to the state-subsidized houses their former privileges and reducing the total number of theatres in the capital, which in the headiest days of free enterprise had risen to forty and more, to a mere eight.

After the Restoration, and again under the July monarchy, these restrictions were relaxed, but if there was no longer any obstacle to commercial entrepreneurialism, the stumbling block of censorship remained, intermittently forsworn only to be quickly reimposed, most commonly in the shape of a pre-emptive measure that required all playscripts to be submitted to the minister of the interior for prior approval. By the middle of the nineteenth century, then, France had a thriving theatrical industry, though one constantly vulnerable to the pressure of market forces and never entirely free of governmental interference.

The liberation of the minor theatres was crucial to the evolution of nineteenth-century theatre in other ways. It conveniently coincided with the advent of spectacular melodrama and nurtured the *comédie-vaudeville*, arguably the two most influential forms of dramatic writing during the period. Melodrama, in particular, possessed a clear-cut narrative momentum and a visual excitement that appealed to a new theatrically conscious popular audience. It took the stage by storm, often literally so, and weakened the long-standing hold of a classical aesthetic on the French dramaturgic imagination, a process of no little consequence to the emergence of an indigenous Romantic drama, and one in which theatres of the boulevards played a key role. In fact, although the presentation of *Hernani* at the Théâtre-Français is usually seen as marking a decisive watershed, it is important to remember that, during the critical years between Dumas's *Henri III et sa cour* in 1829 and Hugo's *Les Burgraves* in 1843, for every play by dramatists of the new generation to reach the stage of the national theatre a further two were performed on the boulevards, most notably at the Porte-Saint-Martin or at the Odéon, then operating under a no less commercial management. In fact, Dumas claimed that he preferred to write for the boulevard theatres, partly for financial reasons but also because the absence of the heavy hand of tradition, both in *mise-en-scène* and in acting, was more congenial to his work.

Almost as potent, perhaps, in their bearing on subsequent developments were the visits of three companies of British actors to Paris between 1822 and 1832, most significantly in 1827–8, when their impact was far-reaching. Audiences were exposed for the first time to *echt* Shakespeare, unmediated by the refinement of French translation or adaptation and given an additional cultural *frisson* by the lingering enmity of the recent wars. Romantic artists and writers found the experience inspiring, while young actors who were then making their way on the boulevards, such as Frédérick, Bocage and Marie Dorval, were profoundly stimulated by this contact with a school of acting that owed nothing to the lessons in received gesture and verse-speaking imparted by the Conservatoire. The Théâtre-Français remained a bastion of the classical tradition in acting as of the classical repertoire which sustained it, but as the drawing-power of the boulevard theatres grew, a degree of cross-fertilization between the two rival camps was not uncommon. Certainly Bocage, Ligier and even Marie Dorval, the current idol of the boulevards, all played at the national theatre for a time during the 1830s, and it is in this context that we can situate the phenomenal success enjoyed from 1838 onwards by Rachel, who seemed to audiences at the Théâtre-Français to embody a wild, exotic, distinctly 'modern' quality in her performances while also displaying the immaculate classical technique she had absorbed from her teachers, thus making her, even to the most conservative, the acceptable face of the revolution in acting that was currently taking place.

These innovations were mirrored, *mutatis mutandis*, by a parallel revolution in scenography. Changeable scenery and the spectacular visual effects facilitated by elaborate stage machinery, which had hitherto been largely the preserve of opera and ballet, became necessary components of melodrama, and boulevard theatres invested heavily in them. At the same time, there was a growing dissatisfaction with the traditional reliance on wing-flats, borders and backcloths, leading to their partial replacement, in the name of a greater realism in the stage picture, by free-standing *décors en relief*, and culminating in the all-embracing box set. A further dimension was added by the importance attached by Romantic dramatists to the physical milieu of the action, entailing an insistence on historical accuracy in the design of settings and the cut of costumes, a process which at times took on a wilfully antiquarian bent. The same approach was extended to plays set in the present: Scribe's comedies, in offering a mildly satirical commentary on contemporary manners, were increasingly dependent on furniture, properties and other paraphernalia aimed at recreating on stage a contemporary domestic interior in the real world. Moreover, the introduction of gas lighting in the theatre in 1822 had contributed a vital ingredient to this transition from a scenic philosophy of presentation to one of representation, the flexibility of gas and its convenience of control making it far easier to replicate the texture and gradations of natural light.

Some aspects of theatre-going were much slower to change. Notwithstanding the freedom of access to France's dramatic heritage promised by the decree of 1791, there was little sign of a consequential shift in audience loyalties. A notional hierarchy of theatres persisted during the period, largely determined by socioeconomic factors: broadly speaking, the Opéra continued to occupy pride of place, favoured by an aristocratic and fashionable élite and the prosperous, upwardly mobile bourgeoisie, while at the opposite extreme a simple show booth such as the Funambules, with its unpretentious repertoire, remained in more senses than one the dedicated stamping-ground of the artisanal and working classes. Finally, throughout these years there was one ubiquitous body of spectators whose primary objective, whatever the performance, was not to seek entertainment: the police maintained a permanent presence in theatres, irrespective of the regime in power, be it republican, imperial or monarchic, and exercised a permanent vigilance towards any aspect of the proceedings that might constitute a threat to public order or to the stability of the state.

---

[1] Documents providing detailed evidence of these and other antecedents may be found in an earlier volume in the present series, William D. Howarth (ed.), *French theatre in the neo-classical era, 1550–1789* (Cambridge: Cambridge University Press, 1997).

I Documents of control

The ailing condition of the theatre in France towards the end of the eighteenth century was a matter of outspoken concern. The restrictive practices arising from the statutory limitation of legitimacy to so few performing companies were clearly not conducive to the development of a healthy dramatic culture, and there had been much agitation for their removal, understandably enough from playwrights in particular. For instance, Cailhava d'Estandoux's pamphlet, *Les Causes de la décadence du théâtre, et les moyens de le faire refleurir*, published, significantly, in 1789, though partly written earlier, made a strong case for the creation of a second national theatre for the purposes of professional competition and public comparison with the first. In politically provocative language he spoke of a 'visible' decline of French theatrical prestige and attributed it to one prime cause, namely 'the exclusive privilege accorded to a single company over what should be the freest, most open and most precious things in any country, that is to say, the enjoyments of its people, its talents and its genius'. In August of the following year his fellow dramatist and respected academician, La Harpe, led a deputation of writers to present a petition to the Constituent Assembly demanding that henceforward all plays by dead authors, especially those in the hitherto inviolable repertoire of the Théâtre-Français, should be freely performable at any theatre, and that the copyright of plays by living authors should remain vested in the author, even after their first performance.

ROYAL ENDORSEMENT FOR A THEATRICAL REVOLUTION

When change did come, early in 1791, it was more radical than either Cailhava or La Harpe had probably envisaged, amounting to a total emancipation of the theatrical profession and extending to actors the same right to exercise their craft as that enjoyed by other citizens.

201 The theatrical profession is emancipated, 1791

Law of 19 January 1791

LOUIS, by the grace of God, etc., to all those present and to come, salutation. The National Assembly has decreed, and we desire and command, the following:

Decree of the National Assembly of 13 January 1791

The National Assembly, having received the report of its constitutional committee, decrees the following:

Article the first. Any citizen is entitled to establish a public theatre, and to have performed in it plays of any genre, on making, prior to its establishment, a declaration to this effect to the appropriate municipality.

2. Works by authors who have been dead for five years or more shall be considered to be public property, and may, notwithstanding ancient privileges which are hereby annulled, be performed at any theatre without distinction.

3. Works by living authors may not be performed in any public theatre in any part of France without the formal, written permission of the authors, on pain of confiscation of the total proceeds of such performances for the benefit of the authors. [. . .]

The excitement generated by these pronouncements was intense. The débutant singer-actress Louise Fusil wrote to a friend in Toulouse: 'The famous decree we have long awaited has just been passed. You can have no idea of the revolution it has produced. The gauze behind which they used to sing at one of the little boulevard theatres [the Délassements-Comiques] has been torn down by some young people. At the Beaujolais, where they mimed on stage to singing in the wings, the performers have started to speak and sing for themselves. Indeed, they're all behaving like mad things.'[1]

A simlar madness was reflected in the sheer proliferation of theatre buildings in the wake of the 1791 decree: the Marais, the Théâtre National Molière, the Vaudeville, the Cité-Variétés, the Liberté, the Concorde and many more in quick succession. At the beginning of 1789 there had been only ten public theatres in Paris; four years later this figure had risen to more than forty, serving a substantially reduced population. 'Scarcely had the decree on the freedom of theatres been promulgated', reported Etienne and Martainville, contemporary chroniclers of the revolutionary period, 'than a host of little theatres were set up, which by their low admission prices attracted citizens from several classes and could not fail to damage the major theatres.'[2] The new establishments were soon beseiged by all orders of society, not least those with little or no experience of theatre-going, who were unfamiliar with the traditional conventions of perfomance and ready to appreciate everything offered to them, including the classic repertory, on its merits. The veteran *forain* Nicolet was quick to seize the initiative by performing Molière's *George Dandin* and scored a huge personal success in the title role. The whole city was gripped by a *frénésie* for theatre, according to Froullé's *Almanach*, which also quoted an epigram by the popular satirist le Cousin Jacques (Beffroy de Reigny): 'Before long we in Paris will be able to count a theatre in every street, an actor in every house, a musician in every cellar and a playwright in every garret.'[3]

Accompanying this expansion, at least initially, was a strong sense of optimism about the future of theatre in France. Recalling a recent time when some theatres were at the mercy of interfering court officials and others were liable to a charge for the mere dispensation to operate, the *Almanach* welcomed their new-found independence.

---

[1] Louise Fusil, *Souvenirs d'une active* (3 vols., Paris: Dumont, 1841–6), vol. 1, p. 154. The comic actor Potier, who was there at the time, recalled that it was the manager of the Délassements-Comiques himself, Plancher-Valcour, who tore down the curtain with a cry of 'Long live liberty!' (*Mémoires de Mlle Flore, actrice des Variétés*, ed. H. d'Alméras (Paris: Société parisienne d'édition, 1903), p. 84).

[2] C. G. Etienne and A. Martainville, *Histoire du Théâtre-Français* (Paris: Barba, 1802), vol. 1, p. 100 n.

[3] *Almanach général de tous les spectacles de Paris et des provinces* (Paris: Froullé, 1791–2), pp. 343, 276.

202   The benefits of freedom, 1791

Almanach général de tous les spectacles de Paris et des provinces, pour l'année 1791 (Paris: Froullé, 1791–2), pp. 5–6, 206

Between the theatres of Paris there used to exist differences of degree and distinction, but now, when all theatres are subject to direct inspection by the municipality, they are all equal in social ranking, and in future will be distinguishable in terms of talent alone [. . .] With this eradication of bias, discerning citizens will no longer be surprised to hear talk of such and such an actor of the meanest theatre if this actor really has ability; if the Associés[1] presents an interesting play, well written and well produced, it will henceforth receive as much publicity as a mediocre piece which through patronage has got itself performed at the Opéra or the Français. Now that people's means are limited, citizens of all classes will visit even the lowliest playhouse; the public is the same everywhere, and that which is capable of entertaining and enlightening them in an auditorium thirty feet square is, in the eyes of the philosopher, just as valid as that which is capable of doing so in one of fifty [. . .]

This dramatist [Mercier], so famous for his philosophical plays, has had all his works performed at the Associés before taking them elsewhere. Among authors of distinction he is the first to have publicly trampled underfoot that lamentable prejudice which would measure the quality of a theatre by the size of its auditorium.

[1]   A minor theatre on the Boulevard du Temple, established in 1774.

But the rejoicing was by no means universal. Within a few years, Grimod de la Reynière, describing himself as a seasoned play-goer, was bewailing the headlong sacrifice of quality to quantity and the consequent adulteration of the theatrical public.

203   The price of proliferation, 1797

A. B. L. Grimod de la Reynière and Fabien Pillet, *Le Censeur dramatique, ou Journal des principaux théâtres de Paris et des départements* (4 vols., Paris, 1797–8), vol. 1, pp. 3, 6

The taste for theatre, which over the past few years in particular has spread to all classes of society, seems to have become even more of a passion than a need. The people of Rome used to demand *panem et circenses*; *circenses* alone has become the cry of the people of Paris. They endured with patience four months of the most appalling famine; we doubt whether they could endure for even one the closure of all the theatres.

[. . .] never has [the theatre-going public] been so obtuse in every respect. One has only to attend a performance to be convinced of it. These spectators, uniformly devoid of the prior knowledge which enjoyment of the drama requires and presupposes, ignorant of the most basic elements of grammar and versification, are incapable of distinguishing prose from verse, comedy from farce, bombast from grandeur, or pathos from sentimentality. The sublimity of Corneille bores them;

they yawn at the poetry of Racine; Molière leaves them cold; Regnard's gaiety repels them; Destouches's sweet reason they find tedious; Dancourt's artlessness offends them. Only *Madame Angot*[1] holds sway and has the power to amuse them. And it is to judges like these, dear God, that the destiny of dramatic art in France is now entrusted!

[1] *Madame Angot, ou la Poissarde parvenue,* an 'opéra-comique' by le Citoyen Maillot (Antoine-François Eve), first performed at Nicolet's theatre, now called the Emulation, in 1796.

OPERATIONAL MEASURES

Proposals were already being put forward under the Directory to curb the number of theatre buildings and to increase the extent of central control over their operations. Article 6 of the decree of 1791 had placed all theatres 'under the inspection of the municipalities', stipulating that they should 'receive orders only from municipal officers' and that the latter could 'require nothing of the players that was not in accordance with the law and police regulations'; any amendments to these restraints would be communicated later. Clearly they were not, for the report of a special commission in 1798 concluded: 'Theatres are under the immediate supervision of the Directory executive, which has the authority to determine their number in each commune in relation to its wealth and population, and to introduce for their organization and policing the regulations announced in the law of 13 January 1791.'[1] Playwrights, too, seem to have undergone a change of heart: whereas in 1790 they had been part of a liberalizing vanguard, some now addressed another petition to the Directory administration on 25 March 1799, protesting at the growth in the number of theatres, though others still argued that to impose any controls would be to contravene the constitutional right of every citizen to pursue his own trade. In the event, no executive decision was taken before Napoleon's personal intervention in the matter in 1806.

In the meantime, legislation was enacted governing the less contentious issues of fire prevention, security and the theatre's contribution to the relief of the poor.

[1] Reproduced in P. Bossuet, *Histoire des théâtres nationaux* (Paris: Jorel, 1909), p. 97.

204 Fire precautions, 1799

'Measures against fire in theatre buildings'. Order of 21 March 1799

Art. 1. The scene dock for a theatre's machines and décors shall be situated in a storehouse separate from the theatre building, in all communes where one exists.

2. Managers and proprietors of theatres are required to equip their buildings with a storage tank always full of water and at least one pump to be continuously maintained in working order.

3. They are required at all times to employ experienced firemen in such a way as to ensure that there is always a sufficient number to provide an adequate service.

4. There shall be one fireman constantly on duty inside the building.

5. A guard post shall be set up in each theatre so that a watchman, who must be relieved every hour, can assist the fireman in keeping the building under continuous observation outside the hours of performance.

6. At the end of a performance, the concierge, accompanied by a guard-dog, shall make a round of the building to ensure that no person is hidden inside and that there is no evidence of a risk of fire.
[. . .]

9. Any theatre in which the precautions and procedures set out above have been neglected or not implemented for one day shall be closed instantly.

Two years later steps were taken to strengthen the provisions for safeguarding public order. By the terms of the 1791 decree there was to be no more than one military guard per theatre, stationed outside the building and not authorized to enter it unless expressly bidden to do so by the 'one or several civilian officers' posted inside, and then 'only in the event of a threat to public safety' (Article 7). The Consulate evidently felt less compunction about the exercise of policing methods.

205   Security of theatres, 1802

Order of 4 October 1802. *Bulletin des lois*, no. 221. Year XI

Art. 45. In addition to the normal police service, the *garde municipale* will be responsible for policing all theatres and public balls; it will supply the guards that may be requested for the protection of balls and private parties. The prefect of police will determine the number of personnel to be assigned to these various services and the payment due to each [. . .]

The so-called *droit des pauvres*, a tax levied on all theatrical takings that had been instituted through royal decree as long ago as 1699, to support a hospice for the poor founded by Louis XIV,[1] was among the impedimenta of monarchy swept away in the aftermath of revolution in August 1789, but on condition that theatres should continue to pay it on a voluntary basis until suitable arrangements could be made for its replacement. On 1 January 1796 the Directory issued a proclamation 'inviting' all commercial managements, as well as the *sociétaires* of state theatres, to give one performance a month in aid of the poor, at which they would be entitled to raise the normal prices of admission by a third and also to collect voluntary donations from members of the audience for the same purpose. This expedient must have been found wanting, for later in the year it was superseded by a mandatory procedure applicable to all performances.

[1] For documents relating to the introduction and subsequent modification of the poor-tax, see W. D. Howarth (ed.), *French theatre in the neo-classical era, 1550–1789* (Cambridge: Cambridge University Press, 1997), nos. 316, 317 and 491.

206   The *droit des pauvres*, 1796

Law of 27 November 1796

Art 1st. One tenth shall be added to the price of all tickets, for a period of six months, at all establishments offering plays, balls, firework displays, concerts, races and exhibitions of horsemanship, for which spectators pay. The same increase will be made in the price of season tickets.

2. The proceeds of this levy will be used for the relief of the poor not accommodated in public poorhouses [. . .]

This measure was extended for a further six months on 21 April 1797, thereafter receiving successive extensions until 1809, when the surcharge was raised to 11 per cent. It was still in force in 1885, when Pougin published his comprehensive theatrical dictionary, in which it is described as 'iniquitous in its principle, disproportionate in its magnitude and predatory in the manner of its collection', primarily, Pougin says, because it had always been calculated on gross takings, before the deduction of daily overheads and authors' royalties.[1]

[1] A. Pougin, *Dictionnaire historique et pittoresque du théâtre et des arts qui s'y rattachent* (Paris: Firmin-Didot, 1885), p. 313.

BONAPARTIST RATIONALIZATION

With the accession of Napoleon as emperor came a total realignment of the theatrical map. Being a devoted patron of the drama in all its forms, as well as a zealot for order, Napoleon did not take long to reconcile these two passions and bring the full weight of imperial authority to bear on the competitive free-for-all into which the French theatre had evolved. By a decree of 8 June 1806 he placed firmly in his own hands and those of 'our minister of the interior' overall control of theatre building, organization and performance, both in Paris and throughout the empire. Henceforward, no theatre was to be established in the capital without his specific authorization, and before this could be obtained, any 'entrepreneur' would have to give proof to the minister that he possessed the necessary funds to meet all his obligations. The minister was to draw up the repertoires of the Opéra, the Théâtre-Français and the Opéra-Comique, and no other theatre in Paris would be allowed to perform works in the repertoire of 'these major theatres' without their permission and without payment of a mutually agreed fee, which would also require the approval of the minister. At the same time, the latter was empowered to assign to every theatre a genre of performance, to which it would be restricted. In the departments, the number of theatres in all large cities would be reduced to two, in all others to one, each of which would need authorization from the relevant prefect, who in turn would be accountable to the minister in Paris. As for itinerant troupes, not one would allowed to function without authorization from the ministers of the interior and police, their respective areas of operation being determined centrally and then communicated to all prefects. Finally, among general provisions, the decree laid down that bankrupted proprietors would be debarred from opening another theatre, and that the owners of *spectacles de curiosités*', such as waxworks, freak-shows, optical and scientific displays, would be subject to separate ordinances and forbidden to describe their entertainments as theatres.

When the minister, J. B. Champagny, produced regulations implementing this decree, they proved to be even more prescriptive, effectively restoring in a modified form the hierarchical ethos that had underpinned the theatre of the *ancien régime*, while infusing it with an almost military sense of strategic purpose.

207   Napoleon's reorganization of the theatre, 1806–7

Directive concerning theatres, 25 April 1807

PART ONE

Of the theatres of Paris

Art. 1st. The following theatres are to be considered as *major theatres* and will enjoy the prerogatives attributed to this title by the decree of 8 June 1806.

(1) *The Théâtre-Français (Théâtre de S. M. l'Empereur)*.[1] This theatre is to be devoted exclusively to tragedy and comedy. Its repertoire will consist of (i) all the plays (tragedies, comedies and *drames*) performed at the old theatre of the Hôtel de Bourgogne, at that directed by Molière and that which was formed by the amalgamation of these two establishments and has existed under various names to the present day; (ii) the comedies performed at the various theatres known as the *Italiens* before the foundation of the Opéra-Comique.

The *Théâtre de l'Impératrice* [Odéon] is to be regarded as an annexe of the Théâtre-Français, for comedy only. Its repertoire will contain (i) the comedies and *drames* written specially for this theatre; (ii) comedies performed at theatres known as the *Italiens* before the foundation of the Opéra-Comique: the latter may be performed only at this theatre and the Théâtre-Français.

(2) *The Théâtre de l'Opéra*. This theatre is devoted exclusively to singing and dance: its repertoire will consist of all the works, operas and ballets alike, which have appeared since its foundation in 1646.[2] It alone may perform pieces composed entirely of music and ballets in an elevated and courtly style, such as all those whose subject matter has been drawn from mythology or history and whose main characters are gods, kings or heroes. It may also, but not exclusively, perform ballets depicting rustic scenes or actions from everyday life.

(3) *The Théâtre de l'Opéra-Comique*. This theatre is intended exclusively for the presentation of all types of comedy or *drame* interspersed with songs, ariettas and ensembles. Its repertoire will consist of all those plays performed at the Opéra-Comique before or after its amalgamation with the Comédie-Italienne, provided that the dialogue of these plays is intercut with song. The *Opéra Buffa* is to be regarded as an annexe of the Opéra-Comique. It may perform plays written in Italian only.

2. Without the authorization of the composers or copyright holders, none of the airs, ballads or other pieces of music performed at the Opéra and the Opéra-Comique may be played at any other theatre in the capital, even with modification to the accompaniment, for five years after the first performance of the work of which they form part.

3. To be considered as *secondary theatres* are:

   1.   *The Théâtre du Vaudeville.* Its repertoire shall comprise only short plays interspersed with songs set to popular tunes, and parodies.

   2.   *The Théâtre des Variétés,* boulevard Montmartre. Its repertoire shall consist of short plays, in the *grivois, poissard* or *villageois* style, at times interspersed with songs also set to popular tunes.

   3.   *The Théâtre de la porte Saint-Martin.*[3] It is intended exclusively for the genre known as *mélodrame* and plays with elaborate spectacle. But the plays in its repertoire, as in those of all other secondary theatres, may make use only of popular melodies for their sung passages.
       [...]

   4.   *The Théâtre de la Gaîté.* It is intended for *pantomimes* of all types, though not incorporating ballets, and for harlequinades and other farces in the manner of those formerly performed by Nicolet at this theatre.

   5.   *The Théâtre des Variétés étrangères.* The repertoire of this theatre shall consist entirely of plays translated from other languages.

4. All other theatres currently in existence in Paris, which were authorized by the police prior to the decree of June 1806, are to be considered as annexes or duplicates of the secondary theatres: the managers of these establishments will each be required to select from the genres allotted to the secondary theatres the one which appears best suited to their own. They will be permitted, as will the secondary theatres, to perform some plays from the repertoires of the major theatres, but only with the authorization of the administrators of those theatres and after payment of a mutually agreed fee, in accordance with article 4 of the decree of 8 June, and with the approval of the minister of the interior.

5. No theatre in Paris will be allowed to perform plays which depart from the genre assigned to it. But a play which has been turned down by one of the three major theatres may be performed at any one of the theatres of Paris, provided that it falls within the genre assigned to it.
[...]

7. In order that theatres may not suffer from this determination and assignment of genres, the minister gives them leave to retain their former repertoires in full, even if they contain plays which depart from the genre allotted to them; but these former repertoires must correspond exactly to those lodged with the office of the minister of the interior and sanctioned by him. At the same time, this article in no way contravenes article 4 of the decree of 8 June, which precludes any theatre in Paris from performing plays belonging to the major theatres without paying them a fee

PART II
Repertoires of theatres in the departments

8. In the departments, *resident* or *itinerant* companies shall be permitted to perform plays either from the repertoires of the major theatres or from those of the secondary

theatres and their duplicates (without prejudice to the rights of authors or copyright holders).

9. In cities where there are two theatres, the *principal theatre* shall be exclusively entitled to present plays drawn from the repertoires of the major theatres; it may also, with the authorization of the prefect, select and perform some plays belonging to the secondary theatres, on the understanding that the other theatre shall not thereby be deprived of the right to perform these same plays. The *second theatre* shall be exclusively entitled to present plays from the repertoires of the secondary theatres; [. . .] In addition, where a city has two theatres, the prefect may authorize the second theatre to present plays from the major repertoires, whenever he considers it appropriate [. . .]

PART III
Designation of the regions allocated to companies of itinerant players

10. Towns where there may be performances for only part of the year have been grouped to form twenty-five regions [*arrondissements*] [. . .]

11. No theatrical entrepreneur may deploy itinerant companies in any of these regions unless, (i) he has been formally authorized to do so by the minister of the interior, to whom he must also show proof of having adequate funds to meet his obligations; and (ii) he has also received the approval of the minister for police coordination.

12. Theatrical entrepreneurs wishing to apply for any given region must, *before August 1st next*, and before the same date in subsequent years, (i) specify the number of persons comprising the company or companies they propose to engage; and (ii) indicate the date on which their companies will arrive and the length of time they will undertake to stay at each of the towns in the region postulated.

13. No authorization will be granted for more than three years at most [. . .]

PART IV
General provisions

17. Theatrical performances being not among the public activities attended by state officials in their professional capacity but entertainments mounted and directed by private individuals who have speculated on the profit they can expect to realize therefrom, no one has the right to enjoy free of charge an entertainment which is retailed by the entrepreneur to the general public. The authorities shall not therefore demand of entrepreneurs more free passes than are required for the number of personnel deemed essential for the maintenance of order and public safety [. . .]

---

[1] See also **368**.
[2] *Sic*. The first *privilège* for the Opéra's foundation was granted in 1669, though performances of Italian opera were given in Paris as early as 1645.
[3] See also **370**.

A further imperial decree, issued later in the same year from the palace at Saint-Cloud, was more draconian still: it is as if any system under which major, state-subsidized cultural establishments might find themselves outnumbered by secondary theatrical concerns subject to the mercenary imperatives of free enterprise could not possibly measure up to the sense of mission with which Napoleon had invested the French theatre.

208   From reorganization to stranglehold, 1807
Decree of 8 August 1807

Art. 3. No new playhouse may be built, and no company may be transferred from one house to another in our fair city of Paris without authorization from us, on receipt of a report from our minister of the interior.

4. The maximum number of theatres in our fair city of Paris is limited to eight; in consequence, apart from the four major theatres referred to in article 1 of our minister's directive of 25 April last, only the proprietors or managers of the following four theatres are authorized to remain open, advertize and present plays:

1. The Théâtre de la Gaîté, established in 1760, and the Ambigu-Comique, established in 1772 in the boulevard du Temple, which will both perform plays of the same genre, as designated in paragraphs (3) and (4) of article 3 of our minister's directive.
2. The Théâtre des Variétés, boulevard Montmartre, established in 1777, and the Vaudeville, established in 1792, which will both perform plays of the same genre, as designated in paragraphs (1) and (2) of article 3 of our minister's directive.

5. All theatres not authorized by the preceding article are to be closed before 15 August. In consequence, no play may be performed at any other theatre in Paris than those designated above, on any pretext, nor may the public be admitted, even free of charge, nor may any playbill be posted, nor any ticket, printed or handwritten, be given out, on pain of the penalties prescribed by the law and police regulations [. . .]

At a stroke, Napoleon had disenfranchised almost a score of legitimately functioning theatrical businesses – and rendered several thousand Parisians jobless[1] – as a means, essentially, of protecting the Théâtre-Français and the Opéra and re-endowing them with exclusive custody of their traditional repertoire. Some of the dispossessed managers went out of business altogether; others, with the characteristic resilience of fairground showmen, simply adapted to the changed circumstances and sought out alternative modes of entertaining the public, from animal acts to *cafés-chantants*, that could plausibly evade definition as drama.

Most notable is the absence from the list of approved theatres of the Porte-Saint-Martin, omitted in favour of the Ambigu-Comique and killed off, no doubt, because its stage possessed facilities for spectacle capable of offering serious competition to the Opéra. After much lobbying and bargaining a passable compromise was found: the minister of the interior wrote back to its proprietors on 11 March 1809 authorizing them to reopen the theatre, though with a modified and strictly defined repertoire, limited to what he described as (i) *jeux gymniques*, i.e. rope-dancing, acrobatic routines, pugilistic or gladiatorial combats and the like; (ii) *tableaux historiques, dans le genre Servandoni*, well-known historical events evoked primarily with the aid of changeable scenery and machinery; (iii) *évolutions militaires*, or foot drill, martial manœuvres, infantry and cavalry charges; and (iv) *prologues*, used simply for the purpose of introducing other items on the programme and delivered by one or at most two actors, the only speaking parts in what had been reduced to little more than a circus entertainment.[2]

Before long the manager, Augustin Hapdé, dared to step out of line and was admonished in unequivocal terms.

---

[1] 'When one considers that the smallest theatre in the capital gives a livelihood to more than thirty families; that the majority support at least a hundred; and that some provide bed and board for more than three hundred, one is tempted to regard as lunatics those who are forever crying that there are too many theatres in Paris. Even allowing no more than four persons per family, it is obvious that our theatres and other entertainments support over ten thousand citizens' (*Almanach général* 1791, p. 10). The same publication goes on to supply exact numbers of all employees, including managerial staff, actors, dancers, musicians, backstage crew, front-of-house personnel and so on, at each establishment, calculating the work-force at Nicolet's theatre, the Grands Danseurs, for example, to be 130, at the Variétés-Amusantes 'about 200' and at the Comédie-Italienne, 316.

[2] The text of this letter is quoted by M. Albert, *Les Théâtres des Boulevards (1789–1848)* (Paris: Société Française d'Imprimerie et de Librairie, 1902), pp. 233–4.

209   Ministerial intimidation, 1811

Letter from the Comte de Montalivet, 11 August 1811. Reproduced in Albert, *Théâtres des Boulevards*, p. 235

I am informed that, contrary to your undertakings, you are giving performances which fall outside the genre assigned to your theatre, indeed that you are presenting, under other names, bona fide dramatic pieces, despite the fact that this category is reserved exclusively for the eight theatres of the capital.

I must warn you that if you persist, under any pretext whatsoever, in giving performances within any genre other than that to which you are entitled, I shall give orders for the closure of your theatre.

Thus constrained, the Porte-Saint-Martin, which was to become such a beacon for the Romantic drama in the 1830s, dragged out its miserable existence for a few months, but was forced to close down in June 1812 and remained dark until after the Restoration.

Heaping Ossa on Pelion, an imperial edict – issued only two days after the above letter – reimposed, as from 1 September 1811, the prerevolutionary system of cash tributes to the Opéra, which were henceforth to be payable not only by the four surviving secondary theatres but also by the proprietors of 'all *cabinets de curiosités*, mechanical shows, model figures, animals, all contests and games, and in general all entertainments of any kind whatever, all those presenting masked balls or concerts in our fair city of Paris', a motley array to which were now added 'the panorama, cosmorama, Tivoli Gardens and other recent establishments' and 'the Cirque Olympique, as a *theatre* where pantomimes are performed'; only *guinguettes* and dances held outside the city walls were exempt. Depending on the nature of the entertainment, fees were set at either one-fifth or one-twentieth of the gross takings, after deduction of the *droit des pauvres*.[1]

The year 1811 still had one last bureaucratic trick up its sleeve, which took the form of a directive from the Paris prefect of police reiterating or reinforcing earlier measures, and introducing some well-intentioned new ones, for the safeguarding of public order and security before, during and after all performances.

[1] Decree of 13 August 1811, Articles 1–3.

210   Policing the theatre, 1811

Order concerning the exterior and interior policing of theatres, 27 December 1811

Art. 2. No theatre may be opened until it has been established that the building is solidly constructed, that the precautions against fire prescribed by the government order of 1 germinal an VII [21 March 1799] have been taken, and that nothing is situated under the peristyles or in the vestibules which might in any way impede freedom of movement.
[. . .]

4. The proprietors of theatres may not issue tickets in excess of the number of persons their auditorium can hold.

5. It is mandatory for proprietors to ensure that throughout a performance the communicating doors remain firmly closed which lead from the auditorium to the wings of the stage, to private boxes and to the artists' dressing rooms, where no one is to be admitted who is not a member of the theatre staff.

6. It is also mandatory for them to ensure that all doors are opened at the end of a performance to allow rapid egress of the public.
[. . .]

8. It is forbidden for anyone to loiter under the peristyles or in the vestibules giving access to theatres (*Order of 27 December 1769*).

9. It is expressly forbidden for anyone to offer for resale tickets which have been bought at the box office, or to sell any which have come from another source.

10. It is forbidden to converse or to circulate in the corridors during a performance in such a way as to disturb the peace.

11. It is also forbidden to disturb the audience's attention, either by calling out or by applauding or by any signs of disapproval before the curtain has risen, or during the intervals.

12. No one may wear a hat while the curtain is up.
[. . .]

15. Carriages may arrive at the different theatres only by the streets indicated in their instructions. Coachmen are expressly forbidden to drop their horses' reins, for any reason whatever, while their passengers are alighting or boarding.
[. . .]

20. At every theatre there must be a guard-room and a bureau for the officers of police.

[. . .]

23. Every person is required to defer to the orders of a police officer, without prejudice (*Law of 10 January 1791*). Consequently, any person requested or summoned by him to leave the auditorium must go immediately to the police-post and provide such explanations as may be demanded of him.

24. Any person arrested, whether at the exit or in the auditorium, must be taken to the police-post by the officer in question, who alone is empowered to determine whether he is to be referred to the competent authority or conditionally released.

The extent to which these various injunctions were in fact heeded may be judged from some of the documents reproduced in chapter 5 below.

A CIRCUMSCRIBED *LAISSEZ-FAIRE*

After the Restoration, in 1814, all the theatres closed by Napoleon reopened one by one, followed by a renewed surge in writing for the stage. Moreover, many of the works banned under the Empire now became freely performable again. But to describe the restored monarchy as a liberal regime where the theatre was concerned would be a gross overstatement: it retained, indeed strengthened, tight imperial controls on theatrical activities in the provinces, and in the capital itself restrictions placed on the choice of repertoire remained unchanged. Some idea of the vigilance with which these restrictions were enforced may be gained from the scribbled draft of a ministerial response to a reported contravention on the part of the Ambigu-Comique, which unmistakably echoes the admonition addressed to the Porte-Saint-Martin some six years earlier.

211   The repertoire is inviolable

(a) Letter from the Minister of the Interior to the manager of the Théâtre de l'Ambigu, 3 September 1817. Archives Nationales, F21 1134; (b) Order of the Minister of the Interior, 19 July 1827. Archives Nationales, F21 1134

(a) Letter from the Minister of the Interior, 1817

Monsieur, the genre of the Th[éâtr]e de l'Ambigu was fixed by the decree of 8 August 1807. Of late you have deviated from it. You have performed works which are the preserve of other establishments.

I have received representations to this effect. I advise you to [rectify?] this by rigorously including in your repertoire only plays of the type that you are authorized to perform.

Any further infringement of the regulations would lead to further complaints and give rise to an investigation which could be very detrimental to you. This matter warrants your full attention.

Ten years later, when the Ambigu burned down, its joint proprietors, the founder's widow, Mme Audinot, and a certain M. Senépart, were compelled not only to seek permission to proceed with the rebuilding but also to apply for a renewal of the licence granted to Audinot in 1815, and the minister took advantage of the occasion to redefine the terms of the theatre's appointed repertoire.

(b) Order of the Minister of the Interior, 1827

Art. 1st. The licence for 15 years accorded to sieur Audinot in 1815, for the exploitation of the Ambigu-Comique, is hereby renewed in the name of the Widow Audinot and sieur Senépart for a period of ten years, to begin on 1 April 1830 and to end on 30 March 1840.

2. Sieur Senépart shall be the managing director of the concern.

3. The repertoire of this theatre shall consist of Melodramas, Pantomimes and one-act Comedies in prose.

4. No Vaudeville shall in future be performed there, other than those already accepted and authorized by us prior to the present order [. . .]

6. All plans relative to the siting and construction of the new theatre may be implemented only in accordance with such sanctions as shall be imposed by us, following the report of M. the Prefect of Police.

The precipitate return to free enterprise on the one hand, coupled with a continuing prescription of the repertoire on the other, had the effect of producing not only a mood of cut-throat competition between theatres but also an internecine obsession with lines of demarcation.

212   Commercial rivalries, 1832

Hippolyte Auger, *Du monopole et de la concurrence des théâtres* (Paris: Everat, 1832), pp. 21–2

As soon as theatre came to be regarded purely as a matter of financial speculation, the theatrical entrepreneurs of Paris saw themselves as enemies, and monopoly was elevated to a right. *You're stealing my audience* became the universal cry that managers bandied at each other, [. . .] So we found the major theatres, the subsidized, spendthrift, aristocratic theatres, reclaiming their exclusive privilege to exploit a particular genre. The Académie Royale de Musique disallowed any *ronds de jambes* on secondary stages except in return for a fee; the Opéra-Comique prohibited new melodies anywhere but at its sanctuary in the rue Feydeau; the Théâtre-Français insisted that no other theatre could perform a play in three acts which was not interlarded with music and did not bear the title of melodrama; and, in retaliation, the melodrama houses thought themselves justified in forcing the Cirque-Olympique and the gaffs [*théâtres à quatre sous*] to have no more than two speaking characters in any one scene. On the other hand, between theatres speculating in the same genre, a struggle to the death. So may it be.

The authorities were well aware of these rivalries, and of the malicious gossip and backstabbing they induced, but turned a blind eye to any mercantile tactics that did not openly bring the law into disrepute.

213   One manager informs on another, 1818

Letter from the Paris Prefect of Police to the Minister of the Interior, 18 September 1818. Archives Nationales, F21 1154

M. le C[om]te, one of the actors whom S[ieu]r Bertrand had engaged, S[ieu] r Bougnol, who according to his statement played the *Cassandre* parts at the Funambules, has just been given notice by the proprietor & wishes to be allowed to rejoin this Establishment. This is not possible; only rope-dancers may appear in the short pieces presented at this theatre. Sr Bougnol is not one of these. His engagement should not have taken place. His departure was the result of orders given by yourself. His return cannot be permitted.

It is evident from the application itself that Sr Bertrand is at last abjuring the delinquencies to which these managers are invariably prone; he must be made to toe the line that has been drawn for him.

I had suggested closing him down. I did so in response to the complaints and remonstrations of Sr Saqui,[1] but you thought that this would be to make a concession to intrigue which would tend to compromise your authority. The grounds you elaborated in your confidential report persuaded me not to insist on the measure. We can, in accordance with your advice, maintain a tolerant approach and, as long as Bertrand does not flout the prescribed rules, leave things as they are. But if he deviates from the genre allocated to him, we could seize the opportunity to tighten the [franchise?] of the establishments where dram[ati]c pieces are performed. We owe protection to those who fulfil their obligations; no claim or allegation that is unfounded should lead us to take a repressive measure; but when a d[irec]tor acts in contravention of his orders, he deserves no quarter. All this class of Th[eatres] needs to be controlled with a firm hand.

---

[1] The acrobat, Jean-Julien Saqui, whose show-booth, the Théâtre des Acrobates, stood next door to Bertrand's Funambules, a proximity that served only to intensify their enmity.

The same inflexibility of attitude was later to confront Casimir Delavigne when in 1829 he canvassed unsuccessfully to have the première of his *Marino Faliero* performed without musical accompaniment: in the event, because it was presented at the Porte-Saint-Martin, music was commissioned from Rossini, scenic design from Ciceri and this five-act tragedy in verse had to be announced on the bills as a melodrama.

THEATRE AS COMMERCIAL SPECULATION

With the advent of the July monarchy, free trade became the watchword as much in the theatre as in any other sphere of business. All restraints in terms of repertoire were removed, and the number of theatres duly increased. Napoleon's favoured eight had steadily multiplied to twenty-two by 1830, including a new circuit of suburban theatres, operated by the Seveste family, in Montparnasse, Belleville, Grenelle, Batignolles and Montmartre; but within months of Louis-Philippe's accession, the figure had risen again to over thirty. Indeed, theatre rapidly became a prime field for venture capitalism, and more than one unwary speculator was made to rue his lack of specialist knowledge. A pamphlet published in 1833 and attributed to Guilbert de Pixérécourt protests bitterly against the *droit des pauvres*, identifying it as the root cause of a spate of theatrical bankruptcies within the preceding few years, and in a period of diminishing profits the writer even regrets the passing of the old embargoes.

214   The hazards of free trade, 1833

[Anon.], *Réclamation de MM les directeurs des théâtres de Paris, au sujet de l'impôt établi sous le nom de droit des pauvres* (Paris: David, 1833), pp. 9, 11–12

Lastly, there is no longer any demarcation between the genres. A theatre which used to be allowed to perform only pantomimes now performs *drame* and tragedy; another, which was limited to mechanical shows, now plays melodramas or vaudevilles; and yet the Proprietor, having contracted substantial obligations under the aegis of legislation which he trusted and which promised him exclusive exploitation of his genre, is still required to honour them, when the protection which the law had encouraged him to expect is lacking. What was a burden to him is retained; what protected him is abolished [. . .]

For [some] theatres, the losses have been so heavy that they have been forced to close. The Odéon has been abandoned by the government. The Opéra-Comique has gone under THREE TIMES. The Nouveautés TWICE. The Porte-Saint-Martin ONCE. The Ambigu-Comique FOUR TIMES. The Théâtre Molière TWICE, and it remains closed. In the theatres of Paris there have thus been TWELVE BANKRUPTCIES since the July revolution.

This is the background against which the repressive legislation of 1835 must be set, aimed at reintroducing some order into the chaos without quite resorting to Bonapartist fiat, but in which the licensing of theatres was made the acknowledged accomplice of censorship.

215   Reassertion of central control, 1835

Law of 9 September 1835

Art. 21. No theatre or entertainment of any kind may be established, either in Paris or in the departments, without the prior authorization of the minister of the interior, for Paris, or of the prefects, for departments. The same authorization will be required for the plays which they present. Any contravention of this article will be punished, through the courts of summary jurisdiction, by a prison sentence of between one month and a year and a fine of between 1,000 and 5,000 francs, without prejudice to any action which may be taken against the offenders on account of the plays performed.

22. The authorities shall be empowered at any time to suspend the performance of a play, and even to order the conditional closure of the theatre concerned, for reasons of public order.

Sadly, no legislation could save from insolvency the grandiloquently named Théâtre de la Renaissance, which was intended to be the home of the new *drame* in verse and which, after robust campaigning on the part of Hugo, Dumas and Casimir Delavigne, finally received ministerial blessing and opened its doors at the former Salle Ventadour in November 1838 with the première of Hugo's *Ruy Blas*. Having soon forfeited the support of its progenitors by wayward programming, it came to an ignominious end in April 1841.

Nevertheless, a fellow Romantic spirit, commenting in January 1849 on a plan to legislate for the future organization of theatres, urged the Second Republic not to contemplate a return to the controls of the previous forty-odd years.

216   Republicanism and the theatre, 1849

Théophile Gautier, *Histoire de l'art dramatique en France depuis vingt-cinq ans* (6 vols., Paris: J. Hetzel, 1858–9), vol. VI, pp. 43–4

A dramatic commission has been appointed to consider the question of whether theatres should operate under privilege or free of any control. That such a question should even be asked in a republic seems extraordinary. It answers itself in the process. Does not the very word privilege sound hollow and artificial under a regime where all privileges have been abolished, in fact or in principle? Why should it not be permissible to open a theatre in the same way as it is to open a shop, or build a house?

The dignity of art will be adduced as an objection; but to what extent is that dignity safeguarded by privilege? Do the vaudeville theatres or the melodrama theatres, despite having a monopoly of their dramatic wares, accord them much respect, and do you suppose that open competition would accord them any less? Besides, do the theatrical proprietors who acquire privileges have any moral, artistic or literary conditions imposed on them?; are they required to provide a certain level of luxury, some attempt at hygiene or comfort? Not in the least. They can perform all the rubbish imaginable in buildings that are cramped, stuffy, evil-smelling and as unhealthy for the spirit as for the body [. . .]

Are we afraid, with the abolition of privileges, of seeing theatres spring up at every street-corner? And where would be the harm in it, for that matter? But have no fear. The meanest theatrical hovel will call for an investment of 500 or 600 thousand francs before the curtain goes up for the first time; and half a million doesn't grow on trees. New theatres that stood any chance of being viable, that responded to some unsatisfied need in the public, would survive, the others would go to the wall, and an equilibrium between theatres and theatre-goers would very soon be established.

CENSORSHIP AND PROPAGANDA

Superficially, the evolution of theatrical censorship during this period follows a similarly alternating pattern of *laissez-faire* and control as that of the licensing of theatre buildings: the apparent effect is that of a political seesaw, as the incoming régime, having made a show of relaxing pre-existing checks on the freedom of expression, found itself compelled by force of circumstances to renew, or indeed to redouble them. In the course of one decade alone, the 1820s, a contemporary journalist would have us believe there was a dizzying succession of policy changes: his laconic jottings in a commonplace book refer to the re-establishment of the *censure théâtrale* in 1821, its suspension in 1822, its reinstatement in 1823, its abolition in 1824 with the accession of Charles X, its recrudescence in 1827 and its suppression in 1830 with the arrival of 'citizen kingship'.[1] However things may have appeared at the time, the reality is quite different: police surveillance of the theatrical event, which shares with all public assemblies a quality of unpredictability and an explosive potential, was never relaxed, and apart from short-lived remissions after the revolution of 1789 and, even more briefly, that of 1830, censorship was covertly maintained throughout the period under the guise of a duty to preserve public order. Consequently, to document the whole process in chronological detail would be repetitious – and possibly redundant in view of the narrative account given by F. W. J. Hemmings in his recent *Theatre and State in France, 1760–1905*[2] – but a selection of exemplary pieces of evidence will suffice to illuminate the various forms, repressive as well as preventive, which censorship assumed.

[1] Charles-Maurice Descombes, *Le Théâtre-Français, monument et dépendances* (Paris: Garnier frères, 1859), pp. 138 ff.
[2] Cambridge University Press, 1994. See in particular chapters 3, 9 and 14. For documents relating to theatre censorship in the seventeenth and eighteenth centuries, see Howarth, *French theatre*, nos. 94 and 304 to 315.

REVOLUTIONARY ZEAL AND PARANOIA

The law of 19 January 1791, which decontrolled the practice of theatre, at the same time made playwrights and players jointly responsible before the law for any work performed on a stage: Article 6 ordained that 'the proprietors or the personnel of the different theatres will, by virtue of their status, be subject to inspection by the municipalities; they will take orders only from municipal officers, who may not suspend or prohibit the performance of any play, without prejudice to the accountability of the authors and actors, and may require nothing of the actors which is not in accordance with the law and police regulations'. This permissiveness encountered its first real test almost exactly two years later, in January 1793, when the Théâtre-Français, under its new title the Théâtre de la Nation, mounted Jean-Louis Laya's *L'Ami des lois*, a comedy extolling the virtues of lawfulness and making a thinly veiled advocacy of the Girondist cause against Jacobin extremism. During the play's initial performances, enthusiastic audience response to its obvious allusions to current issues and personalities, notably in the villain of the piece, Nomophage, a satirical portrait of Robespierre, so incensed the Jacobins that they made a deposition to the Paris commune accusing the national theatre of promoting factional and unpatriotic sentiments, and the fifth performance, on 12 January, was duly banned, allegedly in the interests of keeping the peace but in the event provoking angry public protest. A hastily written appeal by Laya to the Convention occasioned an instant debate, followed by a decision to lift the ban, the text of the resolution reading 'the National Assembly knows of no laws authorizing municipalities to exercise censorship over dramatic works',[1] and the performance went ahead as scheduled, if belatedly.

Later in the year, however, the same company of actors fared hideously less well after a similar charge was laid against them. With France at war abroad and torn by insurrection at home, and with the Jacobins now in control of the Convention, the existence of counter-revolutionaries was suspected under every theatrical bed, particularly at so traditionally minded a house as the former Comédie-Française, and the presentation there of a seemingly innocuous comedy entitled *Paméla, ou la Vertu récompensée*, based by François de Neufchâteau on Goldoni's adaptation of the novel by Samuel Richardson, afforded a pretext for closing the theatre down. On 2 September, towards the end of the play's eighth performance, a speech condemning religious intolerance was greeted with warm applause, whereupon a delegate to the Committee of Public Safety, later described by the *Feuille du Salut public* as 'a patriot in uniform', who was seated in the balcony, jumped up and shouted 'Down with political tolerance! It's a crime!'; with calls for his eviction ringing in his ears, he strode out of the auditorium to report the incident to the Jacobin Club. Accordingly, when the curtain fell on the following night, the entire cast and other *sociétaires* of the company were arrested on a charge of '*incivisme*' and royalist conspiracy and conveyed to prison, where they languished for almost a year and were fortunate to escape the guillotine.[2] The *Feuille* dutifully screamed: 'As for their theatre, let this debauched seraglio be closed forever!'

Shortly before this corporate arrest the *sociétaire* Saint-Prix had been summoned to a session of the Committee, as deputy for his colleagues, to account for their choice of repertoire.

[1] Resolution reproduced in Victor Hallays-Dabot, *Histoire de la censure théâtrale en France* (Paris: E. Dentu, 1862), p. 175.
[2] The episode is recounted by Ernest Legouvé in his *Soixante ans de souvenirs* (4 vols., Paris: J. Hetzel, 1888), vol. II, pp. 256–7.

217   The theatre's accountability to the state, 1793

Minutes of a discussion of the Committee of Public Safety of the Department of Paris, 29 July 1793. Reproduced in Alexandre Tuetey, *Répertoire général des sources manuscrites de l'histoire de Paris pendant la révolution française* (Paris: Imprimerie Nouvelle, 1890–1914), vol. IX, p. 321, item 1112.

2. It having been decided to write to the proprietors of all theatres requesting them to meet the Committee and to perform patriotic plays, citizen Saint-Prix, actor of the Théâtre-Français, appeared before the Committee and declared that at the moment the request was received they were arranging the repertoire and that he could promise satisfaction on this account. 29 July 1793, morning.

This was the first of a series of meetings held in the course of the following week, and Saint-Prix's response was typical of the undertakings entered into by every theatre to present suitable programmes, 'especially', as the Opéra's administrator put it, 'during the sojourn of our brothers from the Departments, on the occasion of the *Fédération*'. The mood of the times was even more clearly reflected in a motion put by Couthon to a full assembly of the National Convention, under Danton's presidency, on 2 August, which called for special performances of 'republican' plays during the ensuing month and ominously added a rider giving authority for the closure of any theatres deemed guilty of peddling reactionary sentiments. 'They have served tyranny all too often,' he argued, 'they must now serve freedom.' His motion was adopted for immediate implementation.

218   Revolutionary propaganda, 1793

(a) Decree of the National Convention, 2 August 1793; (b) Decree of the National Convention, 24 January 1794

(a) Decree of the National Convention, 1793

Art. first. From the fourth of this month until the first of September next, at those theatres of Paris designated by the municipality, there will be performed three times a week the tragedies of *Brutus, Guillaume Tell, Caïus Gracchus*[1] and other dramatic works representing the glorious events of the Revolution and the virtues of the defenders of freedom. One of these performances each week will be given at the expense of the Republic.

2. Any theatre presenting plays tending to deprave the morale of the public and rekindle the infamous superstition of monarchism shall be closed, and its proprietors arrested and punished according to the full rigour of the law. The municipality of Paris is charged with the execution of this decree.

[1] Tragedies by Voltaire (first performed in 1730), Lemierre (1766) and M.-J. Chénier (1792), respectively.

The 'expense' incurred by the Republic for these once-weekly free performances was not inconsiderable, as can be seen from a later decree authorizing the necessary disbursement of public funds.

(b) Decree of the National Convention, 1794

The National Convention decrees that the sum of 100,000 livres shall be placed at the disposal of the minister of the interior, to be divided, according to the schedule attached to the present decree, between the twenty theatres of Paris, which, in conformity with the decree of 2 August (old style), each gave four performances for and in the name of the people.

At the end of the four weeks in question, a further measure was introduced, clearly intended to identify those theatres which were continuing to fulfil their republican duty and those susceptible to reactionary backsliding. The Convention's decree of 1 September 1793, while acknowledging that the 'policing' of theatres would remain the responsibility of municipalities, required all proprietors or *associés* to 'keep a register in which, at every performance, they will enter and have countersigned by the officer of police on duty the titles of the plays given, so as to record the number of performances of each'. A report on the contents of these registers was presented to the Convention in November, while the Committee of Public Safety extended its campaign into the new year, minuting on 21 January 1794 that it had 'welcomed into its midst the managers, actors and actresses of the théâtres de la République, du Vaudeville and de la Cité-Variétés, and requested them, through the performance on their stages of good, stirring plays, to propagate the sound manners from which true patriotism springs'.[1]

These complementary modes of influencing public opinion, by, on the one hand, censoring material considered to be reactionary and, on the other, promoting the revolution itself, were to characterize the remainder of the revolutionary decade. A decree of 26 April 1794, for instance, demanded a close scrutiny of all dramatic texts with a view to eliminating aristocratic titles such as duke, baron, marquis and count, 'those feudal appellations, issuing from a source too impure to sully the French stage any longer', and observers appointed by the minister of the interior kept him continuously informed about the revolutionary credentials of plays in performance, such as *L'Officier de fortune* at the théâtre de la rue Feydeau, where it was reported that the play's 'patriotic passages were applauded with enthusiasm'.[2]

The first formal celebration of the Revolution, *La Prise de la Bastille*, had taken place at Notre-Dame on 13 July 1790 to commemorate the fateful events of the previous July. Described as a *hiérodrame*, a form of oratorio couched in biblical language, it brought together singers and musicians from all the metropolitan theatres, who joined the audience in singing the closing *Te Deum*, and it subsequently became the inspiration for a succession of open-air ceremonies masterminded by Jacques-Louis David, which culminated in May 1794 with the *Fête de l'Etre Suprême*, a ritualized, quasi-theatrical spectacle to inaugurate the new state religion of deism. One of the singers taking part has left a first-hand account of the experience.

---

[1] Reproduced in A. Tuetey, *Répertoire général des sources manuscites de l'histoire de Paris pendant la résolution française* (Paris: Imprimerie Nouvelle, 1890–1914), vol. x, p. 314, item 1517.
[2] Anonymous report to the minister, 21 September 1793. Tuetey, *Répertoire général*, vol. ix, p. 418, item 1373.

219   Festival of the Supreme Being, 1794

Louise Fusil, *Souvenirs d'une actrice* (3 vols., Paris: Dumont, 1841–6), vol. i, pp. 326–8

This festival was without doubt the finest of the age. On the terrace of the château des Tuileries a pavilion had been constructed in the form of an amphitheatre. To either side a flight of steps led down, with a handrail to support the ladies who were grouped in pairs from the top to the bottom and sang the hymns. They were dressed in white tunics with a sash across the breast, a crown of roses on the head and a basket full of rose-petals in their hands. These matching costumes made a very pretty sight. A large orchestra comprising all the capital's musical celebrities and conducted by Lesueur[1] were positioned in front of the pavilion. Deputies from the

Convention, in all their finery, occupied the balcony. Opposite, near the flower-beds, stood the statue of Atheism. Robespierre went with a torch in his hand and set fire to it, producing a kind of pyrotechnic effect. This effigy gave way to a statue of Reason, which emerged quite blackened from the flames of Atheism and Fanaticism. The change of décor was not at all successful.

Once that ceremony was complete, the procession set off, and heaven knows how hot and weary we had become before we reached the Champ-de-Mars. There, under a tree on top of the Mountain, we sang:

> Father of the universe, supreme intelligence,
> Benefactor by purblind mortals unperceived,
> To our apprehension thy being hath been revealed, etc.

This ceremony finished very late. We were dying of thirst and hunger; Talma and David were hard put to find us something to eat, and even then we had to hide it, for fear that it might have seemed too mundane to Robespierre, standing on the mountain-top and no doubt thinking that the incense would afford us nourishment enough.

[1] Jean-François Lesueur (1760–1837), French composer and teacher of Berlioz, who regularly provided music for the revolutionary festivals.

For its part, the Directory, evidently unimpressed by the propagandist benefit to be derived from occasional festivals, sought to impart a regular boost to public morale by legislating for revolutionary songs to be sung at every theatrical performance.

220   Music to revolutionary ears, 1796

Decree of the Directory, 7 January 1796

All managers, entrepreneurs and proprietors of theatres in Paris are charged, on their personal recognizance, with ensuring that every evening before the curtain is raised their orchestras play well-loved revolutionary airs, such as the *Marseillaise*, *Ça ira*, *Veillons au salut de l'Empire* and *Le Chant du Départ*. During the intervals between plays, the *Hymne des Marseillais* or other patriotic songs must always be sung. On every working day the Théâtre des Arts [the Opéra] will give a performance of the *Offrande à la Liberté*, with full orchestral accompaniment, or of other republican pieces.

NAPOLEONIC VIGILANCE

Napoleon adopted a characteristically radical approach to the question of censorship. One of his earliest decisions as First Consul was to entrust his minister of the interior with the examination and approval of all new plays and all plays written since 14 July 1789 'relating to the Revolution', which it was proposed to revive. Without his approval no play could be performed in Paris, and a subsequent ministerial circular made clear that this metropolitan control was to be broadened, by means of the prefectorial system, to encompass the provinces, which could no longer be allowed to enjoy the relative immunity conferred by remoteness from the seat of political power.

221   Extension of censorship to the departments, 1800

Circular from the Minister of the Interior to departmental prefects, 11 April 1800. Reproduced in Pierre Bossuet, *Histoire des théâtres nationaux* (Paris: E. Jorel, 1909), pp. 104–5

Henceforth only those works which I have authorized for performance in Paris may be played in the departments. You will receive without delay a list of the plays, old and new, which may be presented or represented on the stage; and you will see to it that no other is included in the repertoires of theatre managers.

Later, the Emperor made a point of keeping an eye on potentially controversial plays even before they were performed and would advise his minister of police to take appropriate action. Receiving news in Milan of the success of Raynouard's *Les Templiers* at the Théâtre-Français, he had despatched instructions to Paris within weeks of the play's opening.

222   Napoleon manipulates the repertoire, 1805

Letter to Joseph Fouché, 1 June 1805. Reproduced in Bossuet, *Histoire des théâtres nationaux*, p. 116

It would seem that the success of the tragedy *Les Templiers* is directing people's minds towards that era of French history. This is well and good, but I do not think we should allow plays to be performed whose subjects are taken from periods too close to our own. I have read in a newspaper that there are plans to present a tragedy about Henri IV. This epoch is not sufficiently remote not to reawaken strong feelings. What the stage needs is a little antiquity, and without creating too much difficulty for the theatre, I think you must find a way to prevent its performance, while not making your intervention known.

The play in question, doubtless Raynouard's *Les Etats de Blois*, did not in fact reach the stage until May 1814, a month after the Emperor's abdication. Not surprisingly, the wholesale reorganization of the French theatre initiated by Napoleon in 1806 had made explicit provision for the maintenance of centralized censorship. His own decree of 8 June flatly declared that 'no play may be performed without the authorization of the minister of police', and the subsequent ministerial directive of 25 April 1807 made assurance doubly sure by its Article 6: 'The examination of plays by the office of the minister of the interior, and the permission given for their performance, in no way exempts managers from having recourse to the ministry of police, which will examine plays on other accounts.'

CONTINUING WATCHFULNESS UNDER THE RESTORATION

By and large, the Restoration was content to leave in place the control mechanisms established under the Empire, though their targets were no longer necessarily the same. For
example, all overt reference to Napoleon and his military exploits was now banned, and
in 1821 the censor obliged Lucien Arnault to alter the age of the protagonist's son in his
tragedy of *Régulus* so as to avoid any risk of interpretation as an allusion to Napoleon's
10-year-old son and heir, the duc de Reichstadt, now seen as a focus for opposition to the
restored monarchy. This incident is symptomatic of a time when the regime was at its most
paranoid: one year before, a nephew to the King, the duc de Berri, had been assassinated
by a Bonapartist agitator on the steps of the Opéra, and scores of stage works that had
previously been passed by the censor, some of them from the classic repertoire even, were
promptly recalled for further scrutiny to detect either *allusions* of a deliberate nature or lines
of text that might possibly be apprehended in performance as what were called *applications*
to the current political situation. *Application*-spotting, a favoured sport of audiences even
before 1789, was now at its height. What had offered ample opportunity, in the early years
of the Revolution, for an open expression of royalist sympathy and, under the Empire, for a
public, at times conspicuously propagandist, celebration of Napoleon's greatest triumphs,
now became a potential vehicle for Bonapartist dissent, and the state was duly vigilant.
Nowhere was this vigilance more doctrinaire and illiberal than in the activities of the police.

223 Police surveillance, 1827

Circular from the Paris prefect of police, 6 April 1827. Archives Nationales, F21 1046

Monsieur, I have had occasion several times in the past to issue instructions concerning the surveillance with which you are charged in theatres. In referring you
again to the circulars which have been addressed to you on this subject in diverse
connections and in enjoining you to exercise all due regard to the execution of the
measures they contain, I believe I should in particular reiterate the importance
of the reports which I have asked you to submit to me on all occasions when a
new play is performed for the first time, especially when it has given rise to any
circumstances of which the authorities should be apprised. Although my circular
of 6 April 1824 will have sufficiently explained the purpose of these reports, as well
as the points about which I wished to be informed in detail, I must nonetheless
draw your attention once more to this essential part of your service and advise
you to notify me of all first performances, even when the play has not warranted
any particular comment. Thus, any passages liable to offend public decency, any
political or other allusion upon which the subversive might seize, anything that
might strike you as improper either about what is spoken, or about the acting or
costumes of the performers, or about the scenery, in short all those elements that
tend to elicit a response from the audience, any occurrences which may have compromised or disturbed in any manner whatever good public order and harmony,
shall continue to be the subject matter for a circumstantial report, which I would
urge you to forward to me as rapidly as possible.

But it will not suffice to notify me of first performances if I am not also informed of any occurrences which may be occasioned by existing plays, in respect of which the subversive often contrive to make the most improper *applications* and express dangerous points of view.

Consequently any play, whether old or new, whose performance may be marked by some unusual circumstance, from a moral or political standpoint, must henceforward and without exception be the subject of a written communication, in which you will inform me in detail of the effect it has produced on the audience and of the nature of the applause or expressions of disapproval it has provoked. Since it is particularly in places of assembly which are as heavily frequented as theatres are nowadays that subversion endeavours to influence public opinion, you must appreciate, Monsieur, how vital it is for the authorities not to be unaware of anything that you may have occasion to observe [. . .]

In this climate, any deviations from a dramatic text previously approved by the censor, or impromptu additions to it, became especially culpable.

224   The penalties of ad-libbing, 1825

Letter from the Minister of the Interior to the prefect of police, 7 September 1825. Archives Nationales, F21 1134

Monsieur le Préfet, I have received your letter of 29 August last concerning what occurred on the 25th of the same month during the first performance of *Le Cocher de fiacre*[1] at the Ambigu-Comique.

On the following day the management of this theatre informed me that by way of punishing the actor Frédéric [*sic*] for having added certain inappropriate lines to his part they had imposed a fine on him.

In the event of his allowing himself, despite this sanction, a similar outburst in the future, you have authority, in line with your proposal, to suspend his right to appear on the stage for a fixed period, as has happened in his case on a previous occasion, and I suggest that you summon him to give him notice of this decision [. . .]

[1] Melodrama by B. Antier and Naigeon.

For the playwright, the resulting aesthetic claustrophobia was summed up by Hugo.

225   The inhibiting effects of censorship

Victor Hugo, preface to *Marion de Lorme. Œuvres complètes*, ed. Jean Massin (18 vols., Paris: Club Français du Livre, 1967–70), vol. III, pp. 729–30

And indeed, in the last years of the Restoration, the new spirit of the nineteenth century had suffused everything, history, poetry, philosophy, everything except the theatre. And for this state of affairs there was a very simple explanation: the theatre was hemmed in by censorship. No means existed to represent on the stage authentically, seriously and faithfully, with an artist's impartiality but also his rigour, a king, a priest, a nobleman, the Middle Ages, history or the past. Censorship stood in the way, indulgent towards routine, conventional pieces of work, which dress everything up, and thereby distort everything, but merciless towards art which was truthful, honest and sincere.

A CHANGE OF CLIMATE: FROM JULY REVOLUTION TO CITIZEN KINGSHIP

With the overthrow of the restored monarchy in July 1830, censorship was supposedly rendered illegal by the constitutional Charter of 7 August, but the terms of Article 7 applied, by implication, only to the written word in general, the press in particular, and certainly no reference was made to the theatre. In any case, the imperial decrees of 1806 and 1807 had never been formally repealed and could still, if the need arose, be invoked, as could an even earlier edict of 1793 empowering the police to discontinue performances of any play held to be responsible for causing a breach of the peace. Perhaps the most notorious casualty of this loophole was Hugo's *Le Roi s'amuse*, which was suppressed after only one performance in November 1832, despite general agreement that the play had created far less audience disturbance than *Hernani* two years earlier. Conversely, his *Marion de Lorme*, which had been refused authorization at the Théâtre-Français in 1829, was successfully produced at the Porte-Saint-Martin in 1831, thus joining many other plays, which, as he expressed it in his preface, 'the censorship of the Restoration had buried alive' and the July revolution had allowed to burst forth from their tomb. In retrospect, Dumas came to see the brief respite which that three-day revolution had provided from the worst excesses of preventive censorship, as having been crucial for the development of Romantic drama.

226   Censorship is relaxed, 1830

Alexandre Dumas, *Souvenirs dramatiques* (2 vols., Paris: Calmann-Lévy, 1868), vol. 1, pp. 240–1

Then came those three days which, in the process of overthrowing not a few things, overthrew censorship without noticing it. We say without noticing it, because, in point of fact, as soon as it was noticed that censorship no longer existed, it was reinstated. But at least the slumbering hydra lay hidden for two or three years in its ministerial lair, with the result that during this time *Antony, Richard Darlington, La Tour de Nesle, Marion Delorme, Angèle, Lucrèce Borgia* and *Marie Tudor* saw the light of day.[1] Without this interregnum, it is probable that these seven *drames*, which created such havoc in society, would still remain unperformed.

[1] These characteristic new plays, four by Dumas and three by Hugo, were all produced at the Porte-Saint-Martin between May 1831 and December 1833.

Before the interregnum ended, it was served an elegantly worded, and mealy-mouthed, notice of foreclosure, addressed to all theatre managers by the head of the 'division of fine arts and theatres' at the ministry of the interior.

227   Censorship is reimposed, 1834

Circular signed by Hygin-Auguste Cavé, July 1834. Reproduced in *Revue des Deux Mondes*, 3rd series, vol. 3 (1834), pp. 239–40

Monsieur,

Article 11 of the decree of 8 June 1806, still in force today, gives the government the authority to prohibit theatrical productions. Over the last four years it has been found necessary to place an interdict on the performance of several plays. Not having had sight of any manuscripts, the government was unable, for the most part, to take this action until after the managers had borne the costs of production. This has resulted in losses for them and in claims for indemnification which could not be entertained. Appeals from managers have persuaded us of the need to regularize the present situation. It is to this end that I have advised you verbally, and that, *at your request*, I now advise you in writing of what has been decided by the minister of the interior with regard to the implementation of the decree of 8 June 1806.

You have it in your power to avoid any expenditure by submitting the manuscripts of new plays in advance to the division of fine arts and theatres. Plays which have not been submitted will simply be banned when their subject matter warrants the application of the decree, and you will have only yourselves to blame for any losses incurred from production costs which have been rendered superfluous.

This circular led to protests from several managers, notably Pixérécourt at the Opéra-Comique and Harel at the Odéon, and from the recently established Société des Auteurs Dramatiques, but to no avail. A year later, emboldened by Fieschi's attempt on the king's life and at the instance of Thiers as minister of the interior, the government reintroduced both preventive and repressive censorship officially by the comprehensively restrictive law of 9 September 1835.[1]

[1] See **215**.

ACTION REPLAY, 1848–9

All these obstacles were swept away by the Second Republic of 1848. Within days of its proclamation in February, a decree of the provisional administration, dated 6 March, abrogated the law of 1835, and on the 24th the minister of the interior idealistically announced that 'if the state owes its people the work by which they live, it must also enable them to partake of the moral recreations which gladden the soul', including numerous free performances of plays by leading dramatists. Entering into the spirit of the moment, Mlle Rachel chose to mark her return to the Théâtre-Français (now renamed the Théâtre de la République again) after a protracted absence by giving a performance of the *Marseillaise*: having just uttered her imprecations against Rome as Camille in Corneille's *Horace*, she reappeared on stage, her peplum replaced by a plain white tunic, and stepping down to the footlights, half-sang, half-chanted the revolutionary anthem, which culminated, as Gautier reported in an enthusiastic review, when 'she kneeled and enveloped herself in the tricolour folds of the symbolic flag'.[1]

But the euphoria could not, and did not, last. In March of the following year *La Danse aux écus*, a vaudeville by Marc Fournier and Henri de Kock at the Gymnase, was ordered to be taken off after only three performances, eliciting from Gautier a very different commentary, grim with foreboding.

---

[1] *Presse* (20 March 1848) (Gautier, *Histoire de l'art dramatique*, vol. v, pp. 241–3). For a less favourable reaction, accusing Rachel of opportunism and cheap populism aimed at repairing a decline in her audience appeal, see Armand de Pontmartin in *Revue des Deux Mondes*, 22 (1848), pp. 156–7.

228   Suppression for breach of the peace, 1849

Presse (26 March 1849), in Gautier, *Histoire de l'art dramatique*, vol. vi, p. 67

The situation in which theatres find themselves is grave. They are caught between suppression and censorship: of the two evils, suppression seems to us the lesser, because one does not accept it, one submits to it; it is a brutal fact, and no more. Whereas to go and humbly offer to the censor manuscripts which he can score with red marks is to recognize an illegal authority and accord the force of law to an abuse. *La Danse aux écus* has been suppressed because the performances were too rowdy: it seems an inadequate reason. Doubtless, order is a good thing, but order must not be confused with inertia, mutism and inanimation. The most peaceful place in the world is a cemetery, and we trust that this is not the kind of peace to which we are being reduced. Life is noisy and turbulent, and that is why it is called life. For our part, we do not see what harm there can be if, in a theatre, one half of the audience is whistling while the other half is applauding; there is nothing subversive about that, and the public is simply exercising its prerogative. If you are delighted, you clap your hands; if you are disgusted, you apply a hollow key to your lips: this is a privilege which, according to Boileau, the lowest menial enjoyed under the most despotic of sovereigns.

In September another play, Ferdinand Laloue's *Rome*, which dealt with the recent French military intervention on behalf of the Pope against Garibaldi, was banned on similar grounds, also after its third performance.

In the same year a commission was appointed by the Conseil d'Etat to investigate the current state of the theatre and make recommendations for new legislation. Under the chairmanship of M. Vivien, it took verbal evidence from playwrights, actors, managers, critics and other interested parties on a range of issues, among them state control and censorship, on which Hugo's observations were characteristically outspoken.

229   The myth of freedom, 1849

Victor Hugo, speech before the Conseil d'Etat commission, 17 September 1849, reproduced in Victor Hugo, *Actes et paroles. Avant l'exil* (2 vols., Paris: J. Hetzel, [1890]), vol. 1, p. 233

Between these two principles [liberty and authority] you will have to make a choice, leaving aside any beneficent compromises you may subsequently make between what you choose and what you do not choose. You will have to make a choice; which option will you take? Let us consider.

Where theatres are concerned, the principle of authority has both for and against it the fact that it has already been tried. Ever since the theatre has existed in France, it has been dominated by the principle of authority. If its disadvantages have been identified, so have its advantages, they are well known. The principle of liberty has not yet been put to the test.

Chairman: It was put to the test between 1791 and 1806.

Victor Hugo: It was proclaimed in 1791, but not realized; everyone stood in the shadow of the guillotine. Liberty was merely in germ then, it did not flower. One cannot judge the effects of theatrical liberty by what it was able to achieve during the first revolution.

Nor, in the event, could one judge it by what it was allowed to achieve during the 1848 revolution. Although the commission reported in favour of maintaining the status quo, the ensuing bill, when enacted in July 1850, reinstated preventive censorship on a provisional basis, a reinstatement confirmed by the Second Empire, only to be rescinded by the Third Republic in 1870, for the cycle to recommence.

II   *Managerial and contractual documents*

For more than 200 years, since the emergence of professional acting companies in the early sixteenth century, the theatrical year in France had been reckoned to and from Eastertide. Most theatre buildings closed their doors for a period beforehand, at the very least for the duration of Holy Week, including Easter Sunday, and more usually for two or even three whole weeks during Lent. Only musical performances, circuses and fairground displays of acrobatics and rope-dancing were tolerated, except on Good Friday itself.

THE THEATRICAL CALENDAR

Early in 1792, however, in a comparatively mild access of post-revolutionary anti-clericalism, the proprietors of a number of the new theatres that had been set up in Paris in the wake of the edict of the previous January approached the city's magistrates demanding to know whether they should still consider themselves to be bound by the ecclesiastical calendar. With so many rival establishments competing for public favour, all unsubsidized and subject to market forces, they could ill afford to suspend operations for so long a term, and their petition evidently did not fall on deaf ears.

230   An end to doctrinal obeisance, 1792

Letter from the public attorney of the Commune of Paris to the commissioners of police, *Journal de Paris* (28 March 1792), reproduced in Bossuet, *Histoire des théâtres nationaux*, p. 77 n. 1

Certain theatrical proprietors have enquired of the people's magistrature whether they are compelled to close their playhouses for the fortnight before Easter. I owe them a ruling and it is for you, sirs, to adjudicate.

At a time when France was governed by one dominant religion, when we were condemned to do whatever one man required of us, the lieutenant of police was well able to frame a law in collusion with the priests; but when, after a long night, the truth has dawned, putting fools to shame and rogues to flight, when freedom will no longer suffer any tyrants nor equality any slaves, when there is a constitution to protect all creeds at the same time as all opinions, it is now only the people, through its representatives, who can institute holidays, truly national holidays, and all religions must withdraw to their places of worship, if not of refuge. Let those who so wish choose a church, or a synagogue or a mosque. No one will understand better than you, sirs, that if every person is the master of his own skills as of his own thoughts, it can no longer be forbidden to perform a play on Good Friday any more than it is to write one, at least for those who are not in spiritual mourning. Industry enjoys the same rights as commerce, and only the public interest may at any time override them. And on what pretext could a municipality, being the guardian of all prerogatives, consign to idleness a host of citizens for whom the theatre provides a living, and an even larger host to whom it gives entertainment and instruction, above all after a revolution which has proved so conclusively that the tragedies of Voltaire are more apt to forge nations than are the sermons of the abbé Maury?[1] [...] It is greatly to be desired that Rome as a body, gathered in the sacristy, should realize with the end of Lent that it no longer has any privileges; and nothing will more clearly demonstrate the advance of reason than autonomy for the theatres, where, as Christians congregate in darkness, there will be performances for friends of the Constitution of *La Mort de César*.

---

[1] Jean-Siffrein Maury (1746–1817), French prelate, an eloquent apologist of the monarchy, later appointed Archbishop of Paris by Napoleon in 1810.

The conventional Easter closure was duly abolished, and for six years theatres were able to remain open all the year round, until the old tradition was restored by the Consulate, at least for Holy Week itself; thereafter, the break in activity tended to be confined to Maundy Thursday and Good Friday, though the church regained sufficient influence after the Restoration to dissuade many of its flock from visiting the theatre at all during Lent, a severe blow to box office receipts. Business was also notoriously poor in high summer and in the weeks leading up Christmas and the new year, when, as the *Courrier des Théâtres* observed, theatre-goers were more inclined to keep 'the money intended for presents hoarded up in their purses'.[1] In particular, August was characterized by Harel as, at least in Paris, 'the month for *congés*, for new actors to make their débuts and for touring the country. Theatres either close down or, what amounts to the same, are inhabited by mediocre performers; takings fall to nothing.'[2] In 1837, when he brought a suit for damages and loss of earnings against the Théâtre-Français, Hugo went so far as to allege that the theatre had calculatedly reserved the summer months for the contracted revivals of two of his plays in order to increase the likelihood that takings would drop below the figure it regarded as necessary to offset running costs and thus afford a convenient excuse to remove them from the bills.

Traditionally, Easter Day also represented the *terminus a quo* and *ad quem* for actors' contracts: as with other labour markets, notably that for agricultural workers, theatre managers would take advantage of the enforced *relâche* to seek and engage company members for the beginning of the new season, normally on the first Sunday after Easter. Harel described the period as one of 'auditions for the legion of actors requiring to change managers and audiences every year'.[3] These managers, whether based in Paris itself or visiting from the provinces, would foregather to transact their business at one or other of the capital's popular taverns, such as the Café Touchard or the Café de Suède.

---

[1] *Courrier des Théâtres* (15 December 1832).
[2] *Dictionnaire théâtral*, p. 24.
[3] *Ibid.*, p. 22.

231   An employment exchange for actors

Etienne de Jouy, *L'Hermite de la Chaussée d'Antin, ou Observations sur les mœurs et les usages parisiens au commencement du XIXe siècle* (5 vols., Paris: Pillet, 1812–14), vol. III, pp. 192–3

Anyone who wishes to form an idea of the practices and organization of this dramatic fraternity, and of its constituent members, should repair to the café Touchard during the Easter fortnight. This café [is where] Thalia, or rather Thespis, has established a central depot for those actors from the provinces who do not have enough talent or good fortune to obtain an engagement on their native heath; for those whom a cruel audience have prevented from completing their engagements; for those whose debts have obliged them to leave a town where they had only their creditors for spectators; for those, finally, who are hoping to make a début in Paris. Actors of every kind and in every line of business show up at the café Touchard: managers, too, frequent this theatrical bazaar, where all talents are up for auction and can be acquired at knockdown prices.

ADMINISTRATION OF THE THÉÂTRE-FRANÇAIS

One privileged company of artists were spared the indignity and uncertainty of this annual jumble sale. Like the earliest professional troupes, the Comédie-Française still functioned as a covenanted association or partnership of actors and was still organized on the same terms as had governed its formation in 1680, with two categories of members, the *sociétaires* and the *pensionnaires*.[1] The latter, by tradition, had always been a very small group, numbering half a dozen or so and composed of probationers or *débutants*, who were employed on a provisional basis and a fixed salary, to play specified roles for a finite period, usually two or three years, or until such time as it was decided whether to admit them to the partnership or to terminate their engagement. *Sociétaires*, on the other hand, as co-proprietors of the whole enterprise, enjoyed permanent security of tenure and received remuneration in the form of a fee for each performance in which they appeared (known as *feux*) and, at the end of the theatrical year, a share (whether a full share for the most senior members or a *fraction de part*, a half or quarter share) of the net proceeds, after deduction of agreed salaries, production costs and other necessary outgoings.

Under the First Empire this inherited structure was substantially overhauled and precisely codified. By a decree of 1 November 1807 Napoleon had already placed the four state-subsidized houses in the capital – the Théâtre-Français, the Opéra, the Opéra-Comique and the Théâtre de l'Impératrice (or Odéon) – under the supervision of an officer of his household, the Comte de Rémusat, with the title of Surintendant des Spectacles, but it was the Théâtre-Français that he personally valued most, not only as an ornament of imperial authority at home but also as an effective instrument for advancing the prestige of France and French civilization abroad. Before it could be become a truly national theatre, however, it would have to recognize that it had responsibilities to the state in return for state support, and Napoleon was clearly determined to see those responsibilities adequately discharged. Accordingly, the so-called 'Moscow decree', which he signed during the ill-fated Russian campaign but which was doubtless drafted by hands much nearer home, is a remarkably comprehensive document, addressing the entire governance and internal management of the institution. Whilst respecting the underlying principle of partnership between actor-sharers and allowing the *sociétaires* a residual measure of self-determination in the conduct of their purely professional affairs and performance activities, the decree established the post of 'imperial commissioner', who would oversee on a day-to-day basis 'all aspects of the administration and accounting' of the theatre and who would act as a channel for directives from the *Surintendant*, whose function had obvious similarities to that exercised, at times very intrusively, by the gentlemen of the king's bedchamber under the *ancien régime*.

---

[1] For documents relating to the formation and early organization of the Comédie-Française, see Howarth, *French theatre*, nos. 287 to 292.

232   Napoleon reorganizes the Théâtre-Français, 1812

Décret impérial sur la Surveillance, l'Organisation, l'Administration, la Comptabilité, la Police et la Discipline du Théâtre-Français, 15 October 1812 (Bulletin des Lois, no. 469)

PART II

ON THE PARTNERSHIP OF THE THEATRE-FRANÇAIS

Section the First

On the Division into Shares

5. The actors of our Théâtre-Français will continue to be associated as a Society, which shall be administered in conformance with the regulations given hereafter.

6. The proceeds from takings, all costs and expenses having been deducted, shall be divided into twenty-four shares.

7. One of these shares shall be placed in reserve, to be employed by the *Surintendant* to meet any unforeseen requirements: if it is not used in its entirety, the surplus shall be distributed among the *Sociétaires* at the end of the year.

8. One half share shall be placed in reserve, to augment the Society's pension fund.

9. One half share shall be devoted each year to scenery, furniture, costumes in stock, repairs to boxes and upkeep of the auditorium, at the direction of the *Surintendant* [. . .]

10. The twenty-two shares remaining shall continue to be apportioned among the *Sociétaires*, from one eighth of a part to one full part, which shall be the maximum.

11. The shares or fractions of shares outstanding shall be assigned or distributed by our *Surintendant des spectacles*.

Section ii

On Pensions and Retirements

12. Every *Sociétaire* shall, on his admission, contract to play for twenty years; and, after twenty years of continuous service, will be allowed to take his retirement, unless the *Surintendant* considers it advisable to retain him [. . .]

13. A *Sociétaire* retiring after twenty years shall be entitled: 1° to an annuity of two thousand francs from the subsidy allocated to the Théâtre-Français by the decree of 13 messidor year X [2 July 1802];[1] 2° to a pension of equivalent value from the Society's fund referred to in Article 8.

14. If the *Surintendant* considers it appropriate to extend a *Sociétaire's* period of service beyond twenty years, there shall, on his retirement, be added a further sum of one hundred francs per year to each of the pensions referred to in the previous article.
[. . .]

25. Any *Sociétaire* who leaves the Theatre without having obtained the consent of the *Surintendant* shall lose the sum for which he has contributed, and shall not be entitled to any pension.
[. . .]

Section III
On the Retirement of Salaried Actors and of Employees

28. After twenty or more years of continuous service by a salaried actor or actress, or after only ten years in the case of illness, or in the event of an accident, as is prescribed for *Sociétaires* (Art. 15), the *Surintendant* shall have authority to recommend that we award a pension, half to be drawn from the subsidy of a hundred thousand francs and half from the Society's fund, which pension shall not in total exceed half the salary he or she would have received for the last three years of service [. . .]

PART III
Section the First
On the Management of the Society's Interests

30. A Committee composed of male members of the Society, chaired by the imperial Commissioner and with a secretary to maintain a record of its deliberations, shall be charged with the control and management of the Company's interests.

> The *Surintendant* shall nominate the members of this Committee annually. They shall be eligible for re-election indefinitely.
> Three of the members shall be charged with the implementation of its resolutions [. . .]

---

[1] An annual subvention of 100,000 francs, payable through the Ministry of the Interior.

Provision was also made, in Articles 42–44, for general meetings of all the *sociétaires* to be held at regular intervals, convened by the management committee or, exceptionally, by the *Surintendant*, and, in Article 51, for a rota of all *sociétaires* to act as *semainiers*, two per week, to be responsible for calling rehearsals, drawing up the playbills for the week's performances and conciliating the audience in the event of changes of programme or any other untoward occurrence.

The benefits for an actor of elevation to the *sociétariat*, in terms of professional distinction and guaranteed employment were obvious and much coveted; financially, although their income became liable to fluctuation after 1791 in the face of increased competition from the commercial sector, Napoleon's 1807 decree limiting the number of secondary theatres helped considerably to restore their fortunes. At the beginning of the period, in the late 1780s, records show that the average annual yield of a full share amounted to 23,600 livres,[1] and Kotzebue, visiting the French capital fifteen years later – after the reconstitution of the Théâtre-Français with state support but before Napoleon's radical intervention – not only predicated a similar figure but, with a palpable mixture of envy and disapproval, noted the various other perquisites enjoyed by successful *sociétaires*, ensuring 'a level of ease that puts them on a par with the wealthy'.

[1] Figures cited by C. Alasseur, *La Comedie-Française au XVIIIe siècle* (The Hague and Paris: Mouton, 1967), pp. 198–9.

233   Affluence of the *sociétaires*, 1804

August von Kotzebue, *Souvenirs de Paris en 1804*, trans. R. C. Guilbert de Pixérécourt (Paris: Barba, 1805), vol. II, pp. 296–7

The Théâtre-Français is controlled by its members. After the deduction of all costs, the remaining income is divided into twenty-five shares; the leading and longest-serving actors receive a full share, others a half share, and so on. He who has a full share will draw twenty-five to thirty thousand francs a year. [At this point Pixérécourt, as translator, interpolates a disclaiming footnote: Often they would settle for half of that]; but a small amount is held back every month which adds up, for the entire company, to 72,000 livres a year [Pixérécourt's note: Let us say 12 or 15,000 francs at the very most]. This sum is put aside, and invested at an interest. If an actor has served for twenty-five years, he can then live in comfort, even though he were no more than forty years old. He will receive, 1° the proportion of money due to him from that which has been put aside during his years of service, totalling approximately 30 thousand livres. 2° He will be granted a performance at the Opéra, for his benefit, which will bring him a further 30,000 livres, if he is well liked. 3° He will receive from his fellow sharers an annual pension of two thousand *livres.* 4° Lastly, another pension, at least as substantial, from the government. On top of that, he has the right, if still young and in good health, to retain his position, though this seldom happens. [Pixérécourt's note: Yes, but in this event he will not draw his pensions]

Additional rewards were not hard to come by for the leading *sociétaires*. Napoleon was particularly generous towards his favoured players, according Talma, for instance, a monthly gratuity of 1,500 francs and commanding special performances, either for his own entertainment at Malmaison and Saint-Cloud or to accompany important diplomatic initiatives, all of which were liberally funded: for their part in the season of French plays given at Dresden in July/August 1813, in which comedy predominated, the comic specialists Fleury and Mlle Mars each received 10,000 francs, Talma and Mlle George 8,000 apiece, as well as expenses for travel and subsistence. After the Restoration, Louis XVIII, despite Talma's pronounced Bonapartist sympathies, wasted little time before awarding him an annuity of 30,000 francs from his own privy purse in 1816, and six years later, not to be outdone, William I of the

Netherlands offered him a pension of 10,000 francs on condition that he would visit the royal theatre in Brussels annually for the next five years to appear in his most famous roles. Talma's valet, Constant, is on record as estimating his master's annual income to be higher than that of a general, at about 60,000 francs.

However, by far the most reliable means of supplementing routine earnings was the provincial tour, which a *sociétaire* was able to make every summer during his or her two months of *congé*, and which could be taken at any time between May and October. Certain star performers were renowned for capitalizing on this opportunity, to the detriment of both their company colleagues and the Parisian public. Describing provincial departments as the 'favourite abode of the leading actors of Paris', the *Dictionnaire théâtral* of 1824 defines *congé* as a 'licence to levy taxes' in the provinces and claims that the statutory two-month entitlement was usually extended to four.[1] The critic Geoffroy, in replying to a correspondent who had extolled Talma and sought to justify his frequent absences from the stage of the Théâtre-Français, was moved to publish a condemnation of the practice and, through it, a veiled attack on Talma himself, who had become a regular butt of his carping or faint praise.

[1] See p. 85.

234   The venality of touring, 1812

Julien-Louis Geoffroy, in *Journal de l'Empire* (21 November 1812)

My own opinion is that, in the interests of art, leave of absence ought to be regarded, as it was in the past, as a very rare and brief concession; even Lekain was granted a *congé* only with difficulty [. . .] yet Lekain was the greatest tragedian who ever set foot on the stage [. . .]

Great actors sometimes make money and always deteriorate by too long a sojourn in the provinces; too assured of praise from unsophisticated audiences and too certain of the loyal puffing of his supporters, the Parisian prince of tragedy grows careless, yields to bad habits, becomes inflated and absurd. Art's two greatest enemies, pride and excess, together beset him. The laurels he has solicited rain down on his head, the extravagant eulogies of journalists overwhelm him in their embrace, the river of gold flows into his coffers, all these tributes seem to belie his mortal status; he returns to Paris half as rich again and with less than half his talent; now he is merely a bad actor who imagines himself a god.

CONDITIONS OF EMPLOYMENT IN THE BOULEVARD THEATRES

The contrast between this state of affairs and that prevailing in the boulevard theatres was stark indeed. Whatever the uncertainty of their box office returns, the *sociétaires* were spared the daily servitude and unremitting exploitation to which an actor was exposed in the commercial sector, a world dominated by binding contracts and proprietor-managers adept at driving a hard bargain. The *Almanach* for 1809 specifies how most of these theatres were administered at the time – the Vaudeville by a manager answerable to a company of shareholders, the Variétés by a group of 'entrepreneurs', the Gaîté by an executive proprietor, the Ambigu-Comique by a lessee-manager – and confirms that all their actors were engaged on fixed salaries, or *appointements*.[1] Some idea of the rigours of the system may be gained from the terms of a three-year contract drawn up in 1826 between the manager of the Funambules and Deburau, a performer no less vital for success than any *sociétaire*.

[1] *Almanach des Spectacles à Paris, pour l'an 1809* (Paris, 1809), pp. 7–8.

235   Deburau is contracted to the Funambules, 1826

Jules Janin, *Deburau, histoire du théâtre à quatre sous, pour faire suite à l'Histoire du Théâtre-Français* (2nd edn, 2 vols., Paris: C. Gosselin, 1832), vol. II, pp. 6–14

Contract

Between the undersigned, M. NICHOLAS-MICHEL BERTRAND, Director of the Funambules Theatre, domiciled in Paris, No. 18 Boulevard du Temple, for the one part;

And, M. JEAN-BAPTISTE DEBURAU, Artiste, Rope-walker, Mime, domiciled in Paris, No. 28 faubourg du Temple, for the other part, have agreed the following, to wit:

I, BERTRAND, by these presents, engage M. DEBURAU to perform the role of Pierrot, and in general any role which shall be assigned to him by myself or the Stage Manager.

The present Contract is entered into in accordance with the following clauses, undertakings and conditions, to wit:

1° I, JEAN-BAPTISTE DEBURAU, undertake to perform *all the roles* which shall be assigned to me by the Director or his Stage Manager; to dance and walk on in ballets, *divertissements, marches*, pantomimes and all other pieces; to execute stage-fights; to accompany the troupe if it is called to take part in private or public festivities and celebrations, requiring nothing more than the transport necessary for the journey.

2° I promise to attend sectional and general rehearsals, agreeing to any *fines laid down in the rule-book, with which I am familiar* and by which I promise to abide without causing difficulties or disputes; to present myself at the theatre *at three o'clock* on Sundays and holidays and at *four o'clock* on all weekdays, to employ my talents in as many performances as may be determined by the Director or his Stage Manager.

3° I agree to comply with the regulations prescribed or yet to be prescribed for the conduct of performances and *to be satisfied with the lighting, heating* and costumes provided for me by the management.

4° I agree not to absent myself from Paris without the signed permission of the Director, and to be present at the theatre on every performance day, even when I am not due to appear, so as to give the management the opportunity to replace a piece that may have to be withdrawn on account of unforeseen circumstances.

5° *In the event of illness, the Director reserves the right to suspend the Artiste's salary until such time as he resumes work.*

6° In the event of fire, closure of the theatre by a higher authority or any other notable and unforeseen circumstance, the present contract shall be legally null and void, unless the Director signifies his intention to continue payment of the Artiste's salary until further notice.

7° The Artiste will be required to provide his own underwear, suitable for every costume, his hose, footwear, make-up and gloves. The Management is responsible for costumes and properties. Rope-dancers must provide themselves with everything necessary for the practice of rope-dancing, and in acceptable condition.

Any articles supplied by the management which may be lost or damaged through negligence or by design shall be reconstructed in the workshops at the expense and out of the salary of those responsible.

8° In the event of drunkenness, the Director or the Stage Manager shall impose a fine on the culprit in accordance with the tariff; in the event of any recurrence of the offence, the Director reserves the right to terminate the contract without legal remedy for the Artiste.

9° I forgo all use of my talents on public or private stages without having obtained written permission from the Director, on pain of a fine of 300 francs.

Provided that the above clauses are faithfully observed, M. BERTRAND promises to pay to M. DEBURAU the sum of 35 francs per week for the duration of the present contract.

The present Contract shall be for three years, to take effect from the Monday after Easter eighteen hundred and twenty-eight and terminating on Palm Sunday eighteen hundred and thirty-one.

With the consent of both parties, the present Contract shall have the same force and authority as if it had been transacted in the presence of a notary, on pain of a penalty, payable by the initial defaulter to the other party, set at one thousand francs.

Drawn up in duplicate and in good faith between the two parties, in Paris, the tenth day of December eighteen hundred and twenty-six.

That this contract for the renewal of Deburau's engagement should have been signed more than a year in advance is perhaps a measure of his value to the Funambules and the manager's determination to hang on to him, but with the performer already such a firm favourite with audiences, the remuneration offered in return is a mere pittance, less than 1,800 francs for a 51-week year. No doubt Bertrand would have claimed that this was all that his theatre, an inexpensive establishment at the lower end of the popular market, could afford. Legitimate actors at other boulevard theatres fared rather better, but the picture of their professional lives in the 1830s and 1840s painted by George Sand is still a relatively cheerless one.

236   Actors' tribulations and rewards

George Sand, *Histoire de ma vie* (4 vols., Paris: Calmann-Lévy, 1928), vol. IV, p. 216

[. . .] and yet they are poor: the average salary of quite reputable actors in Paris is 5,000 francs per annum. To reach 8 or 10 thousand, one needs to possess a very considerable talent, or what is rarer and harder to achieve (for there are hundreds of unknown or unrecognized talents), one has to score a notable success.

The actor can therefore overcome this difficulty only by dint of painful struggle, and all those questions of inflated *amour-propre* and petty jealousy which he is accused of taking too seriously often conceal great chasms of fear and hurt, and become matters of life and death.

This last consideration was very real in the case of madame Dorval. She earned at the very most 15,000 francs, and did so by never taking a day's rest and living in the most modest style [. . .]

In point of fact, for one brief period she earned rather more than that: at the Gymnase in 1837 her contract specified a salary of 80 francs for each performance of plays in more than two acts and 40 francs for plays in one or two acts, with a guaranteed minimum of 2,000 francs per month and a costume allowance of 200 francs per role. But this starring engagement lasted for less than two years, and for all her popularity, Marie Dorval seems to have been perennially wedded to hardship and misfortune. A year before her early death in 1849, she was reduced to begging the Comédie-Française, to whom she had previously given several years of distinguished service as a *pensionnaire*, to re-engage her on the same footing at a mere 500 francs, unsuccessfully professing herself ready, Dumas tells us, to play any part, 'duennas, utilities, walk-ons'.[1]

Her finest acting partner, Frédérick Lemaître, was captive to the same treadmill of artistic endeavour. When, in 1832, at the height of his powers and celebrity, he accepted an engagement with Harel (who was then running the Odéon and the Porte-Saint-Martin simultaneously), he received the appreciable sum of 60 francs per performance, but for this he had to agree to play 'on demand, at all times, at any hour, and wherever he [Harel] considers fit, even at two theatres in a day if need be, the leading roles in tragedies and *drames*, the said roles to be undertaken as principal, or as co-principal or as understudy [*double*], on the understanding that they may not, on any pretext, be turned down.'[2] In the same year, and for the same management, Juliette Drouet, soon to be Hugo's 'inspiration' and who would appear in his *Lucrèce Borgia* and *Marie Tudor*, was contracted to play the roles of *jeune première* for only 4,000 francs. The increased power of commercial managers over the profession and the relative impotence of actors to challenge it were underlined two years later, when Frédérick sought to place his *Robert Macaire*, a *drame burlesque* he had co-written with the authors of his earliest triumph, *L'Auberge des Adrets*, in which the eponymous character originally appeared. Having fallen out with Harel during the previous season and broken his contract at the Porte-Saint-Martin, he now found that no other manager would look at what promised to be an assured crowd-puller, and he was forced eventually to put the new piece on at the Folies-Dramatiques, a very down-market establishment, amongst the humblest on the boulevard du Temple. Harel, Frédérick was reported as saying in the *Revue de Paris*, 'assimilated the condition of being an actor to the social position of a negro. On the strength of a pact he had concluded with the other Parisian managers, all the theatres of Paris were barred to me, with the exception of that known as the Folies dramatiques. They hadn't considered it worthy of being admitted to the cartel.'[3]

The clearest account of a successful actor's financial trajectory is to be found in the memoirs of the comedian Bouffé, who, alongside his peregrinations from theatre to theatre on the boulevard, details the successive inducements offered him in the course of an increasingly rewarding career, which was cruelly interrupted by illness in his late forties and which he never fully resumed. Beginning at the newly opened Panorama-Dramatique in 1821 on 25 francs a month, 'the pay', he wryly observed, 'of a grade-two cook at the time' and which had to be supplemented by taking a part-time job, he saw his income grow exponentially to 3,000 a year before the management went bankrupt, whereupon he was afforded a bolt hole at the Gaîté, with the relative security of a three-year contract but a drop in salary to 2,000 francs, rising to 2,300 francs a year. Then, in 1825, he signed a four-year contract with the Nouveautés at a salary of 6,000 francs, plus *feux* of 5 francs per performance, where he remained until that theatre too got into difficulties and he moved on to a similar engagement on similar terms at the Gymnase. There Bouffé flourished so prodigiously that on the expiry of the agreement in 1836 he was happy enough to renew it without any increase in salary, though with a doubling of the rate for *feux* and, even more profitably, a guaranteed leave of absence of three months in every year, enabling him to take advantage of the summer round of provincial touring upon which prominent boulevard actors, no less than *sociétaires* of the Théâtre-Français, relied as an annual crock of gold.[4] The one drawback of the new contract was that it made provision for an indemnity (*dédit*) of 100,000 francs to be paid in the event of its revocation. With the proliferation of commercial theatres this penalty clause had become a standard feature of actors' contracts, designed to protect managers against depredation of their principal assets by business rivals: as early as 1791 the *Almanach général* reported that a certain Moras, a 'new actor, who had achieved considerable success at this theatre [Nicolet's Grands Danseurs du Roi], has just been released from it in consideration of a substantial sum which the manager agreed to pay for his *dédit*.' Bouffé was not so lucky: when an attractive proposition was made to him by the Variétés, Delestre-Poirson, manager of the Gymnase, invoked his penalty clause and the actor found himself paying the bulk of a sizeable compensation out of his own pocket. The new deal he struck, however, was well worth it.

[1] A. Dumas, *La dernière année de Marie Dorval* (Paris: Librairie Nouvelle, 1855), pp. 32–3.
[2] Reproduced in L.-H. Lecomte, *Un comédien du xixe siède* (Paris: l'auteur, 1888) vol. i, pp. 314–15. The final clause here represents a routine proviso in all actors' contracts at this time, at least in the commercial sector; Bouffé records in his *Souvenirs* (Paris: Dentu, 1880; pp. 208–9) that 'no-one at the Gymnase was entitled to turn a part down, otherwise God only knows how many times I would have availed myself of the opportunity!'
[3] *Revue de Paris*, 25 (1836), p. 37.
[4] Theatres in the Parisian *banlieue*, too, might be visited: there is a record, for instance, of another celebrated *comique*, Potier, appearing in a benefit performance at the Théâtre Montmartre in July 1830.

237   Bouffé is engaged by the Variétés, 1843

Hugues-Marie-Désiré Bouffé, *Mes souvenirs, 1800–1880* (Paris: E. Dentu, 1880), pp. 229–30

Between M. Nestor Roqueplan, director of the Théâtre des Variétés for the one part And M. Désiré-Marie Bouffé, dramatic artist, for the other part, The following has been agreed, to wit:

The director hereby engages M. Bouffé, to play, with the company, all the roles in his line of business, and in particular to perform the twelve plays in his repertoire at the Gymnase, transferred to the Théâtre des Variétés, comprising *Le Gamin de Paris, La Fille de l'Avare, Michel Perrin, Pauvre Jacques, Les Vieux Péchés, La Maison en loterie, Le Père Turlututu, Les Enfants de troupe, L'Abbé galant, L'Oncle Baptiste, Le Muet d'Ingouville* and *Le Bouffon du Prince.*

M. Bouffé promises to comply with the regulations of the said theatre.

The present engagement is entered into on the basis of the following terms, clauses and conditions, which the contracting parties undertake to observe in full, each as they apply to him, in return for the exact fulfilment of the clauses indicated above. Payment shall be made to M. Bouffé in every year, as a fixed salary, of the sum of 1,000 francs per month; in addition, he will receive a voucher for 50 francs each time he performs. He is assured of a voucher twenty times per month; it is the director's wish that he will have earned thirty by the end of each month.

As for the 60,000 francs advanced by M. Bouffé to redeem his *dédit*, and on which he claimed no interest, this sum shall be refunded to him in the following manner:

The management promises to pay to M. Bouffé's appointed attorney the sum of 100 francs from the takings each time he appears. Be it understood that this sum shall not be paid during his three months of *congé*, June, July and August (unsalaried, of course) [. . .]

The present engagement shall begin on the 1st December 1843, and terminate on the 1st December 1851, and shall therefore hold good for eight years.

Everything agreed above shall be effected on pain of a *dédit* amounting to 50,000 francs, payable in cash.

Drawn up in duplicate, in Paris, the 14th November 1843.

THE PROFESSION OF ACTING

Apart from pay, the consideration uppermost in the mind of today's actor is likely to be the range of parts he or she may legitimately aspire to play, but for much of the nineteenth century, as for many years before, this would have been largely prescribed and circumscribed by his or her *emploi*, or recognized line of business. Although it was not entirely unknown for a performer to be called on to appear as a character outside the scope of his *emploi* (and to receive additional *feux* or a special costume allowance for doing so), the allocation of roles to actors was to all intents and purposes determined – as the French term *distribution* implies – by the existence within any given company of a clear-cut categorization of acting ability. As late as 1885, Pougin's authoritative dictionary of theatrical practice describes as still extant a system derived both in broad outline and, often enough, in precise detail, from long-established tradition.

238   Traditional lines of business

Arthur Pougin, *Dictionnaire historique et pittoresque du théâtre, et des arts qui s'y rattachent* (Paris: Firmin-Didot, 1885), pp. 326–7

A whole category of roles will be associated with a particular genre and will demand, as regards voice, physique and performing style, certain aptitudes or abilities which are inherent in the individual and will render him singularly well equipped to undertake this *emploi* [. . .] Certain actors, born to play comedy, would be quite incapable of filling a serious role, and vice versa. In order, therefore, to assign responsibilities to all concerned with as much precision as is possible in such matters, it became necessary to formulate sets of similar roles and establish what are known as *emplois*.

Pougin then proceeds to itemize the dominant characteristics linked to the various categories of role.

Evidence of the extent to which these expectations might colour both the audience's perception of a performance and the managerial policy is supplied by the veteran patron of the theatre, Pierre-Victor, complaining about conditions at the Odéon in 1830 under the economically minded direction of Harel, and also by the young Bouffé applying in 1821 for his first acting job as a *comique*.

239   The requirements of different *emplois*

(a) Pierre-Victor [Pierre-Simon Lerebours], *Documents pour servir à l'histoire du Théâtre-Français sous la Restauration, ou Recueil des écrits publiés de 1815 à 1830 par Pierre-Victor sur les débats avec l'administration des Menus-Plaisirs et sur les abus qui ont le plus contribué, pendant cette période, à la dégradation des théâtres* (Paris: Guillaumin, 1834), pp. 56, 58; (b) Bouffé, *Souvenirs*, pp. 38–40

(a) Pierre-Victor, 1834

One of the most glaring improprieties of performances at the Odéon is that of casting young people in the roles of confidants. As a rule characters in this *emploi* are men of advanced years, governors or senior ministers. Now how can any illusion be created in such roles by actors who have neither maturity nor authority? [. . .] Another mistake [committed by the Odéon] is that actors are given the opportunity to appear in every *emploi*. If this were to be taken any further, roles would be deprived of any character, the *emplois* of any particularity and whole plays, therefore, of any contrasts or oppositions. And an actor who was versatile enough, and could change his appearance sufficiently to play diametrically opposed roles, would inevitably be doing so at the expense of those he relinquished.

(b) Bouffé, 1880

[M. Allaux, manager of the Panorama-Dramatique,[1] picked up his walking-stick as if to run through a scene from *Le Médecin malgré lui*, but used it instead to] point to a large blackboard similar to those found in schoolrooms.

– Since you're a comedian, he said to me, stand over there, under number 7.

This struck me as so odd that I said to myself: 'No doubt this cove also has special scales to measure the weight of actors before he hires them for his theatre'.

Here is a rough sketch of M. Allaux's artistic yardstick, and I am not exaggerating, word of honour!

Leading roles	*Jeunes premiers*	Lovers	2nd roles	First comedians	Second comedians	Low comedians grimes
No. 1	No. 2	No. 3	No. 4			
				No. 5	No. 6	No. 7

I did as I was told; the whole set-up reminded me of the day I had to draw lots for conscription, but no sooner was I standing under this new sword of Damocles than the manager called out: 'I knew it, you're too short!'

I haven't grown an inch since that day, which means that I'm not very tall – barely five feet – but I was vain enough to imagine that I was of sufficient height to play the *emploi* which is known, I am not too sure why, as low comedians [*bas comiques*]. I made so bold as to say so.

– I tell you you're too short, cried my judge rather heatedly, and I know just as much as you about such things, wouldn't you say?

[1] A speculative minor theatre, which had a brief existence on the Boulevard du Temple from 1820 to 1823.

The day was ultimately saved by the arrival of M. Solomé, the stage manager, who persuaded his superior to engage the would-be *comique* for utility parts. Despite his protestation to the contrary, Bouffé has perhaps gilded the lily of reminiscence, but there is clearly an element of truth in his story, indicating just how rigid the classification of *emplois* might become. It was also tenaciously upheld by the actors themselves, as a guarantee of their relative standing within a company and as a passport to public recognition and favour. Ironically, the formality of the system offered little protection against wrangling or bad feeling when brought face to face with the more amorphous demands of the dramatic text: although plays had been, and continued to be, written with these precise categories of acting in mind, performers could still feel their professional credentials impugned by the process of casting.

240   Disputed roles, 1829

Globe (3 June 1829)

The allotment of roles gives rise to furious quarrels. 'This one falls within my *emploi*', a certain actor will declare. Another will claim it by the authority of the playwright. One will find his part too insignificant and refuse it; yet another will feel it would be humiliating to accept it since a colleague has turned it down; and a host of other complications.

This was the kind of impasse that Napoleon had attempted, and clearly failed, to prevent with Article 46 of his decree, which instructs the *Surintendant* to draw up a list of all plays in the repertoire, 'with the names of all male and female *sociétaires* who are to play roles *en premier*, *en double* and *en troisième* in each of these plays, according to their *emploi* and their seniority, so that there may be no further disputes in this regard'. Some of these internal rivalries persisted from season to season at the Théâtre-Français. As tragic heroines, Mlle George and Mlle Duchesnois were constantly at daggers drawn, while, among their male counterparts, no sooner had Talma overcome all opposition to establish himself as leading tragedian than a new competitor for the heroic mantle emerged in the person of Lafon, who was groomed by Talma's enemies not only for the succession but for immediate pre-eminence. The struggle between them rumbled on for some years, to resolve itself eventually in uneasy compromise and division of the histrionic spoils. In April 1826, a few months before his death, Talma's *emploi* was described as '*premier rôle de tragédie*', whereas Lafon, rather than being referred to as his *double*, was separately bespoken for '*princes de tragédie, chevaliers français*', a partition on which Dumas later put a suitably facetious gloss.

241   Subdivision of an *emploi*

(a) Dumas, *Souvenirs dramatiques*, vol. I, pp. 201–2; (b) A. B. L. Grimod de la Reynière and Fabien Pillet, *Revue des comédiens, ou Critique raisonnée de tous les acteurs, danseurs et mimes de la capitale* (2 vols., Paris: Favre, 1808), vol. II, pp. 212–14

(a) Dumas, 1868

Lafon had a peculiar *emploi* within the company. He played the *chevaliers français*. What exactly was meant by *chevaliers français*?

Firstly, it did mean French knights, that is to say those parts that were played in a black toque, with a white feather, a yellow tunic, skin-tight hose, buff boots and a sword in the shape of a cross [. . .] Now it was accepted once and for all that Talma was better, or to be more precise, had been better as the Hamlets, the Neros, the Macbeths, the Charles the Ninths, the Richard the Thirds and the Othellos, in other words, as men racked by remorse, tyrants, oppressors of innocence, but that Lafon, for his part, had the edge as the French knights. For which, read not only Marigny, Tancred, Raoul, Duguesclin and Bayard, but also Achilles, Britannicus, Pilades, Hippolytus, the orphan of China, the Cid, Zamore and Orosmane, who were not, it is true, French knights, but deserved to be so.

A similar accommodation was reached between Mlle Raucourt and the youthful upstart, Mlle Duchesnois, though in this case, apparently, without undue friction, with the newcomer also acting at times as a *double* for her senior.

(b) Grimod de la Reynière and Pillet, 1808

The dazzling début performances of Mademoiselle Duchesnois momentarily eclipsed the halo surrounding Mademoiselle Raucourt, who even found herself obliged to give up certain prime roles upon which the younger, more tenderly affecting débutante had contrived to set her stamp as on a parcel of acquired or confiscated property. Phèdre was one of them [. . .] a line of demarcation grew up quite naturally between the two rivals; Phèdre and all such passionate roles came to be the portion of the REINE SENSIBLE, while Sémiramis, Médée, Cléopâtre and Jocaste remained exclusively that of the SUPERBE REINE; and this amicable arrangement met with the unqualified approval of public opinion.

Such complaisance was rare, however, even in comedy. Alexandre Ricord condemned the 'despotism' shown by some of the most able *sociétaires* towards the *pensionnaires* and the unhealthy influence they were able to exercise over the choice of programme, not least while they were away from Paris on their annual *congé*. In particular, he pointed the finger of scorn at Mlle Mars, who seems to have been notoriously proprietorial about her chosen roles.

242   Possession of parts

Alexandre Ricord aîné, *Les Fastes de la Comédie-Française, et portraits des plus célèbres acteurs qui se sont illustrés et de ceux qui s'illustrent encore sur notre théâtre, précédés d'un aperçu sur sa situation présente et sur les moyens propres à prévenir sa ruine* (2 vols., Paris: Alexandre, 1821–2), vol. I, pp. 42–3

Just look at the programme of the Théâtre-Français while the great actress is in the provinces harvesting her laurels and her money, and you will realize that the plays in which she normally appears have been excluded. It is forbidden for either mademoiselle Leverd or mademoiselle Bourgoin to touch them. Should one of them request to play a particular role there is always some pretext for refusing it [. . .] Should a dramatist wish to cast some other actress in Mlle Mars's roles so that his plays can be performed during the absence of the jewel in the Théâtre-Français crown, this tyranny extends, I have been assured, to paying him for the performances he requests without actually giving them. Thus, after mademoiselle Mars, there will be no more *ingénues* or *coquettes* at the Comédie-Française.[1]

---

[1] A similar point was made, with no less exasperation, about Marie Dorval's relative inactivity after joining the Théâtre-Français as a *pensionnaire* in 1834: 'We are still impatiently awaiting the appearance in a new role of Mme Dorval, whose exquisite talent has as yet been seen only in *Une Liaison* and who is prevented by certain absurd rules, stubbornly upheld by the interested party, from taking any of the parts in *drames* that have been played by Mlle Mars. *Clotilde* and *Edouard en Ecosse*, in which Mme Dorval would assuredly have achieved great success, are also forbidden to her, even though Mlle Mars no longer performs these plays. The rules of the Comédie-Française, which for twenty years

denied access to all actors of real talent, now inflict unwarranted humiliation on them' ('Chronique de la quinzaine', *Revue des Deux Mondes*, 3rd series, vol. 2 (1834), p. 621).

It is clear that, for Ricord, Mlle Mars's intransigence was in danger of undermining one of the main functions of the *emploi* system, namely the preservation of a tradition of performance and its continuity from one generation of players to the next. Within each *emploi*, be it that of the tragic king or queen, the *jeune premier* or *jeune première*, the *père* or *mère noble*, the confidant(e), the *comique* or the *soubrette*, and so on, there existed a well-defined pecking order, headed by a principal or *premier sujet*, almost invariably a senior *sociétaire*, followed by at least one *acteur secondaire*, with the next claim to a given role, and at the bottom of the pile a number of understudies, who might be called upon at short notice to stand in for indisposed, indolent or simply absent colleagues. Thus, for every young actor, there was a recognizable role model on which he or she might, with perseverance and in the fullness of time, contrive to impose a personal imprint.

Periodically, moreover, on what were popularly known as the *petits jours*, leading actors would cede the stage to their respective seconds or understudies, so that they could be tempered by experience and public criticism, and then become *chefs d'emploi* in their turn, just as, in the previous century, Lekain had understudied Grandval before succeeding him and Mlle Clairon had followed in Mlle Dumesnil's footsteps. This policy was enshrined in the Moscow decree, where Article 54 explicitly forbids any actor to 'reserve for himself any one or more roles of his *emploi*' and requires the management committee to ensure, on pain of a substantial fine, that 'understudies be heard by the public three or four times a month in the principal roles of their respective *emplois*'. However well intentioned, these measures were not immune from abuse. Nerval, for instance, took the management of the Opéra to task for exploiting them deliberately to sabotage the likely appeal of old works, which they were required by the terms of their subsidy to revive but for which they had no stomach.

243   The reception accorded to understudies, 1840

Gérard de Nerval, review of a revival of Spontini's opera, *Fernand Cortez, ou la Conquête de Mexique* (22 June 1840), reproduced in *La Vie du théâtre*, ed. Jean Richer (Paris: M. J. Minard, Lettres Modernes, 1961), pp. 518–19

The behaviour of the managers in this respect is decidedly curious. From time to time they give another performance to an old piece; understudies and utility singers try to look important in the principal roles, the orchestra fool around with the lean score of the period, the theatre's supporting *claque* are allowed to relax into a mood of levity and come out with amusing cracks for the benefit of the provincials sitting next to them. Sometimes even, as on the occasion of the revival of *Le Devin du village*,[1] certain droll spectators toss a wig onto the stage (a theatrical wig, to be sure, for who would dream of such expense for the sake of a bad joke). On the morrow the newspapers loyally sympathize with the management for having been subjected to such exigencies. They find the old masterpiece distinctly lacklustre, extremely dated, out of touch with the *forward movement* of the century, and the administrator immediately trots off to the Minister, the Bureau des Beaux Arts and the Commission Dramatique to say: 'You see! We do what we can, and the public are no longer interested!'

[1] *Intermède* by Jean-Jacques Rousseau, first performed in 1752.

The same ranking principle was prevalent throughout the profession, extending to the commercial theatres of the Paris boulevards and, on a necessarily reduced scale, to the stock companies of the provinces. This much is evident from the *Observation importante* for the guidance of theatre managers, which Albertin, stage manager of the Théâtre-Français, attached to his published notes on the production there in 1829 of Dumas's first *drame historique*. This work broke the neat *emploi* mould adequate for plays of the old repertoire.

244   Casting hierarchies, 1829

Hyacinthe Albertin, *Indications générales pour la mise en scène de Henri III et sa cour* ([Paris]: E. Duverger, [1829]), reproduced in M. A. Allevy (ed.), *Edition critique d'une mise en scène romantique* (Paris: E. Droz, 1938), p. 41

Henri III and the Duc de Guise having been created by two *premiers rôles*, managers may experience some difficulties in casting. To help in resolving them, we record here the opinion of the author and the administrator on this matter. In companies possessing a *premier rôle tragique* and a *premier rôle comique*, the part of the Duc de Guise should be allotted to the former and that of Henri III to the latter, unless individual circumstances make this undesirable. With the same proviso, in companies (and these will be in the vast majority) which contain only one *premier rôle*, the part of the Duc de Guise should be allotted to him and that of Henri III to the *deuxième* or *troisième amoureux*, as the part of Saint-Mégrin will invariably fall to the *jeune premier rôle*. All other parts in the piece can easily be cast according to the *emplois* and aptitudes of the personnel.

Such was the importance attached to these various degrees of eminence that they were not only jealously guarded but often enough clung to well after they had ceased to be realistically compatible with the age of the actor, or more usually the actress, concerned. No less than operatic divas, many a dramatic actress continued to play the *jeunes premières*, the *amoureuses* or even the *ingénues* long after attaining years of discretion, a practice that proved stubbornly resistant to the encroachment of realism in other aspects of performance: as late as 1850, Théophile Gautier saw fit to mention that Marie Favart, making a 'charming *amoureuse*' of Lucinde in Molière's *L'Amour médecin*, was of the right age for her *emploi*, 'a rare event at the Théâtre-Français, where young girls usually take the parts of duennas and nurses, while the *ingénuités* are played by quinquagenarians'.[1] Here again, unsurprisingly, Mlle Mars was a prime culprit. Having passed the age of 30 she considered herself ready to tackle the *grandes coquettes*, but did so without relinquishing her earlier roles, or, as Grimod de la Reynière neatly expressed it, without 'exchanging the simple bouquet of Agnès for the rich aigrette of Céliante'.[2] Continuing to play most of them in her 50s, she could still inspire Auguste Jal to proclaim that 'Mlle Mars will not be too old until the day her dulcet voice has become harsh or tremulous, until the day she can no longer walk',[3] and at the age of

62 her Elmire in *Tartuffe* elicited wild enthusiasm from the 19-year-old Edmond Got.[4] Even an experienced playwright like Ernest Legouvé was impressed by the sheer youthfulness of the two lovers in his *Louise de Lignerolles* as played by Mlle Mars and Firmin, when the combined age of the couple amounted to 125.[5] Other observers were a good deal less generous. Hugo, recording her death in 1847 and recalling her appearance in *Hernani*, made the eloquently non-committal remark: 'Mlle Mars was 52 when she created the part of Doña Sol, who is 17',[6] and Dumas remembered a curtain call in 1841, when, after she had played Célimène in *Le Misanthrope*, a funeral wreath of yellow and black immortelles was thrown onto the stage, adding mischievously that it had been put together in one of the company's dressing-rooms and that he knew which.[7] Perhaps the saddest and most revealing comments, however, came from the pen of Geoffroy, reviewing performances of Collin d'Harleville's *Le Vieux célibataire* and Voltaire's *Zaïre* at the Théâtre-Français in the 1801/2 season.

---

[1] Gautier, *Histoire de l'art dramatique*, vol. vi, p. 144.
[2] A. B. L. Grimod de la Reynière and Pillet Fabien, *Revue des comédiens* (Paris: Favre, 1808), vol. ii, p. 161.
[3] *Revue de Paris*, 3 (1834), p. 220.
[4] *Journal de Edmond Got* (2 vols., Paris: Plon, Nourrit, 1910), 2 March and 16 April 1841.
[5] E. Legouvé, *Soixante ans de souvenirs* (Paris: Hetzel, 1887), vol. ii, p. 70.
[6] Victor Hugo, *Choses vues* (2 vols., Paris: Ollendorff, 1913), vol. i, p. 234.
[7] Alexandre Dumas, *Mes mémoires* (22 vols., Paris: Alexandre Cadot, 1852–4), vol. xii, p. 239.

245   *Emploi* and actor at odds

Julien-Louis Geoffroy, *Cours de littérature dramatique, ou Recueil par ordre de matières des feuilletons de Geoffroy* (6 vols., Paris: Pierre Blanchard, 1825), vol. vi, pp. 196, 264

When an actor has been on the stage for many years, there comes a time when his *emploi*, that for which nature intended him, comes into conflict with his physical appearance. If he moves to a different *emploi*, then the roles which are more in accord with his age no longer accord with his talent; for the talent required for *jeunes premiers* and *petits-maîtres* is not the same as for *pères nobles*, and nature does not endow one man with many different gifts [. . .]

In the theatre it is rare for an actor's physique to be in complete harmony with his role: all too often we are given aged and ill-favoured princesses whom we are compelled to see as young beauties, and unprepossessing lovers who are presented as Adonises; we are expected to lend ourselves to the illusion and not laugh at these grand passions so inadequately justified by their object. But with mademoiselle Bourgoin we have no need either for credence or indulgence; we can very well believe only what we see; she is truly *the young and beautiful Zaïre*.

The hide-bound conventionality of the system was pithily summed up in Harel's dictionary definition of *emploi*: 'Abilities wane, but the *emploi* remains; it is for life.'[1] Increasingly, however, the absurd consequences to which it led became painfully obvious and found the critics and writers of the new movement in literature less tolerant than their predecessors had been. In 1834 Gustave Planche's series of articles under the general title of '*De la réforme dramatique*' contained at least one proposal, prompted by Marie Dorval's recent arrival at the national theatre, that would have struck many, spectators and actors alike, as profoundly revolutionary.

[1] F. A. Harel *et al.*, *Dictionnaire théâtral* (Paris: Barba, 1824), p. 137.

246   Possession of parts challenged, 1834

Gustave Planche, 'De la réforme dramatique. Du Théâtre-Français', *Revue des Deux Mondes*, 3rd series, vol. 4 (1834), pp. 549–51

But why defend as if they constituted an inalienable estate the roles which have enabled one person to register a triumph and might still do so for someone else? Mme Dorval has played Suzanne in *Le Mariage de Figaro* in several of the principal cities of France; she has revealed in the part certain treasurable qualities; she has not copied Mlle Mars, she hasn't even thought of copying her; she has interpreted the character in her own way. Instead of a sly coquettishness, deliberate and controlled in its every motion rather than spontaneous, which Mlle Mars can convey to perfection, she has uncovered in Beaumarchais a young woman who is proud of her beauty, self-assured, mettlesome of speech, alluring without a hint of immodesty, vivacious and playful without compromising herself, full of spirit and charm. Of the two, who is right? Should one compliment Mlle Mars on having reshaped what the author wrote in order to accommodate it to the nature of her own personality? Should one thank Mme Dorval for having penetrated to the heart of Beaumarchais and seized the role in all its sincerity without excising any of its racy impudence? The question is well worth asking; and how can we answer it if no competition is allowed? [. . .]

I can fully understand hierarchy in the military; but I will never accept hierarchy in the theatre. And there is a very simple way of putting an end to its dominance, and that is to insist that all roles be exchanged [. . .] equality among great artistes is one of the necessary conditions of any dramatic enterprise.

Interestingly, Gautier was to make a similar point exactly ten years later apropos Frédérick Lemaître, the other great contemporary actor reared and nurtured independently of the Théâtre-Français and therefore uncontaminated by what he refers to disparagingly as the 'malady' of specialization: 'it is by playing the most contradictory roles, from Robert Macaire to Ruy Blas, and encompassing the entire dramatic scale from top to bottom that he has acquired the remarkable skill we know him to possess.'[1]

Compounding the inherent traditionalism of the *emploi* system, the only formal training available to aspiring thespians was provided by the acting school attached to and staffed by the Théâtre-Français, or by senior (or retired) members of the profession willing to offer private tuition. Founded in June 1786 as the Ecole Royale de Déclamation, with teaching supplied by Dugazon, Molé and Fleury,[2] the school had its funding discontinued early in 1790 and it was closed by order of the Convention on 8 November 1793, only to be partially revived two years later, though merely as a Classe de Déclamation within the Conservatoire de Musique. Napoleon thought it sufficiently important to devote to it one whole subsection of the Moscow decree, redefining it as a dedicated school 'for our Théâtre-Français', with places for eighteen pupils (nine of each sex) selected by the minister of the interior and deemed to be on an equal footing with the the the Conservatoire's music students.

1   Gautier, *Histoire de l'art dramatique* vol. III, p. 229.
2   See Howarth, *French theatre*, pp. 576–8.

247   Re-establishment of a training school for actors, 1812

'Décret impérial sur la Surveillance, l'Organisation, l'Administration, la Comptabilité, la Police et la Discipline du Théâtre-Français', 15 October 1812

PART VIII
On the Students of the Théâtre-Français

92. They may follow classes in music; but they will be more especially trained in the art of declamation, and will scrupulously follow the courses of their teachers, according to the genre [comedy or tragedy] for which they are intended.

93. For this purpose, in addition to the teachers, there will be two *répétiteurs* in dramatic art, one for each genre, who will rehearse and work with the students at set times every day, in the intervals between classes.

94. There will also be a teacher of grammar, history and mythology as they apply to dramatic art, who will specifically teach the students destined for the Théâtre-Français.

The decree also made provision for students to be examined annually and, on successful completion of their studies, to be engaged by the Odéon or one of the provincial theatres, or, if they were particularly promising, at the Théâtre-Français itself, on probation for at least one year with a view to being admitted as *sociétaires*. Though enlightened enough in theory, these measures, which formed the basis of dramatic training for much of the nineteenth century, left much to be desired in practice, for reasons that will be identified in chaper 3 below (**273** and **274**).

CASTING

Within the limits prescribed by the range of *emplois*, it had been traditionally taken for granted that it was the playwright's prerogative to determine the casting of his own plays for performance, though depending on the personalities and circumstances of the individual case, this was routinely done in consultation with the manager of the theatre and perhaps also with his stage manager. Of necessity, such discussions tended to be confidential, and only in the event of a dispute, arising from alleged high-handedness or negligence, are we afforded any insight into the process. When, at the Théâtre-Français in 1829, David, who was playing Cassio in Vigny's version of *Le More de Venise*, developed a throat infection, the author wrote immediately to Albertin opposing his projected replacement by another actor, Bouchet, on the grounds that this part did not accord with 'the nature of his talent' and suggesting that the performance be postponed to the following week. Nonetheless, Bouchet was cast, there was a further enforced reshuffling because the production's Roderigo, Menjaud, had twisted his ankle, and the performance went ahead, whereupon an indignant Vigny wrote again, this time to the management committee, demanding an explanation.

248   Casting at the playwright's discretion, 1829

Victor-Alfred, Comte de Vigny, *Correspondance . . . 1816–1863*, ed. Léon Séché (2 vols., Paris: E. Mignot, La Renaissance du Livre, n.d.), vol. I, p. 46, 9 November 1829

[. . .] I request, sirs, that you give me an answer to these two questions:

1° Does the Comédie-Française consider itself entitled to cast and to change the casting of a play without the express agreement of the author?

2° By which person were parts allotted to the actors who on Saturday, without my knowledge, played the characters of Cassio, the Herald-at-arms and the Officer of Cyprus, and who gave them permission to play them?

The purpose of these two questions is to elicit your opinion and to determine the facts, not to express my own views on the proceeding, which represents an unparallelled lack of consideration towards me.

It was the duty of the Adminstration to discover my wishes. These would have proved so contrary to the casting arrived at that I should have insisted that the performance be deferred rather than expose my play to the complaints which did arise, occasioned by ineptitude in the playing of roles which had been learned in one hour.

Some years later, at the Tribunal de Commerce de la Seine, Hugo brought an action against the Théâtre-Français for breach of a contractual undertaking to stage revivals of *Hernani* and *Marion de Lorme* when they accepted his *Angelo* for performance. In its defence, the theatre's counsel, Me. Delangle, claimed that Hugo had not fulfilled *his* side of the bargain, notably by failing to provide a revised cast list for the revival of *Hernani*, an allegation which the latter immediately repudiated.

249   Casting by consultation

Gazette des Tribunaux (7 and 21 November 1837), reproduced in Hugo, *Œuvres complètes*, vol. v, pp. 354, 359

Me. Delangle: Authors are required to cast *en double* [i.e., specifying understudies as well as principals] 'all parts in their plays'. Now, in the case of *Hernani*, M. Hugo did not do so. An initial casting was made in 1829; but Michelot, who played the part of Charles-Quint has retired; Mlle Mars has relinquished the part of doña Sol. Since then, M. Victor Hugo has not provided any new cast list.

M. Victor Hugo: You are mistaken. A cast list was provided in 1834. It is recorded in the theatre's minute-book, in M. Jouslin de Lasalle's own hand.[1] The part of Charles-Quint was given to M. Ligier, who had earnestly requested it of me.

M. Delangle: I was not aware of the fact. But even if it were so, this would have been a casting of *chefs d'emploi*, and not *en double*, as is stipulated by the decree.

Two weeks later the tribunal found in Hugo's favour, awarding him damages of 6,000 francs, ordering both revivals to be staged within a period of three months and noting

That it is not proper for Victor Hugo to be held to blame for not having cast the roles in *Hernani* both *en premier et en double* in accordance with regulations, since the normal practice is for such casting to be decided by the author and the administrator acting in concert and since, in this instance, the roles were indeed cast.

[1] Armand Jouslin de La Salle was the administrator at that time.

REHEARSALS

It was customary, though by no means *de rigueur*, for authors to be present at rehearsals of their work. In his *Code théâtral*, P. J. Rousseau remarked that the preparation of works for performance was the joint prerogative of theatre managers and authors,[1] but many authors, deferring to the *amour-propre* of their actors or sensing their own inability to offer useful advice, declined all invitations to attend until the very last stages of rehearsal, or even until the opening night. Pixérécourt, in his dual capacity as author and manager, was a significant exception, and Hugo could be very punctilious in matters of staging, making sketches for sets and costumes for submission to the designer and even supervising their execution,[2] though he was sometimes forced to compromise their historical accuracy for practical reasons or to accommodate the vanity of his actresses. Dumas, on the other hand, is reported by the actor Samson as having been diffident to the point of nonchalance about the production of his first solo creation, *Henri III et sa cour*; on being sought out by members of the company for advice on the playing of a particular scene, 'My dear friends,' he exclaimed, 'you understand such things so much better than I. Whatever you do will be well done.'[3] Some eighteen years later, however, when he opened the Théâtre-Historique largely for the presentation of his own plays, he seems to have discovered in himself hidden talent as an autocratic but demonically inspiring *metteur-en-scène*, much to the discomfiture of Hippolyte Hostein, the theatre manager. Laferrière, who was in the cast of *Le Chevalier de Maison-Rouge*, a *drame* set during the early years of the Revolution, with a large cast and a positive army of 300 extras hired locally for 40 sous a day, has left a detailed account of the rehearsals.

[1] Pierre-Joseph Rousseau, *Code théâtral* (Paris: J.-P. Roret, 1829), pp. 77–8.
[2] 'It would be particularly advisable for M. Ciceri and the designer of costumes to call at the theatre on the day of the reading [of *Le Roi s'amuse*] so that I can speak to them' (letter from Hugo to Baron Taylor, reproduced in H. Lyonnet, *Les Premières de Victor Hugo* (Paris: Delavigne, 1930), p. 59).
[3] *Mémoires de Samson, de la Comédie-Française* (Paris: Ollendorff, 1882), p. 262.

250   Dumas directs his own work, 1847

Adolphe Laferrière, *Mémoires de Laferrière* (2 vols., Paris: E. Dentu, 1876), vol. II, pp. 254–5, 257

The early rehearsals, intended to make us word-perfect, took place in the absence of the author: we did what was called 'blocking' [*le dégrossissage*], roughing out a preliminary *mise-en-scène*; we arranged groupings, we agreed on certain moves, and the manager, M. Hostein, whose knowledge of the stage was later to become so comprehensive, would give us advice, contributing particular observations the accuracy of which never ceased to make a deep impression on us. Once the lines were learnt and we could rehearse without scripts, Dumas would appear, and it was like Jupiter emerging from the thunder-clouds. To hear him talk, we had not achieved anything, we would have to start again from the beginning, and it was noticeable that as soon as Dumas appeared M. Hostein retreated into a systematic silence and abstention from activity which had all the appearance of hurt pride [...] Under [Dumas's] direction the most ordinary dialogue or the most trivial situation would be unaccountably transformed and if his wayward imagination periodically led him astray, it has to be said that sometimes it hit the target astonishingly well [...] [With the arrival of the extras,] all recruited at random, in the streets, in garrets, in workshops, not knowing five minutes beforehand what it was all about nor what would be expected of them, the great Dumas now presented an unique spectacle, standing upright in his shirt-sleeves in the midst of this crowd who eyed him with that vacant and distrustful expression which the masses at first affect when confronted by anything out of the ordinary.

Another member of the same cast, Mélingue, emphasized the care which Dumas lavished on the positioning of stage furniture and properties, making the actors 'run through the same scene eight or ten times in succession, placing the sofa left, then moving it right, trying it centre-stage, then left again, and finally right once more'.[1] Looking back over a long theatrical career, Laferrière was in no doubt that Dumas's way of rehearsing represented the first stirrings in France of a new art, which had since become 'the indispensable ally of modern playwrights: the art of *mise-en-scène*'.

As for rehearsal periods, if we are to believe the inveterately hyperbolic Harel, they could vary hugely in length, between the unhurried ease of the subsidized theatres and the frantic but more productive pressure under which their boulevard rivals had to operate.

---

[1] Jules Claretie, *Profils de théâtre* (Paris: Fasquelle, 1904), p. 26.

251   Rehearsal periods

F. A. Harel, P. M. Alhoy and A. Jal, *Dictionnaire théâtral, ou Douze cent trente-trois vérités sur les directeurs, régisseurs, acteurs, actrices et employés des divers théâtres* (Paris: J. N. Barba, 1824), pp. 143–4

The Opéra, which prides itself on a slowness consistent with its majesty, allows not far short of a year for rehearsal of the works it is to perform. The Théâtre-Français, the Odéon and the Opéra-Comique strive to imitate the Opéra. The Vaudeville, the Gymnase and the Variétés, which have no *decorum* to maintain, put a fresh play into rehearsal every week, which is often more thoroughly mastered and better performed than those at the more dignified houses.

Contrariwise, we know from Dumas's testimony that in 1831 his *Antony* was given six weeks' rehearsal at the Porte-Saint-Martin under the management of Harel himself.

It can also be safely assumed that the difference in circumstances between the state theatres and their commercial counterparts led to discrepancies in the working hours of their respective companies. We have already seen that Deburau's contract at the Funambules required him to be present at the theatre even on days when he was not scheduled to perform, to allow for last-minute changes of programme, and Bouffé recalled a normal working day as being of eleven hours, 'continually at the theatre from eleven o'clock in the morning until five in the evening, and from seven o'clock till midnight, without a single day of rest'.[1] Many of his female colleagues had more than just long hours to contend with: George Sand, sympathizing with Marie Dorval's plight in particular, widened her outlook to include all actresses with families of small children.

[1] Bouffé, *Souvenirs*, p. 215.

252   An actress's working day

Sand, *Histoire de ma vie*, vol. IV, pp. 124–5

Nowhere are the ties of blood more closely knit than among theatre people. When the mother is obliged to work for five hours a day in rehearsal and another five in the evening in performance; when she scarcely has the time to eat or to dress, the brief moments when she can cuddle and cherish her children are moments of heady rapture, and days off are veritable holidays. How joyfully, then, does she take them off into the countryside! How glad she is to become a child with them, and for all the indiscretions she may have committed elsewhere, to feel herself pure in thought again and sanctified for a moment by contact with their innocent hearts!

PERFORMANCES

Gautier, too, felt genuine compassion for the hard life led by companies at the more unpretentious of the commercial theatres, like the Petit-Lazary, which he described as 'situated both in hierarchical and in geographical terms at the very bottom of the boulevard' and where performers were contracted to give more than one show a day.

253   Multiple performances

Gautier, *Histoire de l'art dramatique*, vol. II, p. 269

It was the second performance of the evening, for the Théâtre du Petit-Lazary, which, unlike many others, is always packed to the ceiling, presents two performances every day, or even three on Sundays and holidays. Just think what torture it must be for the poor actors, forced to play the same pieces two or three times in quick succession, to get into costume, then into another costume, particularly when the temperature stands at 35 degrees by the thermometer!

Before each performance, the half-hour call for actors was signalled by the tolling of a bell, which Harel likened to the summoning of monks to Matins: 'half an hour before the performance is due to begin, three prolonged clangings of this noisy instrument alert everyone to be at his post. Just as the bell was said to be the voice of the curate, so we might call it the voice of the stage manager; it does not speak in vain; a fine will answer for any disobedience to its commands.'[1]

The precise times of performance were apt to vary from theatre to theatre, those catering for a predominantly working-class audience opening their doors in the late afternoon in deference to the eating and sleeping habits of spectators who had to be at work soon after sunrise, while those relying on the custom of the more leisured classes would opt for early evening to suit their patrons' post-prandial convenience. Among the bourgeoisie and the gentry there was also a tendency for dinner to be taken progressively later during the first half of the nineteenth century, and theatres were obliged to take account of these alterations: thus, any manager anxious to maintain as broad a constituency as possible found himself under conflicting pressures in determining the hour for curtain-up. This tension was evidently being felt as early as 1805, when a letter appeared in the *Courrier des Spectacles* complaining that 'for some time now the majority of theatres do not begin performances much before seven o'clock' and pointing out that 'there are many people for whom it is extremely disagreeable to come out of a show at ten o'clock and not be able to reach home before eleven'.[2] Yet, by 1847 such was the transformation in social habits that Gautier felt impelled to make precisely the opposite complaint on behalf of his readers.

---

[1] Harel et al., *Dictionnaire théâtral*, p. 74.
[2] Quoted by E. D. de Manne and C. Ménétrier, *Galerie historique de la Comédie-Française* (Lyon: Scheuring, 1876), p. 108.

254   The problem of performance times

Gautier, *Histoire de l'art dramatique*, vol. v, pp. 103–4

Theatre managers must realize that in the last few years social habits have undergone a profound change. To begin a performance at 7 o'clock [. . .] is to guarantee that no one will turn up. The influence of English customs, the extension of the city boundaries and the establishment of new housing estates, coupled with the increasing complexities of business life, mean that the dining hour has had continually to be retarded. The working day is growing longer and impinging more and more on the evening. Shortly we shall be dining at the time of day when our ancestors used to sit down to supper. Parliament, offices, workshops, all those places where the affairs of government, commerce, education and industry are transacted, never close before 6 o'clock. How can one expect people to be sitting in an auditorium by 7? They have to get home, change, have something to eat and set out again on the often lengthy journey to reach the theatre.

At whatever time the curtain went up, and whatever the number of items on the bill, from the customary two at the Théâtre-Français[1] to as many as five on the boulevard, performances would end by midnight or thereabouts: certainly, it was considered highly unusual, if not positively unwise, to send the audience home much later. A press report of a special performance given on 15 July 1830 at the outlying Théâtre Montmartre by visiting artistes from the Opéra-Comique noted that there had been 'a full house, dazzling finery, a performance of finesse and expressiveness', all of which had combined to produce a delightful evening, but pointed out to the Seveste brothers, the theatre's joint managers, that the performance had not finished until 'twenty minutes past midnight, an unacceptable state of affairs since it does not allow residents of the capital to reach their homes until an exceedingly late hour and may expose them to unwelcome encounters in the suburb's deserted streets'.[2] Even in the city centre it was not considered advisable to bring the curtain down much after midnight, as Dumas had discovered earlier that year on the opening night of his *Stockholm, Fontainebleau et Rome*, a sprawling *trilogie dramatique* recounting the life of Queen Christina of Sweden, which had been billed by the Odéon as comprising a prologue, five acts and an epilogue and which did not reach the end of Act 5 until after 1 a.m.

---

[1] Where, as Gautier put it in 1843, 'they still retain the practice of giving a happy play after the sad play, so that the audience may go home in a placid and contented frame of mind, and sleep without being haunted by tragic visions, full of ghosts, daggers and poisoned chalices' (Gautier, *Histoire de l'art dramatique* vol. II, p. 325).

[2] Quoted by Maurice Artus in *Le Théâtre Montmartre* (Tours: Arrault, 1904), p. 20. The same source, reproducing an advertisement from *Le Nouveau conducteur de l'étranger à Paris* for 1846, specifies this theatre's performance times: 'Overture at 7 p.m. every day and at 5 p.m. on Sundays' (p. 38).

255   A belated final curtain

Armand-François Jouslin de La Salle, *Souvenirs sur le Théâtre-Français* (Paris: Emile-Paul, 1900), p. 73

The audience was making a dreadful din, afraid that they might not get home at all that night and clamouring lustily for the epilogue, when at last the curtain went up again. Came the moment when Christina, having retired to Rome and knowing that her last hour was near, asked her doctor how long she had to live. 'You have', he replied, 'a quarter of an hour left.' Hearing this, one student jumped up on a bench in the pit and, taking his watch out, yelled: 'It's a quarter past one; if by half past it's not over, we're leaving!' This piece of repartee produced a great roar of laughter and it became impossible to complete the epilogue, which was omitted from the second performance.

The timing of intervals was even less uniform than that of the performance itself. Even allowing for the habitual element of exaggeration in Harel's observations, there was clearly a pronounced, not to say purposive, distinction between the unflagging momentum of the entertainments provided on the boulevard and the more leisurely tempo of an evening at the Théâtre-Français or the Opéra.

256   Intervals

Harel *et al.*, *Dictionnaire théâtral*, pp. 139–40

ENTR'ACTE   The definition of this word varies according to the location. At the Vaudeville, the Gymnase and the Variétés, it means ten minutes; more than half an hour at the Français, and a whole hour at the Académie Royale de Musique; thus, the latter's magnificent foyer is always packed when the performance is not in progress, and often even when it is. There are in Paris well-bred and highly cultivated people whose only visits to the Opéra have been made during the intervals.

PUBLICITY

To announce the time of a performance and give other relevant information, such as the title of the play, names of the leading players and prices of admission,[1] the most common form of publicity was the playbill, copies of which, before the introduction of the eye-catching *colonnes Morris* during the July monarchy, were pasted to the wall at strategic points throughout the city. They were relatively modest in size and discreetly printed in black on coloured paper, green being traditionally associated with the Théâtre-Français, pink with the Comédie-Italienne, yellow with the Opéra and various other shades with the boulevard theatres. Their visual restraint and economy of content appealed to at least one British visitor, John Scott, who described them as 'perhaps the only thing in Paris calculated to make an Englishman blush for the opposite practice of his country. It is a mortifying contrast to the impudent quackeries and lying pretensions which, in all the varieties of a large and small letter are blazoned on the handbills of our two national theatres'.[2] Even so, there was ample scope for the exercise of rank and privilege, both in the design of the playbill and in its positioning.

---

[1] For an informed analysis of price structures and differentials between rival theatres during the period, see John McCormick, 'Joseph Bouchardy', in *Performance and politics in popular drama*, ed. D. Bradby *et al.* (Cambridge: Cambridge University Press, 1980), pp. 34–8.
[2] John Scott, *A visit to Paris in 1814* (London: Longman, Hurst, 1815), pp. 275–6.

257 Playbills

Harel et al., *Dictionnaire théâtral*, p. 12

Before the revolution, the playbill did not include the names of the actors. Nowadays it does, and the vanity of certain performers is very well served by this form of publicity. To have their name printed in big letters on the bill is a distinction to which they aspire as much as to an ovation orchestrated by the *claque*. The playbills of the royal theatres do not allow typographical differentiation of this kind; on them, seniority determines the order of names just as it does that of the bills themselves at street corners and crossroads.

At the same time, other means existed of addressing the public and of recommending one's wares, which tended to be used in inverse proportion to the official status of the enterprise. In the early years of the period some of the minor theatres along the Boulevard du Temple were still employing an *aboyeur aux portes*, a loud-mouthed, fast-talking barker stationed at the entrance door and perpetuating a time-honoured practice of the fairground theatres. Evidently, this was frowned on by other managers and one attempt to suppress it is recorded in the *Almanach général* of 1791, which reported that M. Sallé, the proprietor of the Associés, had been urged to 'remove the barker who still pesters the passers-by outside his theatre, and to substitute playbills freshly printed every day, like those of other theatres, for the advertisements for beer at his door, which are so stained and illegible that it is hard to decipher them'.[1] The *aboyeur* and another inheritance from fairground days, the *parade*, a short sequence of crowd-pulling repartee and knockabout routines performed on a balcony or small fit-up stage in front of the show-booth, gradually became hostages to tighter controls on public order and to the increasing prosperity and prestige of the boulevard theatres themselves. Soon Gérard de Nerval, looking back nostalgically from the sedater perspective of the 1840s, could bemoan the passing of a free and vibrant form of street entertainment that he was too young to have experienced in its heyday.

---

[1] *Almanach général de tous les spectacles de Paris et des provinces* (Paris: Froullé, 1791–2), p. 204.

258   Energetic publicity

Gérard de Nerval, 'Le Boulevard du Temple. Spectacles populaires', *Artiste* (3 May 1844), reproduced in *Variétés et fantaisies*, ed. Jean Richer (Paris: M. J. Minard, Lettres Modernes, 1964), pp. 69–70

There are no more fit-ups [*tréteaux*]! . . . Where has Bobêche's gone? Where is his opposite number, Galimâfré's?[1] A lost art, but names that endure! To tell the truth, the amusements of the people have had their day: local bye-laws have killed them off. The entertainment of the *bagatelle de la porte*, was it not the only entertainment of the poor, the consolation of their evening out, the irresistible attraction that stopped them spending their last sou at the tavern? Was it not even a free performance invariably far more enjoyable than the one inside? Folk from the provinces, half-wits and army conscripts would let themselves be seduced by the latter, rashly responding to the call of the big bass drum and the ironic patter of the *aboyeur*; but the true connoisseurs, the pure-bred Parisians, the veterans of life on the streets, were content to be part of the outside audience, paying for their places, in the last analysis, with laughter and applause [. . .]

---

[1] The stage names of two clowns and buskers *extraordinaires*, Antoine Mandelart (1791–*c.* 1840) and Auguste Guérin (1791–1870), who flourished during the First Empire and the early years of the Restoration.

THE POSITION OF PLAYWRIGHTS

The one item of important information not included in the playbills was the name of the author, at least in the case of a new play. This always remained confidential until, by convention, it was announced from the stage at the end of the first performance by the leading male actor of the company, adjusting his tone to the reception with which the play had met. Even then, it was possible for an author to request that his anonymity be preserved, as is clear from a diffident letter addressed to the administrator of the Théâtre-Français in 1811 by a novice playwright by the name of Adrien de Sarrazin, who, saying that he would not be present at the opening night, proceeded comprehensively to hedge his bets: 'If my play is a triumph, I wish to be named, as I intend to offer further pieces. If it is only half successful, I believe that a mixed reception is best savoured in silence; if it falls flat, I think that failure should remain incognito'.[1] This was an option that Gustave Planche felt Scribe should have taken after the audience's scandalized and mutinous response to his play *Les Mauvais conseils* in 1832: 'I fail to understand how and why M. Scribe, who did not wish to be named after the first performance, amid all the hissing and cat-calling, let his name appear on the bill the following day. The opposite procedure would have seemed more logical'.[2]

Audience response was not, however, the only potential barrier to a playwriting career: before a new play could reach the stage of the Théâtre-Français it had to be accepted by the company's reading committee, a body composed entirely of its most senior actors. In his decree of 1812 Napoleon stipulated a membership of nine, 'drawn from the longest serving *sociétaires*', but, alert to the committee's history of absenteeism, he required the *Surintendant* to nominate three reserves to ensure a full attendance, and added that voting on acceptance should be by simple majority.[3] The voting procedure had about it an appropriate air of ritual, characterized by the soft metallic clink of small colour-coded balls, white for acceptance, black for rejection, being dropped into a zinc bowl. For all this apparent formality and solemnity there was, of course, no means of achieving a dispassionate assessment of the works submitted or of eliminating from the votes cast every vestige of self-seeking, motivated either by the desire to secure a plum role for oneself or to deny one to a rival. Moreover, since the *sociétaires* were explicitly encouraged to present new plays[4] and every aspiring dramatist wished to see his work consecrated by performance at the national theatre, there was at any given time a huge backlog of unproduced manuscripts. Consequently, the whole process of getting a play read, possibly accepted, and then, hopefully, staged was a painfully long one, fraught with hazards and delays, some of which were doubtless unavoidable, others plainly less so. Dumas quipped that 'a man could grow old between the acceptance of his play and its performance; sometimes, he would even die'.[5] The problems are eloquently described both by the playwright Cailhava, in a pamphlet largely written a decade earlier but still pertinent at the time of its publication in 1789, and, in the same year, by the actors of the national theatre themselves, in an unwonted access of self-reproach.

[1] Francois Chéron, *Mémoires et récits de François Chéron* (Paris: Librairie de la Société Bibliographique, 1882), p. 199.
[2] *Revue des Deux Mondes*, 1st series, vol. 6 (1832), p. 128.
[3] Articles 68 and 69.
[4] Decree of 15 October 1812, Article 55: 'Our actors are required each month to perform one full-length work, or at least two shorter works, which are new or revived. Among these plays shall be plays by living authors.'
[5] Alexandre Dumas, *Souvenirs dramatiques* (Paris: Michel Lévy, 1868), vol. 1, p. 392.

259   Selection of plays for performance, 1789

(a) Jean-François Cailhava d'Estandoux, *Les Causes de la décadence du théâtre, et les moyens de le faire refleurir* (Paris: Royez, 1789), pp. 6–8; (b) *Plaintes et doléances de Messieurs les Comédiens-Français* (Paris, 1789), quoted by Maurice Albert in *Les Théâtres des boulevards (1789–1848)* (Paris: Société Française d'Imprimerie et de Librairie, 1902), pp. 49–50

(a) Cailhava d'Estandoux

[. . .] you deliver yourself of a play, you submit it, you request a reading; you wait four years for a reply: impatience sets in; you forswear a career that is so unrewarding, or else uncertainty breeds protracted inactivity [. . .] You are offered a reading; you undertake it in some trepidation. Woe betide you if you haven't taken care to ingratiate yourself with a certain party by promising the best roles; [. . .] It is the hour of judgement; you tremble like a leaf: the votes are cast, a single one holds the balance, the play is rejected; in vain you tell yourself that it is ridiculous for a work of the imagination, on which cultured people could scarely reach a decision after examining it in detail, should be condemned to oblivion on the strength of a mere reading, imperfectly executed in the midst of a noisy gathering: in vain you will argue that your judges may have been mistaken, like those who once turned down La Chaussée's *Mélanide* and Voltaire's *Oedipe*, and many of our best plays; all that is to no avail if you do not have powerful connections [. . .]

Let us suppose that the Theatrical Senate pronounced in your favour; you dream only of the moment when you will see your work on the stage: when will that moment come? A play arriving out of the blue is placed ahead of yours, because the author is titled and wealthy. Feel appalled to see birth and influence acquire privileges in the temple of the arts; [. . .] suffer in secret, but beware of making a fuss if you wish one day to reap the honours of performance and minimize its dangers.

(b) Plaintes et doléances de Messieurs les Comédiens-Français

We would also do well to woo the authors back, who have truly been very shabbily treated, demoralized and alienated. We make them dance attendance on us, we talk to them with an air of condescension, we multiply formalities for the reading and acceptance of plays. There is no ordeal that we do not devise to humiliate those without whom we should not exist. So what happens? A young man will often prefer to work for the minor theatres, where he can earn money quickly and without too much trouble, and this unworthy competition has robbed us of perhaps a score of good dramatists.

This was precisely the disaffection felt by the young Ernest Legouvé, who was later to become a very successful purveyor of comedies to the Théâtre-Français, when the reading committee turned down his first offering, written in collaboration with Prosper Goubaux, in 1836. He subsequently recalled the intimidating and ultimately chastening experience of appearing before an assembly of, it would seem, a dozen *sociétaires*.

260   Ordeal by reading committee

Ernest Legouvé, *Soixante ans de souvenirs* (2 vols., Paris: J. Hetzel, 1887), vol. ii, pp. 11–12

There we were, face to face with this dreadful committee. It was not, as it is today, a sort of council of ten, impassive and taciturn like judges, making the author look like a prisoner at the bar. There used to be some actresses, even young ones, on it. This imparted a note of gaiety to the proceedings. They would laugh at comic

scenes, they would cry at touching scenes, they would applaud purple passages, it
became a kind of final dress rehearsal, making the author aware of the weaker or
stronger points of his play; even their silences could teach him a lesson. This was
the only lesson that I learned from the reading. It lasted an hour; I read with all the
warmth and conviction of my 29 years. Not a reaction! not one! and as a result,
twelve black balls. Rejected unanimously.

Ostensibly, reading committees were also a feature of the commercial theatres. Certainly,
one was appointed at the Montansier in 1791, immediately in the wake of the emancipation
of minor theatres, and this initiative by the actress-manager was enthusiastically welcomed
by the *Almanach général*, which reported that a committee of actors would meet for this
purpose on certain days of the week and that every play, once accepted, would take its
turn for performance, 'without any possibility of unfair precedence'. The writer went on to
suggest that 'this method should be adopted everywhere; it is the best way to improve the
chances of success and to reduce as far as possible the risk of intrigue and partiality'.[1] With
the growth of entrepreneurialism in theatre management, however, and the subjection of
the boulevard to market forces, reading committees were either jettisoned as luxuries or
had to forfeit executive authority to the all-powerful proprietor-manager.

The playwright's work was often compromised by more direct forms of pressure, whether
from actors or from opportunist managers.

[1] *Almanach général*, p. 109.

261   Adaptation of roles to individual performers

(a) Gautier, *Histoire de l'art dramatique*, vol. I, pp. 47–8; (b) *ibid.*, vol. V, p. 273; (c) Bouffé,
Mes souvenirs, pp. 207–8

(a) Gautier writing in 1837

Nowadays we no longer have plays, or even parts in plays; every actor who is
slightly famous, and they are all famous, has his own repertoire of catchphrases
[*mots à effets*], which he will demand of the author. One will say beautifully: 'Oh!
my God! my God! MY GOD!' Another will sob with consummate grace on the
phrase: 'I am so unhappy, believe me.' Someone will utter a medieval oath in an
impeccably chivalric and feudal manner; someone else will possess a positively
Mephistophelian snigger, which is sure to elicit applause and which he is very
keen to place. Whether the role be a happy or sad one, the snigger will have to be
included somehow. Some of Mlle George's roles are miracles of the genre. They do
not contain a single *mot* that has not been applauded on some previous occasion.
Even before writing a play, the author is obliged to go and take stock of the actor.
If the actor is skinny, he will have to be given a skinny role [. . .] Odry has a nose
shaped like a bottle-cork; it is a major part of his talent; and the author is expected
never to lose sight of this magisterial nose.

Here, the bantering tone belies the depth of Gautier's resentment at the enforced subordination of an author's original conception to the realities of performance, a theme to which he returned some years later.

(b) Gautier writing in 1848

The sole concern of the manager, stage-manager, assistant stage-manager, actors great and small, male and female, speaking extras and non-speaking extras, machinists, designer and lighting men is to force on you a different play from the one you have written [. . .] If you resist all their manœuvrings, you are accused of unprecedented obstinacy and disregard for the experience of people who have spent their whole life in the business: theatrical hacks and journeymen predict the collapse of your whole edifice; you give in, and their combined inanities are booed off the stage under your name.

(c) Bouffé, 1880

After playing the exhausting role of Grandet[1] a good many times, I lost my voice and had to take several days' rest.

– It's a great pity, M. Poirson said to me, that you don't have a part for a mute in your repertoire, because then I wouldn't have to take your name off the bill, especially as you're very good at mime, I gather [. . .]

Whatever M. Poirson may think, although you can indeed play a mute when you have a sore throat, it is much more tiring than a speaking role. Nonetheless, I applied myself without delay to finding a suitable subject. My friend Devesne [*sic*] and I soon put together a scenario in two acts which we showed to Bayard, who agreed to collaborate on it. And that is how I came to play *Le Muet d'Ingouville*, a comedy in two acts with songs, in which I didn't sing, needless to say[2] [. . .]

So M. Poirson's prayer had been answered; his actor could lose his voice with impunity, and provided I didn't break a leg or an arm (which would have made it awkward to play mime), they could put my name on the bill every single day: that's just what the manager wanted!

[1] In *La Fille de l'avare*, by J.-F. Bayard and P. Duport, first performed at the Gymnase in 1835.
[2] It was presented by the Gymnase in October 1836.

However, the perennial complaint made by the playwright about his relations with the *sociétaires* or the managers of commercial theatres had to do with the level of his remuneration, which he invariably considered to be disproportionately low and liable to miscalculation. At the Théâtre-Français a system of percentile royalty payments had been in operation since the late seventeenth century, but in practice it afforded authors little protection either against misadventure or deliberate fraud. Not surprisingly, this was one of the factors identified by Cailhava as contributing to the 'decadence' of the theatre in France. After surveying arrangements at the Théâtre des Italiens, the Théâtre de Monsieur and the Variétés, he gave a detailed analysis of the fees payable to playwrights at the national theatre.

262   Performance royalties before the Revolution
Cailhava, *Décadence du théâtre*, pp. 27–8

At the Français the share due to the author for a play in 4 or 5 acts is set at 142 livres 16 sous for every hundred *pistoles* of takings, after deduction of 600 livres for daily overheads and the donation to the poor; it is 107 livres 2 sous for one in three acts, and 71 livres 8 sous for one in one or two acts; that is to say, approximately one-seventh, one-tenth-and-a-half and one-fourteenth; and when a play has, as the saying goes, fallen *dans les règles*, in other words when the takings have dropped below fifteen-hundred livres on two occasions, the author is no longer entitled to any royalty on his work. Protests have been made for quite some time against this injustice: if a play is bad, it should be rejected; if it is good, the author must be allowed a share in the profit it generates. This entitlement is sacred, and its usurpation is all the more dangerous in that it is quite easy to make even a masterpiece fall *dans les règles*: cold weather, hot weather, rain or sunshine can all encourage sharp practice.

Napoleon's Moscow decree endorsed the existing procedure, modifying the share values slightly but offering no further safeguards to the playwright, apart from regularizing his allocation of free passes.

263   Royalties and other privileges after the Revolution
'Decret impérial', (15 October 1812)

72. The author's share in the yield from takings, with a third deducted for over-heads, shall be one-eighth for a play in five or four acts, one-twelfth for one in three acts, and one-sixteenth for one in one or two acts; notwithstanding which, authors and actors may make other settlements by mutual agreement.

73. The author will receive free passes [*entrées*] from the moment his play is put into rehearsal and retain them for three years after its first performance for a work in five or four acts, two years for a work in three acts, and one year for one in one or two acts. Any author of two plays in five or four acts, or three plays in three acts, or four plays in one act which have held the stage is entitled to free passes for life.

In the case of commercial theatres, fees were entirely a matter for negotiation with the individual manager, and it was up to the playwright to secure as favourable a deal as he could, either on the basis of a lump sum on acceptance of his script, or of an agreed rate per performance. When Collot d'Herbois signed a contract with the management of the Théâtre de Monsieur in 1791, after the première of his comedy *Les Portefeuilles*, an on-going collaboration between the two parties seems to have been envisaged.

264   Performance fees in the commercial sector

'Entre les administrateurs du Théâtre de Monsieur, actuellement établi à Paris, rue Feydeau, d'une part, Et, M. Jean, Marie Collot d'Herbois, auteur dramatique, d'autre part', reproduced in Louis Péricaud, *Théâtre de Monsieur* (Paris: E. Jorel, 1908), pp. 122–4

The following agreement has been concluded governing the author's share to which the said *sieur* Collot d'Herbois shall be entitled for each performance of his works:

1° For each one of the first ten performances of his plays given at the said Théâtre de Monsieur M. Collot d'Herbois will be paid 30 livres for every act of which the plays are composed; which ten performances must be given within two months of the première;

2° Payment shall then be made of 24 livres per act of the same plays for each of the next ten performances, that is to say, from the tenth to the twentieth; these ten last to be given within four months of the tenth;

3° And payment shall be made of 18 livres per act for each performance from the twentieth to the thirtieth; these ten last to be given within eight months of the twentieth;

4° The management shall thereafter be free to retain these plays in their repertoire, on payment of 18 livres per act for each performance after the thirtieth, on the understanding that they shall be required to perform the retained plays at least ten times in the course of every year; in which case the author shall not have the right to withdraw his plays.

The management shall also have the authority, if they so wish, to forgo the second category of performances, that is to say, from the tenth to the twentieth, by giving notice to the author before the sixth. In this case, the first category shall be extended, together with the appropriate royalties, to fifteen performances over a period of six months, and thereafter the play shall revert to being the property of the author [. . .]

The above provisions shall be applicable to all plays in one, two or three acts. The author shall be paid one half less for every act of an opera, while the other clauses shall remain identical for all genres.

Mme Collot d'Herbois shall receive the same free passes as M. Collot d'Herbois, from the date of the play entitled *Les Portefeuilles* for a period of four years, beginning on 23 January of the present year, 1791. These shall be continued in perpetuity once M. Collot d'Herbois shall have added one play in three acts, or two plays in one or two acts, to those of his which are already in the repertoire.

M. Collot d'Herbois shall be empowered to assign 12 tickets to the pit, admitting one person each, two to the first gallery, six to the second gallery and four to the *Paradis*, for each of the first three performances of his works. For the ensuing performances, he shall be able to assign two tickets to the second gallery and two to the *Paradis*, each giving admission to two persons.

The present agreement shall have retrospective effect for the play entitled *Les Portefeuilles* only.

So set down and concluded between us in good faith, to be executed in accordance with its form and tenor and to have all force attaching to instruments guaranteeing the property of citizens.

Paris, 17 March 1791.
Signed
For the one part: LEONARD AUTIER, GIOVANNI VIOTTI
For the other part: JEAN MARIE COLLOT D'HERBOIS

The widespread currency of such *ad hoc* conctractual negotiations was formally acknowledged and given legal respectability by an imperial decree of 8 June 1806, in which Article 10 declares: 'Authors and proprietors are at liberty to determine between themselves, by mutual agreement, the remuneration due to the former, either in the form of a fixed sum or otherwise.' The existence of dramatic property, whether in the form of published or as yet unpublished plays, had in fact been officially recognized as early as 1791 by the Constituent Assembly's radical decree of 13 January, which protected an author's rights to his work for the duration of his life and for five years after his death (at which point it became public property and could be performed at any theatre without payment of royalty). A further decree of 19 July 1793 extended the copyright period to ten years, and yet another, issued on 1 September of the same year, explicitly broadened its application to include theatres 'in the departments'.

In theory, these measures were valid throughout the country, but a mere declaration in Paris could do little to resolve the long-standing problem of providing protection for an author's work in the remote provinces. This was another of the evils deplored by Cailhava, who alleged that playwrights were persistently defrauded, both through the pirating of scripts for performance and the withholding of their share in the takings, and who attributed the tolerance of such abuses to a 'covert antipathy which the majority of the so-called aristocracy have always felt towards men of letters'.[1] Also extant is an open letter from the composer André Grétry, dated 2 January 1791, concerning the parallel difficulty of exerting musical control: in it, he says that he is aware that two of his *opéras-comiques* have been in performance at provincial theatres for several months and implores managers to correct from the engraved score the illicit manuscript ones they have acquired 'from treacherous hands', adding plaintively that this is 'the only compensation that I ask of them for having played my pieces WITHOUT MY CONSENT'.[2] However, the promulgation of the Assembly's decrees prompted an enterprising composer-librettist by the name of Nicolas-Etienne Framery to establish an agency for monitoring provincial performances and collecting the royalty payments owing to his fellow victims of exploitation. Its workings so impressed Kotzebue that he described them for the benefit of his fellow countrymen in the published account of his visit to Paris. His French translator, Pixérécourt, with expert knowledge of the facts, frequently had occasion to contradict Kotzebue, giving rise to a lively and informative dialogue between the two men.

---

[1] *Causes de la décadence du théâtre*, p. 30.
[2] Quoted by Charles Maurice [Descombes], *Epaves. Théâtre, histoire, anecdotes, mots* (Paris: chez les principaux Libraires, 1865), p. 15.

265   Levying royalties in the provinces

Kotzebue, *Souvenirs de Paris*, vol. II, pp. 291–3

All this has been set to rights. There exists in Paris an office constituted for this very purpose. The author of a play makes it known to this office, which takes care of everything else. It has correspondents and collectors everywhere, and calculates precisely what is due to every author, for the modest charge of 2 per cent.

[Pixérécourt's note:] M. Kotzebue is again in error. To begin with, authors' royalties in the provinces are not calculated on takings, which would be virtually impossible and give rise to constant abuses and interminable disputes; it is a fixed rate, computed on the basis of the population and resources of the town in question, the capacity of the theatre and the presumed takings. The towns of France are divided into eight categories, the first of which will pay 54 livres per performance of a full-length work, the eighth 3 livres, and the others in proportion.

Furthermore, it is not 2 per cent that dramatic agencies charge to look after authors' interests; to be able to make such a statement, it is necessary either to have given the matter no thought or to have no idea of the trouble and expense which this work entails. Authors make to their agents a remittance of 17 per cent, and although this proportion might seem a trifle excessive, they would be well satisfied and would be party to a very profitable deal if the correspondents brought to this honourable and delicate task all the industry and meticulousness it demands.

Kotzebue then proceeds to paint a very rosy picture of the potential earnings of French playwrights.

As there are in France many more than a hundred theatres (not including the small ones, which are of no importance), one may assume that the author of a play that has been very successful can make 40 thousand livres in the first two years of its performance.[1] Admittedly, this will subsequently decrease, but French repertoires are less subject to change than ours, and consequently an author will continue to enjoy a secure annual income on an equitable basis, since it is determined by the quality of his play. If the excitement of the initial moment was responsible for its success, it will be rarely revived; contrariwise, if the play is a good one it will be performed often. An author fortunate enough to have three or four plays in the repertoire of the Théâtre-Français will not only be well off for the rest of his life but will rejoice in the knowledge that his children will have a living for another ten years thereafter: an honourable legacy! But only in France can one both earn it and collect it.

1. [Pixérécourt's note:] This figure can be reduced by a half, besides which there are few examples of plays making 20,000 livres in two years.

Despite Kotzebue's envy of the prospects enjoyed by playwrights in France, not all of them considered the kudos and steady income accruing from performance at the national theatre to be adequate. Dumas, for one, appears to have been in no doubt that not only his artistic preferences but also his greater financial advantage lay elsewhere.

266   Comparative earnings at the Théâtre-Français and the commercial theatres

Dumas, *Souvenirs dramatiques*, vol. I, pp. 254–6

[M. Thiers, then minister of the interior] had asked me why I worked for the boulevard theatres rather than the Théâtre-Français. I had replied that the genre of plays that I wrote was better served on the boulevard than at the Théâtre-Français. He then urged on me the pecuniary benefits to be gained from working at the Théâtre-Français.

Whereupon, with pen in hand, I proved to him that the Théâtre-Français was the theatre where one earned least. And since M. Thiers is a man of acute intelligence, he immediately understood what I shall now proceed to make you understand.

From its greatest successes the Théâtre-Français may make an average of four thousand francs for thirty or forty performances. Let us assume, at the most, forty performances at 4,000 francs, or 160,000 francs. The Théâtre-Français pays out 9 per cent of the takings. However, it will almost always make a small cut in the 9 per cent. It will play a piece in one or two acts by a dead author, and the living author will now have only 7. Seven per cent on 4,000 francs gives 280 francs. Seven per cent on 160,000 francs gives 11,200 francs. Thus, after forty performances, in other words after three months and eighteen days, a play at the Théâtre-Français will have produced a return of 11,000 francs.

– Why three months and eighteen days? you will ask.

It's very simple: the other theatres will perform a new play every day of the week, including Sundays. The Théâtre-Français will perform it every other day and not on Sundays. As a result, the other theatres will offer the author thirty performances per month. While the Théâtre-Français will give him only twelve.

Now, a play grows old not according to the number of performances it receives but according to the date on the bill. The upshot is that at the end of three months and eighteen days, when a play has had forty performances, it will be as old as if it had been presented daily at another theatre and received a hundred and eight performances.

At the moment, an author is paid 10 per cent at boulevard theatres. Let us say that the hundred and ten peformances have taken an average of 2,000 francs. That is exactly half the average of the Théâtre-Français. The boulevard theatre will have taken 216,000 francs, which at 10 per cent makes a return of 21,600 francs. Ten thousand four hundred francs more than at the Théâtre-Français, or almost double.

Elsewhere, he summed up the occupational hazards of his fellow authors more succinctly by likening the Théâtre-Français to 'a circle of hell overlooked by Dante', where playwrights can be 'decorated in their old age with the cross of the Legion of honour, not for the successes they have achieved but for the sufferings they have endured'.[1] He seems oblivious to the irony of the fact that the fortune which he had once successfully amassed as a boulevard playwright had later been largely dissipated by his own painful speculation in boulevard proprietorship with the Théâtre-Historique.

[1] Dumas, *Souvenirs*, vol. I, p. 238.

III   Actors and acting

In terms of acting, the first half of the nineteenth century was marked by two complementary and interrelated phenomena: on the one hand, an erosion in the credibility of a histrionic tradition that had evolved alongside the repertory of plays long designated as the exclusive preserve of the Théâtre-Français; on the other, the equally gradual acceptance of a new style most typically associated with the recently deregulated, popular theatres of the Boulevard du Temple – in other words, the gradual replacement of an art of acting recognizably governed by precedent and artifice by one that was more freely expressive, more 'true to life' in its representation of human behaviour. To formulate the process thus is, inevitably, to oversimplify. As long as classical plays continued to be performed, 'classical' acting remained a stylistic loadstone and a yardstick against which deviations could be measured. And the acting required by the Romantic *drame* and the melodrama was by no means 'natural'. No stage acting is, or ever can be, natural, and what theatre audiences describe as such usually represents the product of substituting one set of conventions for another. But that a change of quite radical proportions occurred during these years is attested by many commentators. Midway through the period, the playwright and theatre manager J. T. Merle, writing immediately in the wake of the première at the Théâtre-Français in 1829 of Dumas's *Henri III et sa cour*, the first play by one of the young group of Romantic authors to be performed at that shrine of the dramatic establishment, saw the situation clearly and made an explicit prognosis.

267   The Comédiens-Français out of their element, 1829

Jean-Toussaint Merle, *Du marasme dramatique en 1829* (Paris: Barba, 1829), p. 40

I shall say nothing here about the merits of the genres, but subsequent events will prove that the Comédie-Française has need of a different company of actors from those we see there now to play the Romantic drama, and that Joanny, Firmin and Mademoiselle Mars, despite the brilliant and deserved success they gained in *Henri III*, will never come near the level of pathos attained by Frédérick, Gobert and Madame Dorval in the expression of passionate feelings and in the portrayal of the forceful situations and characters of melodrama. I am not blinded by the vogue for *Louis XI*, for *Tasse*[1] and for *Henri III*, I persist in my belief that the Comédiens-Français will be unable to uphold this genre and will forfeit their reputation as actors without achieving that of performers of melodrama.

[1] Two other 'history' plays in prose recently premièred at the Théâtre-Français, a '*comédie historique*' by Mély-Janin (1827) and a '*drame historique*' by Duval (1826).

Not the least interesting aspect of the above comment is that it makes no distinction between the performance style of melodrama and that of Romantic drama.

A TRADITION OF RHETORICAL ACTING

The 'reputation as actors' which Merle here attributes to the Comédiens-Français was of course identified in the public's eyes with a theatrical heritage dating back one and a half centuries to the foundation of their company in 1680, since when their position as official custodians of the nation's repertoire had been stoutly defended. For the Romantic generation, however, the stultifying effect of this responsibility had become a subject of repeated complaint.

268   Gustave Planche bemoans the current state of the national theatre, 1834

Gustave Planche, 'Histoire et philosophie de l'art', in *Revue des Deux Mondes*, 3rd series, vol. 4 (1834), p. 548

What has to be recognized and defined is the unchanging corporate profile of the Comédie-Française. Individual singularities and idiosyncrasies occur too infrequently to make much difference to collective analysis. If there is one maxim which governs the *sociétaires* and consoles them, they say, for the indifference of the public, it is their respect for tradition.

At the moment, not one of them makes any attempt to arrive at a personal understanding of the meaning of Cinna or Britannicus; not one of them endeavours to discern in an acting role written between the time of Richelieu and that of Bossuet any intentions which might lie beyond the comprehension of the multitude. What preoccupies them above all is to know how Lekain or Molé, how Préville or Fleury, how Mlle Contat or Mlle Clairon played the part they are to play. In the name of tradition they have turned dramatic art, the most living and the most dynamic of all the arts, into an inert and static relic.[1]

If this tradition were a genuine and authentic one, such military subservience to the past would be mere foolishness worthy of pity; the slavish fulfilment of commandments that are in themselves obscure warrants nothing but anger.

[1] For documents relating to the acting of Mlle Clairon, Lekain, Préville and Molé, see W. D. Howarth (ed.) *French theatre in the neo-classical era, 1550–1789* (Cambridge: Cambridge University Press, 1997) nos. 630, 631, 633, 634, 635, 636, 637, 638, 639, 648, 649 and 658. See also D. Roy, 'Mlle Clairon' and 'Lekain', in *International dictionary of theatre*, vol. III, *Actors, directors and designers* (London and Detroit: St. James Press, 1996).

Indeed, what had once been a technique of stage performance subscribing to conventions akin to those prevalent in other types of public speaking, in the pulpit or at the bar, and whose purpose was to communicate to an audience by means of formalized diction, gesture, facial expression and posture the stylistic qualities of a dramatic text, had now become overlaid with the accretions of successful practice, the vocal mannerisms and physical business of particular *sociétaires* who were known to have earned the greatest public acclaim during the intervening decades. This state of affairs was exacerbated by the fact that the acknowledged apprenticeship for a young actor or actress aspiring to a permanent place within the company was to seek individual tuition from a leading *sociétaire*, preferably a *chef d'emploi*, and the resulting indebtedness could be all too apparent.

269   Mlle George's début as Clytemnestre, 1802

Review of *Iphigénie en Aulide* at the Théâtre-Français, 30 November 1802. Geoffroy, *Cours de littérature dramatique*, vol. V, p. 468

One recognized in the pupil the manner of the teacher; it could scarcely be otherwise: almost always, in fact, it is the faults that disciples imitate, though when they have talent, they soon create their own manner [. . .] Even if Mademoiselle Georges [*sic*] were no more than a faithful copy of Mademoiselle Raucourt our theatre would still be fortunate, and spectators would have nothing to complain of in being allowed to see Mademoiselle Raucourt at the age of nineteen.

Geoffroy, of the *Journal des Débats*, was among the most conservative as well as the most influential of critics in the early years of the nineteenth century, and it is revealing to note that his great admiration for Mlle Raucourt was based, at least in part, on the fact that she had been the pupil of the pre-eminent tragedienne of the previous century, Mlle Clairon.[1]

[1] For other documents relating to the acting of Mlle Raucourt, see Howarth, *French theatre*, nos. 642 and 643.

270   Geoffroy's assessment of Mlle Raucourt

Geoffroy, *Cours de littérature dramatique*, vol. VI, pp. 207–8

Mademoiselle Raucourt is still the only [actress] of the Théâtre-Français who is capable of representing the great tragic characters, such as Cléopâtre, Médée, Agrippine, Jocaste, etc. She is the great queen *par excellence* because she combines with a profound knowledge of the art the majesty and the loftiness of mien, the superb presence and, if one may so express it, the stuff of tragedy required for such roles [. . .] Mademoiselle Raucourt's diction, her movement, her bearing are all from the best school; one can recognize an actress who has taken lessons from Mademoiselle Clairon and has been able to put them to good use.

That the same was true in comedy and that a *sociétaire*'s lessons could extend to minute details of comportment is confirmed by Legouvé's amusing account of the tuition given by the company's *première coquette*, Louise Contat, to Mlle Mars, who had a habit of gesturing with her left arm.

271 Mlle Mars is taught by Mlle Contat

Legouvé, *Soixante ans de souvenirs*, vol. 1, pp. 85–6

The left arm is always gauche, she said. You must use it only in exceptional circumstances. What's more, I know just how to teach yours to behave. Tomorrow you're playing in *Le Dissipateur*,[1] and in the scene in Act IV, where I'm very happy with you by the way, your miserable left arm whirls itself about like a sail on a windmill. Well, I shall tie a black thread to your wrist, I'll stand in the wings at the side where you play the scene [. . .] and the instant you make a gesture, I shall tug.

The scene began, and on her second line Mlle Mars attempted a tiny rebellious movement [. . .] the thread was pulled. Everything reverted to normal. The scene became more animated, the young actress as well, and at one moment of feeling the left arm twitched and began to shoot forward [. . .] the thread was pulled. The scene continued, became touching, then turned to pathos, and the poor left arm wanted to join in, but the thread kept pulling it back [. . .] It protested [. . .] the thread did, too; with the result that after some moments of struggle, Mlle Mars, overcome by mounting emotion, raised both her hands with such force that the thread broke, and there was the left arm gesticulating merrily away in space! When the scene was over, Mlle Mars made her exit with eyes downcast, not daring to look at Mlle Contat, who went up to her, took her by the hand and said: 'Bravo! Now there's a lesson better than any I could have taught you. Remember, you mustn't use the left arm until it would break the thread.'

[1] Comedy by Destouches, first performed in 1753.

Predictably enough, the lessons which Mlle Mars learned from Louise Contat at the turn of the century were later to be passed on to her own pupils. The début of one such in 1839, by which time Mlle Mars was 60 but still active as a teacher, afforded Gautier an opportunity to comment on the dominance and longevity of this 'classical' influence. Claiming not to be an enemy of tradition as such, he nonetheless counselled against an exaggerated deference to it.

272 The début of Mlle Doze, 1839

Gautier, *Histoire de l'art dramatique*, vol. 1, pp. 316–7

One must venerate the ancients without worshipping them blindly, and profit by what they have achieved; one should make use of them but not copy them. Mademoiselle Doze, whose legitimate admiration for Mlle Mars we commend, has, it seems to us, overstepped the bounds which separate study from imitation [. . .] Mademoiselle Doze is Mademoiselle Mars in daguerrotype.

The same voice, the same intonations, the same gestures, the same postures, the impersonation is complete; Mademoiselle Mars must be very surprised to see herself performing in person, somewhat rejuvenated it is true, a few feet in front of her, in the glow of the footlights and the applause: it must be decidedly odd to hear her own voice issuing from another mouth, and to find herself responding to herself.

It is clear that actor training by regimentation was normalized, if not indeed sanctified, by the very existence of a conservatoire placed under the official aegis of the national theatre and staffed by its *sociétaires*. A mere three years after its establishment the playwright Cailhava d'Estandoux was already disparaging its products, and his strictures were persistently echoed throughout the period.

273   Criticism of the Conservatoire

(a) Cailhava, *Décadence du théâtre*, p. 24; (b) Frédérick Lemaître: *Souvenirs [. . .], publiés par son fils* (2nd edn, Paris: Ollendorff, 1880), pp. 319–20; (c) Dumas, *Souvenirs dramatiques*, vol. II, pp. 182–3

(a) Cailhava d'Estandoux, 1789

[. . .] this wretched *School*, the graveyard of talent rather than its cradle, [from which emerge] every six months one or two little marionettes, very pleased with themselves because they can recite a couple of roles for their début, as children learn to recite 'Maître Corbeau' or 'La Cigale',[1] and because they are being impudently let loose onto the premier stage of Europe with orders to the pit to spend ten years watching over the novitiate of these actor-machines.

(b) Lemaître's *Souvenirs*, 1880

These plays [by Casimir Delavigne] would take on a new lease of life once they were stripped of all the superannuated and mummified traditions of the rue de Richelieu, and above all were liberated from the demoralizing routine of training at the Conservatoire, which consists of transmitting to future generations, as they have been transmitted to us by past generations, every gesture, every vocal inflexion, every look, all of them classified, numbered and stereotyped, without any differentiation for personality, temperament or instinct, a training which, by forcing young people into a strait-jacket of tradition, serves only to produce and to perpetuate a lot of jumping-jacks, all pulled uniformly by the same string, worthy rivals of performing dogs, educated birds and talking parrots.

(c) Dumas's *Souvenirs dramatiques*, 1868

The Conservatoire turns out impossible actors. Give me anybody – a municipal guard discharged in February, a retired shopkeeper – and I'll make an actor of him; but I've never been able to fashion one out of any of the Conservatoire's pupils. They are spoilt for life by the routine and mediocrity of their training; they have never studied nature, they've been confined to copying their teachers more or less imperfectly.

¹ 'Master Crow' and 'The Cicada', two *fables* by the seventeenth-century poet, La Fontaine, which had become standard recitation pieces for generations of French children.

The absence from their curriculum of any opportunity for interactive experience and creative discovery does in fact seem to have marked the average Conservatoire graduate in a way that was depressingly easy to recognize. The habitually acerbic *Dictionnaire théâtral* was not for once overstating the case when it made specific recommendations for combating an evident 'decadence' in the standard of acting at the Théâtre-Français in the 1820s, for its views were corroborated a few years later in the columns of a leading theatrical journal.

274   Proposals for improving actor-training

(a) Harel *et al.*, *Dictionnaire théâtral*, p. 104; (b) *Courrier des Théâtres* (2 December 1827)

(a) *Dictionnaire théâtral*, 1824

Train pupils on a stage set aside for this purpose, and face to face with an audience; reorganize the Conservatoire, which teaches the rules of a profession rather than the principles of an art.

(b) *Courrier des Théâtres*, 1827

They are taught how to *declaim*, how to *recite* speeches, and not how to *play* a scene. The pupils of the School of Declamation ought to have a huge advantage over those who have studied the art of the theatre under a private tutor. The latter can be put through their paces only by their tutor and that is far from adequate. The others ought never to have delivered a single line except as part of a scene, with an interlocutor to consider and by whose expression they may regulate their own gestures, their vocal inflexions. [. . .] Finally, they should *learn nothing by heart* but the words they have to speak, and be accustomed to adjusting everything else to the effect of the scene and in line with their own responses. Is that how one studies at the Royal School? We think not, at least if we may judge by the results.

By the opening decades of the nineteenth century, then, a convergence of self-perpetuating traditionalism and learning by rote had had a debilitating effect on the acting of the classic repertoire, reducing it to a set of conventional prescriptions for giving an acceptable performance, acceptable, that is, to the more conservative members of the audience but of diminishing appeal to the remainder, particularly in the performance of tragedy. To an informed outsider like Kotzebue, making a return visit to Paris in 1804, it appeared desperately mannered, but in many French eyes, too, there was much to criticize about their tragedians, especially in comparison with their German counterparts.

275   Kotzebue on the performance of French tragedy, 1804

Kotzebue, *Souvenirs de Paris*, vol. II, pp. 216–17

I have more than once expounded my way of thinking on the manner in which tragedy is performed in France. I cannot tolerate it, precisely because it is a *manner*.

All French heroes are made to the same model, they all express their thoughts and their passions in the same fashion. To have seen one tragedy is to have seen them all. Talma alone deserves to be excepted; he has himself acknowledged that he is endeavouring to combine the German manner with the French. His rivals censure him for this, but the great effect that he produces every day proves incontrovertibly that his method is the better, in that it can touch the heart.

276   Mme de Staël compares French and German actors, 1810

Mme de Staël, *De l'Allemagne* (Paris: Garnier, 1925), pp. 38–9

In France, the majority of our actors never look as if they are unconscious of what they are doing; on the contrary, there is something studied about all the means they employ and one can predict their effect in advance.

Schröder, whom all Germans regard as an admirable actor, could not bear to be told that he had played such and such a moment well or spoken such and such a line well – Did I play the part well? he would ask; did I become the character? – And, in point of fact, his ability seemed to change in nature with every role he played. No one in France would dare to play tragedy in a conversational tone of voice, as he did frequently. There is a prevailing tone, an agreed sonority that is *de rigueur* for the speaking of alexandrine verse, and even the most passionate of movement must needs be mounted on this pedestal, which is as it were a prerequisite of the art. French actors customarily solicit applause, and earn it on virtually every line; German actors seek it at the end of the play and rarely receive any elsewhere.

Even without benefit of any recorded notation, it is possible to piece together from a variety of sources certain clues as to the nature of this 'prevailing tone' or 'agreed sonority' and of the relationship between acting and declaiming.

277   Deficiencies of the company at the Théâtre de la Nation, 1791

Almanach général (1791), p. 137

However, not all the actors of the Nation, by a long way, are as able as their predecessors. They are taken to task, fairly generally, for their bombast and monstrous affectation on the stage and, in society, for their hauteur, misplaced self-esteem and even a certain pedantry.

278   A declamatory inheritance, 1824

Harel *et al.*, *Dictionnaire théâtral*, p. 105

Did you ever hear Saint-Prix? He was a good declaimer, but not a tragedian; he used to carry his heart in his throat; he was lacking in warmth and excitement; he was cold and monotonous. Listen for a moment to Desmousseaux: he accentuates all the faults of his master, he articulates the full stops and commas, he weighs out the hemistiches, he makes the rhymes resound, he points the cæsuras, he measures the syllables; he does not express himself as a man might but as a compendium of declamation.

279   Vocal mannerisms of the Comédiens-Français

F. R. de Toreinx, *Histoire du Romantisme en France* (Paris: L. Dubreuil, 1829), pp. 49–50

We had ample opportunity to castigate the shortcomings of actors who no longer *breathed* the text and were content to resort to old tricks without much display of intelligence: 'Should one, like M. Lafon, open the eyes and the mouth very wide, and turn our alexandrines into a psalmodic chant more tedious than that of the choristers of Saint Merry? Should one, like Madame So-and-so, regularly bisect the lines with a supposedly dramatic intake of breath [*hoquet*], as if an attack of asthma could add much interest to the situation of Mérope or Iphigénie?' No, that is not how nature speaks.

280   The *hoquet* defined

Harel *et al.*, *Dictionnaire théâtral*, p. 178

HOQUET. Name given quite inappositely to a kind of gasp with which some actors have invested their diction, either from a deficiency of native means or in an attempt to create a greater effect. It is among tragic actors that this lamentable practice of the '*hoquet*' is particularly noticeable: Talma and Mademoiselle George have contrived to avoid it. The ability to disguise one's breathing is not the least important aspect of an actor's art; it is the last thing that tutors at the Conservatoire think of teaching.

Mlle George and her exact contemporary, Mlle Duchesnois, maintained a bitter rivalry in tragic roles throughout their careers, each with a highly partisan following. When, in 1804, they both became *sociétaires* on the same day and Kotzebue, as an impartial outsider, was invited to express a preference, he was forced to admit that he did not greatly admire either, though he was particularly harsh on the intensely studied quality of the latter's performances.

281   The artifice of Mlle Duchesnois, 1804

Kotzebue, *Souvenirs de Paris*, vol. II, pp. 222–4

For one thing, Mademoiselle Duchesnois is much uglier than any actress has a right to be. Secondly, apart from the faults of the French *manner* which are common to all, she has others peculiar to herself, like, for example, a kind of singsong in her way of declaiming and a habit of stressing with all her force several different syllables in the same line, with the result that each is made considerably longer. Everything she does is patently studied; she must be forever before her looking-glass; not one of her intonations is inspired by nature or springs from the heart; one can discern nothing but artifice, in all things and at all times [. . .] [Mlle George] acts well, and does not shout nearly as much as her rival; also, nature occasionally calls forth from her an inflexion which seems heartfelt. She pleased me. Even so, she failed to live up to my expectation.

Consistent with the deliberate cultivation of the voice, which so repelled Kotzebue, was the practice of drawing the audience's attention to certain 'points' in the text and, as Mme de Staël observed, soliciting their applause, particularly that of the body of self-styled *connaisseurs* at the Théâtre-Français, who were all too conscious of their responsibility as guardians of tradition. Evidence of the inevitable consequences of espousing such a priority is not difficult to find.

282   'Effects' in the actor's performance

Harel *et al.*, *Dictionnaire théâtral*, pp. 132–3

EFFECT. A play will always contain a certain number of passages designated by tradition, or by the author himself, or by the actor in whose role they figure, as capable of generating applause, or laughter, or tears, as the case may be. This is what is called an *effect*. There are some actors who, out of jealousy or malice, neutralize their colleagues' effects, which is not difficult to do, either by failing to give the proper cue, or by omitting an agreed piece of business, or by coming in hard after the operative word. Actors have been known to fight duels and actresses, hitherto the closest of friends, to exchange foul-mouthed abuse on account of effects which have been deliberately cut or attenuated.

283   The primacy of forestage acting positions

Legouvé, *Soixante ans de souvenirs*, vol. I (1887), p. 197

Mise-en-scène, particularly in comedy, is still a very modern art. In the old days, an author would write on his manuscript: *The action takes place in a drawing-room*, but nothing took place there as it would in a real drawing-room. To begin with, nobody sat down. One can still recall actors of the Théâtre-Français coming downstage to deliver their speeches, bolt upright, standing next to one another in front of the prompter's box. One enterprising person, who has since become a government official, tried to inaugurate what he called seated comedy at the rue Richelieu. Unfortunately, his play fell flat and the seated comedy ended up on the floor. Scribe was the first to bring to the stage all the animation of everyday life.

284   Mlle Mars plays to the audience, 1838[1]

Stendhal, *Mémoires d'un touriste* (3 vols., Paris: H. and E. Champion, 1932), vol. I, p. 420

Mademoiselle Mars [. . .] is not capable of expressing any emotion in the least heartfelt; she can do nothing but create the impression of a lady who is very well bred. Now and then she will make an effort to behave like a fool, but taking care the while to show you, by means of a delicate little glance, that she has no intention of forfeiting in your eyes her superiority as a person over the part she is playing.

[1] See also **440**.

285   Mme Dorval surprises the traditionalists, 1833

Review of a revival of Monvel's comedy, *L'Amant bourru* (1777) at the Théâtre-Français, in 'Chronique de la quinzaine', *Revue des Deux Mondes*, 2nd series, vol. 1 (1833), pp. 99–100

Madame Dorval of the boulevard! Madame Dorval who with such spirit and such intensity had played Adèle and Marion Delorme,[1] roles not worthy of the French stage, would she be able to speak Monsieur Monvel's verse correctly? Would Madame Dorval walk across these classic boards in the correct manner? Would Madame Dorval make the appropriate gestures? Would Madame Dorval raise her arms to the accepted height, would she give a little kick to the tail of her gown in accordance with sound tradition? Would she, in the interest of greater truth, take up a stately pose as close as possible to the footlights and scarcely look at anyone else on stage, as they did in the old days? – Such were the weighty artistic questions exercising the orchestra pit before the performance, and without going so far as formally to pronounce judgement but by way of betraying an involuntary response, many a contemporary of Monvel inclined and nodded his bewigged head as a mark of incredulity. Madame Dorval did not have to make much effort to dispel these unwarranted suspicions. Her poised bearing, her easy grace and her excellent diction even won over the most exclusive and entrenched devotees of the past.

[1] In Dumas's *Antony* and Hugo's *Marion de Lorme*, respectively, both created at the Porte Saint-Martin in 1831.

Equally evident is the sheer persistence of this tradition, one which united a calculated, intensely self-conscious acting style with an audience dedicated to upholding it. A generation later, long after Romantic dramas had found their way onto the stage of the Théâtre-Français and with melodramas all-powerful in the boulevard theatres, the extraordinary success of Mlle Rachel was seen as a potential salvation for the classical repertoire, though her performances were still closely monitored by her admirers to verify that she was equal to the task.

286   Rachel as Phèdre, 1843

Review of *Phèdre* at the Théâtre-Français, 23 January 1843. Gautier, *Histoire de l'art dramatique*, vol. II, pp. 328–9

The veteran patrons who had seen Mademoiselle Duchesnois and the rest waited in ambush for the young tragedienne at the turn of every notable hemistich, hoping to catch her out, but they were unsuccessful. Speaking for ourselves, we couldn't say whether she spoke well or ill the words:

'*Follow with my eyes a chariot's flight along the course*',

and whether she respected or disregarded tradition; we know only that for two whole hours she gave us Phèdre without once breaking the illusion [. . .]

But veteran play-goers notwithstanding, a revolution in perceptions of acting had occurred in the interim, and no better testimony can be adduced for this than the same critic's account of a perfomance of the same role three months earlier by the archetypal actress of the new *drame*, Marie Dorval.

287   Madame Dorval as Phèdre, 1842

Review of *Phèdre* at the Opéra-Comique, 25 October 1842. Gautier, *Histoire de l'art dramatique*, vol. II, pp. 285–6

[. . .] Madame Dorval seemed to us to be concerned about one thing only, namely to act in a thoroughly classical way, as if she were a tragedienne of the rue Richelieu. It was not what we expected of her. She stressed the lines correctly, sounded the rhymes and marked the hemistiches, so that no one could accuse her of falling back into the prose of *drame*. We thought that she might bring to all this epic stillness some of the turbulence and passion of the modern theatre; on the contrary, she seemed diffident, almost numb, and as if embarrassed [. . .] It is not with such antique roles that the talent of Madame Dorval can develop freely; her distinctive quality is to be modern and of the moment, to be without any tradition, to be able to summon up those sudden cries in whose very inflexion lies their significance, in a word to be *nature*, as is said of an artist's style.

FRENCH AND ENGLISH ACTING COMPARED

A major factor in this revolution had its origin, almost of necessity, outside the French theatrical mainstream, in the organized visits to Paris by companies of English actors, first in 1822, more momentously in 1827, and then again in 1832. The cultural divide that separated the two countries before these visits took place finds ample expression in the accounts of theatre-going recorded by British tourists arriving in Paris after the Peace of Amiens of 1801 had temporarily restored opportunities for European travel, then again some years later, following the conclusion of the Napoleonic Wars, in British reactions to what the *Times* called the 'Grand Concerts of Recitations extracted from the most popular French tragedies' which were given in London by Talma and Mlle George in the summer of 1817.

288 Maria Edgeworth's response to French acting, 1802

Letter to Mrs Mary Sneyd, dated 31 October 1802, reproduced in Augustus J. C. Hare, *The life and letters of Maria Edgeworth* (2 vols., London: Edward Arnold, 1894), vol. 1, p. 99

We have been to the Théâtre Français and to the Théâtre Feydau [*sic*], both fine houses: decorations, etc., superior to English: acting much superior in comedy; in tragedy they bully, and rant, and throw themselves into Academy attitudes too much.

289 The Greatheeds visit the Théâtre-Français, 1803

Journal entry for 19 January 1803, reproduced in J. P. T. Bury and J. C. Barry (eds.), *An Englishman in Paris: 1803. The journal of Bertie Greatheed* (London: Geoffrey Bles, 1953), pp. 31–2

We dined rather early and all went to *Sémiramis*.[1] The wooden columns hinder the view very much and are cut in a very ugly manner by the upper tier of boxes. There was no orchestra but all laid in seats. Three stamps gave notice to raise the curtain. Mademoiselle George and Talma acted. She has a fine person but not much expression of countenance. As in their painting, so in their acting, they are quite over-antique. Talma was constantly Etruscanizing himself. As to the grand air, the strutting bloated pomp, the bombast, gesticulation and declamation, the trembling body and the quivering hands, I cannot bear them and should be inclined to laugh were it not prevented by disgust. In the more impassioned parts they would have acted well if the corruptness of the dramatic school had not prevented them. The death was most correctly grouped. The audience were delighted and Talma and George called for. The curtain was raised and they made a hurried half-dressed appearance at the back of the theatre where they saluted the spectators and hastily retired.

[1] Tragedy by Voltaire, first performed in 1748.

290 Henry Crabb Robinson sees Talma and Mlle George, 1817

Diary entry for 26 June 1817, reproduced in Thomas Sadler (ed.), *Diary, reminiscences and correspondence of Henry Crabb Robinson* (3 vols., London: Macmillan, 1869), vol. II, pp. 60–1

[Talma's] first appearance disappointed me. He has little grey eyes, too near each other, and though a regular and good face, not a very striking one. His voice is good, but not peculiarly sweet. His excellence lies in the imitation of intense suffering. He filled me with horror certainly as Philoctète, but it was mingled with disgust. Bodily pain is no fit or legitimate subject for the drama; and too often he was merely a man suffering from a sore leg. Of his declamation I do not presume to judge. The character of Orestes affords finer opportunities of display. The terror he feels when pursued by the Furies was powerfully communicated and his tenderness towards Pylades on parting was also exquisite. Mdlle Georges [*sic*] had more to do, but she gave me far less pleasure. Her acting I thought radically bad. Instead of copying nature in the expression of passion, according to which the master feeling predominates over all the others, she merely minces the words. If in the same line the words *crainte* and *joie* occur, she apes fear and joy by outrageous pantomime; [. . .] Her acting appeared to me utterly without feeling.

291   Talma's performance as Orestes is appraised by the *Morning Post*, 1817

Morning Post (20 June 1817)

Talma finely displayed the despair of Orestes, but had the same noddings and shakings of the head and slappings of the knee, which were deservedly admired in Talma, been ventured upon by an English Orestes, we doubt if the audience would have refrained from laughter. He presented a most interesting picture of wild emotion, but it was produced by means to which few English actors could safely resort. For such are the differences between neighbours in matters of taste, that what would seem natural and dignified on one side of the Channel, would be thought extravagance and insanity on the other.

THE DISCOVERY OF ENGLISH ACTING

The sense of cultural difference was mutual, to judge by French responses to the performances given by English actors in Paris. Those of 1822 had little chance of a fair hearing from audiences to whom Shakespeare was first and foremost a fellow countryman of Wellington, but by 1827 the cultural climate, together with the political climate, had changed sufficiently to ensure that the impact which Charles Kemble, Macready and Kean[1] (to say nothing of Harriet Smithson) made on French actors and spectators alike was profound, so profound, in fact, that the season of English plays, initially intended to last four months, was extended to more than ten. Even so established a *sociétaire* as Mlle Mars was reported in the press as not having missed a single English performance, and for rising stars of the boulevard theatres such as Frédérick Lemaître and Marie Dorval, who were soon to become the principal interpreters of French Romantic drama, the season must have been as much of a revelation as it was for the Romantic authors themselves. Unable as they were to appreciate Shakespearean poetry for its own sake, to hear dramatic verse spoken with a directness and lack of inhibition inimical to the rigidly generic decorum of French acting, and, moreover, to see it married to energetic stage action and visual expressiveness, can only have served as an object lesson, although some Parisians found such qualities hard to reconcile with the dignity of tragedy.

[1] See **133, 134, 135, 140, 141, 142, 143, 146, 150.**

292   Learning from the English players, 1827–8

(a) *Quotidienne* (3 October 1827); (b) Letter to Frédéric Soulié, dated 28 September 1827, reproduced in Eugène Delacroix, *Correspondance générale* (5 vols., Paris: Plon, 1936–8), vol. 1, p. 197; (c) *Pandore* (19 September 1827); (d) *Pandore* (14 September 1827); (e) *Courrier Français* (13 September 1827); (f) Journal entry for 26 May 1828, reproduced in Robert Baschet (ed.), *Le Journal d'Etienne-Jean Delécluze, 1824–1828* (Paris: B. Grasset, 1948), pp. 491–2

(a) *La Quotidienne*
The assiduity with which our leading lights, tragic and comic, have been following these performances demonstrates conclusively that our literature and our theatre can only benefit from a knowledge of English masterpieces and from a comparison of the two styles of acting.

(b) Eugène Delacroix
The most stubborn classicists are striking their colours. Our actors are going back to school and are wide-eyed. The repercussions of this innovation are incalculable.

(c) *La Pandore*
We would urge Mlle Bourgoin to cry in earnest, as they cry in the English theatre, and have no fear of disordering her toilette or of agitating her pretty face, for a handkerchief to dab her eyes with is not going to be enough to soften the heart of a Turk, however gallant he may be; Orosmane will yield only to real tears.

(d) *La Pandore*
Might not the French art of acting take advantage of this priceless acquisition? It is the English sneer; we in France prefer to weep in the playing of tragedy, but this laughter has nothing cheerful about it; it makes one shudder. The role of Hamlet is often marked by a bitter irony, which affords Kemble many opportunities to make profitable use of this asset.

(e) *Courrier Français*
[...] the monstrous tragedy by Shakespeare which sparkles with such great beauty, alongside which our refined taste regrets to see so much nonsense [...] Nothing could be less tragic on our stage than a hero rolling about on the floor as Hamlet does.

(f) Etienne-Jean Delécluze
Richmond and Richard have a fight with swords for five or six minutes. The latter is finally run through by his opponent. At the moment of receiving the blow Kean staggers but remains standing. He continues to brandish his sword, then lets it fall,

whereupon his disarmed hand again moves in the semblance of a sword-thrust. At the last, Kean falls on his back and in that position, writhing to and fro the while, he delivers half a dozen lines which are no more a part of the play than all the mimed action which has just been described.

TALMA BRIDGES THE OLD AND THE NEW

The art of acting, and, more inscrutably, perceptions of acting, could not remain immune to such prolonged exposure to this alien influence. Over the next two decades, which were to witness the brief flowering of Romantic drama, to say nothing of the ever-burgeoning prosperity of melodrama, some French actors resisted the notion of change, others contrived, consciously or unconsciously, to adapt to it, while still others, particularly in the boulevard theatres, found in it encouragement, perhaps vindication even, for their own approach to performance. Although he did not live to see the Théâtre-Français surrender to the forces of Romanticism, Talma can be considered in retrospect as having formed a bridge between the old, classical tradition of acting and the new: he it was whom Hugo took as the model for his delineation of Cromwell, and the 'pre-Romantic' qualities of his acting, his lack of restraint, his melancholy and nervous intensity, constituted the basis for Geoffroy's persistently hostile comments on his performances, which led eventually to the famous bout of fisticuffs between the two men. More tellingly still, the extraordinary magnetism and unpredictability of Frédérick Lemaître's stage presence, together with Marie Dorval's unparalleled capacity for communicating depth of feeling gave a unique impetus to the emancipation of French acting from the weight of past practice. And it was in large part her ability to learn from their example that allowed Rachel to revitalize the classical tradition and accommodate it to the demands of the mid-nineteenth century. Eye-witness accounts of the work of these star performers and of some of their colleagues make it possible to trace this process of renewal quite closely.

293   Talma challenges tradition, 1800

Review of *Othello*, a tragedy by Jean-François Ducis, Théâtre-Français, 9 November 1800. Geoffroy, *Cours de littérature dramatique*, vol. VI, pp. 220–1

Talma belongs to the new school of acting, created by a few people who had more presumption than experience and taste. These innovators disregard declamation and the correct manner of reciting verse; their delivery is drawling, emphatic and monotonous. On the pretext of coming closer to nature, they demean tragedy by an everyday, commonplace tone of voice, and by gestures taken from comedy; their particular aim is the expression of sensibility and they frequently exaggerate it to the point of impinging on burlesque and the ridiculous. Then they flatter themselves that they have attained to the sublimity of pathos. Without any consideration for established rules and traditions they claim to act by instinct and immediate inspiration: they are the quakers of dramatic art; whence it follows that for a few effective moments, one has to endure a great deal of dullness. It would seem that Talma has made agony and terror his own. His supreme achievement is the depiction of passions carried to a level of frenzy and folly. He is at the head of an association of friends of the macabre, as is Ducis, who is his progenitor in the same way as Voltaire was Le Kain's. There is roughly the same difference between the two actors as there is between the two authors [. . .] Besides, it is too severe a limitation of one's talent to display it only in madness. Such moments on the stage should be only flashes of lightning: once passion is pushed as far as mental derangement, it no longer has a place within the confines of dramatic art. It is true that Talma, impelled beyond nature in these moments of delirium, sometimes discovers extraordinary tones outside the normal gamut that are harrowing; but these encounters are so brief and so rare that he would do well to remain within the bounds of art; instead of astounding us occasionally, he would please us often.

294   The challenge to tradition is defended, 1808

Grimod de la Reynière and Pillet, *Revue des comédiens*, vol. II, pp. 274, 282

Talma was the first actor audacious enough to move about on stage in the same way as the Miltiades and Scipions must have done in the palaces of Athens and Rome. The public has become so accustomed to an innovation no less consistent with natural elegance than with austerity of costume that any tragic actor nowadays who was minded to make his entrance with arched loins and feet in the fifth position would run the risk of being hissed almost as much as if he dared to rig Caesar up in a full-bottomed wig or a Spanish cape [. . .] Some peevish critics have accused [Talma] of playing tragedy solely by instinct and of elevating his own way of thinking above the rules hallowed by tradition; far from regarding this as a subject for reproach, we should applaud him for it. In this respect, instinct may be synonymous with genius and genius has no need to explain itself.

295   Talma as Sylla, 1821
Harvard Theatre Collection

Talma is depicted historically togaed for the title role in Etienne de Jouy's tragedy, first performed in December 1821.

296   Talma is contrasted with Lekain,[1] 1804

Review of Racine's *Andromaque*, Théâtre-Français, 23 June 1804. Geoffroy, *Cours de littérature dramatique*, vol. VI, pp. 229–30

Talma is still receiving enthusiastic applause in the scene of Orestes' madness; he plays it with a frightening conviction which is bound to impress the multitude. Le Kain's method was quite other: imbued with the nobility of his art, he was convinced that it was necessary to preserve a kind of dignity for Orestes even in his moments of insanity. In his view, a tragic hero whose mind is troubled by an excess of passion and suffering should have a different tone of voice and a different manner from an inmate of a lunatic asylum. He did not believe that the madness of Orestes should resemble an epileptic fit. Le Kain therefore endeavoured to ennoble the delirium of a prince whom an appalling fate had sacrificed to the Eumenides. Talma has adopted a different approach; he is more natural and more truthful, but less noble and less interesting even. He accurately portrays an unfortunate person who has lost his reason; he renders faithfully all the symptoms of an average frenzy; he is startling and he is terrifying; Le Kain was more touching and more moving. The success of Talma's approach is reason enough for him not to change it, but it is no reason for *connaisseurs* to think well of it.

[1] For documents relating to Lekain, see Howarth, *French theatre*, nos. 475, 490, 587, 592, 605, 606, 613, 620, 635, 636, 637, 638, 639, 668, 681 and 773.

297   Talma's non-verbal acting, 1821

Ricord, *Fastes de la Comédie-Française*, vol. I, p. 130

Talma is exciting and inimitable in wordless scenes, which he has raised to the highest pitch of perfection; while this indispensable component of the actor's art is completely neglected by lazy or ignorant performers. The mute playing of this tragedian allows the spectator to recognize the sequence of passions which are agitating the soul of the hero he is portraying, and it reveals and sustains the progression of hope, fear or concern which shapes him with a sublimity that invariably arouses the greatest admiration.

298   Mme de Staël admires Talma's power and inventiveness, 1810

Mme de Staël, *De l'Allemagne*, vol. II, pp. 41–2, 44–5, 47

Sometimes he will enter with eyes half-closed, then all at once the emotion he feels will blaze forth from them in rays of light that seem to illuminate the entire stage. The sound of his voice can move you the moment he opens his mouth, before even the sense of the words he is speaking has elicited any response in you [. . .]

Hamlet is his supreme achievement among tragedies from the foreign repertoire. On the French stage audiences do not see the ghost of Hamlet's father; the apparition materializes only on Talma's countenance but is certainly no less terrifying for that. When, in the course of a subdued, melancholy exchange, he suddenly catches sight of the ghost, we can follow all its movements in the eyes that behold it and on the evidence of his stare its existence cannot be doubted. In the third act, when Hamlet enters alone to deliver the famous soliloquy *To be or not to be* in elegant French verse,

> La mort, c'est le sommeil, c'est un réveil peut-être.
> Peut-être! – Ah! c'est le mot qui glace, épouvanté,
> L'homme, au bord du cercueil par le doute arrêté:
> Devant ce vaste abîme, il se jette en arrière,
> Ressaisit l'existence, et s'attache à la terre.

Talma would stand stock still, simply moving his head from time to time to interrogate earth and heaven on the nature of death. We were seeing one man, in the midst of two thousand other men in complete silence, questioning thought about the destiny of humankind!

[. . .] no actor essays more grandiose effects by simple means. In his manner of declaiming verse, Shakespeare and Racine are artistically combined. Why should not dramatic authors, too, endeavour to bring together in their works what the actor has been able to fuse so well in his playing?

That boulevard performers at their best possessed strengths which the Comédiens-Français could not emulate was acknowledged by the latter as early as 1829, when, speaking on their behalf in its issue of 17 May, the *Journal des Comédiens* noted, somewhat condescendingly: 'We are well aware that in terms of rude, untamed energy our colleague Frédérick Lemaître will be able to better us, and that where bitter tearfulness and cries from the heart are concerned, Mme Allan-Dorval will have the advantage over Mlle Mars.' But the relative capacity of the two schools of acting to respond to the demands of Romantic drama is clearly illustrated by juxtaposing critical reaction to Joanny's performance in Vigny's *drame, Chatterton*, at the Théâtre-Français in 1835 with Hugo's tribute to Frédérick's incarnation of Ruy Blas at the Renaissance three years later.

299   Joanny struggles with his characterization in *Chatterton*, 1835

Review by Gustave Planche of *Chatterton*, Théâtre-Français, 12 February 1835, in *Revue des Deux Mondes*, 4th series, vol. 1 (1835), p. 439.

To be sure, Joanny understands with exceptional shrewdness the subtlest implications of his role, but when it comes to communicating them, he finds himself, I believe, in a singular dilemma. On the one hand, the memory of his practice in tragedy makes his voice swell up and imparts to his delivery something of the sonority of the masks of antiquity, and at the same time his sincere desire to throw into relief every intricacy of thought leads him to itemize in the

minutest detail sentiments and images which need to pour forth in a continuous flow. If he were to surrender himself unreservedly to those traditions of
tragedy of which he has a complete command, he would undoubtedly achieve
a unity of conception, but the care he devotes, in the role of the Quaker, to rendering the sort of everyday commonplaces that it has been his lifelong study to
exclude gives to his playing and to his diction an unevenness which, after some
attention, he will doubtless overcome but which it is necessary to point out to
him.

FRÉDÉRICK LEMAÎTRE

300   Frédérick in *Ruy Blas*, 1838

Victor Hugo, note to *Ruy Blas* (1838), reproduced in *Œuvres complètes*, vol. v, p. 777

As for M. Frédérick Lemaître, what can I say? The audience's enthusiastic applause
appropriates him from his first entry on stage and follows him even after the final
curtain. Dreamy and pensive in the first act, melancholy in the second, grandiose,
passionate and sublime in the third, he rises in the fifth act to one of those prodigious
tragic effects from whose lofty eminence the radiant actor eclipses every other
performance of his one can remember. For the old, he is Lekain and Garrick[1]
fused into one; for us, his contemporaries, he represents Kean's physical action
combined with Talma's emotion. And then throughout, amid the lightning flashes
of his acting, M. Frédérick sheds tears, those real tears which make others weep,
those tears of which Horace speaks: '*Si vis me flere, dolendum est primum ipsi tibi*'.
In *Ruy Blas* M. Frédérick realizes for us the ideal of the great actor. There can be
no doubt that his entire career, past as well as future, will be illuminated by this
resplendent creation. For M. Frédérick, the evening of 8 November 1838 was not
simply a performance, but a transfiguration.

[1]   For documents relating to the acting of Garrick, see David Thomas and Arnold Hare, *Restoration and
Georgian England, 1660–1788* (Cambridge: Cambridge University Press, 1989), nos. 160, 324, 328,
330–3, 343, 346–7, 349–50, 352–3, 360–2, 363, 366, 372–3, 376–82, 424–4.

301   Frédérick as Kean, 1842

Review of Dumas's *Kean, ou Désordre et génie*, Porte-Saint-Martin, June 1842. Gautier,
Histoire de l'art dramatique, vol. ii, pp. 249–50

Never was an apter role created by Frédérick, who has much affinity with the
English actor. We doubt whether Kean himself could have played his own part
more successfully. At this moment Frédérick is undeniably the greatest actor in
the world; no performer has ever had so wide a range: at one and the same time
he has at his command laughter and tears, energy and flexibility, passion and
repose, lyrical introspection and violent action, elegance and vulgarity; with equal
authority he can play princes and thieves, marquesses and porters, lovers and

drunkards, prodigal sons and grasping moneylenders. He is a veritable Proteus, a truly Shakespearean player, as great, as simple and as multifarious as nature itself. It is a long time since we have experienced such depth of feeling in the theatre; that evening Frédérick was sublime.

302   Frédérick's 'contemporary' tragic appeal

Joseph Méry in the *Garde Nationale de Marseille*, quoted by L.-H. Lecomte, *Un Comédien au XIXe siècle: Frédérick Lemaître, étude biographique et critique* (2 vols., Paris: chez l'auteur, 1888), vol. 1, pp. 211–12

His tragic genius is even more frightening than that of Talma, at least in my opinion, for this reason: Talma never inhabited the sphere in which we live our lives; he was the bugbear of kings and queens and court poisoners; he sported a gilded dagger, wore a costume that was not like ours, spoke a language that is not heard in everyday life; to be able to quail at his rages one had to imagine one dwelt in castles and palaces, or become a Greek or Roman. But Frédérick dresses like us, he has a jacket and waistcoat; he speaks our homespun language, and he takes care to conceal his dagger. We can meet the middling characters that he plays the very next day, in our town or country abodes, involved by some malign chance in one of our own private affairs or domestic upsets; and it is enough to make us tremble in deadly earnest. We're not really afraid of Nero when he threatens Britannicus; but we might have a Georges de Germany or a Richard Darlington[1] among our relatives or our friends without knowing it. I have long since forgotten what kind of nervous spasm passed across Talma's face when he took hold of the burial urn in *Hamlet*, but I shall remember till my dying day Frédérick's expression in the last act of *Richard Darlington*, when he picked up his wife's hat and contemplated murder [. . .]

---

[1] The protagonists, respectively, of *Trente ans, ou la Vie d'un joueur* (by P. Goubaux, J. Beudin and V. Ducange, Porte-Saint-Martin, 1827) and *Richard Darlington* (by Dumas, Goubaux and Beudin, produced at the same theatre in 1831).

303   Frédérick as Robert Macaire

Bibliothèque de l'Arsenal

A studio photograph of the actor in costume for this characteristically anti-heroic role.

304   Frédérick's instinct for dramatic detail

Legouvé, *Soixante ans de souvenirs*, vol. II, p. 32

Those who attended the first performance [of *Richard Darlington*] can still remember
the wave of horror and fright which swept through the house when an ashen-faced

Richard reappeared on the threshold of the balcony from which he had cast his wife into the ravine [. . .] Do you know what he devised to make his reappearance on the balcony more gruesome? First he had a coloured light set up in the wings which, in shining on his face, would turn it totally green. Then, to complete the effect, he got the actress playing the part of Jenny to drop her muslin veil as she fled from him in terror towards the balcony. This veil lying on the floor was the first thing to catch Frédérick's eye when he came back on stage. Any other actor would have shuddered at the sight, for it was like Jenny's ghost. What did Frédérlck do? He ran to the veil, snatched it up and stuffed it into his pocket as if it were a handkerchief, whereupon, as his new father-in-law knocked on the door, he went to open it with that insolent *sang-froid* that was all his own, and with the end of the veil fluttering from his pocket. It was appalling. In this, Frédérick demonstrated one of the most striking aspects of his genius, the ability to characterize a scene and redouble its effectiveness by the use of a graphic detail.

305   Dickens pays tribute to Frédérick's acting, 1855

Letter from Charles Dickens to John Forster, 13 (or 14?) February 1855, extract reproduced in G. Storey, K. Tillotson and A. Easson (eds.), *The Letters of Charles Dickens* (Oxford: Clarendon Press, 1993), vol. VII, pp. 536–7

Incomparably the finest acting I ever saw, I saw last night at the Ambigu. They have revived that old piece, once immensely popular in London under the name of *Thirty Years of a Gambler's Life*. Old Lemaître plays his famous character, and never did I see anything, in art, so exaltedly horrible and awful. In the earlier acts he was so well made up, and so light and active, that he really looked sufficiently young. But in the last two, when he had grown old and miserable, he did the finest things, I really believe, that are within the power of acting. Two or three times, a great cry of horror went all round the house. When he met, in the inn yard, the traveller whom he murders, and first saw his money, the manner in which the crime came into his head – and eyes – was as truthful as it was terrific. This traveller, being a good fellow, gives him wine. You should see the dim remembrance of his better days that comes over him as he takes the glass, and in a strange dazed way makes as if he were going to touch the other man's, or to do some airy thing with it; and then stops and flings the contents down his hot throat, as if he were pouring it into a lime-kiln. But this was nothing to what follows after he has done the murder, and comes home, with a basket of provisions, a ragged pocket full of money, and a badly washed bloody right hand – which his little girl finds out. After the child asked him if he had hurt his hand, his going aside, turning himself round, and looking over all his clothes for spots, was so inexpressibly dreadful that it really scared one. He called for wine, and the sickness that came upon him when he saw the colour, was one of the things that brought out the curious cry I have spoken of from the audience [. . .] And such a dress; such a face; and, above all, such an extraordinary wicked guilty thing as he made of a knotted branch of a tree which was his walking-stick, from the moment when the idea of the murder came into his head! I could write pages about him. It is an impression quite ineffaceable. He got half-boastful of that walking-staff to himself, and half-afraid of it; and didn't know whether to be grimly pleased that it had the jagged end, or to hate it and be horrified at it. He sat at a little table in the inn-yard, drinking with the traveller; and this horrible stick got between them like the Devil, while he counted on his fingers the uses he could put the money to.

306   Frédérick's magnetism, 1847

Review of Félix Pyat's *drame, Le Chiffonnier de Paris*, Porte-Saint-Martin, 11 May 1847. Gautier, *Histoire de l'art dramatique*, vol. v, pp. 83–4

The creation of a new role by Frédérick Lemaître is the sort of event that can stir even those who are least susceptible to dramatic excitement. That evening, members of high society and artists, critics and poets, duchesses real or imitation, the regular first-night audience in other words, at once eager and *blasé*, enthusiastic and sardonic, on their guard against all surprises, as knowledgeable about the theatre as an old actor turned stage manager, not impressed by any routine effect, and who can tell, from the placing of the furniture, the position of the doors in the set and the precise colour of the costumes, just how the play will end as soon as the curtain goes up, fill the auditorium long before the orchestra have taken their places [. . .] If Frédérick arouses such intense curiosity among the fashionable and the artistic, he has no less a hold on the rough, uncultivated section of the public: as early as three o'clock in the afternoon, those angels in caps and overalls who adorn the 'gods' with a ring of far from seraphic faces are jostling at the door of the theatre; for Frédérick has this immense power of speaking to the highest intelligence as well as to the crudest instinct. Victor Hugo and the lad whose job it is to pick up the apple stumps, Jules Janin and the duty fireman, George Sand and the usherette peeping through the window of a box, are all equally pleased with him and applaud with the same fervour; a breathless, insatiable Rachel, her face a pallid mask, leans out of a stage-box; actors from the other theatres, scarcely pausing to wipe off their make-up, come running after having gabbled their lines or else regretfully depart when the time arrives for them to go on stage themselves: be it only for one act, one situation or one line, everyone wants to experience the emotion and education of a first performance by Frédérick.

MARIE DORVAL

Jules Janin argued that the reason why Frédérick and Marie Dorval acted so well together, bringing about 'a complete transformation in the art of the stage', was that they embodied complementary aspects of the *drame*, he 'tempestuous, passionate, violent, and proud', while she 'with her slightly bowed figure, possessed everything that was needed to evoke the tenderest compassion'.[1]

---

[1]   Jules Janin, *Histoire de la littérature dramatique* (6 vols., Paris: Michel-Lévy, 1853–8), vol. vi, p. 156.

307   Mme Dorval as Adèle d'Hervey, 1831

(a) [Vigny], 'Une Lettre sur le Théâtre à propos d'*Antony*', *Revue des Deux Mondes*, 1st series, vol. 2 (1831), pp. 330–1; (b) Review of Dumas's *Antony*, Porte-Saint-Martin, 3 May 1831, *Le Figaro* (4 May 1831)

(a) All these thoughts and feelings were present in the actress's single cry ['*Mais je suis perdue, moi!*'] and also in her attitude, for on learning of her husband's return, her legs gave way under her, she collapsed onto the arm of a chair and clasped her hands together, staring into the eyes of her seducer as if to force him to behold his victim in her utter abasement and ruin [...] [Mme Dorval] hitherto has seemed like an English actress from Coven-Garden [*sic*] or Drury Lane, with all the brooding, emotional depth of mistriss [*sic*] Siddons,[1] but to this tragic power (the foremost in the theatre) she has now added that of a keen observation of social life; hers is a complete talent, with an immense future, fortunately for Paris and for the art of drama.

(b) [. . .] she wept as one does weep, shedding real tears; she cried out as one does cry out, and cursed in the way that women do curse, tearing her hair, casting her flowers from her, crumpling her dress, at times lifting it, with no regard for the Conservatoire, as high as her knees.

---

[1] For documents relating to the acting of Mrs Siddons, see Thomas and Hare, *Restoration and Georgian England*, nos. 347–9, 363–5, 371.

308   Mme Dorval's realism moves audiences to tears, 1845

Review of *Marie-Jeanne, ou la Femme du peuple, drame* by J. de Mallian and A. Dennery, Porte-Saint-Martin, 11 November, 1845. Gautier, *Histoire de l'art dramatique*, vol. IV, p. 148

Anything we might say by way of describing the effect she produced would fall short of the reality; never has an actress reached such heights: art had no part in it, it was nature itself, motherhood epitomized in one solitary woman. Floods of tears flowed from every eye; the young, the old, men, women, children, everyone, even the *claque* and the press, was moved.– A veritable deluge! Never has our heart been touched so poignantly; our breast shook with sobbing, we were blinded and tears clouded the lens of our opera-glasses. Where does Madame Dorval find such heart-rending tones of voice, such affecting sighs, such despairing attitudes? Someone asked her a few days before the first performance: 'What does your role consist of, and what do you think of it? – I don't know. I have a child and I lose it: that's all.' And indeed that is all there is: but out of that, oh miraculous actress, you have fashioned the greatest drama ever seen. You have combined in one poor woman of the people – Rachel, who remained inconsolable, Niobe, whose marble eyes were forever moist with tears, and Hecuba, who, as the Greek expression has it, barked her grief.

309   George Sand characterizes Mme Dorval, 1855

Sand, *Histoire de ma vie*, vol. IV, p. 211

She created the woman of the new drama, the romantic heroine of the stage, and
if she owed her ascendancy to the masters of this genre, they, in their turn, were
indebted to her for the conquest of a public who sought and found its embodiment
in three great artists, Frédérick Lemaître, Madame Dorval and Bocage. But one
had to see her in *Marion Delorme*, in *Angelo*,[1] in *Chatterton*, in *Antony*, and later in
the *drame* of *Marie-Jeanne*, to experience the fierce jealousy, the chaste tenderness,
the compassionate motherliness that could possess her with an equal intensity. Yet
she had innate shortcomings to overcome. Her voice was harsh, she rolled her *r*s
and her demeanour at first sight lacked a certain nobility and even gracefulness.
Her command of the received mode of delivery was awkward and ill at ease, and
being much too intelligent for many of the roles she was called on to play, she would
often remark: 'I know of no way of saying with conviction things that are false.
In the theatre there are certain conventional expressions which will never come
out of my mouth without sounding wrong, because it has never uttered them in
real life. I have never, in a moment of surprise, said: *What see I?*, or in a moment
of hesitation: *Whither do I stray?* Well, I frequently have entire speeches in which I
cannot find a single word that is sayable and which I should much rather improvise
from beginning to end, if only they would let me.'

[1]   Another *drame* by Hugo, first performed at the Théâtre-Français in 1835.

310   Mme Dorval's gift for improvisation, 1844

Review of *La Comtesse d'Altenberg*, a *drame* by A. Royer and G. Vaez, Odéon, 11 March 1844,
reproduced in Nerval, *Vie du théâtre*, pp. 554–5

Madame Dorval has found in it one of those parts which she plays to perfection
and which so few writers seem able to make to her measure; every day she has new
intuitions about it, and so completely does she put herself in the dramatic situation
that she frequently lets slip the sublimest utterances of a wronged wife and mother,
which the authors receive with gratitude and the audience with acclamation.

311   The modernity of Bocage and Mme Dorval, 1842

Review of *La Main droite et la main gauche*, *drame* by Léon Gozlan, Odéon, 24 December
1842. Gautier, *Histoire de l'art dramatique*, vol. II, p. 320

The actors played a large part in M. Gozlan's success. Bocage and Madame Dorval were back on their home territory again. Whatever talent Bocage may have
been able to display at the Gymnase, whatever intelligence Madame Dorval may
have been able to evince during her excursions into tragedy, neither *vaudeville* nor
tragedy is their true element; essentially they are both modern actors, impetuous,

idiosyncratic, whimsical, their feet planted in the most commonplace reality one moment, their head in the clouds of loftiest reverie the next, full of cries and sudden outbursts, mixing sarcasm with passion, chilling the blood with a jocular tone of voice, and proclaiming the most terrifying of words in precisely the same way as you and I would say them in such a situation.

312   From obituary tributes to Mme Dorval, 1849

(a) Banville, 'Reines de théâtre', in *Critiques*, ed. Victor Barrucand (Paris: Bibliothèque Charpentier, 1917), pp. 360–1; (b) Gautier, *Histoire de l'art dramatique*, vol. vi, pp. 104–5

(a) Who can forget? The evenings she played Ketty [*sic*], when she ran up the wooden staircase leading to Chatterton's room and saw the poet lying dead, who can forget the harrowing cry that rose up from the depths of her being! That was no mere play-acting! She tumbled down the stairs, reeling with despair and delirium, her head striking the banisters, and rolled lifeless onto the floorboards below, while that hideous sound reverberated in the hearts of a stunned audience. In the revival of *Clotilde*,[1] at the Renaissance, she tore her white satin gown, her gloves and her bonnet to shreds, and in an access of frenzy clawed her hair with her bare hands. And in the *Joueur*, do you remember when she caught sight of Frédérick's blood-stained hands, and horror-stricken, clutched her child to her and covered her with kisses! [. . .] But above all in *Angelo*, in the courtesan's speech, that crazed and terrifying oath: '*Ah! Mesdames les femmes honnêtes!*' No, never has such rage, such remorse, such pain and such anger burst forth with such violence from a breaking, embittered heart; she was breathless, wretched, crushed, awesome in her indignation and disdain, and so frighteningly real was it that on one occasion Marie Dorval balked at giving a complete recital of all those profanities before the Queen of England!

(b) Frédérick Lemaître and Madame Dorval made a perfectly matched theatrical couple. She was Frédérick's true wife just as Frédérick was her true husband – on the stage, to be sure. These two artists completed each other and grew in stature when they came together. Frédérick was the man destined to make this woman weep, but by the same token how well she could move him to pity once his rage had passed! what accents she drew forth from him! Anyone who did not see them together, in *Le Joueur* for example, or *Pablo, ou le Jardinier de Valence*,[2] has not seen anything; he does not know the complete Frédérick, nor yet the complete Madame Dorval. Today Frédérick must feel really and truly widowed [. . .]

Madame Dorval's genius was a product entirely of feeling; not that she neglected artistry, but artistry came to her from inspiration. She did not compute her performance gesture by gesture, nor mark out her entrances and exits with chalk lines on the floor; she put herself into the situation of the character, she espoused the character completely, she became one with it, and acted in the way that it would have acted. From the simplest of phrases, an interjection, an '*oh!*' or a '*my god!*', she could generate effects that were electric, unpredictable, that even the author could not have anticipated. Her cries were of an excruciating truthfulness, her sobs enough to burst her breast, her intonations so natural and her tears so genuine that the theatre was obliterated and one could no longer believe her suffering to be a matter of convention. Madame Dorval owed nothing to tradition. Her genius was essentially modern, and this was its most important quality: she lived in her own times, with the ideas, the passions, the sensibilities, the errors and the weaknesses of her times. In sympathy with the *drame* rather than tragedy, she followed the fortunes of the innovators and prospered accordingly. She was a woman where others would have been content to be actresses; never had anything so living, so real, so like the women in the audience appeared on a stage: it was as if we were watching, not in a theatre, but through a peephole into a closed room, a woman who believed herself to be alone.

[1] *Drame* by F. Soulié and A. Bossange, first performed at the Théâtre-Français in 1832 and, with Marie Dorval, at the Renaissance in 1840.
[2] Melodrama by L. Saint-Amand and J. Dulong, first performed at the Ambigu-Comique in 1829.

MLLE RACHEL

A less sympathetic observer of the theatrical scene could claim that this so-called modern acting amounted to little more than a formless, undisciplined display of 'behaving' on stage, totally devoid of art and reaching a peak of iconoclasm in the occasional direct address to individual members of the audience or, most notoriously, Frédérick's offering of snuff to the prompter. Not surprisingly, therefore, the unlooked-for emergence of a gifted young tragedienne at the Théâtre-Français in 1838, and the authority she demonstrated in the plays of Racine and Corneille, seemed to promise a new dawn, a resurgence of the traditional repertoire after the aberration of Romantic *drame* and the style of playing and presentation that went with it. However, at least for Théophile Gautier, arguably her most perceptive as well as most devoted critic, the secret of Rachel's appeal lay essentially in a palpable discrepancy between the eminently classical properties of the lines she delivered and the largely unclassical properties of her own acting (which incorporated even the English 'sneer'), a discrepancy capable of generating tension and a powerful consequential energy. Significantly, these were the very qualities that recommended her to English audiences during her first London season in 1841, and also during her regular return visits in the course of the ensuing decade.

313   Charles Maurice anatomizes 'modern' acting, 1835

Courrier des théâtres (21 June 1835)

Gone is the actor's bearing, gone is nobility, gone is elegance, gone is diction, gone is costume. Gone is everything which made art difficult and success gratifying. Now one comports oneself *naturally* on stage, one sits on tables, on the arms of chairs, one speaks lying down, one turns one's back to the audience, one combs one's hair with one's fingers, one plays without any make-up, one grows a beard and moustache, one talks directly to the occupants of a box in the middle of one's performance, in a word one is now performing '*nature*'.

314   The originality of Mlle Rachel, 1842

Review of *Ariane*, tragedy by Thomas Corneille, Théâtre-Français, 22 May 1842. Gautier, *Histoire de l'art dramatique*, vol. II, pp. 244–6

The curiosity to see Mademoiselle Rachel has been interpreted by certain excessive admirers of the past as a reaction in favour of the old tragedy. This is a mistake, and nothing proves better than Mademoiselle Rachel's success the extent to which the classical instincts and traditions have been lost [. . .] Her mode of diction, clear, clipped, staccato, *intemperate*, if one may put it thus, is at odds with the ample periods, the elegant circumlocutions, the well-draped phrases of classical poetry, and it is from this very contrast that her success stems [. . .] How can this frail girl, with her sombre gaze, her pallid features, her sensitive, febrile countenance, her controlled yet violent gestures, her acrid smile, her nostrils dilated with scorn, her ferocity of diction and her explosions of rage, be said to resemble in any way the marble mask of ancient Melpomene, that great and noble figure who would allow no grief to impair her beauty and who even as she fell, with a dagger in her heart, was attentive to the folds of her toga and maintained her purity of line to the very last convulsion?

315   Mlle Rachel as Hermione, 1843

Review of Racine's *Andromaque* at the Théâtre-Français, 7 January 1843. Gautier, *Histoire de l'art dramatique*, vol. II, pp. 324–5

The role of Hermione is Mademoiselle Rachel's supreme achievement; it allows her to deploy to the greatest effect those fiery qualities which characterize her acting: bitter irony, withering sarcasm, love so violent as to be indistinguishable from hate, all those corrosive feelings whose consummate expression is astonishing in one so young. That we commend these qualities does not mean that we consider Mademoiselle Rachel incapable of expressing tenderness and love, as has been too readily supposed. She has shown in several roles, notably that of Ariane, that she can say things with great warmth and sensibility. But her virile, energetic genius does not incline towards those tearful simperings which so enchant one section of the audience. It is the very sobriety of her means that imparts to all her creations their classical character and sculptural stylishness.

316   Mlle Rachel's London performances are assessed by the *Times*

(a) Review of *Andromaque* at Her Majesty's Theatre, *Times* (11 May 1841, p. 5);
(b) Review of Corneille's *Horace* at St James's Theatre, *Times* (6 July 1847, p. 8)

(a) Review of *Andromaque*, 1841

But her greatest scene was the one with Pyrrhus; many besides Mademoiselle Rachel could have done the most violent parts; but the cool, collected, severe irony with which she addressed her faithless betrothed, the evident force with which rage was confined within her heart, while her speech was fearfully calm and deliberate, was a noble conception and a sign of the highest genius. The burst of passion which followed the touching line –

'Je t'aimais inconstant, qu'aurais-je fait fidèle?'

electrified the audience, but it was in the deliberate irony that the most consummate art was shown. Altogether a more rare combination of intelligence and power has seldom been seen than in this young actress [. . .]

(b) Review of *Horace*, 1847

The hate of Rachel is something withering, withering to the person against whom it is uttered, withering to the person uttering it. When she addresses her brother in the famous speech, '*Rome, l'unique objet de mon ressentiment*', this hate assumes the most compressed form, it is buried in its own intensity. Camille seems driven to search the inmost depths of her soul, that she may find sufficient hatred wherewith to overwhelm her brother [. . .] In the very folds of Rachel's drapery there is something classical, the appearance is statuesque, while her acting is the extreme of vitality.

317   Mlle Rachel's verse-speaking, 1849

Review of *Adrienne Lecouvreur*, '*comédie-drame*' by Scribe and Legouvé, Théâtre-Français (14 April 1849). Gautier, *Histoire de l'art dramatique*, vol. VI, pp. 74, 77–8

The young tragedienne, far from being constrained, as one had feared, by the absence of the alexandrine, seemed, on the contrary, to be more at ease with the short phrases, the irregular periods and the familiar structures of prose. This event appeared to confound some people; it did not surprise us, for Mademoiselle Rachel has never delivered her lines in a metrical or melodic fashion; she has always spoken them according to their meaning rather than their measure (which is not to say that she distorts them). In her mouth poetic periods become sentences, and she utters them without declaiming, without any chanting, more concerned about the words themselves than the music of the line. In short, she gives a speech in verse as if it had been written without any attention being paid to rhythm and rhyme.

[. . .] is she by chance aware that her brooding look, the deep, husky voice, the unhealthy pallor, the brow laden with all the sorrows of our age, the tense by-play, the cold fury, the diction shorn of recitative, making cæsura, rhyme and poetic period barely perceptible, all derive from sheer, unalloyed *drame*, and owe nothing to tragedy as it was understood during the *grand siècle* or in times when the living traditions of the genre still persisted?

This element of *drame*, which the young actress has unwittingly introduced into the severity of form inherited from the past, has over the last decade revitalized a number of masterpieces that had been neglected in favour of plays which are doubtless less accomplished but which reflect our current preoccupations and tastes.

318   The modernity of Mlle Rachel's acting, 1848

Gautier, *Histoire de l'art dramatique*, vol. v (1858–9), pp. 236–7

The temporary regeneration of tragedy that she has brought about derives precisely from the fact that she is so unlike the plays in which she appears. Certainly, Racine could not have envisaged as any of his heroines this slender, tall woman with the sculptural physique, on whom costumes quite naturally arrange themselves in folds exactly as do the raiments on Etruscan figurines. Those intensely dark eyes set amid a marble-like pallor, that prominent brow seeming to exude radiance, that hand so small that it can scarcely grasp the handle of a dagger, yet nonetheless so strong; this whole combination at once fragile and wiry, elegant and untamed, sallow and yet pure-bred, with the ancient blood of the Orient coursing in its Jewish veins, has nothing in common with the conception of the young poet for whom La Champmeslé[1] represented an idol: it is because of this very dissimilarity that she appeals to us. The looks that would have struck the *grand siècle* as somewhat uncivilized, the rasping, mordant diction, the inflexions so natural as to verge on familiarity, the biting irony, the fierce yet repressed passion, things which are all essentially modern and Romantic, are the very qualities which engage us. As a result the actress rejuvenates what might seem innocuous and tame to us about the old tragic plots. She is performing the drama of our time with lines written two hundred years ago, and that is why she enjoys phenomenal success, even among those who dislike the conventional genre of tragedy as we understand it in France.

[1] The actress (Marie Desmares) who created many of Racine's tragic heroines in the 1670s.

IV   Stage presentation

DÉCORS AND MACHINERY

For much of the eighteenth century the use of changeable scenery was to all intents and purposes confined to the Opéra, where multiple chariot-and-pole wings and flown backdrops, controlled by elaborate machinery, had always provided a visually appealing means of decorating the stage. In fact, the Opéra was renowned in this connection for an extravagance which was not always tempered with discretion, if we can believe one of its former dancers, Noverre, who claimed in 1807 that 'the scene-painter, not having a close acquaintance with the text, is often guilty of misapprehension: he will not consult the author but follows his own ideas instead'.[1] Dumas observed ironically that the Opéra was in a class of its own 'because of its machinery' and 'spends prodigious amounts on décors', unlike the Théâtre-Français, 'which goes to the opposite extreme'.[2]

The repertoire which the latter had inherited with its royal patent in 1680, and most of the legitimate drama written for performance there in the intervening hundred years or so, had been governed in form and/or in spirit by a strictly neoclassical aesthetic. The concept of unity of place, in particular, together with the complementary notions of *bienséance* and *vraisemblance*, not only determined the type of setting appropriate for each genre, but also encouraged the stockpiling of 'omnibus' décors that could serve for almost every play, rendering any decorative variety or spectacle largely redundant. In this respect, as in others, a speculative straw in the wind of change was provided in 1784 by *Le Mariage de Figaro*, whose five distinct settings, one for each act, albeit all related to a single location, represented a distinct advance in visual sophistication. However, the decisive impetus came from outside the legitimate mainstream, by virtue of the enormous popularity enjoyed by *mélodrame*, and most notably the runaway success of the plays of Pixérécourt, whose first performed work was given at the Ambigu-Comique in 1797. Three years later, the same theatre staged his highly influential 'drame en trois actes, en prose et à grand spectacle', *Coelina, ou l'Enfant du mystère*, in which, during the climactic scene of the last act, the villain, endeavouring to escape by a narrow wooden bridge over a mountain torrent, struggles with an armed policeman whom he precipitates into the raging waters below.

As commercial managers vied with one another to meet the scenic demands of such action-packed plots, and to impress the audience with settings specific to those plots, a freelance scenographic industry sprang up, led by the example of Pierre-Luc-Charles Ciceri, who, while engaged as chief scene-painter at the Opéra, also opened his own studio in the rue du Faubourg-Poissonnière, where his pupils were able to work under contract for other Parisian theatres. His inspired workmanship, which, after the introduction of gas lighting in 1822, he skilfully adapted to accommodate this new aid to scenic illusion, pointed the way forward to the kind of decorative elaboration envisaged by Hugo in the preface to *Cromwell*:

'Instead of action, we are given narrative; instead of tableaux, descriptions. Grave personages stationed, like an antique chorus, between the play and ourselves come and tell us what is happening in the temple, in the palace or in the public square, so that we are frequently tempted to cry out: Really! well take us there then! . . . it would be good to see!' To this plea Ciceri was well able to respond, but for any such initiative materially to displace the traditional production methods of the Théâtre-Français an act of administrative will was required, provided in the event by the opportune appointment, in 1825, of a sympathetic and free-spending royal commissioner in the person of Baron Taylor.

[1] J. G. Noverre, *Lettres sur les arts imitateurs* (2 vols., Paris: Collin, 1807), vol. I, p. 284.
[2] Dumas, *Souvenirs*, vol. II, pp. 210–11. For documents on eighteenth-century scenery and machines, see Howarth, *French theatre*, nos. 578 to 594.

THE WELL-DESIGNED STAGE

319   Principles of theatre design

Hippolyte Auger, *Physiologie du théâtre* (3 vols., Paris: Firmin-Didot Frères, 1839–40), vol. III, p. 119

The stage is divided into three parts: the first is the space between the upper limit of the proscenium-opening and the roof; the second, that which is visible to the audience, the third occupies the cavity between the stage-floor and the ground on which the building stands. In a well-constructed theatre, these three divisions should be roughly equal in height to provide for operational requirements. The outer, enclosing wall is, and must be, plumb. All walls should be of brick to minimize the effect of fire. The stage-floor is divided into *plans* [transverse sections], each corresponding to a section of wing-space. The width of the proscenium-opening serves as a benchmark for the dimensions of the auditorium and the stage alike. This is the frame upon which the eyes of the spectators converge, and from which all scenic illusion is projected into the auditorium.

320   Working areas of the stage, 1821

Alexis Donnet, *Architectonographie des théâtres de Paris, ou Parallèle historique et critique de ces édifices considérés sous le rapport de l'architecture et de la décoration* (Paris: P. Didot l'aîné, 1821), pp. 161–6

[. . .] it is therefore necessary for the width of the stage to exceed that of the proscenium-opening not only to allow for flats to be withdrawn and replaced by others during a scene change but also to provide room for movement in the wings. Normally the stage has the same overall width as the auditorium; its depth is approximately one and a half times the width of the playing area, that is to say equal to the total width of the building. A backscene, set at this distance, is proportionately far enough removed to create a good perspective effect; but it is always possible to reserve a greater depth for special occasions [. . .] below the stage a sufficiently large space is required to accommodate the winches, levers and counterweights which are used to raise or lower all those parts of the set or temporary scenery which are not moved horizontally. However few decorative effects are envisaged, the stage basement should not be less than ten or twelve feet deep [. . .] The basement is divided into lanes parallel to the front of the stage by the rows of posts supporting the stage floor. The floor itself is not a fixture but composed of a large number of trapdoors and *trappillons* [cuts], built to interlock precisely and to open at will, thus creating at any point an aperture through which to drop into the basement, or to bring up therefrom, objects or personages involved in the performance. To enable one to cross this void at different heights according to the requirements of the action there are a number of flying-bridges consisting of planks suspended by rope. Winches are set up at various levels and pulleys arranged to facilitate the play of counterweights at either side.

The flies, or over-stage areas, call for a height at least as great as that of the stage opening. It is here that is located all the equipment for moving the wing-flats, the backcloths, the *ciels* [sky-borders] and *plafonds* [horizontal sky-cloths], and all the machinery for flights and ascents. This part of the stage is normally bisected by a latticed floor called the *gril*; above this stand the winches, below are hung all the décors intended to be flown in, between which it is possible to cross from one side of the stage to the other by flying bridges similar to those in the basement. Usually there are two or four staircases leading from below to a gallery which runs round the entire stage, a little above the line of the proscenium arch. This gallery communicates with all the flying bridges; if the stage opening is very high, there may be two or even three such galleries. From there one can reach the *gril*, which is always installed approximately level with the spring of the roof vault; occasionally there is even a second floor above the *gril*.

EQUIPMENT OF THE STAGE

Under the entry '*Décoration*', Harel's dictionary contains a useful explanation of the various components that were then used to construct a stage setting.

321   Scenic components defined, 1824

Harel *et al.*, *Dictionnaire théâtral*, pp. 107–9

The term *ferme* is applied to everything which, apart from wing-flats (i.e. those set crosswise at either side of the stage) rests on a *châssis*. The *châssis* are frameworks of wood, of different shapes and sizes, which are covered with canvas and painted to serve as wing-flats or *fermes*. Backgrounds for rooms or palaces which are not lowered from the flies are called *fermes*, as are houses which deviate from the alignment of the wing-flats and occupy an oblique or perpendicular position on the stage.

Everything standing upright which is neither a *ferme* nor a wing-flat is called a *rideau*. Backgrounds of landscape reaching up to the sky-borders fall into this category, and can be wound up into the flies. The need for economy has led to the use of *rideaux* with a sky and seascape painted on them, in front of which can be set *fermes* of landscapes or buildings, depending on the occasion, and thus create a dual-purpose setting. The *montagnes* are composed of *ponts* and *fermes*. The *ponts* are wooden planks arranged to form ramps and supported on trestles which are also called *fermes*. (The use of this term to indicate two different things is a shortcoming of the scenic lexicon.) The points at which *montagnes* level out towards the top are called *paliers*, and the uppermost levels are referred as *praticables*. The wing-flats are attached to vertical poles, which are fitted with iron clamps to hold the *châssis* and coupled together so as to move in unison. This piece of equipment is what is known as a *chariot*. The two poles of each chariot are pierced with iron pins or fitted with brackets to make it easier for the stage hands to work at raised levels.[1] Individual poles which can be taken out of their sockets and moved elsewhere are known as *portants*; they are employed to support all those parts of the scenery which are neither *rideaux* nor capable of being moved on *chariots*.

[1] Alternatively, the poles were fitted with a ladder, enabling 'the stage-hand to climb to the required height and attach the flat' (J. A. Borgnis, *Traité complet de la mécanique appliquée aux arts* (Paris: Bachelier, 1820) p. 284).

The advantages of free-standing *fermes* over the traditional arrangement of retractable wing-flats were soon appreciated and, as the demand for scenic realism grew, they were increasingly used in conjunction with, and at times to the exclusion of, the latter, ultimately in the form of the totally enclosed box set. To avoid congestion in the wings, their component parts were usually winched up from the stage basement.

322   The case for *fermes*, 1809

Colonel [J.-F.-L.] Grobert, *De l'exécution dramatique considérée dans ses rapports avec le matériel de la salle et de la scène* (Paris: F. Schoell, 1809), pp. 136–7

The absurdity of the wing-flat system has been recognized by several leading scene-painters of today; they have been quick to seize every opportunity to make use of a setting which allows them to dispense with or at least reduce the number of wing-flats without being restrained by the complexity of current stage machinery. M. Degotti[1] has never produced a more striking effect than in the last act of *Roméo et Juliette* and the play about Mont Saint-Bernard at the Théâtre Feydeau. Although wing-flats were not entirely eliminated from these settings, their effectiveness derived from free-standing structures concealed behind *fermes* and set at several different levels. Actors made their entrances and exits exclusively by means of the *praticables* of these structures, and wing-flats served only to mask out the off-stage. The public were agreeably surprised by this innovation, for the simple reason that it brought scenic decoration closer to nature and to that relief which is essential for the creation of true illusion [. . .][2]

[1] Ignazio Eugenio Maria Degotti (d. 1824), Italian scenographer who worked in Paris from 1796 and engaged Ciceri and Daguerre as apprentices.
[2] When the Cirque-Olympique mounted a Bonapartist epic entitled *L'Empire et les Cent Jours*, Gautier pronounced himself greatly impressed by a spectacular battle scene in which 'various *praticables* simulating ridges of rock enabled groups to be staggered at different heights and gave depth to the perspective' (Gautier, *Histoire de l'art dramatique en France*, vol. IV, p. 49).

All the elements of staging and their respective functions are fully described in one volume of Borgnis's encyclopaedic series in eight parts, published under the title of *Traité complet de la mécanique*, which also gives an account of the machinery used to operate them.

323   Stage machinery, 1820

J. A. Borgnis, *Traité complet de la mécanique appliquée aux arts. Des machines imitatives et des machines théâtrales* (Paris: Bachelier, 1820), pp. 279–80, 283–7, 289–90

All theatrical décors may be moved by counterweights, which turn winches on which are wound the lines attached to the cloths and *châssis* constituting a setting [. . .] A *théâtre à machines* must be equipped with a large number of winches of different dimensions. Some of these will be located under the stage to direct the movement of *châssis* and *fermes*. The remainder, distributed between the two floors of the flies, control the movement of *rideaux*, backcloths and sky-borders and drive the *gloires* and other machines.

After detailing the workings, whether manual or mechanical, of the *chariots* positioned in the basement, which, he says, as they move their respective poles through *costières* [grooves] in the stage floor, 'serve at once as supports and vehicles' for the wing-flats, Borgnis stresses the importance of the reliability and solidity 'in their closed position' of the various traps and *trappillons*; he goes on to devote several paragraphs to the 'operation of the machines called *gloires*', followed by a further two on the '*machines de travers*'.

Normally a *gloire* consists of 1° a platform to support the actor or actors who are to appear in it; 2° a painted background, either of flats or *rideaux*; 3° a façade to mask the platform; 4° generally, one or several pieces of cloud at either side. The platform may be as much as 36 feet long by 3 or 4 feet wide; it is suspended by 4 metal lines made of brass wire, each of which is customarily 30 lignes [2 $^1/_2$ inches] in diameter and strong enough to bear a load of 1,500 livres without risk [. . .] The *gloire* descends under its own weight and is raised by the action of counterweights.

    Gloires are usually accompanied by groups of clouds coming down at different speeds, which progressively cover the stage before the *gloire*'s descent and then open to reveal it [. . .]

    A *machine de travers* is a type of *gloire* which is lowered from above but crosses the stage obliquely. It may represent a chariot, a formation of clouds or simply consist of a bar to which an actor is attached by hooks and which is held by metal lines of a diameter thin enough to render them almost invisible to the spectators. The actor, thus suspended, appears to fly as he crosses the stage in an upward or downward direction.

    The principal movements made possible by a *machine de travers* are: 1° to cross the stage horizontally at a given height; 2° to cross it while ascending from the right or the left and lifting off from one specific point to arrive at another equally specific point; 3° to cross it while descending from left to right or from right to left;

4° to describe an arc while ascending or descending; 5° to describe an undulating curve.

324   Décors and machinery at the Opéra, 1809

Grobert, *Exécution dramatique*, plate 2

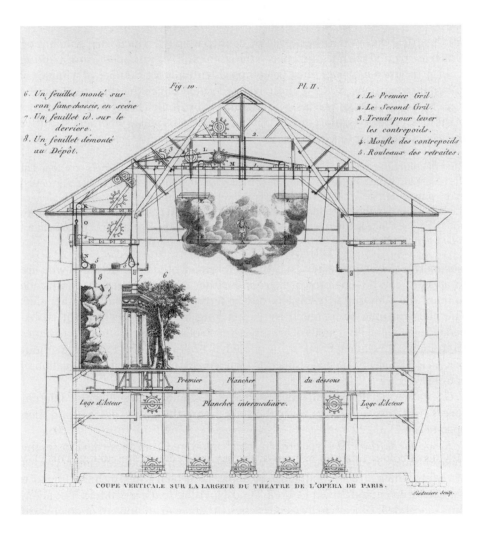

COUPE VERTICALE SUR LA LARGEUR DU THÉATRE DE L'OPÉRA DE PARIS.

Vertical section of the stage, showing the first and second *grils* (1, 2), winch (3), block and tackle for counterweights (4), coiled counterweight lines (5), two wing-flats mounted on chariots and poles (6, 7), another standing in the wings (8), a *gloire* (E) and substage floors and machinery.

In a concluding section to the same volume Borgnis explains the methods currently in use to produce sound effects and a number of composite effects integrating scenery with changes of lighting.

325   Special effects

Borgnis, *Traité complet*, pp. 294–8

Imitation of wind, thunder and lightning

The sound of wind is simulated by a very thin wooden rod, attached to a rope, which is rotated at great speed.

The sound of thunder can be produced in different ways: 1° A number of cannonballs are inserted one after another into a long channel of wooden planks, constructed with several steps and inclined so that the balls will roll rapidly downwards; 2° A large canvas flat is suspended horizontally, on which a stage hand can make a rumbling noise by striking it;[1] 3° A waggon with octagonal wheels and containing stones mixed with pieces of metal is set in motion; 4° Claps of thunder are produced by means of sheets of metal and barrel-staves attached to a rope, which is then dropped onto the floor of the fly-gallery.

To simulate the vivid, instantaneous brilliance of lightning, a stage hand throws rosin onto a burning torch. The effect of lightning flashes can be created by making slits in certain parts of the scenery set for this purpose; behind each slit and covering it is a thin wooden board which can be moved in a groove, each board having a slit in it identical to those in the scenery. Lights are fitted up behind the boards. Once everything is set, and the stage is in darkness, one has only to move a board rapidly in its groove to produce a streak of light, which will reappear every time the slits are opposite each other.

Dawn

To imitate the effect of dawn satisfactorily requires the combination of two means: first, a progressive change in the colour of the sky; second, a gradual and imperceptible intensification in the lighting.

The first object can be achieved by making a backscene of two separate parts, one of them consisting of a lengthy cloth on which are painted the successive shades of colour that can be seen in the sky when dawn is breaking. This cloth is partially wound onto a cylinder which, as it is very slowly turned, will reveal the various shades one by one. The other part consists of a contoured flat which will be outlined against the rear cloth we have just described; this ground-row will represent a landscape or some other feature.

The second object is achieved by means of lamps with movable reflectors. At first, these lamps are set so that the reflector masks the light entirely on the side facing the stage; then, the reflectors are slowly and steadily revolved until the light is exposed in all its brightness.

Lights, flames and conflagrations

[. . .] Frequent use is made in the theatre of a kind of torch which, when shaken, produces a large flame. These torches consist simply of a taper about which is placed a container full of ground rosin or some other highly inflammable powder. The upper part of the container is pitted with small holes, with the result that each time the taper is shaken a certain amount of the powder escapes and produces the desired effect.[2]

To simulate a conflagration, one part of the scenery is made in such a way that it can easily disintegrate into pieces. Stage hands positioned behind the scenery produce flames by shaking torches of the kind we have described; other stage hands use poles to push movable pieces of scenery so that they fall to reveal the seat of the blaze, represented by an endless cloth stretched between two drums which can be turned by a handle. The cloth is semi-transparent, painted to suggest the colour of flames and studded with tinsel and gilt fragments, while behind it are placed reflector lamps emitting a powerful beam. Care is taken to keep all other parts of the stage in darkness. A similar procedure is employed to represent hellfire.

Elysium and paradise

Scenic pieces representing an elysium or paradise are normally set behind a gauze curtain; they must be lit with a soft glow of an unusual colour. One of the simplest ways of obtaining this effect is to use reflector lamps with their burners encased in a coloured glass chosen to produce the radiance that is considered most appropriate. In the same manner it is also possible to simulate the effect of moonlight.

Fountain and running water

The movement of a fountain or of running water is simulated by means of a continuous cloth stretched between two rollers, one of which is fitted with handles turned by two stage hands. The cloth must be painted a sky-blue colour and sprinkled with tinsel and silvery particles.

Movement of waves

The movement of waves is normally represented by *colonnes de mer*. This is the name given to very long drums, fashioned in much the same way as the flour-sieves used by bakers. These drums are in the form of spiral columns, painted to look like waves and dotted with specks of silver. They are supported horizontally by *fermes* on which stand their trunnions and crank-handles operated by stage hands.

When it is desired to represent the sea, a given number of such *fermes* fitted with *colonnes de mer* are hoisted from below stage; once they are at the required height, stage hands begin rotating the handles of the *colonnes de mer* which, as they turn, render the effect of waves very successfully.

In cases where it is necessary for ships to appear and to move on this artificial sea, other *fermes* are positioned between those holding the *colonnes de mer*, the tops of which have an undulating surface over which can be slid the painted flats representing ships.

Should one wish to represent a storm in which the sea swells up, becomes violently agitated, changes colour, then subsides and returns to its former state, one must align under the stage a number of *colonnes de mer* which are different in shape and colour. First, the columns with a gentle spiral and pale in colour are raised up and rotated slowly; then those with a more pronounced twist and darker in colour appear and revolve more quickly; finally, these last are lowered to be replaced by the former [. . .]

---

[1] There is even a suggestion that this effect could be musically 'scored'. Describing the same procedure, Grobert adds: 'the rumbling sounds can be quite convincing when executed by a skilled tympanist; sometimes they are notated and integrated with the sound of the orchestra' (*De l'exécution dramatique*, p. 236).

[2] Harel *et al.*'s *Dictionnaire théâtral* puts a gloss on this combustible device that is suitably jocular, discounting any attendant risks: 'The storm is about to break. Up in the flies the stagehand designated to play the part of Jupiter shakes a torch filled with alcohol while a special bellows blows lycopodium powder over it to burn and sparkle. The heavens are rent with the fugitive blaze of this powder, while the priestess, who is party to the pyrotechnist's secret, steps on to the forestage to speak to us of lightning and thunder on the strength of a flare and a pinch of rosin' (p. 129).

The frequency with which the effect of moving water was called for seems to have exercised scene-painters and machinists particularly, but not to the complete satisfaction either of the critical spectator or at times of the actor concerned.

326   Rough waters

(a) Grobert, *Exécution dramatique*, pp. 234–5; (b) Bouffé, *Souvenirs*, pp. 77–8

(a) Cloths tacked to rods and moved up and down by lines attached to the fly-gallery offer a very imperfect likeness of the sea; one can discern the forms of the same waves as they keep returning, without any variation, to the point from which they started [. . .] If the sea is supposed to become rough, the bands of cloth are moved at greater speed, but the height of each wave remains very much the same.

Sometimes the sea is simulated with the aid of spiral columns turning on a horizontal axis and covered with a silvery cloth. This method is less flawed than the former. It has the advantage of catching reflections of light in the water, but as the same ripples keep recurring at the same points, the problem of uniformity is still present. Uniformity exposes artifice and destroys illusion.

(b) Formerly, to produce this effect [a stormy sea] one simply used what were called *bandes de mer*, placed a metre apart, one in front of the other, and suspended on ropes, which allowed stage hands in the wings to push them to and fro to represent a storm. The public in those days thought it was quite splendid; but the march of progress has continued and every day scene-painters and machinists come up with new marvels. What follows is just a trifling example of their ingenuity [. . .] they had stretched a painted cloth over the floor of the stage under which they positioned a dozen or so men and boys, whose job it was to engage in wild gymnastic exercises, while other men stationed in the wings agitated the cloth by means of ropes attached at various points [. . .]

The staging of *Le Petit monstre* required me to throw myself into this 'ocean' to reach not a ship, as in the full-size *Monstre*[1] at the Porte-Saint-Martin, but a small steamboat. I had performed this nautical manœuvre several times while the 'waves' behaved charmingly, so I launched myself with confidence into this human flood on that night [when the management of the Gaîté had suspended their wages]. I was met with a diabolical turbulence: they were furious, and each time I clambered onto one of them, he shied violently away, casting me into a void, usually head first onto the stage floor. Nonetheless, I still had to reach the boat, where the final scene was set, and I got there in the end, but in quite a state – my body a mass of cuts and bruises!

[1] *Le Monstre et le magicien*, a *mélodrame-féerie* by J.-T. Merle and A. Béraud, which also used child labour to produce the same effect. See J. Lan, *Mémoires d'un chef de claque, souvenirs des théâtres* (Paris: Librairie Nouvelle, 1883), p. 96.

SCENE CHANGES

Bouffé's persecutors were merely unskilled extras, hired by the hour, but this labour-intensive form of presentation also required an army of skilled workmen to man a stage rigged with the complexity of a sailing ship and equipped with a quantity of manually operated machines. Its major strength was its capacity to transform the visual aspect of a performance with great rapidity and with an element of apparent sorcery. By no means the least source of delight for theatre-goers of the day was to see an elaborate stage setting mysteriously change before their eyes into something even richer and stranger. The continuing appeal of the *changement à vue* in the second half of the nineteenth century is attested by a long article devoted to it in Pougin's dictionary.

327 *Changements à vue*

Pougin, *Dictionnaire historique*, pp. 155–6

A change of décor which is effected instantaneously in full view of the audience and without lowering the front curtain [. . .] When a décor that is very ornate, very intricate and in a very precise architectural style succeeds one of a totally different order but just as ornate, just as intricate and just as laden with detail as that which takes its place, the surprise is great and the effect produced so powerful, at times magical and seeming to verge on the miraculous. One sees *fermes* and *châssis* engulfed by the basement and instantly replaced by other *fermes* welling up from innumerable *trappillons*; the *portants* supporting the wing-flats disappear giving way to new *portants* carrying new flats, the backcloth is similarly transformed, the borders of the old décor make room for those of the new, the light from the battens is modified accordingly, and in less than thirty seconds, with the thunderous ringing of a bell, the whole operation is concluded, in full view of a wondering audience, who for all their concentration cannot understand how a change of scene so unexpected, so swift and so complete has been accomplished.

The downside to this complexity, this sense of urgency and profuse deployment of manpower, was a huge potential for misadventure, the acute danger to life and limb and the ever-present threat of fire.

328 Accident-proneness

(a) Grobert, *Exécution dramatique*, p. 195; (b) Donnet, *Architectonographie*, p. 167; (c) Review of *Robert le Diable* (Meyerbeer/Germain Delavigne/Scribe) at the Opéra, 21 November 1831. *Revue des Deux Mondes*, 1st series, vol. 4 (1831), pp. 539–40; (d) Review of Shakespeare's *Le Songe d'une nuit d'été* at the Porte-Saint-Martin, 24 June 1844. Gautier, *Histoire de l'art dramatique*, vol. iii, p. 219

(a) For the sake of speed and economy of space, the wing-flats are always carried upright, sometimes lifted at the rear by a long pole fitted with a hook [. . .] But this way of shifting the décors is fundamentally unsound in that it increases the already high percentage of risks attendant on scene-changing today. A method which depends entirely on the supreme skill and experience of stage hands can go wrong, because these same stage hands may be caught up with the crowd of people milling about on stage, because the grooves for flats, or objects set on the stage, or furniture, or the activities of lighting men may impede their progress. Yet the dropping of one flat can cause serious injury or start a fire.

(b) But the most serious problem about the obligatory layout of a theatre is that everything is made of timber, canvas and rope, and that it is too poorly lit by daylight, thus making it necessary almost always to carry a flaming torch to see one's way through this labyrinth, which a single spark can promptly turn into a sea of fire, against which the stout outer walls of the structure provide the only bulwark. That is the way in which so many such buildings have perished.

(c) What a tragedy if that exquisite ballerina [Taglioni] had had both her legs broken, as might have happened with the fall of the heaviest cloud, which all at once broke loose from the fifth row of borders. Indeed, accidents were plentiful on this particular evening. A tree in the forest, fully loaded with gas-lamps and *quinquets*, all but crushed Mademoiselle Dorus in the middle of a pastoral aria; then, in the final scene of the last act, a *trappe anglaise*[1] swallowed up Nourrit at the very moment that he was saved from the clutches of the demon. Those who know what an abyss separates the floor of the stage from the foundations and that there are fully sixty feet to fall turned pale with fright as they watched Nourrit disappear so suddenly.

(d) It is astonishing that in this day and age when so much progress has been made that the theatre should scarcely be further advanced than it was at the time of the Marquis de Sourdéac.[2] Everything is done by hand, and the stage crew propel the wing-flats in their grooves by sheer strength of arm. It seems to us that by 1844 a theatre should have no more than one machinist, calmly seated in front of a sort of keyboard and striking the keys to move cloths and *portants*. We would not then have those distressing sights of palaces which remain stuck in mid-air or oceans tangled up with forests which sometimes disfigure the noblest of stages;[3] for gear-wheels and levers do not get distracted, they do not read the newspaper or gossip with the supers and the firemen.

[1] The sprung, two-leaf *trappe anglaise* was first used in France for this production. Bouffé recalled a slight *contretemps* with this 'fiendish invention' while playing Clown in a pantomime during his engagement at the Nouveautés in the same year.

[2] An amateur machinist, associated with the first Paris Opéra of 1669.

[3] Elsewhere, he instances a performance at the Opéra in 1838 when the 'Sylphide' was hoisted too violently by a counterweight and struck her foot against the chimney-breast, while at Taglioni's benefit performance two other sylphs were left stranded in mid-air, madly thrashing their arms and legs 'like disorientated toads' (Gautier, *Histoire de l'art dramatique*, vol. i, pp. 177–8).

SCENIC ILLUSION

This forthright comment is one of an infinite number on current productions made by Gautier during his long career as regular drama critic for *La Presse*, a position he took up in 1836 and thereafter made distinctive by devoting no less space in his column to the miscellaneous offerings of the popular playhouses, and even street entertainments, than to the repertoire of the state theatres. With his artist's eye particularly susceptible to the design and other visual aspects of a production, he has left a vivid and discriminating account of the beauties, ingenuities and occasional ineptitudes of stage presentation during this period. The following extracts offer a representative selection.

329   Gautier describes a range of scenic effects

(a) Review of *Bijou, ou l'Enfant de Paris*, 'féerie' (Pixérécourt/Brazier/Duvert), at the Cirque-Olympique, 5 February 1838. Gautier, *Histoire de l'art dramatique*, vol. i, p. 102; (b) Review of *Peau d'âne*, 'féerie' (Van Der Burch/Laurencin), at the Porte-Saint-Martin, 10 August 1838. *Ibid.*, p. 160; (c) Review of *Le Naufrage de la Méduse*, 'drame' (C.L.F. Desnoyer), at the Ambigu-Comique, 6 May 1839. *Ibid.*, p. 258; (d) Review of *Le Tremblement de terre de la Martinique*, 'drame' (Dennery), at the Gaîté, 27 January 1840. *Ibid.*, vol. ii, p. 22; (e) Review of *Les Bohémiens de Paris*, 'drame' (Dennery/E. Grangé) at the Ambigu-Comique, 27 September 1843. *Ibid.*, p. 107; (f) Review of *Eucharis*, 'ballet-pantomime' by Coralli and Deldevez, at the Opéra, 7 August 1844. *Ibid.*, vol. iii, pp. 247–8; (g) Review of *La Chasse au chastre*, 'fantaisie' (Dumas), at the Théâtre Historique, 6 August 1850. *Ibid.*, vol. vi, pp. 197–8

(a) *Bijou, ou l'Enfant de Paris*, 1838

In terms of *changements à vue*, *vols* and other wonders, *Bijou* is not inferior to the celebrated *Pied de Mouton*.[1] Sofas turn into writing-desks; the least suspicious pieces of furniture change shape like Proteuses; portraits yawn in their picture-frames;

signboards unfasten themselves and go for a walk; pies shed their crusts and sprout grinning faces; bottles of champagne discharge fireworks; water from fountains is transformed into a torrent of fire; the most innocuous-looking objects conceal a trap or a trick. None of this prevents the prince from marrying his princess at the end of the play.

(b) *Peau d'âne*, 1838

The fight between Inigo, the clown of the piece, and an elephant which he encounters in a forest is a very original idea. Let me give you an account of this Pantagruelian contest. The elephant uses his great trunk to belabour poor Inigo, who, not knowing how to rid himself of this fearful adversary, decides to stick a pin in it. The elephant, which is made of taffeta and filled with air, deflates, collapses, and shrinks to such tiny proportions that Inigo is able to fold it into four like a banknote and slip it into his wallet.

(c) *Le Naufrage de la Méduse*, 1839

The final tableau, depicting the shipwrecked souls on their raft, is a truly fine piece of work, which all Paris will rush to see. Imagine a sea stretching as far as the eye can see, whose waves lap against the very *quinquets* of the footlights; nothing but sea and sky, no sound but the flapping of the sail, the soughing of the wind, the death rattle of a dying man, while the ground swell comes surging from the distant horizon like a fierce, unbridled mare, her nostrils foaming white and her breath racing: it is dazzling and majestic. Each time the bosom of the Ocean heaves it bears the lurching craft aloft, rising and falling with every wave; this motion is very well rendered. The groupings, arranged like those of Géricault and set off by livid lighting, create an extremely impressive effect and produce a total illusion [. . .] we doubt whether the art of imitation can be taken any further.[2]

(d) *Le Tremblement de terre de la Martinique*, 1840

The decoration of the closing scene is quite good, the change in colour of the sea waters in particular being very well rendered; the sky has some good stormy shades to it, the houses collapse well; in fact, there is only one thing this earthquake fails to do – to quake. But one must always lend oneself to the illusion a little: a machinist is not able to make the floor of a stage move as easily as God can move a planet.

(e) *Les Bohémiens de Paris*, 1843

The Ambigu has incurred enormous expense for the staging of this play, which is clearly inspired by *Les Mystères de Paris*;[3] several of the décors are really magnificent. That for the second act, in particular, which represents a perspective view of the Seine by moonlight, seen from below the Pont Marie, produces an exquisite effect; it is from the brush of Messrs Séchan, Diéterle and Despléchin. A splendid cloth by Messrs Philastre and Cambon[4] also deserves to be commended: it offers a panorama of Paris seen from the heights of Montmartre and serves as a fitting conclusion to this sequence of eight tableaux which, far more than the drama to which they are an adjunct or a pretext, will draw the crowds to the Ambigu for a good three months.

(f) *Eucharis*, 1844

No sooner has the oath been sworn than the storm manifests itself fairly inadequately in the shape of a large black cloth scallopped like the barbel of a crayfish and hoisted up on three thick lines which are perfectly visible. A storm like this would be tolerable at the Théâtre-Français at most, where the neglect of *mise-en-scène* is considered a matter of principle. At the Académie Royale de Musique we had every right to expect a few pinches of lycopodium, a slight rattle of sheet-metal and cobblestones to indicate lightning and thunder. In a purely visual spectacle like ballet the appurtenances and details of production must be the object of very special care.

(g) *La Chasse au chastre*, 1850

The carriage is a real one, and two mechanical hacks with legs that trot are supposed to be pulling it along. The wheels turn, the harness bells jingle, the whip cracks, and at the back of the stage a vast panorama unfurls to represent the route covered. Thus, a lake comes into view, tinged pink by the early light of dawn, then some hills, villages, rocks with a waterfall cascading over them, a town silhouetted high up on top of a crag, forests of parasol pine. To the accompaniment of the bells and the crack of his whip, the driver sings a local folk-song, the melody of which will soon be all the rage [. . .] all of which gives time for the panorama to wind on and for night to fall. The landscape becomes starker and more forbidding. The road narrows as it enters a mountain gorge grotesquely lit by the moon, its pallid escarpments strewn with tufts of fennel and juniper.

[1] A 'mélodrame-féerie comique' by A. L. D. Martainville and C. Ribié, first performed at the Gaîté in 1806.

[2] He had second thoughts a month later, when the Renaissance staged a rival piece under the same title by the brothers Cogniard, reporting that whereas the Ambigu's raft had pitched up and down on the same spot, the Renaissance's 'crosses the stage from one corner to the other' and that the ground swell was improved by the use of 'elastic spirals' (Gautier, *Histoire de l'art dramatique*, vol. I, pp. 262–3).

[3] A novel in multiple parts by Eugène Sue, which appeared in 1842/3.

[4] Charles Séchan, Jules Diéterle, Edouard Despléchin, René Philastre and Charles Cambon were all pupils of Ciceri. Séchan also opened a scenographic studio on similar lines to his master's.

SCENOGRAPHIC ADVANCES

Purely pictorial settings, however realistically painted, could not of course fully answer the requirements of Romantic drama. As Hugo argued in the preface to *Cromwell*, precise location should be regarded as a primary element of reality: 'The place where a given catastrophe occurred becomes its terrible and indispensable witness; and the absence of this kind of mute character would, in the *drame*, leave the greatest scenes of history incomplete.' Stage décors must no longer be considered as merely providing a background to dramatic action, but rather as capable of being inhabited by it; they should be seen as helping to shape and contextualize events and to communicate their significance. In practice, this would mean the adoption of décors *en relief*, the subordination of perspective wings and cloths to free-standing *fermes* and *praticables*. And herein lies the pivotal importance of the performance of *Henri III et sa cour* in February 1829. At this distance it is impossible to quantify the specific extent of Baron Taylor's contribution to the play's production, but two salient facts about his stewardship of the Théâtre-Français cannot have been purely coincidental: first, that as a practised artist and designer he took an active interest in *mise-en-scène* and had already been criticized in certain quarters for allegedly spending too much money on it since his appointment in 1825;[1] and second, that a single period of twelve months, in 1829–30, saw the appearance of Dumas's *drame historique*, Vigny's Shakespearean translation *Le More de Venise* and Hugo's *drame*, *Hernani*. A fortunate convergence of circumstances, therefore, enabled Ciceri, as designer, to give Dumas all the period detail he could have wished for in three quite distinct box sets for Acts 1, 3 and 5, each consisting of a large *ferme* with hinged side-panels, and set up in succession within the larger setting used for Acts 2 and 4, which represented the great council chamber of the Louvre.

[1]   Notably for Pichat's tragedy *Léonidas*, set in ancient Greece and performed with three separate, newly designed settings and period costumes such as had never been seen at the Théâtre-Français, which according to Dumas (*Souvenirs*, vol. I, p. 394), produced 'cries and stampings of feet each time the curtain rose', and Picard's contemporary comedy, *Les Trois quartiers*, with precisely realized, up-to-the-minute domestic interiors.

330   A box set for *Henri III et sa cour*, 1829

Albertin, *Indications générales*, p. 21

Act three

The Oratory of the Duchesse de Guise.
A closed room occupying three sections [*plans*] of the stage.[1] At the rear, in the centre where the door was [in Act 1], a kind of sideboard covered by a white cloth trimmed with white lace; three vases of flowers; above, a picture of a religious subject. These objects are painted.

In the right corner, at the rear, a little door. At either side of the sideboard, a small table covered by a rich cloth. To the right, in the first *plan*, a doorway furnished with a curtain or *portière* attached to a rod. This door leads to the duchess's bedroom. In the second *plan*, a door represented only in paint. To the left, in the second *plan*, an entry door. At either side of the forestage, a table covered by a rich cloth of the period. On the first, to the right, an inkstand, paper, quills, a seal and some sealing-wax; a silver tray, a bowl, an *aiguière*, an antique silver flask. A chair with arms beside the table. In front of the table, a low stool for the page. On the second table, to the left, an antique silver vase on a silver tray, a mask, a domino, two candlesticks, a book. Two chairs for Mesdames de Cossé and Marie.

[1]   Approximately 6 metres deep, each *plan* measuring 2 metres in depth.

In a postscript to his text Albertin acknowledges that 'the taste and erudition which the public was pleased to discern in the details and the ensemble of the *drame* of *Henri III* may be attributed to the enlightened advice rendered by my respected friend, Baron Taylor'.

However, what is of particular interest in his inventory is the juxtaposition of real and painted objects: only those properties and pieces of furniture directly required by the action were provided in physical form and the remainder on flat canvas, partly out of an attachment to old scenographic habits but also, no doubt, in consideration of cost, storage space and the convenience of stage management in a repertory programme such as that of the Théâtre-Français. But, by implication at least, the properties used here are solid articles – indeed, the *aiguière* is described in Albertin's property list as 'made of blue earthenware' – and not the cardboard copies that normally did service for dressing the stage and which Solomé, the *régisseur* of the Opéra, assured sceptical provincial managers among his readers could be assembled quite cheaply, even for an elaborate banquet scene in the *opéra-comique, Zampa*: 'There is a peacock with its tail-feathers extended, the head of a wild boar, a huge pâté, two platters of other items; many bowls of fruit and pastries; all the crockery in gold and silver; everything can be made of cardboard and will not cost very much'.[1]

This hybrid mode of decoration remained common for many years and seems to have been happily accepted by audiences. Indeed, there was a particular aesthetic challenge to be overcome in reconciling not only real objects but also moving actors with their painted simulacra on canvas, and a designer's skill in achieving this was duly recognized. Reviewing the production at the Odéon in 1831 of Dumas's epic *drame, Napoléon Bonaparte*, a contemporary critic found some of its nineteen tableaux, such as the massed deployment of artillery batteries at the siege of Toulon and Napoleon's arrival by ship from Elba, almost 'childishly' over-ambitious, but he was impressed by other aspects of the *mise-en-scène*.

---

[1] *Indications générales et observations pour la mise en scène de Zampa* (Paris: Duverger, 1831), p. 36.

331   Hybrid décors

(a) *Journal des Débats* (13 January 1831); (b) Review of *Les Martyrs* (Scribe/Donizetti) at the Opéra, *Presse* (12 April 1840); (c) Review of *Pierre Février*, 'comédie-vaudeville' (Davesne), at the Variétés, 13 November 1846. Gautier, *Histoire de l'art dramatique*, vol. IV, pp. 372–3

(a) Other tableaux are better conceived. We can readily accept large, well-managed military manœuvres on the stage. Two hundred men can represent twenty thousand, the furthermost columns being imagined as lost in the receding perspective. It is a question of a backcloth and an artistically contrived exit [. . .] similarly for the return to the Tuileries on 20 March and the populace crowding into the salle des Maréchaux. In all these scenes and others like them there is scope for illusion. And I hasten to declare that they are in the majority.

(b) [. . .] an immense crowd covers the square and the painted figures harmonize effectively with the living characters; this transition from representation to reality is accomplished with considerable artistry.

(c) The décor represents a dining-room. A cloth painted to resemble a tiled floor of black and white squares, as in real dining-rooms, covers the boards of the stage [. . .]

Dressers and sideboards in real mahogany furnish this same dining-room. This would perhaps be the moment to initiate a major aesthetic debate. Should properties be real? To address so weighty a subject would have endless ramifications. Real properties might seem, at first sight, to answer the intended purpose far better; but by introducing actuality into convention, are we not committing an error of harmony? If the sideboard is real, how can we accept the canvas wainscotting which abuts it? Will not the illusion one can achieve with the aid of draughtsmanship and colouring be destroyed by the shadows cast by objects of substance? [. . .] On the other hand, one can argue that real properties effect a transition between the reality of the actors and the conventionality of the décor. A man may well walk about in a room or a garden which is no more than an illusion produced by the scene-painter, but he can sit down only on a carpentered chair. Of necessity, practicable properties will violate the laws of perspective. By filling M. d'Estourville's dining-room with irrefutable mahogany, M. Nestor Roqueplan has been daring, but not reckless.

THE ADVENT OF *MISE-EN-SCÈNE*

Despite such aesthetic scruples, the aim henceforward was to be increasingly directed towards strengthening the illusion of material reality, mainly by the more frequent use of décors *en relief* and a greater emphasis on three-dimensionality in dressing the stage. The very publication of production manuals such as those of Albertin and Solomé, which became quite common from 1830 onwards, testifies to a growing concern for the physical and technical details of staging and a desire to ensure that the careful *mise-en-scène* afforded to a play in Paris was less likely to be travestied when it was performed in the provinces. Scribe, for one, welcomed this initiative as a safeguard for playwrights.

332   Closer attention to *mise-en-scène*

Letter from Scribe to Louis Palianti, reproduced in *Collection de mises en scène de grands opéras et d'opéras-comiques*, (36) 'Le Domino noir' (Scribe/Auber, performed 1837) (Paris: E. Brière, 1872)

Monsieur, you ask for my opinion on the *mises-en-scène* published by you up to the present time. First and foremost, I must express my gratitude to you for the service you have rendered me in particular and all my colleagues and dramatic art in general. I consider your work to be executed with such pains and such intelligence that it will make the author's intention clear and unmistakable, that it can be a substitute for his presence at rehearsals, that it must greatly enhance the success of dramatic works in the provinces and that its usefulness is beyond question.

Every manifestation of a desire to mitigate the 'staginess' of the stage picture, whether by disguising its floorboards with some appropriate covering or by littering it with solid articles of furniture, placed and utilized in accordance with the requirements of the action, was welcomed as a precondition of the new 'realism'.

333   Promoting illusion

(a) Review of *Le Songe d'une nuit d'été*, at the Porte-Saint-Martin, 24 June 1844. Gautier, *Histoire de l'art dramatique*, vol. III, p. 219; (b) Henri Monnier, *Mémoires de Monsieur Joseph Prudhomme* (Paris: Dentu, 1892), p. 314; (c) Désiré Nisard, *Souvenirs et notes biographiques* (2 vols., Paris: C. Lévy, 1888), vol. II, p. 229

(a) The curtain rises and reveals an attractive forest setting. The floor of the stage is covered with a cloth spread out like a carpet and speckled with flowers. This is an arrangement that we cannot sufficiently applaud or sufficiently commend. Is it not absurd, in fact, to see trees and shrubs sprouting out of a floor in which every plank and every crack is clearly visible? Elementary common sense tells us that the ground on which the characters stand needs to be represented in some fitting way at the rear of the set; but before we can arrive at the truthful and natural, it would appear that we shall have to put up with all manner of absurdities, and since time immemorial this particular affront to verisimiliude has been flagrantly perpetrated on every stage without anyone noticing it. A no less beneficial innovation would be to substitute *ciels en plafond* [sky-cloths] for those horrible *bandes d'air* [borders] which destroy all illusion and look like dishcloths hung out on the line to dry.

(b) No lies, nothing but the truth, that is how we realists understand art; we want a piece of furniture by Boulle[1] to be a Boulle piece and not any other. I shall never allow a play of mine to be performed on a stage where they still consider it possible to furnish a drawing-room by employing a few daubers at three francs a day.

(c) Before him [Auguste Montigny-Lemoine, manager of the Gymnase from 1844], although we had already seen the back of furniture which was brought on stage for the sole benefit of a conversation and, once the conversation was over, put back against the wall again, and although we had already, thanks to Beaumarchais, who was a great venturer in all things, seen real items of furniture set at specific points, it still remained to enlarge their number, which had until then been restricted to the barest minimum. Thus, we never saw a table, except when it was impossible to do without one; and everything else was painted on canvas. With Scribe, the mock furniture gradually disappeared. A table was permanently set on stage, and on it was everything needed to write with. But this table, in obedience to some immutable law, was consigned to one side of the stage or the other, from which it never moved. Along comes Montigny, he takes hold of it, and plants it in the middle of the stage.

[1] André-Charles Boulle (1642–1732), French cabinet-maker.

Dumas, too, was equally insistent on the provision and, as I have shown, the correct positioning of stage furniture for his plays at the Théâtre Historique, foreshadowing Antoine in his appreciation of the organic relationship between dramatic action and physical milieu. Not surprisingly, therefore, when Balzac submitted the manuscipt of his play *La Marâtre* for production there in 1848, he had already meticulousy annotated it, according to Hostein, with 'everything relating to the period, the location of the action, the furnishing and the décor'.[1]

It is also from the 1840s that one can date an incipient interest in what might be termed an 'archaeological' approach to staging. A first step in this direction was the presentation of Sophocles' *Antigone* in a new translation at the Odéon in May 1844, for which the acting area was extended into the pit to resemble a Greek *orchestra*, marooning the prompter's box at its centre, now camouflaged as an altar with bunches of grapes, crowns of olive-leaves and garlands of ivy. In the same spirit, historically reconstructed costumes had been designed by Louis Boulanger after consultation with Charles Magnin of the Académie des Inscriptions et Belles Lettres.

[1] Hippolyte Hostein, *Historiettes et souvenirs d'un homme de théâtre* (Paris: Dentu, 1878), p. 40.

334   An antiquarian *Antigone*

Review of *Antigone* (trans. P. Meurice and A. Vacquerie), at the Odéon, 21 May 1844.
Gautier, *Histoire de l'art dramatique*, vol. III, pp. 203–4

For this production the stage has been set in an antique style, as far as the unworthy architecture of our present-day theatres will allow, for nothing could be less like those white marble amphitheatres overlooked by an azure sky than our poky little playhouses [. . .]

At the Odéon, a kind of *proscenium*, a thymele or raised platform (which today would be called a *praticable*), communicates with the main stage of the theatre by means of two lateral staircases. In the middle stands the altar of Bacchus.

After a few minutes of tense waiting the curtain falls in the antique manner, disappearing into the floor and revealing the façade, or if you prefer it, the portico of Creon's palace, simple, rugged and severe in design as befits those heroic times. The doors open, and Antigone appears, the urn on her shoulder, accompanied by her sister Ismene.[1]

[1] See also Nerval's review in *L'Artiste* of 26 May (reproduced in Gérard de Nerval, *La Vie du théâtre*, ed. Jean Richer (Paris: Minard, Lettres Modernes, 1961), pp. 568–9), which declares that the performance 'held breathless and a-quiver, for three hours, a whole audience who thought themselves perfectly indifferent to the misfortunes of the race of Cadmus'.

A few years later, in 1850, to celebrate the anniversary of Molière's birthday, the Théâtre-Français (then, de la République) offered a production of *L'Amour médecin*, played uncut, with its original music, songs and *entrées de ballet*, and in an environment purporting to recreate that of its first performance before Louis XIV in 1665. Candles were lit, musicians took up their places on the stage and aristocratic spectators were led in ones and twos to the three rows of armchairs facing them, to constitute an on-stage audience.[1]

Here then, paradoxically, in the name of realism one sees the resurrection of historical conventions. Nothing could illustrate more tellingly the emergence of *mise-en-scène* as a theatrical discipline in its own right, independent of the text, and with it, the arrogation of a place alongside author and actor of an influential newcomer, the director, who on this occasion, interestingly enough, was Alexandre Dumas *fils*. However, the indispensability of a close regard for the details of staging had been registered as early as 1830 as a novel, and not altogether welcome, prerequisite for the performance of legitimate drama.

[1] See Gautier, *Histoire de l'art dramatique*, vol. vi, pp. 142–4.

335   *Mise-en-scène* in the ascendancy

(a) E. L. N. Viollet-le-Duc, *Précis de l'art dramatique* (Paris: Bachelier, 1830), p. 220;
(b) Gustave Planche, 'Le Théâtre en 1853', *Revue des Deux Mondes* (Oct.–Dec. 1853), p. 11

(a) Although the material aspect of *mise-en-scène* did not at first seem to us an integral part of a treatise on dramatic art, we subsequently came to the conclusion that to have disregarded this adjunct altogether might be a subject for reproach. And there would certainly be no point in attempting to justify such an omission by reference to the absence of comment on the part of earlier writers on dramatic art; spectacle *proprement dit*, the verisimilitude of décors and the accuracy of costumes, were not then as rigorously demanded as they have since become. It is no longer even a question of whether this improvement in *mise-en-scène* represents an artistic advance. It is a necessity to which one must submit, and it is undeniable that to mount a play well is to afford it some chance of success [...] Usage has prevailed, and today the fate of a dramatic work would be jeopardized if it were to depend on the capability of its author alone, without seeking assistance from the scene-painter, the machinist, the costumier and the walk-on supernumeraries.

Other theatrical commentators were less inclined to acquiesce in what they saw as a progressive abasement of poetry to visual effect, of dramatic substance to mere show. An article of 1834 in the journal *L'Artiste*, blaming Hugo in particular, accuses contemporary playwrights of placing such excessive reliance on a 'mania' for décor and machinery as no longer to concern themselves with truthfulness or even plausibility in their writing, of betraying modern drama to 'seductive accessories', and the author goes on plaintively to ask whether, amid the current entrepreneurial stampede to secure theatre licences, one speculator could perhaps be found who, 'anxious to preserve the French language and the sublime mysteries of French art, might not seek permission to open a new theatre called the "Theatre without Décors"'.[1] Two decades later dissenting voices could still be heard, even from quarters not necessarily unsympathetic to Romantic drama itself, calling into question the revolution that had overtaken stage practice in the interim.

(b) We have seen walking about on stage cuirasses and hauberks that gladdened the eyes of antiquaries; we have seen the boards of our premièr theatre swept by togas; but what change has there been? There is certainly much intelligence and much erudition in the reforms to which I refer; only I consider this intelligence to have been ill employed and this erudition wasted. Whether we are dealing with antiquity or the Middle Ages, with a ribbed vault or a Corinthian capital, décor will never be more than an ancillary part of dramatic art.

[1] *L'Artiste*, 1st series, vol. 8 (1834), p. 13.

But what change there had been was irreversible, and even more significantly perhaps, the day of the *metteur-en-scène* was dawning, as Janin's ironic tribute to his influence, written a few years after the preceding passage, attests.

336   The pre-eminence of the *metteur-en-scène*

Jules Janin, *Histoire de la littérature dramatique* (6 vols., Paris: Michel Lévy, 1853–8), vol. vi, p. 88

Once the manager has spoken, up comes the *metteur-en-scène*, a person of importance and perhaps the first in the hierarchy. Alas! nothing can be achieved without him. Take him away from the theatre, and there will be no more comedy, and with greater reason, no more *drame*. There is no point in saying that minute detail is the province of small minds, minute details represent precisely the genius and the value of the *metteur-en-scène*. It is he, in the last resort, who decides entrances and exits, it is he who allocates to each actor that portion of stage on which he has to cover at least ten leagues in three hours; without his sanction not one of those actors so ready of response and so quick of cue would even address one another. He sets up conspiracies, organizes riots, acts as master of ceremonies for every slightly complicated bit of revelry. Before the drama erupts, the *metteur-en-scène* has visualized the whole play in the camera obscura of his mind; he does not necessarily know what is happening or what is being said, but he can see the whole picture in action, the positioning of the characters, of the chairs, the table, the gueridon, the bell-rope. Ah! how many famous plays, thanks to this gifted man, have been successes in detail that would have been failures overall, through the shortcomings of the actors or the ineptitude of the author.

LIGHTING

The period immediately before and after the turn of the eighteenth century was one of profound and quite rapid change in the means of lighting the stage and auditorium alike. After centuries of performances accompanied by the flickering of wax and tallow candles, or the odorous fumes of primitive oil burners, the 1780s witnessed a welcome improvement with the advent of the argand lamp, pioneered in England by the Swiss physicist Aimé Argand but refined and promptly marketed in France by the pharmacist Antoine Quinquet, by whose name it became generally known.[1] Its hollow cylindrical wick, tall flute-glass chimney and gravity-fed supply from an oil tank placed higher than the flame combined to produce a stronger, steadier and comparatively smoke-free light. The *quinquet* was quickly appropriated for theatrical purposes and with considerable success, usually in conjunction with some residual candlelight. Despite several drawbacks – the continuing susceptibility to draughts, the frequent necessity to replace charred or unevenly burning wicks, and a tendency for the very brightness of the lamp, when used with a reflector, to cast visible roundels of light on any surface – it remained the norm for upwards of four decades, until the introduction of coal-gas in the 1820s further revolutionized the possibilities of stage lighting.

---

[1] For documents relating to earlier stage lighting, see Howarth, *French theatre*, nos. 385, 386 and 610 to 618.

LIGHTING BY OIL

337   The *quinquet* lamp

J. A. Kaufmann, *Architectonographie des théâtres [. . .] Seconde série. Théâtres construits depuis 1820. Détails, et machines théâtrales* (Paris: L. Mathias, 1840), pp. 101–2[1]

In 1783, the lighting of playhouses was greatly improved by the utilization of lamps with a dual air-draught, invented by Argand, Meunier and Quinquet. This invaluable invention, now familiar to everyone, consists of fashioning wick-holders that are circular in shape and extremely thin, leaving an inner channel which allows air to pass on both sides of the flame; a glass tube, taller than the flame, encloses it. This tube, devised by Quinquet, is tapered, that is to say, it has a diameter narrower at a height of one inch than at its base: the effect of this is to accelerate the draught passing through the flame, in much the same way as do the pipes attached to chemical furnaces.

A rack and meshing pinion are fitted to the wick-holder, serving to raise or lower the wick and make the light more or less intense.

[1]   See also Borgnis, *Traité complet*, p. 269.

338   *Quinquets* and candles in parallel, 1817

Illumination du Théâtre-Français. Traité pour les années du 1er juillet 1811 au 30 juin 1817. Messieurs Empaire & Cie, Entrepreneurs (Bibliothèque de la Comédie-Française)

[. . .] 1° That Messrs Empaire & Co. undertake to supply and maintain the lighting of the said Théâtre-Français, rue de Richelieu, as it is at present arranged and fitted, for all performances and rehearsals, whether individual or *générales*, taking place in the said theatre, as well as for the regular service by night and day, whether for the brigade of firemen, the interior of the auditorium or the booking and ticket offices.

2° To use for this purpose only the best oil, without odour or smoke, and of the same quality as that of the sample deposited under seal at the office of the Committee.

3° To supply each month fine wax candles for the stage, those for the orchestra, as well as tallow candles for the box offices, the quantity of which to be determined each month by the requirements of service but amounting approximately to

– Fine wax candles. Twenty-six livres.
– Orchestra candles. Forty livres.
– Tallow candles. One hundred and eight to one hundred and twenty livres.

The quality of the said wax and tallow candles to conform with the samples deposited with the Committee.

4° To employ at their expense workmen to dispense the oil, the wax candles and the tallow candles, who will be responsible for servicing the lighting for the footlights, the orchestra, the great chandelier and the peristyle. The two workmen employed to service the lighting of the stage, the auditorium and the corridors to be appointed by the Committee and paid by them, the Administration having resolved to pay only two workmen concerned with lighting.

5° A Chief Lamp-man also at the expense of Messrs Empaire & Co. for the upkeep of the ironmongery of the lighting.

6° To be careful to ensure that the lighting up of the great chandelier, together with the peristyle, the corridors and the stage, be complete at the hour specified by the Administration of the Théâtre-Français.

[...]

9° To manufacture from new, and instal at their expense within two months from the date of signing this contract, all the lamps or *quinquets* fitted to the great chandelier of the auditorium, and further, to supply as quickly as possible, also at their expense, seventy *quinquets* identical to those employed at the theatre of the Château des Tuileries, of which number forty-eight to be allotted for use on the stage and twenty-two for use in the corridors. Subject to the faithful execution of the above clauses, the members of the Committee, on behalf of the Administration, undertake to pay to Messrs. Empaire & Co. punctually the sum of twenty-four thousand francs for each year of the contracted service [...]

LIGHTING BY GAS

As early as 1818 Louis XVIII had despatched his Intendant des Menus Plaisirs, M. de la Ferté, to London to investigate the use already instituted there of gas lighting, with a view to adopting it for his own royal theatres. The envoy's report led to the appointment of engineers, the establishment of a factory and the construction of Paris's first gasometer in the rue Richer, at the northern end of the Faubourg-Montmartre. And when a new building for the Opéra opened in the rue Le Peletier on 16 April 1821, it offered its patrons an auditorium comprehensively lit by gas, with a large central chandelier, made up of seventy burners, suspended from the ceiling and a further seventy-two in eight sconces attached to the pillars. Such was the unwonted brilliance of the lighting, in fact, that ladies were apt to complain of its unflattering effect on their complexion, its reddening of eyes and hardening of features, so globes of frosted glass had to be added to the burners to temper their effulgence. The Opéra's lead was soon followed by the Théâtre-Français: in his well-known account of the first night of *Hernani* in 1830, Gautier evokes the anticipatory tension of the occasion by describing the progressive illumination of the house lights.

339   The auditorium lit by gas, 1830

Théophile Gautier, 'Première représentation d'*Hernani*', reproduced in *Ecrivains et artistes romantiques* (Paris: Jules Tallandier, 1929), p. 23

Meanwhile, the chandelier descended slowly from the ceiling with its triple crown of gas and its prismatic iridescence; the footlights rose up, tracing a luminous boundary between the ideal world and the real. Candelabra were fired in the stage boxes and little by little the house filled up.

If the sheer resplendence of gas lighting was not universally welcomed, there could be no doubt about its reliabilty or, above all, its controllability, and it was quickly adopted for use on the stage itself. Less than a year after irradiating the auditorium the Opéra presented, on 6 February 1822, its first fully gaslit performance, the appropriately named opera by Nicolo Isouard, *Aladin, ou la lampe merveilleuse*, with fairy-tale dioramic décors executed by the young Louis Daguerre, including a 'Palace of Light' with a moving sun, for the effectiveness of which the versatility of gas represented a key factor. Press comment in *Le Miroir* some ten days later was symptomatic of the response it provoked: 'The success of the new opera comes as no surprise. By turns, partisans of the new lighting and lovers of the old darkness can find in it scenes that are to their taste.' Later in the same year, a retired dancer and choreographer, publishing his suggestions for improvement at the Opéra, was quick to grasp the possibilities of gas lighting and spoke in suitably glowing terms of its capacity for promoting illusion.

340   The dramatic potential of gaslight, 1822

A. J. J. Deshayes, *Idées générales sur l'Académie de Musique* (Paris: Mougie, 1822), p. 35

This lighting is perfect for scenic effect. By means of gas, it would become possible to create a truly magical gradation of luminescence and one would not be obliged to commit glaring implausibilities when the action requires a change from daylight to night; it could also be turned to account for illuminations, for gauzes, etc. This innovation would be beneficial for the management and verisimilitude of stage scenery as well as for its cleanliness, in that it would no longer be coated with smoke or stained with oil.

Significantly, Deshayes had immediately identified ease of dimming as the major advantage of gas, as did the ever-pragmatic Harel, who welcomed the new invention with the jubilant remark that 'a half-turn of the tap on the gas pipe and the effect of night is produced instantaneously'.[1] In retrospect, there seems to be something providential about the arrival of gas lighting in the theatre on the very eve of the Romantic movement in French drama, as if it had been preordained to facilitate and to enhance that supremely characteristic feature, the scene by twilight or by moonlight. It did so to memorable effect, for instance, in Act 3 of Meyerbeer and Scribe's opera *Robert le Diable* in 1831, as Dr Véron, who was never renowned for modesty about his achievements as administrator of the Opéra, was at pains to point out.

[1] Harel *et al.*, *Dictionnaire théâtral*, p. 258.

341   The stage lit by gas, 1831

Louis-Désiré Véron, *Mémoires d'un bourgeois de Paris* (6 vols., Paris: Gabriel de Gonet,1853–5), vol. III, p. 338

The lighting of the stage constitutes an extremely important resource. It was under my direction that gas was used for the first time to light the scenery at the Opéra, whether in the form of enclosed boxes hanging from the flies to produce the effect of moonlight in the cloister set for *Robert le Diable*, or attached to vertical poles [*portants*], or in banks hidden by the borders. During my directorship, the painting, setting and lighting of stage decoration made enormous strides, under the detailed supervision of M. Duponchel.

More than a decade later, Gérard de Nerval was still sufficiently impressed by the lighting of a moonlit tryst between lovers to single it out for favourable comment in his review of the performance of Dumas's comedy, *Une Fille du Régent* at the Théâtre-Français: 'and, while they exchange their secret vows, up comes their pale confidant, the moon, bathing this love scene in light and casting the young gallant's shadow upon the wall'.[1] But for a fuller and more functional assessment of the progress that had been made, one must turn again to Kaufmann.

[1] *L'Artiste* (5 April 1846), reproduced in Nerval, *Vie du théâtre*, p. 677.

342   The design and advantages of the gas lamp, 1840

Kaufmann, *Architectonographie*, pp. 109–11

The ring burner has a raised flange, broader in diameter, which holds a glass chimney, and the flame is aerated, as in the case of argand wicks, by a double air current. However, the chimney enclosing the flame, which is often made of frosted glass, is intended to reduce the glare of the light and protect it from the effect of draughts rather than to speed up the flow of air. The flame is thus quite different from that of the oil lamp, being much wider and much less tall.

The application of the form of lighting we have just described to the illumination of theatres has eradicated many of the problems to which we referred earlier. Everyone is aware how much care and attention is required for the raw material of oil lighting; the regular cleaning, the oil to replenish, the wicks to mount, the necessity of regulating every flame, all of which demands a great deal of time and manpower. With gas lighting, everything is set in an instant; there is only one tap to turn, only one taper to apply and immediately a flame shoots forth which is pure, clean, strong and brilliant, and whose intensity one can increase or diminish at will. Moreover, the flame produced by gas is almost totally devoid of odour, despite the fact that before combustion the gas itself has a quite unpleasant smell. Another advantage of the gas flame is that it can be deployed in any direction. As nothing is wasted in this form of lighting and as the gas flows from the supply pipe at a constant pressure, the flame burns just as well horizontally as vertically, and two substantial drawbacks which other forms of artificial lighting could not overcome disappear of their own accord. These were, 1° that the least luminous part of the flame was directed low, where most light is needed, and 2° that the flame-holder or mounting would cast a shadow.

The height, shape and intensity of the flame being adjustable by means of taps attached to the supply pipes, it is possible to flood the auditorium or the stage, or both areas at once, in the most dazzling light, or to plunge them into the utmost darkness. The changing shades of daylight, various nocturnal effects and blazing, fiery meteors can now be simulated with great ease and conviction.

343   Types of gas-lighting equipment, 1860

Clément Contant and Joseph de Filippi, *Parallèle des principaux théâtres modernes de l'Europe et des machines théâtrales* (New York: Benjamin Blom, 1968), part 2, plate 15

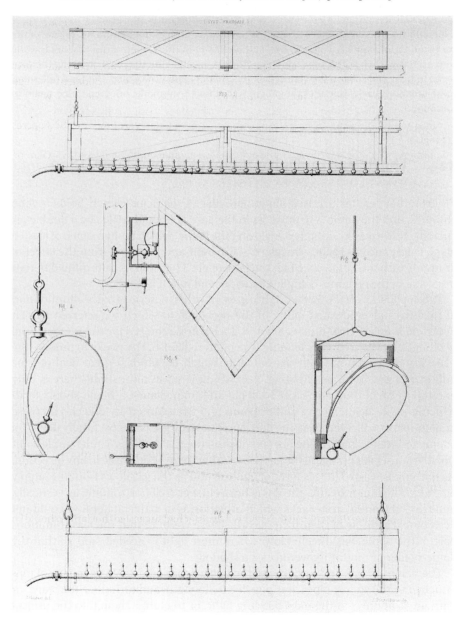

Illustrated are a pinewood batten, top, rear (1) and profile (2), a cast-iron batten (3,4) and a cone-shaped transportable lantern with plated-metal reflector (5).

By the time Kaufmann's treatise appeared in 1840, all Parisian stages were equipped with gas, though the oil lamp had not been completely abandoned: it was still commonly used during the day for rehearsals, fit-ups and maintenance, and at the Théâtre-Français, where old habits died hard, *quinquets* were retained for the footlights during performance until 1873, a quarter of a century after the Opéra, once more in the van, had made a first experiment with electricity. Culminating a period of extraordinary development in stage lighting, the battery-powered arc lamp made its début there on 16 April 1849, when it was used, in another example of prescient appropriateness, to represent a radiant sunrise accompanying an *hymne triomphal* at the end of Act 3 of Meyerbeer and Scribe's opera, *Le Prophète*.

Kaufmann also provides certain basic information about techniques currently in use for lighting the scenery, but his observations are by no means exhaustive and to amplify them one needs also to refer to a later work, Moynet's well-known *L'Envers du théâtre*, which, though not published until 1874, gives an account of practices dating back several decades, at least as regards gas lighting.

344 Lighting the set, 1840

Kaufmann, *Architectonographie*, pp. 90–1

Lighting of the stage and the scenery is effected by means of lamps attached to the side wings, so that each one casts light on the one immediately behind it, and so on to the rear of the stage. By fitting efficient movable reflectors, which make it possible to direct the beam towards those areas it is thought necessary to illuminate, one can make considerable savings in fuel and at the same time make use of a quantity of light that would otherwise be squandered where it was not required.

In our theatres the back-scene is seldom adequately lit, particularly centre-stage, which is too remote from the lamps attached to the wings. This part of the stage which is always viewed from the front and represents perspectives and long vistas, is one of the most important in terms of the illusion it can generate for an audience. It is therefore vital to be able to light it more or less at will in order to render convincingly the different times of day, the glare of the sun, the gloomy light of a storm or tempest, a sunrise or sunset, night, moonlight etc., etc.

By way of overcoming this problem the chemist Lavoisier had suggested that lamps should be installed behind the proscenium arch and beneath the rigging-floor, all fitted with movable reflectors so as to permit optimum directionality of the beam, and their luminosity controlled by means of coloured gauzes of varying thickness dropped upstage of them to intercept more or less of the light. Althougth advanced as far back as 1781,[1] this proposal had evidently made little impression on theatre practice, perhaps for reasons of cost or of operational difficulty. With the greater flexibility of gas, however, and possibly inspired by the sensation created by over-stage lighting for the moonlit scene of disgorging tombs in *Robert-le-Diable*, the use of battens suspended from the flies soon became standard. Moynet, having dealt with the footlights, then goes on to describe the gas-batten and other staple items of lighting equipment in some detail.

[1] In his 'Mémoire sur la manière d'éclairer les salles de spectacle', published in *Mémoires de l'Académie des Sciences* for the year 1781.

345   Other means of lighting the set

J. Moynet, *L'Envers du théâtre. Machines et décorations* (3rd edn, Paris: Hachette, 1888), pp. 106–8

After the footlights come the battens [*herses*], elliptical metal cylinders stretching across the stage, one section of which is open and fitted with wire netting so as to expose the flames from a row of gas jets inside. This appliance is suspended by chains, which are in turn attached to ropes, at a sufficient distance not to be in any danger from the heat of the batten. All this is mounted on a drum and counterweight, so that the batten can be lowered or flown.

There is one batten for each section [*plan*] of the stage: a threaded gas conduit leads to a small cubby-hole [*logette*] under the forestage, where the lamp-man is positioned; from this *logette* he can raise or lower the level of combustion by turning a tap, enabling him to dim the stage progressively, beginning with the footlights, the batten of the first stage section, and so on; he also has taps for the *portants*, of which we are about to speak, thus placing the entire lighting system under his control.

The *portants* are tall wooden uprights to which copper pipes may be fastened. Fitted to these pipes are three, four, five or even ten gas jets with glass chimneys. At the top, these uprights are provided with a large hook, allowing them to be suspended, either from a set of upper grooves or from a chariot-pole. Once the *portant* is in position, a lamp-man proceeds to attach a leather or rubber tube to the bottom of the copper pipe, where there is a tap. This leather or rubber tube passes through the stage floor and connects with a system of pipes leading from the central conduit, where the gas-cock is situated. These uprights can be used with all sections of the stage and there is a sufficient number of pipes to bring a concentration of light to bear on a particular point, if the requirements of a scene demand it.

To these three appliances must be added a fourth, called *les traînées*, which have no fixed position: they are set up according to need. When the décor is of uneven height and there are low flats occupying several sections, at times extending the entire width of the stage, such as ground-rows, water-pieces and small landscapes, these set pieces would throw one another into shadow and remain imperfectly lit, were one not to position lights on the stage floor between them. These consist of fairly lengthy slats fitted with hollow cylinders that are studded with tiny holes, from which issue rows of long, thin flames, not unlike the illuminations decorating monuments on public holidays; these *traînées* can produce a splendid effect within certain settings.

We should add that moving pieces of scenery such as clouds and the platforms used to elevate and lower the characters in *féeries*, are also lit by gas, the ease with which the supply pipe can be shortened or lengthened making it possible to use it anywhere on stage.

Of equal, if not greater, importance was ensuring that the moving actor would be fully visible at all times, and, for as long as the forestage was regarded as the dominant acting area, this remained the primary function of footlights. Kaufmann was clearly in no doubt about their indispensability, nor indeed about their shortcomings.

346   Lighting the actor, 1840

Kaufmann, *Architectonographie*, pp. 92–4

If it is important adequately to light the stage and the scenery, and to cast sufficient light overall to create and sustain the illusion, it is a great deal more important to light the actor; it is he who animates a scene, it is through him that emotion is communicated to the heart of the spectator: the slightest movement, the slightest alteration of his features, everything must be apprehended, nothing should be lost, and everyone knows that it is in such details that the quality of acting resides, that it is on them that the interest of a scene, and often the success of a whole play, depends.

As the actor has no need to see the audience, only to be seen by them, there can be no objection to illuminating him from the front, nor would there be any disadvantage if the brightness of the lighting made the remainder of the theatre appear dark to him. It will be appreciated, moreover, that the actor should be lit from approximately the same angle as that from which he is seen; whence follows the necessity to situate the source of light between him and the spectator [. . .]

The practice adopted for this purpose is to place a row of lamps very low down along the edge of the forestage, known as the footlights [*rampe*]. But the glare of the footlights is detrimental to the charms of the performance and just as tiring for the actors as for the audience seated in the boxes, and particularly for those in the balconies. They fill the auditorium with smoke, and produce a kind of fog which comes between actor and spectator. Besides, nothing could be more artificial than this light shining on the actor from below, it disfigures him, imparts a grimace to all his features and, by inverting the dispostion of shadows and highlights, it dismantles, as it were, the entire physiognomy and robs it of its mobility and expressiveness. Daylight strikes all bodies from above: such is the natural order of things, and in order to produce the same effect, it is advisable to make use of a kind of artificial sunshine.

PROBLEMS OF LIGHTING

The disadvantages inherent in footlights had long been recognized, and they continued to exercise the ingenuity of practitioners. Among suggested expedients for lighting the actor less artificially was that of placing front-of-house lanterns facing the stage at either end of each tier of auditorium boxes, which, the architect Pierre Patte had argued,[1] by casting light from above, would not only replicate the 'natural' effect of sunshine but also cover the forestage in all directions. The solution propounded by the celebrated dancer and choreographer Jean-Georges Noverre was to design the two columns of the proscenium arch so as to incorporate on their upstage side long hemispheroid indentations, lined with a polished, reflective material on their curved inner surfaces, into which vertical banks of lanterns could be fitted. Lavoisier, on the other hand, while acknowledging their drawbacks, could see no viable alternative to footlights, since lateral lighting was incompatible with the demands of stage management and overhead lighting of the forestage, by illuminating the actors perpendicularly, simply shrouded their faces in even uglier and more intrusive shadows than did lighting from below. This was also the pragmatic conclusion reached by theatre managers, and footlights continued to be routinely used and just as routinely condemned, on various grounds, by generations of commentators.

[1] In his *Essai sur l'architecture théâtrale, ou de l'Ordonnance la plus avantageuse à une salle de spectacles, relativement aux principes de l'optique et de l'acoustique* (Paris, 1782).

347   The curse of footlights

(a) Jean-Baptiste Pujoulx, *Paris à la fin du XVIIIe siècle* (Paris: B. Mathe, an-IX [1801]), p. 128; (b) Grobert, *Exécution dramatique*, p. 5; (c) Review of *Le Songe d'une Nuit d'été*, at the Porte-Saint-Martin, 24 June 1844. Gautier, *Histoire de l'art dramatique*, vol. III, p. 219

(a) Faced with this blaze of light at the feet of the actor, one would think that it was from Tartarus that sprang the flames which illuminate him. How ridiculous! Whether in our fields or in our homes, light always comes from the heavens, and in the theatre we are forever condemned to receive it from hell! No, this procedure smacks of nothing but obstinacy and it is adhered to still merely because everything is subordinated to that part of the house where the audience come to make a mutual exhibition of themselves, whereas everything should be subordinated to theatrical illusion.

(b) Few people realize that the torrent of light emanating from the *rampe* is an absurdity sanctioned by the desire to show off the charms of actresses, the postures of dancers, and the splendour of elegant costumes. If the public could experience for once the effect of light shining from above on objects below, in accordance with the order of nature, they would no longer see in the images presented to us by today's theatres anything but extravagant caricatures as far removed from any notion of beauty as a painted screen from a work by Raphaël.

(c) [. . .] it will soon be time to have done with that idiotic form of lighting which contradicts the most obvious laws of physics, displaces shadows and lends to the human face an aspect quite different from that which it should possess.– How can you expect stage scenery painted with top light and lit with bottom light to create the desired effect?

The other notable feature of theatrical lighting to attract frequent comment was the *lustre*, or auditorium chandelier. Traditionally it, like all other house lights, remained lit throughout the performance, for the compelling reason that, just as traditionally, the principal object of theatre-going for many members of the audience was not to watch the events on stage.

348   The intrusive *lustre*

(a) Grimod de la Reynière, *Censeur dramatique*, vol. ii, p. 165; (b) Pujoulx, *Paris*, p. 128

(a) First nights are never adequately lit in the estimation of the ladies, whose main concern is less to see than to be seen. For the true enthusiasts, they are always too well lit, because the darker the house is the more the stage stands out, to the extent that, were it not contrary to propriety, it would be preferable for the house to remain in total darkness for the duration of the performance; the stage would benefit in more ways than one.

(b) So greatly has the intensity of lighting been increased in our auditoria that to be able to light the stage in relative proportion it has been necessary to double the number of *quinquets*, and still our décors appear less well lit than in the past. I believe, and I said long ago, that it would be possible to reconcile the brightness of the auditorium with the level of light needed for the décor by fitting to the *lustre* a simple mechanism whereby it could be masked during the performance, so as to shed only a subdued glow. This would restore to the stage all the radiance that it requires. This mechanism, which would cost the Opéra scarcely 300 francs, would save more than 3,000 francs a year in oil and upkeep of the *quinquets*.

The advent of gas made it much simpler – and no doubt more cost-effective – to maintain the requisite differential in intensity of light, but 'true enthusiasts' still had many years to wait before the total darkening of the auditorium was achieved.

Such was the manifest superiority of gas lighting, and so keen the desire not to be competitively outdone in exploiting its potential, that the serious disadvantages that it presented were all too readily overlooked. The excessive heat it generated, the rapid vitiation of the atmosphere of stage and auditorium alike, the steady discolouration and erosion of furnishings, fittings, even stock scenery, were all tolerated. The ever-present threat of fire, for which the accidental combustion of dancers' dresses in the naked flames of the footlights provided a regular, at times gory, reminder, was seen as an acceptable risk. Looking back years later, from the comparative safety of a time when all Parisian theatres were converted to electricity, Georges Moynet gave a graphic account of the dangers faced in the age of gas.

349   The risk of fire

Georges Moynet, *La Machinerie théâtrale. Trucs et décors. Explication raisonnée de tous les moyens employés pour produire les illusions théâtrales* (Paris: La Librairie Illustrée, n.d. [1893]), pp. 237–9

The chief stage-manager of a major theatre, one of the most senior in his profession, said as he showed me the incandescent lanterns of his lighting rig: 'Nowadays I can sleep more or less peacefully; but with that confounded gas, for thirty-five years of my life, I could never arrive for work at the theatre without wondering: Will it be tonight that everything goes up in smoke?'

[. . .] if one looks at the sad catalogue of theatrical disasters, one will see that the number of fires increased with the use of wax candles, that it declined with the use of oil, and that it rose again, but with a terrifying escalation, with the introduction of gas. Gas was so convenient, so easy to use, instead of those heavy, unmanageable *quinquets*! No one could resist the temptation of offering the public vivid décors enlivened by this joyous flame, whose only drawback was that it turned blues into greens. Competitiveness took a hand, and it became a question of who could dazzle his audience the most. Behind the scenery, on all sides, gas burned furiously, often with a naked flame, darting its tongue to within a few centimetres of the overheated pine of the traps or the dessicated canvas of the flats.

The first consequence of this riot of light was to transform the flies into an oven. In the fly-galleries, tropical temperatures of 40 or 50 degrees centigrade were recorded. And this heat had an alarming quality of dryness. Timber, canvas and hemps retained not the slightest trace of humidity. Once a set of curtains had been rigged, no one could touch them again [. . .]

That was not all. A substantial amount of gas would escape, during rapid scene changes or through faulty connections. Anyone who set foot on a stage during this period will remember the pervasive and persistent smell of gas, which saturated the atmosphere from top to bottom.

The gas, mixed with air, spread more or less everywhere; it lodged in the dried up fibres of the timber, it accumulated in nooks and crannies, it formed pockets here, there and everywhere. So, when by some mischance a flame leapt out, it was all over, everything caught fire like a bowl of punch. The conflagration started instantaneously, on all sides at once. We saw this happen in the dreadful accident at the Opéra-Comique,[1] a theatre well insulated against air from the outside so as not to expose its singers to the risk of colds, where the unburned gas had built up insidiously, impregnating cloth and timber, and for many a long year.

---

[1] In 1887, when it was razed to the ground, with the loss of hundreds of lives.

COSTUME

The notion of costume design as an integral part of *mise-en-scène* and inseparable from the world of the individual play took a very long time to gain acceptance.[1] At the end of the eighteenth century actors possessed their own wardrobe as a necessary item of professional equipment, governed to some extent by the style of dress conventionally associated with their chosen line of business but otherwise a product of personal taste. In any case, for plays set in the present day all members of a company were expected by the management to provide suitable contemporary attire. Essentially, stage costume, at all times the actor's closest ally, was seen in a purely functional light, as a means of ready identification and, for the leading performer at least, an opportunity for self-enhancement, irrespective of what other members of the cast were wearing. The credit for being the first actor to conceive of costume in terms of period as well as character is normally given to Talma: he is known to have sought advice from artists and antiquarian authorities and his historical reading was reputedly very wide. In retrospect, the fruits of his vestimental research may strike us as unduly contrived, and he was certainly exercising it in isolation, without reference to his colleagues, whose response was rarely supportive. Among the earliest documented examples of costumes designed specifically as a coherent set, derived from historical models and taking due account of the age and relative status of the *dramatis personæ*, were those for the production of Dumas's *Henri III et sa cour*, and they created a precedent for other Romantic dramatists to follow. Despite their success with audiences and critics, however, performers remained unconvinced and many continued to dress with more of an eye to tradition and personal vanity.

[1] For documents relating to seventeenth- and eighteenth-century stage costume, see Howarth, *French theatre*, nos. 204, 205, 206, 207, 226, 227, 228, 229, 230, 231, 388, 389, 390 and 595 to 607.

DRESS SENSE AND NONSENSE

350   Sartorial anarchy at the Théâtre-Français, 1803

Joseph Lavallée, *Lettres d'un mameluk, ou Tableau moral et critique de quelques parties des mœurs de Paris* (Paris: Capelle, 1803), p. 112

[. . .] a Spartan hero makes a dignified entrance, conversing with a Babylonian confidant. And here comes the guard to a king of Assyria wearing the uniform of a lictor for a Roman consul. In comedy, a fop will be clad arbitrarily in a Louis XV outfit or else that of one of today's *muscadins*, while the plays of Molière will show us old men from the period of Louis XIII, attended by valets from no period whatever, and talking to young men in Louis XV garb in the company of ladies dressed in the very latest fashion, like Mme Récamier or Mme Tallien at Tivoli. Thus, between a father and his sons there can be a gap of three hundred years, and the oddest thing about it all is that no one seems to notice.

351   Old 'habits' die hard

Ricord, *Fastes de la Comédie-Française*, vol. II, pp. 142–3

The Comédie's wardrobe master Dublin, a man of taste, had simplified the costumes for tragedy with a view to rendering them less heavy and easier to wear. 'Ah! Monsieur Dublin,' said Vanhove to him, 'so you think yourself a scholar; but your improvements are a nuisance! In the past, when I played Agamemnon, I used to be able to blow my nose and take a pinch of snuff; now, there's nowhere to stuff my handkerchief or my snuff-box.' Monsieur Dublin has purged the Greek costume of pockets [. . .] Oh, how famous the great man will be for it!

Vanhove, an actor of the old school, whose daughter Caroline became Talma's second wife shortly before her father's death in 1803, was the subject of several such anecdotes, ironically so in view of what his son-in-law was to be renowned for in the field of costume.

Seeing in Paris a performance of *Misanthropie et repentir*, a translation of his own drama *Menschenhass und Reue*, Kotzebue was disconcerted by the costume adopted by Saint-Fal for the leading role of Meinau.

352   The constraints of long tradition and current fashion, 1804

Kotzebue, *Souvenirs*, vol. II, pp. 227–8

Saint-Phal [*sic*] should not be dressed as a workman. He wears an old-fashioned, dark-blue jacket with yellow buttons, a scarlet waistcoat with large square pockets, black breeches, and boots that come above the knee. When I expressed astonishment at seeing such a bizarre costume, I was told that it was German. However much I protested and showed them my own frock-coat, which was made in Germany, they would not have it otherwise and kept insisting that this was the German costume.

Kotzebue was equally dismayed by the blatant inconsistencies of appearance in Fabre d'Eglantine's comedy, *Le Philinte de Molière, ou la Suite du Misanthrope*, which is set contemporaneously with Molière's original, in the 1660s.

In this play [the actor Fleury] still wears shoulder ribbons on a rich costume in the style of the period. If the dress indicated by Molière had been observed throughout, I would have had no objection; but, alongside this, the ladies appear on stage attired in the Grecian mode and the height of current fashion, which produces a ludicrous and disagreeable hotch-potch.

No less than actresses, many male performers regarded costume above all as the surest means to be seen to best advantage on the stage. Dumas tells an amusing anecdote of an encounter that took place in the wings of the Théâtre-Français during the first night of the tragedy *Pierre de Portugal*, in which Lafon, playing the part of Don Pierre, had a costume change between acts 1 and 2.

353   Costume as a form of display

Dumas, *Souvenirs dramatiques*, vol. I, pp. 204–5

He had to doff his princely robes and pay a visit to Inès disguised as a common soldier. Lucien Arnault, the play's author, saw him approaching in a costume embroidered all over and with a sun emblazoned on the breast. Lucien, panicking, assumed that Lafon had put on the wrong costume and would hold up the second act in making good his mistake. He rushed up to him.

- Oh! my dear Lafon! he said, what have you done?
- How do you mean, what have I done?
- Well, what costume is this?
- Don't you like my costume? You're very difficult to please, my dear Lucien; it's quite new and shiny.
- Rather too shiny, in fact! that's what bothers me.
- What have you got against it, then?
- Well, I feel that for a soldier, really . . .
- Well, what?
- There's too much embroidery about you, and satin and velvet; and as for the sun . . .

Lafon interrupted Lucien, putting his hand on the other's shoulder.

- My dear Lucien, he said with a smile I can still see, there's one thing you should know; I want people to feel envy, not pity.

With that he turned his back, and he had the satisfaction of playing the second act not as a Portuguese soldier, not even as a French chevalier, but *en troubadour*, as we used to say at the time.

354   Political correctness in costume, 1793

La Feuille du Salut public (24 November 1793)

We exhort all citizenesses, especially those attached to theatres, to refrain from wearing crucifixes when playing the parts of village girls. This token of religious zeal, which has been ostentatiously adopted as an adornment, must be outlawed in perpetuity.

355   An actor's wardrobe before Talma

Fusil, *Souvenirs d'une actrice*, vol. I, p. 72

In tragedy, a costume of white satin with red stripes for Romans, a cuirass, a buff under-garment and a helmet for knights, a Spanish costume, and a ridiculous Turkish outfit, such was the wardrobe of actors in the provinces, and even in Paris. When I arrived in Paris in 1789, Love, in *Psyché*, still wore hose and knee-breeches of flesh-coloured taffeta, with jewel-encrusted buckles for the garters and black pumps embroidered with sequins. In the *Jugement de Midas*, an opera by Grétry, Apollo descended from the clouds in a snow-storm of powder [. . .]

[. . .] thanks to the advice of this famous artist [David], Talma was the first actor to dispense with the idiotic use of hair powder, hip-pads, plumed hats, and countless other absurdities adopted by his predecessors. In this he was supported by antiquaries and scholars. His own research into the Greeks, Romans and medieval monuments enabled him to assemble a wardrobe that was remarkable for its accuracy. His cuirasses, his helmets, his weapons were priceless. Julie[1] thought that she could make no better use of her wealth than by seconding her husband in everything that might help him to appear to advantage on stage. The long room of her house was decorated entirely with Turkish yataghans, Indian arrows, Gaulish helmets and Grecian daggers; all these trophies were hung up on the walls.

[1] Julie Careau, Talma's first wife, whom he divorced in 1801 to marry Caroline Vanhove.

At the poorer theatres, where actors were frequently called on to play parts outside their normal lines of business, the need for a capacious *magasin de costumes* was paramount. Jules Janin was struck by the range of attire available to members of the company at the Funambules during Deburau's time there.

356   A well-stocked costume store, 1832

Janin, *Deburau*, vol. II, pp. 87–8

No doubt you were greatly amazed to read *La Mère l'Oie*. You regarded this work as an unparalleled sequence of changes of scene and of scenery that you would not think possible except at the Opéra. What would you say if you were to enter into the detail of this vast undertaking? What if Mme Carpon herself, she who is so generous with trousers towards those who have no stockings in their shoes, were to take you by the hand and lead you into her costume store? How astonished you would be at the sight of all these dresses hanging up, these silk scarves, these embroidered tunics, costumes for clowns, magistrates, harlequins, gypsies, noblemen, pickpockets, the eighteenth century and the seventeenth century, gold and spangles, the Middle Ages and '93, the armour for a knight and the carmagnole jacket for a revolutionary, the entire history of France and of Rome, the history of Germany and of Italy, the history of Europe *in toto*, portrayed in costume by Mme Carpon, for a twopenny-ha'penny theatre.

TALMA'S PREOCCUPATION WITH COSTUME

Talma's earliest attempts at historically appropriate costume, apparently motivated by his frustration at being condemned to play only *les troisièmes rôles*, were confined to the 'classical' personages of French tragedy.

357   Talma shows his true colours

(a) Grimod de la Reynière and Pillet, *Revue des Comédiens*, vol. II, pp. 260–3; (b) Mme de Staël, *De l'Allemagne*, vol. II, p. 43

(a) Grimod de la Reynière and Pillet, 1808

[. . .] unable to distinguish himself by his acting in very minor roles, [Talma] resolved at least to earn the approval of people of taste by the fastidiousness of his dress; he therefore bravely forswore all the frippery of the costume store and had all his Greek and Roman garments made in accordance with the strictest historical designs. Before this a Roman consul had been dressed just like a hero of the siege of Troy, both having the same cuirass and satin chiton in common; but Talma reserved the cuirass for the parts of warriors, varying its form according to period, rank and location, and was the first to dare to assume a toga to play the Roman magistrate.

When he did so for the first time, as Proculus in Voltaire's tragedy of *Brutus*, his fellow actors derided his appearance in the wings, but the moment he stepped on stage

the audience, agreeably surprised by this authenticity of costume, expressed their satisfaction with four or five rounds of applause; his spirits quickly revived, and although he had been assigned the smallest part in the play, the entire honours of the evening were his.

On another occasion, playing an equally minor role and

having no more than ten lines to say, [he] appeared swathed in antique robes of the strictest historical accuracy. One actress, in point of fact an extremely amiable one, whom we shall refrain from naming out of deference to her talent, could not contain her laughter, and exclaimed: Oh, how ridiculous! he looks like an ancient statue. Could this dear lady have paid a sweeter compliment to the person she intended to make fun of, or administered a stronger rebuke to the conventionally minded actors whose routine ways Talma was rejecting?

Encouraged by the favourable response of audiences, Talma extended the same approach to other eras of dramatic subject matter.

(b) Mme de Staël, 1810

In du [*sic*] Belloy's play[1] he rendered Bayard the service of divesting him of those airs of the braggart soldier which other actors had felt obliged to lend him; thanks to Talma, this Gascon hero became once more as straightforward in tragedy as he is in history. His costume for the part, his simple, contained gestures recall those statues of knights that one can see in old churches, and one is astonished that a man who has such a feeling for the art of classical times should also be able to cast himself back into the temper of the Middle Ages.

[1] *Gaston et Bayard*, a tragedy by P. L. de Belloy, first performed in 1771.

358   Items from Talma's personal wardrobe, 1827

Catalogue de costumes, tableaux, dessins, gravures, et autres objets d'art composant le cabinet de feu François-Joseph Talma, artiste sociétaire du Théâtre-Français, to be sold at his house, 22–4 March 1827, pp. 3–8

LEICESTER (role of), in MARIE STUART, by *Lebrun*

A complete costume, consisting of a cape of deep-violet velvet, with gilt brocade, and a jerkin of imitation velvet embroidered in gold; a sword-belt of black velvet; decorations of gilt-brass, with the garter of the order of that name.

HAMLET (role of), by *Ducis*

Two costumes, comprising one tunic of black wool-cloth, the other of silk; one pair of silk trousers; one pair of silk hose: all these items of the same colour; a dagger with a hilt of gilt-brass, inlaid with paste stones; one chain *idem*; one pair of black half-boots; a wooden urn.

MACBETH (role of), by *Ducis*

A complete costume, consisting of a coat of mail in steel and iron-wire; a tunic and cape of cashmere; a toque of blue cloth; a sword with steel handle; a pair of red hose, with greaves of brass [. . .]

NERON (role of), in BRITANNICUS

Two cloaks, one purple and the other sky-blue, with gilt brocade; two tunics of white floss-silk embroidered in gold; two white kerchiefs and a waistband of blue cloth picked out in gold. Nero's crown [. . .]

MEINAU (role of), in MISANTHROPIE ET REPENTIR

A jacket of blue cloth; three pairs of trousers of pale grey, yellow and white cassimere; a waistcoat of white piqué and a black silk *cravate* [. . .]

JOAD (role of), in ATHALIE

A costume consisting of two long tunics of white calico, and a sleeved waistcoat with gold brocade; a short tunic of sky-blue merino wool, decorated with little gold bells; a tunic of deep-violet merino wool, with gold embroidery and fringes; two clasps set with paste stones; a sash of white muslin, with two gold tassels; a cap of white muslin, with head-band and gilt-brass chain, of the order of the Twelve Tribes, in a mount of paste stones.

ORESTE (role of), in ANDROMAQUE

A pallium of white cassimere, with embroidery of lilac wool; a long tunic of white calico embroidered in like manner [. . .]

CHARLES VI (role of), by *Delaville*

A long tunic of purple velvet, trimmed with fox fur; waistcoat of gold material; breeches of bright red silk; waistband of black velvet, embroidered in gold and adorned with colourful stones; black velvet mules. Wig.

LADISLAS (role of), in VINCESLAS [*sic*], by *Rotrou*

A dolman of scarlet cloth; cap with white fur; a sleeveless surcoat of gold cloth, brocaded in silk, brown fur trimming; a tunic of purple cloth, embellished with black lace, fur *idem*; two pairs of sandals of purple cloth, embroidered in gold [. . .]

OTHELLO (role of), by *Ducis*

A costume of scarlet cassimere, decorated with embroidery and black velvet, with white lining; enriched with gold; another waistcoat of yellow beaver-cloth, a waistband and its cord of silk, with gold brocade.

GENGISKAN [*sic*] (role of), in the ORPHELIN DE LA CHINE

A cap of green satin, decked with coloured ribbons; two pairs of sleeves, one of which in green satin, enriched with embroidery appliquéd in gold; a surcoat of printed cretonne; another with stripes; a velvet toque with white plumes; a tunic of sky-blue cloth, embroidered in gold; a tunic of merino wool, decorated with embroidery, jewels and pearls; a pair of knee-breeches *à la turque*; two lengths of muslin for turbans.

359   Talma argues for an historicist approach to the actor's performance, 1819

(a) Letter to Mme de Staël, dated 5 April 1819, reproduced in F. J. Talma, *Correspondance avec Mme de Staël* (Paris: Editions Montaigne, 1928), p. 22; (b) J. J. Regnault-Warin, *Mémoires historiques et critiques sur F. J. Talma* (Paris: Henry, 1827), p. 519

(a) One must read history in such a way as clearly to picture in one's imagination the manners and comportment of the characters or the peoples one has to represent. This will give one an ease far superior to that of the average player [. . .] One is then in the same province as one's character.

(b) [. . .] the theatre somehow must offer to young people a living course in history. Does not such negligence [by actors careless of historical detail] rob it, in their eyes, of its true nature? Does it not give them altogether false ideas about the life of peoples and about the characters tragedy seeks to recreate?

360   A more sceptical view of Talma's achievement

Théodore de Banville, *La Comédie-Française racontée par un témoin de ses fautes* (Paris: E. Albert, 1863), p. 41

Banville describes a portrait hanging in the foyer of the Théâtre-Français showing the actor as he appeared in the role of Hamlet.

Attired in a frock-coat of black velvet, drawn in about his waist by a silk cord with tassels, and a pair of close-fitting white trousers, against which stand out a pair of boots *à la* Souvarow,[1] adorned with tassels and hearts; wearing a broad plumed hat, of the sort they used to wear under the First Empire for less formal court occasions [. . .] his expression ecstatic, his eyes fixed on heaven, and his face smooth-shaven except for very short side-whiskers to the tips of his ears, Talma holds in his hands the ballot-urn of bronzed tin! All of which will not prevent compilers of anecdotes from repeating until the end of time that credit for the reform of theatrical costume belongs to Talma.

[1] Count Aleksandr Vasilyevich Suvorov, a Russian soldier who fought against the French armies in northern Italy.

THE CALL FOR AUTHENTICITY

361   The case for a costume designer, 1829

P. J. Rousseau, *Code théâtral, physiologie des théâtres, manuel complet de l'auteur, du directeur, de l'acteur et de l'amateur* (Paris: J.-P. Roret, 1829), p. 85

Since not all actors have sufficient concern or sufficient regard for their art to trouble themselves with such details, which are nonetheless so important, it would be advisable for every theatre to engage an artist for this purpose. We have seen several works for which the costumes had been designed by the precise and elegant hand of M. Henri Monnier and we have been won over by the considerable appeal which his historical authenticity added to the performance.

To complement Ciceri's historically precise settings for Dumas's *Henri III et sa cour*, Duponchel was commissioned to design a range of period dress extending even to the six royal pages, the court ushers and the halberdiers.

362   Historical costumes for Romantic drama, 1829

(a) Albertin, *Indications générales*, pp. 15, 17–18; (b) *Quotidienne* (13 February 1829)

(a) Henri III (27 years of age).– Black velvet toque, decorated with a panel composed of pearls, jewels and white plumes. White collar in the Italian style. Pearl-shaped earrings. Hair very short. Beard and moustaches. Doublet, trunk-hose and breeches of purple gros-de-Naples. Cape of purple velvet, embroidered in gold. The doublet very long and the cape very short. Purple silk hose. Purple shoes with white slashes. The order of the Holy Spirit hanging from a blue ribbon and embroidered on the cape. A sword.

The Duc de Guise (31 years of age).– First costume. (Headpiece as for the king.) Pear-shaped earrings. White ruff. Cape of grey cloth embroidered in gold, lined with crimson silk. Doublet and trunk-hose of smooth, heavy broadcloth, green foliaged with gold. Knee-breeches of grey cloth, hose, garters of buff-coloured hide, chamois boots with spurs. A sword. Second costume: helmet known as sallet, gilded; a tuft of white plumes at the rear. (The first page wears this helmet in Act II.) Cuirass of pasteboard coloured as iron, damascened in gold, armlets and cuishes of the same [. . .]

The Duchesse de Guise (34 years of age).– Hair drawn up straight in a chignon *à la* Marie Stuart. Large ruff *à la* Medici. Chemisette of gold fabric, trimmed with pearls and jewels. Bodice and stomacher of white satin, embroidered in gold. Puckered sleeves of the same.

Catherine de Médicis (52 years old).– Widow's weeds of the late XVIth century. Bonnet *à la* Marie Stuart fringed with a tippet of black crêpe. Standing bodice of black velvet with white turn-down collar. Sleeves and stomacher of black satin damasked with floral patterns.

King's pages.– Black velvet toques garnished with pearls and plumes. Doublets, trunk-hose and knee-breeches of buff-coloured broadcloth, garnished at the front with gold braid and buttons. Over-doublets of sky-blue broadcloth, garnished with braid of the royal livery; buff-coloured silk hose. Shoes of white prunella.

(b) Not for a long time have the beauty, the richness, the variety and the authenticity of costumes joined so powerfully together to complete the theatrical illusion.

Despite the personal example of Talma and the enlightened management of Baron Taylor, the manner in which productions were dressed at the Théâtre-Français continued to attract criticism throughout the period – and beyond – on the grounds of inconsistency, casualness or incorrigible vanity.

363   Continuing resistance to innovation in costume

(a) *Courrier des Spectacles* (30 April 1797); (b) Harel *et al.*, *Dictionnaire théâtral*, p. 93; (c) *Courrier des Théâtres*, 14 January 1833; (d) Review of *Marie Stuart*, a tragedy by P. A. Lebrun, at the Théâtre-Français, 28 December 1840. Gautier, *Histoire de l'art dramatique*, vol. II, pp. 88–9; (e) Review of *La Péri*, a *ballet fantastique* by Gautier and Jean Coralli, with music by Burgmüller. Nerval, *Vie du théâtre*, pp. 652–3; (f) Gautier, *Histoire de l'art dramatique*, vol. VI, p. 260; (g) Review of *Otello*, opera by Rossini, Théâtre des Italiens, 20 March 1843. Gautier, *Histoire de l'art dramatique*, vol. III, p. 21

(a) *Courrier des Spectacles*, 1797

Talma and his associates may strive to promote classical costume as much as they like, their example is not followed by everyone, and while the leading players are willing to pay for costumes conceived in accordance with historical models, the supporting roles are neglected and the costumes in which those playing them are rigged out bear no relation whatever to the period in which the action is supposed to take place.

(b) *Dictionnaire théâtral*, 1824

COSTUME. Talma may be regarded as the creator of the costume for tragedy. Before his time, the most absurd contradictions and ludicrous anachronisms were commonplace in this most vital aspect of theatrical art: many old habits still remain to be changed. Is it not preposterous to see dramatic roles which are rooted in contemporary manners played in the formal dress of the court of Louis XV?; is it not incongruous that a comic plot exclusively featuring characters of the present day should confront us with a notary swathed in a long black robe and a full-bottomed wig on his head? And the ladies! is not their craving for extravagant costumes risible?

(c) *Courrier des Théâtres*, 1833

In the sorry state in which our former premier theatre finds itself, scarcely any attention is now paid to historically correct dress. Every day we can see a garment of 1833 alongside a costume in the style of Louis XIV, and one of Corneille's heroes moving and talking with all the easy informality of an *habitué* of the Café Tortoni.

(d) Gautier in 1840

Rachel's performance as Marie Stuart had been greeted with the customary wild enthusiasm and floral bouquets.

Despite the torrent of flowers, we shall still take the liberty of pointing out to Mademoiselle Rachel that she has not read her part very attentively or, at least, not given much thought to it. In the scene between Elizabeth and Marie Stuart one finds the lines:

> Within these dungeon walls you have confined me now,
> Bereft at once of every trace of majesty,
> Without help, without friends, all but without servants,
> To the vilest need, in prison, am I reduced . . .

which has not prevented Mademoiselle Rachel from attiring herself with dazzling opulence, from having a bodice bristling with precious stones and a necklace with three rows of pearls. The first thing a woman will do when she imprisons her rival is to disarm her, in other words to strip her of her finery: to remove a woman's jewel-case is the same as taking a man's sword; and since Marie died for the capital crime of beauty, one can well imagine that the jealous Elizabeth did not neglect to do so. This rich and elegant costume, historically correct to be sure, and making Mademoiselle Rachel resemble the portrait of Anne Boleyn, is out of place; by its sheer magnificence it obliterates that of Queen Elizabeth, and it renders Queen Mary herself less interesting. A woman so well dressed is not an object of pity [. . .]

The part played by costume in the overall *mise-en-scène* was equally compromised by the vanity of performers at the Opéra.

(e) Nerval in 1845

This review first appeared in *La Presse* on 4 August 1845, while Gautier himself was away travelling in Algeria.

How I wish the costumiers of the Opéra would undertake the same voyage! What a quantity of errors and oversights in the finery of their almahs and in the apparel of the slaves and the odalisques! And is it not supremely outrageous to see the noble Turk in the leading role burdened with an Albanian outfit? As far as the actresses' costumes are concerned, we shall say not a word: no one has ever been able to persuade a woman on the stage to wear a correct costume; there are always pieces of lace or gauze, flounces and ghastly Parisian furbelows to add to the basic costume; always a waist to be taken in, hair to be arranged in a particular way, shoulders to be bared, countless little details of fashion to conform with which completely destroys its character. But nothing can be done about that.

The indignity he suffered on this occasion was painful enough for Gautier to recall it some years later when finding similar fault with *Sainte-Geneviève, patronne de Paris*, a spectacular production at the Cirque in September 1851.

(f) Gautier in 1851
The chorus has been dressed with much more care [than the principals]. A certain degree of historical accuracy has been attempted; though does it not destroy the effect to see young ladies in bouncing crinolines walking with head-dresses consisting of a gold band and the dried skins of guinea-fowls?

At all events, the strictures we have made are not addressed to the management: we are well aware that every actor will refuse to let himself be dressed; the only influence one can exercise is on the chorus, who are obliged to put up with the historical costumes assigned to them; this is something of which we ourselves have had personal experience. For *La Péri*, in fact, all the costumes had been designed by Marilhat. Only one performer was intelligent enough to accept hers, namely Mademoiselle Delphine Marquet; all the other dancers chose to bedizen themselves like carnival Turks or fairground mountebanks.

As with ballet, so hide-bound was the opera in this respect that as late as 1843, when one principal soloist chose to introduce an element of historical realism into his costume for Othello, he was, as Gautier reports, roundly admonished, even by certain critics.

(g) Gautier in 1843
Mario, making an innovation of which we approve but which several newspapers have condemned, on account, as ever, of this exaggerated devotion to tradition, makes his first appearance dressed as a Venetian general of the XVIth century, with gilt armlets and gauntlets, a coat of mail, and a surcoat of floral damask, like those painted by Paolo Veronese or Giorgione; this alteration is entirely logical. Othello, having entered the service of Venice, must of necessity wear the uniform of his rank. That he should then revert, for the domestic scenes, to his caftans, his embroidered waistcoats and his Middle Eastern manners makes perfect sense. Mario has thus given proof of his good taste.

364   Mlle Mars remains a law unto herself, 1837

(a) Review of *Le Château de ma nièce*, comedy by Mme Ancelot, Théâtre-Français (8 August 1837). Nerval, *Vie du théâtre*, p. 355; (b) *Revue des Deux Mondes*, 4th series, vol. 10 (1837), pp. 142–3

(a) Mlle Mars played the role of the judge's wife in powdered hair and a period costume. This represented a great effort on her part, we know; but to what purpose? Mlle Mars felt called upon to pay the author of *Marie* a compliment which she does not pay Marivaux. Normally Mlle Mars plays Marivaux in a costume in the style of the Restoration and Molière in a costume of the Empire, by way of preserving the necessary differential. Now why do that? We can assure her that the powder suits her very well, as does the historically correct dress. Let us hope that in future Marivaux will have Mme Ancelot to thank for being played in costumes of his period. Then it will simply remain for us to petition the theatre to provide a setting other than the inevitable red drawing-room from the time of Louis XIII, which at present serves for performing the entire repertoire dating from Louis XIV and Louis XV, or else its alternative, the lamentable striped drawing-room, which is from no time whatever [. . .]

Gustave Planche, reviewing her performance as Mlle de la Chausseraie in *La Vieillesse d'un grand roi*, a *drame* by Lockroy and A. J. F. Arnould set in the closing years of Louis XIV's reign, makes a somewhat different point, though its thrust is essentially the same.

(b) Mlle Mars, as is her wont, dispensed with any accuracy of costume; whatever the location or the period of the play which she is performing, she persists in wearing the same cut of dress; her outfits are deemed resolutely fit for all eras of history; I am sure that if she were to play Queen Clotilde, she would change neither the bodice nor the skirt which served her as Mlle de la Chausseraie. Does not the author of a play have the right to insist that his characters be dressed in accordance with historical fact?

365   The importance of authenticity in costume, 1843

Review of *Phèdre*, tragedy by Racine, Théâtre-Français, 23 January 1843. Gautier, *Histoire de l'art dramatique*, vol. II, p. 328

[Rachel's] costume was of an austere elegance and exemplary style. Anachronisms in dress are excusable in a primitive artist. We smile indulgently at the players of bass viols and the Venetian clothes in the *Cena* of Paolo Veronese; but today, it is no longer permissible to be inaccurate, because it is no longer permissible to be ignorant.– The actor's task is not confined to speaking his lines well, he must recreate the character's appearance and external aspect; the audience must be able to imagine that it is the character himself speaking; otherwise one would be far better employed reading plays in one's armchair, one's feet warmed by the glowing embers and a more or less philosophical cap on one's head. Here, the diadem, the veil, the peplum speckled with flashes of gold, the tunic, the cloak of imperial purple, everything was in the most exquisite taste.

366   'Antiquarian' costumes for Greek tragedy, 1844
Bibliothèque de l'Arsenal, fonds Rondel

Costumes :   Ismène, Mlle Vollet.   Tirésias, M. Rouvière.   Eurydice, Mlle Dupont.   Créon, M. Bocage.   Antigone, Mlle Bourbier.   Hémon, M. Miton.

Designs by Louis Boulanger, 'after mosaics', for Sophocles' *Antigone*, in a translation by P. Meurice and A. Vacquerie, Odéon, May 1844: Ismène (Mlle Vollet), Tirésias (Rouvière), Eurydice (Mlle Dupont), Créon (Bocage), Antigone (Mlle Bourbier), Haemon (Miton).

367   The aesthetic principle of realism is questioned
(a) François-René de Chateaubriand, *Mémoires d'Outre-tombe*, ed. Maurice Levaillant (4 vols., Paris: Flammarion, 1947), vol. II, pp. 38–9; (b) Gautier, *Histoire de l'art dramatique*, vol. I, pp. 45–6

(a) Chateaubriand, 1848
We have Talma to thank for perfecting the actor's outward appearance. But are verisimilitude on the stage and authenticity of costume as essential to art as is supposed? Racine's characters owe nothing to the cut of their dress: in the work of early painters little attention is paid to background and costumes are inaccurate. The 'mad scene' of Orestes or the 'prophecy' of Joad, as read by Talma wearing a frock-coat in a drawing-room, have produced just as much effect as they did when declaimed on stage by Talma in a Grecian cloak or a Jewish robe [. . .] Such precision in the representation of inanimate objects exemplifies the spirit of the arts in our time: it betokens the decline of high poetry and of true drama; we make do with small beauties when we are incapable of great ones; we copy the appearance of chairs and velvet so well as to deceive the eye, when we can no longer paint the countenance of the man seated on the velvet and in the chairs. However, once we have sunk to this perfection of the material form, we find ourselves forced to keep reproducing it, for the public, who have themselves become materialistic, demand it.

That Chateaubriand was not alone in his scepticism is attested by the fact that even so staunch an advocate of the visually correct and convincing as Gautier could still at times appear equivocal about its value and regret the crass literalism and imaginative poverty into which it could so easily degenerate.

(b) Gautier in 1837

What is lacking, by and large, in today's theatre is ideality, or poetry. The prosaic is invading everything; no longer is there room anywhere for fantasy. Actors appear on stage in the same clothes as they wear in the street, adopting the same expressions and the same attitudes as they employ in their daily lives, which is scarcely interesting and far from diverting; one drawing-room in pistachio-green and one in nankeen-yellow are adequate for the needs of the repertoire. I confess that I have often longed to see a red drawing-room or a sky-blue drawing-room, and that the black frock-coat or puce redingote of the leading man have made me pine for the cloak with red stripes like a tulip that used to be worn by the cheeky Neapolitan valets of the old comedy; is present-day dress so attractive to look at that it deserves to be replicated on the stage? I cannot understand why actors who are free to dress up in silk and velvet, to deck themselves out in glittering embroidery, to sport great scarlet plumes three feet high in a felt hat, to dangle a cape from the tip of one shoulder with a rapier scraping the heavens, should be content to hang on to their pantaloons with foot-straps, their floppy-collared jackets and their high-belled toppers; though it is true that, with their absurd pretension to become bourgeois and national guards, they consider it beneath their dignity as citizens to trick themselves out like carnival mummers every night.

Art cannot exist without convention; the absence of convention will bring about the theatre's ruin . . .

V   Audiences and auditoria

Unless special performance requirements dictated otherwise – as, for instance, at Astley's Cirque-Olympique and some years later at Daguerre's Diorama – the new generation of theatre buildings unleashed by the legislation of 1791 all tended to follow the same basic plan: a roughly rectangular structure, housing a flat-floored pit overlooked by multiple galleries and tiers of boxes arranged elliptically or in a horseshoe to face the stage, and with a proscenium arch set back behind an array of *loges d'avant-scène*, or forestage boxes. Indeed, the extent of any theatre's pretensions could be crudely gauged from the number of private boxes it provided for the better class of patron, each new establishment adding a further tier as it became more prosperous. In Paris, a paradigm for its successors had been created by the construction in the rue de Richelieu of what was soon to become the new Théâtre-Français, opened in 1790 as the Variétés-Amusantes and described in the following year as 'the finest in the Kingdom, after that of Bordeaux',[1] the same architect, Victor Louis, having been responsible for both. This assessment of its quality was subsequently endorsed by no less a tourist than Kotzebue, who reported admiringly, if not quite uncritically, on its auditorium.

[1] *Almanach général de tous les spectacles de Paris et des provinces* (Paris: Froullé, 1791–2), p. 155.

368   The new Théâtre-Français, 1804
(a) Kotzebue, *Souvenirs de Paris*, vol. II, pp. 235–6; (b) Bibliothèque de l'Arsenal, fonds Rondel

(a) A vast and imposing edifice; there are six tiers of boxes and galleries, one above the other, and extending all the way to the ceiling. One can hear well from all parts of the house, but in several places the sight-lines are poor, with pillars for the boxes blocking one's view of the stage.

(b) View of the auditorium from the stage in 1790, showing the six tiers of boxes which so impressed Kotzebue, including those in the dome. Note, too, the actors occupying forestage positions, a pair of masking wing-flats and one ground-row.

Kotzebue's one reservation is amply supported by the evidence of native commentators, some of whom also professed themselves to be far less satisfied than he with the quality of acoustics in certain recently completed auditoria.

369   Common design faults

(a) Auger, *Physiologie du théâtre*, vol. III, pp. 122, 124; (b) Pierre-Victor, *Documents*, p. 60; (c) Review of a benefit performance at the Opéra, 27 October 1845. Gautier, *Histoire de l'art dramatique*, vol. IV, pp. 131–2

(a) Hippolyte Auger, 1840

It is imperative for spectators to be so positioned as to be able to see well and hear every word. Unfortunately, architects often have more regard for the profit motive of the speculators in drama than for the good of the art itself: they are intent on accommodating more people than the space can reasonably hold, and above all on gratifying the vanity of those spectators who come to the theatre to be seen rather than to see. Hence the need for forestage boxes, for balconies and galleries, which impair the sonority of the auditorium [. . .] for nothing can compare with the insatiable cupidity of theatrical entrepreneurs, unless it be their parsimony when incurring expenditure which is essential for the public's enjoyment.[1]

[1] The relationship between auditorium design and the maximization of profits had been remarked on by Kotzebue in 1804. Having noted the Ambigu-Comique's 'three tiers of boxes, with galleries at the rear, placed behind the boxes', he comments: 'This type of construction, which appears to have been adopted at a number of Parisian theatres, is highly advantageous for takings in that there is no wasted space.' August von Kotzebue, *Souvenirs de Paris en 1804* (Paris: Barba, 1805), vol. II, p. 260.

(b) Pierre-Victor, 1834

The actors of the Odéon [as rebuilt in 1820] are criticized for shouting; but they are encouraged to do so by the dimensions of the space that they have to fill. Frequently, too, they appear to be shouting when speaking without effort; sometimes they can bawl at the top of their lungs and scarcely be heard. These divergent effects arise from the direction taken by the voice, growing stronger or weaker in proportion as it strikes the relief of the roof vaulting or loses itself in the recesses of the boxes, as it is reflected or absorbed, so that it is impossible to give it any distinct or precise direction. It follows that this theatre is favourable to actors who are not afraid to resort to yelling, and inimical to those who are less concerned to hit hard than to ring true [. . .] Another mistake is to have given the stage too pronounced a rake, making it difficult for the actor to strike a pose or to walk, and spoiling the effects of perspective.

(c) Gautier in 1845

In *Les Horaces*, and especially in the fourth act, Mademoiselle Rachel scored an enormous success, far greater than at the Français. This is because the Opéra's auditorium, although larger than that of the rue de Richelieu, imparts a much sharper vibrancy to the voice, being designed and constructed according to certain laws of acoustics which are too often disregarded in theatres not intended for specialized singing. The clear, strong and incisive voice of the young tragedienne reverberated powerfully in this ample space; not one syllable, not one rhyme, not a single intonation was lost, whereas at the Théâtre-Français the most sustained concentration and the profoundest silence are required to hear words spoken on a dimmed stage or delivered *sotto voce*.

Gautier was here describing a performance at the opera house in the rue Le Peletier, opened in 1821, but his opinion of the superior acoustical properties of operatic architecture in general is interestingly corroborated by Banville's nostalgic account of the old Porte-Saint-Martin, which had been built as a home for the Opéra in 1781 before becoming a theatre associated with spectacular melodrama.

370   The Porte-Saint-Martin

(a) Théodore de Banville, *Petites études. Mes souvenirs* (Paris: Charpentier, 1882), p. 226;
(b) Kaufmann, *Architectonographie*, plate 8

(a) Its proportions had been so skilfully calculated that emotion or laughter was instantly communicated from the performer to the furthermost spectator in the highest gallery [. . .] all the actors have told us as much, and we have in any case seen for ourselves how well every voice carried in this magical auditorium [. . .] and every genre could be played there with equal success, from tragedy and epic *drame* to drawing-room comedy, so easy was it to enlarge or reduce the cleverly designed proscenium opening and enable the work performed to be seen and heard to its optimum effect and in the most congenial conditions.

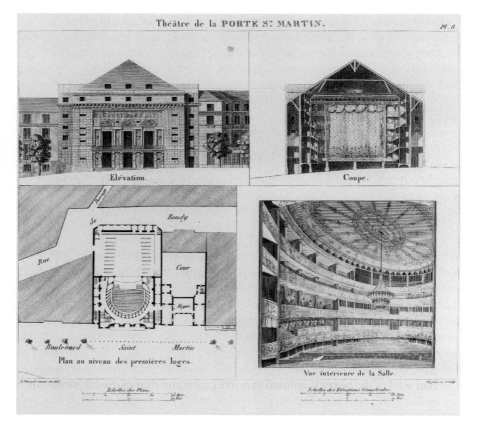

(b) Elevation, vertical section, plan at the level of the first tier and view of the auditorium from the stage.

Theatres without these intrinsic advantages were obliged to compensate for poor audibility or visibility by exhibiting a rich, inviting appearance. Welcoming the opening in June 1807 of the Variétés, Mlle Montansier's new playhouse on the boulevard Montmartre, the *Journal de Paris* reported that its 'auditorium presents a most attractive sight', with its four tiers of boxes set off by decorations in pale-green, 'enriched with arabesques of gold' against a background of 'marble of variegated colours'.[1] When commercial competition between the boulevard theatres became intense after the Revolution, and even more so under the July monarchy, their interior design reached a peak of extravagance. The managers of the Opéra-Comique, refurbished in 1834, and the Gaîté, reopened in November 1835, a mere nine months after its destruction by fire, seem to have vied with one another in terms of opulence and cosiness.

[1] Quoted by M. Albert, *Les Théâtres des Boulevards (1789–1848)* (Paris: Société Française d'Imprimerie et de Librairie, 1902), p. 213 n. 3.

371   The Opéra-Comique of 1834

Le Figaro (21 May 1840)

Picture a delightful playhouse, where oriental luxury is combined with the most exquisite comfort. In the corridors, soft carpets absorb the sound of footsteps; in the foyer, gold and velvet drip on all sides; in the auditorium, cascades of mellow gaslight cast an amorous glow; the cramped stall seats have given way to broad, well-cushioned armchairs [. . .] At present, this theatre is quite simply the most commodious, the most elegant and the best appointed of all.

372   The Gaîté of 1835

Kaufmann, *Architectonographie*, pp. 270–2

The splendid overall design of the interior decoration creates a dazzling effect. The style chosen is that of the period of Louis XIII and early Louis XIV, with all its sumptuousness. Perhaps it is even too rich for a secondary theatre, but we make no complaint, since art benefits thereby. The first gallery, on a level with the pedestals of the forestage boxes, is adorned with brightly painted satyrs surrounded by scrollwork and flanked by nymphs in grisaille playing various instruments, all on a ground of gilded leather [. . .] The auditorium ceiling is largely painted in imitation of the ceilings of Fontainebleau and Versailles and to striking effect [. . .] The rear wall of the boxes is painted in a soft green and that of the forestage boxes in crimson. The curtain is made to resemble a red cloth drape, framed in a rich border. Its base is trimmed with a fringe and gold braid.

In a report on the reopening of the Gymnase after a decorative facelift, Nerval gives a vivid impression of the internal aspect of Parisian theatres at this time and of the cosmetic repairs undertaken in an effort to woo back audiences during the dog days of summer.

373   Theatrical spring-cleaning, 1840

Presse (13 July 1840). Reproduced in Nerval, *Vie du théâtre*, pp. 526–7

Now that winter has left us, the theatres, like nature itself, outdo one another in the act of renewal, and anxious to bring back the crowds now scattered over fields and footpaths, they compete in display with the springtime. The greensward of stall-seats and benches has grown everywhere greener and is dotted with shiny gilt studs; pillars, balconies and galleries are entwined with golden acanthus, liana and palm leaves, climbing, twisting and spreading out – tropical flowers that have opened in the sunshine of the *lustre*, fabulous flowers of fairyland dreams, gilded scallops, sculpted wreaths, marble balustrades writhing with ivy, where aloes and cactus sprout from Chinese vases; and higher still, a firmament glittering with candlelight, where clouds rise into the ether, bearing aloft amid garlands all the powdered deities of Vanloo! This is what three or four theatres have to offer the passer-by, the dreaming poet, the ladies in their best dresses fearful of a summer shower; two or three others are about to close in order to contrive similar marvels; nature is routed; this year's pale sun recedes and fades before the refulgent gaslight, and captive breezes issue only from theatre ventilators with the aid of horsepower.

The Gymnase itself has repainted its smoky auditorium, which was last cleaned before the triumphs of M. Scribe began. Four days were enough to complete this new toilette, a trifle less glossy than that of the Variétés and the Opéra-Comique, but perfectly acceptable nonetheless, and the reopening has got under way with two new plays.

A SEGREGATED PUBLIC

The edict of 1791, which emancipated the theatrical profession, giving leave for the opening of new theatre buildings and abolishing the notion of repertorial monopoly, had relatively little lasting effect on the habits of theatre audiences. The Théâtre-Français and the Opéra by and large retained the loyalty of the more literate and more prosperous sections of society, while the hoi polloi continued to seek out the hitherto 'illegitimate' entertainments that had grown out of the fairs and now flourished under the arcades of the Palais-Royal or along the boulevard du Temple. Napoleon's 1807 order limiting their number, draconian though it may have been, was nonetheless predicated on the existence of a de facto division between different types of theatre serving different types of audience. That this situation had not materially changed a generation later is borne out by Auger's observations on play-going in the late 1830s, which offer a quasi-sociological analysis of audiences in the capital and are worth reproducing at some length.

374   The stratification of Parisian audiences

Auger, Physiologie du théâtre, vol. III, pp. 269–70, 273–4, 276 and 278–80

The Théâtre-Français – for it is there that one must always begin, not only because it is the doyen of theatres but also because it represents the noblest and loftiest expression of dramatic art – by its very past inspires the kind of respect that history demands of educated people. No sooner does the orchestra strike up its overture (chosen with more care nowadays, and at times even adapted to the tone of the play to be performed) than a feeling of solemnity is aroused, and faces will immediately take on a serious expression, betokening a religious frame of mind, the involuntary alertness that takes possession of one at the recollection of great names and fine things, even if one is about to see a farce by Molière.

There will be a larger or smaller house at the Théâtre-Français depending on the ability and reputation of the actors who are playing a piece from the old repertoire or on the current vogue of a new piece; but a good hearing is always guaranteed, except on days when a play is entrusted to understudies [*doublures*] and elicits no more than indulgent laughter. But for grand occasions and even for day-to-day performances, the entire audience, in the pit, the stalls, the balconies and the galleries, seem to be united in the importance they attach to what they are experiencing [. . .]

[At the Opéra] the public is a special one, with a majority firmly rooted in the aristocracy, the immensely rich and the fashionably idle, among whom the feeble contingents of pit and amphitheatre, where the audience is apt to change and re-form, are completely lost [. . .] Has turmoil or uproar ever threatened to disrupt the fundamental elegance of this bastion of the arts? The shrillness of a whistle would be an almost unprecedented event. Here, France is observed and attended to by the rest of Europe; here, etiquette alone determines the rules and subdues individuality under a yoke of decorum. One acts as others do, one models one's demeanour on theirs, one registers the pitch of the place and adjusts one's thinking accordingly. It becomes, as it were, a magical excursion to foreign climes: one might be at St Petersburg, London or Vienna. The theatre in the rue Le Peletier is the capital of the world; it is Europe in patent-leather boots and civilization in white gloves. Such travel educates the young. Hence, however overawed the bumpkins from our commercial neighbourhoods may feel, they will observe, and observe themselves in relation to, these alien manners, and the spectacle in the auditorium will remain in their memory even longer than that on the stage [. . .]

[. . .] one comes here [to the Opéra-Comique] in a sense for a singing lesson; one can follow the performer by humming in one's head, if not under one's breath, those catchy popular ballads which are so easy to remember; later, everyone murders them out loud, each in his own way and in his own voice: a *la la la la* will be heard at the interval and at the final curtain, an universal ululation, in the foyer, in the corridors and in the neighbouring streets, testifying to the popularity of the genre and of those who uphold it. The simperings of MM. Auber and Adam represent a nonpareil for lady shop assistants; and the Opéra-Comique provides every shop with the wherewithal for romantic intrigues and proposals, just as the shops provide the theatre management with handsome takings [. . .]

In the melodrama theatres, it is never hard to tell what is in people's hearts: the audience will leave you in no doubt whatever in the course of the performance;

and when the curtain falls, their cries and comments will show how much interest this crowd has taken in what they have seen and heard. Not that they are hushed with concentration: this would be beyond them, for they cannot contain their indignation or their joy, nor withhold their tears, their sighs or their alarms [. . .] What they ask of a play is that it should provide some respite from their troubles, an escape from their own sorrows in the depiction of imaginary distress: they will take pity on the suffering of others as if to forget their own. With a heaving breast, a tightening of the throat, a moistening of the eye and a face contorted by the conflicting emotions of fear and hope, every woman will put herself in the place of the heroine, every man will feel himself inflamed by a desire to defend the oppressed; the involvement which they all experience in the plot will find expression in an involuntary stirring, at times even an universal shudder [. . .]

The taste of the lower classes may be called into question, but never their common sense. It is rare to find wanting that warm-heartedness which sustains the patience of the poor. In the theatre, as we have said, collective mankind is honest and upright; it will tolerate crime only on condition that it is seen to be punished; it is necessary for every particle of this multiple being to carry away in his heart a devout belief in the reparations of providence that will bring a momentary glow to his domestic fireside; otherwise what might these passive forces do, if they were to rise up against the injustices of society?

Generalized though they may be, the validity of these observations is borne out by the fact that occasional departures from the norm were remarked upon. The free performances for all citizens which the Théâtre-Français was required to present during the early years of the Revolution provided a case in point, and seem to have lived on as a traumatic memory in the collective consciousness of the theatre-going public.

375   Popular audiences in privileged surroundings

Pier-Angelo Fiorentino, *Comédies et comédiens. Feuilletons* (2 vols., Paris: Michel Lévy, 1866), vol. ii, pp. 226–7

Those who can remember the productions that used to be given *gratis* maintain that there was something alarming about them. All one could see were bare arms, hairy chests, shaggy tresses, dangling legs, a mass of rags and tatters. The aspect was sinister, the smell unbearable. The actors went in fear and trembling before this hideous audience. They were met with coarse words, crude jokes, raillery and abuse. They had objects hurled at them. Once some vinegar was thrown over an actress's dress. Yet at the same time, beauty and talent could tame and fascinate this gaping mob. When Talma appeared, they would cry out: 'Long live the Emperor!' Then there would be a profound silence, as if the auditorium were completely empty, and after the speeches of the great artist, huge roars. The lion of the people had been quelled by his firm hand and powerful voice. One day, Madame Paradol had just come on stage, playing Agrippine, I believe. She was extremely beautiful and superbly dressed. There followed a quarter of an hour of clapping and shouting. They frequently demanded patriotic songs, or the entire house would burst out with vulgar choruses or make animal noises. At the exit doors there were riots. Look at the difference now! There is no possible comparison between that disorderly rabble and the public of today.

Similar perceptions of what constituted fit and proper behaviour for a given audience can be discerned in the adverse criticism directed at Dr Véron for lowering the tone of the Opéra by changing its production style and thereby attracting a different class of spectator.

376   Upheaval at the Opéra

'Chronique de la quinzaine', *Revue des Deux Mondes*, 4th series, 3 (1835), p. 232

Every day the Opéra is becoming rowdier and more boisterous in the pit. People now whistle[1] at the Opéra, they stamp their feet for all the world as if they were at the Folies-Dramatiques or the Funambules; and if you want to know the reason for this debasement you need look no further than the mistakes made by the administrator. In sacrificing art to meretricious effect, the pleasures of the mind to other, more facile ones, he is aping the managers of minor theatres and, by aping them, attracting their audience.

[1]   At this time, 'whistling' might refer either to the sound produced by pursing the lips or, more commonly, the shriller noise of blowing through the hollow shaft of a door key.

On the other hand, Talma was quick to defend these proletarian spectators against any charge of crude philistinism towards the performance itself. Notwithstanding their rough manners and grimy working clothes, once the curtain was up, he assured Hilarion Audibert, they were capable of exemplary attentiveness.

377   The challenge of unsophisticated audiences

Hilarion Audibert, *Indiscrétions et confidences: souvenirs du théâtre et de la littérature* (Paris: Dentu, 1858), p. 13

Such an audience brings out the best in me. You should come along on one of the free admission days, and see how they respond to every hint, how they applaud in all the right places, how warmly and to the proper extent. They seize every nuance, nothing escapes them; they are nature in the raw, if you like, but nature all the same, and as long as the actor is truthful, the working-class audience, that personification of truth, will respond immediately.

AUDIENCE INTERVENTION IN THE PERFORMANCE

Even under normal conditions, however, the supposedly civilized tenor of performance at the Théâtre-Français could be upset by an untoward reaction on the part of the audience.

Particularly vulnerable in this respect were the trial appearances by newcomers to the company, a state of affairs illustrated by the mixed reception accorded to Mlle George's début, at the age of 15, as Clytemnestre in Racine's *Iphigénie en Aulide*.

378   Mlle George is admonished, 1802

Geoffroy, *Cours de littérature dramatique*, vol. v, pp. 468–9

The public certainly did not indulge mademoiselle George; they even elevated rigour to the level of injustice when they tut-tutted the tone of voice in which she delivered the lines:

You know, and Calchas told you many times, etc.

[. . .] Mlle George was brave enough to start the speech again three times, until at last an affecting look in the direction of the pit, as if to reproach them for their intolerance, disarmed her severest critics and the liveliest applause atoned for their muttered disapproval.

Ostensibly in the name of aesthetic disputation, there were also occasions when disturbances in the auditorium became physically violent, as when the flames of a putative rivalry between Mlle George and her fellow débutante, Mlle Duchesnois, were fanned by rival press critics, and their partisanship then spread to members of the public.

379   A confrontation between rival fans, 1802

Ricord, *Fastes de la Comédie-Française*, vol. i, pp. 159–61

[. . .] the young people who frequented the theatre fell into line under the banners of these opposing critics: separate factions were formed, and the pit of the Théâtre-Français became a theatre of war.

After several minor skirmishes, which were scrupulously reported in the newspapers of the two parties, Mlle George appeared for a second time in the role of Phèdre [in which Mlle Duchesnois had recently made her début]; and it was on this memorable evening that the major battle occurred which was to determine the fate of the theatrical powers who had provoked the war. The army of Mlle Duchesnois took control of the front benches of the pit and set up its headquarters under the *lustre*, a position that was well chosen, as we shall see. That of Mlle George extended its lines and occupied more territory. As soon as Mlle George appeared, she was greeted by a triple salvo of applause which reverberated through all parts of the house. Each time that Phèdre took a breath, the applause began again with greater fervour and this running fire was renewed and sustained until the end of the play. Already shouts of victory could be heard, when Mlle Duchesnois's contingent, which one assumed had been put to flight, made the auditorium resound with its cries, summoning the *semainier* of the Comédie-Française. The latter appeared at once and was ordered to arrange for Mlle Duchesnois to play the role of Phèdre the next day, the actress being called for with a vehemence verging on frenzy. The company, taken aback both by the noise and by the demand, which betokened an even stormier performance on the following day, temporized by saying that *Phèdre* was playing in repertoire [. . .] The excitement reached a peak: words of abuse flew thick and fast and were followed by blows. At this point the army of Mlle Duchesnois, taking advantage of its position, covered the approaches to the barrier separating the pit from the orchestra and, while fighting continued, a column was detached to climb onto the stage and take it by storm. The confusion was matched only by the ferocity of the combatants, whereupon the military entered the auditorium. The arrest of a number of young men served only to aggravate the disturbance; and it would have become difficult to restore order without resorting to methods that would subsequently have been regretted if the actors had not made a solemn promise that Mlle Duchesnois would play Arménaïde (in *Tancrède*[1]) for her reception, and that in order not to delay the reception of Mlle George, the latter would play Mérope[2] immediately afterwards for hers. Tempers cooled, each of the two factions claimed victory and withdrew from the battlefield, leaving it strewn with hair, scraps of headgear and shreds of clothing.

[1] A tragedy by Voltaire, first performed in 1760.
[2] In Voltaire's tragedy of the same name, first performed in 1743.

The position was further complicated by the regular distribution of free passes to friends and sympathizers, a privilege jealously guarded not only by actors but more particularly by playwrights, intent on ensuring a favourable reception for their work. Harel took a typically caustic view of a practice, which to his commercial manager's mind had got progressively out of hand.

380   Free tickets galore

Harel *et al.*, *Dictionnaire théâtral*, pp. 44–5, 55

TICKET. For many years authors were only entitled to a fixed number of seats for first performances. Nowadays they can hand out virtually as many as they like. In the crown theatres above all this privilege has exceeded all bounds. It would not be difficult to name tragedies which have been given a first performance in the presence of large crowds without being seen by thirty paying customers. As a result, it has become extremely rare, and almost impossible, for a play to fail at its première. To boo on such an occasion is now, in the full sense of the term, an act of courage. Those who stood up for *Le Maire du palais* and *Maxime* maintain that it took even more courage to applaud [. . .]
BOX-OFFICE. Place where tickets are sold every evening to those members of the public who do not possess either mandatory passes, or complimentary passes, or courtesy passes, or management passes, or police passes, or authors' passes, acquired at half price or allocated free.

In this context, the clamorous demonstrations that accompanied the early performances in 1830 of *Hernani* (and two years later, of *Le Roi s'amuse*), and were seen as representing a decisive breach in the citadel of classicism by the forces of Romanticism, may be regarded as simply one more example of a long-standing tradition of critical intervention on the part of the audience, one that Hugo carefully engineered for maximum strategic effect and deliberately prolonged by his liberal distribution to supporters of tickets, which he pressed Baron Taylor to supply him with long after the author's customary entitlement to free passes had been exhausted.

381   The 'battle' of *Hernani*

(a) Joanny [Jean-Baptiste-Bernard Brisebarre], *Journal manuscrit* (Collection Rondel, Bibliothèque de l'Arsenal). Reproduced in Maurice Descotes, *L'Acteur Joanny et son journal inédit* (Paris: Presses Universitaires de France, n.d. [1956], pp. 66–7); (b) Contemporary caricature by Jean-Ignace-Isidore Gérard, known as Gran[d]ville. La Maison de Victor Hugo; (c) Letter from Hugo to Paul Lacroix, 27 February 1830, midnight, reproduced in Hugo, *Correspondance*, vol. I, p. 467; (d) C. A. Sainte-Beuve, letter to Adolphe de Saint-Valry, 8 March 1830, reproduced in *Correspondance générale*, ed. J. and A. Bonnerot (16 vols., Paris: Stock, Privat, Didier, 1935–7), vol. I, pp. 181–2

(a) Joanny

First performance: Hernani, Thursday 25 February 1830 – This play was a complete success, despite a well-organized opposition to it. And despite the original manner of its treatment, the beauties it contains will always elevate it above the low machinations of ill-will. I played my old *Duc de Silva* as well as I could possibly have done at a first performance. Perhaps in time this role will earn me some prestige.

Saturday 27 February 1830 – The work is vigorously attacked and vigorously defended. We shall see.

Monday 1 March 1830 – The conflict continues. What's good about it is that it brings in lots of people.

Wednesday 3 March 1830 – A merciless cabal. Ladies of quality are taking part in it; their style is to make a lot of noise at the most interesting moments and particularly during the final scene of the fifth act; only the noise they make is one of *laughter* . . . Bravo, my ladies!

Friday 5 March 1830 – The house is full and the whistling increases in hostility. There is something of a paradox about this: if the play is so bad, why do people come? if they are so anxious to come, why do they whistle? . . .

Saturday 6 March 1830 – Just the same; they've made up their minds. People are coming to see *Hernani* in order to make fun of the play and the actors, but they are coming, which they certainly wouldn't do for a good piece of work. Such is the public of today.

Monday 8 March 1830 – They're coming to hiss *Hernani*, but they're coming; if we were playing *Cinna*, the house would be empty.

Wednesday 10 March 1830 – A little rowdier still . . . fisticuffs . . . interruptions . . . police . . . arrests . . . shouts . . . bravos . . . whistles . . . uproar . . . crowds . . .

Friday 12 March 1830 – A large audience and still the same din. It's fun only for the box office.

Monday 15 March 1830 – Still the same old story. Huge crowd and huge commotion. Act in the middle of all that, and act well . . . if you can [. . .]

(b) Caricature by Gran[d]ville

(c) Letter from Hugo to Lacroix

The classicist cabal were intent on biting, and did so, but thanks to our friends, broke their teeth in the process. The third act was treated roughly, and will continue to be for some time yet, but the fourth reduced the house to silence, and the fifth was admirably [received], better even than on the first night. Mlle Mars was miraculous. She was recalled, and acclaimed, and overwhelmed with applause. She was exhilarated.

It will go well, I think. The takings for the first two performances have already reached 9,000 francs, *which is unheard of at the theatre*. Let us not sleep, however. The enemy are still watching and waiting. The third performance must demoralize them, if that is possible. So, in the name of our precious literary freedom, summon up our whole battalion of firm and faithful friends for Monday. I'm relying on you to help me pull this final tooth from the old classical warhorse. Back me up, and let us press forward!

(d) Letter from Sainte-Beuve to Saint-Valry

This evening we come to the seventh performance of *Hernani*, and things are beginning to become clear; they haven't always been. The first three performances, buoyed up by friends and the Romantically minded spectators, went very well; the fourth was stormy, although victory ultimately belonged to the brave; the fifth, only so-so; the cabal fairly restrained; the public indifferent, somewhat sarcastic, but allowing themselves to be won over at the end. The takings are excellent, and with a little more assistance from our friends we shall have rounded the Cape of Good Hope; that's the news report. Victor in middle of it all, cool, his eye to the future, trying to find time to write another play, a veritable Caesar or Napoleon, *nil actum reputans*, etc. [. . .] In short, the whole Romantic question has, by the very fact of *Hernani*, been advanced by many a mile, and the arguments of its opponents have been thrown into confusion; they will have to go to the trouble of constructing new ones, which Victor's next play will demolish in their turn.

Some two years later, in November 1832, the equally stormy reception that greeted *Le Roi s'amuse* was symptomatic of the undiminished scorn harboured by reactionary elements of the regular audience at the Théâtre-Français for Hugo's revolutionary approach to verse drama. Indeed, this may have been at least as responsible as any imputation of politically inflammatory sentiments for the play's sudden withdrawal from the repertoire at the express order of the minister of the interior, after only one performance.

382   Another embattled première

'Chronique de la quinzaine', *Revue des Deux Mondes*, 1st series, vol. 8 (1832), pp. 602–3

Besides, while awaiting the war of parliamentary portfolios and the outbreak of hostilities in Belgium, we have had the great battle of *Le Roi s'amuse* in the rue de Richelieu.

On the one hand, M. Victor Hugo entered the arena with some deplorable actors, but with a drama audacious both in thought and conception. He also had some auxillary battalions in the orchestra stalls, in the first gallery and in the pit. The remainder of his army commanded the heights of the second gallery and the amphitheatre. All these contingents, made up of young soldiers full of ardour and enthusiasm, fought bravely and with no weapons other than their stout hands.

The opposing army, deployed in small detachments, occupied the majority of the boxes, the balcony, and the *baignoires*. This was where it had positioned its artillery of whistles; from here it directed its treacherous broadsides of derision and yammering.

The fracas was appalling, the conflict long and unremitting. At last, after four hours of combat, it appeared that the poet's colours had carried the day. M. Victor Hugo was left in possession of the field.

However, if this one evening belonged to him, the enemy host swore to take its revenge two days later, and this war would doubtless have lasted an entire winter, as did that over *Hernani*. But hereupon M. d'Argout,[1] showing no respect for the sacred right of non-intervention, took it upon himself to become embroiled in the affair and prohibited all subsequent performances of *Le Roi s'amuse*.

The consequence has been, as in a comedy by Molière, that the defeated army has taken the side of M. Victor Hugo against the minister. And this is no more than justice. In this century of sovereign liberty, can we not at the very least be allowed to tear each other apart in peace within the lists of drama and poetry?

[1] Antoine, baron d'Argout, Minister of the Interior.

It is equally clear that even when there were no serious grounds for controversy the comportment of the Théâtre-Français audience was not always one of respectful attentiveness. Applause could be both delirious and sustained, expressions of disapproval every bit as demonstrative as those more commonly associated with the popular theatres, which were unburdened by any sense of theatrical pedigree. Moreover, the passage from one type of response to the other could be unpredictable as well as abrupt. The visiting German playwright, Kotzebue, whose observations on the post-revolutionary Parisian scene were as acute as they were sometimes condescending, has left a vivid description of the antics of some of his fellow spectators.

383   Audience reaction and counter-reaction

Kotzebue, *Souvenirs de Paris*, vol. II, pp. 225–30

A new play by Longchamp, *Le Pauvre Garçon malade*,[1] was interrupted by a fearful din and could not be played to its conclusion. The décor, representing two rooms side by side, was very fine and was much applauded when the curtain rose [. . .] I have been told that some young men go to first nights with a pair of bellows under their arms to which they attach a whistle so that while appearing to clap their hands they set these confounded bellows in motion and produce an unholy noise. It's said that they also put one in their shoes, arranged in such a way that as they rock forward on the balls of their feet and back onto their heels, the whistling reverberates throughout the house [. . .]

Some of the applause [for Mlle George's performance in Le Franc de Pompignan's tragedy, *Didon*] was marred by the sound of a whistle; this was certainly unmerited: the audience sensed its injustice and the applause which had at first been partisan and rather sparse, became universal. The whistler remained unabashed; no sooner had silence been restored than he began again. At this point the whole pit rose up quite spontaneously and shouted for several minutes: *Outside!* [*A la porte*]. But as the whistler could not be located, the pit turned towards the actress and compensated her for this minor unpleasantness with cries of *bravo* fit to shake the building. For the duration of this scene, which lasted at least five minutes, poor Mlle George suffered more than I can say. She stood throughout, holding her hands together and with her eyes and head lowered. The blood rising to her face obliterated her make-up. She indeed looked ravishingly beautiful.

[1] A play by Charles de Longchamps, which remained not only unfinished in performance but unpublished as well.

Unsettling it may well have been for the relatively inexperienced Mlle George, but at the same time the very stridency of such contradictory reactions could act as a source of inspiration to the performer, if we can believe Pierre Ligier, Hugo's original Triboulet in *Le Roi s'amuse*, who found himself driven to the limit by the warring salvoes of cheers and jeers during the play's première.

384   Ligier in the crossfire

Charles Monselet, *De A à Z: portraits contemporains* (Paris: Charpentier 1888), p. 197

I know not by what miracle I contrived to reach the end of my big soliloquy, with my foot on the sack holding my daughter. I think that the howling of the audience had made me over-excited. They told me I had been magnificent, that I had shown a touch of genius. The truth is that I must have looked like someone possessed. Whenever I recall that incomparable moment of my life, I feel a terrible malaise. I was carried away despite myself. It was no longer a performance. I was crying in earnest, I was screaming, I was hanging onto the bell of the ferry for dear life [. . .] Believe me, I wouldn't want to live through those hellish sensations again for a fortune.

There were those among the theatre-going public who were dismayed by these excessive displays of pleasure or displeasure. Looking back with nostalgia to the days of the *ancien régime* and to visits to the old Comédie in the Faubourg Saint-Germain, the antiquary and theatrophile Pierre-Victor bemoaned what he saw as a coarsening in critical attitudes, which had occurred under the successive impacts of revolution and restoration, and the part it had played in an allegedly general decline in theatrical standards.

385   A less discriminating public

Pierre-Victor, *Documents*, p. 32

At that time there was none of the howling or noisy protesting which all too frequently disrupt the performance and leave little room for doubt as to what the public wants. Spectators had only two ways of indicating their satisfaction or their dissatisfaction; to put their hands together for the one and their lips for the other constituted, as it were, their sole means of expression.

This clear-cut, forcible language was as readily understood as it was respected; and an actor was more sensible of a tribute thus awarded him than of the cries of *bravo* lavished by thoughtlessness and ignorance [. . .]

The major speeches in an actor's part still receive their due applause; but are people equally able to appreciate the whole, to grasp the essence and all the finer points? A lapse of memory or an unfortunate stress are condemned out of hand, while the crassest misapprehensions are frequently allowed to pass.

As for the final curtain call, it had until now been reserved for individual actors and normally invoked only as a way of recognizing an exceptional performance. After the Revolution, as audiences became more demonstrative and more demanding, a general call uniting the entire company was gradually introduced, an innovation resented by some actors as an intrusive chore and deplored by the arch-conservative Geoffroy as 'an excessive, meaningless, burdensome and even shameful demand made of good performers, tending to reward mediocrity and to promote cabals. It is nothing but a humiliating charade for the actor, whose reputation it in no way enhances and who is simply made to feel his subservience to the audience.'[1] In time, however, the mutually ingratiating rituals of actor–audience engagement began to proliferate. Leading players were applauded and encouraged to take a bow, not only at the end of a performance but also after each act and, not infrequently, after an important scene or single speech. The most popular might be greeted by a burst of clapping on their first (and every subsequent) appearance, while floral tributes soon ceased to function as a spontaneous gesture of delight, becoming consecrated as an expected, not to say mandatory, homage to star quality.

[1] *Journal des Débats* (21 July 1804).

386   The irrepressibility of applause

(a) Kotzebue, *Souvenirs de Paris*, vol. ii, pp. 253, 221; (b) Bouffé, *Souvenirs*, p. 266; (c) 'Chronique de la quinzaine', in *Revue des Deux Mondes*, 2nd series, 4 (1833), p. 119; (d) Gautier, *Histoire de l'art dramatique*, vol. ii, p. 88; (e) Gautier, *Histoire de l'art dramatique*, vol. v, p. 91

(a) Although it [a performance of Corneille's *La Suite du Menteur* at the Théâtre Louvois] was very indifferently played, the actors were nonetheless much applauded, not only as they walked on stage and before opening their mouths but again at their second or even third entrance. This irritates me [. . .]

Both of them [Mlle Volnais and Lafon in a production of Voltaire's *Zaïre* at the Théâtre-Français] were recalled after the performance. The noise went on for over a quarter of an hour before Mlle Volnais appeared; she took scarcely one pace onto the stage, bowed very sweetly, and walked off. Lafond [*sic*] did not come back at all, despite the bawling of the pit. The music started; people were still shouting; the curtain went up for the second play, but the performers could not make themselves heard; eventually, one of them stepped forward and said to the audience: 'Gentlemen, our colleague is indisposed.' People then calmed down, and things returned to normal.

(b) The evening [in June 1848, while he was on tour in Nantes] ended with all the actors being recalled, which in the provinces is not as commonplace as it is in Paris, where we see the spear carriers, the elephants and even the performing dogs recalled with the same enthusiasm as our foremost artistes.

(c) Not once did she [Mme Dorval, on tour in Rouen in September 1833] play *Antony*, *Les Enfants d'Edouard*,[1] *Clotilde* or *Le Joueur* without being recalled and being detained on stage by protracted volleys of applause, by cries of admiration and garlands of flowers tossed from all the boxes, or posies torn from ladies' waistbands.

(d) The applause for the young tragedienne [Mlle Rachel, playing the lead in Lebrun's tragedy *Marie Stuart* at the Théâtre-Français in December 1840] was enough to bring the house down; there was a deluge of flowers and gigantic bouquets; none of the outward tokens of a success had been neglected. On the subject of bouquets we would venture to make the following observation: that, in a moment of excitement, a woman should throw the spray of flowers she is holding in her hands, or the single bloom tucked into her hair, is perfectly understandable, or indeed that a man should pluck the rose or camellia from his buttonhole to manifest his pleasure to a singer or actress who has played her part well: this is natural and understandable; but we do not see why anyone should arrive at the theatre with his or her admiration already arranged in bunches and wrapped up in white paper; if by chance (a not uncommon chance at that) the *diva* should sing off key or perform badly that night, what should one do? Take the premature bouquets home again or present them at an unfortunate moment! Such displays ought to be reserved for exceptional triumphs; bestowing them so liberally only diminishes their value, and encourages inordinate vanity in the idols to whom they are addressed.

(e) Never has an actor received such applause [as Frédérick, starring in Félix Pyat's *drame*, *Le Chiffonnier de Paris*, at the Porte-Saint-Martin in May 1847]. Nonplussed, the *claqueurs* allowed the audience to have its head, full of admiration for the strength of the clapping, the echoing of the *bravos*, the unanimity of this entire house, even though they had been able to rehearse their own enthusiasm the night before. On this occasion they will have had to acknowledge the superiority of nature over art. Frédérick was recalled three times, between the acts and again at the end of the play.

---

[1] Tragedy by Casimir Delavigne, first performed in May 1833.

THE *CLAQUE*

As the preceding extract makes clear, applause was not exclusively, or even chiefly, the preserve of the paying public. By and large, the louder and more sustained the expression of pleasure, the likelier it was to have come from those professional guarantors of approval, the *claque*. Of ancient, if questionable, lineage, this practice first attracted notice as a venal trade under the First Empire, and after the Restoration it became progressively more entrenched in the Parisian theatre, if not in the provinces, ultimately operating as a fully-fledged commercial service, contracted to theatre managers to stimulate a favourable audience response or, if need be, to make good its absence. Pougin devotes a long entry to it in his dictionary, describing the *chef de claque* as 'a person of consequence', who by his day was also known to act as a backer or financial investor by offering to purchase in advance a certain number of performances of a production in return for the entire takings resulting therefrom. But there is ample corroborative evidence from the first half of the century too, including inside accounts by retired *claqueurs*, such as the pseudonymous book of memoirs by Louis Castel, who recalled the training he had received under an experienced *chef de claque* by the name of Mouchival before he himself rose to a similar position at the Opéra.

387   Organization of the *claque*, 1829

Robert [Louis Castel], *Mémoires d'un claqueur, contenant la théorie et la pratique de l'art des succès* (Paris: Constant-Chantpie et Levavasseur, 1829), pp. 34–5 and 39–42

Every *claqueur* enrolled in one of the brigades on duty at the Théâtre-Français must first provide himself with a decent suit of clothes, as it is possible for him to be detailed to *officiate* in the orchestra pit, the first gallery or even a reserved box. At all events, he is expressly forbidden to wear gloves for fear that he might, either absent-mindedly or from sheer laziness, neglect to take them off and the quality of his work would suffer in consequence.

Every *sociétaire* of the company is entitled to a round of applause on making an entry; except that the cheering must be more sustained for those who are members of the committee of management, as it is they who determine the number of tickets issued [to the *claque*]. The two *semainiers* must also be given a slightly warmer welcome than other *sociétaires*; this is a custom which has the force of law. An absolute silence is to be observed towards those *pensionnaires* who have not been *recommended* [for promotion to the *sociétariat*]; and even for those who have made good, the number of *claques* must not be allowed to exceed twelve, or the principal in their line of business may be disconcerted. There is no objection, however, to bestowing a thirteenth on the young ladies among them, as this may at a pinch be ascribed to chivalry on the part of the public.

The same drill is to be implemented for *exits*, with the proper gradations due to the status of each *artiste*. For the rest, it is sufficient to keep an eye on the group leader who, knowing the countersign, will make all the agreed gestures in accordance with long-range signals from the commander-in-chief [. . .] It is also necessary to be keenly on the lookout for lapses of memory. When an actor blusters and stamps his foot, there is not a moment to lose; quick, applause to the rescue; meanwhile the prompter will give him his cue and he will pick up the thread of his speech [. . .] Once inside the auditorium, Mouchival drew up his plan and specified the points at which his men would be stationed. The orchestra benches and the pit having been ceded to him in their entirety, he disposed his cohorts in such a way as to occupy the ends of rows; by this means, the spectators to whom he intended to sell tickets would of course find themselves surrounded on all sides, and disapproval on their part could be smothered if need be. He also went the rounds of the first and second galleries, where emotion was reckoned to be at its most intense. It was here that he normally placed his *dames-claque*, who were instructed to become moved at given moments and to make liberal use of their handkerchiefs in compliance with the *ars poetica* of success.

The advantages accruing to the playwright, the actor and above all, perhaps, the theatre manager from a well-disposed and well-primed *claque* were obvious; no less so, of course, was its potential for abuse. In a review of 1846 recording his 'profound admiration for the gentlemen *claqueurs* of the Gymnase', their 'swooning with joy' and 'convulsive' reception of a new comedy by Scribe,[1] Gautier's irony does not conceal the contempt he felt for this practice, and other writers were even more outspoken in condemning its parasitical influence and the scope it offered for intimidation of an audience, both in a psychological and, at times, alarmingly physical sense.

---

[1] Gautier, *Histoire de l'art dramatique*, vol. IV, pp. 379–80.

388   Bargaining with the *claque*, 1821

Ricord, *Fastes de la Comédie-Française*, vol. I, pp. 39–40

Nowadays, true patrons of the drama, neutral spectators and young people who are well bred have almost all deserted the pit, and more often than not the pit's voice is merely the product of a cabal: the shoddiest piece of work, provided it is supported by a body of *claqueurs*, will always attain the greatest vogue.

This mob has usurped the privileges of a public to which dramatic art was so deeply indebted and it arbitrarily controls the fate of those entering on a theatrical career; it determines the future of actors who, after playing for many years in the provinces, have a laudable desire to reap the fruits of their labour on the stage of the Théâtre-Français; and it dispenses the acclaim which mediocrity, by means of a protection it has bought, wrests from the genuine merit it oppresses.

The mob is made up of several different companies, whose leaders are known and who undertake contracts to secure the success or failure of a particular play or actor. Those who serve the major theatres are organized into gangs, and when there are various new plays or more than one actor to applaud or to subvert they will give each other mutual support [. . .] Authors are forced, on pain of being booed off the stage, to come to terms with these redoubtable gangs [. . .] Applause is regulated according to the financial sacrifices they have made, the gang-leaders pledging to puff [*mousser*] a piece in strict proportion to the money or the number of tickets they receive.

389   The *claque* in control

(a) Letter from the Paris prefecture of police, dated 31 May 1830, *Circulaire aux Commissaires de Police pour la répression des cabales dans les Théâtres* (Archives Nationales, F$_{21}$ 1046); (b) Review of *Les Belles Femmes de Paris* at the Variétés, 21 July 1839. Gautier, *Histoire de l'art dramatique*, vol. 1, pp. 279–80

(a) Letter from the Paris prefecture of police, 1830

Sir, the persistent complaints which have been reaching me for some time about a very serious offence which has found its way into the diverse theatres of the capital make it incumbent on me to issue certain directives in this connection: I refer to the cabals initiated by certain individuals who, under the name of *claqueurs* and in return for payment, undertake to ensure the success of plays which do not appeal to the public or to bring down those which rival interests and partisan feeling have singled out for retribution. Since the tyranny and brutality with which they exercise the prerogative they have assumed of imposing their views on respectable and enlightened members of the audience is one of the most potent factors in the disturbances which are troubling performances, as your own experience will have shown, it has become necessary to notify you of the action you should take in such circumstances, whether to uphold freedom of expression or to restrain its abuse when it oversteps the bounds within which it should reasonably be contained [. . .] when you see the auditorium transformed into an arena in which differing opinions have entered into veritable conflict, where it has become dangerous for the minority freely to voice their sentiments on the merits of the dramatic works submitted to the judgement of the public, and where, indeed, the paying customers, having to contend with these large gangs of paid *claqueurs*, are unable to defend the interests of good taste or protest against successes so shamefully procured without exposing themselves to assault and outrageous provocation, it then becomes imperative for you to intervene, and you are in duty bound to assert your authority to prevent any such acts of violence. In this eventuality, it is particularly important to identify the authors of the offences and to eject them forthwith from the auditorium, without prejudice to any charges that there may be grounds for bringing against them in the courts.

(b) Gautier in 1839

At the first performance [. . .] some people who had ventured to hiss a truly lamentable and highly improper scene were insulted and abused, then set upon, beaten black and blue and thrown out by the wretched *claque*, on the pretext that they represented a hostile cabal; nowhere in the world but in a Parisian audience would such an affront be tolerated. Incidents such as these recur all too often, to the shame of the public and the management alike; an auditorium ought not to be a boxing ring; it is extremely tiresome to arrive home with a bloody nose and an eye all the colours of the rainbow; no vaudeville is worth taking so many risks for. Might it not be possible to set up a machine with a wheel or a crank-handle that could activate a sufficient number of hammers and flaps to imitate the sound of the *claque* at those moments when it was necessary to warm things up? It would not cost much, it would be cleaner and it would smell less; as for the ethical implications, they would be absolutely identical, for there can no longer be a single dolt in Paris or bumpkin from Brives-la-Gaillarde who is so benighted as not to recognize rented applause: the real public do not wear alpaca jackets buttoned to the neck, neckerchiefs and cab drivers' capes at the height of summer. The *claque* doesn't fool anyone; it is an outdated, corrupt and barbaric device.

These sentiments were widely shared. Even the poor actor, often the beneficiary of their support, could at times feel threatened by the *claque*: Bouffé recalled in his memoirs an evening at the Gaîté when, having included in his performance a reference to the insufferable behaviour of the *chevaliers du lustre*, as they were dubbed, and having received an appreciative round of applause from the audience, he was accosted outside the theatre and remonstrated with by an irate bunch comprising the *chef de claque* at the Gaîté and his opposite numbers from five other boulevard theatres. In point of fact, a number of attempts were made to eradicate the practice: the journalist Charles-Maurice Descombes recorded a proposal by the Théâtre-Français's royal commissioner to impose a formal ban there as early as 1825,[1] and almost three decades later another newspaper critic announced its long-overdue demise and prematurely obituarized some of its unmourned iniquities in an article published in 1853.

---

[1] Charles Maurice [Descombes], *Le Théâtre-Français, monument et dépendances* (Paris: Garnier Frères, 1859), p. 143.

390   Reports of the *claque*'s demise are greatly exaggerated

'Plus de Claqueurs', reproduced in Fiorentino, *Comédies et comédiens*, vol. 1, pp. 126–9

The upshot of all this is that the official, organized, I was about to say legal, if I was not afraid of profaning the word, *claque* is under formal notice of liquidation. The order was communicated on Thursday to all theatre managers, the prefect of police, in association with the director of the office of Beaux-Arts, having resolved to abolish an infamy which has dishonoured the theatre for too long [. . .] No more will those doughty battlers form their tight, serried phalanxes; no more will they utter their stupid cries, their inane howls of laughter, their bellowing of enraged bulls. No more will they curse the audience or show them their fists simply for declining to take part in their frenzied joy or inconsolable grief. Nor will they, in fine, in defiance of the law, of decency and of morality, traffic in that sordid influence they can wield and enter into contracts of all kinds with theatre managers which the courts have to declare *illicit and contrary to public order*.

The *claque* has until now been an instrument of violence and oppression, a double-edged sword forever suspended over the heads of audience and performers alike. Decent people, repelled by the ignoble spectacle in the *parterre*, no longer dare to show any sign of approval, or else at moments of wild enthusiasm they will bring their hands together as gently as possible and without making a sound, for fear of being mistaken for *claqueurs*.

The *claque* survived this serious threat to its existence. After a week of unwontedly, almost lugubriously quiet performances, which pleased no one, because, as Fiorentino said later, 'the public were being asked to do what they never do, to make up their own minds, commit themselves and take an initiative, which is what people are most afraid of doing in Paris', the director of Beaux-Arts, Auguste Romieu, was petitioned by a deputation of playwrights and composers to restore the status quo. It still flourished, in as highly organized and irresistible a form as ever, some thirty years later, when Pougin was compiling his dictionary, and it was as a part-time member of the *claque* at the Théâtre-Français in the 1870s that André Antoine was exposed at first hand to the theatrical ethos against which he subsequently resolved to set his face.

A PROFILE OF AUDIENCE BEHAVIOUR

Apart from the noise made by *claqueurs*, there were countless other sources of distraction and disruption in the course of a performance. The respectfully and attentively hushed auditorium of today could not be taken for granted in the early nineteenth century, even at the grandest theatres; at the more popular, it was unthinkable, and arguably undesirable. Spectators were prone to indiscipline, exuberance or extra-dramatic priorities.

391 The irritation of latecomers

(a) Harel *et al.*, *Dictionnaire théâtral*, pp. 201–2; (b) Jouy, *Hermite de la Chaussée d'Antin*, vol. III, pp. 239–40; (c) Bouffé, *Souvenirs*, pp. 298–9

(a) RESERVING boxes. This is a privilege of the gilded aristocracy. The plebeians sit in the parterre and the galleries; the patricians, so as not to have their cosy way of life upset or not to be confused with people *who are not of their sort*, reserve boxes; they thus acquire the advantage of being able to arrive late for a performance, to acquaint everyone of their presence by the racket they make as they come in and to be harangued by the public when the noise they contrive to augment by moving their chairs and slamming their doors disturbs its calm enjoyment.

(b) Up goes the curtain.– *Shush! be quiet there!* . . . – Futile endeavour! Not ten lines can be heard during the first two scenes. Why do people have to dine at six o'clock? Why is it *du bon ton* to arrive late at the theatre, to talk loudly in the corridors, in a word, to create an effect when entering one's box? The first act is over, and we haven't been able to hear the exposition, which could well make the rest of the piece somewhat confusing, unless the author has taken care to devise another exposition for the following act; there are examples.

The boxes are full for act two: the ladies occupy the time by making sure they are noticed, by catching sight of one another, by scanning every part of the house through their lorgnettes; they lean out of their boxes from the waist up, make signs to each other with a nod of the head or a wave of the hand; and the plot has already reached a climax before these ladies have even discovered the names of the characters.

As for late arrivals to the parterre, the potential for annoyance and discomfort was even greater, given a theatre manager's natural propensity to maximize takings at every opportunity. Bouffé recalled a touring engagement at Rouen in 1837, at a time when not all provincial theatres were equipped with benches in the pit.

(c) It sometimes happened that, on days when the house was full, late-comers hoping to find room despite the crush were hoisted up over the heads and shoulders of spectators and passed from hand to hand until a gap presented itself which enabled them to land on their feet. I often witnessed these gymnastics, and the manager's delight, too, as he watched them; he much preferred a standing parterre to benches, as it allowed him to admit a hundred more paying customers.

392   In-house banter, 1804

Kotzebue, *Souvenirs de Paris*, vol. II, pp. 256–7

The audience here [at the Vaudeville] have adopted a singular custom. One cannot afford to leave the tiniest portion of a wrap dangling over the edge of a box without the parterre immediately calling out: 'Take the wrap away'. If the lady does not comply at once, the noise is redoubled and the shout becomes: 'Sling the wrap! off with it!' Almost always the ladies are compelled to give in to these riotous demands. When they do resist, the rumpus will continue until the police take a hand and enter the lady's box to request her to accede to the wishes of the public, or else there is a cry of 'Out you go!' Likewise, no one in a box can turn his back on the audience without hearing them cry: 'Don't turn your back, it's rude!'

393   Gossiping during the performance

(a) Press report, dated 18 July 1830, reproduced in Artus, *Théâtre Montmartre*, p. 20;
(b) Gautier, *Histoire de l'art dramatique*, vol. III, p. 44

(a) Press report, 1830

Furthermore, we would advise Messrs Seveste [the directors] that at every performance a little out of the ordinary at the Théâtre Montmartre there are seated in the orchestra benches two or three people (always the same ones, and we suspect them of being shareholders or subscribers), who take the auditorium to be a parlour, chatting away like magpies, especially when the curtain is up, and preventing their neighbours from following the thread of the play, and who take not a scrap of notice of the word *quiet* spoken in their ear, unless it be to step up the pace of the conversation and raise their voices by half an octave. In Paris itself, the management of theatres is far better; shareholders and subscribers do, it is true, make a lot of din banging doors in the corridors, but once the play has begun, they can be relied on to hold their peace.

But not, apparently, at all theatres within the city boundaries, for the *Courrier des Théâtres* was still complaining on 12 March 1828 about so-called ladies in the audience at the Porte-Saint-Martin who, showing little interest in the performance, 'talk at the tops of their voices [and] laugh in an immodest fashion'. That even devotees at the shrine of classical tragedy could be equally guilty of worldly considerations once their high-priestess had left the stage of the Théâtre-Français, is indicated by Gautier's wry comment on the disservice done to serious theatre-going by the cult surrounding Mlle Rachel.

(b) Gautier in 1843

Make no mistake, the interest attaching to Mademoiselle Rachel does not extend to the plays in which she appears: in *Phèdre*, for example, while she is on stage and delivering a speech, the entire house is intent, handkerchiefs remain in pockets, colds are extinguished, one can hear a pin drop. As soon as she has finished and disappeared into the wings, the talking starts up again, people turn away from the stage, or have a good laugh, or read the newspaper, in much the same way as they do in the Italian theatres once the *prima donna* has sung her big aria. Yet the lines being spoken are still Racine's, and every bit as fine as those which were applauded a moment before.

394   Eating and drinking in the auditorium

(a) Harel *et al.*, *Dictionnaire théâtral*, p. 167; (b) 'Le Boulevard du Temple. Autrefois et Aujourd'hui', *Artiste* (17 March, 3 and 12 May 1844), reproduced in Nerval, *Vie du théâtre*, pp. 73–4; (c) *Revue de Paris*, 13 (1835), p. 270; (d) Kotzebue, *Souvenirs de Paris*, vol. II, p. 265

(a) It is *de bon ton* to eat ice cream at the theatre. I know ladies from the best society who would not dream of touching any at Tortoni's[1] but cannot do without it at the Bouffes.

(b) A pungent odour of sausages and fried fish beckons the stroller further [along the Boulevard] to esconce himself at a table in the *Père de Famille* [. . .] it is here, too, that the patrons of the uppermost gallery, commonly known as the *poulailler*, come to lay in their supplies. These ample provisions, particles of which often end up on our jackets in the orchestra pit, usually constitute the evening meal for this discerning crowd, who start forming queues at four in the afternoon or turn up eagerly for the first of the two or three performances given at the minor theatres. Rousseau was at his happiest when reading during dinner; may it not be just as enjoyable, when you cannot read, to eat your dinner while giving ear to an interesting play? The common people have their fancies, no less than great men and great lords.
[. . .] Now what can you do with the remains of a sausage when you dine in the gallery? You drop it nonchalantly onto the gentlemen in the orchestra pit or the

balconies: that's how people behave everywhere [. . .] And what, you may ask, is the apple core collector doing all this time? This official applies himself diligently to his job; an apple core is more than a piece of refuse, it is an offensive weapon; note the distinction, and let us move on.

(c) At the Folies-Dramatiques, the public's exuberance made any display of taste impossible. When questioned by the police, one individual gave as his occupation: 'Superintendent of apple cores at the Folies-Dramatiques': his duties consisted of restraining, by any manner of persuasion or duress, the propulsion of these grubby leftovers. The use of the apple core is so ingrained at this address that the poor superintendent died, they say, of overwork.

(d) Also in the box [at the Ecole-Dramatique] where I was sitting was a party of ladies and gentlemen who ordered some beer; unfortunately for me, it was good beer and blew its bung, instantly covering my entire outfit with froth.

¹ Fashionable café on the Boulevard des Italiens.

It is equally certain that the private boxes of some theatres could be used for the satisfaction of other physical appetites in the course of the performance; what is less clear is just how widespread the immemorial symbiosis between theatre and prostitution remained at this time and for how long the habit of publicly flaunting it was tolerated. Whereas the theatrical almanac for 1791 seems to suggest that the practice was not only strictly localized but rather had been on the decline since the Revolution, Kotzebue was specific enough ten years later about the continuing availability of sexual transactions, and with the connivance of the management, to elicit indignant disclaimers from his translator, Pixérécourt. A further twenty years later Harel evidently thought it still prevalent enough, if discreetly secluded, to warrant one of the cynically amused comments in which his dictionary abounds.

395   Catering for other appetites

(a) *Almanach général* (1791), p. 182; (b) Kotzebue, *Souvenirs de Paris*, vol. 1, pp. 302–4; (c) Harel *et al.*, *Dictionnaire théâtral*, p. 201

(a) Les Grands Danseurs du Roi, ou Théâtre du Sieur Nicolet: This playhouse is of a totally different stamp from the others; formerly, people would go there in order to enjoy a degree of licence that could not be found anywhere else. You could sing, you could laugh, you could make someone's acquaintance [. . .] and sometimes a lot more, without anybody objecting; everyone could be as uninhibited there as in his own bedroom. Nowadays a better class of clientèle is beginning to change the tone of the theatre somewhat.

(b) Those of the girls who are a little higher up the scale exhibit themselves in the boxes of the Théâtre Montansier as they did before [i.e. at the time of his first visit to Paris in 1791]. They pay a very good price for these boxes, though you never see two of them in the same box; and depending on how generous they are in tipping the box-keeper, she will bring them knuckleheads and foreign visitors, eager for pleasure.[1] During the intervals, those who have not yet received any custom will stroll up and down in an elegant saloon known as the *foyer*, where one can look them over and bargain with them at one's ease[2] [. . .] One night during my stay in Paris I saw a very heated quarrel break out between two of these charmers, which ended with their dresses all torn and in shreds. This fracas, which became the talk of Paris for a whole day, persuaded the police to outlaw the display of such merchandise inside the foyer; but the ban was not effective for more than a few days.

Note 1 There is not a word of truth in all this, unless M. Kotzebue be one of the greenhorns of whom he speaks.

2 At the time when M. Kotzebue came to Paris, orders had been given prohibiting their admission to the foyer and not one of them could be seen there.[1]

(c) BOX. A respectable lady, when she goes to the theatre, will not sit anywhere but in a box. There are several kinds of box; boxes with lattices, for persons who want to see the play; open boxes for those who want to be seen; boxes in the roof void for those who want neither the one nor the other.

---

[1] Kotzebue's version of events receives some support from the testimony of a visitor from England, who describes the Montansier's foyer as a place where 'the ladies of the "Palais royal" roam at large, as at Covent-garden and Drury-lane' ([J. G. Lemaistre] *A rough sketch of modern Paris* (London: J. Johnson, 1803), p. 129).

Most exuberant of all, and most numerous, were the audiences who flocked to the theatre on Sunday, a day of rest and distraction for all classes of spectator. Managers could be assured of a good house and of substantial takings at the box office, whatever the play advertised: indeed, billing a play for the Sabbath came to be symptomatic of its relative lack of commercial appeal, no play being pressed into service in this way before its twentieth performance unless it was doing very poor business during the remainder of the week. But by the same token, Sunday audiences were known to be less easy to please: they were demanding and inflammably critical. Some actors dreaded having to appear on Sundays, while others positively relished the challenge, a challenge to which not all plays were equal: by way of illustration, Harel mischievously instances the unfavourable reception of a comedy by François Ancelot, *Le Maire du palais*, which, he says, merely 'fell flat on a weekday' but would have been 'hissed off the stage on a Sunday'.[1]

Irrespective of the day of the week, however, it would be true to say that the lower the social class of an audience the more demonstrative their response was likely to be. Auger's generalization about the unconstrained reactions of melodrama audiences in the course of a performance cannot be doubted, but his further assertion, that 'it is above all in the theatres intended for the working classes, from the Porte-Saint-Martin to the Porte-Saint-Antoine, that the behaviour of the public shows a frankness of gesture and of language which confirms the importance of dramatic art as a means of influencing these classes',[2] requires some qualification. It would be a mistake to conclude that the effect of a performance on such uncultured audiences was simply to induce a naïve acceptance of illusion as if it were reality, together with an unthinking proclivity to identify with the situations and personages of the play. On the contrary, passivity of this kind was tempered by an active appreciation of the skill displayed in presenting that illusion and an alertness to the almost metatheatrical dimension in the act of performance itself. When, for instance, a slight mishap jeopardized the dramatic effectiveness of a moment in act I of *Lucrèce Borgia*, Frédérick's instantaneous improvisation of additional business, perfectly in character, was suitably acclaimed by the Porte-Saint-Martin audience (and sufficiently admired by Hugo himself to be incorporated in the published text of the play).

[1] Harel *et al.*, *Dictionnaire théâtral*, p. 119.
[2] Hippolyte Auger, *Physiologie du théâtre* (Paris: Firmin–Didot, 1839–40), vol. III, p. 267.

396   The rewards of improvisation

Adèle Foucher, Mme Victor Hugo, *Victor Hugo raconté par un témoin de sa vie* (2 vols., Paris: A. Lacroix, Verboeckhoven, 1863), vol. II, p. 343

Frédérick's presence of mind rescued a delicate situation: when Gennaro [played by Frédérick] discovers that his colour-sash has been sent him by Lucrèce, he casts it from him. The sash became tangled up in his sword and in a snood that he had seen fit to wear on his head. Some derisive laughter could be heard [. . .] M. Frédérick drew his sword, seized hold of the sash and the snood and trampled them underfoot with so lordly and irate a gesture that he was applauded by all parts of the house.

A similar observation was made by Thackeray on a visit to Paris in 1840. Noting the current vogue in the boulevard theatres for melodramas based on biblical subjects, he was apparently struck less by the performances themselves than by the readiness of the public to respond overtly and proactively to the pseudo-evangelistic spirit of the occasion.

397   Audience participation

W. M. Thackeray, *The Paris sketch book. The works of William Makepeace Thackeray* (26 vols., London: Smith, Elder & Co., 1895–1900), vol. XVI, pp. 267–8

Vast numbers of schoolboys and children are brought to see these pieces; the lower classes delight in them. The famous 'Juif Errant', at the theatre of the Porte St. Martin, was the first of the kind, and its prodigious success, no doubt, occasioned the number of imitations which the other theatres have produced.

The taste of such exhibitions, of course, every English person will question; but we must remember the manners of the people among whom they are popular; and, if I may be allowed to hazard such an opinion, there is, in every one of these Boulevard mysteries, a kind of rude moral [. . .] Vice is vice on the Boulevard; and it is fine to hear the audience, as a tyrant king roars out cruel sentences of death, or a bereaved mother pleads for the life of her child, making their remarks on the circumstances of the scene. '*Ah, le gredin!*' growls an indignant countryman. '*Quel monstre!*' says a grisette, in a fury. You see very fat old men crying like babies; and, like babies, sucking enormous sticks of barley-sugar. Actors and audience enter warmly into the illusion of the piece [. . .]

For supposedly unsophisticated audiences, these would seem to have been perfectly well aware of their allotted role in the theatrical equation.

Part Three: Italy

Edited by KENNETH RICHARDS AND LAURA RICHARDS

Introduction

We cannot strictly speak of an Italian theatre at this time. Italy was not unified until 1860, and for much of the second half of the eighteenth century the political order remained that which had been settled by the treaty of Aix-la-Chapelle in 1748: the peninsula was divided into a number of small- or medium-sized states, and much of it was governed by foreign powers, particularly Bourbon or Habsburg. Even those states officially independent were either subject to foreign influence or potential prey to foreign territorial ambitions: thus Genoa, although autonomous, had its independence circumscribed by French protection, and Venice, for a long while one of the most admired of the small Italian states, by the mid-century was a shadow of her former self politically and economically, her *terra firma* territories coveted by Austria. The tiny republics of Lucca and San Marino, which had managed to retain their independence through numerous vicissitudes, were more curiosities than models for any future political development in the peninsula.

For much of the eighteenth century the Italian peninsula was considered by most English and continental commentators, and until recently by most later historians, as politically quiescent and economically and culturally backward, endlessly fascinating as a stamping ground for the educated and well-heeled on the Grand Tour in pursuit of the antique or the paintings of the Venetian *vedutisti*, but contributing little to the explorations of the European Enlightenment or to the main patterns of political and economic development in the period.[1] In fact, there was more of interest and innovation in mid- and late eighteenth-century Italy than there appeared: it included lively and challenging journalism modelled on the English examples of the *Tatler* and the *Spectator* and pioneered by Gasparo Gozzi and others in Venice and by the founders of the highly respected and influential journal, *Il Caffe*, in Milan; original thinkers such as Beccaria, who posited highly original ideas about the treatment of crime; savants who assembled invaluable collections of artistic, historical and popular cultural records; and influential treatises written by political economists and thinkers such as Antonio Genovesi (1713–69) and Ferdinando Galiani (1728–87), while polymaths and theoreticians such as Francesco Algarotti (1712–64) and Francesco Milizia (1725–98) explored topics including art and architecture, theatre buildings and the function of theatrical activity in the community.[2]

Yet it must be acknowledged that the last decades of the eighteenth century produced little of great theatrical or dramatic significance. As will be seen below, by the end of the century the long, 300-year domination of European theatre by Italian architects, stage and scene designers and machinists was coming gradually to an end. As far as playwriting was concerned, Goldoni left Venice for Paris in 1761, and was to remain there to his death in 1793, the most interesting centre of dramatic activity in the century, Venice, thereafter being dominated by the work of decidedly lesser dramatists such as Gozzi and Chiari. Elsewhere there were no dramatists of note until the emergence of Alfieri in the last two decades of the century. These final decades of the century also saw the activities of the last travelling companies of the *commedia dell'arte*, the departure from the Comédie-Italienne of virtually all the Italian players by 1782, and the death of many of the great actors of the age, such as Antonio Sacchi (Truffaldino) and Carlo Bertinazzi (Carlino), and of company managers such as Girolamo Medebach.[3] Some elements of improvised playing lingered on, particularly in Naples and southern Italy, in the work of early to mid-nineteenth-century popular performers such as Antonio Petito. The penultimate decade of the eighteenth century also saw the publication of a major work of Italian theatre history, *Notizie istoriche de' Comici italiani che fiorirono intorno all' anno MDL fino a' giorni presenti* (two volumes, 1782), by the former actor, Francesco Bartoli (1745–1806).

All the while the peninsula remained divided and in thrall to foreign political, economic and cultural influences and interests. Nor did things change substantially with Napoleon's invasion of Italy in 1796: where at that time there were ten states in the peninsula, following the Congress of Vienna settlement in 1815 there were still eight. Inevitably, then, these independent states, while they undoubtedly had much in common, have not only rich and complex, but inevitably somewhat diverse histories, for there were wide divergences between them in political organization, social and even religious attitudes and cultural interests and emphases. Of course, notwithstanding this diversity some general observations are applicable to the peninsula as a whole, both before and after the entry of Napoleon on the scene, and some conditions can be said to have been widespread, even if they did not necessarily apply in all territories. Thus most Italian rulers were still absolutist and authoritarian and power was concentrated in a few hands; the influence of affluent and conservative forces in the Church remained strong; a potentially powerful middle class was emerging and the most successful in the trades and professions enjoyed ever more favourable standards of living. Poverty, however, was widespread and the gulf between rich and poor remained substantial; social services, policing and the like outside the main cities were patchy and generally primitive; opportunities for education were limited, and illiteracy among the poor was ubiquitous, while crime, as in any society where life for the majority is harsh and precarious, was widespread and travel not always safe or easy. Finally, nearly all regions showed traces, indeed many of them quite magnificent records, of the great civilizations of the remote past.

The most obvious broad difference in the peninsula as a whole, and one which had hardened since the Renaissance, was that between the comparatively prosperous north and a markedly poorer agricultural south, where an essentially feudal system survived. There were many differences between the major cities of the north, however, such as Venice, Florence, Genoa and Parma, all of which had been shaped by different economic and geographical conditions and by many different kinds of foreign occupation or influence, so that they were politically, socially and culturally distinct. Their theatre activities inevitably reflected those distinctions. For one thing, language remained divisive, both in the sense that the literary language was a rather arbitrary construct, rooted in the Tuscan, and in that a significant amount of cultural expression found outlet in local dialect not readily comprehensible elsewhere. Dialect drama was one obvious example of the cultural exclusivity of a region, for while it could be vital in its own locale, it did not always translate well to theatres elsewhere in the peninsula. Nor, of course, was local rooting merely a matter of language: the situations, characters and stage 'business' of a play could as much reflect the *mores* of a community as its dialogue could. Furthermore, different cities and regions tended to display different kinds of dramatic and theatrical tone, interest and expertise for reasons far from easy to calculate: what took in Naples might well not appeal, or might make quite a different impact, in Florence or Turin, and vice versa.

Many of the characteristics and differences remarked above were to persist long into the nineteenth century, notwithstanding the impact made by the French Revolution, the Napoleonic conquest of Italy, the Risorgimento and Unification. For example, the Risorgimento was largely driven, and Unification achieved, by a minority consisting of the urban, middle class, educated and politically active; the vast majority of the people, in what was still a predominantly agricultural peninsula, were little engaged, even if, in due course, they were to be significantly affected, by the great political events of the time. One can distinguish roughly two key periods during the period of Napoleonic domination: that from 1796 to 1799, the period of the first Napoleonic campaign, which saw the creation of the Cisalpine Republic and events through to the treaty of Campoformio in 1799, including the episode of the Partenopean Republic in Naples; the second from 1800 to 1814, when most of Italy was under French rule, either direct, as in the Kingdom of Italy based on Milan, or indirect, as in some of the small dependent states or in the Kingdom of Naples. Even before the invasion local revolutionary groups had begun to emerge in the northern Italian states, most of them pro-French, and the invasion at first attracted little popular hostility. But the tendency of the French army to live off the land changed sympathy to resentment, and the occupation in its turn bred an Italian nationalism that was to persist after the restoration of much of the old order, fuelling opposition to foreign presences and inherited structures, encouraging the formation of urban opposition, issuing eventually in insurrections in the major towns and leading finally to the Unification of 1860.

Of course, Italian theatre, being essentially urban and, even in its more popular dimensions, dominated by bourgeois values, in the early nineteenth century reflected that burgeoning sense of national consciousness. Many of the decades which concern us here saw great political ferment as the movement towards unification gathered momentum, driven too by the sentiments of the Romantic movement that had by now begun to penetrate the Italian arts, and which were, in complex ways, a revolt not only against French-oriented classicism but also against foreign domination, political fragmentation, economic retardation and intellectual obscurantism. As far as Italian theatre is concerned, this is a period often regarded as one of dismal inadequacy, a judgement largely but perhaps not wholly true; for it was also a period of fermentation, the possibility of political change for many presaging the possibility of significant reform in the theatre. Many actors and actresses were quick to associate themselves with the mood and activities of the Risorgimento: some, like Gustavo Modena, were so activist that for periods they had to live in exile; others, like Tommaso Salvini, helped to stimulate political unrest and were actively engaged in the insurrections of 1859 and 1860. Many dramatists, too, were committed nationalists, and patriotic themes dominated in many plays from 1796 through to the 1860s.[4]

Yet although these political events excited great cultural ferment and a sense of engagement in a great cause, they did not generate any strikingly original or vital new drama. For much of the first half of the nineteenth century, indeed, the Italian theatre was dominated by translations, adaptations or imitations of French melodrama and the well-made play, when it was not in the shadow of Goldonian comedy and Alfierian tragedy. Comedy in particular was the Italian forte, invariably with a bias to the farcical, and to the real, the natural, as Goethe remarked; yet even comedy, although rooted in native traditions, showed little inspiration. Moreover, if dramaturgic talent was in short supply, general working conditions in the Italian theatre did little to encourage it. Throughout the late eighteenth century and the first half of the nineteenth century most acting companies remained, as they had been in the past, itinerant, touring the major cities, renting theatres for short seasons and transporting props and scenery as they moved from place to place. Dramatists might supply the companies almost on a house-dramatist basis, but they could not be sure their work would receive either considerate staging or sympathetic critical notice.

But models for possible future change were becoming available. The early decades of the nineteenth century saw the establishment of a number of acting companies in major cities, who enjoyed official approval and state subsidy, and who were located in their own permanent theatre buildings. The most considerable of these companies, and the one that holds a special place in nineteenth-century Italian theatre history, was the Compagnia Reale Sarda; one of the first in the peninsula to be formally constituted as a state-subsidized municipal theatre, its lengthy and important activites will be examined in more detail below.[5] The privileged companies promised significant change, for the Napoleonic occupation had provided the occasion to pilot notions of radical theatrical reform; and even if few of these attempts were realized, or, if realized, lasted for any length of time, that so many programmes for reform were formulated both focused attention on the need for significant change and gradually gave impetus to the attempts of those who sought to effect it. However, the emergence of these companies, and the presence in them of actors and actresses of considerable ability, cannot conceal the generally poor condition of the Italian theatre in the early decades of the nineteenth century: for most, the emergence was a brief one and, as in the second half of the eighteenth century, the lyric stage flourished in the first half of the nineteenth while the *teatro di prosa* languished.[6]

By the later 1850s the social and financial status of some great players had improved enormously, and there was more generally an improvement in the discipline and morale of many companies. Yet much, too, remained as before. The quality of the scripted drama remained low: the language problem was unresolved, dependence on foreign imports persisted, even the better native plays were heavily imitative of foreign example or were limp reworkings of Goldonian and Alfierian motifs, marked by excessive rhetoric, lachrymose sentiments, unpersuasive situations and implausible characters. Regular theatrical activity continued to be financially precarious, and the theatrical infrastructure – front-of-house and backstage facilities and organization, and technical accoutrements such as machinery and lighting – even in the major cities remained backward compared to many other parts of Europe, and was to remain so until the end of the century. Furthermore, at least as far as organization and infrastructure were concerned, much in the lyric theatre was comparable to the regular stage. We are primarily concerned here with the regular theatre, but it is difficult when discussing that to make a clear and firm distinction between the *teatro di prosa* and the *teatro lirico*, and perhaps at no time is that more the case than in the period covered by this volume, for two reasons: first, the sheer variety of dramatic and theatrical forms; and second, a marked tendency among theatre and company managers to mix different dramatic and theatrical genres. If one looks for a reason for this variety of forms and promiscuous mixing of genres, it may lie in the fact that the Italian theatre had never traditionally been, with a few distinguished exceptions, a theatre of dramatists, but one in which the visual rather than the literary predominated, a theatre of performers and scenographers.

Many visitors to Italy during the period remarked on the many different kinds of theatrical entertainment encountered, from live street performers to puppet theatres, from dance and mime and improvised drama, to comic and serious opera, and they noted too how ballets often punctuated the acts of an opera, rather as *intermezzi* divided the acts of a Renaissance *dramma erudito*; how plays and musical pieces were mingled in a programme or how a single theatre housed indiscriminately musical and dramatic performances. The writings of these English and continental visitors, perforce more numerous in the decades following the fall of Napoleon, provide some of the most lively and detailed accounts of theatre in this period. Most notable, of course, are Goethe's account of his two-year-long visit in the 1780s and the descriptions provided by Stendhal, who lived for many years in Italy, of life in Milan, Rome and Naples, and whose *Vie de Rossini* is one of the most stimulating biographies of an opera composer ever written. If we have drawn on them here only very slightly, it is because we have preferred to cite from many whose writings are little known; and there are good modern translations of both Goethe and Stendhal to which we would direct the reader.[7]

The selection of short documents below is inevitably personal and impressionistic and, in the limited space available, much has had to be omitted. But this selection has at least tried to achieve fairly broad coverage, to mix familiar and less well-known passages, to include some texts unfamiliar to Italian, let alone English, readers, and to point up how, in some notable respects, conditions in the Italian theatre were different in this period from those found in many other parts of Europe, even if many of the performed plays were the same or similar. Undoubtedly the period surveyed here saw a distinct improvement in the condition of theatre in Italy: players began to find larger and more regular audiences; 'star' players emerged who were to bestow distinction on the stage; the art of acting came to be taken more seriously than it had been hitherto; and if there were no great new dramatists, at least the work of Shakespeare was beginning to be discovered.[8] But none of that must be exaggerated: towards the end of the century we find the greatest Italian actor of the age, Tommaso Salvini, warning his son off an acting career, and Luigi Bellotti-Bon, one of the most ambitious of actor-managers, committing suicide after going bankrupt.[9] Hard times were always just around the corner, and, in a system dominated by touring, there were many corners.

NOTES

1. Recent studies in English of eighteenth-century Italy include D. Carpanetto and G. Ricuperati, *Italy in the age of reason, 1685–1789* (London: Longman, 1987) and Franco Venturi, *Italy and the Enlightenment: studies in a cosmopolitan century* (London: Longman, 1972), while a work of broader scope is Stuart Woolf, *A history of Italy, 1700–1860: the social constraints of political change* (London: Methuen, 1979). Extremely useful are the relevant volumes in collections like *La civiltà veneziana del Settecento* (Florence, 1960). For the history of the Risorgimento period, standard English texts are Harry Hearder, *Italy in the age of the Risorgimento, 1790–1870* (London: Longman, 1983), and Denis Mack Smith, *The making of Italy 1796–1866* (2nd edn, London: Macmillan, 1988).

2. Franco Venturi in particular, in essays like those gathered in *Italy and the Enlightenment*, provides a seminal revaluation of the Italian contribution to the period.

3. For broad overviews, see, in English, M. Carlson, *The Italian stage. From Goldoni to D'Annunzio* (Jefferson, NC and London: McFarland, 1981), and in Italian the relevant

chapters in Roberto Tessari, *Teatro e spettacolo nel Settecento* (Bari: Laterza, 1995), and Claudio Meldolesi and Ferdinando Taviani, *Teatro e spettacolo nel primo Ottocento* (Bari: Laterza, 1991). Also extremely useful are the relevant sections of Federico Doglio's *Teatro in Europa*, 3.1 (Milan: Garzanti, 1981). We are throughout indebted to three major resources: Luigi Rasi, *I comici italiani* (2 vols., Florence, 1897–1905); N. Leonelli, *Attori tragici, attori comici* (2 vols., Milan, 1940–4); and the volumes of the *Enciclopedia dello Spettacolo* (Rome, 1960–62).

4. For the drama of the period, see Federico Doglio (ed.), *Teatro e Risorgimento* (Bologna: Cappelli, 1961), and Giorgio Pullini, *Il teatro in Italia*, vol. III, *Settecento e Ottocento* (Rome: Edizioni Studium, 1995).

5. The best study remains Lamberto Sanguinetti, *La Compagnia Reale Sarda (1820–1855)* (Bologna: Cappelli, 1963).

6. The Italian lyric stage has received much attention recently in English, notably by David Kimbell, *Italian opera* (Cambridge: Cambridge University Press, 1991), and two studies by John Rosselli, *The opera industry in Italy from Cimarosa to Verdi: the role of the impresario* (Cambridge: Cambridge University Press, 1984) and *Singers of Italian opera* (Cambridge: Cambridge University Press, 1992).

7. Goethe, *Italian journey*, translated by W. H. Auden and Elizabeth Mayer (Harmondsworth: Penguin, 1962), and later editions; Stendhal, *Rome, Naples and Florence*, translated Richard Coe (London, 1959), and Stendhal, *Life of Rossini*, translated Richard Coe (New York, 1970).

8. See in particular Laura Caretti (ed.), *Il teatro del personaggio. Shakespeare sulla scena Italiana dell'800* (Rome: Bulzoni, 1979).

9. See Laura Richards, 'Italy, 1886–1919', in *Theatre in Europe: a documentary history. Naturalism and symbolism in European theatre, 1850–1918* (Cambridge: Cambridge University Press, 1996).

I   *After Goldoni*

The eighteenth-century Italian comic stage was dominated by the work of Carlo Goldoni (1707–1793), perhaps the greatest, as he was the most prolific, of Italian dramatists. It was Goldoni who reformed the comic stage, gradually eliminating the crudities and excesses into which too many of the traditional improvising masked comedians had fallen, and substituting for their plot and action *scenarii*, carefully crafted plots and fully scripted dialogue, in effect establishing the authority of the dramatist in the theatre. Among his many enduringly successful plays are *I due gemelli veneziani* (The Venetian twins, 1747), *La vedova scaltra* (The artful widow, 1749), *La locandiera* (The mistress of the inn, 1753), *La bottega del caffè* (The coffeehouse, 1750), the *Villeggiatura* trilogy (1761), *I rusteghi* (The Boors, 1760) and *Le baruffe chiozzotte* (The Chioggian squabbles, 1762). Most of Goldoni's work falls outside the *terminus a quo* of this account, but must be mentioned here for the powerful influence it exercised on nearly all Italian comic drama and theatre in the late eighteenth and early nineteenth centuries. Goldoni's theatrical work in Italy was in large measure completed by 1761, when he left his native Venice, for whose theatres most of his plays had until then been written, to try his fortune in Paris with the Comédie-Italienne. Although later he occasionally sent back plays to Venice for production there, as was the case with one of his very best, *Il ventaglio* (The fan, 1764), by the 1780s he had retired from the theatre and, after a spell as tutor to the French royal children, had settled down at Versailles on a state pension to write his engaging *Mémoires* (1787).[1] Although in the latter decades of the eighteenth century his popularity with audiences waxed and waned, his influence was ubiquitous in Italian comic drama, particularly in the early and mid-nineteenth century, and today he remains the most frequently performed Italian dramatist in Italy.

In 1748 Goldoni, whose involvement with theatre had hitherto been intermittent, was persuaded by the actor-manager Girolamo Medebach (1706–90) to commit himself full-time to a theatrical career by contracting as house-dramatist to the Medebach troupe at the Teatro Sant'Angelo in Venice. It was here that he began his reform of comedy. Yet it is perhaps no exaggeration to say that the great resurgence of theatre, particularly comic theatre, in Venice in the middle decades of the eighteenth century owed as much to the influence of Medebach as it did to the work of Goldoni. Medebach was in his thirties when he took up with a company of rope-dancers led by Gasparo Raffi, married Raffi's actress daughter, Teodora, took over the direction of the company, trained its performers in the methods of the 'straight' theatre, and established them in the little San Moisè Theatre in Venice. He was an astute impresario with a good business sense, an eye for talent and a professional buoyancy that enabled him long to survive in a rough market. The combination of those talents and the play-crafting skill of Goldoni helped to make Venice for several decades the centre of regular theatre activity in Italy. In the seventies and eighties Medebach's fortunes declined and his last years seem to have been gloomy, but as much might be said of many of the century's actors and actresses. Acting troupes proliferated: in addition to those of Sacchi and Medebach, there were companies led by Giuseppe Imer, Giuseppe Lapy, Pietro Rossi, Luigi Perelli, Carlo and Maddalena Battaglia, and many others, the majority probably of mediocre quality, although their history has never been adequately investigated.[2] But there were, too, many outstanding performers, and in certain respects one might say that in Italy, as much as elsewhere in Europe, the second half of the century saw the beginning of a great age of actors and actresses. Reading the waspish or despairing comments of the comic dramatist Carlo Gozzi and the tragic dramatist Vittorio Alfieri on the moribund state of Italian theatre, one might doubt that to be the case, but their disappointment was occasioned less by the paucity of fine acting talent than it was by the frustrating inadequacies of the theatrical superstructure in Italy – the vagabond status of the profession, the often ramshackle or obsolete facilities, the financially precarious nature of theatrical activity, the lack of official support, the dependence upon foreign, particularly French drama, the ascendancy of the lyric stage – all of which helped to foster casualness and indiscipline in the companies and a reluctance to experiment or innovate. Equally disheartening was the hard fact that much of the finest Italian acting talent in the eighteenth century was much more frequently found abroad than at home: not only at the Comédie-Italienne in Paris, but in the German States, Poland, Russia and elsewhere.

Supposed by some to be in part responsible for Goldoni's departure from Venice was his great rival, Carlo Gozzi (1720–1806). Where Goldoni seems to have taken up playwriting because it was a more entertaining and potentially more rewarding profession than that of advocate, Gozzi was of aristocratic lineage, a conservative and a traditionalist, hostile to the bourgeois spirit he detected in many of Goldoni's social comedies. Gozzi for a time resuscitated the stock masks in a comedy of fairy-tale-like fantasy and spectacle in his *fiabe*, the best known of which today are the first, *L'amore delle tre melarance* (The love of three oranges, 1761), a gauntlet deliberately thrown down to challenge Goldoni, and the pieces which followed through to 1765, such as *Turandot*, *La donna serpente* (The serpent woman) and *Il mostro turchino* (The blue monster). These won success abroad, later lent themselves to adaptation for opera and today are occasionally revived. Gozzi's later plays, although they enjoyed a certain success, are of much less interest today: based on Spanish models, perhaps the best known is *Droghe d'amore* (Love potions, 1777). Gozzi's work remained prominent in the Venetian theatres through to the 1780s, after which, in Italy at least, his popularity and influence quickly began to fade.

Venetian theatrical life was intense and competitive, and the polemics between Goldoni and Gozzi extended to include the third important dramatist who worked there in the eighteenth century, Pietro Chiari (1712–85). Little read or performed today, Chiari, a native of Brescia, and for a time a priest, settled in Venice in 1747 and wrote a number of very popular plays and novels, such as *La scuola delle vedove* (The school for widows, 1749) and *La francese in Italia* (The French girl in Italy, 1759). Some of his work was translated into English.

For the second half of the eighteenth century Gozzi's *Memorie inutili* (Useless memoirs, 1797–8), along with Goldoni's memoirs, are a rich mine of information about the Venetian theatre, notwithstanding the author's frequently caustic comments on the selfishness and self-centredness of players. Although in the passages cited below Gozzi writes primarily about the Sacchi company and the Venetian theatre, much of what he says has a bearing on the wider eighteenth-century theatrical scene. But his reminiscences bear most on comedy and on exotic and spectacular theatre. What they also incidentally bear witness to is that for all the Goldonian reform of comedy and the increasing emergence in Italy of the professional dramatist, improvised drama, often with dialect connections, persisted to the end of the century and beyond. In the nineteenth century traditions of masked and improvised drama took on even more distinctly regional characteristics, notably in Naples and southern Italy.

[1] The best introduction to Goldoni's life and work remains the memoirs themselves. There is no modern long study of Goldoni in English, although Chatfield-Taylor's biography of 1914 remains useful. A good recent account in Italian is Franca Angelini, *Vita di Goldoni* (Bari: Laterza, 1993), and useful studies of the Venetian theatre in Goldoni's time are Carmelo Alberti, *La scena veneziana nell'età di Goldoni*, (Rome: Bulzoni, 1990), and Marzia Pieri, *Il teatro di Goldoni* (Bologna: Il Mulino, 1993). For Gozzi, the memoirs are the best English account: see bibliography below.

[2] For eighteenth-century Italian theatre in general, see *Il teatro italiano nel Settecento*, ed. G. Guccini (Bologna: Il Mulino, 1988), and Roberto Tessari, *Teatro e spettacolo nel Settecento* (Bari: Laterza, 1995). An interesting study of the later improvising companies is provided by Orietta Giardi, *Comici dell'arte perduta* (Rome: Bulzoni: 1991).

398   Gozzi on actors and actresses

The memoirs of Count Carlo Gozzi, trans. J. A. Symonds (2 vols., London: J. C. Nimmo, 1890), vol. II, pp. 218–20

In what concerns the practice of their art, all that these people[1] know is how to read and write; one better, and one worse. Indeed, I have been acquainted with both actors and actresses who have not even had that minimum of education, and yet they carried on their business without flinching. They got their lines read out to them by some friend or some associate, whenever a new part had to be impressed in outline on their memory. Keeping their ears open to the prompter, they entered boldly on the stage, and played a hero or a heroine without a touch of truth. The presentation of such characters by actors of the sort I have described abounds in blunders, stops and stays, and harkings back upon the leading motive, which would put to shame the player in his common walk of life.

Barefaced boldness is the prime quality, the chief stock-in-trade, the ground-element of education in these artists. Assiduous use of this one talent makes not a few of them both passable and even able actors.

These are the reasons why a civil war is always raging in our companies about the first parts in new pieces. The conflict does not start from an honest desire to acquire or to manifest theatrical ability. The players are actuated wholly by ambition, by the hope of attracting favourable notice through the merit of their role, by the wish to keep themselves continually before the public, performing ill or well as their blind rashness prompts them.

Notwithstanding all these disadvantages, Italy would be able to make a good show in comparison with other nations if our theatres were better supported and remunerated.[2] These are not wanting persons of fine presence, of talent, sensibility, and animation. What we do want are the refinements of education, solid protection, and emoluments sufficient to encourage the actor in his profession.

[1] Gozzi wrote his *fiabe* and other plays for such actors and actresses, but he has for them a certain patrician disdain. The main troupe he worked with was led by Antonio Sacchi, for whom see below (**400, 401**).

[2] Gozzi's observation is accurate, and it is one frequently repeated in his time and later, when the condition of the stage further declined, and inevitably it attracted even less support.

The 1780s were something of a watershed in the Italian theatre, for the decade also saw the death of one of the most celebrated actors of the eighteenth century, Antonio Sacchi (1708–88), whose work in Italy is above all associated with that of Goldoni and Gozzi: the former wrote a number of *scenarii* for him, including *Il servitore di due padroni* (The servant of two masters) and the latter both comic *fiabe*, using the masked figures of the improvised drama, and plays in imitation of Spanish romantic drama. Sacchi was born into the profession, and from the beginning worked with Venetian companies, travelling with them to Russia, Austria and Portugal, where his agility, ready wit and imaginative skills in improvisation won him a considerable following. Sacchi's death in 1788, while sailing from Genoa to Marseilles, is often taken to mark the demise of improvised playing, as too does the Italian departure from the Comédie-Italienne by 1782.

399   A scene from a Goldoni's dialect comedy, *Sior Todero Brontolon*

Sior Todero Brontolon (Master Theodore the Complainer), first performed in 1761. Picture from the collected edition by Zatta, published from 1788; Biblioteca Teatrale Burcardo, Rome

400   Goldoni on the actor-manager Antonio Sacchi

Memoirs of Goldoni, trans. John Black and Henry Colburn (2 vols., London, 1816), vol. I, pp. 280–I

This actor, known on the Italian stage by the name of Truffaldino,[1] added to the natural graces of his action a thorough acquaintance with the art of comedy and different European theatres.

Antonio Sacchi possessed a lively and brilliant imagination; he played in comedies of intrigue; but while other harlequins merely repeated themselves, Sacchi, who always adhered to the essence of the play, contrived to give an air of freshness to the piece, by his new sallies and unexpected repartees. It was Sacchi alone whom the people crowded to see.

His comic traits, and his jests, were neither taken from the language of the lower orders nor that of the comedians. He levied contributions on comic authors, on poets, orators, and philosophers; and in his impromptus we could recognize the thoughts of Seneca, Cicero, or Montaigne:[2] but he possessed the art of appropriating the maxims of these great men to himself, and allying them to the simplicity of the blockhead; and the same proposition which was admired in a serious author, became highly ridiculous in the mouth of this excellent actor.

[1] Hence the name of the main comic character in Goldoni's play *Arlecchino, servitore di due padroni* (Arlecchino, The servant of two masters); the piece was originally devised as a scenario for Sacchi, and Goldoni wrote it up later, after he had seen Sacchi perform the part. He thus in all likelihood used some stage action and dialogue that Sacchi himself had improvised.

[2] This was a common strategy of improvising actors; for a good account of the practice see P. M. Ceccini, *Brevi discorsi intorno alle comedie, comedianti e spettatori* (Venice, 1621).

401   Gozzi on Sacchi

Carlo Gozzi in *Prefazione alla tragedia il Fajel*, cited in F. Bartoli,[1] *Notizie Istoriche de'comici italiani* (2 vols. Padua, 1781–2), vol. II, pp, 146–7

Sacchi, the famous Truffaldino, is today the only one among the Italian Players who understands the nature of the times; and how to manage a Theatrical Troupe well [. . .] He keeps his company trained in the improvised drama, and well supplied with the most suitable actors for that kind of performance; but he also ensures that it is well stocked with players extremely skilful in acting in any good written or translated Tragedy, Tragicomedy or Comedy which may be offered to him by any kind person.[2] In that way he gives a breathing space to the improvised drama and strengthens its semblance of novelty, which is indispensable if it is to survive fruitfully in the theatre throughout the year [. . .]

[1] Francesco Saverio Bartoli (1745–1806) was an actor, and later a bookseller and theatre historian. He was for a time married to the actress Teodora Ricci, until she left for Paris.

[2] This had long been considered the mark of a good *capocomico* (actor-manager); see, for example, the remarks of Gabrielli on this ability to perform in both scripted and improvised drama, cited in K. Richards and L. Richards, *The commedia dell'arte: A documentary History* (Oxford: Oxford University Press, 1990).

The late eighteenth century produced one Italian dramatist in the tragic genre whose work was to be as influential as that of Goldoni and whose plays were to remain as firmly embedded in the Italian theatrical repertory as the comedies of the Venetian. That dramatist was Vittorio Alfieri (1749–1803), an aristocrat like Carlo Gozzi, but of more considerable social standing; also, like Gozzi he wrote an important *vita* (life). Turning to dramatic writing in the late 1770s, he produced some twenty-one tragedies and six comedies, and theorized much about drama and theatre. Much of his work interestingly reflects a mingling of Enlightenment notions, including the questioning of the absolutist status quo, Romantic sentiment and a classical taste for firm structure, Roman subject matter and heroic rhetoric. Alfieri's plays have never acquired a reputation on international stages, but they made up a considerable part of the repertoires of many of the leading performers of the nineteenth century, were toured internationally by actors such as Rossi and Salvini, and several are regularly performed in Italy today. Perhaps most notable of them in the nineteenth century were *Mirra*, *Saul* and *Virginia*. In their time, and for some decades into the nineteenth century, they were particularly important for their political engagement, which was in tune with the Risorgimento mood, making them 'classic' pieces for players to perform in and for dramatists to seek to emulate.

402   Alfieri on his problems as a dramatist in Italy

Vittorio Alfieri, *Epistolario (1767–88)*, ed. L. Caretti (Milan, 1963), pp. 106–7

Everything is against me: the times, the country, my own situation, the language I want to write in, the kind of literary work I have chosen, the blindness of the spectators, the bestiality and barbarity of the actors, etc. I could go on for ever; I close by saying that those whose misfortune was to be born in Italy should make shoes and not write tragedies, for all wear shoes, while no one reads tragedies, no one understands them, no one values them.

403   Alfieri on the lack of a theatre in Italy

Vittorio Alfieri, *Risposta dell'autore a Ranieri Calzabigi*, in *Le tragedie*, ed. P. Cazzani (Milan: Mondadori, 1966), pp. 972–3

Among the many miseries of our Italy, which you so well point out, is the fact that we lack a theatre. It is fatal that in order to create a theatre one needs a ruler. This very cause contains in itself a hindrance to the true progress of this sublime art. I strongly believe that men must learn in the theatre to be free, strong, generous, driven by virtue, intolerant of any kind of violence, lovers of their country, truly aware of their rights, and ardent, upright and magnanimous in all their passions. Such was the theatre of Athens; and such a theatre can never be that grows in the shadow of a ruler. If love is presented on the stage, it must be in order to show how far that terrible passion, in one who has actually experienced it, can push its lethal effects: seeing it thus represented men will learn to avoid it, or to pursue it, but in all its vastness and capacity; and very great things are always born from either extremely passionate or bitterly disillusioned men. All this seems to me to exclude real theatre from a good part of Europe, but especially from the whole of Italy; therefore it is better not to think of it, and I do not. I simply write under the illusion that possibly, given the resurgence of the Italians, these tragedies of mine will one day be performed: I shall not be there then; thus this is but an altogether ideal pleasure on my part. Besides, even allowing that rulers could allow a theatre to develop, if not an excellent one, at least a good one, and exclusively concerned with love, I still do not see the dawn of such a day in Italy. In order for a theatre to exist in a modern nation, as it was among the ancients, there must first be a true nation, and not a division into ten small states which, even if they were unified, would find themselves different in every respect. Moreover, it would also need to have private and public education, customs, culture, armies, commerce, wars, ferment, fine arts, life. And let the examples tell us: the Greeks and the Romans had a theatre, the French and the English have a theatre. But the best patron of the theatre as of any noble art and virtue, would still be a free people. The tears, the approval, the enthusiastic praise of the Athenian people were and would be, I think, still a warmer incentive and a more generous reward to any tragic author, and actor, than the pensions and honours granted by rulers, who give and take everything except fame.

404 A scene from Alfieri's tragedy *Oreste*

Biblioteca Teatrale Burcardo, Rome; a scene from Alfieri's 1777–8 play, as depicted in an early illustration

405   Alfieri speculates on an ideal Italian theatre

Vittorio Alfieri, *Parere dell'autore sull'arte comica in Italia*, in *Tragedie*, pp. 1095–9

In order for theatre to be born in Italy, first there must be authors of tragedies and comedies, then actors, then spectators.

The greatest authors can be hampered, but not created, by either a prince or an academy.

When there are great authors, and let us suppose there are, the actors, always provided they do not need to fight hunger by today being Brighella and tomorrow Alexander, will easily, little by little, form themselves, spontaneously, by pure force of nature. They will have no rule regarding their art save that they should know their parts so well they can rehearse without a prompter; that they should speak slowly in order to understand themselves and to think about what they are saying (an infallible method in order to make listeners understand and hear); and finally, that they know how to speak and pronounce the Tuscan language, without which anything will always be laughable. Aside from any dispute about the primacy of a particular language in Italy, one thing for certain is that theatrical pieces are always written, as far as the author is aware, in the Tuscan language; consequently, they must be spoken in the Tuscan language and accent. If in the Parisian theatre an actor were to speak just one French word in Provençal or some other regional accent, he would be booed, not tolerated, even if he was an outstanding performer.

Spectators too will gradually form their own taste, and their appreciation will become as sharp as the art of the actor becomes subtle and precise; and the actors will become subtle and precise to the extent that they are educated, civilized, affluent, respected, free and dignified; this means, for a start, that they must not be born paupers or come from the dregs of society.

Finally, authors will be able to improve themselves when, interpreted by such actors, they can see in the theatre the actual effect of even the slightest of their directions, and from this effect judge where they need to make changes, where to cut and where to add. When authors, actors and spectators, all three, know and do what is required, they will very soon proceed in agreement; and not only with each syllable and full stop, but also with even the subtlest intention of the author which has its effect, and shows that effect, on the spectators through the actor. These three hold each other by the hand, and are at the same time, and in turn, the cause and effect of the perfection of the art.

Briefly to sum up, I say that when there are great authors, and when actors are highly paid in order to be good, there will be spectators enough. An actor who says good things well, will perforce be listened to; and those who have listened to them for but a year, without interruption, will then no longer want to see mediocre or badly acted pieces; on the contrary, by getting ever better and better, by perfecting their criteria, spectators will be able to control both authors and actors.

So let authors come forward and write well; let actors speak from the beginning, sincerely and with intelligence (by which is meant slowly), and in the

Tuscan manner; let spectators listen in a reverent silence; then the theatre will be born.

Alfieri's wish for theatrical reform was reflected in the many attempts, particularly following the French Revolution and through to *circa* 1800, to improve the condition of the stage in its main Italian centres. A governing idea was the need to change theatre from a private activity to a public service, thus giving birth to the notion of a national theatre that would serve to educate the citizenry. This was, of course, an idea imported from France, whose subsidized theatre was to provide the model for later Italian developments. Dramatists and legislators alike sought to foster such a theatre, calculated, as Alfieri had wished, to educate the theatre-going populace in Roman virtues: a theatre that was to be noble, austere, moral and independent. In 1796 the Teatro Patriottico was established in Milan to affirm republican principles. In the same year, on 26 July, the activist Francesco Salfi published in Brescia the programme below.

406   Project for a national theatre, 1796

F. Salfi, 'Political thermometer, 6th thermidor, year IV' (26 July 1796), in A. Paglicci Brozzi, *Sul Teatro Giacobino e Antigiacobino in Italia, 1796–1805* (Milan: Luigi di Giacomo Pirola, 1887), pp. 48–50

1. A director might be established who has the talent, the knowledge and the practical experience of theatrical art, and is capable of drawing up a plan of dramatic projects which would be most appropriate for current needs.
2. This person might work in association with others willing and able to collaborate on the same objective, namely to compose new plays, and translate and adapt existing material. France is rich in such work, particularly since the Revolution. A collection of such work could be brought together rapidly, in order to fill the current gap.
3. Give these people total control of the choice, execution and, particularly, the delivery of the plays, which at present is totally lacking in the Italian theatres, where decency, passion and truth are unknown.
4. To the same academy others might contribute with new plays, which they have either written or translated, or which they perform. The director and his colleagues should have the right to bring them into the academy, and the public should have the right to acclaim them as people who have done well by the national theatre, but subject to the approval of the director and his colleagues.
5. Let a company be formed of honest and able national actors, free of the vices and weaknesses of ordinary actors. A company of amateurs observing the above-mentioned regulations, and clearly of patriotic inclination, might initially fill the void, and open the way to the emergence of the kind of company ideally sought.

6. The patriotic entertainment of these amateurs should serve as a model and example to those who would seek to practise professionally. The Greeks used to admire unreservedly those who, after having fought in a war, appeared on the stage to perform in their own tragedies. Roscius, Aesop and their fellows were applauded in the theatre, but were not without respect in society. What has belittled the art of acting, especially in Italy, where baseness and infamy are rewarded, is not the business of acting itself, but the behaviour of both the actors and the public.

7. The same academy should include ordinary professional actors, that is salaried actors, but they should be chosen from among those who have the rare fortune of being characterized by a certain talent and probity, and therefore of being susceptible to influences calculated to further advance the art of the theatre. Thus the increased number of actors will allow each sufficient time to work on the roles most suited to their particular aptitudes; and thus one will no longer see the same actor vulgarly chirrup now Brutus, now Arlecchino.

8. They should all be considered highly effective instruments of public education, and should behave responsibly in their conduct, so as not to deny by their actions the moral principles they should inspire on the stage.

9. The public should be educated into having the greatest respect for the theatre. The institutions established should all collaborate to this end, but this same end might also be obtained if lectures were given in the same theatre by the most respected academics, who could illustrate the merits of theatrical masterpieces and the worth of writers and actors who have excelled in this field.

10. Audience admission charges should be reduced to a minimum in order to increase the size of the public, which would in its turn make up for any box office losses.

11. A fund should be established under the guarantee and administration of the municipality, or whoever is acting on behalf of the municipality, to cover the costs of the upkeep of the theatre.

12. The main theatre of the republic should be the dramatic theatre. Other theatres, given over to music and dance, should be in a subordinate position, because their unfortunate influence has made Aspasias and Frines triumph on the stage, before they found rest from their triumph in hospitals.[1]

13. A national theatre thus constituted, or differently constituted, as long as it has the same objectives, must immediately be promoted, administered and protected by the municipality, or by whoever is in charge of the national welfare. If the theatre is to be a most important school for the public, its administration must be removed from the venal hands of impresarios, who make the most scandalous commerce from abhorrent theatrical vulgarities.

---

[1] Notorious Greek prostitutes.

A year later, in 1797, a manifesto was published in Venice urging the establishment of a civic theatre of educational intent, and many writers at this time were fired up by a sense of the potential social and political utility of theatre. The following report issued in Brescia in 1798 reflects many of the idealistic sentiments then still current.

407   Report of the Committee on Theatres, 1798

'13th messidor, year VI (1 July 1798)', in Paglicci Brozzi, *Sul Teatro*, pp. 179–84

The history of the theatre in every civilized nation clearly shows that theatre has always gone hand in hand with government: on the one hand, it is a free censor of manners, and lethal to the enemies of democracy; on the other, under a tyrannical government it is a vile adulator and teacher of corruption. It provides the most faithful picture of the spirit and moral character of a people.

This observation teaches us that theatre, which takes its physiognomy from government, by virtue of its very nature determines the physiognomy of a people. It is one of the most powerful instruments of politics. By means of it despotism perverts souls, and plunges them further and further into servitude, but with it, a democratic Constitution reinforces in them strong feelings of freedom and virtue.

Freedom, which now reigns among us, must finally resume its control over the theatre. It is time for the theatre to purge itself of the infamies committed under the rule of tyrants, and return to the glorious days of Athens. The Cisalpine people loudly demand regeneration in this sector [. . .]

The Great Council, considering that in a free people theatre should be a school of freedom and of manners, and considering that the state of political servitude under which Italy has been for so many centuries is the only cause of the corruption of the theatre, thus resolves:

1. In the Cisalpine territory it is intended that the theatre should serve the purpose of making public education an object of pleasure for the people.
2. All forms of spectacle – that is, tragedies, comedies, music, balls and displays – have this same aim.
3. Musical works, both serious and comic, will be performed for no more than three months in the year, according to the conditions of Article 2; for the remaining nine months patriotic comedies and tragedies will be performed.
4. *Castrati* will be banned from the stage. Foreign *castrati* will not be allowed to sing, even in private, under penalty of six months' imprisonment.
5. When tragedy is performed it should inspire hatred of tyrants, courage, republican sentiments and commiseration for oppressed innocence.
6. Comedy should unmask the brutal pride of aristocrats, the imposture of hypocritical superstition, the absurd ambition of the rich, the caball-like interference of busybodies, the avarice of *provisioneri*, the venality of

magistrates, the infamy of false patriots. It should have universal powers of censure over the manners of the age.

7. Ballets, and all other shows, should regularly follow these principles.

8. Between one act and the next patriotic hymns will be sung, or at least will be played.

9. On days of national celebration performances will show some past event relevant to the celebration.

10. Foreign comic companies are banished from the Cisalpine soil.

11. The existing national companies will be dissolved at the latest within two years.

12. In the main towns of each department national companies will be formed. Teachers of speech in the central schools will teach theatrical declamation to those young people of either sex who, having considerable talent, wish to enter the companies.

13. Instruction in declamation will take place three times every ten days. Parents, or any person representing them, will be allowed to accompany young women to this training. All others are expressly forbidden to enter the theatres on such occasions.

14. No pupil of either sex will be admitted into the national salaried companies without a certificate of competence acquired according to the instruction given in the central schools.

15. Those actors and actresses who for whatever reason have an indecent lifestyle are immediately expelled and will be severely punished according to their circumstances. As far as this matter is concerned, the police are directly responsible for surveillance.

16. The executive power is responsible for securing a theatre for the main town of each district, and for any other town with at least eight thousand inhabitants.

17. These theatres are to be directly administered on behalf of the nation by the local administration according to norms which will be prescribed.

18. Every year the district administrations will be obliged to publish the theatre management's accounts, including expenses incurred, both ordinary and extraordinary, and revenues received.

19. This budgeting will serve as a guide to the expenditure permitted for performances, and the national companies in the respective districts and communes will be indemnified according to the net sum.

20. In all those theatres designated national property all divisions between boxes will be eliminated, and there will be only one *loggia* open to all the people.

21. In each theatre there will be a separate place for citizens who have made themselves noteworthy in the republic, either for military distinction, or some invention, or some useful deed, or for some tragic or comic composition which has received a prize, as will be indicated below.

22. The executive power will issue to the local administrations appropriate regulations according to which the admission price to performances will be set at the lowest possible in order to encourage better attendance from citizens.

23. One evening in each *décade*,[1] and on each evening of a national holiday, the theatre will be open free. The administrations will distribute on such evenings tickets giving preference to those citizens who, because of their particular situation, are least able to attend the theatre at other times.

24. In the theatres not named as national the boxes will be uniformly decorated and only in the national colours.

25. Each year the executive authority will appoint a committee of theatrical discipline composed of ten citizens of well-known patriotism and ability, and this committee will be charged with regulating every kind of theatrical representation in relation to public education, manners and good taste.

26. This committee will publish each year a list of the productions which will be performed in the whole of the republic, and will prescribe the kind of music, the décor and the subject of the ballets which will be part of the spectacle. This committee is also authorized, however, in the course of the year to prescribe the performance of any new composition it thinks worthy of being shown to the people.

27. Teachers of speech in the central schools of the various districts will ensure the plans of the committee are neither violated nor altered.

28. A competition will be announced for theatrical compositions intended to educate the public according to Articles 5 and 6. Each year the executive power, on receipt of the report of the committee for theatrical discipline, will choose six compositions, and these will receive as prize a gold medal worth 500 lire. The authors will receive civic crowns at a national celebration in which their compositions will be performed.

This function, which will be held only once, will follow the performance and will take place with the décor prescribed by the commission.

[1] *Décade*: a period of ten days, which replaced the seven-day week in the French Republican calendar.

But while such ideas were never abandoned, and some later underpinned the work of patriots such as Gustavo Modena, there emerged all too soon an unbridgeable gulf between the dreams of the reformers and social, political and theatrical realities. By the end of the century the early reform movement was in large measure exhausted. Many of the ideas expressed above were replaced by somewhat different notions of the way theatre should be organized and the purposes it should serve. Again, these were brought from France: French-subsidized acting companies were sent into Italy for the Italians to imitate and emulate, and the Compagnia Reale Francese was duly established at the Teatro Carcano in Milan in 1806. Greater emphasis on discipline, regulation and financial and political control were characteristics of the new wave.

II   *Carnival,* feste *and street theatre*

In the late eighteenth and early nineteenth century festivals remained, as they had been in the high Middle Ages and the Renaissance, a marked feature of Italian life, although whether or not they fulfilled quite the same social functions and carried the same quasi-ritualistic significance as earlier are moot points. Certainly, they continued to be of many kinds, marking important weddings and funerals, visits by the illustrious, community celebrations, particularly those in honour of a patron saint, such as John the Baptist at Florence, as well as significant dates in the Church calendar, while Carnival, with its pre-Lenten associations of freedom and licence, remained the most conspicuous occasion for revelry and the one most frequently remarked on by commentators. Carnival clearly reflects the influence, if at some remove, of Roman festivals, but was offically established, or re-established, in 1466 by Pope Paul II (1464–71). Most festivities were still communal activities and consisted of types of entertainment which appealed to all social groups; indeed, if anything, the more prosperous middle ranks of society seem to have taken more of a leading role than the lower social groups, at least to the extent that their enthusiastic endorsement, ubiquitous presence and semi-participatory engagement, as spectators on balconies or celebrants in carriages and processions, were a crucial part of the atmosphere of revelry.

Public festivals were essentially urban, drawing many to the cities from the countryside and attracting the interest of foreigners. They were theatrical by their very nature, entailing masquerade and role-playing. But they could include many specific forms of theatre: varieties of musical and dance drama, from *seria* to *buffa*, productions of new and classic, secular and religious plays by amateur and professional groups in purpose-built or temporary or makeshift theatres and performance places, spontaneous or unstructured offerings, comic skits, burlesques and farces, and serious and comic puppet stagings, whether performed in theatres or halls or in main streets and squares, and a range of virtuoso and spectacular entertainments from rope-dancing, through feats of strength and agility to firework displays and exhibitions of verbal and mental skill.

Some of these shows were, of course, part of the regular professional theatre fare available throughout the year, but specific offerings were frequently targeted with an eye to an audience's likely festive mood, its preferences and composition. One or two instances of such are given here, but others are to be found, too, in chapter 3 below. But what dominated at street level during festivals was popular theatre, in the sense not of a theatre by and for a particular social group, but a theatre that appealed to, and often permitted the participation of, virtually all social groups and, by virtue of being public and *al fresco*, was even available to those in the lowest reaches of the social scale. Below are brief notices which reflect the variety and vitality of that street theatre: amateur and professional, prearranged and spontaneous, performed by actors and actresses, mimes, rope-dancers and singers, maskers, clowns and puppets. Italians invariably took this range of spectacle and these kinds of entertainment for granted, which in part explains why the best accounts have traditionally been provided by foreigners. We have not included here a passage from the most celebrated and extensive report of Carnival in Rome ever penned, that by Goethe, who encountered it during his travels of 1786–8, for his long and vivid account is readily available in English.[1] But other, less well-known passages we cite below clearly indicate that Carnival in Italy, what Goethe called a 'festival the people give themselves', persisted long into the nineteenth century.

[1] Notably in the translation by W. H. Auden and Elizabeth Mayer of J. W. Goethe, *Italian journey* [1786–88] (Harmondsworth: Penguin, 1962).

408   A Swiss traveller sees Carnival in the Corso in Rome, 1816

James Aug. Galiffe,[1] *Italy and its inhabitants; an account of a tour in that country* in 1816 and 1817 (2 vols., London, 1820), vol. 1, pp. 428–9

Many of the crowd are masked, and exhibit some very comical figures and amusing groups; but on the whole, they are rather noisy than gay, and their dresses are more gaudy than elegant. A great many coachmen and some of the tallest footmen are dressed in women's clothes. The chief part of the general amusement consists in throwing at each other small figures of plumbs [*sic*] made of chalk or of plaster – which imitations have succeeded to real sugar-plumbs, as modern has succeeded to ancient Rome. They do no hurt to anyone, unless they are purposely and violently thrown at the face; a species of brutal sport, of which I am sorry to acknowledge I have seen some English travellers guilty. As these missiles whiten every thing they strike, black clothes are usually the principal objects of attack. But in carrying on this warfare against the ladies of their acquaintance, it is the fashion for gentlemen to use real sugar-plumbs. Nor are the ladies wholly idle, many of them being engaged in throwing similar substances at the balconies and into the windows of their friends on the Corso. However trifling this amusement may appear in description, it is really not unentertaining when carried on (as it invariably is by the natives) with cheerfulness and good-humour.

[1] Jacques Augustin Galiffe was a Swiss historian and genealogist who published work in Geneva and Paris as well as in London.

409   An illustration of Carnival in Rome

Biblioteca Teatrale Burcardo, Rome

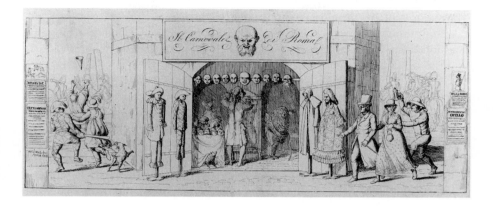

410   Carnival in the Piazza di Spagna and in the Corso, Rome, 1847

Mrs Butler,[1] *A year of consolation* (2 vols. London, 1847), vol. I, pp. 151–5

Passing trough the Piazza di Spagna we found it filled with soldiers on horseback, and every street was sending up to the great rout its string of carriages and stream of eager hurrying pedestrians; groups of masks went dancing and laughing by; Harlequins and Pantaloons, Turks, Albanians, Spanish Dons, and girls in short white skirts and coloured bodices, with blue or pink silk boots and very freely shown legs. Most of these groups had their faces covered either with grotesque masks or the classical black silk visor: in passing the carriage, they threw us confetti or nosegays, or merry words.

Later she watched from a balcony on the Corso.

The long irregular street presented the most singular and animated scene; every window was filled with spectators, every balcony or jutting window from which a convenient view could be obtained was adorned with hangings either of crimson and gold, or gay rose colour and white; the little balcony in which we stood was all festooned with the latter colours, and tapestry and curtains and carpets were put in requisition [. . .]

---

[1] The married name of the actress and writer Fanny Kemble (1809–93), daughter of Charles Kemble, manager of Covent Garden Theatre, where she made her acting début in *Romeo and Juliet* in 1829. In 1834 she married an American Southern plantation owner, Pierce Butler, in Philadelphia, but separated from him in 1845 and stayed for a year with her sister in Rome; hence the title of this volume of reminiscences.

411   Carnival in Florence, 1821

A journal of a tour in Italy in the year 1821, with a description of Gibraltar, by an American (New York, 1824), pp. 403–5[1]

The majority of the throng was composed of an endless variety of masks and dominos; and among these mingled, here and there, whole families of hale and laughing peasants from the neighbouring farm-houses: the men usually in short jackets, and the women in round black beaver hats, decorated with sable plumes [. . .] Harlequins, in their parti-coloured suits, were as usual performing their pranks, brandishing their magical wooden swords, and spending as much time as possible off the ground; while Pulcinella, or Punch, with his white gown and sugar-loaf cap, poured out his wit as fluently, and with as much effect, as if he had been still on the stage, and acting on a preconcerted scheme.

Three men in the antiquated dress of students, went about with huge illuminated volumes pressed under their arms, holding abstruse disquisitions on literary subjects, and frequently stopping to refer to disputed passages, or even to indulge in a brown study, in the very thickest of the crowd, from whom they received many a rough though undesigned thrust and buffet. Nothing, however, could avail to discompose the gravity of their faces, and I believe a thunderstorm would not have interrupted the thread of their discourse; for the tricks and railleries of the Harlequin and Pulcinella were entirely wasted on them, although they raised shouts for a wide extent around. But even this noisy mirth was occasionally drowned by the notes of four or five musicians, who were constantly changing their place [. . .] plying without mercy their jangling strings, in the most savage symphony I ever heard. Their leader was a tall, ragged personage, who performed in the part of an *improvisatore*,[2] but in so high a style of burlesque, that I think I can never lose the recollection of his looks and actions. He was painted in such a manner as to give his countenance an expression of the utmost self-complacency, and yet to counteract all the kind designs of nature in rendering it agreeable. These itinerants were entirely abstracted from everything except their own immediate concerns. Whenever they stopped, it was with their faces fixed on their leader; and though in the thickest crowd, paid not the least regard to anything about them. The poet would sometimes assume the air of one in the highest regions of poetic rapture, looking into some distant cloud, and trilling till he shook in his shoes; while his conceptions were often of the most ludicrous kind, and his lines ran on and halted in a style quite irresistible. This seemed to transport his companions, who would gaze upon him in silence through their hideous masks, and then exchanging looks of approbation, open their throats, and join their hoarse voices in a thundering chorus.

---

[1] This visitor saw the tail end of Carnival in Florence on 6 March 1821. He gives a vivid but rather sour account. With a puritanical sense of cost-effectiveness he thinks it would be better to spend money improving social conditions than on 'extravagant but unmeaning scenes', and thinks the Carnival revellers to have 'heads as hollow as the masks they wore', p. 403.

[2] *Improvisatori* had long been, and remained, a feature of Italian urban life, performing either in the streets and piazzas or in private houses.

412 The St John the Baptist Day Festival in Florence, 1854

George Foxcroft Haskins, *Travels in England, France, Italy and Ireland* (Boston: Patrick Donahoe, 1856), pp. 164–5

On the eve of the feast [of St John] there is always a chariot race, a remnant of the ancient Etruscan games. The exhibition took place as usual in the piazza of Santa Maria Novella. The square was surrounded with rows of seats, tier above tier, in the manner of an amphitheatre. These seats were let for about sixpence each, and were soon all taken. At each end of the piazza was a column, connected by a rope, its centre being held up by six men dressed in ancient costumes. Around these columns was the course. At the foot of the scaffoldings were posted bodies of cavalry and infantry. At the upper end of the piazza was the royal box, elegantly decorated. It contained the grand duke, his consort, and the royal children, besides ambassadors and ministers of foreign courts, and other strangers of distinction, with their families. All the windows, balconies, and even roofs of the surrounding houses, were crowded with spectators. There must have been from ten to fifteen thousand individuals, spectators of the races. The chariots were four in number, and the charioteers were arrayed in ancient costume. At a given signal they all started off, with a prodigious racket. They passed several times around the course, when, the one that was victorious having received a long and tremendous shout of applause, all was ended, and the spectators retired without further noise or confusion to their homes. I was particularly struck and gratified at witnessing the perfect good order, and good nature too, that prevailed among this multitude of people. It was infinitely the most interesting part of the exhibition. While the race continued, they were frequently pressed back by the guards, and almost trampled on by the multitudes of horses, but not an angry word did I hear, nor an impatient remonstrance [. . .]

In the evening there was to have been an illumination of the Arno, and of some of the principal squares, streets, and public buildings, and also a display of fireworks from one of the bridges; but a terrible squall of wind, which came in the morning like a thunderbolt, and blew like a hurricane, demolished the scaffoldings that had been a week in building, and overthrew and shattered so large a portion of the lamps, that both designs were necessarily abandoned.

413 Carnival in Messina, Sicily, 1813

Journal of an officer in the King's German Legion: comprising an account of his campaigns and adventures in England, Ireland, Denmark, Portugal, Spain, Malta, Sicily and Italy (London, 1827), pp. 282–3

The season of the Carnival, in February, is passed with great glee, and gives occasion to many ludicrous occurrences. Daily are men and women to be seen parading the streets in the wildest and most grotesque garbs, in which masquerading the holy priesthood do not disdain to join, but on the other hand, get up numerous processions in which the prevailing object appears to be to make themselves look as ridiculous as possible. The crowds of boys who are let loose at this period exhibit a practical commentary on these laudable efforts of the pious fathers, and run about in parties dressed as Catholic priests and wearing masks representing *sheep's heads*! Other persons, likewise, with an apparent and no doubt a proper consciousness of their own deserts, scruple not to parade the streets habited as criminals with ropes round their necks.

414   A Carnival scene in Venice

Biblioteca Teatrale Burcardo, Rome

LE CARNAVAL DE VENISE

415   The Bucentoro[1]

Thomas Martyn, *A tour through Italy* (London, 1791), pp. 460–2[2]

The Bucentoro, or state galley of the republic, is laid up here. It never goes out, but when it carries the Doge to the espousals of the Adriatic. It is loaded with ornaments, gilding, and sculpture; and is a heavy-bottomed vessel, that draws little water, and might easily overset in a gale of wind. Of this however there is little danger; for not only the patriarch pours some holy water into the sea, as soon as the vessel is afloat; but the admiral has a discretionary power of postponing the marriage ceremony when the sea shows any signs of being boisterous.

When the weather however is favourable, the ceremony of the espousals is performed on Ascension-tide day. The solemnity is announced in the morning by the ringing of bells, and the firing of cannon. About noon the Doge, with the Pope's nuncio and the Patriarch on each side of him, and attended by a numerous party of the Senate and Clergy, goes on board; the vessel is rowed a little way into the sea, accompanied by the splendid yachts of the foreign ambassadors,[3] the gondolas of the Venetian nobility, and an incredible number of small vessels of every kind, many of them covered with canopies of silk or rich stuffs, with the gondoliers in sumptuous liveries. A band of music plays, while the Bucentoro, and its train, slowly move towards the Lido. The Doge drops a ring into the sea, pronouncing these words – *desponsamus te mare in signum veri perpetuique dominii.*[4] He then returns in the same state, inviting those who accompany him in the galley to dinner. The day following, the Fair begins at St Mark's place, which lasts ten days.

[1] A decorated galley used in the traditional ceremony in which the Doge cast a ring into the Adriatic to symbolize wedding to the sea on Ascension Day (forty-six days after Lent). The last Bucentoro was built in 1729 and was destroyed by March 1798 for its gold decoration.
[2] Martyn (1735–1825) was a distinguished botanist who became professor of botany at Cambridge. He made his tour of Italy between 1778 and 1780. His account was first published in 1787.
[3] Venice was still at this time an independent state.
[4] 'We marry you, sea, in the name of the true and eternal god.'

416 A puppet theatre in Milan, 1826

N. H. Carter, *Letters from Europe, comprising the journal of a tour through Ireland, England, Scotland, France, Italy and Switzerland in the years 1825, '26, and '27* (2 vols., New York: Carvill, 1827), vol. II, pp. 502–3

At another minor theatre,[1] we witnessed a perfect burlesque upon the Italian stage. The players were marionettes, made of wood, about three feet in height, with imperceptible wires fixed in their heads, and moved by persons above the scenes, who by dint of ventriloquism threw their voices into the consequential actors. By a contraction of the stage, and the illusion of the perspective, they appear like real persons at a distance. The principal piece for the night was the Rape of Proserpine, a very classical production, in which the infernal regions were disclosed to view! Pluto appeared in his flaming car, driven by Cupid bearing a blazing torch. Peter Quince and his corps did not raise a storm half so tremendous, as these Lilliputians produced. Then came the ballet, which was an admirable satire upon the dancing at the Scala.[2] Minikin actresses hopped, reeled, and span like tops, showing wooden legs with as much dexterity, as 'children of a larger growth'. An exhibition of this kind was witnessed at Lodi; but there the marionettes were *contadini*,[3] displaying the rusticity of a country life, and not to be compared with the gay dresses and fashionable manners of city puppets.

[1] Probably the Teatro Girolamo, for which see below (**417**).
[2] Satire with an economic and class emphasis was traditionally a feature of much popular theatrical entertainment in Italy.
[3] Peasants.

417 A puppet theatre in Milan, 1827

J. D. Sinclair, *An autumn in Italy* (Edinburgh, 1829), p. 54[1]

Another evening I passed a couple of hours most agreeably at the theatre of Gerolamo,[2] where puppets of about three feet high are made to represent men and women in the most amusing manner. Many living actors whom I have witnessed would suffer from a comparison with these wooden performers. So complete is the delusion, from the admirable manner in which they are managed, that one would absolutely imagine the dialogues to proceed from the mouths of the puppets. A comedy, or rather farce was performed, called 'Il Vapore di Lago Maggiore', a piece full of humour, which afforded the greatest display of the roguish qualities of Gianduja, a Piedmontese valet, who by his playful wit atoned for the want of interest in the plot. This was followed by a *ballet* with the same actors, whose *aplomb* and *möelleux* were nearly equal to those of a Vestris or a Biggotieri.[3] One can form no idea of an Italian Polcinella until he beholds these acting puppets. Although I had often heard of its excellence, this exhibition even exceeded my expectations. Gerolamo's theatre is quite a fashionable resort, nothwithstanding the trifling price of admittance; and I was told that the late manager left a fortune of 300,000 livres, an amazing sum in that country, particularly to be gained by keeping a puppet-show.

[1]   An evening or two before seeing this puppet play he had been to a play by Goldoni at the Teatro Re. He thought the Italian theatre generally to be in a low state – particularly the drama, and especially at Genoa. Other travellers thought it poorer in Florence. The centres where theatre seemed to flourish best were Milan, Venice and Naples, and occasionally at Rome, although only at certain times of the year.

[2]   It is thought that such a theatre existed as early as the seventeenth century; however, the specific theatre referred to here seems to have been established in the first decade of the nineteenth century. It was named after the central figure of the puppet plays, Gerolamo (or Girolamo della crina), who was accompanied by his wife, Giacometta, and other members of his family. The theatre had quite a substantial repertory of plays, some of them sympathetic to the nationalist cause.

[3]   It is less than clear to whom Sinclair refers here, but he may intend the French dancer Emilia Bigottini (1784–1858), who was at the height of her career in the 1820s, and either Gaetano Vestris (1729–1808) or, and more likely, his illegitimate son, and a dancer who performed occasionally with Bigottini, Augusto Vestris (1760–1842). In the 1780s father and son appeared together at the King's Theatre in London.

418   Street theatre in Venice, 1826

Carter, *Letters from Europe*, vol. II, p. 459

At the square of St Mark's, we found an immense crowd, and witnessed a great deal of buffoonery, probably much in the style of the Carnival. The first object that attracted attention, was a mountebank standing in the midst of a throng, in the dress of a priest, with a black cap upon his head, a profusion of rings upon his fingers, and a farthing candle in his hand.[1] He recited a long prospectus of what he was about to write on scientific and literary subjects, in the character of a Caleb Quotem,[2] and deliver for the edification of the public. A young poet, in a more serious vein, walked back and forth in front of a coffeehouse, and spouted half-a-dozen of his latest sonnets, to amuse a circle of both sexes, who were all the while eating ice-cream. An old ballad-singer, accompanied by a young girl on the guitar, attracted another audience. The Austrian band played natural airs, the Greeks played cards, and others played the fiddle. It was the oddest compound of amusements, as well as of population, that I have ever witnessed.[3]

[1] Mountebanks had been a traditional feature of street life in St Mark's Square in Venice since at least the Middle Ages. There are brilliant accounts of them during the Renaissance in Thomas Coryate's *Crudities* (1611) and in Tommaso Garzoni's *Piazza universale delle professioni del mondo* (1585), and Goldoni gives a detailed description of the mountebank the Anonymous, who was active in the eighteenth century. In the sixteenth century links between such trestle-stage performers and actors proper could be close, and they remained so: the company Goldoni knew managed to translate itself from a group of street performers to a company operating in a regular Venetian theatre.

[2] The main character in S. Arnold's comic opera, *Throw Physick to the Dogs!* or *Caleb Quotem and his Wife* (1798).

[3] As an indication of the persistence of certain kinds of popular street theatre one might compare the scene described here with the illustration of performers in St Mark's Square given in Giacomo Franco's *Habiti d'Huomeni et Donne Venetiane* (Venice, 1610).

419   A fireworks display in Rome, 1854

George Foxcroft Haskins (1856), p. 77

On Easter Monday evening we witnessed the display of fireworks on the Pincian Hill.[1] They were the most brilliant and the finest not only that we had ever seen, but that we had even conceived of. There were silvery cataracts; fountains and jets of gold; emerald palaces and gorgeous temples, glittering with innumerable lights; vast candelabra of seven branches; an emerald atmosphere dissolving into one of a rich crimson; the booming of cannons; a wild and rapid discharge of innumerable pieces of ordnance, the smoke of which ascended in heavy, sluggish clouds, and instantly caught different hues – red, crimson, scarlet, green, and violet; and hundreds of rockets, as though shot from a fountain, and descending as they burst, throwing out different coloured lights in overwhelming showers, illuminating the whole scene, and discovering the presence of the immense multitudes packed together in the Piazza del Popolo.[2]

[1] Il Pincio, a small hill above the Piazza del Popolo in Rome and part of the Borghese Gardens.

[2] A main square in the heart of Rome.

III   Theatres, scenic design and audiences

Although from the early sixteenth century the work of Italian architects, designers and artificers had dominated European theatre architecture, scenic decoration and stage machinery, by the late eighteenth century that domination had begun to wane. In Italy itself, however, throughout the peninsula, the late eighteenth and early nineteenth centuries saw a considerable increase in the number of theatres newly built or substantially refurbished, and a steady increase in the numbers of people who went to the theatre regularly, even if much of that increase related to the lyric theatres. In part, the building and refurbishment was a response to spectator demand, but in part, too, it was a reflection of the degree of civic and regional pride invested in public monuments. The last decades of the old century and the first decades of the new saw the building of such theatres as La Scala in Milan (1778), La Fenice in Venice (1792), the Teatro San Carlo in Naples (1810), the Teatro Ducale (later Regio) in Parma (1828), and the Teatro Carlo Felice in Genoa (1828). The interiors, and sometimes the exteriors, of some older theatres were redesigned and refurbished, often with a view to providing more and improved seating and increased auditorium comforts. In general, the tendency in Italy, as elsewhere in Europe, was for larger theatres with horseshoe-shaped auditoria and ever more rows of boxes.

As earlier, books on theatre architecture continued to appear, while by the second half of the century the social significance of theatre buildings was attracting the attention of academicians and intellectuals: Francesco Milizia, for example, in his *Trattato completo, formale e materiale del teatro* (1794), advanced a notion of theatre as an integral part of the cultural life of a city. One outcome of this emphasis on the formal significance of theatre buildings was the increase in regional community theatre provision, even if the focus was primarily institutional, the buildings being seen as imposing civic monuments, for emphasis on civic splendour inevitably led to the erection of ever more architecturally imposing emblems of local pride. Thus Milizia observed of Venetian theatres of the mid-eighteenth century that all 'their magnificence is confined to the interior'; but when La Fenice was built in 1792 the intention was very clearly to erect a theatre as elegant without as it was within.

Many of the new or revamped theatres were, of course, designed more particularly to house opera.[1] But important features of much of the period in most parts of the peninsula were, first, the sheer variety of theatre available, whether *al fresco* or in purpose-built or adapted venues, and second, the promiscuous manner and frequency with which the various dramatic genres were mingled. A theatre could readily accommodate opera, *seria* and *buffa*, along with ballet, and regular serious scripted drama together with farce, either sequentially over a period of years or as part of a regular weekly programme of theatrical offerings. Thus, although La Scala in Milan was then, as it is now, associated particularly with opera, at the same time we find Fabbrichesi with his *teatro di prosa* company performing there for some years. As can be seen below, many of the comments on theatre by foreign visitors bear witness to the variety of theatrical fare available in Italian theatres and the apparently casual manner in which the serious, the farcical, music, song, mime and dance could be intermixed.

As far as scenic design is concerned, the great period of experimentation in the work of innovative figures such as Ferdinando, Alessandro, Antonio and Giovanni Galli da Bibbiena and Filippo Juvarra was past, a general passing signalled by the death in Rome in 1778 of the late eighteenth-century master of stage design, Giovan Battista Piranesi.[2] But emphasis on the opulent in designs for opera and ballet remained characteristic, and although the extravagances of late baroque scenic decoration were much toned down, the exotic, more particularly perhaps in ballet design, remained popular. Throughout the period, such stage decoration for regular drama as there was seems to have shown an increasing tendency towards the naturalistic, but compared to the musical or dance stages, the regular professional theatre was nearly always very modest in its use of decorative and mechanical means. Certainly in the last decade or so of the eighteenth century and the first decades of the nineteenth, most productions of even the more important acting companies consisted of not much more than modest painted backdrops and essential utilitarian properties, both tending to the stock and recyclable. In the period some striking design work was certainly done in Italy for the musical stage, and by Italian designers working abroad, but Italians no longer dominated scenic design, any more than the design of theatre buildings, to the same extent as they had done since the late Renaissance. That hegemony was now passing to the Parisian stage. Through the early decades of the new century, however, their reputation persisted, and there is a continuation of the eighteenth-century practice of leading stage designers publishing collections of their designs, as the illustration to document 431 bears witness.

The behaviour of Italian audiences at both the *teatro lirico* and the *teatro di prosa* seems to have been much as it was when visitors such as the Frenchman the Abbé De Brosses and the Englishman Samuel Sharp visited the peninsula in the mid-eighteenth century: noisy, boisterous, talkative, often ambulatory and frequently indifferent to the activities on stage. At the upper social levels, *palchetti* (boxes) became increasingly important, serving in effect as small salons in a public place, which could be made the more private by drawing a curtain to conceal the interior of the box from the eyes of spectators in other boxes or in the pit. Again, as comment below bears witness, individual behaviour could be as eccentric, obnoxious and unresponsive to theatrical art, as was at times collective conduct. There were, then, quite substantial audiences for many different kinds of theatre. Unfortunately, what many Italian commentators and foreign visitors were agreed on, as were many in the acting profession, rarely were the tastes of those audiences such as to encourage the intellectually ambitious and theatrically innovative. Most theatrical entertainment throughout much of this period attempted to do little more than entertain audiences, who sought primarily what they were easy and familiar with and who delighted in local fads and fashions.

---

[1] A good, illustrated overview of Italian theatres is Giuliana Ricci, *I teatri d'Italia* (Milan: 1971). A useful short account is Antonio Pinelli, *I teatri* (Florence: 1973).

[2] For an overview of design activity see Valerio Mariani, *Storia della scenografia italiana* (1930).

420   La Scala, Milan, 1790

Biblioteca Teatrale Burcardo, Rome; La Scala Milan, designed by Piermarini between 1776 and 1778, in an early nineteenth-century illustration

GRAND THEATRE DE LA SCALA
Teatro della Scala

Although the Teatro alla Scala in Milan is one of the world's great opera houses, and in the late eighteenth and early nineteenth centuries was a key point of interest for any visitor to Milan, when built it was not considered particularly original architecturally, save perhaps for its size, and for the sheer amount of space and attention accorded the front-of-house facilities, such as the foyers, salons and offices. The work of the architect Giuseppe Piermarini, it was built, together with the Teatro Cannobiana (destroyed in 1894), to replace the old Teatro di Corte in Milan, which was gutted by fire on 26 February 1776. Designed according to the now standard horse-shoe shape, the auditorium had tiers of *palchi*, a large open gallery above them, and an open ground floor entered from the back, and had some eighteen rows of benches and a railed-off space between these and the stage for the orchestra. It was later refurbished a number of times, and although it retained many of its essential characteristics, a distinctive feature of the original, the elaborate interior decoration to the boxes, was for the most part removed. In 1814 the whole was substantially extended by Canonica and Giusti, the stage and off-stage area at the rear being given several scene-painting rooms and storage rooms. It was further altered in 1830. Early lighting was by candles, followed by the installation of gas in 1860 and electricity in the 1880s. It was, of course, built for the presentation of opera, but in its earlier years La Scala could also on occasion house regular drama, Salvatore Fabbrichesi having his privileged company there, as well as at the Cannobiana, when the opera was not performing.

421   A visit to La Scala, Milan, 1816

Galiffe, *Italy and its inhabitants*, vol. 1, pp. 38–41

Our impatience was naturally great to see the theatre of La Scala, the finest in the world; and to hear an Italian opera in Italy. Upon learning of our intention to visit it the same evening, our *laquais de place* assured us, that we could not possibly find a seat in the pit, and that we ought to hire a box, which, he said, would cost us twelve or fifteen franks; and he offered, of course, to run to the theatre to engage one. But I have an habitual distrust of these gentry; so we stopped him, and, going quietly ourselves, at eight o'clock, we succeeded in hiring a box for seven franks. The tickets are a separate charge, and cost each a frank and a half: this is astonishingly cheap, in comparison with English prices; but the subscriptions are still cheaper, and do not amount to more than 5 soldi, or French sous, for an evening. It is true, that what are called the house-expenses of this theatre are comparatively trifling. There are, for instance, no other lights than those on the stage. Those are, however, quite sufficient; and the effect of the decorations is even improved by this mode of illumination [. . .]

In size it appeared to me to be twice as large as the largest theatre in London. There are five tiers of boxes, and above them a gallery called *Loggione*: each tier is composed of thirty-nine boxes,– except the second and third, which have only thirty-six, the middle of both these being occupied by that of the imperial family; and each box may contain eight or ten persons. In the pit, there are seats for about 600 persons, and standing-room for 400 more; the proportion of space for the latter is larger than in French or English theatres, because the pit, in those of Italy, like the Exchange in a commercial town, is a place of general resort, where you can hardly fail to find at some hour of the evening whomsoever of your acquaintance you may wish to speak to. Hence there is a great deal of intercourse and circulation amongst this part of the audience; which would not be easily practicable, if the whole space were occupied by benches. This constant moving and talking, is very unpleasant to a stranger, who comes to the theatre for the purpose of listening to the performance; but it may be observed, on the other hand, that as the same opera is usually performed every evening for a whole month, the plot of the piece ceases, after the second or third representation, to excite any interest; and further, that those parts of the musick, which really deserve attention, always command a general silence.

The theatre is not decorated in an ostentatious manner; but it is more truly elegant and grand, than all the gilt ornaments in the world could render it. Every box has a drapery of green silk, with curtains of the same; which, being drawn in front, convert it into a neat little closet, where you may sit as comfortably as if you were at home.

The performance consists of an opera in two acts (this is, at present, the new and universal fashion) and two ballets, a serious one between the two acts of the opera, and a comic dance to close the evening's entertainment. Sometimes, the second act is performed before the first; sometimes you have the first act of one opera, and the second of another, or *vice versa*; or two first, or two second acts:– all which seems very strange to an English spectator [. . .]

422   Theatres in Turin, 1819

Lady Morgan, *Italy* (3 vols., London: Henry Colburn, 1821), vol. I, pp. 81–2[1]

The two small Theatres, which were open when we were at Turin, had nothing to recommend them. They were dark and dirty, with no other attraction than what the excellent acting of the *Marcolina*[2] lent to the comic opera, of which she was the *prima donna*. The Grand Opera, in the absence of the court, was shut. Long deemed the private property of royalty, it has undergone the general purification which followed the Restoration,[3] and is exclusively set apart for the *noblesse*; the Queen presiding over the distribution and prices of the boxes. Her list decides the number of quarterings requisite to occupy the aristocratic rows of the first and second circles, and determines the point of *roture*, which banishes to the higher tiers the *piccoli nobili*. We visited this theatre by day; and as we had not yet seen the theatres of Milan and Naples, it struck us by its splendour and extent. In fact, it rates as the third *salle de spectacle* of Italy.

[1] Lady Sydney Morgan (1776–1859), *née* Owenson, Irish novelist and daughter of an actor, best known for her novels *The Wild Irish Girl* (1806) and *O'Donnell* (1814). She wrote a study of France that was controversial for its bluntness.

[2] Marietta Marcolini (*c.* 1780–?), Italian contralto, who was a notable early interpreter of Rossini.

[3] The reference is to the restoration of the French monarchy after the Napoleonic period.

423   Teatro Carlo Felice, Genoa, 1847

Biblioteca Teatrale Burcardo, Rome

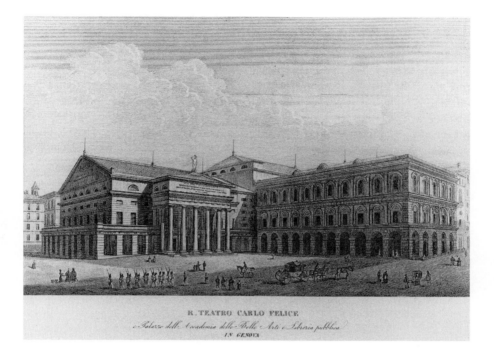

R. TEATRO CARLO FELICE
Palazzo delle Accademia delle Belle Arti e Libreria pubblica
IN GENOVA

424   Theatres in Venice, 1780

Martyn, *Tour through Italy*, p. 459

There are no less than seven *Theatres*[1] at Venice; two of these are commonly appropriated to the serious opera, two to comic operas, and the other three to plays; but they are all open only during the Carnival, which begins on S. Stephen, and continues till Lent; and then they are all full every night. In autumn the houses are open for the comic opera and plays: and at the Ascension there is a serious opera.

[1] This was the case for much of the eighteenth century, although most were for the musical stage and the number of theatres actually given over to the regular drama varied from time to time, but was rarely more than three.

An outstanding opera house built in this period was the famous La Fenice in Venice. Designed by the architect Antonio Selva, it was one of the last major architectural works of the independent Venetian Republic, being commissioned in 1788 and opened in 1792. Nearly all theatres in Venice had been pressed for space and La Fenice was no exception, but Selva succeeded in producing a simple but highly utilizable building that included an entrance for patrons arriving by gondola and a simple, but neat and attractive façade. Greatly damaged by fire in 1836, it was reconstructed by the Meduna brothers.

425   Theatres in Florence, 1780

Martyn, *Tour through Italy*, pp. 384–5

There are several *Theatres* in Florence, all open during the Carnival, which begins the day after Christmas-day, and lasts till Ash-Wednesday: at other times also one of them is open, except in Lent and Advent. The two principal are the *Pergola*,[1] finished in 1755; and the new Opera house,[2] first opened in the year 1779. This is very elegant; but the stage is not so spacious as in the Pergola: it has five rows of boxes, 106 in all; the pit will scarcely hold 400. There is a little theatre, *di Santa Maria lata*,[3] for burlettas; and another, which is larger, wherein comedies are performed.

[1] The most celebrated post-Renaissance Florentine theatre, the Teatro della Pergola, was established by the Academia Immobili and first opened in 1656. It had a very long and distinguished history, in the seventeenth century presenting opera by composers such as Melani and Cavalli. It then had close links with the Medici family. In 1755 it was substantially reconstructed, as Thomas Martyn's dating indicates, being given eighty-four boxes set out in four rows; the interior was decorated by one of the great designers of the age, A. Galli da Bibbiena. For most of its long history the theatre was dominated by *opera seria* and *buffa* and by dance.

[2] This reference is to the Teatro Nuovo, founded by the Societa degli Intrepidi in the summer of 1778 and opened just over a year later, and thus decidedly new when Martyn visited it. At that time it catered for lyric theatre, but later became a house for regular drama.

[3] The Teatro Santa Maria was both established and then thoroughly refurbished in the mid-eighteenth century. It housed mainly regular drama, with generally only modest stage decoration. In the nineteenth century it was several times refurbished and amplified, notably in 1828, when it was given ninety-six boxes set in five tiers and renamed the Teatro Alfieri.

426   Theatres in Rome

Galiffe, *Italy and its inhabitants*, vol. 1, pp. 416–25

The Theatres at Rome are never open except during the Carnival, that is to say, from Christmas to Lent. There are several of them, but only one – the *Argentina*[1] – that is much frequented by people of fashion. It is spacious and handsome. It has six rows of boxes, and may contain about fifteen hundred spectators; the ornaments are in good taste, and it is less gloomy than the Italian theatres we have hitherto seen,– being lighted by a large chandelier. Each of the tickets for the pit bears a number corresponding with that of the particular seat to which it entitles the possessor; and being marked at the two extremities, they are torn down the middle when delivered,– the doorkeeper retaining one half, and returning the other to the visitor, to enable him to find his proper place; there is besides a person within the theatre, whose business it is to guide the company to their seats. All this is well arranged; but the theatre is built of wood, and in case of sudden fire, a great part of the audience must inevitably perish. Two companies of players performed at it this winter. The first was an indifferent set; and the music of Tancredi,[2] which they pretended to perform, was so sadly mangled, that it could hardly be recognised. I saw only the first act, which was bad enough; but Rossini who saw the second, assured me that it contained only one piece of his composition; and that the rest, though it bore his name, was perfectly unknown to him. The second company was infinitely better, and performed *Quinto Fabio*, with excellent music. The price of a ticket is 5 paoli for the evening, and 3 paoli afterwards.[3]

The next theatre is called *La Valle*,[4] and has room for eighteen hundred or two thousand spectators. The performances were mixed, comedy and opera: and the singers much better than the first company at the *Argentina* [. . .] The price of tickets at *La Valle* is only 2 paoli.

The theatre of *Apollo*[5] is the largest of all; there is very convenient room in it for two thousand spectators, and it is built of stone; so that I was rather surprised at its being given up to the lower classes. But I afterwards learnt that people thought it very unsafe, on account of its situation on the Tiber, which they fancied might some time or other carry it off. The performances here were likewise diversified; but dramas, comedies, farces, and operas were all equally bad. The price of a ticket is only 1 paolo.

The theatre *Della Pace*[6] is the ugliest I ever saw: it is long and narrow; there are only eleven places in the whole breadth of the pit,– ten sitting, and one, in the middle standing; and there are four rows of twenty-one boxes each. Nothing can be imagined more wretched and vulgar than the performances, unless it be the audience that applauded them, and who seemed delighted with their entertainment: the latter consisted of such ill-looking, ill-dressed, dirty people, that it was really no indifferent part of a stranger's amusement to see *such* an assemblage sitting at a play. Here also the ticket cost 1 paolo.

The theatre *Capranica*[7] is large, and may contain about sixteen hundred spectators. There are six rows of boxes, the uppermost of which forms the *Loggione*, or gallery. This theatre is the most dangerous of all in case of fire; it is not only built entirely of wood, but there is not the least mixture of plaster on the walls, and the passages are so low, that a tall man could not stand erect with his hat on; and so narrow, that we were obliged to remain stationary for more than ten minutes, without the least possibility of moving on, until those who were before us had cleared the only outlet that there is. The company was not good, but they sometimes performed entertaining comedies,– such as *Le Donne Avvocate*,[8]– and some strange farces [. . .]

The theatre of *Pallacorda*[9] is just of the same form as the theatre Della Pace, but much smaller, having only two rows of boxes. Its passages are abominable, being exceedingly narrow and low; and the staircase is a mere assemblage of broken planks. It really is a horrid place, but the puppet-show which occupied it was highly admired by the connoisseurs. I certainly thought it far superior to that which I had seen at Milan, but tiresome for a whole evening's amusement.

There is another very small theatre on the ground-floor of the *Palazzo Fiano*, where the admission costs only 3 baiocchi:[10] it was not so very bad as the lowness of the price had led me to anticipate. The performances were abbreviations of well-known pieces, and were tolerably adapted to the size of the theatre; not so the actors,– who looked preposterously tall, and were obliged to exert considerable dexterity in order to cross the stage without pulling down the scenery.[11]

The theatre *Aliberti*,[12] which is by far the handsomest of all, was not made use of in my time; and I only saw it on the evening of the Carnival balls [. . .]

One thing is truly shocking in all the theatres of Rome,– their disgusting filth-iness, and the horrible stench which pervades them,– of which no one who has not experienced them, can have any idea.

---

[1] This theatre, in the Piazza Argentina, is still Rome's principal theatre. Built in 1732 with six rows of thirty-one *palchi* or boxes, it was dominated for much of the century by musical drama. At the turn of the century it began to offer performances of prose drama more regularly.

[2] *Tancredi*, an opera, or, more accurately, a 'melodramma eroico', by Rossini, first presented at La Fenice, Venice, in 1813.

[3] A *paolo* was a measure of currency.

[4] Constructed in the courtyard of the Palazzo Capranica in the 1720s and later thoroughly refurbished several times, as in the 1760s and the 1820s. In the nineteenth century it enjoyed a rich musical repertory. It was there that the actor-manager Ermete Novelli attempted to establish the first *stabile* in Rome early in the twentieth century.

[5] Formerly the Teatro Tor di Nona and dating from the late 1660s, it was largely destroyed by fire in 1781, but rebuilt and renamed the Apollo.

[6] A minor theatre dating from the late seventeenth century, which had been quite substantially ren-ovated in the early eighteenth century. By the early nineteenth century it had declined and become a home for dialect drama, puppet plays and rope-dancing. It was closed in 1844 and demolished in 1858.

[7] Likewise dating from the late seventeenth century, it had been thoroughly refurbished on a number of occasions in the eighteenth century and in the early years of the nineteenth century by architects of distinction, such as Juvarra and Marescotti. It was closed in 1817 as a fire hazard, and its later fortunes were punctuated by periods of opening and closure.

[8] A play by Sografi, written in 1801.

[9] A wooden theatre built in 1714, it had a long history as a house for musical theatre and serious drama. In the later eighteenth century it gradually declined and became a house for dialect plays and popular farces. This tradition was sustained throughout much of the first half of the nineteenth century, but the theatre fell into disuse and was finally demolished at the time of the First World War.

[10] Another currency measure.

[11] Reminiscent of English *interregnum* and later seventeenth- and eighteenth-century mainly fair-ground practice, this is an interesting indication that drolls were a feature of the poorer and simpler kind of Italian theatre at this time.

[12] Dating from the early eighteenth century, in its heyday this was one of the largest and most splendid theatres in Rome, boasting seven tiers of balconies, each with thirty-two boxes. It was substan-tially renovated twice in the course of the first half of the nineteenth century, was demolished in 1859 and rebuilt, opening a year later, but survived only three years, being destroyed by fire in 1863.

427   The interior of the Teatro Apollo in Rome
Biblioteca Teatrale Burcardo, Rome

This nicely illustrates the *palchetti* (boxes), which in the major theatres in the late eighteenth century, not only in Rome but also in most of the important cities, were often embellished according to the tastes of the prosperous spectators who occupied them on a regular basis: they were social meeting places, and activities might well go on in them other than that of just watching the performance; in some theatres occupants could be on view when they so wished, the box openings presenting them to the audience in the other boxes and in the pit, rather like figures framed in a painting; but curtains could be drawn across the opening to provide complete privacy.

When built in 1737, the Teatro San Carlo in Naples was a large and splendid theatre, noted for being one of the largest and most elegantly appointed in Italy, and it was certainly the dominant musical theatre in southern Italy throughout the period. Its horseshoe-shaped auditorium had six tiers of boxes, amounting to 184 *palchi*. As nearly half of these belonged to noble Neapolitan families, who were required by royal edict to hold them, the clientèle at San Carlo invariably presented an impressive show, as was remarked on by visitors. In 1810 it was fitted with an imposing façade by Antonio Niccolini, who later rebuilt it after it was destroyed by fire in 1816.

428   The Teatro San Carlo, Naples, 1780

(a) Martyn, *Tour through Italy*, pp. 282–3; (b) Biblioteca Teatrale Burcardo, Rome

(a) The great *Theatre of S. Carlo*, adjoining to the royal palace, is vast, noble and elegant. The form is a truncated ellipse, like the other Italian theatres. There are six ranges of boxes, thirty in each row, except the three lowest, out of which the king's box is taken: this, as usual, is in front of the stage. In the pit are fifteen rows of seats, thirty in a row, separated by broad rests for the elbow: they are mostly let for the season; and turn up, and are locked in the absence of the proprietor. The price of admission into the house is 3 carlini, about thirteen-pence half-penny. The stage is of an immense size: the scenes, dresses, and decorations, are magnificent. On public nights, such as the king's and queen's name-day, etc., the house is superbly illuminated: in the front of each box is placed a large mirror, before which two large wax tapers are set; these, with the lights within the boxes, and on the stage, make a prodigious splendor. The size of the theatre, and the noise of the audience, are such that neither voices nor the instruments can be heard distinctly: but the Italians consider the opera so much as a place of rendezvous and visiting, that they seldom attend to the performance, except when a favourite air is singing. It is common not only to receive company in the boxes, but to take ices and other refreshments, to sup, and to play at cards. The opera generally begins on the 5th of November, and lasts till September.

(b)

At the opposite extreme to the grand Teatro San Carlo opera house was the small theatre that housed some of the most brilliant comic performers of the early and mid-nineteenth century, the Teatro San Carlino. There was little of the architectural grandeur of the great houses here, and few of their front-of-house comforts, but there was a great deal of enthusiasm and vitality among performers and audiences alike.

429   The Teatro San Carlino, Naples

Paul de Musset, *La Course en voiturin* (1845; Paris, 1953), pp. 129–30

On the Piazza di Castello, facing the cannons which through the bars are aimed at the passers by, you will see a modest building, which you would never mistake for a theatre. The entrance resembles rather that of a shabby cabaret. A low and winding corridor down a steep slope takes you into a basement where a small but a proper and well-lit *salle de spectacle* can be found. You are in the Teatro San Carlino. Not far from it, on the same *piazza*, there is another tavern of similar appearance, called the Teatro la Fenice.[1] The ancient comic spirit, the genius of which Italy will never lose, plays which treat of the here and now, the representation of well-known ridiculous characters and of popular types, direct audience address, as in the times of Scaramouche or Gros-Guillaume,[2] all have found refuge in these two booth theatres [. . .]

[1] Not to be confused with the Teatro la Fenice in Venice, which was of course a great opera house.

[2] The latter was a popular French theatre and street comic performer in the seventeenth century; the former the celebrated Tiberio Fiorilli, an actor of the *Commedia dell'arte*, who first visited Paris in the 1640s and largely settled there from 1660 onwards, his troupe, which became the Comédie-Italienne, sharing a theatre for a time with Molière, who was said to have been much influenced by the Italian actor. Scaramouche came to London several times in the 1670s and performed at the English court.

430   Teatro San Carlino, Naples

Biblioteca Teatrale Burcardo, Rome

Although considerable caution is needed in relating book illustrations to actual stage designs, we can perhaps see something of the gradual shift in the last decades of the eighteenth century, from stylized stage settings to the more overtly representational in the illustrations to the two late eighteenth-century collected editions of Carlo Goldoni's plays: depiction of scenes in the Pasquali edition is refined and decorative, reflecting mid-century French taste; that in the later Zatta edition rougher, more familiar and quasi-naturalistic. But one may doubt that even the most important acting companies actually used scenes and props in quite the detail shown here, much decoration probably being at best stock and schematized. Spectacular scenery was a feature of the musical rather than the dramatic theatre.

431   Romantic scenery

Biblioteca Teatrale Burcardo, Rome. Lorenzo Ruggi, *Raccolta inedita di cinquanta scene teatrali le piu applaudite nei teatri* (Bologna, n.d.)

In its depiction of the towers, battlements and steps of a castle seen through an arch, the emphasis of this early nineteenth-century design is distinctly Romantic. Designed for an opera, it illustrates the continuing practice of leading designers of publishing collections of their work.

432   Interior of the Teatro San Carlo, Naples

Biblioteca Teatrale Burcardo, Rome

Interno del R.º Teatro, di S.Carlo.

Several of the contemporary observers cited below make it clear that theatre-going was popular among many social groups, and the theatre often functioned as a convenient meeting place. As the range and variety of popular street theatre indicates, audiences were socially heterogeneous, and this seems to have applied to audiences in many of the theatres as well: even at the more socially exclusive the audience was drawn from a number of different social levels. At some theatres this was conspicuously the case, as at the San Carlino in Naples, which attracted spectators from all classes and, as is indicated below, provided regular secular and religious entertainment for whole families.

433   A socially heterogeneous audience for opera at La Scala, Milan

Lady Morgan, *Italy*, vol. I, pp. 161–4

The vast pit was crowded; the women were nearly as numerous as the men; and though none but the *cittadini*[1] go to this part of the house, they were perfectly Parisian in their dress; and had exchanged the far more elegant Milanese costume of the morning, in which they are seen tripping to mass, for the overloaded bonnets and overwhelming ruffs of the French toilet. The resemblance, however, of the two nations was confined to dress: there was none of the petulance, the smartness, the mannerism, which pervades the female *bourgeoisie* of Paris. The women were *posées*, graceful, indolent, and at rest. Whenever a female face *could* be seen, it rarely happened that it was not a handsome one;– the eyes never failed. The men who filled the alleys of the pit, were separated into dusky groups, and engaged in animated though whispering conversation. Many, in spite of their great coats and round hats, had a military air. Thinly scattered through the whole, appeared the sky-blue and silver, or white Austrian uniform; and here and there a yellow-whiskered phlegmatic German face edged itself among the dark expressive heads of the Italians, in marked and curious contrast. Every door was doubly guarded by foreign soldiery, and the *gens-d'armes* were conspicuous among the audience in the pit. In the upper boxes a few lights twinkled, where *Tarocco*[2] is played, in cadence to Rossini's delightful symphonies.

The fronts of the boxes almost uniformly exhibit a *tête-à-tête*: sometimes a lady and gentleman, sometimes two ladies: for two only appear in front, though the back of the box may be crowded. The ladies take off their large bonnets and hang them in the box, exactly as at Paris; and the elegant *demi-toilette* prevalent in the Scala, would not have shamed the inventive genius of Mademoiselle Victorine of Bourbonite memory. The most scrupulous ladies of the highest ranks come alone in their carriage to the opera. As soon as they enter their box, and have glanced their eye along the circles, giving or returning the Italian salutation, which has something at once infantine and coquettish in its beckoning gesture, they turn their back to the scene, and for the rest of the night, hear and see nothing out of their own society; except when apprised by the orchestra that some scene in the ballet, or some *aria* or *duo* in the opera is about to be performed which it is good taste or good fashion to listen to and admire [. . .]

The Scala is the evening home of almost all ranks, the recreation of the trades-man, the exchange of the merchant, the closet of the critic, and the rendezvous of the politician. For there alone, amidst the openest publicity, can privacy find an asylum against the intrusions of espionage. The box is sacred – none can intrude there but the intimate friends of the lady or her husband [. . .]

[1] Ordinary citizens.
[2] Taroc or tarot, a card game played with seventy-eight decorated cards.

434   Attending the theatre in Venice, 1780

Martyn, *Tour through Italy*, pp. 459–60

A trifle is paid at the door for admittance; this entitles a person to go into the pit, where he may look about, and determine what part of the house he will sit in. There are rows of chairs towards the front, the seats of which fold back, and are locked; they who choose to take them, pay a little more to the door-keeper for unlocking the seat.* Very decent people occupy these chairs; but the back part of the pit is filled with servants and gondoliers.[1] The nobility and better sort of citizens hire boxes by the year; and there is always a sufficient number for strangers. The price varies according to the season and the run of the piece.

* In the playhouses 10 soldi at going in, and 5 more for a seat.
   At the comic opera 40 or 50 soldi; and 20 more for a seat.
   At the serious opera 80 soldi at entrance, and as much more for a seat.

[1] The gondoliers were, of course, awaiting their customers. Goldoni refers to these in several of his comedies, notably *La buona figliuola* (The respectable girl).

435   Behaviour in the opera auditorium in Venice, 1789

Arthur Young, *Travels in France and Italy during the years 1787, 1788 and 1789* (London, 1915), p. 260

There is between the front row of chairs in the pit and the orchestra, in the Venetian theatre, a space of 5 or 6 feet without floor: a well-dressed man, sitting almost under a row of ladies in the side boxes, stepped into this place, and made water with as much indifference as if he had been in the street; and nobody regarded him with any degree of wonder but myself.

436   A Roman audience, 1808

Baron d'Uklanski, *Travels in upper Italy, Tuscany and the ecclesiastical states; in a series of letters written to a friend in the years 1807 and 1808* (2 vols., London, 1816), vol. II, pp. 89–90

The uncleanliness, however, which prevails there [the Teatro della Valle] is truly surprising; the noxious smell is so great that I nearly fainted away. The same public, besides, who are so polite in private intercourse, are here rather ill-behaved. They chat, laugh, and talk aloud; so that there is no chance of knowing what is said or sung on the stage; but when a favourite air is introduced, they will become silent, or even join in the chorus. For a fortnight past has been continually performed the opera *Griselda, or La Vertu al Cimento*,[1] in the intolerable practice of first regaling the public with one act of a play, and then with another of an opera; continuing alternately with declamation and song, and concluding with vocal harmony. The *prima donna* is at present Signora la Festa. She has a pleasing diction, and an insinuating voice, but without compass. She is, besides, in the habit of spying round the boxes, and nodding or bowing to her acquaintance; in which many more performers imitate her.

[1] Opera in two acts by A. Anelli.

437   The audience at the San Carlino in Naples, 1820[1]

Lady Morgan, *Italy*, vol. III, pp. 293–4

We observed on this occasion, that the theatre was filled with women and their children; and that many of the boxes included the whole family of the lower *cittadini* class, even to the livery-boy and the baby; for it seems to be a sort of duty to attend these sacred dramas in Lent; and all that appears so singular and even profane in these exhibitions to the foreign spectator, is by them attended to with reverence and interest. When the false prophet was praying to his false gods, and Elijah kept crying in a taunting tone, *'più forte! – non t'ascoltano!'* ('Cry louder! – they don't hear you!') – the audience clapped their hands and exclaimed, 'Bravo Elijah! bravo!'

[1] Lady Morgan was at Naples during Lent, when at the Teatro San Carlino Pulcinella plays had given way to religious drama for the period. Although in her box they were disappointed not to experience one of the traditional Pulcinella plays, she saw a piece about the prophet Elijah, called *Acabe*.

438   Actor–audience relations at the Teatro San Carlino, Naples, 1845

Musset, *Course en voiturin*, pp 129–47

The Neapolitan public, much more amenable than the Parisian, accepts anything as long as the play is amusing; it does not have, unlike us, a particular dislike of the fantastic [. . .] one does not entertain the Neapolitans with subtle humour or sophisticated wit. One must feed them a more substantial repast [. . .]

During the forty days of Lent, the masks being strictly forbidden in the theatres in Naples, Pulcinella transforms himself into *Pascariello*. He is also a cunning servant, absent-minded, lazy and gluttonous, but he is less fantastic than Pulcinella. He wears a livery [. . .] His pleasantries lose some of their strength because of the missing half-mask. The other roles remain the same all through the season.

The old and naïve habit of addressing the audience has been preserved both at the San Carlino and La Fenice. During the last interval, the troupe's orator presents himself between the stairs and the toilet, and announces the following day's spectacle or the benefit performances. Once upon a time in France, the actor most beloved by the public was expected to make these speeches; in Naples, Don Pancrazio, who is a man of wit and comic to the tip of his fingernails, every evening, together with Altavilla, invents an amusing address which is eagerly awaited. The day the theatre closed, before Holy Week, I was at San Carlino in the box of a Neapolitan lady. Don Pancrazio addressed the audience in these terms:

'Ladies and Gentlemen, I have plenty of children, who have all their teeth, and who devour a *rotolo* of macaroni as if it were a fig. They have broken so many glasses at home that I have been obliged to make them drink from the palm of their hands. Next week I shall have to give them some Easter eggs. My colleagues and the signor *impresario* wish to help me by giving a performance for my benefit on the day of reopening. We shall present the new play of the *Guappi*, and I recommend myself to your generosity.'

After making this speech, the actor went round the auditorium in order to persuade important people to keep their boxes for the benefit performance.

IV Early nineteenth-century acting companies and theatre conditions

In discussing the general state of the regular theatre in Italy at the end of the eighteenth century and in the first decades of the nineteenth, we can say with some confidence that technical means were poor, organization was often chaotic, rehearsals left much to be desired and finances were for the majority of players and companies nearly always precarious. Its moribund state was variously ascribed at the time to a lack of dramatists with imagination, intellect and theatrical flair, the unavailability of a language that might permit the growth of an attractive national repertory, the excessive dependence on French drama and dramatic models, the vulgar, undemanding tastes of audiences interested more in spectacle and displays of physical skill than in wit or ideas, the pettily restrictive censorship operating in many cities and the generally debased state of the acting profession. At the end of the eighteenth century Alfieri had tried, both in his critical and theoretical writings and through the influence he was able to exercise in the theatres, at least to address this last problem, seeking to reform both the preparation and performance of plays by emphasizing the need for careful study and the disciplined control and shaping of a production. But he had little effect. Writing of conditions in the second decade of the new century, the actor and writer Francesco Augusto Bon complained bitterly of the 'crass ignorance' and 'widespread dissipation' of actors whose reading was confined to their parts. Many in most companies were slack in learning lines and dilatory in rehearsal, and few managers were able to exercise effective regular control over performance practices. The profession enjoyed little social standing, was ill-rewarded and artistically was accorded scant respect. There were, of course, distinguished exceptions, and they were to increase significantly in the later decades of the century, but the tendency of the best players in the early and middle years of the eighteenth century to take their talents abroad, attracted by richer financial pickings and official subsidy, had a debilitating effect on the Italian theatre until well into the nineteenth century.

No less debilitating had been the progressive decline throughout the later seventeenth and eighteenth centuries in patronage of the regular theatre in Italy. Whilst theatrical activity had always been financially precarious, and acting a mercenary profession dependent on success in the marketplace, in the past some leading acting troupes in the peninsula had invariably enjoyed patronage, particularly in the later sixteenth and for much of the seventeenth century, when their support came from rulers or members of the social or religious élite, some of whom took an active interest in company personnel and repertoires, and who often saw the troupes as emblems of state prosperity and artistic refinement, even using them as quasi-political emissaries: thus in 1678 the Duke of Modena sent his acting company to the court of the English king, Charles II, as a gesture to his sister, Maria d'Este, wife of James, Duke of York, and to help cement a specific political policy. But such companies were very much the hobbies, even the playthings, of particular rulers. By the eighteenth century patrician patronage and interest had waned, and, where it was available, opera rather than *teatro di prosa* was invariably the recipient. What is more, with the decline in patronage any real sense of stability evaporated, even for the major troupes. To a considerable extent the eighteenth-century *embourgeoisement* of theatre had led elsewhere in Europe to the establishment of new theatre buildings, with acting companies attached, a concomitant shift from touring to resident or semi-resident companies and, where touring persisted, to more confined and well-defined circuits. In the Italian peninsula, however, throughout the eighteenth and nineteenth centuries regular touring remained the norm, and the stability of being theatre-based, with the luxury of some civic support, was in the early decades of the nineteenth century the prerogative of a mere handful of companies, and often for only a few years (see chapter 5 below).

In the first decades of the nineteenth century opera, which could boast the music of Rossini, Bellini, Donizetti and the young Verdi, and the texts of able librettists such as Felice Romani and Salvatore Cammarano, dominated the Italian theatre, and even leading players such as De Marini, Belli Blanes and Anna Fiorilli Pellandi were, and felt themselves to be, of an inferior art and profession. Most acting companies were independent and most lived hand to mouth. The principal companies, employing perhaps as many as fourteen or fifteen actors and actresses, for the most part managed to confine their touring to the major cities, and generally performed in theatres, even if not all of those were technically well equipped. But, almost certainly, the majority of companies operated at a much lower financial and artistic level, had probably no more than seven or eight members, performed mainly in the provinces, and appeared before predominantly uneducated audiences in halls, open-air arenas and town and village squares. What scenery and props they used would have been basic and of a kind they could deploy in a variety of plays, and would have been easy to modify, repair and transport from place to place. Unsung by commentators, many of these players may well have been of limited education themselves, for poverty and unemployment certainly continued to encourage some to take up the profession, as had been the case in the past. This may in part account for the fact that they have left few records. However, many must have been not unlike some of the companies briefly mentioned by visitors to Italy (see chapter 2 above).

As has been said, most theatre companies in this period were independent, and survived or went under according to their ability or failure to compete in a tough marketplace. In the early nineteenth century, however, and under the impact of the Napoleonic invasion, a new kind of stable, privileged company emerged: one supported more as a civic facility, legally constituted and intended to serve the interests of the community as well as local political policy. All these companies were important, not so much perhaps for their particular theatrical achievements, as for their inauguration of the long, slow process of giving a degree of financial stability and artistic dignity to the regular Italian theatre, which had reached its nadir in the last decades of the eighteenth century. The Compagnia Reale Francese, established by Napoleon on 10 July 1806 and housed in the Teatro Carcano in Milan, set the pace for this new development, being expressly set up to please and instruct the populace by presenting masterpieces from the French dramatic repertory.

The first Italian *capocomico* to obtain a privilege was Salvatore Fabbrichesi, the French Viceroy of Milan authorizing a warrant on 12 August 1807 for a company of Italian players to perform tragic and comic drama from the national repertory: it included one of the finest actresses of the early decades of the century, Anna Fiorilli Pellandi, and excellent actors such as Pellegrino and Belli Blanes. On the restoration of Austrian hegemony in 1814 the troupe became, first, the Compagnia de' Commedianti Italiani, and then the Compagnia Comica Nazionale. In 1815 Fabbrichesi moved with a number of his players to Naples, and was supported there at the Teatro dei Fiorentini by Ferdinand IV of Bourbon. Other subsidized companies followed, including in 1821 the Compagnia del Re di Sardegna, in 1827 the Drammatica Compagnia at Parma, and in 1823 the Compagnia Ducale di Modena, patronized by Francesco IV and for a time under the direction of Francesco Augusto Bon. But few of these companies survived for very long, and in addition their subsidy fluctuated and their artistic quality was in the main modest. The exception was the Compagnia Reale Sarda: what set the Reale Sarda apart was that while it too found its subsidy sparse and subject to cuts and its functioning and repertoire fettered by political regulation, it nonetheless managed to enjoy a long and artistically successful history.

The first passage quoted below, a piece from the memoirs of the actor and dramatist Francesco Augusto Bon, indicates that the conduct of Italian companies left much to be desired, and invited negative comparison with foreign troupes. But all was not negative. Other visitors cited below, well informed about theatre elsewhere in Europe, such as Stendhal, Galiffe and Paul de Musset, were able to find much of value on the Italian regular stage. Local dialect theatre, still rooted in many of the old ways of the *commedia dell'arte*, and the example set by the practices and aspirations of some of the major actor-managers of the early years of the century, such as Fabbrichesi, De Marini, Righetti, Domeniconi and Modena, came in time to rejuvenate the stage. It is no accident that many of the leads of the 1820s and 1830s, such as Carlotta Marchionni and Maddalena Pelzet, came out of the Morrocchesi stable, that the Compagnia Reale Sarda gave schooling to such important figures of the mid-century as Ristori, Rossi and Luigi Bellotti-Bon, and that Modena's Compagnia dei giovani included the talents of the young Tommaso Salvini and Fanny Sadowsky. The reform of the theatre, at least in terms of company operations, was slow but came increasingly to be felt, and the middle decades of the nineteenth century were to constitute the great age of the Italian 'star' players, the most outstanding of them, from Ristori to Salvini and Rossi, touring beyond Italy and achieving international reputations. Several of these bear witness, in the passages from their memoirs cited here, to conditions they experienced when young and touring through the peninsula: Ristori to the subordination of the drama to opera and dance, and to the rigours and vagaries of censorship, Salvini to the sort of dangers travelling players might encounter. What emerges from many of the accounts is that, notwithstanding numerous tribulations, theatre in Italy retained much vitality and never wholly lacked either champions or enthusiastic recruits to the profession.

439   French and Italian companies in Naples, 1814

Francesco Augusto Bon, *Scene comiche, e non comiche della mia vita*, ed. Teresa Viziano (Rome: Bulzoni, 1985), pp. 89–94, and *Teatro Archivio*, 1 (1979), pp. 63–7

During the first five or six months of my stay in Naples I became friendly with the French actors,[1] and especially with the company director [. . .]

The days allowed to the Italian drama were Sunday, Tuesday and Thursday, the French actors having Monday, Wednesday and Saturday [. . .]

The repertoire of the French company was excellent [. . .] but the company was not strong enough to wear the cothurn with confidence, and so staged few tragedies. Unlike the French, the Italian company turned to *Ottavia, Virginia, Filippo, Oreste, Saul, Mirra, Polinice, Sofonisba* and almost all their sisters; with the exception only of the two *Bruti, Timoleone, Maria Stuarda, La congiura de' Pazzi* and *Agide*.[2] They added to these Monti's *Aristodemo* and *Manfredi*[3] and other works by contemporary Neapolitan authors. With respect to comedy, our director had nothing in his repertory but sentimental pieces, dreadful comedies calculated to entertain the plebs, and not one of Goldoni's masterpieces. The actors were poorly trained in a false mode, and being used to dialogue cast in a barbaric style, full of reticences, and epithets, and pleonasms, overloaded with long words and adverbs of four and five syllables, all declaimed their lines with a chant, accompanying their words with mannered gestures and affected contortions. Yet despite this, those few who had a degree of good taste did their best to improve themselves, to abandon false ways and follow a more correct path. Signora Perotti,[4] who was gifted enough to be as fine a tragic actress as she was a comic one, and who possessed sound judgement, set a good example, and she was followed by all the rest who wished to change and were capable of so doing. Goldoni's *Un curioso accidente* and *La vedova spiritosa* were the first steps the company took on the right path. *Molière* and *Tasso*[5] helped them to progress. *La bottega del caffè, Zelinda e Lindoro, La donna bizzarra, Pamela, Il ventaglio* and *Il burbero benefico*[6] propelled the actors even further: and much more might have been achieved had the director, who was obstinate and enthusiastic about the false mode, been more keen on the initiative and willing to listen to the advice of those who saw better, and if he had done from the beginning what two years later he came to see was the correct thing to do [. . .]

Many new comedies were offered to the company by various Neapolitan authors, among whom was a certain Barone di Cosenza.[7] What that man had in mind when he wrote plays I couldn't say, and few could guess by reading his compositions: the fact is that having set out on a false path, he got what always happens to those who walk on uneven ground. To make matters worse for him, the Perotti Company was succeeded by the Fabbrichesi Company,[8] in which the most talented actor in Italy, Giuseppe De Marini,[9] was making a name for himself. He was an artist who showed us how far human anomalies can go. This excellent player had stopped acting in tragedy, judging it to be an exalted poetic *genre* that in performance required an approach going beyond the simplicity of comedy. But what kind of comedy did he perform most of the time? That which degenerated into the most heart-rending drama. Every evening he would appear either as an exile, or a hardened criminal tortured by remorse or madness, or a victim of misadventures and disasters worse than those endured by King Theodore's ghost, or with an adulterous wife, or with a prostitute daughter: sometimes he had a son who was a thief or a brother charged with treason to the state [. . .] anyway he was always immersed in a farrago of crime, misfortune, lunacies terrible to watch and hear. What happened as a consequence? The worst evil that could have happened. Bad writers began to comply with his taste, and among them the one I have just mentioned. What do both good and bad writers want? Applause. In order to obtain applause, what is required? The enthusiasm of De actor and the vote of the public. The leading Italian actor wanted that: therefore one had to go along with him. The public, who love what is extraordinary, applauded, and moved further away from what is true and beautiful and from its golden simplicity. Good comedy went back to sleep; the finest Italian actor was furthering the demise of our theatre, while at the same time new authors trod the same path with him.

However, Nota did not do likewise.[10] When he began to write, with the exception of two or three lively plays by Giraud,[11] and two or three by Sografi,[12] the rest of the repertory was a heap of detestable rubbish. A few old and boring plays by Federici,[13] a mish-mash of vulgar pieces, melodramatic historical spectacles by Avelloni,[14] innumerable translations of the worst French and German plays; to sum up, Nota found the repertory to be a rubbish dump revolting to common sense. As a wise man, possessed of good taste, he was the first to go against the grain, and it is thanks to him that young students of dramatic art are now back on course. Although his plays lack invention, and their best scenes imitate Goldoni, or French theatre, and although the plots are rather contrived or novelettish, taken as a whole his first works gained him a reputation; and they very much helped to reinstate true comedy.

[1] Naples at this time was under French control. For more detail, see the introduction and notes to Teresa Viziano's edition of Bon's account.
[2] These are mainly plays by Alfieri.
[3] Vincenzo Monti (1754–1828) was an Italian poet and dramatist. Influenced by Goethe and Alfieri, he turned to dramatic writing from the mid-1780s. In 1791 he married the actress Teresa Pichler.
[4] Assunta Nazzari (c. 1780–1852), wife of the actor-manager Gaetano Perotti (fl. c. 1790–1820), who played amorosa roles and was launched as primattrice in her husband's company.
[5] Plays by Goldoni.
[6] Also by Goldoni.
[7] Giovanni Carlo Barone di Cosenza (1765–1851), a prolific Neapolitan dramatist.
[8] Salvatore Fabbrichesi (1760–1827), though by no means a great actor, gave one of the earliest Italian stage performances of a version of Shakespeare's Hamlet and was an important company manager.
[9] Giuseppe De Marini (1772–1829), an actor-manager with a fine stage presence and strong voice, was one of the leading Italian players of the generation that preceeded Modena.
[10] Alberto Nota (1775–1847), a minor but not insignificant dramatist, whose many works included comedies, bourgeois dramas of sentiment and historical plays.
[11] Giovanni Giraud (1776–1834), minor dramatist of the school of Molière and Goldoni.
[12] Simeone Antonio Sografi (1759–1818), a prolific dramatist and librettist.
[13] Probably meant here is Camillo Federici (1749–1802).
[14] Francesco Antonio Avelloni (1765–1851), a minor dramatist, also known as Il Poetino.

440   Stendhal on the De Marini company, 1817

Stendhal, Rome, Naples et Florence (Paris: Delaunay, 1826), vol. II, pp. 220–23

4 April, 1817. I was at the Teatro Nuovo. The de' Marini company was giving its one hundred and ninety-seventh performance. The stocky Vestri[1] is the best actor in Italy, indeed in the world; he is the equal of Molé and Iffland[2] in Il Burbero benefico,[3]

in l'*Ajo nell'imbarazzo*,[4] and in I don't know how many dismal rhapsodies to which he gives distinction. He is someone you can see twenty or more times without being bored. If Mademoiselle Mars[5] plays the role of a fool or a feather-brain, a casual glance, enough to seduce a vain public, indicates she is the first to ridicule her role and the foolish gestures she will permit herself. That is a defect never exposed by Vestri or Madame Pasta.[6]

Italians, and more particularly Italian women, place in the first rank de'Marini, whom I have seen in *Li Baroni di Felsheim*, a play translated from Pigault-Lebrun,[7] and in *I due Paggi*. For reasons of which I am well aware, natural simplicity does not charm in Italian books; they always require the florid and emphatic. The *Eloges* of Thomas,[8] the *Génie du Christianisme*, the *Gaule poétique*, and all the poetic writings on which, after ten years, our reputation rests, seem to have been devised expressly for the Italians. The prose of Voltaire, of Hamilton, of Montesquieu, seems not to affect them. There is the principle on which rests the immense reputation of de'Marini. He observes nature, but in moderation; and the emphatic always has pride of place in his heart. In young lead roles he bewitched all Italy; today he plays dignified fathers. Those last permit flamboyance, and have always given me pleasure.

Naïveté is something unknown in Italy, and scarcely anyone can endure the *Nouvelle Héloïse*. Such slight traces of naïveté as I have come across I have found in Mademoiselle Marchioni [*sic*],[9] a young woman possessed by passion, who performs every day, sometimes twice a day: at four o'clock in the open air for the people; and in the evening, by oil lamps, for the great company. I was bewitched by her today first at four o'clock, in the *Pie Voleuse*, and then at eight in *Francesca da Rimini*.[10] Madame Tassari,[11] an actress in the de' Marini company, plays rather in the same style. Her husband, Tassari,[12] is good in the role of a tyrant.[13]

Blanes,[14] before he enriched himself with a good marriage, was the Talma[15] of Italy. He lacked neither naturalness nor force: he was terrifying in the part of Almachilde in *Rosmunda*.[16] In this play the Queen, unhappy and dominated by passion, was interpreted by Madame Pelandi,[17] who has always bored me, but who was warmly applauded.

Pertica,[18] whom I saw tonight, is a fine comedian, particularly in heavier roles. He made me yawn in the *Poeta fanatico*,[19] one of the most boring of Goldoni's plays, but which is frequently performed. Certainly it is *realistic*,[20] but how vulgar it is! and it degrades, in the eyes of the grossest kinds of people, one who should be the noblest thing in nature: a great poet. This actor was much applauded in the part of *Brandt*, and he deserved his success, especially at the end, when he says to Frederick II: '*I shall write you a letter.*'

[1] Luigi Vestri (1781–1841) was, like De Marini, a leading actor of the early decades of the nineteenth century.
[2] Molé and Iffland. The former was an actor at the Comédie-Française in the early years of the century; the latter was August Wilhelm Iffland (1759–1814), a German actor, dramatist and theatre director.
[3] One of Goldoni's last comedies, written during his period in France, and known in English as *The Beneficent Bear*.

[4] Play by G. Giraud, written in 1807; it provided the plot for several opera *libretti*, notably for Donizetti in 1824.

[5] Mlle Mars (1779–1847), a French actress renowned in the early nineteenth century (see **242**, **246**, **271**, **284**, **364**).

[6] Giuditta Maria Costanza Pasta (1797–1865). Italian soprano with an international reputation.

[7] Charles Antoine Guillaume Pigault de l'Epinoy, known as Pigault-Lebrun (1753–1835), a French actor, director and dramatist.

[8] A minor French writer.

[9] Carlotta Marchionni (1796–1861) was born into the profession and became one of the greatest Italian actresses of the early nineteenth century. Early in her career she worked with such major figures as Luigi Vestri and Gustavo Modena and quickly became established as a leading player. She entered the Compagnia Reale Sarda as *primattrice* in 1823, and was noted for the versatility of her playing, more particularly in Goldonian comedy and Alfierian tragedy, and in the plays of Silvio Pellico. One of her finest performances was as the title part in Alfieri's *Mirra*, and in this, as in other parts she undertook, she was much commended by the leading theatre commentators of the age, such as Colomberti and Francesco Righetti.

[10] *La Pie voleuse, on La servante de Palaiseau*, a melodrama by Caigniez and d'Aubigny, first performed in Paris in 1815; *Francesca da Rimini* (1815) is the play by Silvio Pellico (1789–1854).

[11] Carolina Cavalletti-Tessari (1794–c.1850) was born into the profession and worked with such distinguished players as Fabbrichesi, Anna Fiorilli Pellandi and Paolo Belli-Blanes.

[12] Probably Alberto Tessari (1780– ?), described by Rasi as an 'ottimo padre nobile e tiranno tragici', was also a *capocomico*.

[13] That is, in the kind of role taken by an actor who specialized in playing 'heavies'.

[14] The Belli-Blanes were a family of Italian actors and actresses. Here is meant Paolo (1770–1823), one of the best tragic actors of the early nineteenth-century stage and noted for his performances in the plays of Alfieri.

[15] For documents relating to the acting of Talma, see **290**, **291**, **293**, **294**, **295**, **296**, **297**, and **298**. See also D. Roy, 'Talma', in *International dictionary of theatre, vol. III, Actors, directors and designers* (London and Detroit: St. James Press, 1996).

[16] Play by Alfieri, written 1779–80.

[17] Anna Fiorilli Pellandi was the distinguished actress-wife of the minor actor Antonio Pellandi; they were together in the Compagnia Vicereale Italiana.

[18] Nicola Pertica (1769–1821), for a time a member of the Compagnia Vicereale Italiana, played *caratterista* parts and at one time or other acted with most of the leading performers of his day.

[19] Goldoni's *Il poeta fanatico* (1750) is a rather insipid comedy that mocks in a good-humoured way the excesses of the Arcadian Academy.

[20] Literally *vrai*; many of Goldoni's comedies were noted for their seeming truthfulness to nature.

One of the great acting companies of the first half of the nineteenth century was the Compagnia Reale Sarda, which was established in Turin by Victor Emmanuel I on 28 June 1820 and which opened at the Teatro Carignano on 29 April 1821, led by two experienced actor-managers, Gaetano Bazzi and Domenico Righetti; it survived, if towards the end only precariously, until 1855. It is a reflection of the instability of pre-unification theatre that the company broke up on its return from what had been a triumphant three months in Paris, where Ristori first acquired her international reputation, and a no less successful tour of several months through the French provinces, followed by visits to Belgium, Dresden and Berlin. Many of the most distinguished actors, actresses and company managers of the early and middle years of the nineteenth century were at some time members of the Reale Sarda. Some were with it only briefly, such as the actor and author Francesco Augusto Bon, a member in 1821; others for many years, such as the actor-manager Luigi Vestri. Some spent more than one period with the company: Ristori joined it in 1837, when she was a young actress, and remained for four years, then returned in 1853, staying through to its closure. Young actors and authors acquired their early experience with the troupe, as did Gaetano Gattinelli and Ernesto Rossi.

441   The Compagnia Reale Sarda–the Victor Emmanuel patent, 1820[1]

Cited in Sanguinetti, *Compagnia Reale Sarda*, pp. 13–14

There has been presented to us, in order to receive Our Sovereign approval, the laudable project of a Society which would have as its purpose to institute in this Capital city a permanent Company, made up of excellent Italian Dramatic Actors. Since We consider Dramatic Art, when well regulated and appropriately favoured and protected, likely to refine manners at the same time as it provides honest entertainment for the Inhabitants of the Capital; and since We are in accord with other Princes in Italy in wishing to preserve the purity of Our beautiful language, and raise to a higher degree of splendour an art once so illustrious and so purposeful, in which outstanding Italian Talents provide instances of singular value, We have willingly decided to approve the execution of such a plan, convinced that the most efficient way to improve and perfect Dramatic Art is by the institution of a Company of Excellent Actors. And since We wish such an institution the more easily to achieve its aim, and since We wish to ensure it endure, We have decided to effect this at the cost of the Royal Treasury; and the execution of the plan is entrusted to the Noble *Direzione*[2] of the theatres.

In order to allow the above more easily to achieve its purposes, we wish that five people named by Us be added to the same. To this end, the above-mentioned *Direzione* will present a plan of execution, and will suggest the necessary sum to be paid by the R. Treasury, which sum, however, shall not exceed fifty thousand lire;[3] and finally it is Our will that the Repertory of Dramatic actions[4] to be performed by such a Company, be prepared and decided by the Noble *Direzione*, and then presented to the First Secretary of Police for his approval.

Turin, 28 June 1820

Victor Emmanuel – of S. Marzano.

[1]   The interest of this patent lies in the extent of the support offered. However, Vanda Monaco has argued that the terms on which the company was established in fact fell far short of what the reformers and idealists had hoped for. See *La Repubblica del teatro* (Florence, 1968), *passim*.
[2]   The committee that ran the theatre.
[3]   Although it did not stay at this fairly generous level for very long.
[4]   In other words, plays.

442   Bon on the Compagnia Reale Sarda, 1820

Bon, *Scene comiche*, pp. 171–84

Its direction was entrusted to a certain Gaetano Bazzi,[1] a Piedmontese, who was already an actor-manager. He suggested I should take the leading *brillante* role,[2] and as he offered me a suitable honorarium I signed a contract with him, but for one year only. [...]

The new royal company was not well organised. It was lacking in various respects, and notably in its repertory. Bazzi, an old-fashioned actor, counting, as they

say, on his old hits, from which he had always had some profit, had no intention of relinquishing them. Turin's *Direzione dei teatri* had delegated as its representative the Count
of Piossasco, an erudite, witty man, who was quite an expert in business and theatrical
matters: he took care of the choice of productions to be staged, and did well, as far as he
could: but one cannot do everything at once.

After giving a few performances in Pavia, with fair success, the royal company moved to
Turin in order to begin its service in the theatre of Prince Carignano.

Here things got decidedly confused. The Turin public disliked all the actors who had been
educated in Bazzi's school. Indeed they were mannered, self-conscious and inhibited. Those
actors who were new did not like Bazzi's old repertory, and things were not going at all
well. Soon after the first performance there was talk of changing the *prima attrice*, and in
the rush of the moment replacing her with the *seconda attrice*.[3] This cure was no worse
than the problem, but nor was it much better. The *Direzione* delegate left immediately in
order to engage the actress Carlotta Marchionni; but she managed a company of her own,
had engaged actors and had also leased some theatres for the following year, and so could
only commit herself for two years hence. Not knowing where to find a *prima donna* who
was available immediately, Piossasco decided to engage signorina Marchionni for the period
indicated and to return to Turin with this good news, although in the interim the company
would have to limp precariously along, in danger of falling into a crevasse from which there
would be no escape.

As there was no *prima attrice*, one had of necessity to stick to comedies of intrigue and
those plays where male characters predominate; in consequence, we poor comic actors had
to study new comedies continuously, rehearsing for four or five hours daily, and with only
one day's rest per week.

We staged a few tragedies, and, to tell the truth, Madama Bazzi,[4] who was not accepted
as *prima attrice* in comedy and drama, did not displease in tragedy, and more than once
succeeded in attracting the applause of the public. This actress had some merits, and she
would have revealed more, had she not been so discouraged at her first appearance.

A spirited young actress began to achieve prominence in the course of the year; this was
madama Rosa Romagnoli,[5] who later succeeded admirably in the comic parts of the maid,
the so-called *servetta* roles. This actress, without any study or training had instinctively
adopted a simple and spontaneous acting style. Her manners were not at all affected: she
possessed a good voice, a clear diction and, if at times she lacked a little colour, spoke her lines
with an excellent rhythm which never sounded monotonous. While not beautiful, she had
attractive features which, though not very mobile or capable of many shrewd expressions,
in her smile and joyful manner served her very well. She was of average height, and agile
of limb. She too came from the Perotti company, where she had begun her career. I acted
for several years with this actress, and always with pleasure, for our artistic talents were so
much in accord that in performance they created an excellent effect.

---

[1] Gaetano Bazzi (1771–1843), a Torinese actor and *capocomico*, born into an established theatrical
    family. In 1821 he helped form the Compagnia Reale Sarda, which he directed for more than twenty
    years.
[2] A light comedy role, invariably with some underscoring of the lively, the witty and the self-assured;
    in many companies there were both a *primo* and a *secondo brillante*.
[3] The leading lady and the second lead female role.
[4] Anna Maria Bazzi (1790–1860), niece of the Gaetano Bazzi referred to above, was a very competent
    actress, particularly in tragedy, and a member of the Reale Sarda at least between 1821 and 1828
    and possibly for longer.

5 Rosa Romagnoli (1806–86), wife of the actor Luigi Romagnoli, was born into the profession and, as Bon says, specialized in *servetta* roles, notably those of Goldoni.

443   Actors and actresses of the Compagnia Reale Sarda

Biblioteca Teatrale Burcardo, Rome

This illustration shows leading members of the company at the height of its success.

444   Rossi joins the Compagnia Reale Sarda, 1852[1]

E. Rossi, *Quarant'anni di vita artistica* (3 vols., Florence, 1887–8), vol. I, pp. 61–2

When I joined the Compagnia Reale, Bazzi was dead; Righetti,[2] who had been a good actor, was old, sick and dejected, and no longer performed. His lawyer son was the Company administrator. Giovanni Borghi,[3] one-time a member of the Company and its *brillante*, was the technical director. An extremely erudite man, gifted with an infallible memory, he was almost a walking library: in a position to advise on the art of acting, able to indicate how a character should be interpreted, to explain a concept, to illustrate an historical event – to be precise about its epoch. However, to control a group in every detail, to direct an ensemble so that all was in harmony and moved with regularity and precision, that was not for him: perhaps because he was old and was easily tired [. . .] But he never neglected direction, and Borghi would sit by the prompter's box from the moment rehearsal began to the moment it ended. During rehearsal no conversation was allowed in the wings or at the back of the stage, no actor would wear his hat or carry a cane in his hand or [. . .] a cigar in his mouth, as is nowadays the practice among Italian companies, including the so-called *primarie*,[4] which the reform created. One never failed to respect the ladies, one was not over-familiar, one did not use *tu* – as if to say, we have eaten together. One rehearsed and acted one's part to the best of one's ability, because nobody wanted to do to others what they did not want done to themselves. Borghi rarely acted, and when he did so it was always to replace somebody who was unwell. Whatever part it was, whether comic or serious, that of a young man or an old one, he was always ready. I remember how one evening Tessero[5] was ill, and his part was that of the Pontifex in *Ester d'Engaddi*,[6] done for Ristori's benefit; a long, difficult part which allowed for no expedients. Borghi went into the dressing-room, put on Tessero's costume, gave a quick glance at the part, appeared on stage and – I tell no lie – did not botch a line. When he had to replace someone, he was a better actor than when he acted in his own right [. . .]

I had signed a contract to be *primo attore*; not *primo attore assoluto*,[7] with choice of parts: once upon a time when absolutism ruled, the absolute was not very fashionable; today, with freedom, any Tom, Dick or Harry can be *assoluto* [. . .] and with choice of parts [. . .]

It was natural that I should be *assoluto* with my actors, who were all young and without pretensions, eager to learn, and that I should be Martha or Magdalen, Christ or Longinus, Herod or Barabbas, today Paolo, tomorrow Louis XI.[8] But it would have been improper, egotistical and ridiculous, had I pretended to exercise such absolutism in a semi-permanent *compagnia primaria*,[9] in which all the characters were assigned by the director to each individual actor.

---

[1] For Ernesto Rossi, see **460**.
[2] Domenico Righetti (1786–1859) was a Veronese actor and company manager. Of noble birth, he was a member of a number of acting troupes, including those led by Fabbrichesi and Blanes, before he and his wife, Vincenza Pinotti, joined forces with G. Bazzi, with whom he shared the fortunes of the Reale Sarda from 1821.

3 Giovanni Borghi (? – 1870), an actor and company manager, was married to the actress Elisabetta Bazzi.
4 The *primarie* created by the reform were the major acting companies that emerged in the early nineteenth century and enjoyed some degree of subsidy and stability, as did the Compagnia Reale Sarda.
5 Pasquale Tessero (1797–1887) came from a distinguished acting family. Although much of his career was spent in second-level companies, he and his wife, Carolina Ristori, sister of Adelaide, were members of the Reale Sarda from 1836. Their daughter, Adelaide (1842–92), was to enjoy great success in Italy as a player of romantic roles.
6 Play by Silvio Pellico.
7 A *primo attore* was a lead actor in a company, expected to play principal male roles when needed; a *primo attore assoluto* was one who was contractually free to chose the roles he played.
8 Lead roles in the stock dramas, melodramas and romantic plays of the time: thus Paolo was the lead role in Silvio Pellico's *Francesca da Rimini* and Louis XI the lead in Delavigne's play of the same name.
9 An established and state-supported stable company.

445   The company at the Teatro San Carlino in Naples, 1845

Musset, *Course en voiturin*, pp. 130–2

The San Carlino company is composed of about a dozen excellent actors, authentic Neapolitans by virtue of their facial expressions, their vivacity, their expressive gestures, their energy, and the ease with which they improvise. They understand one another like thieves, and are immensely popular. In all the plays one constantly finds the four classic roles: Pancrazio, Pulcinella, the *bègue* (gabbler) who wears enormous glasses, and the old woman Pangrazia, who is all the time convinced that young men adore her.[1] These four characters have the privilege of making the stalls laugh. They speak the Neapolitan dialect, while other parts vary according to the play, and are ordinarily written in Italian.[2] The old Don Pancrazio represents naïveté, good nature, the credulous ass, while Pulcinella represents cunning, gluttony, sloth, all the low and material instincts. When the old pedant with the large glasses is not Pancrazio's crony, as the French Orgon is Géronte's friend, he plays the lawyer, the bailiffs or the police commissioner. The character of the old woman is similar to that of Pancrazio, with in addition the weaknesses of the weaker sex. Often these four characters work out together a comic plot which is grafted on to another more serious plot. In those plays entirely *da ridere*,[3] the whole story rests on them. The theatre bill announces the double plot with a double name. Don Pancrazio and his foil the pedant wear black breeches and a wig with a tail and without powder. Pulcinella is not, like the Pulcinella puppet, a hunchback dressed in glad rags. He does not have physical deformities. His costume consists of a shirt and a large pair of white linen trousers, gathered at the waist with a hem. His cap of white wool is straight like a bishop's mitre; a black half-mask with a long nose covers half of his face, giving his features an intriguing contrast of immobility and grimace. The old woman, in an extravagant manner, colours her cheeks, affects the pretensions and the parures of youth, and covers her fingers with rings and her neck with necklaces. At the San Carlino, these character parts, especially those of Pancrazio and the old woman, are performed by truly talented and exquisitely natural artists; even their most outrageous farces never reach the point where laughter and merriment give way to fatigue or disgust.

In the rest of the company there are other actors of merit: three men of odd physique who represent familiar types, a lover altogether too good-looking for the place, a young *prima donna*, well endowed and with abundant hair, the exact type of the Neapolitan brunette, warm-hearted and hot-headed; another young and beautiful actress, with lively looks, who admirably fills the roles of *servetta* or *popolana*.[4]

[1] Stock comic roles.
[2] That is, in the literary Italian.
[3] Exclusively for laughter, purely farcical.
[4] A servant girl or working-class woman.

446   Ristori on the competition of opera and French drama and the power of theatre censorship

Adelaide Ristori, *Studies and memoirs* (London: W. H. Allen, 1888), pp. 18–21

[. . .] although the *repertoire* of the Company [the Reale Sarda] was most varied, well chosen and rich in the production of our best and most celebrated authors [. . .] yet it was impossible to fight against the growing rivalry of the lyric stage. The muse of melody seemed alone in favour with the public.

In order to provide for the expense of the Opera, the managers, or directors, or theatrical academies spent enormous sums, and the prices of admission were, of course, in proportion. A great performance was an event. Everything was sacrificed to it, and it was necessary to make Herculean efforts to prevent poor dramatic art from being left altogether in the background.

During the early years of my career, the preference of the public for the works of French writers, which were at the height of fashion then, was such that, in order to be certain of a full audience for several consecutive evenings, it was enough to announce a play of Scribe, Legouvé, Mélesville, Dumas, &c. in the bills. It was not that the productions of our native geniuses had no chance of finding favour with the public, who appreciated their literary merit, the spontaneity of the dialogue, and the purity of the language. But, with very few exceptions, all the applause was reserved for French pieces.

Besides, it should be remembered that the censorship then exercised in Austria and the Papal States had a great share in the decay of our native productions. Thus patriotic subjects were absolutely forbidden. Morality was expressed in the most fantastic way. In consequence our native dramas were reduced to a mass of absurdities when they escaped being utterly silly and without any interest whatever.

I will give a few examples of the absurd changes made by the ecclesiastical censorship in these years.

It was forbidden to an actor to utter the name of *God*, or to use the words *Angel* or *Devil*. Actors were forbidden to take on the stage the names of Gregory while Gregory XVI was Pontiff, and of John and Pius during the pontificate of John Mastai, Pius IX. The word 'fatherland' (*patria*) was likewise prohibited as a blasphemy!

One day a certain play was submitted to the Censor, in which the principal character, who was dumb, returned to his native land after a long exile. The book of the piece contained certain directions which were to be reproduced in dumb-show. Among them was the following: 'Here the actor must convey to his audience the joy he feels in once more seeing his own country.' Well, actually the word *patria* (fatherland) was erased by the Censor, and *paese* (country) substituted, as though the change of words could be indicated to the public by gestures!

On another occasion, when *Macbeth* was given at Rome, and one of the three witches says in the second scene of the first act:

> 'Here I have a pilot's thumb,
> Wrecked as homeward he did come,'

the Censor cancelled the lines.

'Why?' asked the manager of the company.

'Because,' was the answer, 'the public will probably find an allusion in them to the vessel of St Peter, which is in danger of being submerged by the wickedness of the times.'

What can be said in defence of such absurdities?

Nor did the operas fare any better than the plays.

447   Salvini on a peril encountered when touring, 1855[1]

Tommaso Salvini, *Leaves from the autobiography of Tommaso Salvini* (London: Fisher Unwin, 1893), pp. 87–8

We [the members of the Astolfi company[2]] went to Bologna just as the cholera was beginning to appear there; it was threatening at the same time several other cities in Italy. I advised all to leave Bologna at once, and to go to some place that was free from infection; but neither manager nor company would accept my advice, being unwilling to incur the unforeseen expense of a new journey. To mask their stinginess, they declared that my advice was dictated by fear, and Astolfi[3] diverted himself hugely at my expense, and ridiculed the timidity of my proposal. In the meantime the disease was becoming more and more serious, and one day when I saw an expression of grave anxiety on the faces of my late opponents, I said to them: 'You refused my advice, and said that it was due to my being afraid. Now all I have to say to you is that I shall be the last of us all to leave Bologna.' Soon the victims of the pestilence numbered 500 a day. The city was in consternation, and business was forgotten or neglected. At many street corners temporary altars were set up, and the people would kneel down before them and pray, and seek to conjure away the danger. One night I myself stumbled over the body of a person who had been suddenly stricken down. In a short time the city became a desert, and only then did my companions decide to go away. They hired carriages by the day to make the journey; and when they had all gone, I took a place in the public coach, and reached Leghorn before them. Our manager, Astolfi, upon his arrival at Pistoja [sic], was taken with the epidemic, and lost his life.

[1] One tends to associate the closure of theatres by pestilence mainly with stage activity in the sixteenth and seventeenth centuries, although it is occasionally found in the eighteenth century in cities with warm climates and many foreign visitors, such as Marseilles and Venice. Salvini's account is a useful reminder that well into the mid and even late nineteenth century in some parts of Europe a hazard like cholera could still threaten individuals and disrupt the practice of playing.

[2] Salvini joined this company in 1854.

[3] The Astolfi were a family of Italian actors, the leader of the company referred to here being Giuseppe (1795–1855). After acting in a variety of companies, and working in partnership with Sadowski, he formed his own company in 1854, in which Salvini appeared as *primattore*.

The passage below relates to the career of Gustavo Modena, but may serve to illustrate a number of factors bearing on the condition of the theatre in the early and middle decades of the nineteenth century, and indicates the great detail informing a legal contract entered into by an actor-manager when taking over the lease of a major theatre. Almost every eventuality had to be accounted for, as both parties sought to protect their interests.

448   Modena takes a lease of the Teatro Carignano in Turin, 1853

Cited in Claudio Meldolesi, *Profilo di Gustavo Modena* (Rome: Bulzoni, 1971), pp. 127–9, from material in the Biblioteca Teatrale Burcardo, Autografi 1, cart. 46

With this private agreement which the parties intend should have the force and weight of a legal document drawn up by a Public Notary, Sig. Domenico Righetti manager of the Carignano Theatre in Turin, grants the lease of the said Theatre from the first of September to the end of October of the current year, eighteen fifty three, to sig. Gustavo Modena, director and manager of the Drammatica Compagnia Toselli e Colombino[1] on the following conditions which are now being fixed and agreed upon, and which must be observed fully and in good faith.

Art. 1 Sig. G. M. assumes the obligation to be in Turin on the thirty-first day of the coming month of August with the whole of his aforementioned company, made up according to the list to be submitted to this *R. Direzione Teatrale* for suitable approval, and with all his equipment, scenery, costumes etc., in order to begin his performances on that day and daily until the aforementioned thirty-first of October. The performances should be divided for subscription purposes as is customary, and there should be only one day of rest per week.

Art. 2 Sig. G. M. will pay all the ordinary and extraordinary expenses of the company, and will give the Camerino del Teatro[2] one Tenth of the revenue from the daily sale of the Boxes, and the fixed tax for those Boxes which are sold for the Season, because of the rent due for the use of the Furniture.

Art. 3 Sig. G. M. will be expected to provide the maximum possible number of Novelties in his Repertoire, and will have to send notification of this to Sig. Righetti in good time, and will be obliged to accept all the cuts and all the demands made by the *Censura Teatrale*,[3] to observe and enforce the Regulations of the *Regia Direzione*,[4] and during the Season to give one performance for the benefit of the *Cassa di Soccorso degli Artisti Teatrali*.[5]

Art. 4 In return for such obligations, Sig. Righetti will hand over to the above-mentioned Sig. G. M. the profit of all revenue from admission tickets, subscriptions, and Boxes throughout the already mentioned two months, after the deductions specified in the following Articles.

Art. 5 Sig. G. M. will remit to Sig. Righetti as payment for the lease one Sixth of the gross revenue from admission tickets, subscriptions and Boxes.

Art. 6 In addition Sig. Modena will have to pay each evening 90 francs to defray the ordinary evening expenses, upkeep and cleaning of the Teatro; this sum of 90 francs will cover the Orchestra, the Lighting, the Employees, the Support Staff, and the printed bills – the latter, however, will have to be in the format customarily used for the Bills of the Regia Compagnia Sarda. Therefore with respect to the bills for a *Serata* or *recita Straordinaria*,[6] the bulk of the expense will be to the charge of Sig. Modena; stagehands, walk-on actors, and any other extraordinary expenses are not considered to be included in the said 90 lire.

Art. 7 In addition to the Royal Box, and the two Lateral boxes under no. 10 which belong to the Royal Court, and no. 10 in the first row to the left for the Police, and the Proscenium box in the first row to the right, which is reserved for the *Regia Direzione*, Sig. Righetti reserves for personal use box no. 8 in the third row to the right, and the proscenium box in the first row to the left; all the other boxes are at Sig. Modena's disposal, as per Art. 4.

Art. 8 During the said season, Sig. Modena will be free to use up to six back-cloths which belong to the *Regia Compagnia*, and will be responsible for them as well as for all the Furniture, Tools, Equipment, Apparatus, Machinery etc., which are made available to him. All of which things, in the way in which they have been agreed and arranged, the parties promise wholly and faithfully to respect, against the surety of their present and future possessions, with the commitment to replace any missing part, pay for any damage and expenses. In execution of the above the parties have signed the present contract (in two original copies) in the presence of the Witnesses noted below. In good faith, Turin, 16th May 1853,* in which Sig. Modena will personally give no less than three Performances.

Domenico Righetti
Gustavo Modena etc.

* Reserving to myself the right of up to two days' rest per week, given that in the holiday season there are many slack days in the theatre.

[1] Giovanni Toselli (1819–86) played *amoroso, brillante* and *generico* roles, and joined forces in management with Napoleone Colombino.
[2] The theatre authorities.
[3] The theatre censor.
[4] The royal authorities.
[5] The fund to help theatre artists.
[6] Unscheduled performance.

V   Players and playing

If theatre in the Italian peninsula was for much of the period examined here at a low ebb, undoubtedly the tide began to turn more in its favour in the middle decades of the nineteenth century: it has been noted that whereas in 1850 Modena could lament the fact that as an actor he was stranded on the fringes of theatrical life, by 1860 Ristori was requested by the Teatro San Carlo to pay 2,000 lire indemnity to the opera house for its loss of earnings during the period she performed in Naples.[1] Improvements in the condition and status of the theatre were to continue: by the last decades of the century not only was regular reviewing firmly established in much of the press, but the activities of 'star' players such as Ristori, Salvini and Duse were considered national news.

For the most part, however, the heyday of the 'stars' lay in the decades after 1860, which might suggest that Unification did effect some change in the theatre, for the very achievement of uniting the peninsula, at least in formal geographical and political terms, gave a fillip to the national self-confidence of the educated and the artistic: at least something of what they had striven for had been achieved.[2] Of the actors and theatre managers who were at the forefront of the struggle for unity, most notable was the actor and company leader Gustavo Modena, to whom most of the leading Italian players of the mid- and late nineteenth century acknowledged a debt. In important respects Modena must be considered a founding father of the modern Italian theatre, for his influence and example were powerful and of several kinds. First, he was an important teacher of the art of acting, stressing the need to acquire and refine technical skills, physical and vocal, and to adopt an easy, natural style of performance. Second, his respect for simplicity in performance was carried over into a preference for a comparatively economic use of stage decoration, which was widely imitated. Third, he sought to dress plays, particularly costume drama, with much greater attention to period accuracy than had prevailed hitherto. Fourth, he urged the social functions and indeed, at that particular juncture in Italian history, the revolutionary responsibilities of theatre. Fifth, he saw theatre as having a clear educational function, reclaiming for it the classical conception of the purpose of all art: to entertain and instruct.[3] Few who worked with him were not influenced by his practice, ideas and reform projects, as the many tributes of his collaborators, like that of Salvini below, testify.

When discussing the importance and influence of a figure like Modena we are on fairly sure ground, but much more problematic is an assessment of the quality of performance provided in this period by both notable players and the ruck of performers. Reformers, then as now, inveighed against particular performance styles and practices, and some in due course saw their demands for reform realized in some of the ways they sought. But the likelihood is that, notwithstanding the complaints of reformers, most players most of the time gave their public what it wanted; their livelihoods, after all, depended on their so doing. This simple fact needs to be borne in mind when considering some of the extravagances and excesses of movement, gesture, grimace and vocal delivery that seem to have characterized nearly all Italian acting for much of the period. The early nineteenth century in Italy saw the publication of a large number of books on acting, many of them attempts to examine the business in a semi-scientific way by codifying stage gestures, expressions and physical movements in order to relate what was said or implied in dialogue and dramatic action to what was visibly performed by the performer. Performance attempted to exteriorize in physical actions human conditions and psychological states, and commentators attempted to draw up a catalogue of performance means for so doing. By far the best known of these studies was Antonio Morrocchesi's *Lezioni di declamazione e di arte teatrale*, which was published in Florence in 1832. Although influenced by an earlier German study by Johann Jacob Engel, Morrocchesi's work is the more significant in that it was not a mere piece of academic theorizing: Morrocchesi had himself been a successful actor, had thought carefully about the subject, had established a school for actors in Florence and had taught the art for some years before publishing his book.[4] The publication attempted to relate human physical expression in all its variety to the equal variety of human moods, passions and mental states; it sought to elaborate a kind of compendium of movements, gestures, glances and grimaces appropriate to specific states and emotions.

What is perhaps significant is that Morrocchesi, like several of those who produced such works, had considerable experience of the stage.[5] The kind of stage language he and others endeavoured to define strikes us as fantastically extravagant and over-rhetorical, but their stage experience suggests first, that it was probably not far removed from how actors and actresses of the time actually moved, posed and expressed emotions in physical terms, and second, that it was a mode of performance most spectators were comfortable with. It is notable that foreign observers such as Stendhal are by no means wholly condemnatory. This stage language implies a very theatrical theatre – stylized, demonstrative, vigorously and purposefully expressive. The purposefulness may have been occasioned by the need in most performance places, whether theatre buildings in major towns or stages in arenas or streets, to impress the presence of the performer, and the fundamental moods and significant dramatic actions of a play, on the minds and imaginations of audiences whose attention span was limited and whose readiness to be distracted from what was happening on the stage was considerable. It was too, in part perhaps, the instinctive response of the players of the *teatro di prosa* to the undeniably successful and up-market, but manifestly artificial, convention-bound, emotionally extravagant and grandly theatrical delivery of performers on the opera stages.

If attempting to judge the quality of performance is difficult, no less so is assessing whether in the dialect theatres it was in any significant ways different. The appeal of the plays acted was more local, accommodating many familiar traditions, character types, kinds of stage business and particular references to figures, habits and institutions. But whether or not declamatory styles, the penchant for expressive poses and the disposition to chant dialogue was as common on regional stages is problematic to ascertain. What we can say with confidence is that the first half of the century saw in Naples and the adjoining regions the continuation in modified, transmuted forms of many of the traditions of the *commedia dell'arte*, including the use of masks and the emergence there of a number of popular farce actor-writers, such as Pasquale Altavilla and Antonio Petito.[6] What also seems clear is that on the regular stages and in the major companies there was a gradual shift away from the highly stylized and formal use of gesture, posture and delivery to something the age saw as more natural and more realistic. The reasons for this shift are, of course, complex and not confined to Italy – the influence of scientific empiricism, an increasing emphasis on the individual in society, a fascination with particulars – nor was naturalism at any stage taken as far in the Italian theatre as it was elsewhere. The acting of Modena, Alamanno Morelli, Ristori, Rossi, Clementina Cazzola and Salvini would certainly seem to us highly artificial, if not grotesque, and quite remote from actual behaviour. But there is ample evidence that their contemporaries found their playing to be more truthful to life as observed and lived than were the performances of their predecessors. Also intricately allied to this shift was a new way of perceiving dramatic characters: on the one hand, an increasing personalization of the stage figure, with an emphasis upon psychology and the underscoring of individual traits; on the other, and perhaps particularly in the interpretation of female characters, an ever greater requirement to highlight moral virtue in performance. Giovanna Ciotti Cavalletto has interestingly drawn attention to the losses as well as gains, especially for actresses, in the progressive march of the acting profession towards social respectability and status.[7]

Finally, no account of this period would be complete without reference to the fact that it was in the early and middle decades of the nineteenth century that Italian performers and spectators began to discover the work of Shakespeare, the Roman plays and the great tragedies being the first to appeal, and via French translations or adaptations: thus in 1791 Antonio Morrocchesi, acting under the pseudonym of Alessio Zaccagnini, presented Ducis's *Hamlet* at the Teatro Borgognissanti in Florence. Early in the nineteenth century Italian translations were made, and between 1810 and 1820 versions of *Othello* were given by Carlo Cosenza and Francesco Lombardi, while in 1842, in a notoriously controversial production in Milan, the same play was staged by Gustavo Modena, who later directed *Romeo and Juliet*, with Salvini as Romeo. In 1849 Alamanno Morelli acted Macbeth and followed it in 1850 with Hamlet, and adaptations of *Macbeth*, *Othello* and *Romeo and Juliet* may have been given in or before the 1840s. It was not until the middle decades of the nineteenth century, however, that a few of Shakespeare's plays, mainly the tragedies, began to appear at all regularly, and in fairly respectable texts (notably those of Giulio Carcano), in the repertoires of leading Italian players.[8] Perhaps the year that signalled particular interest in Shakespeare was 1856, when two of the most distinguished young actors of the age appeared in the tragedies for the first time: on 16 June Ernesto Rossi acted Othello at the Teatro Re in Milan, and fifteen days later played Hamlet; also in June, although possibly after Rossi had appeared in the part in Milan, Tommaso Salvini played Othello at Vicenza. In the next few years both these actors added other Shakespearean tragic roles to their repertoires, and they were joined by the leading Italian actress of the day, Adelaide Ristori, who assumed the role of Lady Macbeth in a version that reduced the role of the male protagonist to that of a support. The major tragedies and the Roman plays were undoubtedly the most popular, and few of the comedies were attempted at any time in the century. But Salvini, Rossi, Ristori and other Italian players, such as Emanuel, included the great Shakespearean tragic roles as key elements in their international touring repertoires.[9]

The discovery of Shakespeare also contributed to the dignity of the profession, for by mid-century he had begun to acquire an international reputation as a great writer and thus the inclusion of his work in the repertoire raised the artistic status of the Italian stage in the second half of the century, as did the tendency of several leading players, such as Ristori,

Rossi and Salvini, to publish their critical and interpretative responses to the plays.[10] But those activities, like their performances outside Italy, lie after 1860.

[1] In a letter written by the actor Vincenzo Torelli now in the Ristori archive, Museo del attore, Genoa.
[2] For actors in this period see Giovanni Calendoli, *L'attore, storia di un'arte* (Rome, 1959).
[3] A good account of Modena is Claudio Meldolesi, *Profilo di Gustavo Modena. Teatro e rivoluzione democratica* (Rome, 1971); see also K. Richards, 'Modena', in *International dictionary of theatre*, vol. III, *Actors, directors and designers* (London and Detroit: St. James Press, 1996).
[4] Engel's *Ideen zu einer Mimik* (1785–6) was translated into Italian in 1818, as it had been eleven years before into English; the wish to establish a kind of vocabulary of movements and gestures was not just an Italian preoccupation, but was in part a European-wide product of the emphasis in Enlightenment science upon definition and tabulation.
[5] Texts like D. Buffelli, *Elementi di mimica* (1829) and G. Bazzi, *Primi erudimenti dell'arte drammatica* (1845); such leading actors as Salvini and Rossi wrote later on interpretation.
[6] For Petito, see Laura Richards, 'Un Pulcinella antico e moderno: Antonio Petito and the traditions of the *Commedia dell'arte* in nineteenth-century Naples', in *The Commedia dell'arte. From the Renaissance to Dario Fo*, ed. Christopher Cairns (Lampeter, 1989), pp. 277–96.
[7] See her *Attrici e società nell'Ottocento italiano* (Milan, 1978). Vanda Monaco points out how the actor at this time sought to advance socially and win acceptance in bourgeois society by accepting the moral codes of that society, *La Repubblica del teatro* (Florence, 1968), p. 176.
[8] The first comprehensive translation of Shakespeare into Italian was made by Michele Leoni and published 1814–19. Both players and writers were influenced by the discovery of Shakespeare's work, notably the greatest Italian novelist and dramatist of the early nineteenth century, Alessandro Manzoni (1785–1873) – see his plays *Il conte di Carmagnola* (1820) and *Adelchi* (1822).
[9] For an account of the tours of nineteenth-century Italian players with Shakespeare, see M. Carlson, *The Italian Shakespeareans* (Washington, DC: 1985), Henry Knepler, *The gilded stage* (London, 1968), and K. Richards, 'Italian actors in Victorian London', in *Shakespeare on the Victorian stage*, ed. R. Foulkes (Cambridge: Cambridge University Press, 1986).
[10] For some passages from these in English, see Leigh Woods, *On playing Shakespeare: advice and commentary from actors and actresses* (New York and London, 1991), and *Actors on acting*, ed. Toby Cole and Helen Krich Chinoy (New York, 1949).

449   Two synoptic views of the quality of Italian acting

(a) L. Simond, *A tour in Italy and Sicily* (London: Longman, Rees, Orme, Brown & Green, 1828), p. 18; (b) M. Valery [Antoine Claude Pasquin], *Historical, literary and artistical travels in Italy*, trans. C. E. Clifton (Paris, 1839), p. 66

(a) An English view of Italian players, 1817

Another evening we went to the theatre *Re*,[1] where we had a melodrama in the Kotzebue style, extremely improbable and absurd, launching at the very outset into the grand pathetic. Notwithstanding all this and the overacting, and our imperfectly understanding what was going on, we were all caught at *attendrissement*, according to our various capabilities of feeling, and half the house had their handkerchiefs to their eyes.– Italian actors are less genteel than the French; their sense of the *bienséances théâtrales* is not half so nice; they give way awkwardly but strongly to the impulse of the part they are acting, and do not mince the matter in point of demonstration. The consequence is that they are often ridiculous, but at times very impressive.

[1] The Teatro Re in Milan was the leading house in the city for the performance of regular drama.

(b) A French view of Italian players, 1839

Were the several actors of that country united, who are now dispersed and belong to different companies, they would compose probably the best comic troop in Europe. Demarini was an excellent comedian, Vestris is very natural and lively; Bon, an esteemed dramatic author, is original and piquant; Modena is noble and pathetic; Domeniconi[1] is full of warmth; signoras Marchionni, Luigia Bon,[2] Internari,[3] Pasqualini,[4] Belloni-Colombelli,[5] Polvaro-Carlotta,[6] have sensibility, grace, and delicacy, and I doubt whether there exists a more genteel *soubrette* than signora Romagnoli. It is true that none of these actresses equal mademoiselle Mars, but the talent of that inimitable actress would be scarcely adapted for Italian comedy and the characters it represents [. . .]

The difference of dialects[7] is another obstacle to the improvement of the Italian stage: the pieces which are written in the dialects, are the only merry and popular ones, but they are not intelligible to the whole nation; the others, written in the book style, a kind of dead language not resembling the vernacular tongue,[8] cannot supply those spirited and natural expressions which excite the laugh peculiar to good comedy [. . .]

---

[1] Luigi Domeniconi (1786–1867), after some years in small travelling companies, acted for a long period with Carlotta Marchionni. In the 1830s he assumed the management of the company and in 1845 was a leading member of the Reale Sarda, working subsequently with many of the up-and-coming younger players of the time, such as Ristori and Salvini.

[2] Luigia Bellotti, actress-wife of the dramatist Francesco Augusto Bon and stepsister of the actor-manager Luigi Bellotti-Bon.

[3] The Internari were a family of Italian actors and actresses.

[4] Albina Pasqualini (1801–54) was one of the major comic actresses of the first half of the nineteenth century, *prim'attrice assoluta* in several companies before forming her own troupe in the later 1830s; Luigi Rasi remarks that she was particularly successful in the comedies of Goldoni, notably *La Locandiera*.

[5] The actress meant here is probably Isabella Colomberti, wife of the actor Antonio Colomberti.

[6] The actress Carlotta Polvaro (1800–51).

[7] The language question, object of intense discussion and activity since at least the Renaissance, persisted in the nineteenth century. Dialect theatre in some parts of Italy, like Naples and Venice, produced work of considerable quality; comparatively little drama of worth was written in the approved literary language.

[8] Based on the Italian of Dante and Boccaccio and essentially Florentine.

---

450   Theory of acting: Morrocchesi on anima or sentiment, 1832[1]

A. Morrocchesi, *Lezioni di declamazione e di arte teatrale* (Florence, 1832), cited in Giovanni Calendoli, *L'attore, storia di un'arte* (Rome: Edizioni dell'Ateneo, 1959), pp. 356–7

Do we wish to switch easily from one mood to another? Then if necessary, let us retire to a lonely place, let us concentrate, let us meditate, let us keep silent for a while, then let us read a book with a fine style on an appropriate subject, and gradually we shall reach our goal. Let us exercise our soul often in such a way and try, by taking an interest in other people's misfortunes, to render it acutely responsive. Let us in imagination conceive of a man wounded and dying; the languor expressed in his posture and depicted on his countenance penetrates us, moves us. Let us imagine a pretty country-maid who, while cavorting carelessly in the grass, is about to tread on a snake, or some other poisonous creature. Let us contemplate a good family, sleeping serenely within walls surrounded by flames. In short, let us rapidly in imagination survey the whole vast range of human disasters, and thus we shall acquire that expansion of soul which is so necessary to any public performer who would aspire to fame.

It will not be inopportune in this context to give the example of the famous classical actor Polo,[2] of such renown in the annals of theatrical history. He had to simulate Electra's cries, sobs and groans over the corpse of her dead brother, Orestes. What art could ever have taught a perfect way to imitate so unfortunate a sister in such a terrible predicament? What method could ever be suitable for such a purpose? But the illustrious actor proved equal to the task. Having ordered the ashes of his beloved son, but recently deceased, to be brought to him, he studied them, brooded over them, was so moved and overcome by a mood of despondency, mingling his heartfelt paternal tears with the feigned tears of Electra, that by such means he profoundly moved the spectators too.

After such observation one cannot recommend too highly that ever admired rule of Horace:

> You must first cry if you want me to cry

Such an approach gives to the actor's face, and to his gestures and expressions, all the turmoil of the passion which dominates him, takes possession of him, and makes him become his own feelings. In this way one can portray deeply both Ariadne and Dido, who deploy all the eloquence of their passion to move and summon back an ingrate; thus we shall make the air echo with our lamentations along with Philoctetes, Merope, Hecuba and Oedipus.

These rules, which we may call the wellspring of sentiment, would be useless if used by a cold and sterile soul, but they acquire great strength and efficacy when used by a genius; that is, by a mind whose lively imagination feels itself roused by any feeling, and which, animated by the soul, does not see but is moved, does not become agitated but communicates its agitation to others and, vehement as a tempest, penetrating as lightning, rapid as a torrent, wounds, demolishes, transports, none able to resist its drive and power.

Having exhausted as best I can the subject of this difficult lesson, my fortunate young pupils, please bear with me a little longer, for I wish to recount an incident, appropriate in this context, which occurred to me during the fourth or fifth year of my theatrical career: it was in Bologna, at the Zagnoni Theatre,[3] where out of friendship, which friendship meant so much to me, I had pledged myself to present a new tragedy: *I conti di Malbiano.*

The author of the play had great faith in me, although I had very little confidence in his work; and his learned compatriots had even less confidence in it, indeed perhaps none at all. The part I was to interpret was long and pathetic: it was of a passionate young man who has suddenly lost his beloved bride. The day of the wretched performance arrived, a day I shall always carry in my heart and memory! At about ten that morning a letter arrived announcing a sudden loss – alas! all the more painful for being so little expected – of a dear sister of mine. I fainted and remained unconscious for a long time. Yet despite this, because of circumstances beyond our control the performance had to take place that evening. In imitation of the Greek Polo, I took with me onto the stage, as you can well imagine, the actual mourning of a brother, together with that of a make-believe widower; and my emotion was so great and so strong at every moment, that I carried along with me the souls of the listeners, so that they concluded by rewarding with applause that which they had planned to punish with contempt. At that, the celebrated Marquess Francesco Albergati Capacelli,[4] a very renowned author of comedies, and a distinguished man of letters, said to the author in the presence of various people: the death of Morrocchesi's sister was the salvation of your tragedy. From that instant I believed even more strongly that the greatest gift of any speaker consists in feeling very powerfully those sentiments he wishes to awaken in others; and the most efficacious lesson experience has confirmed for me, and that can be added to those I have already mentioned in order to educate one's soul to emotion is: systematically to avoid any hard, painful, sorrowful, tearful spectacle, in short, as far as the vast number of human misfortunes are concerned, pity them and relieve them by all means, but from as far a distance as possible; I can assure you that in this way you will soon be able to fortify your soul to the most exquisite sensibility [. . .]

---

1 Antonio Morrocchesi (1768–1838), who first appeared under the pseudonym of Alessio Zaccagnini in Ducis's version of *Hamlet* in 1791, played lover roles in a number of companies, rising to the rank of principal, and was particularly noted for his interpretation of Alfierian parts. He gave up the stage in 1811 in order to fill the chair of declamation at the Florence Academy of Fine Arts, and in 1832 published his important *Lezioni*, from which this passage and the illustrations below are drawn.

2 The fifth century BC Athenian actor Polos, noted by classical authorities for his interpretation of the role of Sophocles' Oedipus.

3 Dating from 1641, when it was the Teatro Formagliari, it had a long and chequered history as a house for regular drama, until in the 1770s it was taken over by the Zagnoni and renamed after the proprietor. It was destroyed by fire in 1802.

4 Francesco Albergati Capacelli (1728–1804), comic dramatist and friend of Goldoni and Alfieri.

451   Figures from Morrocchesi's *Lezioni di declamazione e di arte teatrale*, Florence, 1832

Biblioteca Teatrale Burcardo, Rome

Gustavo Modena (1803–61), one of the most admired and influential Italian actors of the first half of the nineteenth century, was born into the profession, and after reading law at Padua and Bologna universities and acting occasionally on an amateur basis, became a member of the troupe of Salvatore Fabbrichesi. He then joined other travelling companies and toured widely in the peninsula, developing his skills in comedy, tragedy and romantic drama and winning particular success in the role of Saul in Alfieri's play of the same name. In 1829 he formed his own company, with his father and Carlotta Polvaro, and began increasingly to emphasize in his repertory plays of a distinctly patriotic nature, such as Silvio Pellico's *Francesca da Rimini* and Hippolyte Romand's *Il Cittadino di Gand*, which reflected his own intense sympathy with the cause of Italian independence. In fact, his political involvement became ever more pronounced: he formed friendships with political activists such as Mazzini, agitated for radical change, and in the later 1830s was forced into exile, travelling in France, Switzerland and Belgium and surviving in a variety of ways, as teacher, proof corrector, grocer and lecturer, while writing political pamphlets and professional studies such as *Il teatro educatore* (1836), an essay that addressed the role of theatre in society. In 1839 he went to London and gave Dante recitals at the Queen's Theatre, and later in the same year returned to Italy, acting wherever he was granted permission but never renouncing his political engagement. In 1843 he formed a company of young actors in Milan, the Compagnia dei giovani, that included the 14-year-old Tommaso Salvini, Luigi Bellotti-Bon, Fanny

Sadowsky and Gaetano Vestri, all of whom were later to profess many of his theatrical, and indeed political, ideals. He is credited with a number of important attempts to reform the Italian stage (see the introduction to this section, above). In 1847 he staged Shakespeare's *Othello*, in a much adapted text, but without success, and this failure deterred him from attempting *Hamlet*. His later years were marked by a political and professional uncertainty that perhaps betrayed the disillusionment of an idealist, and he died on 21 February 1861 in Turin, a month before the new unified Kingdom of Italy was officially inaugurated.

452   Gustavo Modena

Figure from *The autobiography of Tommaso Salvini*, London, 1893, opposite p. 16

453   Modena and the art of acting, 1861

F. Dall'Ongaro, 'Studi drammatici: Gustavo Modena', *Rivista contemporanea* (August 1861), pp. 285–6, 293

Modena did not instruct his pupils. He would read them the part; he would explain the nature of the character he thought most appropriate to their capabilities, then he would leave them free to interpret it according to the dictates of their own heart. Only after watching the pupils try this or that way, would he say, if he thought they had not got it right: 'I would do it this way.' But his advice was never presented as irrefutable: nor would he say: 'one must do thus because that is how it is done' or 'how it has always been done'. He would say, nature is varied and multiform. Sorrow and pleasure, disdain and prayer can take and do take as many tones and as many colours as there are varieties of characters, of which the human species is formed. There is nothing absolute in the world. The beautiful is as much varied as the aspect of nature; what is true in art does not consist in a straight line but in the correspondence of the idea with the external image which must express it and make it accessible to all [. . .]

In dramas and in tragedies he looked for that passage in which the nature of the character most clearly and truthfully would shine [. . .] such a passage is like the tail which suffices to give an idea of the lion.

Once Modena had found this fundamental point, this typical trait of the character, he would consider himself master of his subject. With this flash of light he would illuminate the whole picture: and whenever the word was missing he supplied it with gesture, silence, facial expression. He did not pay very much attention to details, to fortuitous incidents, to the padding that necessarily abounds in the five acts apparently indispensable to modern tragedies. It sufficed to maintain the unity of character in his subject: and everything, his expression, his costume, his movements, his intonation, all was harmonious, all was related. One might say, this was how to create a character.

454   Salvini on Modena

Tommaso Salvini, *Ricordi, aneddoti ed impressioni dell'artista* (Milan, 1895), p. 60

Gustavo Modena's teaching method was more practical than theoretical. Today this method would be criticized. Nowadays artists claim to know a lot, they talk a great deal, but they study and work much less. Very rarely would Modena expatiate in order to explain the nature, the physiognomy, the aesthetic importance of the character, to underline the meaning of the calm, the vehemence, the passion, with which to colour the dramatic *persona*, according to the various events and intrigues of the plot. He preferred to say instead: 'Do it this way', and teach by example.

[. . .] most of Gustavo Modena's pupils, not excluding those who acquired some reputation, copied him more in his defects than in his good qualities. Thanks to a wound in one of his arms, acquired during a political uprising, he found it difficult to stretch it fully; and so you see the incomplete and awkward gesture adopted by many of his pupils. Because Modena had a bad habit in the way he moved one of his legs, his imitators would raise a heel as if spurring a horse; and in attempting to imitate his voice, which had become nasal after an illness when he was young, you would hear his pupils modulate sound through their noses like so many rabbis in a synagogue.[1] These physical defects, which in him were not noticeable thanks to his innumerable merits, would become quite evident in his pupils and in his imitators – also because they were artificial and forced – and reduced the value and efficacy of their few talents. That: 'Do it like this' was good and valid for those who perceived and guessed the reasons why he would do it so. Gustavo Modena was a great innovator in the Italian theatre. It was he who introduced the audacious but restrained sincerity of gesture, the vigorous boldness of the soul, the leap of the phrase, the freedom in action, and more than anything else the genuinely sincere impersonation of the character; all traits that belonged to him and in which he had very few rivals.

The first great Italian 'star' of the international touring circuit in the nineteenth century was Adelaide Ristori (1822–1906). Born into the profession, she was acting important roles in her early teens, including the title part in Pellico's *Francesca da Rimini* in 1836. At the age of 16 she entered the Compagnia Reale Sarda in Turin, working with the influential and experienced manager of the troupe, Gaetano Bazzi, and its leading actress, Carlotta Marchionni. She then joined the company of another of the leading actor-managers of the age, Luigi Domeniconi. On her marriage to an Italian marquis she left the stage for a year or so, before returning to play lead roles in a number of companies before rejoining the Reale Sarda in 1853. She made certain roles very much her own, such as Francesca da Rimini, Alfieri's Mirra, Schiller's Maria Stuart and Goldoni's Mirandolina. In 1855 she went with the Reale Sarda to Paris where, playing with Ernesto Rossi as her leading man, she secured the first of many international triumphs, prompting critics to compare her performance to that of the French favourite, Rachel.[2] Between 1856 and 1866 she returned every year to perform in Paris. She visited London and the main British provincial towns several times between 1856 and 1882, and from 1866 played in the United States on four occasions. Three years before she retired from the stage, in 1885, she acted the role of Lady Macbeth in English at London's Drury Lane, a feat perhaps admired more for its audacity than for its achievement.

---

[1] It is interesting to compare Modena in these respects with another highly influential actor, Henry Irving, who similarly had certain distinct peculiarities of gait and vocal idiosyncrasies.
[2] For documents relating to the acting of Rachel, see **314**, **315**, **316**, **317** and **318**.

455   Contract with Righetti for Adelaide Ristori to join the Compagnia Reale Sarda, 1853

Giovanna Ciotti Cavalletto, *Attrici e società nell'Ottocento italiano* (Milan: Mursia, 1978), pp. 136–8, citing the Ristori archive, Museo-Biblioteca dell'Attore, Genoa

With this private written agreement, which at the wish of the parties should have the force and power of a legal contract drawn up by a chartered notary, signora

Adelaide Capranica del Grillo[1] *née Ristori*, remains engaged by, and firmly a member of, the Dramatic Company in the service of S. S. R. M. the King of Sardinia etc. etc. in the capacity of *prima attrice and associate of the Reale Compagnia*, for the coming three years, beginning on the first day of Lent 1853 and terminating on the last day of Carnival 1856; under the following fixed terms and conditions.

First: The above-mentioned *Signora Adelaide Capranica* shall be obliged to act all the parts of *prima attrice assoluta for five evenings a week; excluding those parts which may be considered immoral like Il Fallo, Clarissa Harlowe, Stifelius, etc. and those which would require her to wear male attire* (they will be assigned) without further dispute or refusal.

Second: The above-mentioned *Signora Adelaide Capranica* shall be obliged to dress with elegance and decency when interpreting all the individual characters assigned to *her*, according to the historical period, and similarly shall make sure that she punctually attends rehearsals at the the time and place *she* is advised (consistently), *acting in agreement with the artist in charge* of direction (signor), *from whose advice she might profit*, or whosoever is appointed by him: she shall besides comply with all the orders and rules of the *Regia Direzione*.

Third: *Signora Adelaide Capranica* shall be bound to follow the company to wherever is indicated by the manager of the same, and she shall travel at her own expense on the appointed day, in order to be ready to begin rehearsals, and she shall not be allowed throughout the duration of the contract to lend her services to others either publicly or privately, nor shall she leave the performance place without permission from the management. *However in the case of any ascertained, dangerous illness of signora Capranica's parents-in-law, the aforementioned shall obtain permission to be absent for 10–12 days maximum, and during the rest of the year she shall make good the performances which she has missed during those days*.

Fourth: The *aforementioned signora Adelaide Capranica* shall also be obliged always to carry with her what is necessary, at least for the first four performances which will be indicated to her from performance place to performance place, in order to avoid any inconvenience which may arise from a delay in transport.

Fifth: The company manager is bound in his turn to take all possible care of the theatrical effects handed over to him by the *above-named signora Capranica*, and to provide for their transport as appropriate, *but not by boat* and in the forms and ways employed for the transport of his own effects, although he is not responsible for the damage that might occur from bad packaging, bad weather, *force majeure* and suchlike.

Sixth: *Signora Adelaide Capranica* shall be bound to maintain herself, both as far as food and lodgings are concerned, to abide by all the cuts or restrictions of the censor; (to be each evening in the theatre one hour before the performance, and to let people know where she can be found in case of emergency, even if she has no part in the performance, as well as never to add any sentence of her own or of others to the part assigned to her, absolutely without exception).

Seventh: *However, signora Adelaide Capranica shall not* be bound to act (every evening) in the farces, (although if the company manager finds it convenient, she will have to), *or* to perform (besides) in two (complete) spectacles in the same evening: (and in case of a double performance in two different theatres, she will be paid half of the daily honorarium in compensation, according to the practice).

(Eighth: in the case of an actor falling ill, she is bound to supply acting, so that the performance is not impaired).

(Ninth) *Eighth*: In return for her conscientious work and all her above-mentioned obligations, *signor Domenico Righetti, as* director of the COMPAGNIA DRAMMAT-ICA AL SERVIZIO DI S. M, is obliged *each year* to pay *signora Adelaide Capranica* the sum of *twenty thousand* (20,000) new Piedmontese lire, *in addition to a third of the Management profits*. The *salary shall* be paid in two-weekly instalments in advance, the first of which shall be on the first day of Lent. In addition, each year, *signora Capranica* shall be entitled to *half a* benefit evening, *of which two in Turin, one during Carnival, the other during Lent, in each performance place*, and in the following way. The box office receipts for the evening (after deduction of what is rightly due to the Spettacolo Regio, and to the theatre proprietors for the rent or other), shall be divided into two equal portions, one for the *Actress* and the other for the management so that the company expenses and the usual evening expenses are paid. The choice of performance days shall depend (on the company Manager with the consent of the) *on the actress*, but always on a non-festive or non-solemn day, and always *after the 13th performance in the place* and not on subscription days. Any presents shall rightly go to the actor [. . .]

(Eleventh) *Tenth*: The present contract shall last for the duration of the agreed time: (unless the *Regia Direzione* had reasonable motives for) *however it shall be possible for each party* to dissolve it from year to year, having previously given six months notice [. . .]

The editor, Giovanna Ciotti Cavalletto, notes that the parts above which are hand-written in the text of the contract are put in italic, those crossed out in the text are here put in brackets.

---

[1] In 1847 Ristori married a nobleman, the Marquis Giuliano Capranica del Grillo, retired from the stage for a time, but later returned, an indication in itself of the extent to which the theatre was gradually winning respectability.

456   Ristori in the role of Mary Stuart

Figure from *The autobiography of Tammaso Salvini*, London, 1893, opposite p. 48

457   The actor Altavilla at the Teatro San Carlino, 1845

Musset, *Course en voiturin*, pp. 132–3

[The actor-dramatist Altavilla[1]] is the life and soul of the San Carlino Company. He fills both the roles which correspond to those of Gontier[2] in our vaudevilles and other more comic or caricatural roles, because he is an excellent mime, and his face, of an extraordinary mobility, lends itself to all kinds of buffoonery. What allows Altavilla to rise above his colleagues is the fact that he is the Molière of the company. For several years now, although he appears hardly older than 35, he has been staging exclusively his own plays, and it is no simple affair to supply the San Carlino, for a new play is needed every Saturday during the winter season. The first night of a new play has never failed to take place on the agreed date. In the course of a week he writes, learns and rehearses a play, all the while performing that of the previous week. The prolific Lope de Vega himself would have tired of such a job, and would perhaps have handed in his resignation. Mr Altavilla is as fresh in spirit and as active as on the first day.

You will easily guess that with so little time to devise and prepare a play, it is impossible to write a new work, that is, to put it entirely down on paper. Only a scenario is prepared, a series of roughly drafted scenes, and hints of direction to the actors, while the rest is achieved in discussion and during rehearsal. A great deal is left to improvisation, to Pulcinella's wit, to Pancrazio's good nature, to the delightful *minauderies* of the old woman, to the gabbling of the man in glasses, and to the last-minute inspiration which at the moment of the performance may come to the author. One does not know precisely if the sequence of scenes is right, how things should go. Already Saturday is here, and the audience fills the auditorium; the orchestra has played the overture, the three knocks have been heard, the curtain is up. Pancrazio appears, the stalls burst into laughter. The prompter is very good; the exposition successful; each actor is clear about his part. The actors understand one another, support one another. The play proceeds: suddenly in the wings the lover seizes Altavilla by the arm.

'What can I say?', he cries; 'What shall I do? I've missed my cue. My love scene can no longer be done.'

'Don't worry, my boy,' responds the author. 'You must change your part like this and like this. In place of this speech you will say what I am going to tell you . . .'

And in a haste he cobbles together a new passage, different from the previous one. Meanwhile Pulcinella, not seeing the actor make his entrance, guesses he is reworking things and preparing it all. He fills in the time with *lazzi*. The lesson is over, the stalled carriage is off again and proceeds beautifully. The audience has perceived nothing; the denouement takes place as planned, and the evening ends amid laughter and applause.

---

[1] Pasquale Altavilla (1806–72), a Neapolitan dialect actor and dramatist, began his career at the San Carlino in 1835, writing sketches in which he also performed. He began to publish collections of his pieces from 1849. In 1852 he surrendered his mask to Antonio Petito, assuming instead a kind of *promiscuo* role, in his case marked by the regular playing of a guitar.

[2] Stage-name of Georges Belloste (1785–1841), French actor noted for his performances in the plays of Scribe.

Often considered by the more discerning mid- and late nineteenth-century theatre critics and commentators as perhaps the greatest Italian actor of the period, Tommaso Salvini (1829–1915) was born into the profession. Apprenticed to Gustavo Modena in 1843, he then moved on to the company of Luigi Domeniconi as juvenile lead, acting with Adelaide Ristori. A true pupil of Modena, he fought in the Rome uprising of 1848 and was for a time imprisoned. He first played Othello in 1856 and another of his great parts, that of Corrado in Paolo Giacometti's powerful social drama, *La morte civile*. In 1869 he successfully toured Spain and Portugal, thus initiating the international touring he regularly undertook for much of the rest of his life: this took him to all parts of Europe, north and south America and north Africa. Shakespeare was an important element of his international repertoire, including, in addition to Othello, Hamlet, Macbeth, King Lear and Coriolanus. He acted several times in England, like Ristori making tours of the British Isles in 1876 and 1884, and four triumphant visits to the United States. His great part was Othello, which when first seen in London and in American cities stunned audiences with its powerful animality and physical and emotional realism, though his Hamlet was also a brilliant interpretation, the critic of London's *The Athenaeum* observing that 'no actor of our day has brought to the part of Hamlet equal intelligence and mastery of art, equal rigour of judgement and profusion of effort'.

458   A letter contract from Modena engaging the young Salvini, 1843

Cited in Celso Salvini, *Tommaso Salvini nella storia del teatro italiano e nella vita del suo tempo* (Rocca San Casciano: Cappelli, 1955), pp. 48–50

Trieste, 30th January 1843.

Signor Giuseppe Salvini[1]
dramatic actor
Forlì (Romagna)

    From your letter of the 24th January, I understand that you and your son pledge to be members of the dramatic company I manage for the year 1843–1844, that is from Easter 1843 to the end of Carnival 1844.

    In consequence you pledge yourself, in the week before Easter, to be in the city that I shall in advance, and in good time, have indicated; and to come there with your own costumes and effects, which you will have acquired at your own expense.

    You pledge to learn, to rehearse and to act all those dramatic parts which will be assigned to you by the Director, both in matinées and evening performances, and if need be twice daily. Bear in mind, though, that in those productions in which I, Giacomo Modena, do not perform you will always take the principal serious role, the role I would have taken had I been in the production. Your son will have no right whatsoever to expect this or that part.

    You pledge, still both for yourself and for your son, to wear your own costumes suitable to the parts you will be given, and exactly in conformity with the Director's instructions.

    To take yourself to all the Cities which the Director will have indicated. To attend all the rehearsals in their entirety, and not just only one part of them. To take the place of any colleague who may fall ill.

    You will be so kind, too, as to pledge to appear on stage in walk-on parts when productions require many persons decorous in their deportment. Where you yourself are concerned, this applies in cases of extreme necessity; where your son is concerned this applies in all cases.

The praise that the public gives to the perfect execution of the play is given to the whole Company.

You will not keep with you dogs or parrots or pets of any kind, since I have so decided in order to put an end to the scorn such a practice procures for us in cities and villages, and also so that there will be no distraction during rehearsals.[2] The old, improper practices of comic actors will not be followed by us if they run counter to justice and common sense.

In return for your work and your son's work, I pledge to pay travel expenses to you both, and the expenses for the transport of both your personal and theatrical effects. In addition, I shall pay you 3,000 (three thousand Austrian lire) for the whole period, as indicated above, payable in weekly instalments (in the form of local money). In addition 400 (four hundred) Austrian lire on your arrival in the first performance place. In the event of suspension of performances through *force majeure*, payment will be withheld in proportion to the number of days until performances are resumed.[3] In the case of disagreement over the interpretation of our reciprocal obligations and duties, the official authority shall have the final word.

Your very affectionate Gustavo Modena.

This letter shall serve as the agreed contract until a regular contract can be drawn up.

I cannot indicate to you at present what will be the first performance place. I shall do this before the end of Carnival. I believe you can come to Piacenza without wasting a journey. I came to Trieste to give a few performances: the Impresario is doing his best to keep me here because until now the box office has been good; but to be stuck in this remote place is very inconvenient for dealing with performance venues. It is certain we shall stay a long time in Milan from September on. Meanwhile you can study [the part of] Achimelech in *Saul*, and whichever parts you choose in Alfieri's *Filippo*; I shall be the protagonist; but in the event of me being ill or of any other difficulty, you shall have that part as well. In *Polinice*, Eteocle or Creonte, just as you please. In *Attilio Regolo*[4] the part you choose; I shall be Attilio. Lusignano in *Zaira*, Andron in *Pamela nubile*, Leidanno in *Il vagabondo*.[5] The father in Iffland's *Il giocatore*.[6]

Please acknowledge receipt of this letter as a binding agreement.

---

[1] Giuseppe Salvini (? –1844), the head of a prominent nineteenth-century acting family, whose second son was Tommaso.

[2] This little detail, the ban on dogs and parrots, gives a vivid glimpse of what one of the less prosperous touring companies might have looked like when on the road.

[3] This nicely points up the precariousness of acting as a profession for most of the nineteenth-century, as indeed earlier; players had little protection against unforeseen hazards.

[4] The plays mentioned here are by Alfieri and his imitators.

[5] *Zaira* was an Italian version of Voltaire's tragedy *Zaïre*; *Pamela nubile* (Pamela unmarried, 1753) was a comedy by Goldoni based very loosely upon the character in Richardson's novel *Pamela*.

[6] Iffland's version of Goldoni's play *Il giuocatore* (The gamester).

459   Salvini in the role of Orosmane in an Italian version of Voltaire's *Zaïre*

Figure from *the autobiography of Tommaso Salvini*, London, 1893, opposite p. 208

The other great Italian actor of the middle decades of the nineteenth century was Ernesto Rossi (1827–96). Like Salvini, early in his career he worked with Gustavo Modena, who encouraged him to develop a more natural technique than was then common in Italy. His performances of Shakespeare are among the first given on the Italian stage in respectable translations: in June 1856 he acted Othello at the Teatro Re in Milan, and fifteen days later Hamlet. As was the case with Salvini, Shakespeare came later to underpin his international touring repertory, although he never toured as regularly as Salvini. He did, however, play more Shakespearean roles than his great contemporary, notably Romeo, Macbeth, Lear and Julius Caesar, and he translated *Julius Caesar* into Italian. Although in his heyday he was a great romantic lead, he was very much a technical actor and was inclined to resort to tricks for theatrical effect. He remained on the stage too long, and his style of playing came to be regarded as old-fashioned: Duse, after seeing him as Hamlet and Lear, called him 'a tooth-puller'. But in his great days he did much to focus the interest of educated Italians on the legitimate theatre.

460   Ernesto Rossi in the role of Hamlet

Biblioteca Teatrale Burcardo, Rome

ERNESTO ROSSI

la sera della sua beneficiata al teatro Re di Milano
24 Settembre 1869

Bibliography

BRITAIN

Works of reference

Altick, R. *The shows of London*. (Cambridge, MA: Harvard University Press, 1978)

Arnott, J. F. and Robinson, J. W. *English theatrical literature, 1559–1900. A bibliography*. (London: Society for Theatre Research, 1970)

Avery, E. L., Scouten, A. H., Stone, G. W. and Hogan, C. B. (eds.). *The London stage, 1660–1800*: Part V, *1776–1800*. (Carbondale and Edwardsville: Southern Illinois University Press, 1960–5)

Bolitho H. (ed.). *Further letters of Queen Victoria*. (London: Thornton Butterworth, 1938)

British parliamentary papers, stage and theatre 1. Introduced by M. L. Norstedt. (Dublin: Irish University Press, 1968)

Cole, T. and Chinoy, H. K. (ed.). *Actors on acting*. (New York: Dover, 1949)

Hall, Lilian A. *Catalogue of dramatic portraits* in *The Theatre collection of the Harvard College Library*. 4 vols. (Cambridge, MA: Harvard University Press, 1930–4)

Howard, Diana. *Directory of theatre research information resources in the UK*. 2nd edn. (London: Society for Theatre Research and Library Association, 1986)

Howard, Diana. *London theatres and music halls, 1850–1950*. (London: Library Association, 1970)

Mackintosh, Iain and Ashton, Geoffrey. *The Georgian playhouse – actors, artists, audiences and architecture*. (London: Arts Council of Great Britain, 1975)

Mayhew, H. *London labour and the London poor*. 4 vols. (London: Griffon, 1864)

Nicoll, Allardyce. *A history of English drama, 1660–1900*, vols. III–IV. (Cambridge: Cambridge University Press, 1959)

The Revels history of drama in English, vol. VI. General editors Clifford Leech and T. W. Craik. (London: Methuen, 1975)

Sheppard, F. H. W. (gen. ed.). *Survey of London*. Series on-going. (London: Athlone Press). Vol. XXIII, *South Bank and Vauxhall* (1951); vol. XXIX, *St James's, Westminster* (1960); vol. XXXV, *The Theatre Royal, Drury Lane, and the Royal Opera House, Covent Garden* 1970)

Thomas, David and Hare, Arnold. *Restoration and Georgian England, 1660–1788*. (Cambridge: Cambridge University Press, 1989)

3 William IV cap. XV. *Collection of the public general statutes passed in the third and fourth years of the reign of HM King William IV*. (London: Eyre & Strahan, 1833)

6 & 7 Vict. cap LXVIII. *Collection of the public general statutes passed in the sixth and seventh years of the reign of HM Queen Victoria*. (London: Eyre & Strahan, 1843)

Manuscript sources

British Library

Theatre. Cuttings 47–48 Olympic Theatre
Crach 1. Tab.4.b.4 – Percival Collection. Sadler's Wells
Add. MS 29643 – Covent Garden Theatre Letterbook of H. Robertson 1823–49
Add. MS 18590 – A collection of printed play bills from 1762 to 1836 formed by B. P. Bellamy

Add. MS 29709–11 – Accounts of Drury Lane, 1772–1826
C. I 2 o.h. I – A collection of material relating to Drury Lane Theatre
Eg 2273–2319 – Ledger of Covent Garden Theatre 1767–1822. 47 vols.

Lord Chamberlain: petitions

PRO LC7/4 part 1

Lord Chamberlain: theatres

PRO LC7/10
LC7/5 1843–4 scrapbooks
LC7/6 1844–5 scrapbooks

Minutes, depositions and letters

PRO LC7/5
PRO LC7/6

Theatre Museum

Enthoven Collection

Covent Garden, Drury Lane, Haymarket theatre boxes.
H. R. Beard Collection

Published sources

Adolphus, J. *Memoirs of John Bannister, comedian.* 2 vols. (London: Bentley, 1839)
'An Old Stager' [Matthew Mackintosh]. *Stage reminiscences.* (Glasgow: Hedderwick, 1866)
Archer, W. *William Charles Macready.* (London: Kegan Paul, 1890)
Archer, William and Lome, R. W. (eds.). *Dramatic essays.* (London: Walter Scott, 1895)
Baker, David Erskine, Reed, Isaac and Jones, Stephen. *Biographia dramatica: or, a companion to the play-house.* 3 vols. (London: Longman, Hurst, 1812)
Baker, H. B. *History of the London stage, 1576–1903.* 2 vols. (London: Allen, 1889)
Baker, H. B. *Our old actors.* (London: Bentley, 1878)
Baynham, W. *The Glasgow stage.* (Glasgow: Forrester, 1892)
Bedford, P. J. *Recollections and wanderings.* (London: Routledge, Warne, 1864)
Bernard, J. *Retrospections of the stage.* 2 vols. (London: Colburn & Bentley, 1830)
Boaden, James. *The life of Mrs Jordan.* 2 vols. (London: Edward Bull, 1831)
Boaden, James. *Memoirs of Mrs Siddons.* (London: Gibbings, 1893)
Boaden, James. *Memoirs of the life of John Philip Kemble Esq.* 2 vols. (London: Longman, Hurst, 1825)
Booth, J. B. *Memoirs of Junius Brutus Booth.* (London: Chapple, Miller, 1817)
'Boz' [Charles Dickens]. *Memoirs of Joseph Grimaldi.* 2 vols. (London: Bentley, 1838)
Brayley, E. W. *Historical and descriptive accounts of the theatres of London.* (London: Taylor, 1826)
Britton J. and Pugin, A. *Illustrations of the public buildings of London.* 2 vols. (London: Weale, 1825–8)
Bulwer-Lytton, E. *England and the English.* (London: Bentley, 1833; ed. Standish Meacham, Chicago: University of Chicago Press, 1970)
Bunn, A. *The stage, both before and behind the curtain.* 3 vols. (London: Bentley, 1840)
Cole, J. W. *The life and theatrical times of Charles Kean, FSA.* 2 vols. (London: Bentley, 1859)
Coleman, J. *Memoir of Samuel Phelps.* (London: Remington, 1886)
Coleman, J. *Players and playwrights I have known.* 2 vols. (London: Chatto & Windus, 1888)
Coleridge, E. H. (ed.). *Letters of Samuel Taylor Coleridge.* (London: Heinemann, 1895)
Colman the Younger, G. *Random Records.* (London: Colburn & Bentley, 1830)

Cook, Dutton. *A book of the play: studies and illustrations of histrionic story, life and character.* 2 vols. (London: Sampson, Low, Marston, Searle and Rivington, 1881)

'Cornwall, Barry' [B. W. Procter]. *The life of Edmund Kean.* 2 vols. (London: Moxon, 1835)

'Cowell, Joe' [Hawkins Witchett]. *Thirty years passed among the players of England and America.* (New York: Harper, 1845)

Cumberland, Richard. *Memoirs.* (London: Lackington, Allen, 1806; reprinted New York: Blom, 1969)

Decastro, J. *The memoirs of J. Decastro, comedian.* Ed. R. Humphreys. (London: Sherwood, Jones, 1824)

Dibdin, C. I. M. *History and illustrations of the London theatres.* (London: Proprietors of *Illustrations of London Buildings*, 1826)

Dibdin, James C. *The annals of the Edinburgh stage.* (Edinburgh: Cameron, 1888)

Dibdin, Thomas. *Reminiscences.* 2 vols. (London: Colburn, 1827)

Dickens, C. (ed). *The life of Charles James Mathews.* 2 vols. (London: Macmillan, 1879)

Donaldson, W. A. *Recollections of an actor.* (London: Maxwell, 1865)

Doran, J. *Annals of the English stage from Thomas Betterton to Edmund Kean.* 3 vols. Ed. R. W. Lowe. (London: Nimmo, 1888)

Dyer, R. *Nine years of an actor's life.* (London: Longman, Rees, 1833)

Ebers, J. *Seven years of the King's Theatre.* (London: Ainsworth, 1828; reprinted New York: Blom, 1969)

Egan, Pierce *The life of an actor.* (London: Arnold, 1825; reprinted Pickering & Chatto, 1892)

Faucit, Helen. *On some of Shakespeare's female characters.* (London: Blackwood, 1885)

Foote, H. *Companion to the theatres.* (London: Marsh & Miller, 1829)

Foulston, J. *The public buildings erected in the west of England.* (London: Williams, 1838)

Galt, J. *The lives of the players.* 2 vols. (London: Colburn & Bentley, 1831)

Genest, John. *Some account of the English stage from the Restoration in 1660 to 1830.* 10 vols. (Bath: Carrington, 1832)

Gilliland, T. *The dramatic mirror.* 2 vols. (London: Chapple, 1808)

Goede, C. A. G. *The stranger in England; or, travels in Great Britain.* 2 vols. (London: Mathew & Leigh, 1807)

Goodman, W. *The Keeleys: on stage and at home.* (London: Bentley, 1895)

Grant, J. *The great metropolis.* (London: Saunders & Otley, 1837)

Hawkins, F. W. *The life of Edmund Kean.* 2 vols. (London: Tinsley, 1869)

Hazlitt, William. *Dramatic essays.* Ed. W. Archer and R. W. Lowe. (London: Walter Scott, 1895)

Hazlitt, William. *A view of the English stage.* (London: Robert Stodart, 1818)

Hunt. Leigh *Critical essays on the performers of the London theatres.* (London: John Hunt, 1807)

Hunt, Leigh. *Dramatic essays.* Ed. W. Archer and R. W. Lowe. (London: Walter Scott, 1894)

Kelly, Michael. *Reminiscences* (compiled by Theodore Hook). 2nd edn. 2 vols. (London: Colburn, 1826)

Kemble, F. A. *Further records, 1843–83.* 2 vols. (London: Bentley, 1890)

Kemble, F. A. *Record of a girlhood.* 3 vols. (London: Bentley, 1878)

[Knight, Charles] *Penny cyclopaedia.* (London: Charles Knight, 1841)

Lewes, G. H. *On actors and the art of acting.* (London: Smith, Elder, 1875)

Macready, W. C. *The diaries of William Charles Macready, 1833–51.* Ed. W. Toynbee. 2 vols. (London: Chapman & Hall, 1912)

Macready, W. C. *Reminiscences.* Ed. Sir F. Pollock. 2 vols. (London: Macmillan, 1875)

Marshall, T. *Lives of the most celebrated actors and actresses.* (London: Appleyard, 1847)

Marston, J. W. *Our recent actors.* 2 vols. (London: Sampson, Low, 1888)

Martin, Theodore. *Helena Faucit, Lady Martin.* (London: Blackwood, 1900)

Mathews, Mrs A. *Memoirs of Charles Mathews.* 4 vols. (London: Bentley, 1838–9)

Mayhew, E. *Stage effect.* (London: Mitchell, 1840)

More, Hannah. *Strictures on the modern system of female education.* 2 vols. (London: Cadell & Davies, 1799)

Munden, T. S. *Memoirs of Joseph Shepherd Munden, by his son.* (London: Bentley, 1844)

Murdoch, James E. *The stage, or recollections of actors and acting.* (Philadelphia: Stoddart, 1880)

Oulton, Walley C. *The history of the theatres of London, 1771–95.* 2 vols. (London: Martin & Bain, 1818)

Pascoe, C. E. *The dramatic list.* (London: David Bogue, 1880)

'Paterson, Peter' [J. G. Bertram]. *The confessions of a strolling player.* (London: Bertram, 1852)

Peake, R. B. *Memoirs of the Colman family.* 2 vols. (London: Bentley, 1841)

Penley, B. S. *The Bath stage.* (London and Bath: Lewis, 1892)

Phelps, W. M. and J. Forbes-Robertson. *The life and life-work of Samuel Phelps.* (London: Sampson, Low, Marston, 1886)

Planché, J. R. *Recollections and reflections.* 2 vols. (London: Tinsley, 1872)

Pollock, Lady J. *Macready as I knew him.* (London: Remington, 1884)

Pueckler-Muskau, H. L. *A tour in England, Ireland and France.* (1832; reprinted Zurich: Massie, 1940)

[Pyne, W. and Combe, W.] *Microcosm of London.* 3 vols. (London: Ackerman, 1808–11)

Raymond, G. *The life and enterprises of Robert William Elliston, comedian.* (London: Routledge, 1857; published as *Memoirs of Robert William Elliston, comedian,* London: Mortimer, 1844)

Rede, Leman, T. *The road to the stage.* (London: Smith, 1827)

Rees, A. *Cyclopaedia, or universal dictionary of arts, sciences and literature,* vol. xii. (London: Longman, 1803–19)

Reynolds, F. *The life and times of Frederick Reynolds.* (London: Colburn, 1827; reprinted New York: Blom, 1969)

Robson, W. *The old playgoer.* (London, 1845; reprinted Fontwell, Sussex: Centaur, 1969)

Russell, W. Clark. *Representative actors.* (London: Frederick Warne, 1872)

Scharf, G. *Recollections of the scenic effects of the Covent Garden Theatre.* (London: Pattie, 1838–9)

Scott, Walter, Sir. *Prose works.* Vol. vi, *Essays on chivalry, romance and the drama.* (Edinburgh: Cadell, 1834)

Siddons, Henry. *Practical illustrations of rhetorical gesture and action.* 2nd edn. (London: Sherwood, 1822)

Stirling, E. *Old Drury Lane: fifty years' recollections.* 2 vols. (London: Chatto & Windus, 1881)

Tomlins, F. G. *A brief view of the English drama.* (London: Mitchell, 1840)

Vandenhoff, G. *Leaves from an actor's notebook.* (London: Cooper, 1860)

'Veteran stager' [G. Grant]. *An essay on the science of acting.* (London: Cowie & Strange, 1828)

Wallack, L. *Memories of fifty years.* (New York: Scribner's, 1889)

Webster, B. (ed.). *The acting national drama.* 6 vols. (London: Chapman & Hall, 1837)

Whyte, F. *Actors of the century.* (London: Bell, 1898)

Wilkinson, R. *Londina illustrata.* 2 vols. (London: Wilkinson, 1819, 1825)

Williams, M. *Some London theatres past and present.* (London: Sampson, Low, 1883)

Winston, James. *The theatric tourist.* (London: T. Woodfall, 1805)

Wyatt, B. *Observations on the design of the Theatre Royal, Drury Lane.* (London: Taylor, 1813)

Young, J. C. *A memoir of Charles Mayne Young, tragedian.* (London: Macmillan, 1871)

Studies

Allen, S. S. *Samuel Phelps and the Sadler's Wells Theatre.* (Middletown, CN: Wesleyan University Press, 1971)

Appleton, W. W. *Madame Vestris and the London stage.* (New York: Columbia University Press, 1974)

Armstrong, C. F. *A century of great actors, 1750–1850.* (London: Mills & Boon, 1912)

Armstrong, M. *Fanny Kemble: a passionate Victorian.* (New York: Macmillan, 1938)

Arundell, Dennis. *The story of Sadler's Wells, 1683–1964.* (London: Hamish Hamilton, 1965)

Baer, Marc. *Theatre and disorder in Georgian London.* (Oxford: Clarendon Press, 1992)

Baker, M. *The rise of the Victorian actor.* (London: Croom Helm, 1978)

Barker, Kathleen. *The Theatre Royal, Bristol, 1766–1966.* (London: Society for Theatre Research, 1974)

Bergman, Gosta M. *Lighting in the theatre.* (Stockholm: Almqvist & Wiksell, 1977)

Booth, M. R. *English melodrama.* (London: Jenkins, 1965)

Booth, M. R. *English plays of the nineteenth century.* 5 vols. (Oxford: Oxford University Press, 1973–6)

Booth, M. R. *Theatre in the Victorian age.* (Cambridge: Cambridge University Press, 1991)

Broadbent, R. J. *Annals of the Liverpool stage.* (Liverpool: E. Howell, 1908)

Brown, Eluned (ed.). *Selections from the diary of Henry Crabb Robinson – the London theatre, 1811–66.* (London: Society for Theatre Research, 1966)

Burley, T. L. G. *Playhouses and players of East Anglia*. (Norwich: Jarrold, 1928)

Butler E. M. (ed.) *A Regency visitor*. (London: Collins, 1957)

Conolly, L. W. *The censorship of English drama, 1737–1824*. (San Marino: Huntington Library, 1976)

Crane, Harvey. *Playbill: a history of theatre in the West Country*. (Plymouth: MacDonald & Evans, 1980)

Cunningham, J. E. *Theatre Royal: the history of the Theatre Royal, Birmingham*. (Oxford: George Ronald, 1950)

Davis, J. *John Liston, comedian*. (London: Society for Theatre Research, 1985)

Disher, M. W. *Greatest show on earth: Astley's*. (London: 1937; reprinted New York: Blom, 1971)

Disher, M. W. *Mad genius: a biography of Edmund Kean*. (London: Hutchinson, 1950)

Dobbs, B. *Drury Lane: three centuries of the Theatre Royal, 1663–1971*. (London: Cassell, 1972)

Donohue, J. W. (ed.). *The theatrical manager in England and America*. (Princeton, NJ: Princeton University Press, 1971)

Downer, A. *The eminent tragedian: William Charles Macready*. (Cambridge, MA: Harvard University Press, 1966)

Findlater, R. *Joe Grimaldi: his life and theatre*. (Cambridge: Cambridge University Press, 1978)

Fothergill, B. *Mrs Jordan: portrait of an actress*. (London: Faber, 1965)

Foulkes, R. (ed.). *Scenes from provincial stages*. (London: Society for Theatre Research, 1994)

Furnas, J. C. *Fanny Kemble: leading lady of the nineteenth century stage. A biography*. (New York: Dial, 1982)

Fyvie, J. *Comedy queens of the Georgian era*. (London: Constable, 1906)

Fyvie, J. *Tragedy queens of the Georgian era*. (London: Constable, 1903)

Grice, E. *Rogues and vagabonds, or the actor's road to respectability*. (Lavenham: Dalton, 1977)

Hadley, Elaine. *Melodramatic tactics: theatricalized dissent in the English marketplace, 1800–1865*. (Stanford, CA: Stanford University Press, 1993)

Hibbert, H. G. *A playgoer's memories*. (London: Grant Richards, 1920)

Hillebrand, H. N. *Edmund Kean*. (New York: Columbia University Press, 1933)

Hodgkinson, J. L. and Pogson, R. *The early Manchester theatre*. (London: Blond, 1960)

Houtchens, L. H. and Houtchens, C. W. *Leigh Hunt's dramatic criticism*. (Oxford: Oxford University Press, 1950)

Joseph, B. *The tragic actor*. (London: Routledge & Kegan Paul, 1959)

Kelly, Linda. *The Kemble era. John Philip Kemble, Sarah Siddons and the London stage*. (London: Bodley Head, 1980)

Leacroft, R. *The development of the English playhouse*. (London: Methuen, 1973)

Lowndes, W. *The Theatre Royal at Bath*. (Bristol: Redcliffe, 1982)

Macqueen-Pope, W. *Haymarket: theatre of perfection*. (London: W. H. Allen, 1948)

Macqueen-Pope, W. *Theatre Royal, Drury Lane*. (London: W. H. Allen, 1945)

Mander, R. and Mitchenson, J. *London's lost theatres*. (London: Hart-Davis, 1968)

Mander, R. and Mitchenson, J. *The lost theatres of London*. (London: New English Library, 1975)

Manvell, Roger. *Sarah Siddons, portrait of an actress*. (London: William Heinemann, 1970)

Marshall, H. and Stock, Mildred. *Ira Aldridge: the Negro tragedian*. (London: 1958; reprinted Washington, DC: Howard University Press, 1993)

Merchant, W. M. *Shakespeare and the artist*. (Oxford: Oxford University Press, 1959)

Morley, M. *Margate and its theatres, 1730–1965*. (London: Museums Press, 1966)

Murray, C. *Robert William Elliston, manager: a theatrical biography*. (London: Society for Theatre Research, 1975)

Nalbach, D. *The King's Theatre, 1704–1867: London's first Italian opera house*. (London: Society for Theatre Research, 1972)

Nicholson, Watson. *The struggle for a free stage in London*. (London: Constable, 1906; New York: Blom, 1966)

Odell, M. T. *The Old Theatre, Worthing, 1807–55*. (Aylesbury: Jones, 1938)

Oswald, Harold. *The Theatres Royal in Newcastle-upon-Tyne*. (Newcastle-upon-Tyne: Northumberland Press, 1936)

Pearce, C. E. *Madame Vestris and her times*. (1923; reprinted New York: Blom, 1969)

Playfair, G. W. *The flash of lighning: a portrait of Edmund Kean.* (London: Kimber, 1983)
Playfair, G. W. *The prodigy: a study of the strange life of Master Betty.* (London: Secker & Warburg 1967)
Rees, T. *Theatre lighting in the age of gas.* (London: Society for Theatre Research, 1976)
Rhodes, R. C. *The Theatre Royal, Birmingham, 1774–1924.* (Birmingham: Moody, 1924)
Rosenfeld, Sybil. *Georgian scene painters and scene painting.* (Cambridge: Cambridge University Press, 1981)
Rowell, G. *Queen Victoria goes to the Theatre.* (London: Elek, 1978)
Saxon, A. H. *Enter foot and horse.* (New Haven: Yale University Press, 1968)
Saxon, A. H. *The life and art of Andrew Ducrow and the romantic age of the English circus.* (Hamden, CN: Archon, 1978)
Shawe-Taylor, D. *Covent Garden.* (London: Max Parrish, 1948)
Sheridan, P. *Penny theatres of Victorian London.* (London: Dobson, 1981)
Sherson, E. *London's lost theatres of the nineteenth century.* (London: Lane, 1925; reprinted New York: Blom, 1969)
Southern, Richard. *Changeable scenery.* (London: Faber, 1952)
Southern, Richard. *The Georgian playhouse.* (London: Pleiades Books, 1948)
Speaight, George (ed.). *Memoirs of Charles Dibdin the Younger.* (London: Society for Theatre Research, 1956)
Sprague, A. C. 'A Macbeth of few words', in *All these to teach (Essays in honour of C. A. Robertson),* (Gainesville, FL.: University of Florida Press, 1965)
Sprague, A. C. *Shakespearian players and performances.* (New York: Russell & Russell, 1953)
Stephens, J. Russell. *The censorship of English drama, 1824–1901.* (Cambridge: Cambridge University Press, 1981)
Trewin, J. C. *Mr Macready: a nineteenth-century tragedian and his theatre.* (London: Harrap, 1955)
Troubridge, St Vincent. *The benefit system in the British theatre.* (London: Society for Theatre Research, 1967)
Waitzkin, L. *The Witch of Wych Street: a study of the theatrical reforms of Madame Vestris.* (Cambridge, MA: Harvard University Press, 1933)
Watson, E. B. *From Sheridan to Robertson.* (Cambridge, MA: Harvard University Press, 1926; reprinted New York: Blom, 1963)
Williams, C. J. *Madame Vestris: a theatrical biography.* (London: Sidgwick & Jackson, 1973)
Williamson, J. *Charles Kemble, man of the theatre.* (Lincoln, NB: University of Nebraska Press, 1970)
Wilmeth, D. B. *George Frederick Cooke, Machiavel of the stage.* (Westport, CN: Greenwood Press, 1981)
Wilson, A. E. *The Lyceum.* (London: Yates, 1952)
Wyndham, H. Saxe. *Annals of Covent Garden Theatre from 1732 to 1897.* 2 vols. (London: Chatto & Windus, 1906)

Articles

Barker, C. 'The audience of the Britannia Theatre, Hoxton'. *Theatre Quarterly,* 9, 1979, pp. 27–41
Butler, James H. 'Early nineteenth-century stage settings in the British theatre'. *Theatre Survey,* 6, 1965, pp. 54–64
Carlisle, C. J. 'Helen Faucit's acting style'. *Theatre Survey,* 17, 1976, pp. 38–56
Carlisle, C. J. 'The other Miss Faucit'. *Nineteenth-Century Theatre Research,* 6, 1978, pp. 71–88
Carlisle, C. J. 'Two notes on Helen Faucit'. *Theatre Notebook,* 30, 1976, pp. 99–103
Cowhig, R. M. 'Ira Aldridge in Manchester'. *Theatre Research International,* 11, autumn 1986, pp. 239–46
De Felice, J. 'The London theatrical agent'. *Theatre Notebook,* 23, 1969, pp. 87–94
Donohue, J. W. 'Kemble and Mrs Siddons in *Macbeth*: the Romantic approach to tragic character'. *Theatre Notebook,* 22, 1967–8, pp. 65–86
Donohue, J. W. 'Kemble's production of *Macbeth* (1794)'. *Theatre Notebook,* 21, 1966–7, pp. 63–74
Downer, A. 'Players and painted stage: nineteenth-century acting'. *PMLA,* 61, June 1946, pp. 522–76
Fahrner, R. 'The second Sans Souci Theatre, 1796–1835'. *Theatre Notebook,* 29, 1975, pp. 69–73

Foulkes, R. 'Helen Faucit and Ellen Terry as Portia'. *Theatre Notebook*, 31, 1977, pp. 27–37
Hogan, C. B. 'The MS of Winston's *Theatric Tourist*'. *Theatre Notebook*, 1, 1946–7, pp. 86–90
Irvin, Eric. 'More drawings from Winston's *Theatric Tourist*'. *Theatre Notebook*, 19, 1964–5, pp. 64–6
Larsen, Orville K. 'A commentary on the "Historical development of the box set"'. *Theatre Annual*, 1946, pp. 28–36
Lorenzen, R. L. 'The old Prince of Wales's Theatre: a view of the physical structure'. *Theatre Notebook*, 25, 1971, pp. 132–45
McDonald, J. 'Lesser ladies of the Victorian stage'. *Theatre Research International*, 13, 1988, pp. 234–49
McDowell, J. H. 'Historical development of the box set'. *Theatre Annual*, 1945, pp. 65–83
Ranger, P. 'A matter of choice: a comparison of locations and repertoire in some English provincial theatres'. *Nineteenth-Century Theatre Research*, 10, 1982, pp. 61–84
Rosenfeld, Sybil. 'The theatrical notebooks of T. H. Wilson Manley'. *Theatre Notebook*, 7, 1952, pp. 2–12
Steadman, J. W. 'General utility: Victorian actor-authors from Knowles to Pinero'. *Educational Theatre Journal*, 24, 1972, pp. 289–301

FRANCE

Works of reference

Bulletin annoté des lois, décrets et ordonnances depuis le mois de juin 1789 jusqu'au mois d'août 1830 . . . mis en ordre et annoté par M. Lepec. 18 vols. (Paris, 1834–9)
Joannidès, A. *La Comédie-Française de 1680 à 1900. Dictionnaire général des pièces et des auteurs.* (Geneva: Slatkine Reprints, 1970)
Recueil général des lois et ordonnances depuis le 7 août 1830 (– décembre 1847). 17 vols. (Paris, 1831–47)
Recueil général des lois et ordonnances depuis le 24 février 1848 (– décembre 1852). 5 vols. (Paris, 1848–52)
Tuetey, Alexandre. *Répertoire général des sources manuscites de l'histoire de Paris pendant la révolution française.* 11 vols. (Paris: Imprimerie Nouvelle, 1890–1914)
Wicks, Charles Beaumont. *The Parisian stage: alphabetical indexes of plays and authors (1800–1900).* 5 vols. (Alabama: University of Alabama Press, 1950–79)

Manuscript sources

Archives Nationales. F21 1036; F21 1042; F21 1046; F21 1134; F21 1154; F21 1159; F21 1165
Bibliothèque de la Comédie-Française. Illumination du Théâtre-Français. Traité pour les Années du 1er Juillet 1811 au 30 Juin 1817. Messieurs Empaire & Cie, Entrepreneurs

Published sources

Albertin, Hyacinthe. *Indications générales pour la mise en scène de Henri III et sa cour* (Paris: Duverger, [1829]), in M. A. Allevy, *Edition critique d'une mise en scène romantique.* (Paris: Droz, 1938)
Alhoy, Maurice. *Grande biographie dramatique, ou silhouette des acteurs, actrices, chanteurs, cantatrices, danseurs, danseuses, etc. de Paris et des départments.* (Paris: chez les marchands de nouveautés, 1824)
Allard, Louis. *Esquisses parisiennes en des temps heureux, 1830–1848.* (Montreal: Editions Variétés, 1943)
Almanach général de tous les spectacles de Paris et des provinces, pour l'année 1791. 2 vols. (Paris: Froullé, 1791–2)
Almanach des spectacles à Paris, pour l'an 1809. (Paris, 1809)
[Anon.] *Réclamation de MM les directeurs des théâtres de Paris, au sujet de l'impôt établi sous le nom de droit des pauvres.* (Paris: David, 1833)
Arago, Jacques. *Foyers et coulisses, panorama des théâtres de Paris.* (Paris: Librairie Nouvelle, 1852)
Arago, Jacques. *Mémoires d'un petit banc de l'opéra.* (Paris: D. Ebrard, 1844)
Arago, Jacques. *Physiologie des foyers de tous les théâtres de Paris.* (Paris: chez les marchands de nouveautés, 1841)

Audibert, Hilarion. *Indiscrétions et confidences: souvenirs du théâtre et de la littérature.* (Paris: Dentu, 1858)

Auger, Hippolyte. *Du monopole et de la concurrence des théâtres.* (Paris: Everat, 1832)

Auger, Hippolyte. 'Mémoires inédits d'Hippolyte Auger (1810–1869)'. *Revue rétrospective,* 13 (1890), 14 (1891) and 15 (1891)

Auger, Hippolyte. *Physiologie du théâtre.* 3 vols. (Paris: Firmin-Didot, 1839–40)

Banville, Théodore de. *La Comédie-Française racontée par un témoin de ses fautes.* (Paris: Albert, 1863)

Banville, Théodore de. *Petites études. Mes souvenirs.* (Paris: Charpentier, 1882)

Banville, Théodore de. 'Reines de théâtre', in *Critiques,* ed. Victor Barrucand (Paris: Charpentier, 1917)

Bawr, Mme Alexandrine Sophie de. *Mes souvenirs.* (Paris: Passard, 1853)

Bernier de Maligny, Aristippe. *Nouveau manuel théâtral théorique et pratique nécessaire à tous les acteurs; aux directeurs, régisseurs et employés des théâtres; aux auteurs et aux critiques.* (Paris: Roret, 1854)

Blagdon, Francis. *Paris as it was and as it is; or a sketch of the French Capital illustrative of the effects of the Revolution.* 2 vols. (London: Baldwin, 1803)

Borgnis, J. A. *Traité complet de la mécanique appliquée aux arts. Des machines imitatives et des machines théâtrales.* (Paris: Bachelier, 1820)

Bouffé, Hugues-Marie-Désiré. *Mes souvenirs, 1800–1880.* (Paris: Dentu, 1880)

Bouilly, Jean-Nicolas. *Soixante ans du Théâtre-Français, par un amateur né en 1769.* (Paris: Gosselin, 1842)

Brazier, Nicolas. *Chroniques des petits théâtres de Paris, réimprimées . . . par Georges d'Heylli.* 2 vols. (Paris: Rouveyre & Blond, 1883)

Brazier, Nicolas. *Histoire des petits théâtres de Paris, depuis leur origine.* 2 vols. (Paris: Allardin, 1838)

Brifaut, Charles. *Souvenirs d'un académicien sur la Révolution, le Premier Empire et la Restauration.* 2 vols. (Paris: Albin Michel, 1921)

Cahier. Plaintes et doléances de Messieurs les Comédiens-Français. (n. p., 1789)

Cailhava d'Estandoux, Jean-François. *Les Causes de la décadence du théâtre, et les moyens de le faire refleurir.* (Paris: Royez, 1789)

Carr, John. *The stranger in France, or a Tour from Devonshire to Paris.* (London: Johnson, 1807)

Catalogue de costumes, tableaux, dessins, gravures, et autres objets d'art composant le cabinet de feu François-Joseph Talma, artiste sociétaire du Théâtre-Français. (Paris: n.p., 1827)

Chastenay de Lanty, Louise Marie Victorine de. *Mémoires de Mme de Chastenay, 1771–1815.* 2 vols. (Paris: Plon-Nourrit, 1896–7)

Chateaubriand, François-René de. *Mémoires d'outre-tombe.* Ed. M. Levaillant. 4 vols. (Paris: Flammarion, 1947)

Chaulin, N. P. *Biographie dramatique des principaux artistes anglais venus à Paris, précédée de souvenirs historiques du théâtre anglais à Paris en 1827 et 1828.* (Paris: chez les marchands de nouveautés, 1828)

Chéron, François. *Mémoires et récits de François Chéron.* (Paris: Librairie de la Société Bibliographique, 1882)

Claretie, Jules. *Profils de théâtre.* (Paris: Fasquelle, 1904)

Claudin, Gustave. *Mes souvenirs. Les boulevards de 1840–1870.* (Paris: Calmann-Lévy, 1884)

Contant, Clément, and Filippi, Joseph de. *Parallèle des principaux théâtres modernes de l'Europe et des machines théâtrales françaises, allemandes et anglaises.* (New York: Blom, 1968; first published 1840–2)

Couailhac, Jules. *Physiologie du théâtre, par un journaliste.* (Paris: Laisné, 1841)

Courtois, Clément [P. D. Lemazurier]. *L'Opinion du parterre, ou Censure des acteurs, auteurs et spectateurs du Théâtre-Français.* 10 vols. (Paris: Martinet, 1803–13)

[Descombes], Charles Maurice. *Epaves. Théâtre, histoire, anecdotes, mots.* (Paris: chez les principaux libraires, 1865)

[Descombes], Charles Maurice. *Histoire anecdotique du théâtre, de la littérature et de diverses impressions contemporaines.* 2 vols. (Paris: Plon, 1856)

[Descombes], Charles Maurice. *Le Théâtre-Français, monument et dépendances.* (Paris: Garnier, 1859)

Delacroix, Eugène. *Correspondance générale.* 5 vols. (Paris: Plon, 1936–8)

Delécluze, Etienne-Jean. *Journal de Delécluze, 1824–1828.* Ed. Robert Baschet. (Paris: Grasset, 1948)

Deshayes, A. J. J. *Idées générales sur l'Académie de Musique.* (Paris: Mougie, 1822)

Donnet, Alexis. *Architectonographie des théâtres de Paris, ou Parallèle historique et critique de ces édifices considérés sous le rapport de l'architecture et de la décoration.* (Paris: P. Didot l'Aîne, 1821)

Dumas, Alexandre. *La dernière année de Marie Dorval*. (Paris: Librairie Nouvelle, 1855)

Dumas, Alexandre. *Mes mémoires*. 22 vols. (Paris: Alexandre Cadot, 1852–4)

Dumas, Alexandre. *Souvenirs dramatiques*. 2 vols. (Paris: Michel Lévy, 1868)

Dumas, Alexandre. *Une vie artiste [Mélingue]*. 2 vols. (Paris: Alexandre Cadot, 1854)

Dumersan, Théophile. *Manuel des coulisses, ou Guide de l'amateur*. (Paris: Bezou, 1826)

Etienne, C. G. and Martainville, A. *Histoire du Théâtre-Français, depuis le commencement de la Révolution jusqu'à la réunion générale*. 4 vols. (Paris: Barba, 1802)

Fiorentino, Pier Angelo. *Comédies et comédiens. Feuilletons*. 2 vols. (Paris: Michel Lévy, 1866)

Fleury [J. A. Bénard]. *Mémoires de Fleury, de la Comédie-Française*. Ed. J. B. P. Lafitte. 2 vols. (Paris: Delahays, 1847)

Flore, Mlle [Flore Corvée]. *Mémoires de Mlle Flore, actrice des Variétés*. Ed. Henri d'Alméras. (Paris: Société Parisienne d'Edition, 1903)

Foucher, Adèle, Madame Victor Hugo. *Victor Hugo raconté par un témoin de sa vie*. 2 vols. (Paris: A. Lacroix, Verboeckhoven, 1863)

Framery, Nicolas-Etienne. *De l'organisation des spectacles de Paris*. (Paris: Buisson, 1790)

Fusil, Louise. *Souvenirs d'une actrice*. 3 vols. (Paris: Dumont, 1841–6)

Gautier, Théophile. *Ecrivains et artistes romantiques*. (Paris: Jules Tallandier, 1929)

Gautier, Théophile. *Histoire de l'art dramatique en France depuis vingt-cinq ans*. 6 vols. (Paris: Hetzel, 1858–9)

Gautier, Théophile. *Histoire du romantisme*. (Paris: Charpentier, 1874)

Gautier, Théophile. *Portraits contemporains. Littérateurs, peintres, sculpteurs, artistes dramatiques*. (Paris: Charpentier, 1881)

Gautier, Théophile. *Souvenirs de théâtre, d'art et de critique*. (Paris: Charpentier, 1883)

Geoffroy, Julien-Louis. *Cours de littérature dramatique, ou Recueil par ordre de matières des feuilletons de Geoffroy*. 6 vols. (Paris: Pierre Blanchard, 1825)

Géréon, Léonard. *La Rampe et les coulisses: esquisses biographiques des directeurs, acteurs et actrices de tous les théâtres*. (Paris: chez les marchands de nouveautés, 1832)

Gosse, Etienne. *De l'abolition des privilèges et de l'émancipation des théâtres*. (Paris: Delaunay & Barba, 1830)

Got, Edmond. *Journal de Edmond Got, sociétaire de la Comédie-Française*. 2 vols. (Paris: Plon-Nourrit, 1910)

Grimod de la Reynière, A. B. L. (ed.). *Le Censeur dramatique, ou Journal des principaux théâtres de Paris et des départements*. 4 vols. (Paris, 1797–8)

Grimod de la Reynière, A. B. L. and Pillet, Fabien. *Revue des comédiens, ou Critique raisonnée de tous les acteurs, danseurs et mimes de la capitale*. 2 vols. (Paris: Favre, 1808)

Grobert, Colonel [J.-F.-L.]. *De l'exécution dramatique considérée dans ses rapports avec le matériel de la salle et de la scène*. (Paris: Schoell, 1809)

Guilbert de Pixérécourt, René-Charles. *Guerre au mélodrame!!!* (Paris: Delaunay, 1818)

[Hapdé, J. B. Augustin]. *De l'anarchie théâtrale, ou De la nécessité de remettre en rigueur les lois et les règlements relatifs aux différens genres des spectacles de Paris*. (Paris: J. G. Dentu, 1814)

Hare, Augustus J. C. *The life and letters of Maria Edgeworth*. 2 vols. (London: Edward Arnold, 1894)

Harel, F. A., Alhoy, P. M. and Jal, A. *Dictionnaire théâtral, ou Douze cent trente-trois vérités sur les directeurs, régisseurs, acteurs, actrices et employés des divers théâtres*. (Paris: J. N. Barba, 1824)

Hervey, Charles. *The theatres of Paris*. (London: John Mitchell, 1846)

Hostein, Hippolyte. *Historiettes et souvenirs d'un homme de théâtre*. (Paris: Dentu, 1878)

Hostein, Hippolyte. *La Liberté des théâtres*. (Paris: Librairie des Auteurs, 1867)

Hostein, Hippolyte. *Réforme théâtrale [. . .]* (Paris: A. Desesserts)

Houssaye, Arsène. *Les Confessions. Souvenirs d'un demi-siècle*. 6 vols. (Paris: Dentu, 1885–91)

Hugo, Victor. *Actes et paroles. Avant l'exil*. 2 vols. (Paris: Hetzel, [1890])

Hugo, Victor. *Choses vues*. 2 vols. (Paris: Ollendorff, 1913)

Hugo, Victor. *Œuvres complètes*. Ed. Jean Massin. 18 vols. (Paris: Club Français du Livre, 1967–70)

Janin, Jules. *Deburau, histoire du théâtre à quatre sous, pour faire suite à l'histoire du Théâtre-Français*. 2nd edn. 2 vols. (Paris: Gosselin, 1832)

Janin, Jules. *Histoire de la littérature dramatique*. 6 vols. (Paris: Michel Lévy, 1853–8)

Joanny [J. B. Brisebarre]. *Ma confession.* (Paris: Imprimerie de Lacrampe, 1846)

Jouslin de la Salle, Armand-François. *Souvenirs sur le Théâtre-français (1833–1837).* Ed. M. G. Monval and le Comte Fleury. (Paris: Emile-Paul, 1900)

Jouy, Etienne de. *L'Hermite de la Chaussée d'Antin, ou Observations sur les mœurs et les usages parisiens au commencement du XIXe siècle.* 5 vols. (Paris: Pillet, 1812–14)

Jouy, Etienne de. *L'Hermite en province, ou Observations sur les mœurs et usages français au commencement du XIXe siècle.* 14 vols. (Paris: Pillet, 1818–27)

Kaufmann, Jacques-Auguste. *Architectonographie des théâtres . . . commencé par Alexis Donnet et Orgiazzi et continué par Jacques-Auguste Kaufmann, architecte.* (Paris: Mathias, 1840)

Kotzebue, August von. *Souvenirs de Paris en 1804.* Trans. R. C. Guilbert de Pixérécourt. 2 vols. (Paris: Barba, 1805)

Lablée, J. *Du Théâtre de la Porte-Saint-Martin, de pièces d'un nouveau genre et de la pantomime.* (Paris: Blanchard, 1812)

Lacan, Adolphe and Paulmier, Charles. *Traité de la législation et de la jurisprudence des théâtres.* 2 vols. (Paris: Durand, 1853)

Laferrière, Adolphe. *Mémoires de Laferrière.* 2 vols. (Paris: Dentu, 1876)

La Harpe, Jean-François. *Correspondance littéraire.* 6 vols. (Paris: Dupont, 1801)

Lan, J. *Mémoires d'un chef de claque, souvenirs des théâtres.* (Paris: Librairie Nouvelle, 1883)

Laugier, Eugène. *De la Comédie-Française depuis 1830, ou Résumé des événements à ce théâtre depuis cette époque jusqu'en 1844.* (Paris: Tresse, 1844)

Laugier, Eugène. *Documents historiques sur la Comédie-Française pendant le règne de S. M. l'Empereur Napoléon Ier.* (Paris: Firmin-Didot, 1853)

Lavallée, Joseph. *Lettres d'un mameluk, ou Tableau moral et critique de quelques parties des mœurs de Paris.* (Paris: Capelle, 1803)

Legouvé, Ernest. *Epis et bleuets: souvenirs biographiques, études littéraires et dramatiques.* (Paris: Hetzel, 1893)

Legouvé, Ernest. *Soixante ans de souvenirs.* 2 vols. (Paris: Hetzel, 1887)

[Lemaistre, J. G.] *A rough sketch of modern Paris; or, Letters on society, manners, public curiosities and amusements, in that capital.* (London: Johnson, 1803)

Lemaître, Frédérick. *Souvenirs, publiés par son fils.* 2nd edn. (Paris: Ollendorff, 1880)

Léon d'Amboise [Léon Guillemin]. *Physiologie du parterre. Types du spectateur.* (Paris: Desloges, 1841)

M. D***, ancien directeur et artiste. *Notice sur les causes de la décadence du théâtre en province et des moyens de le régénérer.* (Paris: Tresse, 1852)

Merle, Jean-Toussaint. *Du marasme dramatique en 1829.* (Paris: Barba, 1829)

Monnier, Henri. *Mémoires de Monsieur Joseph Prudhomme.* (Paris: Dentu, 1892)

Monselet, Charles. *De A à Z: portraits contemporains.* (Paris: Charpentier, 1888)

Moreau, F. J. *Souvenirs du théâtre anglais à Paris.* (Paris: Gaugain, Lambert, 1827)

Moynet, Georges. *La Machinerie théâtrale. Trucs et décors. Explication raisonnée de tous les moyens employés pour produire les illusions théâtrales.* (Paris: Librairie Illustrée, n.d. [1893])

Moynet, J. *L'Envers du théâtre. Machines et décorations.* 3rd edn. (Paris: Hachette, 1888)

Musset, Alfred de. *Mélanges de littérature et de critique.* (Paris: Charpentier, 1867)

Nerval, Gérard de. *La Vie du théâtre.* Ed. Jean Richer. (Paris: Minard, Lettres Modernes, 1961)

Nerval, Gérard de. *Variétés et fantaisies.* Ed. Jean Richer. (Paris: Minard, Lettres Modernes, 1964)

Nisard, Désiré. *Souvenirs et notes biographiques.* 2 vols. (Paris: C. Lévy, 1888)

Noverre, J. G. *Lettres sur les arts imitateurs.* 2 vols. (Paris: Collin, 1807)

Olivier, Juste. *Paris en 1830. Journal.* Ed. André Delattre and Marc Denkinger. (Lausanne: Payot, 1951)

Paccard, Jean-Edmé. *Mémoires et confessions d'un comédien.* (Paris: Pougin, 1839)

Palianti, Louis. *Collection de mises en scène de grands opéras et d'opéras-comiques.* No. 36, 'Le Domino noir'. (Paris: Brière, 1872)

Pierre-Victor [Pierre-Simon Lerebours]. *Documents pour servir à l'histoire du Théâtre-Français sous la Restauration, ou Recueil des écrits publiés de 1815 à 1830 par Pierre-Victor sur les débats avec l'administration des Menus-Plaisirs et sur les abus qui ont le plus contribué, pendant cette période, à la dégradation des théâtres.* (Paris: Guillaumin, 1834)

Pierre-Victor [Pierre-Simon Lerebours]. *Idées sur les deux Théâtres-Français, sur l'École royale de déclamation*. (Paris: Brianchon, 1819)

Pillet, Fabien. *La Nouvelle lorgnette de spectacles*. (Paris: Imprimerie Durat, 1801)

Pujoulx, Jean-Baptiste. *Paris à la fin du XVIIIe siècle, ou Esquisse historique et morale des monuments et des ruines de cette capitale*. (Paris: B. Mathe, an-IX [1801])

Regnault-Warin, J. J. *Mémoires historiques et critiques sur F. J. Talma*. (Paris: Henry, 1827)

Rémusat, Claire-Elisabeth de. *Mémoires de Madame de Rémusat, 1802–1808*. Ed. Paul de Rémusat. 3 vols. (Paris: Calmann-Lévy, 1880)

Ricord aîné, Alexandre. *Les Fastes de la Comédie-Française, et portraits des plus célèbres acteurs qui se sont illustrés et de ceux qui s'illustrent encore sur notre théâtre, précédés d'un aperçu sur sa situation présente et sur les moyens propes à prévenir sa ruine*. 2 vols. (Paris: Alexandre, 1821–2)

Robert [Louis Castel]. *Mémoires d'un claqueur, contenant la théorie et la pratique de l'art des succès*. (Paris: Constant-Chantpie et Levavasseur, 1829)

Robinson, Henry Crabb. *Diary, reminiscences and correspondence*, ed. Thomas Sadler. 3 vols. (London: Macmillan, 1869)

Rochefort, A. de. *Mémoires d'un vaudevilliste*. (Paris: Charlieu & Huillery, 1863)

Rousseau, Pierre-Joseph. *Code théâtral: physiologie des théâtres, manuel complet de l'auteur, du directeur, de l'acteur et de l'amateur*. (Paris: Roret, 1829)

Ruggieri, Claude. *Précis historique sur les fêtes, les spectacles et les réjouissances publiques*. (Paris: l'auteur, 1830)

Sainte-Beuve, C. A. *Correspondance générale*. Ed. J. and A. Bonnerot. 16 vols. (Paris: Stock, Privat, Didier, 1935–7)

Sainte-Beuve, C. A. *Portraits littéraires*. 3 vols. (Paris: Garnier, 1862–4)

Samson, Joseph-Isidore. *Mémoires de Samson, de la Comédie-Française*. (Paris: Ollendorff, 1882)

Samson, Mme Joseph-Isidore. *Rachel et Samson: souvenirs de théâtre par la veuve de Samson*. (Paris: Ollendorff, 1898)

Sand, George. *Correspondance inédite de George Sand et Marie Dorval*. Ed. Simone André-Maurois. (Paris: Gallimard, 1953)

Sand, George. *Histoire de ma vie*. 4 vols. (Paris: Calmann-Lévy, 1928; first published 1854–5)

Sand, George. *Questions d'art et de littérature*. (Paris: Calmann-Lévy, 1878)

Sanderson, John. *The American in Paris*. 2 vols. (London: Colburn, 1838)

Scott, John. *A visit to Paris in 1814, being a review of the moral, political, intellectual, and social condition of the French capital*. (London: Longman, Hurst, Rees, Orme & Brown, 1815)

Séchan, Charles. *Souvenirs d'un homme de théâtre, 1831–1855, recueillis par Adolphe Badin*. (Paris: Calmann-Lévy, 1883)

Ségaud, Emile. *Question d'honneur littéraire et artistique. A bas la claque!* (Paris: chez les principaux libraires, 1849)

Seveste, Edmond. *De la situation du Théâtre-Français et des améliorations à introduire dans son administration*. (Paris, 1839)

Simonet, Claude-Hubert. *Traité de la police administrative des théâtres de la ville de Paris*. (Paris: Thorel, 1850)

Staël, Mme de. *De l'Allemagne*. 2 vols. (Paris: Garnier, 1925; first published 1810)

Stendhal [Henri-Marie Beyle]. *Mémoires d'un touriste*. 3 vols. (Paris: Champion, 1932; first published 1838)

Storey, G., Tillotson, K. and Easson, A. (eds.). *The letters of Charles Dickens*. (Oxford: Clarendon Press, 1993)

Talma, François-Joseph. *Correspondance avec Madame de Staël, suivie de toute la correspondance léguée à la Bibliothèque Mazarine*. (Paris: Editions Montaigne, 1928)

Thackeray, William Makepeace. *The Paris sketch book of Mr M. A. Titmarsh*. (London: Smith, Elder, 1897; first published 1840)

Toreinx, F. R. de. *Histoire du Romantisme en France*. (Paris: Dubreuil, 1829)

Trollope, Frances. *Paris and the Parisians in 1835*. 2 vols. (London: Roger Bentley, 1836)

Vacquerie, Auguste. *Profils et grimaces*. (Paris: Michel Lévy, 1856)

Vallier, J. P. *Recherches sur les causes de la décadence des théâtres et de l'art dramatique en France.* (Paris: Appert, 1841)

Véron, Louis-Désiré. *Mémoires d'un bourgeois de Paris.* 6 vols. (Paris: Gabriel de Gonet, 1853–5)

Viennet, Jean-Pons-Guillaume. *Journal de Viennet, pair de France, témoin de trois règnes, 1817–1848.* (Paris: Amiot-Dumont, 1955)

Vigny, Victor-Alfred, Comte de. *Correspondance . . . 1816–1863.* Ed. Léon Séché. 2 vols. (Paris: Mignot, Renaissance du Livre, n.d.)

Viollet-le-Duc, E. L. N. *Précis de l'art dramatique.* (Paris: Bachelier, 1830)

Vivien, Auguste and Blanc, Edmond. *Traité de la législation des théâtres, ou Exposé complet et méthodique des lois et de la jurisprudence relativement aux théâtres et spectacles publics.* (Paris: Brissot-Thivars, 1830)

Vulpian, Auguste and Gautier. *Code des théâtres, ou Manuel à l'usage des directeurs, entrepreneurs et actionnaires de spectacles, des auteurs et artistes dramatiques, etc., etc.* (Paris: Warrée, 1829)

Studies and articles

Alasseur, Claude. *La Comédie-Française au XVIIIe siècle: étude économique.* (The Hague and Paris: Mouton, 1967)

Albert, Maurice. *Les Théâtres des Boulevards (1789–1848).* (Paris: Société Française d'Imprimerie et de Librairie, 1902)

Allevy, Marie-Antoinette. *La Mise en scène en France dans la première moitié du dix-neuvième siècle.* (Paris: Droz, 1938)

Artus, Maurice. *Le Théâtre Montmartre.* (Tours: Arrault, 1904)

Bailey, Helen Phelps. *Hamlet in France from Voltaire to Laforgue.* (Geneva: Droz, 1964)

Baldick, Robert. *The life and times of Frédérick Lemaître.* (London: Hamish Hamilton, 1959)

Bayet, Jean, *La Société des auteurs et compositeurs dramatiques.* (Paris: Rousseau, 1908)

Beaulieu, Henri. *Les Théâtres du Boulevard du Crime de Nicolet à Déjazet, 1752–1862.* (Paris: Daragon, 1905)

Bergman, G. 'Les Agences théâtrales et l'impression des mises en scène aux environs de 1800'. *Revue d'Histoire du Théâtre,* 8, 1956, pp. 228–40

Berthier, Patrick. *Le Théâtre au XIXe siècle.* (Paris: Presses Universitaires de France, 1986)

Boncompain, Jacques. 'Les Deux cents ans de la Société des Auteurs et Compositeurs Dramatiques'. *Revue d'Histoire du Théâtre,* 29, 1977, pp. 57–70

Bonnassies, Jules. *Les Auteurs dramatiques et la Comédie-Française aux XVIIe et XXIIIe siècles.* (Paris: Léon Willem, 1874)

Bonnassies, Jules. *Les Auteurs dramatiques et les théâtres de province aux XVIIe et XVIIIe siècles.* (Paris: Léon Willem, 1875)

Bonnassies, Jules. *Les Spectacles forains et la Comédie-Française. Le droit des pauvres avant et après 1789. Les auteurs dramatiques et la Comédie-Française au dix-neuvième siècle.* (Paris: Dentu, 1875)

Borgerhoff, Joseph-Léopold. *Le Théâtre anglais à Paris sous la Restauration.* (Paris: Hachette, 1913)

Bossuet, Pierre. *Histoire des théâtres nationaux.* (Paris: Jorel, 1909)

Boudet, Micheline. *Mademoiselle Mars l'inimitable.* (Paris: Perrin, 1987)

Brenner, Clarence D. *The Théâtre-Italien, its repertory 1716–1793; with a historical introduction.* (Berkeley and Los Angeles: University of California Press, 1961)

Bury, J. P. T. and Barry, J. G. (eds.). *An Englishman in Paris: 1803. The journal of Bertie Greatheed.* (London: Godfrey Bles, 1953)

Cain, Georges. *Anciens théâtres de Paris: le Boulevard du Temple; les théâtres du boulevard.* (Paris: Charpentier & Fasquelle, 1906)

Carlson, Marvin. *The French stage in the nineteenth century.* (Metuchen, NJ: Scarecrow Press, 1972)

Carlson, Marvin. *The Theatre of the French Revolution.* (Ithaca, NY: Cornell University Press, 1966)

Challamel, Augustin. *L'Ancien Boulevard du Temple.* (Paris: Société des Gens de Lettres, 1875)

Chauveron, Edmond de. *Les Grands procès de la Comédie-Française depuis les origines jusqu'à nos jours.* (Paris: Rousseau, 1906)

Chevalley, Sylvie. 'La Comédie-Française et l'avènement de l'Empire'. *Europe*, 480–1, 1969, pp. 263–70

Chevalley, Sylvie. *La Comédie-Française hier et aujourd'hui*. (Paris: Didier, 1979)

Collins, Herbert Frederick. *Talma: a biography of an actor*. (London: Faber, 1964)

Copin, Alfred. *Etudes dramatiques. Talma et l'Empire*. (Paris: Frinzaine, 1887)

Daudet, Ernest. *Conspirateurs et comédiennes. Episodes d'histoire d'après des documents inédits, 1796–1825*. (Paris: Juven, 1902)

Descotes, Maurice. *L'Acteur Joanny et son journal inédit*. (Paris: Presses Universitaires de France, 1956)

Descotes, Maurice. *Le Drame romantique et ses grands créateurs*. (Paris: Presses Universitaires de France, 1955)

Des Granges, Charles-Marc. *Geoffroy et la critique dramatique sous le Consulat et l'Empire (1800–1814)*. (Paris: Hachette, 1897)

Des Granges, Charles-Marc. *La Comédie et les mœurs sous la Restauration et la monarchie de juillet (1815–1848)*. (Paris: Fontenoing, 1904)

Estrée, Paul d' [Henri Quentin]. *Le Théâtre sous la Terreur (théâtre de la peur) 1793–1794*. (Paris: Emile-Paul, 1913)

Foucher, Paul. *Les Coulisses du passé*. (Paris: Dentu, 1873)

Fouque, Octave. *Histoire du Théâtre Ventadour, 1829–1879. Opéra-Comique, Théâtre de la Renaissance, Théâtre-Italien*. (Paris: Fischbacher, 1881)

Froger, Béatrice and Hans, Sylvaine. 'La Comédie-Française au XIXe siècle: un répertoire littéraire et politique'. *Revue d'Histoire du Théâtre*, 1984, pp. 260–75

Gascar, Pierre. *Le Boulevard du Crime*. (Paris: Hachette, 1980)

Genty, Christian. *Histoire du Théâtre National de l'Odéon (journal de bord), 1782–1982*. (Paris: Fischbacher, 1982)

Gourret, Jean. *Histoire de l'Opéra-Comique*. (Paris: Publications Universitaires, 1978)

Guibert, Noëlle and Razgonnikov, Jacqueline. *La Comédie aux trois couleurs: le journal de la Comédie-Française, 1787–1799*. (Paris: SEDES, 1989)

Hallays-Dabot, Victor. *Histoire de la censure théâtrale en France*. (Paris: Dentu, 1862)

Hamiche, Daniel. *Le Théâtre et la Révolution. La lutte de classes au théâtre en 1789 et en 1793*. (Paris: Union Générale d'Editions, 1973)

Hemmings, F. W. J. 'Co-authorship in French plays of the nineteenth century'. *French Studies*, 41, 1987, pp. 37–51

Hemmings, F. W. J. *Culture and society in France, 1789–1848*. (Leicester: Leicester University Press, 1987)

Hemmings, F. W. J. 'Playwrights and play-actors: the controversy over *comités de lecture* in France, 1757–1910'. *French Studies*, 43, 1989, pp. 405–22

Hemmings, F. W. J. *Theatre and state in France, 1760–1905*. (Cambridge: Cambridge University Press, 1994)

Hemmings, F. W. J. *The theatre industry in nineteenth-century France*. (Cambridge: Cambridge University Press, 1993)

Hérissay, Jacques. *Le Monde des théâtres pendant la Révolution, 1789–1800*. (Paris: Perrin, 1922)

Howarth, W. D. *Sublime and grotesque: a study of French Romantic drama*. (London: Harrap, 1975)

Howarth, W. D. (ed.). *French theatre in the neo-classical era, 1550–1789*. (Cambridge: Cambridge University Press, 1997)

Hugot, Eugène. *Histoire littéraire, critique et anecdotique du Théâtre du Palais-Royal, 1784–1884*. (Paris: Ollendorff, 1886)

Isherwood, Robert M. *Farce and fantasy: popular entertainment in eighteenth-century Paris*. (Oxford: Oxford University Press, 1986)

Jones, Louisa E. *Sad clowns and pale Pierrots: literature and the popular comic arts in nineteenth-century France*. (Lexington, KN: French Forum, 1984)

Jones, Michèle H. *Le Théâtre national en France de 1800 à 1830*. (Paris: Klincksieck, 1975)

Krakovitch, Odile. *Hugo censuré. La liberté au théâtre au XIXe siècle*. (Paris: Calmann-Lévy, 1985)

Krakovitch, Odile. *Les Pièces de théâtre soumises à la censure (1800–1830)*. (Paris: Archives Nationales, 1982)

Krakovitch, Odile. 'Les Romantiques et la censure au théâtre'. *Revue d'Histoire du Théâtre*, 36, 1984, pp. 56–68

Laplace, Roselyne. *Mademoiselle George*. (Paris: Fayard, 1987)

Lassabathie, Théodore. *Histoire du Conservatoire Impérial de musique et de déclamation*. (Paris: Michel Lévy, 1860)

Lecomte, Louis-Henry. *Un comédien du XIXe siècle: Frédérick Lemaître. Etude biographique et critique, d'après des documents inédits*. 2 vols. (Paris: l'auteur, 1888)

Lecomte, Louis-Henry. *Histoire des théâtres de Paris: les Jeux Gymniques, le Panorama-Dramatique*. (Paris: Daragon, 1908)

Lecomte, Louis-Henry. *Histoire des théâtres de Paris: les Nouveautés*. (Paris: Daragon, 1907)

Lecomte, Louis-Henry. *Histoire des théâtres de Paris: le Renaissance*. (Paris: Daragon, 1905)

Lecomte, Louis-Henry. *Histoire des théâtres de Paris: le Théâtre de la Cité*. (Paris: Daragon, 1910)

Lecomte, Louis-Henry. *Histoire des théâtres de Paris: le Théâtre Historique*. (Paris: Daragon, 1906)

Lecomte, Louis-Henry. *Histoire des théâtres de Paris: le Théâtre National; le Théâtre de l'Égalité*. (Paris: Daragon, 1907)

Lecomte, Louis-Henry. *Histoire des théâtres de Paris: les Variétés-Amusantes*. (Paris: Daragon, 1908)

Lecomte, Louis-Henry. *Napoléon et le monde dramatique*. (Paris: Daragon, 1912)

Loliée, Frédéric. *La Comédie-Française. Histoire de la maison de Molière de 1658 à 1907*. (Paris: Lucien Laveur, 1907)

Lough, John. *Paris theatre audiences in the seventeenth and eighteenth centuries*. (Oxford: Oxford University Press, 1957)

Lyden, E. M. de. *Le Théâtre d'autrefois et d'aujourd'hui. Cantatrices et comédiens, 1532–1882*. (Paris: Dentu, 1882)

Lyonnet, Henry. *Dictionnaire des Comédiens-Français (ceux d'hier). Biographies, bibliographie, iconographie*. 2 vols. (Paris: Jorel, 1908–12)

Lyonnet, Henry. *Les Premières de Alfred de Musset*. (Paris: Delagrave, 1927)

Lyonnet, Henry. *Les Premières de Victor Hugo*. (Paris: Delagrave, 1930)

McCormick, John. 'Joseph Bouchardy: a melodramatist and his public', in *Performance and politics in popular drama*, ed. D. Bradby, L. James and B. Sharratt. (Cambridge: Cambridge University Press, 1980)

McCormick, John. *Popular theatres of nineteenth-century France*. (London and New York: Routledge, 1993)

Manne, Edmond Denis de. *Galerie historique des comédiens de la troupe de Talma: notices sur les principaux sociétaires de la Comédie-Française depuis 1789 jusqu'aux trente premières années de ce siècle*. (Lyon: Scheuring, 1866)

Manne, E. D. de and Ménétrier, C. *Galerie historique de la Comédie-Française*. (Lyon: Scheuring, 1876)

Manne, E. D. de and Ménétrier, C. *Galerie historique des acteurs français, mimes et paradistes qui se sont rendus célèbres dans les annales des scènes secondaires depuis 1760 jusqu'à nos jours*. (Lyon: Scheuring, 1877)

Manne, E. D. de and Ménétrier, C. *Galerie historique des comédiens de la troupe de Nicolet. Notices sur certains acteurs . . . des scènes secondaires depuis 1760 jusqu'à nos jours*. (Lyon: Scheuring, 1869)

Martinet, André. *Histoire anecdotique du Conservatoire de musique et de déclamation*. (Paris: Kolb, 1893)

Melcher, Edith. *Stage realism in France between Diderot and Antoine*. (Lancaster, PN: Lancaster Press, 1928)

Monselet, Charles. *Les premières représentations célèbres*. (Paris: Achille Faure, 1867)

Muret, Théodore. *L'Histoire par le théâtre, 1789–1851*. 3 vols. (Paris: Amyot, 1865)

Ozouf, Mona. *La Fête révolutionnaire, 1789–1799*. (Paris: Gallimard, 1976)

Pailleron, Marie-Louise. *François Buloz et ses amis: la 'Revue des Deux Mondes' et la Comédie-Française*. (Paris: Firmin-Didot, 1930)

Péricaud, Louis. *Le Panthéon des comédiens, de Molière à Coquelin aîné, notices biographiques*. (Paris: Fasquelle, 1922)

Péricaud, Louis. *Théâtre de Monsieur*. (Paris: Jorel, 1908)

Péricaud, Louis. *Le Théâtre des Funambules: ses mimes, ses acteurs et ses pantomimes, depuis sa fondation jusqu'à sa démolition*. (Paris: Léon Sapin, 1897)

Pierre, Constant. *Les anciennes écoles de déclamation.* (Paris: Tresse & Stock, 1895)

Plunkett, Jacques de. *Cent soixante ans de théâtre. Fantômes et souvenirs de la Porte-Saint-Martin.* (Paris: Ariane, 1946)

Pollitzer, Marcel. *Trois reines de théâtre: Mademoiselle Mars, Marie Dorval, Rachel.* (Paris: La Colombe, 1958)

Porel, Paul and Monval, Georges. *L'Odéon. Histoire administrative, anecdotique et littéraire du second Théâtre-Français.* 2 vols. (Paris: Lemerre, 1876–82)

Pougin, Arthur. *La Comédie-Française et la Révolution.* (Paris: Gaultier, 1902)

Pougin, Arthur. *Dictionnaire historique et pittoresque du théâtre et des arts qui s'y rattachent.* (Paris: Firmin-Didot, 1885)

Richardson, Joanna. *Rachel.* (London: Max Reinhardt, 1956)

Rodocanachi, Emmanuel. *Le Sifflet au théâtre: étude de mœurs et d'histoire.* (Paris: Ollendorff, 1896)

Rolland, Romain. *Le Théâtre du peuple.* (Paris: Hachette, 1913)

Root-Bernstein, Michèle. *Boulevard theater and revolution in eighteenth-century Paris.* (Ann Arbor, MI: University of Michigan Research Press, 1984)

Soubies, Albert. *Le Théâtre-Italien de 1801 à 1913.* (Paris: Fischbacher, 1913)

Soubies, Albert and Malherbe, Charles. *Histoire de l'Opéra-Comique: la seconde salle Favart.* 2 vols. (Paris: Flammarion, 1892–3)

Thierry, Augustin. *Mademoiselle George, maîtresse d'empereurs.* (Paris: Albin Michel, 1936)

Thierry, Augustin. *Le Tragédien de Napoléon: François-Joseph Talma.* (Paris: Albin Michel, 1942)

Thomasseau, Jean-Marie. 'Le Mélodrame et la censure sous le Premier Empire et la Restauration'. *Revue des Sciences Humaines,* 162, 1976, pp. 171–82

Tissier, André. *Les Spectacles à Paris pendant la Révolution. Répertoire analytique, chronologique et bibliographique.* (Geneva: Droz, 1992)

Treille, Marguerite. *Le Conflit dramatique en France de 1823 à 1830 d'après les journaux et les revues du temps.* (Paris: Picart, 1929)

Warnod, André. *L'Ancien Théâtre Montparnasse.* (Paris: Editions O. Lieutier, 1930)

Welschinger, Henri. *Le Théâtre de la Révolution, 1789–1799.* (Paris: Charavay, 1880)

Worms, Fernand. *Le Droit des pauvres sur les spectacles, théâtres, bals et concerts, etc. . . . législation, doctrine et jurisprudence.* (Paris: Larose, 1900)

ITALY

Works of reference and published sources

Alberti, A. *Quarant'anni di storia del teatro dei Fiorentini in Napoli.* (Naples, 1878)

Alberti, Carmelo. *La scena veneziana nell'età di Goldoni.* (Rome: Bulzoni, 1990)

Alfieri, Vittorio. *Epistolario (1767–88).* Ed. L. Caretti. (Milan, 1963)

Alfieri, Vittorio. *Le tragedie.* Ed. P. Cazzani. (Milan: Mondadori, 1966)

Alonge, Roberto. *Teatro e spettacolo nel secondo Ottocento.* (Rome, 1988)

Andrei, V. *Gli attori italiani da Gustavo Modena a Ermete Novelli e alla Duse.* (Florence, 1899)

Angelini, Franca. *Vita di Goldoni.* (Bari: Laferza, 1993)

Antonini, Trisolini Giovanna. *Rivoluzione a teatro. Antinomie del teatro giacobino in Italia (1796–1805).* (CLUFR, 1985)

Antonini, Trisolini Giovanna. *Teatro della Rivoluzione. Considerazioni e testi.* (Longo, 1984)

Apollonio, Mario. *Storia del teatro italiano.* 2 vols. (Florence, 1950 and 1981)

Artioli, U. *Teorie della scena dal naturalismo al surrealismo.* (Florence, 1972)

Azzaroni, Giovanni. *Del teatro e dintorni. Una storia della legislazione e delle strutture teatrali in Italia nell'800.* (Rome, 1981)

Bartoli, F. *Notizie istoriche de'comici italiani.* 2 vols. (Padua, 1781–2)

Bon, F. A. *Scene comiche, e non comiche della mia vita.* Ed. Teresa Viziano. (Rome: Bulzoni, 1985)

Bosisio, Paolo. *Tra ribellione e utopia. L'esperienza teatrale nell'Italia delle Repubbliche Napoleoniche (1796–1805).* (Rome, 1990)

Boutet, E. *Nel centenario della nascita di Gustavo Modena.* (Rome, 1903)

Bracco, R. *Tra le arti e gli artisti.* (Naples, 1918)

Brocca, A. *Il teatro Carlo Felice di Genova.* (Genoa, 1898)

Butler, Mrs [Fanny Kemble]. *A year of consolation.* 2 vols. (London, 1847)

Calendoli, G. *L'attore, storia di un'arte.* (Rome: Edizioni dell'Ateneo, 1959)

Caretti, Laura (ed.). *Il teatro del personaggio, Shakespeare sulla scena italiana dell'800.* (Rome: Bulzoni, 1979)

Carlson, M. *The Italian Shakespearians. Performances by Ristori, Salvini and Rossi in England and America.* (Washington, DC, 1985)

Carlson, M. *The Italian stage. From Goldoni to D'Annunzio.* (Jefferson, NC and London: Macfarland, 1981)

Carpanetto, D. and Ricuperati, G. *Italy in the age of reason, 1685–1789.* (London: Longman, 1987)

Carter, N. H. *Letters from Europe, comprising the journal of a tour through Ireland, England, Scotland, France, Italy and Switzerland in the years 1825, '26, and '27.* 2 vols. (London: Carvill, 1827)

Cauda, G. *Chiaroscuri di palcoscenico.* (Savigliano, 1910)

Cauda, G. *Figure e figurine del teatro di prosa.* (Chieri, 1925)

Ciotti Cavalletto, Giovanna. *Attrici e società nell'Ottocento italiano.* (Milan: Mursia, 1978)

Corsi, M. *Maschere e volti sul palcoscenico e in platea.* (Milan, 1945)

Cosentino, G. *Modena, Lombardi e Vestri a Bologna.* (Bologna, 1901)

Costetti, G. *La Compagnia Reale Sarda.* (Milan, 1893)

Costetti, G. *I dimenticati vivi della scena italiana.* (Milan, 1893)

Costetti, G. *Il teatro italiano nel 1800.* (Rocca San Casciano, 1901)

Curti, P. A. *Adelaide Ristori.* (Milan, 1855)

D'Amico, S. *Storia del teatro drammatico.* (Milan, 1953)

D'Amico, S. (ed.). *Mostra dei costumi di Adelaide Ristori.* Official catalogue of the Venice Biennale, the 26th International Festival of Theatre and Plays, 1967

Di Martino, G. *Adelaide Ristori attrice drammatica.* (Florence, 1908)

Di Stefano, C. *La censura teatrale in Italia.* (Bologna, 1964)

Doglio, F. (ed.). *Teatro e Risorgimento.* (Bologna: Cappelli, 1961)

Doglio, F. *Il Teatro pubblico in Italia.* (Rome, 1970)

Doglio, F. *Teatro in Europa,* vol. 3/1. (Milan, 1981)

D'Uklanski, Baron. *Travels in upper Italy, Tuscany and the ecclesiastical states; in a series of letters written to a friend in the years 1807 and 1808.* 2 vols. (London, 1816)

Enciclopedia dello Spettacolo. 10 vols. (Rome, 1950–62)

Galiffe, James Aug. *Italy and its inhabitants; an account of a tour in that country in 1816 and 1817.* 2 vols. (London, 1820)

Goethe, J. W. *Italian journey.* Trans. W. H. Auden and Elizabeth Mayer. (Harmondsworth: Penguin, 1962)

Grandi, Terenzio. *Epistolario di Gustavo Modena.* (Rome, 1955)

Grandi, Terenzio. *Scritti e discorsi di Gustavo Modena.* (Rome, 1957)

Grandi, Terenzio. *Gustavo Modena attore patriota.* (Pisa, 1968)

Grandi, Terenzio. 'Gustavo Modena in Piemonte'. *Miscellanea del centenario,* 1.3. (Turin, 1949)

Haskins, George Foxcroft. *Travels in England, France, Italy and Ireland.* (Boston: Patrick Donahoe, 1856)

Hearder, H. *Italy in the age of the Risorgimento, 1790–1870.* (London: Longman, 1983)

International dictionary of Theatre. 3 vols. (London and Detroit: St. James Press 1994–7)

Jarro [G. Piccinni]. 'Gustavo Modena, ricordi e aneddoti'. *Rivista Teatrale Italiana,* February–March 1903

Jarro [G. Piccinni]. *Vita aneddotica di Tommaso Salvini.* (Florence, 1908)

Journal of an officer in the King's German Legion: comprising an account of his campaigns and adventures in England, Ireland, Denmark, Portugal, Spain, Malta, Sicily and Italy. (London, 1827)

A journal of a tour in Italy in the year 1821 with a description of Gibraltar. By an American. (New York, 1824)

Kimbell, David. *Italian opera.* (Cambridge: Cambridge University Press, 1991)

Leonelli, N. *Attori tragici, attori comici.* 2 vols. (Milan, 1940–4)

Lettere inedite di Gustavo Modena e di Giulia Modena. Ed. Cesare Agostini. (1902)

Mack Smith, D. *The making of Italy, 1796–1866.* 2nd edn. (London: Macmillan, 1988)

Mangini, N. *Gustavo Modena e il teatro italiano del primo Ottocento*. (Venice, 1965)

Mangini, N. *I teatri di Venezia*. (Milan, 1974)

Martini, F. *Al teatro*. (Florence, 1895)

Martini, F. *Confessioni e ricordi*. (Florence, 1922)

Martyn, Thomas. *A tour through Italy*. (London, 1791)

Meldolesi, Claudio. 'Modena e la Ristori'. *Bollettino del Museo-Biblioteca dell'Attore*, Genova, January–April 1970

Meldolesi, Claudio. *Profilo di Gustavo Modena. Teatro e rivoluzione democratica*. (Rome: Bulzoni, 1971)

Meldolesi, Claudio and Taviani, Ferdinando. *Teatro e spettacolo nel primo Ottocento*. (Bari: Laterza, 1991)

The Memoirs of Count Carlo Gozzi. Trans. J. A. Symonds. 2 vols. (London: J. C. Nimmo, 1890)

Memoirs of Goldoni. Trans. John Black and Henry Colburn. 2 vols. (London, 1816)

Mineo, Nicolo and Nicastro, Guido. *Giusti e il teatro del primo Ottocento*. (Bari, 1981)

Monaco, V. *La Repubblica del teatro*. (Florence, 1968)

Monaldi, G. *Ricordi viventi di artisti scomparsi*. (Campobasso, 1927)

Montazio, E. *Adelaide Ristori*. (Paris, 1855)

Morgan, Lady. *Italy*. 3 vols. (London: Henry Colburn, 1821)

Morley, Henry. *Journal of a London playgoer*. (London, 1891)

Morrocchesi, Antonio. *Lezioni di declamazione e d'arte teatrale*. (Florence, 1832)

Musset, Paul de. *La Course en voiturin*. (1845; Paris, 1953)

Nicastro, Guido. *Vittorio Alfieri*. (Bari, 1974)

Paglicci Brozzi, A. *Sul Teatro Giacobino e Antigiacobino in Italia, 1796–1805*. (Milan: Luigi di Giacomo Pirola, 1887)

Pandolfi, V. *Antologia del grande attore*. (Bari, 1954)

Pieri, Marzia. *Il teatro di Goldoni*. (Bologna: Il Mulino, 1993)

Pullini, G. *Il teatro in Italia*, vol. III, *Settecento e Ottocento*. (Rome: Ediciones Studium, 1995)

Rasi, Luigi. *I comici italiani*. 3 vols. (Florence, 1897–1905)

Rava, A. *I teatri di Roma*. (Rome, 1953)

Regli, F. *Dizionario biografico*. (Turin, 1860)

Ricci, Giuliana. *I teatri d'Italia*. (Milan, 1971)

Richards, Kenneth. 'Italian actors in Victorian London', in *Shakespeare on the Victorian stage*, ed. R. Foulkes. (Cambridge: Cambridge University Press, 1986)

Richards, Kenneth and Richards, Laura. *The Commedia dell'arte. A documentary history*. (Oxford: Oxford University Press, 1990)

Richards, Kenneth and Richards, Laura. 'Italy', in *The Cambridge guide to world theatre* (Cambridge: Cambridge University Press, 1988)

Richards, Laura. 'Italy, 1868–1919', in *Theatre in Europe. A documentary History. Naturalism and symbolism in European theatre, 1850–1918*, ed. C. Schumacher. (Cambridge: Cambridge University Press, 1996)

Richards, Laura. 'Un Pulcinella antico e moderno: Antonio Petito', in *The Commedia dell'Arte. From the Renaissance to Dario Fo*, ed. C. Cairns. (Lewiston, 1989)

Righetti, Francesco. *Studi sull'arte drammatica*. 3 vols. (Turin, 1834)

Ristori, Adelaide. *Studies and memories*. (London: W. H. Allen 1888)

Ristori, Adelaide. *Ricordi e studi artistici*. (Turin-Naples, 1887)

Rosselli, John. *The opera industry in Italy from Cimarosa to Verdi: the role of the impresario*. (Cambridge: Cambridge University Press, 1984)

Rosselli, John. *Singers of Italian opera*. (Cambridge: Cambridge University Press, 1992)

Rossi, Ernesto. *Quarant' anni di vita artistica*. 3 vols. (Florence, 1887–8)

Rossi, Ernesto. *Studi drammatici*. (Florence, 1885)

Ruggi, A. *Raccolta inedita di scene teatrali le più applaudite nei teatri*. (Bologna, n.d)

Salsilli, A. *Tra un atto e l'altro*. (Milan, 1914)

Salvini, Celso. *Tommaso Salvini nella storia del teatro italiano e nella vita del suo tempo*. (Rocca San Casciano: Cappelli, 1955)

Salvini, Tommaso. *Discorso in commemorazione di Adelaide Ristori*. (Florence, 1906)

Salvini, Tommaso. *Leaves from the autobiography of Tommaso Salvini*. (London: Fisher Unwin, 1893)
Salvini, Tommaso. *Ricordi, aneddoti ed impressioni dell'artista*. (Milan, 1895)
Sanguinetti, L. *La compagnia Reale Sarda (1820–1855)*. (Bologna: Cappelli, 1963)
Sarcey, F. *Quarante ans de théâtre*. (Paris, 1900)
Simond, L. *A tour in Italy and Sicily*. (London: Longman, Rees, Orme, Brown & Green, 1828)
Sinclair, J. D. *An autumn in Italy*. (Edinburgh, 1829)
Stendhal [Henri-Marie Beyle]. *Rome, Naples et Florence*. (Paris, 1817; 2nd edn, Paris: Delaunay, 1826)
Stendhal [Henri-Marie Beyle]. *Vie de Rossini*. (Paris, 1823)
Talfourd, T. N. *Supplement to vacation rambles*. (London, 1854)
Tessari, Roberto. *Teatro e spettacolo nel Settecento*. (Bari: Laterza, 1995)
Tommaseo, Niccolò. *Diario intimo*. Ed. Raffaele Ciampini. (Turin, 1939)
Tonelli, Luigi. *Il teatro contemporaneo italiano*. (Milan, 1936)
Valery, M. [Antoine Claude Pasquin]. *Historical, literary and artistical travels in Italy*. Trans. C. E. Clifton. (Paris, 1839)
Venezia e lo spazio scenico. Catalogue, Mostra a Palazzo Grassi. (Venice, 1979)
Venturi, F. *Italy and the Enlightenment: studies in a cosmopolitan century*. (London: Longman, 1972)
Vianello, Carlo Antonio. *Teatri, spettacoli e musiche a Milano nei secoli scorsi*. (Milan, 1941)
Villiers, A. *La Psychologie de l'art dramatique*. (Paris, 1951)
Woolf, S. *A history of Italy, 1700–1860: the social constraints of political change*. (London: Methuen, 1979)
Yorick. *La morte di una musa*. (Florence, 1885)
Yorick. *Per l'ottantesimo genetliaco di Adelaide Ristori*. (Florence, 1902)
Young, Arthur. *Travels in France and Italy during the years 1787, 1788 and 1789*. (London, 1915)

PERIODICALS

L'Arte Drammatica. Ed. Polese Santarnecchi. Milan, 1871–1929
Il Barbiere di Siviglia. Ed. G. Battaglia. Milan, 1832–34, then *Il Figaro*, Milan, 1835–48
Il Corriere delle Dame, Milan, 1803–72
Corriere della Sera, Milan, 1876–
Il Piccolo Faust. Ed. A. Lambertini. Bologna, 1874–84
Il Pirata. Ed. F. Regli. Milan, 1835–48, then Turin, 1849–91
Il Ricoglitore di notizie teatrali, Florence, 1839–45
Teatro Moderno Applaudito, Venice, 1796–1809
I Teatri, Bologna, 1824–63

Index

Persons, places or institutions referred to in the text but having no significant bearing on theatre practice during the period are not included.

DARK
WATERS

DARK
WATERS

★ ★ ★ ★

BY RICHARD DANSKY

UBISOFT®

625 3rd St, San Francisco,
CA 94107, U.S.A.

Published by Ubisoft.
The publisher does not have any control over and does not assume any responsibility
for author or third-party websites or their content.

Special thanks:
Yves Guillemot, Laurent Detoc, Alain Core, Geoffroy Sardin, Yannis Mallat,
Gérard Guillemot, Kate Papacosma, Arin Murphy-Hiscock, Andrew Heizt, Holly
Rawlinson, Virginie Gringarten, Joshua Meyer, Marc Muraccini, Léo Rébillaud,
Charles-Thomas Pélissier, Faceout Studio, Paul Nielsen, Jeff Miller, Torrey Sharp,
Emma Delage, Damian Dale, Diana Da Costa, Romain Foucher De Brandois,
Alexis Kosciuszko, Bailey McAndrews, Sam Strachman, Heather Pond, Joanie
Simms, Michael Kwan, Hector Rodriguez, Clémence Deleuze, François Tallec.

ISBN 978-1-945210-03-7

10 9 8 7 6 5 4 3 2 1 17 18 19 20 21

First printing 2017. Printed in the U.S.A.

Book design by Faceout Studio, Jeff Miller and Amanda Kreutzer
Map artwork created by Diana Da Costa

For my mother, Irene Dansky, who

always wanted me to write something

with a happy ending.

GHOST, n. The outward and visible sign of an inward fear.

-Ambrose Bierce

GHOSTS, THE: Designated The Group for Specialized Tactics, they stand at the tip of the spear of the US Army's unconventional warfare response forces. Highly specialized and incredibly skilled Special Forces soldiers, they are called The Ghosts. This reconnaissance and direct action unit is made up of the absolute best of the best of the US military. They are the first unit deployed into dangerous situations and the last ones to leave when things get rough. And if they do their job right, no one will ever know they were there. Over the years, the faces have changed, but the unit – and its legend – has endured.

PROLOGUE

There weren't supposed to be Vympel in Ukraine.

That was Nomad's first thought as a hail of bullets scythed through the air over his head. Then again, he thought, as he slid down into a roadside drainage ditch for cover, there weren't supposed to be any Ghosts running around Donetsk, either, so in a weird way, that made things even.

Which, of course, wouldn't help him stay alive if the Russian special forces got the drop on him again. Up on the right was a vast, overgrown field, grass and weeds poking through a parking lot's worth of burned-out and shelled cars. On the left was a field command center for "independent" pro-Russian forces in eastern Ukraine. It was built out of a jacked-up doublewide and a couple of piles of sandbags. On the roof was a jury-rigged satellite dish; out back was a laboring generator.

And inside, where Joker and Sage were supposed to rendezvous with the objective, he could see muzzle flashes.

He tapped his PTT button. "Sage. Joker. I've got multiple contacts out here." Another barrage of bullets passed overhead, punctuating his statement with a series of sharp cracks as they flew by. "Gimme a sitrep. Do you have the package?"

"Negative, Nomad, package is down, Joker's hit but not bad." Sage's voice was calm, even as Nomad heard gunfire and breaking glass crackling over the link. He was the squad leader, by dint of experience and because he never got rattled by anything, up to and including having a tank drive through his front door. That's what had earned him his callsign, which he insisted on using instead of Ghost Lead. "Got contacts of our own. Can you cut us an exit out the back door?"

"Sage, this is Weaver. I'm seeing a half-dozen hostiles closing on your position from the east, another two moving toward Nomad. Exfil vehicle is in position, route Bravo to exfil is still clear." Weaver was the squad's sniper, a laconic, matter-of-fact presence currently parked a half-klick away up a wooded hillside. A scarred and shaven-headed African-American man, Weaver was the team's pessimist. Tall and lean, with a close-cropped beard and graceful piano-player's fingers, he was a former SEAL. He was also fond of telling everyone how easy he found serving in the Ghosts—"At least it's dry most of the time"—and how he found his current assignment a vacation, all things considered.

"Roger that. Bravo it is. Get the company off Nomad's back, then you two cover us. We'll hold here till you do."

"Copy that. You gonna need Nomad's help with the package?"

Sage's voice was grim. "Not unless he brought a sponge."

Behind him, Nomad heard a splash and then hurried footsteps. A quick look over his shoulder told him that one of the Russians had leapt down and was pursuing him directly. He turned and fired wildly. None of the shots hit, but the Russian soldier had to dive for cover in the dirty water that covered the bottom of the ditch. Nomad turned and ran.

"Weaver? What have you got for me?"

"Bad news. Guy behind you is picking himself back up and climbing out of the ditch. His buddy's headed up the left side along the road so he's picking up ground on you— oh hell, grenade!" he called out. "Get out of there, now!"

Even as Weaver gave the warning, Nomad saw the tumbling grenade arc overhead to land maybe twenty feet ahead of him. It hit with a muddy splash, and Nomad made a desperate lunge over the side of the ditch. He cleared the top and pressed himself flat against the dirt just as an explosion rocked the trench, sending shrapnel screaming down its length and a geyser of muck and water into the air.

"Nomad! Status!"

"I'm fine." He rolled to his feet and saw his original pursuer barreling down on him, already firing. Clumps of yellowed grass and mud kicked up as Nomad ducked behind one of the burned-out cars that dotted the field. Metal sparked and screamed as more rounds bounced off or punched through. Nomad returned fire, but out of the corner of his eye he saw the second Vympel leaping the ditch and moving toward his flank. If he stayed where he was, one or the other would get a clean shot.

He turned and squeezed off a round at the grenade thrower, causing the man to drop to the ground. As he did so, the first Russian advanced, closing within thirty yards of Nomad's position. Nomad ripped off a couple of shots in his direction, enough to make him duck behind the chassis of a thoroughly dismantled Lada before returning fire. Taking advantage of the respite, Nomad fell back, angling away from the ditch to get as much of the wrecked car's bulk between him and his pursuers as he ran.

"Weaver! Got a shot?"

"Negative, you keep dropping them into cover every time I draw a bead. Got an ace up my sleeve, though."

A tire half-hidden in the grass nearly caught Nomad's toe. Instead, he leaped over it, exposing himself for an instant to hostile fire. Both pursuers missed the opportunity he gave them, squeezing off long bursts that once again went high. Bad marksmanship for Vympel, Nomad thought, and then a chilling realization struck him.

"Hey, Weaver, how big's a Vympel squad?"

"Usually six, but it varies. Why?"

"How many you got eyes on?"

"Eight . . . . Oh, hell."

And then there were four more Russians, all wearing the uniform of a local "independent" unit, rising out of the grass ahead and shouting in Russian at him to surrender. That's why the chasers had been aiming so poorly; they'd been herding him to where their friends could wrap him up. A Ghost captured on the ground where no US troops were supposed to be would be a huge PR coup for the Kremlin and a black eye for the Pentagon, and God help the poor sap who got taken.

Like he was about to be.

"Weaver, you got anything?"

"Get down."

"What?"

"I said, *get down*!"

Nomad threw himself on the ground, praying he wasn't going to land on the jagged end of an antique gear shift. In front of him, the Russian soldiers began shouting, some aiming at him, some turning to the right . . .

. . . where a quadrotor drone, moving at speed along the top of the grass, was zeroing in on their position. Even as the Russian spotted it, it rose and then trained a vicious-looking barrel on them. Before they could scatter, the drone opened fire, blasting away on a strafing run just above the heads of its targets. Before the first had hit the ground, the last was already falling.

More shots rang out, the two pursuers shifting their aim from Nomad to the drone. With their attention elsewhere, Nomad popped up to a crouch and took careful aim at the first soldier, partially hidden by rusting metal cover. A moment of calm, a squeeze of the trigger, and down the man went.

The second Russian realized the danger of his position. One last burst clipped the drone, making it wobble in its flight. A thin stream of smoke leaked out of one of the rotors and the device sagged in mid-air.

"Weaver?"

"The runner's yours. Let me bring baby back in so the Donetskis don't grab her for salvage."

Nomad was already in full sprint. The Russian had a good head start on him and was running smart, zigzagging erratically and using what cover he could.

Nomad didn't pursue him directly. Instead, he ran straight for the nearest wreck, the remnants of an SUV, and crouched behind it. "Weaver, where is he?"

"Cutting left," came the reply. "He'll pass through the opening between the Lada and the Renault in about five seconds."

"That's all I need." Nomad picked out the Lada, pivoted right, and sighted down the barrel.

A running figure appeared, silhouetted in the space between the two cars.

Nomad squeezed the trigger.

The Russian fell.

"Clean kill, Nomad."

"Thanks, Weaver. Drone landed?"

"Yes."

Sage's voice cut through. "We need to get out of here."

"Do it quick, Sage. I'm seeing two moving on the door you want to bust out through." Weaver sounded unusually grim. "And what looks like three rooster tails from vehicles a couple klicks east-northeast. Roads are shitty, but they're still gonna be here in five minutes, tops."

"Nomad, wait till they close on the door, then open fire. Weaver, target whichever one is further from the door. On my mark, you drop him, then haul ass for transportation."

"Roger that. The truck's 300 meters upslope."

"Get there fast. We'll be coming out that door like a bat out of hell. Nomad, you cover us till we can all rendezvous with Weaver, and then we head for Bravo. You copy?"

A chorus of "Rogers."

"Okay, then, we're moving. Come on, Joker, time to go."

The Russians were moving, too, a pair creeping up on the side door of the bullet-riddled trailer. One nodded to the other, who carefully shot out the windows next to the door. The other reached down to his belt and pulled out a grenade.

"Incoming!" Nomad barked into the comm. "Looks like tear gas, not frag!" A tinkle of broken glass punctuated the alarm, and then the hissing of escaping gas fuzzed over the channel.

"Weaver, take the shot! We're coming out! Nomad, open up!"

Dangerously exposed, Nomad unleashed a long burst at the two Vympel soldiers. They immediately turned to return fire as Nomad crouched and ran, bullets mowing down the long grass around him. At the same time, the door of the trailer burst open, billowing clouds of white tear gas. Before the Russians could open fire, they both dropped; one from a sniper's bullet from behind and the other from a stream of fire from inside the door. Then two figures came staggering out, one supporting the other, who was bleeding from a leg wound.

"Weaver, you got visual on us?"

"Negative, Sage, I'm getting that truck you asked for."

"Roger, we'll move to the road. Nomad, status?"

"Pretty busy right now!" A burst of enemy fire drove him back against the far end of the mobile HQ, and he ducked around a corner. "They're waiting for their friends to show up."

"Keep 'em honest as long as you can. Weaver, ETA?"

In response, the roar of an engine came over the comms. "On my way." A red Toyota pickup, its sides marked with gray primer, burst out of the trees on the hillside above the site, bucking down a shot-up road that was as much dirt as chewed-up asphalt. Sage and Joker, coughing like fiends, hurried toward the road.

"Nomad! Thirty seconds! Say goodbye and fall back to the road!"

"Roger that!" He peered around the corner and nearly got his head taken off by a burst of enemy fire. He returned blind fire, then pulled back his weapon and grabbed a frag grenade off his belt.

The truck was almost to their position now, fishtailing wildly on the rutted road. Nomad pulled the pin on the grenade and tossed it around the corner, then threw another one into the now-deserted HQ for good measure as he ran. Up ahead, he could see the truck slowing to a stop, the passenger-side door already open and Sage getting ready to drag Joker inside.

"Come on, come on!" Weaver was shouting as Sage lifted the groaning Joker, then slammed the door and settled into firing position. Nomad ran for the truck, the twin explosions behind him shoving him forward as something inside caught and blew the satellite dish clear off the roof. Weaver swore furiously as he negotiated the truck into a three-point turn, then Sage opened fire as the pair of surviving Russians came around the corner Nomad had abandoned, guns blazing. They both dropped, one of his own accord, the other with a pair of holes in his chest, then Nomad was vaulting himself into the back of the truck. He landed hard, then sat up and reached out to pull Sage in.

"We're in! Go! Go! Go!"

Weaver floored it, dirt and rocks spitting up from the rear wheels. The enemy trucks were getting closer now, men hanging out the windows and firing wildly, but the uneven road didn't do their aim any favors and the bullets went whizzing harmlessly past.

"We've got five kilometers to a friendly checkpoint." Sage ticked it off as matter-of-fact as if they'd been going for a Sunday drive. "Even Vympel aren't going to push that, not right now."

"You say so," Weaver replied. "You go with that theory, I'm just going to drive fast. And Joker's out of commission."

"Copy that." Sage and Nomad hunkered down in the back of the pickup, the rear gate offering some protection as they lobbed grenades out to cover their retreat.

The last Russian stood his ground even as the shrapnel from the grenades blew past him. He opened up with a final, desperate burst at the fleeing truck before the blast took him and he fell backwards, gun firing wildly into the air.

The hollow sound of metal punching through metal rang out through the truck, and then Nomad was rising up from behind cover to see what, if anything, was left behind them.

What he saw was dust, and bodies rapidly fading in the distance.

"The pursuit is over," he said without turning. "Looks like it's a clean run to—" and then Sage groaned and went down.

"What the hell's going on back there?" Weaver demanded.

Nomad turned and dropped to get a closer look at the squad leader. What he saw was blood, and Sage clutching his side in pain. "Sage is hit! Just go!"

It was bad, Nomad could see at once. A round in the side, another in the shoulder. Body armor had stopped a couple more, but the two that got through were going to be more than enough if Sage didn't get medical help immediately.

"Evac helo is inbound on that LZ!"

"Tell them we've got two wounded, one urgent, and they need to be ready to dust off as soon as we get there."

Nomad began stripping Sage's gear off him. If he could get to the wounds, if he could apply direct pressure, if they got to the LZ fast enough . . . .

He looked up over the cab for a moment, his fingers red with his squad leader's blood. Safety seemed very far away indeed.

CHAPTER 1

A gentle hand on his shoulder nudged Nomad awake. He looked around, seeing not the withered grass of a blasted Ukrainian field, but rather the interior of a hospital room. Off-white walls, pale winter light coming in through tall vertical windows, masses of beeping equipment hooked up to an unconscious figure in a hospital bed with a dozen tubes running in and out of him.

Landstuhl Regional Medical Center, his memory supplied. The hospital in Germany where they sent the emergency cases. And that was Sage in the bed, with enough holes in him to let him do a serviceable impression of a character in a blockbuster movie plot.

"Major Perryman. How's he doing?"

Nomad turned. He hadn't heard anyone refer to him by his title and actual surname in awhile. Standing in the doorway was Coray Ward, better known as Weaver, his face a mask of concern. He looked as tired and haggard as Nomad felt.

"What's this major bullshit, Ward? Sage was in surgery for eight-plus hours. I've been with him since he got out. Docs say he's got a fighting chance, but . . . ." Nomad's voice trailed off. "Fighting chance" was doctor-speak for "Hell if we know," which was a long way from "He's gonna make it."

Weaver nodded. "Best thing for him to do is sleep, then. Sorry I can't say the same for us."

"Hmm?" Nomad stood and stretched, his back making popping noises like a kid shooting off a cap gun. They made an odd counterpoint to the electronic beeps and hums coming off the machines keeping Sage alive.

Weaver gestured down the hall. "The Old Man wants to talk to us. To you, really, but he knows it's a package deal."

Nomad rubbed the sleep out of his eyes. "The Old Man's in Georgia. Or did we get airlifted back to Benning while I was asleep?"

"Nope. There's a room down on the first floor set up for teleconference, on the entirely sane notion that people here might want to talk to people back home without a nine-hour flight as a prereq. We've got priority on the room as soon as you finish your Sleeping Beauty routine." He made an exaggerated sniffing sound. "And maybe take a shower. You smell like the bottom of a Ukrainian sewer."

"Drainage ditch," Nomad replied tiredly. "All right. Meet you down there in twenty."

"Sounds reasonable." Weaver turned to go, then looked back over his shoulder. "I'm sorry, man. I would have let you stay there and sleep, but if the Old Man's calling us here, after what just went down, it's not because he wants to hear about the weather."

"Just for once, it would be nice if he did." Nomad stooped and grabbed his backpack from where it sat on the floor next to his chair.

"Shower's down the hall to—"

"To the right, and then you make a left. Not my first time here, Coray."

Ward put up his hands in a gesture of mock defensiveness. "Okay, okay. I'll see you in twenty. Just hoping I don't smell you before then." He turned and walked off.

Nomad watched him go, then headed towards the bed. Sage's eyes were closed, his breathing was shallow, and his skin was a clammy bluish-white.

"You look like shit, buddy," Nomad said softly. "Now get better so you can get up and kick my ass for saying that, okay?"

The only response was the slow hiss of the air compressor and the quiet beeping that promised Sage was still alive.

The briefing room at Landstuhl was nicely decorated, which led Nomad to think it wasn't normally a briefing room at all. One wall was dominated by a huge television screen. There was a table with a couple of chairs set up in front of it, and then behind that, a few couches and chairs in haphazard array. Everything in the room was beige, except the walls, which were pale green, and dotted with landscape photographs from various places where American forces were deployed.

When Nomad arrived, he felt almost human. His riotous beard, already showing a couple of gray hairs here and there, was neatly combed, and his cheeks were practically red from all the scrubbing he'd done to get the stench of the mission off him. He'd changed into clean fatigues, if not neat ones, and a pair of cheap sunglasses protected his weary eyes from the harsh fluorescent lighting.

Weaver was already seated at the table, in fatigues so neatly pressed they looked like they'd just come from the dry cleaner. His boots were spotless, unlike Perryman's, and he had a cup of tea in front of him. Ward was reading something on a Military Rugged Tablet and snickering. To Perryman's raised eyebrow, he said, "*Financial Times*. It's always good for a laugh."

"Gotcha." Perryman dropped into the seat next to him. "How do we turn this thing on?"

In response, Weaver put down the MRT, swung his feet to the ground, and picked up a remote control. He mashed a few buttons, and then the screen filled with the familiar sight of Lt. Col. Scott Mitchell, the Old Man. Mitchell had led the Ghosts through more missions than Nomad could count before the Pentagon had kicked him upstairs. Now he headed the Group for Specialized Tactics, watching over the Ghost teams like they were his own children.

"Major. Master Sergeant." Mitchell acknowledged both men with a curt nod. He still looked like he could roll in the field at a moment's notice, but there were lines around his eyes now, and there was an increasing amount of gray in his close-cropped hair.

"Lieutenant Colonel. What can we do for you?"

"You can give me an update on Sage, for starters. How's he doing?"

"Still out, sir. Doctors think he's got a chance."

Mitchell sat back in his chair. "That's better than I was expecting, at least. He's a good man. And Joker?"

Weaver leaned in. "His leg's torn up pretty thoroughly. He's not going to be walking for a while, but he'll recover."

Frowning, Mitchell consulted a sheaf of papers on the desk in front of him. "Glad he'll be all right, but that timetable's not what I was hoping for. You want to tell me what happened out there, Major Perryman?"

Nomad coughed. "It's all in the preliminary report, sir."

Mitchell slapped the papers in his hand against the table. "I know what's in the report. And I asked you to tell me, in your own words, what happened to put Joker and Sage out of action, and one of them at death's door.

Now talk to me."

Nomad shot a look at Weaver, who was keeping his eyes straight ahead, the barest hint of a smile tugging at the corner of his mouth. *Son of a bitch had already talked to Mitchell's CSM, I'll bet.* Nomad grimaced. *He's gonna enjoy watching me squirm now that it's my turn.*

"Sir. Our objective was to exfil a colonel in the Donetsk Separatist Sparta Battalion, said colonel having expressed interest through channels in switching sides and providing intel confirming an active and formal Russian presence in and around the DPR." Nomad coughed once. "I mean, we knew they were there, but bringing back formal proof would have made it a whole new ballgame."

"It would have given Moscow something new they could deny and would have left the strategic analysis for the eggheads who get paid to do it. Continue."

Nomad stiffened in his seat. "We reached the rendezvous point. Did a sweep of the area and it read all clear. Everything looked green."

"Joker and Sage advanced into the field HQ to meet with the package and escort him to safety, while Weaver and I secured the perimeter. Our contact had assured us prior to deployment that he'd order hostile patrols out of the area before our arrival, making this a clean and easy exfil."

"And was it?"

"Negative. When our people got there, the package refused to come along with Sage. He attempted to subdue the package to enable transport, at which point the package chose to shoot himself instead. At the same time, we had contact with enemy personnel who had presumably been tipped off by the package and who had been waiting to ambush us from prepared positions."

"Interesting." Mitchell leaned forward. "And you didn't spot them during your sweep?"

Nomad grimaced. "No. They were well hidden, and the majority remained at safe distance until we arrived. Clearly the ambush had been planned well in advance, and their positions had been extensively prepared." He thought for a moment. "We're lucky they didn't just boo-by-trap the field, or that would have been that."

"If they did that, they wouldn't have been able to take you alive. And that did seem to be their aim, yes, Major?"

Nomad nodded. "That's what it seemed like. On the bright side, I was able to confirm these troops were in fact Russian Vympel operators wearing Sparta Battalion kit and insignia." He stopped and turned to Ward. "Did I leave anything out?"

Weaver shook his head. "Nope. They knew we were coming; they were in place and well camouflaged. Drone sweep didn't see them either, so like you said, they'd taken the time to do some serious prep—and they waited until we were at our most vulnerable to hit us. In my opinion, sir."

Mitchell sighed. "I'll start hunting for leaks on our side, but it sounds like someone with a Moscow mailing address got to the package before we did. Wouldn't be the first time."

"Yessir." Nomad sat for a moment in uncomfortable

silence. "Shall I continue?"

Mitchell shook his head. "Not necessary at this time. The rest, like you say, is in the report. I was more interested in seeing how you described a mission that, by any reasonable definition, turned into a soup sandwich. We'll do a more thorough debrief when you get back, but right now, we've got something else on our plate."

"Sir?"

"I'm sending a package through to your MRTs. You'll want to study it on the flight back home. In the meantime, how much do you know about southwestern Venezuela?"

Weaver raised an eyebrow. Nomad coughed. "Not much, sir. Am I going to need to correct that?"

"You might want to. The short version is that in 2008, Venezuela and Colombia nearly had themselves a shooting war down that way, and while everyone kissed and made up for the cameras, the real deal was a lot messier."

"Define 'messy'?"

"Venezuelan regulars dressed as rebels hooking up with FARC irregulars and moving into permanent encampments on the wrong side of the border messy. They've mostly been laying low, but they've never gone away. And now, they're starting to make themselves interesting."

Nomad and Weaver exchanged worried looks. "'Interesting' usually means someone shooting at us, sir."

"With all due respect," Weaver chimed in, "why is this our problem?"

Mitchell smiled, lips pressed together. "I'm getting there, Master Sergeant. As you might have noticed, the Venezuelan government isn't terribly fond of the United States right now. It's also dealing with an economy that looks like Godzilla just walked through the middle of it, which means that certain things are falling off the table. Like, say, paying the soldiers nobody knows about who aren't supposed to be there. And once those soldiers stopped getting paid, they got other ideas, because they had numbers and guns in a place that's damn near impossible for any legit authority to project force into. Basically, they're looking to carve out an autonomous state down there for reasons passing understanding, and there's no one available to stop them."

Weaver leaned forward. "I repeat my question, sir. What the hell does this have to do with us?"

"The good news is that we're not being tasked with solving this. As far as the Pentagon's concerned, this is an internal dispute, and we're not getting involved. The bad news is, though, that there's a couple of groups of American citizens in the territory these jokers are claiming, and they're being held for ransom. All quiet and back channel stuff, you understand, but somebody down there wants some hard currency to tide them over until the narco-cash starts rolling in."

"What sort of hostages are we talking about here?"

"Two small groups. A small biological research lab's scientists trying to find a cure for cancer by dissecting rare orchids and an archaeological expedition looking for God knows what. Washington wants them both back before the story explodes all over the news and people start screaming for full-bore intervention. The remoteness of the region where the hostages are being held has helped us keep a lid on this thing—not a lot of good cell reception down there for Snapchat selfies—but it's not going to stay buttoned down forever. Which means someone has to go in and get those people out."

"Sir." Nomad stared at the screen, his face carefully neutral. "Half this squad is fighting for their lives. Weaver and I have not yet even been formally debriefed on our previous operation. You cannot be seriously telling me that we are going to be tasked with getting those people out."

"Not the squad, Major. You. And Master Sergeant Ward. And the rest of the squad—your squad—will be filled out when you get here."

"Sir, I am happy serving under—"

"Zip it." Mitchell suddenly looked very tired. "This is not optimal, and we all know it. You've been bucking for your own team for a while now, but this sure as hell wasn't the way you wanted to get it. But right now we're stretched thin. Every single one of our teams is deployed, but when the White House calls, you don't turn to NCA and say 'Sorry, we're busy.' I've the greatest confidence in you. Your flight leaves at 1100 hours. Read the package. We'll talk more when you get to Benning."

The monitor switched off, leaving Weaver and Nomad facing a blank screen.

"Congratulations?" Weaver raised an eyebrow. "I guess you're the man now."

"This is bullshit," Nomad replied. "You don't throw a squad together like this and send them in-country on something this hot, and you don't do it when half your operators are still washing dust off their boots from the last op."

"Are you saying you didn't earn this?"

"I'm saying this shouldn't be happening. Doesn't matter what I earned or didn't. You saw the Old Man. He's not happy about the op either, and if he's not happy, you and I should be scared shitless."

Weaver shrugged. "Oh, I am. But we're still doing this. Which means I'd rather go in thinking about the mission than about how we're potentially getting screwed. It's not like we haven't been dropped in some shit before."

The two men stared at each other, and then the tension was broken by a small ping. "I'm betting that's the briefing report," Weaver said, as he stood and stretched. "I hope it's long. Cause it's a long-ass flight to Georgia."

Weaver only snored when he wanted to. Nomad had come to that conclusion long ago, and the flight back to the States was backing it up with more evidence. Put Weaver in the field, and he slept like a cat, one eye open and barely breathing. Put him someplace where it was safe to annoy a friend—say, during a ten-hour ride on a C-17 back to the US—and he suddenly turned into a two-legged sawmill. It was, Nomad decided, a gift.

He, however, was not so blessed. The last time he'd slept on a plane, someone had tried to introduce a Stinger missile to one of the plane's engines with extreme prejudice over Anbar province. The pilot had pulled a heroic maneuver and dodged the missile, but the resultant chaos had convinced Nomad that the best way to spend a flight was wide awake and with his seat belt firmly fastened.

Lt. Colonel Mitchell had been as good as his word. The package that had been pushed to his MRT before takeoff was depressingly thorough in terms of the tactical and strategic importance of the operation Mitchell had suggested he'd be leading, and it also came with the jackets for the two additional Ghosts who'd be attached to the squad.

Looking them over, Nomad didn't recognize one of the names. That in and of itself was mildly unusual. While there were more operators now than there had been before they'd been shuffled under JSOC, it was still a small, elite group, and sooner or later everyone trained—and drank—with everyone else. Squads were squads and you didn't go in-country with everyone, but you at least put in the time back at base to gain a basic familiarity.

But Rubio Delgado, callsign Midas, was new to him.

Nomad read his file carefully. Midas reminded him of Sgt. Scott Ibrahim, a first-generation American who'd been serious about love of country and giving back through service. According to the jacket, Midas had a strong spiritual side, and at one point had seriously considered joining the Roman Catholic priesthood. The desire to do more than he could from the pulpit, however, was too strong to resist, and he'd sworn a different oath instead. Most of his deployments had been in Central and South America, and Midas was known to prefer negotiation to gunplay. Not that he was bad in a fight—there was a cheerfully gruesome report of his skill with his preferred sidearm, the Serbu Super-Shorty sawed-off shotgun, tucked into the file—but he was definitely more thoughtful, both about what he was doing and about collateral damage to civilians, than most. Midas's preferred weapon was a Magpul ACR with an M203 underbarrel grenade launcher, an odd choice considering how many Ghost operations relied on stealth, but the jacket indicated he'd just been elevated to the unit. Maybe he'd learn.

Then again, Nomad would have killed for an M203 on the last op. Maybe the kid was onto something, after all.

Dominic Moretta, callsign Holt, was a whole other kettle of fish. Nomad was familiar with him, though they'd never been on an op together, and for that at times he'd been grateful. Holt was older than Midas. He'd enlisted at eighteen and earned his Sapper and Ranger tabs in the Ranger regiment before he'd been legal to drink. He was a gearhead and had a bit of a rep as a practical joker and more of one as a ladies' man. The trick with Holt, one of his previous commanders had helpfully mentioned, was to have someone shooting at him at all times. Then, he'd take things seriously. If not, God help anyone trying to give him an order. He came from a military family, with his father and both grandfathers having served. Holt had decided early on he wanted to do the same, a resolve that was only strengthened when it became clear that enlisting was the fastest and safest route out of the crumbling Louisiana town where he'd grown up. Defensive as hell about his roots, Holt had long since made it plain he was never going back.

Weaver cracked one eye open. "You been through the scouting reports yet?"

In response, Nomad held up his MRT, with Midas's picture prominently displayed. "Just going over them now. It's going to be an interesting fit, especially with the fresh meat. I'd prefer going in-country with someone a little saltier."

"I don't think we've got the time to wait for Holt to settle down or Midas to get more experienced. But like you said, there's some talent there. I made a couple of calls before we climbed on board, tried to get the unofficial word on these guys, and what I got back was good. Holt's a goddamned wizard with a drone, and Midas, well, the guy's a total straight arrow but he's got drive like a stock car on a straightaway. You get these two to buy in to your dubious leadership skills, and we're going to be just fine."

Nomad laughed. "I like it better when you're snoring. The sounds coming out of your mouth make more sense."

Ward harrumphed. "If you don't wish to take my wise counsel, Major, that's on you. But it could be a lot worse. A hell of a lot worse."

"Thanks for checking." Nomad unbuckled his seat belt, then stood and stretched. "Believe it or not, that does make me feel a little better about all this."

"Well, that's what I'm here for, isn't it?" Weaver gave a huge, theatrical yawn. "You going to get any shut-eye before we hit ground?"

"Naah. You know I can't sleep on planes."

"Then aren't you going to be a bundle of joy when we touch down in South America. I'm half tempted to go full B.A. Baracus on you."

"Who?"

"Television character from the eighties. Don't look him up. I want this to be a surprise. Now if you'll excuse me." Ward closed his eyes and turned his head, and loudly resumed snoring.

"Lucky bastard," Nomad muttered. He cast a jealous glance at his sleeping friend, then went back to studying the report.

CHAPTER 2

The two newcomers to the team were already in the room when Weaver and Nomad arrived, still shaking off the weariness of the flight. Nomad instantly recognized each of them from the photos in their jackets. Midas, the taller of the two, was seated at the far end of the room, looking about as relaxed as an overwound watch spring. Clean-shaven, dark-eyed, and with his hair tied back in a ponytail, he looked the two late arrivals up and down with detached assessment.

Holt, on the other hand, was thoroughly at ease. Physically imposing with piercing blue eyes and sharp features, he had his feet up on the conference table. A pair of scratched Oakleys sat next to Holt's footgear, the sort of shades Nomad knew from experience were equally useful in the field or for disguising bloodshot eyes and life-threatening hangovers.

"Nice boots," said Weaver, and sat down next to Holt. "Kicked a lot of shit in those?"

Holt stared at him appraisingly. "Four continents' worth. Hoping we'll get sent to Antarctica this time so I can make it to five."

"No such luck, gentlemen." Lt. Col. Mitchell walked into the room, trailed by his intelligence officer, First Lieutenant Kirk Graham. The two had been working together so long that at this point, it seemed like Mitchell didn't even have to ask questions out loud; whatever he needed, whether it be tactical field reports from Balochistan or market analysis of Chinese pork belly futures, Graham had it in his hands instantly. As such, despite the fact that he hadn't done fieldwork in years, Graham had acquired the callsign Wizard, lovingly bestowed in recognition of his skills.

Mitchell took a seat at the head of the table, Graham sliding in next to him with his laptop already open and fingers dancing furiously. Nomad settled in on the left side halfway down, folded his hands and waited.

"First things first, people. Holt, feet off the table. Save the badass act for the new recruits who are impressed by that sort of thing. We've got business to attend to." There was an unusual edge to Mitchell's voice, frustration that filled the room with tension. "Any bullshit about taking out penguins so Holt can get another stamp on his luggage is sadly off the mark."

"I take it the situation hasn't changed, sir?" Nomad asked. Out of the corner of his eye he saw Holt's eyeroll, an expression that eloquently said "ass-kisser."

"We've got less time, if that counts as a change." Mitchell rubbed his eyes. "Look, I know in a perfect world Weaver and Nomad would be rolling off active right now to recover from that shit show in Donetsk. And Midas, you'd have a very different assignment for your first time out as a Ghost. But we don't deal in wishful thinking. As much as I'd love to leave you four alone to meet cute, there's no time for that. This isn't a permanent assignment, so no one get their shorts in a twist, but considering the situation we're in and the manpower we've got available, this is how it's going to have to play out. Anybody has a problem with that, they can walk—and keep on walking—right off base. Do I make myself understood?"

"Sir." It was Midas who spoke. "Is there a chance this will become a permanent assignment?" His glance took in the room, lingering briefly on Weaver and much longer on Nomad.

"There is a chance. There is also a chance that by the time we pull you back out of the jungle, intelligent dinosaurs will have reclaimed the earth. Let's just say that for this op, I'm grading on a curve. Lieutenant?"

Graham smoothly picked up where Mitchell left off. "Ghost lead for this op will be Major Perryman. You've got twenty-four hours to bone up on what you're getting

into, then we're putting you on a cargo jet bound for
Manaus, Brazil. In Manaus, you'll be transferred to a
light aircraft that will drop you in Amazonas State along
the Rio Negro, a town in the Cucuí district where you'll
rendezvous with Captain David Protasio of C Op Est.
He'll be your support on this mission. Brasilia's made it
very clear to the White House they do not want a shooting war popping up on their northern border, particularly
since there's a good chance it could spill into their territory. Moving force en masse into that part of the country is like trying to force-feed tofu to an alligator. We've
already got a man in the city—town, really—arranging
logistics and coordinating with Protasio's people. There
will be a craft waiting for you. Your ammo, fuel, and kit
are already headed upriver from Manaus."

"Craft? You mean 'boat,' right?" Holt didn't sound
impressed. "We're crossing the border by boat?"

"The other options were, A: March sixty miles
through trackless and impassible jungle with zero land-
marks and spotty satellite connectivity with the hope
that you could then march the hostages back out that way
before they dropped dead of exhaustion, or B: Swim up
the Rio Negro while keeping your powder dry. There's
one airstrip in that whole region; it's in hostile hands; and
it's not long enough to take anything bigger than a Piper
Cub anyway. Anything else, or can I continue?"

Holt opened his mouth to retort but Weaver beat him
to it. "First rule of standing in a hole is 'stop digging.'
Holt, put the shovel down."

That earned Weaver a glare, but Holt said nothing,

and after a minute, Wizard tapped a couple of keys on his laptop and nodded. Behind him, a giant screen flared to life, showing a satellite image of terrain so green it looked like AstroTurf. "The good news is, you're not being tasked with shutting this down by yourselves, taking out separatist command structures, or really doing anything that could end up on the front page of the morning papers in Caracas or Bogota." The map refocused; this time there were borders drawn, and the image centered on the long, dark line of the Rio Negro as it ran south toward the Amazon. Two red dots appeared on the map, close to the water. "We've got credible intelligence of American citizens being held here and here by the soldiers of what's now calling itself the Revolutionary Free State of Amazonas."

"Begging your pardon, Lieutenant, if these guys are such a threat, why have I never heard of them?"

"Good question." Wizard sounded pleased for the chance to expound. "One, media's crap at reporting anything international, double crap for reporting anything in South America that isn't about sports, and triple crap for reporting on international politics unless the US is directly involved. Two, intel from that deep backcountry is incredibly difficult to come by. Best you can do is have stringers in Manaus and wait for locals to come in along the river and talk. There's no infrastructure, no comms network, nothing. Hell, there's barely any people. So it's a big dark spot on the intel map most of the time simply because you can't get an asset out there except under dire circumstances."

"But now they've decided to kidnap Americans, which will put them on the map." Nomad frowned. "I don't see the percentage in it."

"We've got two possibilities. The first is the one Lieutenant Colonel Mitchell relayed to you, which is that they're taking a page from their neighbors in FARC and moved into the kidnapping-for-ransom business. Hard currency for hostages is a sweet deal. And then there's the one we're really sweating."

"Which is?"

"That it was a mistake. That they took those hostages by accident, maybe some local commander deciding to be a hero, and now they're stuck with them. They can't let them go because that shows weakness and they can't keep them. Which means that sooner or later some-one's going to make a bad decision, and then this thing blows up all over the news." Graham rubbed his eyes in unconscious imitation of the Old Man. "We've been able to convince the families to stay quiet so far, but if anything happens—or if someone gets antsy—then all bets are off."

"This is a goat rodeo." Weaver pushed back from the table. "You're sending us down there half-prepped with a Frankenstein's-monster squad just to avoid some bad press? That's not what any of us signed up for, Colonel."

"We're sending you in because this thing could very easily blow up into a regional war on our door-step." Mitchell's voice was cutting. "If we don't do any-thing and the hostages are killed, then suddenly we've got half the country pushing us to send a significant military presence to yet another part of the map we've got no interest or business being in, antagonizing both Venezuela and Colombia in the process. Those two have a hard enough time getting along, and now we'd be adding a possible US incursion to the mix? No thank you, Master Sergeant. That's what we're really racing to stop—the cascade of interconnected crap that's going to grow out of this if things go bad."

Holt frowned. "And if the op goes bad and we get caught, it all blows up anyway."

Nomad turned to him. "Then I guess we'd better not screw it up. You up for that?"

"You've got no idea what I'm up for."

"Enough." Mitchell stood and stared each man down in turn. Holt looked away, grinning. The rest met his eyes. "I cut you a bit of slack because you're Ghosts and I expect you to know how to be grownups when the time comes. I remember Buzz Gordon drinking Klaus Henkel under the table, and then Susan Gray doing the same thing to him. I remember Astra Galinsky kicking Joe Ramirez in the balls so hard he walked around cross-eyed for a week after he made some dumb-shit crack about Russian training methods. And I remember being a young smartass and trying to tell Will Jacobs his business and getting my head handed to me on a plate with a side of fries because of it. But it was always about the mission, no matter what else went down. If you knuckleheads can't get that straight, then the hell with you. I'll go to Venezuela myself and get this done. Alternatively, you can get your heads out of your collective asses, stop the pissing contests, and actually get ready for this double-decker soup sandwich I'm handing you. Do I make myself clear?"

"Sir."

"Yes, sir."

"Yessir."

"Roger that."

There was silence for a moment, then Mitchell glared ferociously. "No more digressions. Just give them the basics and let them have the rest for homework."

"Colonel." The Wizard cleared his throat. "These suggested positions correspond to last known locations for the hostages. This," he said, highlighting the one farther south, zooming in on the image to show higher resolution images of trees, "is a biomedical research station. Small team, largely involved in sample collection in hopes of squeezing new drugs out of the local plants."

Three pictures popped up on the screen, two women and a man. The image at the left, a headshot of a sharp-faced African-American woman with graying hair, was highlighted. "Dr. Kathleen Crotty's the head of the team. RIT undergrad, Stanford PhD, taught at UMich and Notre Dame before landing a tenured position at Washington U in St. Louis." The other two images lit up in turn, a younger African-American man with a round face and a serious expression, and a slender, smiling blonde woman with hazel eyes and a tasteful stud in her nose. "Gilbert Stanton and Melanie Carpenter. Dr. Crotty's graduate assistants. He's in charge of logging the specimens and prepping them for transportation, she's logistics. They've been in-country for about two months, brought there by a local guide who's been resupplying them at a rendezvous point on the east side of the Rio Negro. A week ago, Carpenter failed to show for the meet. Instead, there were a couple soldiers with a message—Crotty and her team were prisoners of the Revolutionary Free State of Amazonas, and that someone needed to send along a lot of money to free them." A new picture popped up, the three researchers looking very frightened standing in front of a small row of tents, while armed soldiers with casually slung weapons framed them in the shot.

"The guide went back downriver with the message and the pic, and our friends at the base in São Gabriel de Cachoeira got it back to us. The interesting thing in this image, though, isn't the hostages. I mean, they're interesting and they're important, but there's something else here. Specifically, this guy."

The screen zoomed on one of the soldiers on the left, a tall man with a hatchet face and a thin mustache. He seemed relaxed and in control, unlike the other soldiers who were obviously tense, clutching their weapons with white-knuckled fingers. They looked like amateurs. This other guy looked like he'd been there before.

"Who's that?" Holt drawled.

"Glad you asked. That, near as we can tell, is Colonel Gilberto Urbina, ranking officer for the Amazonas group. Ex-SEBIN, ex-509th Special Operations Battalion. A real charmer. A couple of years back he got crosswise with his superiors and the next thing you know, he drops off the radar. Turned out they'd assigned him to sloth-watching duty down in Amazonas, presumably to get him as far away from the seat of power as possible."

"SEBIN?" Nomad asked.

"Secret police. Very unpleasant people." It was Midas who responded. "I don't know what you have to do to get kicked off that squad, and I don't want to think about it."

"Right in one." Wizard plowed on. "That they didn't just disappear him says a few things about his capabilities. That they sent him off to rot in the jungle says more. But if he's running the show for Amazonas, they just got a little more worrisome."

Weaver cleared his throat. "So we're to assume that he's on-site? And that the hostages are still there?"

"No and yes. We've gotten a couple of other images, all with the hostages in the same location. So as of twenty-four hours ago, they're still where they were captured. On the other hand, none of the other pictures—" He paused to rapidly flick through a series of photos of the hostages. "—show Colonel Urbina. Best guess is that he's moved on to another site, which is good news. He's dangerous and well-guarded. If he's in camp, the number of potential defenders goes way up."

"Noted." Nomad tapped the screen of his MRT impatiently. "What about the other site? The archaeologists?"

"Ah. Yes." The grim images from the bioresearch lab vanished, replaced by two more portraits, a heavily tanned older man with a shock of white hair, and a younger, slightly heavyset man of Asian descent wearing round John Lennon glasses and sporting a shaved head.

"The two we've got here are Doctors Andrew Messina and Herbert Kwan, respectively. Both specialists in pre-Columbian cultures. One teaches at DePaul, the other at Penn, and by all accounts, they hate each other's guts. Figuring out why they agreed to go on an expedition together is beyond my department's capabilities, but a very large check from an anonymous donor underwriting the whole thing might have gone a long way toward smoothing that rift. They headed upriver with about fifteen porters, guides, and bodyguards a month and a half ago, looking for evidence of a lost city a grad student claimed to have located on Google Maps." He shrugged. "Go figure. In any case, they stopped making their regular satphone check-ins ten days ago. Instead, a couple members of the traveling party came drifting out of the jungle scared out of their minds and claiming they'd been taken by armed men. Protasio's people got ahold of them and sat them down, and this is the best guess as to the location where they were being held."

Nomad studied the map. "There's some miles of hard jungle between those two locations. We can't shepherd civilians, especially not ones who've been in captivity, over that much ground and put them in range of a firefight before we pull them out."

"That's correct." Mitchell's expression was grim. "We're looking for a pair of clean exfils. Hit the first site, pull the hostages out, and then go back and hit the second."

"Shouldn't we be doing this with two teams simultaneously?"

"In a perfect world, yes. With what we've got to work

with, you're going to have to make that first outpost go quiet so they don't know you're going for the second. That means quick turnaround. You get the hostages from site Alpha, run them to the border and do a handoff to the Brazilians, resupply and go back in for the clincher at site Bravo."

"And if the Free Amazonas types start shooting at Protasio while we're doing the handoff?"

"Then he'll shoot back. I don't think they're dumb enough to start a war with Brazil, no matter how mad they'll get at you, and I know Protasio. By the book, formal as hell. He's not going to move one inch across the border and risk being accused of a provocation, but if someone threatens his people he'll get up on his hind legs."

Nomad grimaced. "I'm liking this guy more and more all the time."

"You'd better like him. He's your lifeline. Any other questions?"

"What support can we expect in-country?"

Graham looked pained. "Comms are shit out there. We'll have a bird going overhead twice a day so you can check in, but constant data's feed's a no-go. Local commlink will work fine up to about a mile, but mainly, you'll be on your own. Any others?"

"About a million, but I'm not going to like any of the answers, so, not at this time, Colonel."

"Then I guess we'd better go pack."

"You've got twenty-four hours. I don't care what you do with that time as long as you're on that plane."

With that, Mitchell stood, Wizard following his lead and snapping his laptop shut. The four Ghosts were left sitting in silence, looking one to the other until finally Weaver spoke.

"That went well."

Despite themselves, Nomad and Holt chuckled.

"All right, fair enough." Perryman put his hands in the air. "Not the best first impression we could have made as a team. But these are the cards we're dealt. If we can't win straight up, we'd better get real good at bluffing together."

Holt stood. "Twenty-three hours, fifty-two minutes. Plenty of time for us to pull together as a squad." But there was a lightness in his tone that hadn't been there previously. "With your permission, Major?"

Nomad nodded. "Dismissed. See you tomorrow." Holt walked out of the room without a backward glance.

"That goes for you, too." Nomad stretched out of his chair and looked from Midas to Weaver and back. "Me, I need to go over the gear Wizard's decided we needed for this op and then requisition the stuff we're actually going to need and pray the Old Man can get it for us. And then I'm gonna get some shuteye."

"You do that," Weaver uttered. "See you on the other side."

Midas watched Nomad go, his face impassive. When the major had left the room, he turned to Weaver. "Master Sergeant, a question?"

"Ask away. But I'm guessing you want to talk about Nomad."

Midas flushed faintly. "He seems a little . . . unsure."

"He's still coming down a bit from what happened in Donetsk, and this is his first time leading the squad. Can't blame him for nerves, but he's going to be fine." Weaver hooked a thumb in the direction of the doorway. "Also, your buddy Holt is what we in the head-shrinking business clinically diagnose as an asshole."

Midas laughed. "I'm sorry. I know it shouldn't be my place to ask, but I'm new to the unit. New to all of this. And to see things start out like that, it was a little worrying."

"It's always like this, even when it looks like it's perfect." Weaver looked away for a moment, lost in memories. "You know what really makes a Ghost?"

"Professionalism? Mental toughness?"

Weaver shook his head. "Nope. Being able to take the most screwed-up, unexpected, five-alarm tire fire imaginable in stride and turn it into a tactical advantage. Hell, the way I look at it, we're ahead of the game on this one—we know which brand of tire's on fire going in for a change."

Midas laughed again, and then stood. "I admire your confidence, Master Sergeant. And I look forward to working with you."

"You say that now," Weaver replied, walking away.

CHAPTER 3

The runway in Cucuí was short, rough, and uneven, which made it a perfect match for the flight in from Manaus. The plane itself was a beaten-up EMB 121 Xingu, its rough paint job only partially obscuring old Brazilian Air Force markings and what looked to be a couple of duct-taped bullet holes. There were two other passengers on board, one a telecom executive sent to the Cucuí branch office as punishment for some infraction or other, the other a local returning from a trip to see family in the big city. They chatted amicably in Portuguese as the plane bounced up and down over the jungle. Midas joined in on occasion. His Portuguese wasn't great, but it was good enough for him to be included in the conversation.

The cover story they'd been provided for travel was that they were going fishing on the Rio Negro, looking to catch big peacock bass and piraiba. The telecom executive asked once, got the answer from Midas, and then promptly ignored Holt, Weaver, and Nomad the rest of the trip.

Which, to be fair, was what Nomad wanted.

Weaver had shut his eyes as soon as they'd climbed on board, and Holt had long since joined him in dreamland. *Professionals*, Nomad thought. *Get your sleep where you can.* That, and Midas's joining the other men's conversation, left Nomad the chance to simply look out the window and watch the endless green unfold below. Occasionally, small cleared patches broke through, small towns or even single buildings, often on the banks of rivers whose names he didn't know. But the jungle covered everything, its canopy leaning over roads and stretching from horizon to horizon in an unbroken sea of green.

It was going to be a problem once they hit the ground, he reflected. Wizard had made it clear that the canopy was so thick and did such a good job of diffusing heat sources that there was basically no way to get any idea of what was going on under the leaves. If Nomad and his team wanted intel, they couldn't send a drone out and wait for results. They'd have to go out and get it the hard way. And as for what was under the canopy, the advance reports didn't look promising, either. The Old Man could talk all he wanted about quick in and out, but nothing about the jungle suggested that "quick" was even an option.

The plane landed with more force than was absolutely necessary, and the much-abused landing gear whined in protest. The plane bounced once, twice, a third time, then settled in and lurched down the runway with propellers whirring and brakes screeching. Ahead, a wall of greenery marked the end of the runway and the start of the jungle, and both looked disturbingly close.

The pilot shouted something in Portuguese, Midas crossed himself, and the two other passengers looked deeply unconcerned as the plane skidded to a halt maybe a half dozen yards from the edge of the makeshift airfield. There was silence in the cabin for a moment, then Weaver sat up and asked, "Did we make it?"

"Yeah, we made it," said Nomad. A lone man ran out of the dusty trailer that served as both tower and terminal, pushing a cart for bags. The pilot kicked open the door, providing a staircase down to the ground, and the hot, humid air flooded into the cabin.

"Jesus, you could drink this stuff with a straw," Holt muttered.

"You want to catch the big bass, you go where it's wet," Midas replied without skipping a beat. "Or would you rather be back home going after crappies and snakehead?"

Weaver hid a smirk while Holt sputtered something about alligator gar, and, grabbing their bags, the squad deplaned. They'd worn civvies for the flight in keeping with their cover, jeans and shorts and whatever the hell else Wizard said rich jerks going fishing wore, and Nomad could feel the sweat already starting to soak through his black t-shirt. Weaver, on the other hand, looked immaculate in a garish Hawaiian number, while Holt wore a rumpled and faded Drive-By Truckers t-shirt that had enough sweat rings under the armpits that you could cut the shirt open and count its age. Midas seemed not to mind the heat at all, his blue cotton shirt unmarred by any sign of perspiration.

All of them wore sunglasses.

"Where's our guy?" Weaver asked, as the porter slung the bags out of the plane and onto the cart. "Hey, easy there, we'll take those."

Nomad put a wad of reais in the man's hand to forestall any protests, and the Ghosts grabbed their packs and cases. The porter rumbled off across the dusty field with his mostly empty cart, the other two passengers following. The local turned, said something to Midas, and then walked off.

"What did he say?" Weaver asked.

"He said if we were going fishing, not to go too far upriver. The river's running a little high, and it's dangerous. A couple of other fishermen didn't come back."

Holt laughed sarcastically. "Yeah, can't imagine why."

"There's our guy," Weaver interrupted, and pointed. Standing in the scant shade offered by the side of the terminal building and sipping a bottle of water was a short, deeply tanned man wearing cargo shorts, a linen shirt, and a shapeless fishing hat loaded up with pins and lures.

"What makes you so sure?" Nomad asked.

"Got a Group for Specialized Tactics insignia pin in there on his hat with all the flies and World Cup stuff." Weaver pointed at the man, who stood up at the gesture. Nomad couldn't see a damn thing.

"And you can see it?" he added doubtfully.

Weaver nodded. "I've got good eyes."

The man waited for Weaver to finish speaking, and then waved them over. "Oscar DeScalso," he introduced himself. "Uncle Mitch sent me to make sure you boys had a good time. I got a car around the other side. Come on." Without stopping to see who was following, he turned and trundled off. The Ghosts, after a moment's hesitation, followed.

DeScalso's car turned out to be a Range Rover of early '80s vintage painted bright orange, with the legend OSCAR'S FISHING TOURS painted on the sides in both English and Portuguese. The Ghosts slung their gear in the back and then climbed in, Holt squeezing in between Weaver and Midas in the back while Perryman sat up front.

"You got air conditioning in this thing?" Nomad asked.

"Yeah, not that it does a lot of good. There's a cooler in the back with water and beer. That'll help more." With expert precision, the man wheeled the vehicle out of the parking lot, weaving around pedestrians, pedicabs, and other drivers. Horns blared, but he ignored them, turning right and accelerating.

"Welcome to the ass end of Brazil, guys," he said. "I've

rented a boat for you for the trip upriver and your gear's either already stowed or waiting with Protasio. He'll see you tonight after sundown."

"I was hoping we could roll out immediately," countered Nomad. "Time's tight, or so Uncle Mitch kept saying."

"Negative on that." DeScalso swerved around a chicken that had suddenly run out into the street and its equally focused owner. "Never hit a chicken down here. You never hear the end of it. You get away with hitting a human with less paperwork than if you hit a goddamn chicken." He shook his head, stopped for a nanosecond at a dusty stop sign, then continued. "You're fishermen, you play the part. I take you to see Protasio right off, people ask questions. You put in on the river after noon, people ask questions. So, I'm taking you to the local hotel, and then tonight I'll take you to meet Protasio, and tomorrow before dawn, you hit the river like any other bunch of rich assholes looking for something to mount on their wall. *Capiche*?"

"Where the hell are you from, man?" Holt demanded.

"Canarsie. Y'know, Brooklyn. But I've been down here fifteen years, setting up ops for jamokes like you all over South America. So trust me, and everything's gonna be just fine."

"You get us a river pilot along with that boat?" That was Weaver.

"You really want to depend on a civilian in the type of shit you're likely to get into? Not happening. Your jacket said you could pilot riverine craft, so you got the job,

Weaver." He hit the callsign with a little more emphasis than necessary, a reminder that he did in fact know what the hell he was talking about.

Weaver sank back in his seat, grumbling. "Great. Why do all you army pukes think that the only job in the navy is drive the big damn boat?"

Descalso chuckled. "Because that's the only interesting thing you do."

Weaver started to reply, but DeScalso slammed on the brakes in front of a white two-story building that smelled faintly of fresh paint. "We're here. Grab your shit, I've already checked you in, and Protasio will meet you in the hotel bar at 1900 hours."

"Hell of a way to win an argument," Weaver muttered, but he got out like the rest.

The room Weaver and Nomad shared was surprisingly large, with twin beds and photos of successful fishermen holding up oversized catfish of various varieties hung on the wall. A tiny window-mounted air conditioner wheezed as it kept the heat somewhere less-than-unbearable. Weaver stretched out on one of the beds. "How much time we got to kill?"

"Five minutes less than the last time you asked." Nomad was at the one small desk the room offered, engrossed in his MRT. "I'm reading up on this Colonel Urbina. He's a piece of work."

"You think he's behind the hostage-taking?"

Nomad rubbed his eyes. "I think Wizard's right and

this was a panic move on somebody's part. I think he came in to take control, make sure things didn't get out of hand."

"Ah." Weaver swung himself into a sitting position. "Makes sense. That means he's probably got some of his better people in place. It would be stupid to clean up the mess and then turn it right back over to the turkeys who caused it."

"Right. Hey, I don't know about you, but I'd feel a lot better if you got a look at our ride up-river."

Ward stood. "Are you trying to get rid of me?"

Perryman shook his head. "No, I'm trying to make sure we don't end up at the bottom of the Rio Negro because we tried to cram too much gear into a two-man canoe. Take Holt with you. Delgado and I will stay here and watch the gear."

"If you say so." He walked over to the door. "Don't go anywhere. I'm pretty sure my key only works if there's someone already in the room opening the door."

"You got it. Now grab Holt and go."

Weaver went out into the hall and shut the door behind him. Holt and Midas were in the next room over, debating fish stories loudly enough to be heard in the hall. He rapped on the door, "Knock it off, you two. The little old lady in 2-B doesn't want to hear it."

The door opened, revealing a barefooted Holt. "Yes, Mom. What do you want?"

"Put some shoes on. I was going to go for a walk, and you look like you can use the exercise."

They shared a look, and then Holt turned away.

"Gimme one second." He reappeared a minute later wearing ratty flip-flops. "Let's go."

They were out in the street before either of them said another word, and it was Holt who broke the silence. "Didn't want to talk in the hotel?"

"Nomad did a sweep for bugs, but better safe than sorry. Thought we'd check out our transportation like good little fishermen." They turned right, heading for the river.

"You been down this way before?" Holt asked.

"Nope. First time. Here's hoping we make the catches we're looking for." The streets were relatively quiet in the heat of late afternoon. Cars and bicycles were whizzing by in equal numbers. In the distance, thunderheads rumbled over the forest, promising rain sooner rather than later.

"Do we know where the boat is?"

"Nomad got the location from Oscar. The guy's a full service fishing trip coordinator, you know what I mean?"

Holt snickered. "Just wait till we get out on the water. You want fishing, you come to Louisiana."

"Yeah, I heard you and Midas going at it with the fish stories. I thought all you had up the bayou were gators and catfish."

Holt spat on the ground. "Piraiba's nothing but a big catfish, right? But let me tell you, growing up, getting a boat out and going off to do a little fishing, that was as good as it got. All the crap going down around me—my family, my friends, you name it—I could push off, and in ten minutes, I was in a whole other world. Prehistoric.

No human troubles allowed. You just put your line in the water and waited for something to bite, and then it was may the best critter win."

"Did you win a lot?"

"More than I lost. But losing was okay, too. If a fish put up a good fight, I was okay with it getting loose. If it was my own damn fault, then I'd get mad."

Weaver nodded. "Fair enough. And you didn't end up as gator chow."

"Naaah, once you learn the rules with gators, they're no problem. Treat 'em with respect, and don't go dipping your toes in the water when they're hungry."

They hit a broad intersection. Weaver consulted a scribbled note, then shoved it back into his pocket. "Left," he said, and they crossed against the light. "Hope the same rules apply for caimans."

"What's a caiman?" Holt's tone was quizzical.

"I thought you said you'd been in-country before. Black caiman's like an alligator's meaner cousin, and the Rio Negro's full of them. Word is they get up to twenty feet long, which means a short guy like you is a snack."

"Well, ain't that a kick." Holt sunk into thoughtful silence for a moment. "They attack people?"

Weaver nodded. "Oh yeah. They'll hit boats, too. Knock the passengers into the water where they can snap 'em up."

An edge of irritation crept into Holt's voice. "Now you're just messing with me."

"Probably," Weaver agreed. "Turn right here. We're almost to the water."

They turned and walked another block, and then the river stretched out in front of them. It was wide and black, with only the passage of a leaf or branch caught up in the current revealing how swiftly it was flowing. The far side was nothing but forest, trees crowded up to the water's edge and exposed roots sticking out into the air where the mud of the riverbank had eroded.

On their side of the river, a sandy beach stretched tenuously out into the water, a couple of docks extending out beyond it into the flow. A small boat emblazoned with the insignia of the *Policia Federale* bobbed up and down at the end of one, its duties done for the day. A pair of elderly men fussed over a canoe, hauling it up onto the sand and squabbling in Portuguese.

"What are they saying?" Weaver asked.

"Arguing over which one of them pays for the repairs. Apparently they hit a snag when they were out this morning."

"Fair enough, I guess. There. That one's ours." Weaver pointed.

It was long and low and out of the water, covered up with a tarp to protect it from the incipient rain. The sides showed wear, silver aluminum peeking through a jungle camo paint job. Only the engine looked new, a gleaming Yanmar diesel that promised more power than was strictly necessary to propel a boat of that size.

"Welp," said Holt. "It's definitely a boat."

"It's a boat that's going to be no fun at all if we bring in a big catch and hit some rough waters. Those sides are awful low."

Holt shrugged. "Guess we'd better be careful, then," he said softly. "Anything else you wanted to see?"

"Yeah." Weaver clambered down onto the beach. "I want to get a closer look."

"The beer cooler comes later, if that's what you want to know."

Weaver whirled. DeScalso stood at the edge of the street, holding a fresh bottle of water and shaking his head. "What's the matter, you don't trust your trip coordinator?"

"Just hoping we'd gotten one of those nice bass boats like you see in the brochures." Weaver stared up at him. "Wanted to see if it was big enough for everything we're going to catch."

"You've got enough fuel in the tank to do one hundred ninety-five miles, give or take, with a couple of cans of diesel on board just in case. Boat seats a dozen, got more than enough room for all your gear and supplies and anything you happen to catch, and you get a top speed of about thirty MPH. You've got a draft of two feet, and with the river this high that should get you over most of the snags and sandbars. Beam's six and a half feet, give or take, so don't go wedging her into too many tight spots. Remember, she's a rental."

"Heh. I couldn't forget that if I tried." Weaver frowned. "You're sure we're good here?"

"You're good," DeScalso answered firmly. "Now head back to the hotel. I'll see you tonight in the bar. Be on best behavior. Protasio had a stick surgically implanted in his ass the day he was born."

DeScalso stood there and stared at them pointedly until Weaver and Holt started walking back. When they were out of earshot, Holt turned to Weaver. "You know what I hate most about this gig?"

"I couldn't imagine."

"Putting up with all the smug assholes who know more than you do about what you're about to do."

"I imagine you meet a lot of those," Weaver said blandly, and they walked the rest of the way back in silence.

The hotel bar had a lot of overhead fans. It was dimly lit, as seemed appropriate, and packed lightly with patrons sitting in ones and twos at the small wooden tables scattered around the room. In the corner, a television showed a football match, Taruna playing Olimpico, with the sound turned up just enough to interfere with any other conversation. The bartender, an older man with a shock of gray hair and hands that looked big enough to palm a bowling ball, nodded when Nomad's team walked in and shouted "What do you want?" at them before they'd finished entering the room.

"Four Xingu," Perryman responded. The bartender looked at him with a combination of pity and disappointment, then ducked behind the bar and re-emerged with four cold bottles. He put them down on the counter and muttered something Nomad didn't catch, then waved him off when Nomad went for his wallet. "No, no, already paid for. Your friend, he has a tab." He jerked a thumb toward the corner of the room, where Oscar DeScalso was sitting with two figures Nomad didn't recognize. Oscar turned and raised his beer in their direction, then motioned them over.

The scarred wooden table was barely big enough for all of them, the elderly chairs creaking under their weight. "Good choice on the beer," Oscar said as they sat down. "Xingu's the beer of choice of the American fishing tourists who come through here."

"It's that good?" Weaver asked, the bottle halfway to his lips.

"It's the only Brazilian beer most Americans have heard of," said the man sitting across from Oscar. He was deeply tanned, with a neatly trimmed mustache and a black crew cut that was showing the first hints of gray at the temples. Sharply angled eyebrows gave him an expression of permanent surprise. He wore a white shirt with the sleeves rolled up, revealing an impressive collection of scars along his forearms, and, incongruously, a pair of reading glasses were tucked into his shirt pocket.

"Captain Protasio, I assume?" Perryman reached across the table to shake his hand. The man's grip was firm. No jockeying for position and going for the maximum squeeze, just a quick shake and then he let go.

"A pleasure," Protasio said. "No need for introductions on your side. Oscar's made me quite aware of the details of your fishing trip. But allow me to introduce my aide, Lieutenant Marta Correa. You can thank her for your equipment and supplies."

DeScalso coughed. "Captain Protasio is our point of

contact with the Brazilian authorities. He oversees all the fishing expeditions in this part of the country, and if you run into trouble, he's the one who'll come bail your boat out."

"I hope that won't be necessary," Nomad said. "Any more word on the fish upriver?"

"Someone brought in a picture of three this morning. They looked a little underfed, but they still put up a fight. In the morning, there'll be a map in the boat showing you where the big ones can be caught."

"Good, good. I'd hate for this trip to be for nothing. If we don't come back with a lot of catches, my old man will never let me hear the end of it."

A smile quirked at the corner of Protasio's mouth. "A couple of years ago, and he would have tried to take the trip himself. He's a real go-getter, as I recall." He pronounced the words precisely, one after the other, his accent so faint as to be barely noticeable. "Now, Marta, have you prepared the charts for these gentlemen?"

Correa was short but not slender, with the build of an athlete and the no-nonsense attitude of every logistics officer everywhere. She wore a short-sleeved yellow blouse, and there was a sheaf of papers on the table next to her glass. Water, Nomad noted, not beer.

"Gentlemen. You'll want to be on the water by four-thirty to get to the best fishing spots upstream before anyone else decides to take an interest."

"Are we likely to run into trouble at the border?"

"There's a Venezuelan outpost at the border, but they're not stopping anyone these days." She looked annoyed. "It's good for fishing, better for other business, if you know what I mean."

Nomad nodded, and she continued. "Now, if you get in trouble north of the border, technically we can't help you. The last thing we want is to create a border incident. That's still Venezuelan territory, even if they're not doing much with it. But unofficially, these days, the actual location of the border may be open to some debate. In any case, river charts, tackle, bait, and every-thing else you need will be delivered to the boat shortly before you leave. We'll be stowing your kit in false-bot-tomed lockers. You'll be able to gear up once you get in-country, but when you get on the water, we'll want you looking like tourists."

"She'll supervise the loading herself," Protasio said. "You'll have everything you need to make this a success-ful expedition."

"Sounds good to me." Perryman raised his beer, and the others clinked theirs against his. "To a good fishing trip."

"To a good trip," the rest echoed. Holt drained his beer in one long pull, then put the bottle down on the table. "Need a refill. Anyone else want anything?"

"I think we're fine, thanks." Perryman took a small sip of his, the beer heavy and strong on his tongue. "Got to get an early start, remember?"

"Lightweight," was Holt's response. He turned to Lt. Correa. "So, Marta, if only tourists drink Xingu around here, what do the locals drink?" She glanced at Protasio, then opened her mouth to reply, but before she could,

Holt interrupted again. "No, no, show me. Come on." And then somehow she was walking with him to the bar, and the two were conversing intently.

"I think I'll be turning in," Midas said, and put his mostly full bottle back down on the table. "Like you said, we've got an early start." He rose from the table, nodded to Nomad and Protasio, and, without another word, made his way out of the bar.

"Quite an eclectic bunch of friends you've decided to go fishing with," Protasio commented as Midas left the room. "Have you done a lot of fishing together?"

"Not as much as you're doing now," Perryman replied. "I'm sure it's going to be a good trip."

"I have no doubts." Protasio leaned forward. "But I confess, I'm a little disappointed in one of your friends' failure to keep his mind on business." He nodded toward the bar, where Holt and Correa were now engaged in an animated discussion. "If his behavior crosses a line, that could impact how well my team can support your expedition."

"Are you threatening me, Captain?"

"No, merely pointing out that on something as . . . *delicate* as this trip of yours, we want to make sure there is no confusion about what everyone's role is and where everyone's focus should be. Your team should be looking upriver."

"I see. Well, I'll have a little talk with him."

"That would be most appreciated." Protasio rose. "And now, if you will excuse me, I'll be turning in as well. You're not the only fishermen on the river, I'm afraid." He gave a tight grin, then wandered over to the bar in a clear effort to extract Correa from her conversation with

Holt. Somewhat reluctantly, she acceded, and then the two Brazilian officers were walking out the door.

"Hell of a start, guys," DeScalso said, swirling the last dregs of beer around the bottom of his bottle. "Trust me, you do not want to get on Protasio's bad side. Not out here."

"I get it, I get it." Nomad shook his head disgustedly. "Anything else we need to know?"

"Get down there at four to make sure Correa's still handling the loading. Other than that, you're no longer my problem until you show up with your fish. Good - hell, what do you say? Not hunting, cause you're fishing."

"Good luck," Weaver said. "I'll settle for good luck."

DeScalso chuckled. "Wouldn't we all?" He finished the last of his beer and stood. "You want anything else? I'm gonna go settle the tab."

"We're good," Perryman said.

"Yup," Weaver added. "Actually, I need to let some out more than put anything else in right now. If you'll excuse me." He wandered off in search of the bathroom as DeScalso headed to the bar, leaving Nomad alone for a moment. A quick look at the soccer game told him nothing of interest, so he turned back to the bar. Holt was talking earnestly with DeScalso, probably trying to get one more round out of the man, and DeScalso was having none of it. Unsure whether to laugh of sigh, Nomad settled instead for walking over to the bar himself. "A word?" he asked Holt.

"Since this cheapskate's cutting us off, that word's not going to be beer." Holt grimaced. "What can I do for you?"

"Outside." The two men walked out, cutting through the hotel lobby and out into the street. A few steps away from the building and out of earshot, and Holt nodded.

"So, what can I do for you, Major?"

"You can start by acting like a goddamned professional. We're not down here twenty-four hours and you're putting moves on one of the officers we're going to be relying on to get us out of this green hell? Now her CO's pissed, and out here he's the only friend we've got."

Holt took a deep breath. "Major, I don't know what Protasio told you, but it's all bullshit. And if you're really worried, go talk to the lieutenant and see if she's upset with our little confab."

"That's not the point. You've got a rep, Holt, for being a player. Lieutenant Colonel Mitchell assured me that was overblown, and that you had your head screwed on straight, but what happens as soon as we get down here? I've got local senior staff calling you out on that. What's your excuse, Holt? What's the explanation that I can take back to our friend and have him believe it?"

Holt didn't answer immediately. Instead, he pulled a pack of cigarettes out of a pocket, took one out and lit it, then inhaled slowly before letting the smoke stream out his nose. "Nasty, these things. Local brand. Traded with one of the hotel staff for 'em cause I always got to try the local flavor. You want to learn about a place, smoke the local cigarette. You'll get more about the people who live there from one puff than you will from all the reports and all the briefings and all the dossiers

HQ's ever put together." He took another drag. "Now, I admit I have a certain rep. But so do you, Major, and that's for being a tightass. Loosen up a bit, and we'll get along just fine. Keep up this spit and polish bullcrap and you're gonna get us both killed."

Nomad could feel his face flushing red with anger. "I'm not here to get along with you. You're here to fill out my squad so we can do this mission as clean and as quick as possible."

Holt took a long drag, then flicked the butt onto the ground. "Look, Major, I know this is your first time taking point on an op, so I'm gonna cut you a little slack, but here's a tip for you. You're leading the squad. That means you get your squaddies' backs, especially when some local thumbdick on a power trip comes after one of us. You get our backs here, we'll have yours out there. But trust has got to start somewhere, Major, and if you're not trusting your guy did the right thing in a bar here, it's gonna be hella hard for me or Midas—or your buddy Weaver, once he figures out you're clenched up tight enough to turn coal into diamond—to trust the shots you're calling out there." He ground out the cigarette with his heel, took a couple of steps back toward the tents, and then turned. "And for the record, Lieutenant Correa and I were discussing navigation on the river. Specifically, how to get past that checkpoint without being seen and having our fish confiscated. Thought that might be useful." And with that, he walked off.

Nomad watched him go, fists unconsciously clenching. There were a million things he could say in response but following Holt, calling him out would just make him look unsure of his leadership, weak and petty.

"The kid's right, you know." Weaver moved out of the shadows behind Perryman. "A bit overassertive in the way he phrases things, but his argument's on point."

Nomad turned. "How long were you there?"

"Long enough to hear the whole thing. And before you go full Captain Queeg, no, I did not follow you to eavesdrop. Came back from the can and the party was over, so I thought I'd grab some air."

Despite himself, Perryman chuckled. "Okay, fine. But I need some backup here, Weaver. First op, this guy's got the word 'horndog' splashed all over his jacket, and the next thing I know our POC is screaming a blue streak over Holt macking on his number two."

"I think the good captain wishes he were her number one, if you take my meaning. And Holt's a good-looking guy. But come on, you really think the Old Man's going to saddle us with a couple of dandruff factories on an op like this? They're Ghosts, and that counts for something. Maybe our two new friends aren't quite Alicia Diaz-level yet, but hell, neither are me and thee. You're going to lead, trust your people and trust that you're the right guy to lead them. You get my meaning?"

Nomad nodded. "Yeah. Just don't want to screw this up, and it looked like we were headed there with speed."

"I think you'll be fine. Just remind Protasio who's here to help whom, and that'll be that." Weaver yawned hugely. "Right, I'm for bed. Got a boat trip tomorrow, or so I hear. You going to do bed checks at curfew, Nomad?"

Nomad shook his head. "Not necessary, I think. Thanks for the advice."

"Don't mention it. Now get some sleep yourself, or you're going to be even more worthless tomorrow than Holt is afraid you might be. You'll want to demonstrate different, I suspect." And with that, he ambled toward the hotel entrance.

After a minute, Nomad took a deep breath and followed.

Correa was already at work with a crew, all dressed in civvies, down at the river when the Ghosts arrived in the predawn darkness. Fishing gear was conspicuously displayed as the lieutenant directed men shifting crates of supplies into the boat. Despite the weight, it rode high in the water, straining at the rope that anchored her to shore as if eager to get underway. Other boats were already moving out onto the water, fishermen yelling greetings at one another as they headed to their separate fishing grounds. The old men Weaver and Holt had seen the day before were midstream, yelling at each other with undiminished ferocity that faded only as they drifted downstream.

"Everything shipshape?" Nomad asked.

Correa stopped yelling at a man pulling a cooler with the heft of an ammo box off a flatbed truck marked with DeScalso's company name and turned to face Perryman. "You're early," she said.

"I wanted to see your work," he replied. Down by

the boat, the other Ghosts were lending a hand, helping move gear while Weaver clambered on board and started fussing with the engine.

"Everything Mr. DeScalso specified will be on board in five minutes. River charts are in a waterproof pouch near the helm. I've uploaded them for you as well, but on the river it's best to have tools you can touch."

"Understood. Have you been upriver where we're going?"

She nodded once. "The thing you have to understand is that the territory you are going into, it is not tame. The river seems calm. The jungle, because of the black water, is actually sparse enough that you can walk easily most places. There's less wildlife than you'd think, at least on shore. But that doesn't mean that it's friendly, or that it's safe. The jungle is merciless, and it's more dangerous to you than the men you're going after."

"We're going after hostages," Nomad corrected her. "They'd better not be dangerous."

"You get into the jungle, everyone's dangerous," she replied. "Hold on a moment." Without waiting for his response, she walked over to the truck, which was nearly empty, and snagged a small cooler, the sort of thing fishermen would bring with them. Without ceremony, she handed it to Nomad. The contents clanked slightly as she did so.

"For your friend. Better than Xingu. I'd recommend being polite to him. He might just share. Godspeed, fisherman." She turned and issued a set of orders in Portuguese. The last of the boxes went on the boat, and the work gang headed up the beach to the truck. Three jumped in the back, while another got in the passenger side and Correa took the wheel. Then the truck was gone in a cloud of barely visible dust, and Weaver was waving him on board.

Shaking his head, Nomad walked down the beach to the boat. Holt was already on board, and Nomad handed him the cooler.

"What's this?"

"A present from your debate partner. She said to share."

Holt popped the cooler lid open and grinned. "The hell she did." He stashed the cooler under one of the benches that served as seats, and offered his hand to Perryman. Perryman took it and hopped in. Behind him, Midas undid the hawser tying them to the ramshackle pier and then they were floating free.

"Take us upriver, Weaver."

"Yessir." Weaver gunned the engine, which had been idling, and the boat leapt forward against the dark waters.

CHAPTER 4

"You got your night eyes on?" Holt asked.

"Don't need NVG," Weaver replied. "Sun's already on its way up."

Holt shrugged, and went back to watching the shoreline, an endless run of trees, vines and other, less identifiable, plant life. The air was alive with bird calls and the alarmed hoots of howler monkeys, spreading the word that something was making noise on the river, and it just might be a predator.

Midas crouched in the prow, constantly scanning the river ahead. Occasionally he'd call out "snag" or "sandbar" to Weaver, and the boat would shift course slightly as they steered around the obstacle, and then continued on.

Nomad sat in the middle of the boat, port side, scanning some of the maps that Lt. Correa had provided with a hand-held flashlight. "Okay, Weaver, how's it looking back there?"

"She's handling fine. I'm staying in the center of the channel. Deepest run, cleanest water. And out in the open like this . . . ."

"We're sitting ducks?" Holt interrupted. Weaver ignored him.

"Out in the middle, we've got that much less of a chance of something dropping out of a tree into the craft with us. Or do you want to have to deal with a tree viper or a Brazilian wandering spider dropping down into the boat to say hello?"

"The what spider?" Holt asked. "That can't be real."

"Can, and is," Weaver assured him. "The world's most venomous spider. It comes in bright orange. And we're getting further from the nearest dose of antivenom every second. Once one of those suckers gets its fangs into you, the poison starts—"

"Enough!" Nomad interrupted. "Weaver, I trust you to not get us eaten, bitten, or constricted by anything along the river. God knows it's wide enough; nothing's going to jump off the bank and take a bite. Holt, keep an eye out for anything orange and poisonous, and we'll be fine. Understood?"

"Yeah, yeah," Holt grumbled. Midas whistled, and Holt turned.

"Here." Midas threw Holt a can, which the man caught one-handed. "Mosquito spray. Put it on. Unless you want to go home with something unpleasant. They're particularly bad along the river."

Holt was already spraying himself down, then passing the can of repellant to Nomad. Perryman took it and hosed himself down, then offered it to Weaver.

"You do me. I've got my hands full. The current's a bear."

"Right." Nomad got to work. "What's our timeline?"

"Border's coming up sooner than I'd like. There's a couple of estates—fishing lodges, mostly—on the west bank of the river. That's my real reason for not hugging the shore. Then it's all jungle for a good long way. The border between Venezuela and Colombia actually runs right down the middle of the river, so that could make things interesting."

"Colombia's not our problem. Okay, Holt, get the fishing gear out. We're going straight up the gut. Gonna play it straight until we can't anymore."

"You sure?" Weaver sounded dubious. "Charts say there's an island on the west side of the main channel, its point extending over the border. With the river high, we can cozy up behind there and sneak across, no worries."

"Negative. Wizard said these guys wander into town sometimes. The last thing we need is them hearing about a fishing boat that went upriver that they never saw. Besides," he grinned, "Oscar went to all the trouble to get us this nice gear. It'd be a shame to let it go to waste."

"Roger that," Weaver said dubiously, and held course in the center of the channel. "Can we go over the plan if we get stopped?"

Nomad nodded, and pivoted in his seat. "Always worth another run-through. Midas, if we run into company, you get to do the talking. You're taking your buddies fishing, feel free to play up the rich idiot angle. Holt, it's been made clear you actually know what to do with this crap. Do it, and make us look good. Weaver, if it looks bad, you get us out of there."

"And what will you be doing, Major?" Midas asked, half-smiling.

Nomad popped open the small cooler Correa had given him. He pulled out a beer, then placed a pistol in with the bottles. "Pretending to be a rich idiot on a fishing trip. And watching all our asses."

Holt immediately got busy with the fishing gear, planting a piece of his own under the seat and in easy reach while he pulled out the ostentatiously large tackle boxes DeScalso had provided for them. He filled a bait bucket with water, and when Midas looked at him quizzically he explained, "Piraiba mainly strike live bait. We're gonna look like assholes if we're not prepped for them." An examination of the fishing gear met with grunts of approval, and he made sure multiple eight-foot rods were good to go with sixty–five-pound test line and circle hooks bound with wire.

"Hell of a complicated rig," Weaver noted, watching in spite of himself.

"Gonna need to add sinkers if we're going after the big boys," Holt replied. "Apparently all this crap keeps the piranhas off it."

"You say so." Weaver eased the throttle down. "Major, how are we doing?"

"Coming up on the border. Midas, you see anything?"

Midas scanned the river. "Nothing on the water. I can see the border station coming up to starboard."

"Slow and steady, Weaver," Nomad said. "Let's see how this goes."

As they got closer, more of the morning mist boiled off, and the station hove into view. It was an ugly two-story blockhouse, big enough for offices and barracks alike. An empty flagpole sat out front. Part of the beach had been paved in concrete, now cracking, and a series of riverine boats like the one the Ghosts were using were drawn up on shore. They looked old and had clearly seen hard use, and someone had done his level best to scrub away evidence of the Venezuelan flag on the paint. Nomad was pretty sure that even with four of them, even fully loaded, their boat could outrun anything he saw there, except that each boat also had a jury-rigged machine gun mounted at the prow.

There were lights on in the station, and as the boat approached the border, a figure in Venezuelan army fatigues came tumbling out of the front door, an AK-103 slung over his back. He began waving immediately, yelling at them in Spanish to pull in to shore.

"Major?" Weaver asked.

Nomad shifted in his seat, moving the beer to his left

hand. "Take us in, but not too close. Midas, you're up."

Midas nodded. Weaver gently changed the boat's direction, swinging them in a graceful arc toward the eastern shore.

The soldier had reached the river's edge by the time Weaver got them into shallow water. He was a short man with a round face and a bushy mustache and a nose that looked like someone had broken it for him several times. Every breath was a faint wheeze, and he had unslung his rifle as he'd advanced. "Who are you?" he demanded in Spanish. "Don't you know this is an international border crossing? You can't just come through here." He looked ready to boil over with indignation.

"I have to apologize for my friends." Midas stepped smoothly into the conversational breach. "They're from the States, they're down here to fish, and they don't know the rules. I'm taking care of them, but you know how those Americans are." He let his voice trail off, a little expression of camaraderie in the face of hopeless companions.

"Shit," the soldier said. "They know nothing. They just come down here with their dollars and think that will make everything all right. What are you fishing for?"

"Piraiba," Midas answered. "Peacock bass. Arapaima, if they can find it."

"Of course. The big fish and the fancy ones." The soldier scowled. "Illegal to catch arapaima, isn't it?"

"They know that," Midas said. "They don't care."

Knowing his cue, Nomad turned to Midas. "Hey, man, what's the hold up? We gotta get up river!" Midas looked at the soldier with a *see-what-I've-got-to-deal-with* expression, and the man nodded.

"How long are you stuck with them?" he asked.

"We have food for a week. Beer for three days."

"So three days?" He gave a humorless chuckle. "Okay, let me see one of their rigs," he said. Midas reached back and grabbed one of the poles. Holt protested, but Midas ignored him and handed the rod to the man onshore. The soldier took it and examined it with a professional's eye. "Hmm. A little worn, but good quality. Nice reel. Hasn't been used much. The line's a little light for piraiba, too heavy for bass. Your friend's going to catch nothing but piranha." He took a step back and waved them on. "Okay, you can go. Happy fishing."

"Hey, that's my rig!" Holt sputtered convincingly. Midas elbowed him perhaps slightly harder than necessary to sell the moment. "It's a show of respect. Let's get out of here." He looked at Nomad, who gave a small nod. Weaver said nothing, but steered the boat back out into the current. Behind them, they could see the soldier standing on the bank, making a couple of experimental casts into the current before turning and marching back inside.

They waited until the station was almost out of sight before anyone said a word. "Nice going, Midas," Nomad said, and raised the beer bottle in his direction before tucking it back into the cooler.

"Thank you, Major. It wasn't too hard. He didn't really want to stop us. Just wanted a little something for his trouble. It's the toll on river traffic."

"If he's got early morning duty, I'm guessing he doesn't get a lot of take," Weaver mused. "We still got enough rods back there?"

"Yeah, yeah." Holt sounded grumpy. "Five bucks says our buddy Oscar bills us for the damn thing."

"What do you care," Weaver needled him. "You heard the man. You weren't going to catch a damn thing anyway."

"You want some of that action? Twenty bucks says I catch more than you do."

"You win, because I'm not here to fish." He turned his attention to Nomad. "What's the plan?"

"According to Correa's map, we still have a ways to go upriver before we can pull in and start looking for an approach to the camp. We'll keep heading upriver, pull in when the satellite's overhead so we can check in with the Old Man, and then gear up."

Holt nodded. "We going to hit them tonight?"

"If we can. If not, you get to catch us dinner."

"Twenty bucks," Holt asserted to Weaver. "Just you wait."

CHAPTER 5

It was around noon when they pulled in at a low spot on the western bank, a beach that was more mud than sand and more water than either. Weaver and Nomad hopped out and pulled the boat out of the river while Holt started unpacking gear and Midas scouted the area. After a few minutes, he returned. "All clear. The underbrush isn't too thick. I'll clear us an area to gear up."

Nomad nodded. "Roger that. I'll call the Old Man. Weaver, keep an eye out for company. Holt, give Midas a hand, then grab something to eat."

"Roger that," Holt said, lugging a heavy box ostentatiously marked with the DeScalso logo and the silhouette of a leaping fish. "Give the colonel my love."

"I'll try to remember that," Nomad said dryly, pulling the comms rig, a lightweight Harris 117G, out of the boat and firing it up. "OVERLORD, this is BLUECAT. OVERLORD, do you copy?"

"Loud and clear, BLUECAT," came Mitchell's response. "Status?"

"In-country and upriver. Maybe halfway to optimal pull-in point. Oh, and you owe Oscar a rod and reel."

Mitchell's amusement came through loud and clear. "Do I even want to know?"

"Negative, sir."

"I didn't think so. How's the team?"

Nomad hesitated for a second, then answered. "All lights are green so far. Haven't seen action yet, so as of now, everything's frosty."

If Mitchell noticed the pause, he didn't say anything. "Good. No further intel on the targets. Was hoping for another proof of life, but I'll settle for no corpses. Anything else?"

"No, sir. Kudos to Captain Protasio's logistics officer. She's solid." Nomad thought for a minute. "Nothing else to report. Will check in tomorrow when we've got a bird overhead."

"Roger that, BLUECAT. I know it's hard down there, but keep your powder dry. The rest of your gear, too, while you're at it. They keep on making everything for desert ops and forget there's still a couple of places in the world where it rains."

Nomad chuckled. "Yes, sir. BLUECAT out."

He cut the connection, stowed the radio, and headed in off the river. A thick scrim of trees greeted him, but once he squeezed through he could see. Holt and Midas had already finished eating. Midas was halfway into his battle rattle—helmet, eyepiece, wrist comm unit in place—while Holt stood guard, scanning the jungle.

"Anything exciting out there?" Nomad asked.

"Negative. I'd like to keep it that way." He looked back at Nomad, who had started slipping into his jungle camo. "You sure it's a good idea kitting up now?"

"Yeah. We're too far in-country for the fishing trip act to hold any longer. Trouble comes, it's going to come in force, and I want to be ready for it. And I don't want to take the time to prep when we're on their doorstep."

"Understood. As long as we don't have to mess with any of Weaver's caimans, I'm good."

"Put your plates in and the caiman will break their teeth on you. All we've really got to worry about is snakes and bugs."

Holt groaned theatrically. "Why'd it have to be snakes?"

"You're disgracing a classic," Midas said, now kitted out. "Swap?"

"Gladly." Holt went over to one of the crates and started pulling out his gear.

"When you're done, relieve Weaver."

"Got it." The rest of Holt's answer was lost as he stuck

his head inside the crate, looking for something.

"Do you want me to throw out a sensor?" Midas asked as he walked up next to Nomad. "Make sure we're clear?"

The sensors weren't usual Ghost gear. Wizard had talked Holt into taking them along for a field test. In theory, when activated and tossed out like a grenade, they'd paint a friend-or-foe picture of everyone moving within their range on the Ghosts' HUDs. In practice, they'd been erratic when Holt had tested them on base, and neither he nor the rest of the team could afford to count on them.

"Negative. No sense wasting them. Besides, we're still not sure how well the damn things work. And keep the gear on minimum until it's go time. Correa was nice enough to pack us a JENNY and a power manager, so we can do a couple of rounds of recharges, but I don't want to risk running low on juice."

"Understood." He relaxed and watched the forest, rifle slung, machete held lightly against whatever the jungle offered.

It didn't offer much. Correa had been right; black-water jungles were less dense than their brown-water counterparts, though there were still plenty of patches of dense undergrowth. The sounds of life were everywhere, echoing down from the impenetrable green up above, but motion was limited to occasional explosions of color as some bird or other was startled out of cover and burst into flight. Off in the distance, a tapir snorted; a bunch of howler monkeys answered with scorn.

"Peaceful, isn't it?" Midas asked.

"I suppose," Nomad answered. "Not really my kind of thing. Too close. Sightlines are too short. Not enough convenience stores."

"I enjoy the quiet," Midas said, smiling, as something else set the monkeys off.

"You call this quiet?"

"It's a different sort of quiet."

Weaver tapped Nomad on the shoulder. "You're up, Major. Get something to eat and get into your jammies."

"Where's Holt?"

"Down by the river, watching the boat. I think he's fishing."

"Tell him we are not stashing a two–hundred-pound catfish in the boat."

"I don't think we have to worry about him catching one."

"Point." Nomad moved towards the gear. "All right. Let me do this, and let's get back on the river."

Holt had in fact caught several fish, all of them small, spiky, and inedible-looking. He'd tossed them all back by the time the team was ready to head back upriver. There was no more pretense. The fishing gear was packed away, and Weaver pushed the pace as fast as he dared.

"I think we're in good shape," Nomad said, taking another look at Correa's map. "We keep up this pace and—"

A loud crack of thunder drowned out what he was

going to say next. "God damn!" Holt shouted. "What the hell was that?"

Midas pointed upstream, where a wall of black clouds was boiling up behind them. Thick daggers of lightning cut through the clouds, followed closely by more explosive thunder.

"Where did that come from?" Weaver demanded.

"Storms blow up quick down here," Midas answered. "It's headed our way."

"Shit." Nomad could swear the clouds were visibly gaining on them. "Already. Weaver, bring us in to shore. We don't want to be sitting out here in a thunderstorm."

"Looking for a good place to bring us in," Weaver shouted over the rising wind. "Nothing on either side where we can put in!"

"Find something!" Nomad ordered, and then the rain was on them.

It hit the water with a sound like a thousand snare drums beating rapid time, sweeping up the river like a solid wall. The light changed from golden to gray to near nothing, the banks of the river vanishing. When the water hit exposed flesh, it hit so hard it stung, and the wind screamed along the channel.

Already there was an inch of water in the bottom of the boat, with more pouring in every second. Overhead, a bolt of lightning snaked upriver before burying itself in a tree at the river's edge. There was a sharp cracking noise, and the treetop exploded in flames and wooden shrapnel. A deafening peal of thunder rolled along the river, making it almost impossible to hear Weaver, but his actions were clear. Muttering a prayer under his breath, he gunned the engine and the boat surged into the rising flood of the main channel.

"Clear to starboard!" Holt reported, eyes just over the gunwale. The customs station might as well not have existed, so heavy was the curtain of rain blocking it from view.

"Visibility's maybe five meters! I can barely see the shore!" Midas chimed in from the other side.

"Not worried about the shore," was Weaver's reply, and then they were out in the middle of the river and everything was gray rain. Holt was already bailing, and after a minute, Midas joined him. Nomad squatted down in the prow, trying to stay low enough to avoid getting hit by lightning while keeping an eye out for river obstacles. A darker blob loomed on the water, faintly visible through the spray. "Got a tree trunk heading for us," he shouted. "Hard to starboard!"

"Hard starboard!" Weaver repeated, and flung the boat into a sharp turn. The river surge slapped up against the side, pushing toward capsizing even as a giant tangle of torn roots and trailing branches went sweeping past, then Weaver adjusted course and they were headed upriver again. There was another flash of lightning and the tortured groan of wood giving way, as another massive tree toppled into the river. "Hang tight!" Weaver yelled, his voice swallowed by the thunder, and then the trunk was caught in the current, barreling downstream at them. Weaver slammed the boat hard right. "Ahead!" Nomad yelled, but it was too late; the boat shuddered as a floating branch slammed into it, the impact pushing the vessel back toward the main channel. Up ahead, the roots of the toppled tree loomed large, clawed fingers scrabbling at the rain as it careened downriver.

"We're not gonna make it!" Holt bellowed.

"Trust me!" Weaver yelled back, and cut the engine.

The current seized them immediately, pulling them back downriver at speed. Just ahead, the massive tree trunk surged after them, its bulk seemingly blocking half the river as it spun in the current.

"What the hell? We're gonna go right past that checkpoint!"

"I said, trust me!"

And he slammed the throttle forward again.

The roots of the tree surged up, closer and closer as the boat roared upriver. Nomad threw himself flat as they passed overhead, a few scraping the side of the boat as it pushed past. Then they were clear, the tree tumbling into invisibility behind them as Weaver pulled them close to the eastern riverbank.

"What the fuck?" Nomad turned and yelled. "How close were you going to cut that?"

Weaver beamed like a madman. "Leaves had more drag than the roots. I knew it would straighten out enough for us to get past . . . eventually."

"You're out of your mind! Just . . . take us upriver slow and don't pull any more stunts like that!"

"Yessir, next time I'll let us get sunk." Weaver bent to his work, a cheerful Charon on a rain-swollen Styx.

INTERLUDE - WEAVER

"This," said Coray Ward to himself, "is pointless."

The target was Salim al-Rahman, nicknamed the Salesman, a senior ISIS figure and a key man in the Islamic State's financial operations. Al-Rahman was the man who coordinated illicit money transfers to ISIS through thriving black markets in Turkey and Lebanon, and he also oversaw the underground trade in supposedly destroyed antiquities that kept the group's coffers brimming. It had been he who came up with the idea of destroying sites like Palmyra, the better to raise the price for the surviving artifacts—carefully gathered and catalogued beforehand—on the unscrupulous collector's market, and it was he who had carefully identified the dealers and auctioneers who would willingly trade in such items for a price. When not engaged in looting the past for profit, he oversaw the network of complex financial transactions between ISIS and its far-flung group of affiliates, making sure that the money was always flowing in the right direction.

He had not earned the notoriety of an Abu Salef or the battlefield legend of Abu Sulemein al-Nasser, but analysts agreed that he was one of the most dangerous members of ISIS, and that his activities netted the group hundreds of millions of dollars a year.

And now he was in Uzbekistan, and someone at the Pentagon thought that this would be the perfect opportunity to take him out.

One would think, Ward mused, that the Uzbek government would be more than happy to help dispose of The Salesman. An ISIS-affiliated *wilayat* had taken root in Uzbekistan, stubbornly resisting efforts by the country's largely disinterested military in rooting them out. But the Uzbek government's relationship with Washington had deteriorated of late, making drone operations or any sort of large-scale response impossible.

That meant boots on the ground. Quiet ones. Because, the analysts said, the odds of getting another crack at al-Rahman were minimal. If they didn't take him out now, they might not get another chance. And the impact of taking him off the board could be devastating.

"Or," Weaver muttered to himself, "they could just promote another guy who'd do the same damn thing."

He lay on a rocky outcropping overlooking a hastily constructed airstrip east of Tepar, his body occupying a shallow trench he'd dug out himself after arriving here two nights previously. SIGINT intercepts had suggested a three-day window when the target would be arriving along with a best guess at a destination, and then Weaver and his team had been on the move, dropped on the Kyrgyz side of the border and hoofing it through brutal terrain to reach the target zone. The rest of the squad was under cover, prepared to assist if things went bad, but Weaver was front and center, and all he could do was wait. He'd amused himself by calculating targeting solutions to every inch of the airfield and the surrounding area, but that had gotten old, fast. Now there was nothing to do but be patient.

He stretched and then tugged at the camo netting overlaying his Remington MSR to make sure there were no telltale reflections off the metal of the barrel. The weapon was painted matte black to avoid just such an occurrence, but Ward was a great believer in attention to detail. All it took was one paint chip to expose polished metal and he'd be made, and then the best thing that could happen would be scrubbing the mission.

The worst, well, he didn't feel like thinking about that.

"Weaver, this is Buccaneer, do you copy?" The voice of his squad leader came crackling in over his headset.

"I hear you, Buccaneer. What's up?"

"One, I'm pretty sure I just saw a scorpion the size of

a small dog walk past our position. Two, Ajax claims he's picking up chatter from a plane inbound on your position. Engine noise indicates civilian transport. It may be showtime."

"Roger that. Can you get eyes on the bird?"

"Will do. Bearing is one-six-niner . . . and we've got visual. It's a Cessna Caravan. No markings. Altitude is angels three, coming down rapidly. Cannot get a visual on the passenger."

"I hear you." Ahead of him, the runway shimmered in the morning heat. It was a mirage, there'd been no rain here for weeks, and the slightest breeze kicked up vast billowing puffs of orange dust.

Now he, too, could hear the plane, the high propeller whine cutting through the intermittent sound of the wind. Its approach to the runway was straight, which meant it would be traversing from his right to his left to touch down on the unpaved and absurdly short strip. A lone windsock hung at the end of it, its fitful attempts to flap in the breeze punctuated by long stretches of dangling against the post. An unpainted shack stood at the side of the runway, its windows caked with dust, and three vehicles sat beside it. One was a technical pickup with a gleaming .50 cal mounted in the back, while the other two were beaten-up Land Rovers in dust-covered white.

As he watched, a small group of men emerged from the building. The one in the middle of the group wore a gray business suit, incongruous in the surroundings, while the rest wore fatigues and sported AKs slung over their backs. The entire group stood, looking off into the distance toward the direction of the inbound plane.

"Buccaneer, this is Weaver. I've got eyes on the Salesman's welcoming party. I'm seeing four armed outside, an unknown number inside, and one VIP who I'm guessing is the reason for the meet."

"I hear you, Weaver. Can you get an image on the VIP?"

"Working on it," Weaver replied. He put his eye back to the EOTech Vudu 3.5x 18 scope, centering the image on the man in the suit. The scope itself had been jury-rigged by one of the geniuses back at Coronado for just such a circumstance. Somehow, he'd attached a small digital camera to the scope itself, allowing Weaver to take pictures of targets at multiple kilometer range. He could then upload the images to the rest of the squad, an invaluable asset on operations like this.

"Turn around, you beautiful bastard," he urged the man in the suit, but the man stubbornly refused to oblige. Bodyguards kept passing in front of him, ruining the shot, and the din of the approaching aircraft got louder. "Running out of time here," Weaver told himself, then steadied his breathing and waited . . .

. . . and the man in the gray suit turned, his expression faintly impatient, as Weaver got a quick series of three snapshots. "Buccaneer, this is Weaver. Uploading images now."

"Roger that. Receiving and patching them through on the satellite uplink. Maybe we got lucky and caught two fish today."

"But I only brought one bullet."

Buccaneer laughed, even as another voice broke in on the link. "This is Ajax. We have confirmation the target is on the flight. Repeat, chatter between the plane and the tower indicates the target is on board."

Weaver blew out a deep breath, slowly. "So that's the good news. The bad news is that the plane's coming in on a vector where I'm not set up for the shot. I'm going to have to wait for him to move to the vehicles, and even that's not going to be clean."

"Should have brought two bullets," Buccaneer replied. "Getting comeback on the images. HQ confirms your man in the suit is a British expat named Harris Abernathy. They call him 'al-Britani,' the Brit, and he's a dirty-money specialist with links to terrorist sponsors in Qatar. If he's meeting al-Rahman here, that means ISIS is going to be ramping Uzbekistan up as a theater. Alternatively, they're going to be moving some key people here from Raqqa cause the heat's been turned up in Syria."

"Well, goddamn. What does the brass want me to do about this? Take out Abernathy? Abort the mission? Keep on keeping on?" The buzzing of the plane was louder now, and Weaver glanced over to see a small single-engine aircraft crest the series of low ridges that bounded the western edge of the plain where the airfield was located, and start its descent.

"Brass are having themselves a slapfight over what to do. Until you hear otherwise, Weaver, the original op is still a go. I repeat, original op is still a go."

"Roger that." He hunkered back down and put his eye to the scope, scanning the makeshift parking lot for the best angle. The Salesman would almost certainly be riding in the back of one of the Range Rovers. He was an honored guest, and besides, he'd probably want to be talking business with his opposite number. Mentally, Weaver started ticking off the routes and doors the target wouldn't be using, finally settling for one path that would leave a shooting lane in the gap between building and vehicle. It wasn't much—at a brisk walking pace the target would only be in his field of fire for a couple of seconds—but that was what Weaver had trained for: Patience. Precision. And ultimately, results.

"Weaver." Buccaneer sounded exasperated. "Bigwigs can't decide on who's the bigger target, or if you should just switch to photo surveillance and bring back evidence of the meet."

"They wanted that, they could have sent a high-altitude UAV and saved the need for you to have scorpions crawling all over your jock."

"Preach it. But there has been no call to abort, so unless I hear differently, you are to hit the target, and only the target."

Weaver thought for a second. "So we're going to leave al-Britani free to go?"

"Until they tell us otherwise, that is correct."

"I find that outcome unsatisfactory."

"Orders, Weaver."

"I know, I know."

The plane was approaching the runway now, dropping

speed and coming in at a sharp angle. In seconds, they'd be on the ground, then the bodyguards would be hustling the target away and, as good as he was, Weaver knew the realistic odds of him pulling off the shot were low. There were too many variables and the window was tiny. He could do it—his ratings were off the charts—but it was still a gamble.

On the other hand, he knew exactly what path the plane was taking.

It was the longest of long shots, of course. Hitting a moving aircraft, even a slow-moving one, even one coming in for a landing and thus on an eminently predictable flight path, was tough enough. Hitting someone *inside* the aircraft, that was the sort of thing only madmen would try.

He'd heard Pepper, a sniper he'd done some training with, had brought down a Hind on an attack run, and had asked the man about it when he ran into him once in a bar. "First of all," Pepper said, "It was a truck, not a helo. Second, I was aiming for the engine block. Son of a bitch hit a pothole and I caught him in the neck instead."

What the hell . . . ?

"I'm taking the shot," Weaver heard himself saying.

"Come again, Weaver? They're not on the ground yet."

"I said, I'm taking the shot."

"What shot?"

And then he squeezed the trigger.

A thunderous boom rolled out, swallowed by the immensity of the plain below. The bullet smashed through the glass of the plane's cockpit and took the pilot just behind the ear. The man slumped forward, taking the stick with him, and the plane suddenly dove straight down.

The men on the ground were professionals. Two grabbed al-Britani and pulled him away from the airstrip, while the others dove for cover as the airplane hit with a sickening crunch of twisted metal and shattered glass. The nose plowed into the airstrip, digging a trench as the wreck drove forward, and then the back end of the plane tumbled over the front and it began sliding down the rest of the runway upside-down. A minute later, it shuddered to a stop right next to the hut that served as a tower. Small flames burst out along the now-jagged lines of the fuselage, and then the two unattached bodyguards were running for it, hoping to pull the Salesman out while the other two hustled al-Britani toward one of the Land Rovers.

Weaver waited until they were all in place—al-Rahman getting into a Land Rover, the two men pulling at the fractured door of the plane—before carefully sighting and firing another bullet into the plane's fuel tank.

It went up with a roar, sending flames skyward and pieces of burning metal raining down. One smashed the windshield of the Land Rover the Salesman was in, another hit a free-standing propane tank next to the shed. There was another explosion, and then another, and then there was just scorched metal and flame and dust and nothing moving on the ground at all.

"Weaver, what the hell did you just do?"

"I found a second bullet."

There was silence on the channel for a long moment, then Buccaneer broke back in. "Ajax, Golem, go down there and confirm the kills. Weaver, I sure as shit hope you brought at least three bullets so you can cover them. Once the kills are confirmed, rally at Hector-two-nine for evac."

"Roger that."

"And Weaver, when we get home, some army puke from Benning wants to talk to you. He wants to talk to you real bad." Buccaneer's tone was full of ominous threat, which Weaver failed to acknowledge.

"Let's not keep the man waiting, then. Ajax, Golem, pick it up."

CHAPTER 6

A half hour and a couple more close calls later, Midas spotted a place along the bank to pull in for the rest of the storm. Weaver steered the boat in under the thick cover of the riverine jungle canopy, keeping a sharp eye out for more flotsam that could put a permanent dent in their transportation.

Eventually the rain slackened, and then sunshine burst through and the jungle was transformed. The wet leaves were a vibrant, glistening emerald, while wisps of steam drifted out of the jungle to curl, smoke-like, on the still-raging river. In the distance, birdsong started up again, a final sign the deluge was over.

"River's going to keep rising for a while, Major. We might as well go now before it crests. Otherwise, who knows how long we'll be sitting here."

Nomad nodded. "Right. Take us back out, nice and easy. It gets rough, we pull back in. How far to our pull-in point?" Midas studied the GPS. "About fifteen klicks."

"It's a long way to walk," Holt countered.

Midas looked at him. "Seriously?"

Holt gave an exaggerated stretch. "Much better to be traveling in this kind of luxury." He patted the side of the boat while Midas rolled his eyes. Nomad suppressed a chuckle and looked away. "Let's get started. Weaver, let's go."

They pulled back into the river, its black waters stained with blooms of muddy brown. Gone was the placid, slow current of the morning. Now the river pushed back against them, trying to drive them downstream. Shrubs, branches, and the occasional tree trunk crashed past, but Weaver maneuvered around them with ease. "You know, this is going to eat up our fuel a lot faster than we planned." Weaver tapped the fuel gauge with one finger, just for emphasis.

Nomad shook his concern off. "We'll refuel back in Brazil. Just keep pushing."

"You're the boss. I'll just drive the big damn boat."

"I heard that," Nomad said, but he was smiling. "Holt,

you've got navigation duty."

"What's that mean?"

"Watch out for trees." Nomad clambered back toward the rear, while Holt took his place, sitting with predatory stillness at the prow, weapon at the ready. They cruised in silence for an hour, and then Holt held up his hand in warning.

"What the hell is that?" Using his weapon, Holt gestured upstream to where a section of the river appeared to be boiling. The water roiled and frothed, and bloody spray pulsed into the air.

Weaver eased back on the throttle. "Feeding frenzy. We don't want to get in the middle of that. Gonna just hold right here until whatever's out there gets itself flensed."

Holt leaned forward. "Gimme the binos." Wordlessly, Midas handed them over. Holt took them and scanned the disturbance up ahead.

"What have you got?"

Holt frowned, then passed the gear to Nomad. "Take a look for yourself."

Nomad lifted his shades, then peered through the binoculars. At first all he saw was the bloody froth, filled with silvery fish darting back and forth so fast they were little more than blurs in the reddened water. Then he adjusted focus and realized what the scavengers were devouring.

"That's a floater."

"Two, at least," Holt disagreed. "I don't like it. There's a whole lot of nothing since we crossed the border, and then suddenly we see this? At the very least, we ought to get a closer look at the bodies."

"GPS says there's no village within at least thirty klicks." Holt sounded disgusted. "Which leads to the obvious question: Where'd those bodies come from?"

"Real close by. The way those fish are going at them, there's no way they could have lasted long."

Nomad put the binos down. "Holt's right. This stinks. I know we can't get the bodies out of the water—"

"Not without losing a hand," Weaver added blithely.

"—but we need more to go on."

"I am *not* driving us into that," Weaver said.

"Don't need you to." Nomad stared out across the water. "Steer us in to shore, eastern side. I want us under cover of the canopy. Midas, keep an eye out for anything that might try dropping out of the branches. Holt. Do your thing."

"Roger that." With practiced ease, Holt pulled a quad-copter drone out of a waterproof bag. Matte black and sporting a .9 gigapixel camera, it leapt into the air and buzzed out over the choppy water. "Pushing you the feed," Holt said, and the image from the camera, muddy waves rolling past at high speed, popped into focus on Nomad's HUD.

"Got visual."

"Roger. Moving her into position. Gotta keep her low or one of the big fucking birds they've got around here will decide she's a snack." There was a soft shudder as the side of the raft bumped up against a massive tangle of tree roots that marked the riverside. Bright sunlight gave way to cool green shade as the forest canopy loomed over them. Midas leapt out onto the bank, weapon ready, and scanned the deep woods.

"Something's wrong," he announced. "Nothing's

moving back there."

"Hush." Holt was hunched over the controls of the drone, now zeroing in on the rapidly subsiding disturbance in the river. "Couple more feet and . . . we . . . are . . . there." An angry whine cut through the thick jungle air, the sound of the drone hovering at dangerously low altitude. On Nomad's HUD, the scene in the water came into focus. The bodies had been savagely worked over by scavengers, many of whom were still at it. Rags of clothing marked them where the ravenous fish hadn't gnawed it away, part of a t-shirt here, mostly undamaged denim from a pair of jeans there.

"Locals," Nomad said, and Holt nodded. "Guess there's a village around here after all."

"Probably. Let me see if I can get in a little closer . . . ." Holt cursed as a particularly energetic blast of foam surged up from the feeding frenzy and temporarily rendered the drone view a crimsoned blur. "There we go. There. There, you see it?"

As the image resolved, one of the torsos came into view, rolling over lazily in the water. Much of the meat was gone. But even where piranha and other scavengers had been at it, there was still unmistakable evidence of what had happened before. A line of bullet holes stitched across the body, plainly visible for a moment before the waters surged over it and it was lost to view beneath the spray.

"Those look like exit wounds to you?" Holt was all business as he brought the drone back into the boat.

Nomad nodded. "Yeah. Which means at least one of them was caught by surprise."

"Or running away."

"Or running away." They paused for a moment to consider the implications while the drone settled back down into the craft ahead of where Holt sat cross-legged. "Good girl," he said, wiping it down with a microfiber cloth. "Don't want any of that nasty-ass river mud on your lenses, no ma'am."

Nomad and Weaver shot each other a glance, with one of Weaver's eyebrows slowly going up. "Permission to speak?"

Nomad nodded.

"Something bad's going down around here. But our mission's upriver. The people we've got to rescue, they're a long way from here. This isn't our op, and if we get caught up in whatever's going down, then we put those other people, the ones we're supposed to be getting out, at risk. We can't get involved here."

Midas suddenly sniffed. "You all smell that?"

"Smoke?"

"Smoke."

"Shit."

Nomad frowned. "All right, Holt. Back onboard. We're pulling out before the fight finds us."

"Sir." Midas pointed into the deep woods. "I think it already has."

They all heard it then, even as Midas ducked behind a fallen log covered in shelf fungus and creeping vines.

Footsteps. The sound of someone running for their life, crashing through vegetation as they went. And behind it, gunfire in three round bursts and the sounds of pursuit.

"Headed our way." Holt unlimbered his weapon with easy confidence and slithered onto the bank. "We run, we got nowhere to hide on the river."

"Get back in the damn boat! I can get us out of here!"

Nomad looked from river to forest and back again. Holt was right, there was no cover on the river, and if they pulled out now, there was every chance they'd be spotted and drawn into a running gun battle along the banks. On the other hand, if they stayed put, they were signing up for a slugfest against an unknown enemy force on bad terrain, on behalf of locals who might not be friendlies.

A bad call was the best call.

"All right. If we're gonna do this, we're gonna do it right. Holt, move left and find some cover. Midas, flank right. Weaver, you've got our backs. Hunker down, don't let yourself be seen, line up a shot but don't take it unless I give the word or whoever's out there starts shooting first. We still don't know what's going on." He clambered onto the riverbank, Holt jumping lightly ahead of him before disappearing into the underbrush.

"Weaver?"

"Right behind you."

The comm link crackled. "In position," Holt said.

"Roger that. Midas?"

"Good to go."

Nomad spotted a fallen log overgrown with greenery and slithered behind it. The soil was soft, and he dug down a bit, maximizing the cover of the wood behind the curtain of vines. His weapon he rested on top of the trunk, trusting the leaves to conceal the telltale gleam of gunmetal. Shooting over the top was risky, but there was too much undergrowth to line up a clear shot if he were setting up prone.

He took a deep breath, calming himself. Anywhere he went, the moment before combat was always the worst part. Once the bullets started flying, there was just reaction, a calm space where his body knew what to do and his mind worked with what was in front of it. Before the first shot, though, there was too much possibility, too many chances to overthink or to talk himself into the idea he'd made a mistake.

This was his first firefight where he was in charge. If things went south, it would be on him. His decisions. His mistakes.

Most of him hoped the runner would turn around and his people wouldn't have to engage.

The rest of him just wanted to squeeze the trigger and end the wait.

"You good, Nomad?" That was Weaver, friendship and support showing through his brusque tone.

He thought about it for a second. "Yeah. Let's do this."

And then the first man burst into view, eyes wide with terror. He wore a sweat-soaked navy t-shirt that read "New England Patriots—Super Bowl XLII Champions," torn here and there from the brambles he had run through, and he kept looking back over his shoulder as he ran. He ran blindly, not sticking to a given path but instead blundering through whatever foliage lay in front of him in his mad dash toward the riverbank.

Nomad spoke first. "One of the locals; hold your fire."

"Roger that," Holt muttered. "Guy's scared as hell."

Midas's reply was succinct. "Who's he running from that's gonna scare him this bad on his home turf?"

"Better question. You realize he's headed straight for us?"

And it was true: The man's zig-zagging path was bringing him closer to the water, but in a way that he was likely to hit the bank halfway between Holt and Midas.

"Shit. He's gonna bring whoever's chasing him right down our throats." Weaver sounded resigned. "I knew I shoulda pulled in on the west side."

"Little late for that now." Nomad propped his gun on top of the log and motioned to Holt to head to the cover of a large tree to his left. "Fire on my mark. Whoever's coming, we want to drop them all at once. Nobody gets off a warning, nobody gets away." A chorus of "Roger that"s echoed in his ear. "And Midas, the local's your responsibility. Get him safe but keep him quiet. Doesn't do us any good to shut down the pursuit if he gives us away."

"Copy that." Midas sounded grim. "Moving into position."

The man was closer now, drops of sweat flying everywhere as he ran. Behind him, staccato barks of gunfire could be heard, and bullets whined harmlessly through the trees. One clipped a leaf off one of the branches overhanging the river, and it drifted down to land next to Weaver in the boat.

"They're lousy shots."

Nomad shook his head. "They're driving him toward the river. Don't care if they hit him or not. He's dead either way."

"Unless someone comes along to rescue him." Holt's tone was flat.

"Well, yeah, what are the odds of that?"

The man had nearly reached the fallen tree trunk Midas was using for cover. He reached for it, but his foot caught on a creeping vine and he fell.

Before the man hit the ground, Midas had him, one arm under his shoulder. His eyes widened as he stared into Midas's face. "Shhh," Midas hissed, and clamped a hand over his captive's mouth as he lowered him to the ground. In Spanish, he continued, "We are friends. Stay down and don't make a sound."

Before the man could respond, his pursuers burst into view. There were three of them, laughing and joking as they advanced. Two of them carried the standard issue AK-103s, while the one in the center, apparently an officer, carried only a large pistol. Every few steps one of the flankers would raise his weapon and fire off a short burst, while the other two made mocking catcalls.

On the ground, the fugitive's eyes bulged with fear and he squirmed frantically in Midas's grip. A quick look at the man showed blood on the back of his leg where he'd been hit multiple times. How he'd managed to run so far was a mystery, but Midas could see the wound was a bleeder.

"Drop them?" Weaver whispered.

"Not yet."

"They're stopping."

And they were, the officer in the middle holding up a hand to slow the other two. They turned to face him and he immediately began yelling in accented Spanish, "What do you mean we lost him? Where the hell could he have gone?"

Just turn around, Nomad said to himself. *Just turn around and walk away* . . . .

The bigger of the two men with an AK, a hulking, muscular figure with a shaved head and a ferocious mustache to make up for it, gave as good as he got. "Use your fucking eyes if you're so smart, you were with us the whole time."

The officer's face turned purple. "You'll obey orders, you disobedient son of a bitch, or I'll—"

"Or you'll what? Court-martial me? Piss off, we're in the jungle!"

"Pick your targets," Nomad breathed.

"Got a shot on the one on the left." That was Holt.

Weaver: "Got me a shot on the one on the center. Right's yours, Nomad."

"Not yet. Too much foliage in the way. Let them get a little closer."

"Nomad!"

"Read you. What's the situation?"

"Our local's been hit. Bullet in the calf, another one in the thigh, looks like he's bleeding pretty good. We don't do something quick, he'll bleed out."

"Can you knock him out until we take care of business?"

"Not in his condition."

"Shit." Nomad lined up his shot. The man on the left, the giant, was clearly unconcerned with the possibility of opposition. He'd slung his weapon over his back and was arguing, complete with aggravated hand gestures, with the officer. The one on the right, meanwhile, pressed ahead oh-so-cautiously, weapon ready as he followed the trail of broken foliage the runner had left behind.

"Tango three's headed your way, Midas. Can you take him?"

"Negative, Nomad. Got my hands full with the local. Good news is, we rolled under the tree trunk so we got that between us and them. Bad news is that it's not much of a tree."

"Copy that." *Turn around,* he thought hard at the lone man stomping his way through the jungle while his friends argued. *Just go back to base and forget the whole thing and—*

From behind the downed tree, there was a short, startled yell. The arguing soldiers froze, then turned and brought up their weapons. The man on the right gave a yell of triumph and started charging forward, spraying bullets indiscriminately. Clouds of splinters exploded into the air.

"Midas?"

"Local banged his leg. Couldn't stop him. Keeping him low."

"Roger that. Right. Everyone, on my mark!"

The lead enemy soldier jumped up on the fallen log. "Got you!" he shouted, and then his face crumpled into a mask of surprise as he realized Midas was with his quarry. He moved to raise his weapon, but as he did so, a single shot rang out. The bullet entered underneath his chin and he fell backwards, convulsing wildly.

"Marco!" the officer called.

"God damn it, fire!"

Two more weapons barked as one and the remaining men dropped in unison.

"All targets down!"

"Midas, status on the civilian?"

Midas's response was terse. "Stabilizing him now. He's losing blood. Could use a hand."

"Roger that. Weaver, you've got—"

And then four more hostiles burst into view. A quick look at their downed comrades told them all they needed to about the situation, and then they opened fire.

"Shit! Down!" Weaver dropped as a hail of bullets ripped through the space where he'd been. More bullets shredded the vines over Nomad's position, while the gunmen retreated to cover.

"Midas! Stay with the civilian and do what you can! We've got this!" Nomad squeezed off a round over the top of the log, driving the hostiles back for a moment. As soon as he fired, Holt was on the move, worming his way along the edge of the river. One of the Amazonas soldiers popped out from behind a tree to open up on Nomad's position, causing explosions of sawdust and splinters as his rounds smacked into the log. Before he could pull himself back behind cover, a single round caught him in the shoulder. He cried out as the impact spun him around, then took another bullet square in the middle of the back. With his AK falling from nerveless fingers, he dropped to the jungle floor.

"I always bring two bullets," Weaver said. "Where's the other three?"

"One to the left of the path, two to the right. I'm closing on the lone target." Holt paused. "Any chance you can buy me a distraction?"

"We'll get their attention," Nomad promised, then squeezed off another burst. "Just let me know when you're in position, then watch out for my banger."

"You're gonna throw a flashbang? Are you nuts? You're gonna set the whole damn jungle on fire!" Weaver was incredulous.

"It just fucking rained! Banger on my mark!"

"Roger that."

More bullets slammed into the tree, the last of which produced a solid cracking noise. Time to move, Nomad decided. He squeezed off another burst, then crawled right.

"One of them's on the move," Weaver called out. "Midas, he's headed your way."

"Don't see him. Can you keep him off me?"

"Roger that." Weaver uncoiled from behind a tree stump half his height and fired. The ground exploded at the soldier's feet and he hastily dove for cover. Another shot sent him scurrying back the way he came, then Weaver had to drop as another spray of suppressive fire raked his position. "How's it going, Holt?"

"Almost there." He looked up and saw the enemy

soldier at the same moment the man saw him. Too late, the rebel brought his rifle to bear. In the time it took him to turn, Holt had put three rounds into his chest. "Now!" Holt yelled.

"Banger! Get down!" A single grenade soared from Weaver's position as Holt and Nomad flung themselves into the dirt. The two remaining soldiers shouted in alarm, and then with a scream, the world went white.

One of the two rolled away from behind the stumps he'd been using for cover, rubbing his eyes. Nomad dropped him with a single shot.

The other ran.

"Shit. Must have been looking the other way." Nomad glanced left, then right. "Weaver, get to Midas. Holt, he's yours."

"You say the nicest things, Major." And then Holt was flying after the man, and then he was gone from sight.

INTERLUDE - MIDAS

In high school, Rubio Delgado remembered, they told you extracurriculars were a good thing. *Go out and do stuff besides study*, the guidance counselors said. *Make yourself a more attractive candidate for college admissions. Become a more well-rounded person.*

In the army, though, things were a little different. Extracurriculars were frowned on. You stayed within the lines, you didn't do anything to stand out, and you especially didn't do anything they didn't tell you to do.

So what, he wondered, was he supposed to think about his current activity, definitely extracurricular and way outside the lines, but also a chance to do some real good in the world. Was it the right thing to do? Should he even be here? One thing was for certain, there was no way in hell this was going to help him get into a better college.

He turned and looked out the window. Orange-reddish dirt and rocks on the left, orange-reddish dirt and rocks on the right, and ahead and behind was a dusty two-lane track that pretended to be a highway. Overhead, the sun was an angry white eye staring down at the little two-car convoy, daring them to break down out here far from help or shelter.

Delgado adjusted his keffiyeh and checked, for the thirtieth time this trip, the safety on the shotgun in his lap. The Serbu Super-Shorty wasn't exactly a regulation weapon, but this wasn't a regulation op. He sat in the passenger seat of the second car in the convoy, a beaten-up white Toyota Land Cruiser that the driver, a cheerful Kurd named Hari, had insisted on calling a "Wanawsha." Another one, still showing the remnants of a light-blue paint job that suggested it had been liberated from UN forces, led them by a few hundred yards. Both vehicles had forged license plates, and each carried precious cargo: Yezidi women and children kidnapped by ISIS and forced into servitude. The operation was part of an ongoing attempt, funded by Yezidi expats in Europe, to liberate them from their captors and get them to safety in Kurdistan.

The job was dirty and dangerous, and the men and women behind the operation understood that. Most of the men they'd hired to run the exfil ops were hard-bitten smugglers, many of whom charged the desperate escapees every dinar they had. But the alternative was worse, so they paid.

Delgado had refused any money to be a part of this. He'd been approached a week prior about doing a ride along, providing protection and muscle for an op taking two families out of Mosul, he'd volunteered instantly.

He turned to Hari, whose unflappable, cheerful pessimism had informed the entire trip, and asked, "How much farther till we cross the border?"

Hari shrugged. "Don't know. Depends on what kind of day the ISIS sons of bitches are having. If we're lucky, we cross soon. If we're not, then maybe another hour. Or, we could hit an IED and get blown up and then we'll never get there, *inshallah*." He took a moment to fiddle with the rearview mirror. "You should fasten your seat belt," he added. "It's much safer."

Instead, Delgado twisted in his seat to face the passengers in the back. A woman in her late twenties with two small children huddled up against her stared back at him. She had removed the veil she'd been wearing when they'd rendezvoused for the pickup, but still wore a black abbaya and hijab. The two children, both boys, sucked ferociously on juice boxes Delgado had handed them when they'd gotten in the car. Neither had said a word the entire time.

"We'll be there soon," Delgado said, only to be met with silence.

"She doesn't speak English, you know," said Hari

cheerfully. "Kurdish, Arabic, Farsi—she's a very smart woman. She was a teacher before ISIS, you know."

Delgado sighed. "Can you tell her we're almost there, and that she and her kids will be safe?"

Hari shot him a look. "You want me to lie to her?" Then, "Oh, shit."

Up ahead, the first car was slowing down. The reason was obvious: a group of ISIS soldiers standing behind a makeshift checkpoint composed of sandbags and salvage. One stood in the middle of the road, arms waving in clear instructions for the vehicles to stop.

"Hari?"

"Don't ask me. This wasn't here last time."

"What is the first car doing?"

In response, Hari tapped his cell phone and started speaking rapidly in Kurdish. The answers came back just as quickly. "They're going to stop. They don't have a choice. And if we're lucky, they'll take bribes. If we're not . . . ." His voice trailed off.

In the back seat, the woman had already replaced her veil. The tension in her body was unmistakable. She met Delgado's eyes for a moment, and then shook her head slightly. She wasn't going back.

Delgado turned to Hari. "All right. If things go south, here's what you do: gun it. Don't look back, don't slow down, just go. Tell the lead car that, and tell the woman in back to get down and cover her kids."

Hari stared at him. "You're insane. Are you trying to get us killed?"

"No. Maybe just me. Now tell them."

"It's your funeral." But he uttered a few short sentences to the woman in the back, who responded by holding her children closely. There was some energetic back and forth with the other car, and then the conversation was cut off abruptly as one of the checkpoint soldiers strode up to the driver's side window and began hammering on it. Behind him, one of the others leveled a dusty AK at the driver, while two more soldiers began the walk back to where Hari's car sat, idling in the dust.

"Let me talk first," Hari said softly. "There's a chance we can get out of this without anyone getting hurt."

Delgado nodded, then quietly thumbed the safety off on the Super-Shorty.

One of the soldiers walked up to the car and knocked on the window. For emphasis, the second soldier cocked his weapon.

Carefully, Hari rolled down the window. "Where are you going?" the soldier asked in heavily accented Arabic.

"My cousin and I are taking my sister to visit family. Our mother is unwell and wished to see her only daughter."

The man scanned the back seat, decided he approved of what he saw, and then turned to Delgado. "Your cousin. Where is he from?"

"Batnay. He thought it would be best if he came with us, as the roads are dangerous."

"And what does he do there? Let him answer for himself."

Hari turned to face him, desperation in his eyes. Delgado did not speak Arabic or Kurdish, and Hari knew it.

"I serve under al-Hamduli," Delgado said in Arabic, keeping his eyes firmly forward.

Hari bit his tongue. The soldier at the window blinked in surprise, then smiled and turned to Hari. "You must be a strong fighter. You are well protected here, my friend."

For a second, Hari said nothing, and then he stammered, "It is good of you to say so. He honors us by—"

The sound of a single gunshot exploded into the air. Both the ISIS soldiers and Hari turned toward the source of the sound, the first car in the convoy. One of the soldiers there was standing next to the driver's side window, weapon raised. The rear window was spattered with blood.

Hari's eyes widened in horror as the soldiers near the second car began to turn back towards him, their weapons raised.

Delgado acted first. Raising the AOW in his lap, he squeezed off two shots. The first took the man nearest the car full in the chest. He tumbled backwards, arms flailing wildly. The second caught the second soldier in the right shoulder, spinning him around. He cried out with the impact and dropped his weapon. "Just go," he shouted, and threw himself backwards out the door.

Delgado hit the ground and rolled as the car swerved right off the road and accelerated, spewing a massive cloud of dust. The first car's horn started blaring as the driver collapsed onto the steering wheel, while the first two soldiers tried to figure out where to look: at their downed allies, at the escaping car, or at the man rising up out of the dust at them.

Delgado slammed himself against the side of the stationary car, then ducked as bullets ripped through the car's windows, sending broken glass everywhere. He could hear screaming from inside the car and he prayed for an instant that none of the passengers had been hit. Then he dropped down even lower and squeezed off a round underneath the car's chassis.

One left, he told himself. Here's hoping this one counted.

The shot took out the shooter next to the car at the ankles. He shrieked, then toppled over backwards, still firing. The second man, cursing, threw himself on the ground to dodge the spray, and Delgado took advantage of the opening. He dodged around the hood of the car, firing as he went. The shot went wide, but it kept the man down and scrambling as Delgado came around the far side of the vehicle. Letting go of the Super-Shorty, he reached down and snagged the dying man's AK. A line of bullets stitched along the ground toward him as the downed man frantically fired. Delgado threw himself to the right just in time and returned fire. The AK barked three times in rapid succession, and then the man on the ground slumped again.

Delgado let himself exhale, then checked each of the downed men. Two were dead, and two were bleeding and unconscious.

He walked over to the remaining vehicle. The driver was slouched in the front seat, his face a bloody ruin. Blood was spattered everywhere: on the windows, the seats, the floor, and the passengers in the back. There were two of them, a woman and a child, and when he looked into the vehicle through the shattered window, they simply stared at him. Bullets had stitched through all of the vehicle's windows and several of the doors. There was a bright smell of burned plastic in the car, mixed with fresh blood and smoke, and broken glass was everywhere. A bullet had caught the driver's dash-mounted cell phone and punched right through the center of it. It still sat there, weirdly poignant evidence of the carnage that had passed too close.

"I'm not going to hurt you," Delgado said softly. He let the AK drop and raised his open hands. "I don't know if you can understand me, but I'm here to help."

The child—a girl, he saw now—burrowed into her mother's side. The woman kept staring at him.

Outside, the radio at the hip of one of the dead men crackled, a voice calling out for a response that was never going to come. In the distance, Delgado could see the rooster tail left by Hari's car, long gone and with no way to make contact.

The radio squawked again, more urgently this time. Soon, Delgado knew, they'd get tired of not getting responses and come looking. If he and the passengers were still there when that happened, nothing would save them.

There was only one thing to do.

He reached into the car and popped the trunk. Somehow, miraculously, it still worked.

Moving quickly, he scoured the scene of the fight. The enemy's brass, he left on the hard-packed dirt.

His own shells, he picked up. Let those who found the bodies wonder what had happened here. The remaining firearms, he picked up and threw in the front seat on the passenger side, so that there would be fewer pieces for ISIS to work with when they found the bodies. One of the dying men had already bled out by the time he got to him. The other, he decided, might make it with medical attention. He looked back at the car and thought about the mercy that had been shown the driver, about the mercy that would have been shown the woman in the back. About the very thin line between self-defense and retribution.

Then he knelt and bandaged the man's shoulder as best he could, and picked him up in a fireman's carry. The man moaned, but Delgado ignored him. Mercy had its limits. Then he put the man in the trunk and shut the lid. A harsh way to travel, perhaps, but he wasn't going to put the man in the car, and it beat a slow death under a hot sun.

Resolved, he went back to the driver's seat. The dead man was still there, a big guy with an unruly beard and a face that looked like it had once had laugh lines.

"I'm not going to leave him here," Delgado said, knowing his words weren't understood, hoping the tone made all the difference, hoping the woman had seen what he had done and understood what he was trying to do for them now.

As gently as he could, he moved the dead man's body over to the passenger seat, awkwardly arranging him around the piled weapons. He wasn't going to leave the man here for enemies to find and vultures to feed on. Maybe Hari's people could get him back home to his family for burial. Maybe someone who knew his name could find them.

The driver's seat was sticky with drying blood when Delgado slid into it. He could feel it slowly seeping through his shirt and pants and onto his skin. The steering wheel was wet, as well. He ignored it. The key was still in the ignition, the motor idling noisily. It was a small favor, he decided, a note of benediction for what he had done. Quietly, he recited a small prayer of thanks, then put the car in gear. It leapt forward, as eager as he was to be out of that place and away from the carnage he'd helped create.

Only once they were underway did the little girl start crying.

Much later, Hari asked him how he had known what to say in that moment. Delgado looked away. "That was what one of the prisoners we brought in would say when we would interrogate him. It was the only thing he would say. The translator told me it was his unit designation, and a badge of honor."

"Interrogate?"

"Not like that," Delgado said. "Not while I was there. I . . . objected when the man from the CIA arrived to take over. I was suspended from duty, which is what allowed me to ride with you that day. God moves in mysterious ways."

"God is great," Hari responded. *"Allahu akbar."* The two men sat there, drinking coffee in a quiet shop in Duhok, sitting for a moment in companionable silence.

Eventually, Hari finished his cup and set it down. "You are going home?"

"Back to the United States. Not home. There's a man who wants to speak to me. He finds what I did interesting. And perhaps admirable. Or, at least, useful."

"Those are very different, very dangerous words, my friend. Take care of yourself."

"I will." Delgado rose to leave and tossed some money on the table. "The women and children, they are . . . ."

"As well as can be hoped, considering. Sabeen and her children are on their way to Hungary. They have a patron there, a Yezidi man who is wealthy and sponsoring as many refugees as he can. Amira and her daughter, Sanaa, they are in Kirkuk. They have family there, other refugees, but at least they are together."

"And the man I brought in?"

"Died on the operating table. Or so they tell me."

"Ah."

"It was a generous and merciful thought. You will be rewarded for it, I am sure."

"That makes one of us who thinks that, perhaps. Goodbye, Hari."

"Goodbye."

When Delgado had left, Hari ordered another cup of coffee and wondered how long it would take to get the first car repaired. There were so many others still waiting for a way out, with or without the strange American.

CHAPTER 7

The path wasn't a path, just a rough slash torn through the jungle by a fleeing man and his pursuers. Now the pursuit ran the other way, and the hunter had become the hunted.

The soldier had a good twenty-yard head start on Holt, but the zig-zag nature of his route, combined with the rough terrain, made it hard for him to sprint all out. Holt, on the other hand, had no such issues, running surefooted over the damp jungle floor.

"Holt! You got him?" Nomad's voice crackled in his ear.

"Working on it!" He skidded around a bend and was nearly cut in half by a burst of automatic fire.

"Shit!" Holt let his momentum carry him off the trail and into the deeper undergrowth as the bullets stitched into the greenery behind him. There was a final burst, and then the sound of footsteps rapidly receding.

"Idiot," Holt cursed himself under his breath as he rolled to his feet and resumed pursuit, trading a handful of speed for caution. "Should have expected him to try an ambush."

He'd probably try it again, too, Holt decided. Only dumb luck had saved him the first time; no way was he going to let this guy have another shot.

For an instant, he stopped. The sound of the fleeing soldier crashing through the undergrowth was clearly audible, ahead and to the left. "Gotcha," Holt said, and then abandoned the path for the jungle.

And if there's one thing Mama Moretta's boy knew how to do, it was run in the woods.

Truth be told, he decided, there wasn't too much difference between here and the cypress swamps he'd done runners through growing up. The ground was a little more stable, the vegetation a little different, but the principle was the same: Keep moving, watch where your feet land, slide through the green instead of running straight up against it. Up ahead, he heard another burst of fire, his prey firing blindly at an unseen pursuer. Holt smiled. *Good. Let him slow himself down.* He jumped a small creek, the splash of the rivulet hiding the sound of his landing, and kept running. The sounds of the soldier were getting close now, his labored breathing audible even through the green and the heavy damp air. Another pause, another burst, and then a curse. He started running again, his footsteps more ragged, his pace slower.

And Holt ran past him.

There was another sound now, a confused hubbub. Yelling, screaming, the crackle of flames and the pop of small arms fire. That would be the village, Holt decided, and if the runner made it that far, things might get a little sticky.

Not going to happen.

Holt slowed for half a second, then shifted direction toward where he guessed the path would be. A curtain of green rose up in front of him, and he crashed through it, wishing for an instant that he had Midas's machete. Then he was through and on the path, and the footsteps were headed his way. Holt could almost see him now, weary, stumbling, out of breath. He slowed, fired one last burst behind him, and then came round the bend to where Holt was waiting.

The man's eyes widened in panic. He scrambled to bring up his weapon, almost falling backwards as he did so, and opened his mouth to call for help.

Holt dropped him with three to the chest. The yell became a sigh as he sank to the ground.

Holt didn't wait for him to hit the path before he was moving. A couple of steps, and he was at the dead man's side, kicking his weapon off the trail into the forest and then grabbing hold of the corpse to do the same. If help was coming, there wouldn't be anything in the path to warn them.

Besides, Holt had learned long ago that a suddenly missing comrade was a hell of a lot more unnerving for a patrolling soldier than a visibly dead one.

He pulled the body well off the path, far enough away and behind sufficient vegetation that only a concerted search was going to find him.

"Holt." Nomad's voice broke in again. "You got the runner?"

"Roger that. Looked like he was trying to call for help. Might be some more Tangos in the village. I'm hearing what sounds like combat. Can't be more than a half a klick from where I'm standing."

"Recon. Do not engage unless fired on. Weaver is headed your way."

Holt grinned faintly. "Tell him to hurry or I'm not going to leave him anything."

Nomad sounded like he failed to see the humor in the situation. "You've got your orders, Holt. Go see what's shaking and call it in, but I don't want you taking on a whole village full of hostiles solo."

"Oh ye of little faith. The civilian make it?"

There was a pause. "Working on it. Still touch and go."

"Gotcha. Holt out."

He turned to the dead man and nodded, a farewell gesture to a fellow soldier, then started loping toward the village.

The jungle thinned out quickly as Holt approached, and he was able to see the village. There were maybe a dozen loosely arranged houses, one of which was burning fiercely. On the far side of the clearing, a deep gouge in the earth indicated a side channel that no doubt drained into the Rio Negro, and series of manioc fields stretched off away from the direction of the river. A single road, more of a rutted dirt track really, led across the creek on a rough bridge and into the jungle. Holt could see a battered old Toyota pickup sitting in the middle of the square, guarded by a pair of very nervous-looking soldiers. The villagers were gathered in a loose knot about ten meters from the two guards, and only the guns the men held were holding them back. A couple of villagers were down, Holt saw now. Bullet wounds or blunt trauma, and their neighbors crouched over them to try to help them.

"Holt, this is Weaver. Inbound on your position. Do not start the fun before I get there, you copy?"

Holt looked back at the jungle. No telling how long it would take Weaver to cover the ground, no telling how quickly things might go south.

"Can't promise that, Weaver. Better move." He dropped to one knee and sighted his rifle on the soldier on the left. The crowd was getting restive, the scents of blood and smoke in the air. The other soldier shouted something indistinct at them, and they didn't react well. The murmur of discontent got louder, and the crowd edged forward. The soldiers took a step back toward the cab of the truck. The one on the right raised his weapon, swinging it back and forth wildly as the villagers pressed in.

Holt risked a quick glance over his shoulder. "Weaver, you'd better hurry." Before he could look back, the crack of gunfire split the air.

"Holt! Status!"

Holt turned back to the village, finger on the trigger. The soldier on the right, the jumpy one, had fired a burst into the air as a warning. It didn't seem to be working. The crowd was still edging forward. One of the women cradling a body on the ground was weeping, and her grief had fed the villagers' anger.

One word, one gesture, and all hell could break loose. Holt figured he could only drop one of them before the bullets started flying and the bodies went down in heaps.

"Situation's fragile, nobody's down yet. Got two armed hostiles and a truck, and a whole lot of angry locals closing in on them."

The soldiers took another step back. They were scared, eyes wide enough that Holt could see it from where he crouched. One of them bumped up against the back of the truck. His comrade turned to him and barked something. The other man nodded and started edging toward the cab.

He reached the driver's side door and swung it open, then emptied another burst into the trees. That was the signal for the second man to start moving toward the cab. Clearly, they weren't going to wait around for their buddies who'd gone running into the bush and hadn't come back.

Which was a whole different kind of problem.

"Come on, Weaver, pick it up." Holt whispered. The second soldier reached the cab and pulled the door open, then gestured to his friend. He climbed in, and the truck roared to life, belching a cloud of thick, black smoke.

Someone in the crowd coughed and stumbled onward.

And that was all it took.

Holt could see the gun coming up, could see the squeeze on the trigger start to happen, and he fired.

The single shot took the soldier right under the ear. He spun and dropped, his rifle barking angrily into the air as his fingers spasmed in death.

The villagers scattered. Some threw themselves to the ground, others broke left or right or covered up the wounded. The other soldier slammed his door shut and jammed his foot down on the gas. Plumes of muddy dirt spewed into the air as the tires grabbed for traction, and then the truck was moving, clipping a man who'd gotten too close and sending him spinning. Holt squeezed off a couple more shots. They smacked into the side of the truck with a series of metallic thumps as the soldier slewed the wheel left, putting some of the stumbling villagers between himself and Holt.

Holt burst out of the woods at a dead run. Some of the villagers saw him and started shouting, afraid of the new stranger with a gun. Holt ignored them. All that mattered was getting clear of the civilians so he could get a shot at the driver before the truck could get away.

A house loomed in front of him and he cut left, sprinting around the corner. The truck's engine roared from the other side, an unfair advantage in the race. Up ahead, Holt could see part of the opening where the road dove into the jungle, not enough for him to have a good angle. He shifted direction, rifle cradled against his chest.

And the truck came barreling around the corner. It skidded, digging deep furrows in the mud, then leapt forward straight at Holt.

There was no time to get out of the way. He raised his weapon and started firing, first at the tires and then at the cab. The driver ducked down as glass shattered all around him; the vehicle kept coming. It veered sharply left, then right, running on rims as the shredded tires tore away. Bullet holes crawled their way up the hood and into the cab; steam and upholstery exploding in equal measure, but still it plowed forward.

Holt squeezed off one last round and then braced himself for impact.

From the jungle, another shot boomed out. There was a brief fountain of red from behind the wheel, and then the truck swerved right. Holt threw himself out of the way just in time, and then the truck plowed into a tree with a terrible crunch.

"You okay, Holt?" Weaver's tone suggested he damn well knew the answer. "Sorry I took so long."

"Fuck you, too." Holt picked himself up and started dusting himself off. "Keep covering me. Don't know if the locals realize we're friendlies yet." And the crowd was already drifting toward him.

Weaver's voice was calm in his ear. "Gun down, hands up. Show 'em you're not a threat."

"You sure this is a good idea?" Slowly, Holt raised his hands, letting his weapon dangle. "I mean, you're covering me, right?"

"You bet your sweet ass I am. Now, smile."

Holt forced himself to smile. "Hey there. I'm a friend," he said, nodding and grinning as the locals got closer.

And then they flowed around him and rushed to the truck. It hadn't caught fire, at least not yet, but the front was pretty well wrapped around a tree, and what was left of the hood was bent and folded like rough terrain. The door still worked, though, and they pulled it open and dragged the dead man out. They laid him out, as if to make sure he was really dead, though the ruin Weaver's shot had made of his head attested that the job had been done thoroughly and fast.

Only after they were satisfied did they turn to Holt.

He took a step back. In English and then in Spanish, he tried, "Like I said, people, I'm a friend."

One of the men, balding and heavyset, pointed to the man on the ground, then at Holt, and responded in Spanish. "Soldier? You're an American? What are you doing here?"

Holt gave his best friendly smile. "The men who attacked your village, they've, uh, I'm here to do something about them. And . . . Midas? Help?"

In answer, there was a shout from across the village. Everyone turned as Midas stepped out of the brush, hands in the air, speaking rapid-fire Spanish. The man who'd been questioning Holt immediately trotted over to him for a brief, intense conversation, and then he turned and shouted some orders. A couple of the other men ran off into one of the houses, re-emerging a moment later with a bedsheet and a couple of knobby wooden poles. They paused long enough to build a makeshift stretcher out of the components, then set off into the jungle at a trot. The village elder watched them go. He turned back to Midas for another quick exchange, and then he gathered Midas into an embrace. The other villagers scattered, some seeing to the wounded, some rushing to the creek to form a bucket brigade to deal with the burning house.

Eventually, Midas broke free and walked over to where Holt was watching. "That's the chief of the village. He's named Erubiel, and he and his people are Baniwa. He says thank you for the help, and that he is happy to repay the favor."

"I can speak Spanish, and that is not exactly what he said. Half of it wasn't so friendly," Holt sputtered as Weaver laughed over comms.

Midas looked faintly embarrassed. "The man we helped out by the riverside is Erubiel's son. The chief is grateful but explaining what actually happened was a little tricky."

"I'll bet it was." Holt looked around. "So now what? Sooner or later, someone's going to realize that truck didn't come back to wherever it was going."

Nomad cut into the conversation, just as Weaver emerged from the trees. "Stretcher bearers just arrived, Midas. Thanks for sending them. Holt, I want you back here with me. We need to take care of the boat and hump the gear."

"You sure do like making me run."

Midas cut in. "We've got more wounded at the village. Requesting permission to assist."

There was a pause. "Granted. Weaver, you watch his back and keep an eye out in case more hostiles show up."

"Got it." The men separated, and Holt disappeared back under the trees.

Holt passed the stretcher bearers on the way back to Nomad's position. They didn't see him, as he was moving parallel to the trail and not on it. But he got a good look at the headman's son, thoroughly bandaged and pale, but alive. The bearers were clearly doing their best to make speed without jostling him.

Nomad was at the boat, blood on his sleeves and his pants. "Holt," he acknowledged. "Get the drone, get anything else you're going to need. Then we pull her up and make sure she's camoed from the river. "

"We're hoofing it to the hostages from here?"

"Yeah. We're close enough to the site, and the more I think about being out on the water, the less I like it. C'mon, let's move."

Together, they pulled Holt's drone out of the boat as well as supplies for a couple days' worth of hard travel over rough terrain, a couple of small toolkits with gear for dealing with various constraints hostages might be held with, and spare ammo.

Holt also took Correa's beer cooler.

"Really?"

"Running's thirsty work," Holt replied defensively. He pulled one beer out, then put the cooler back in the boat. "I'm not sharing," he said, and Nomad didn't push it.

With the gear out, they dragged the boat onto the bank as best they could and tied lines to the thickest trees they could find, insurance against another storm sweeping it away. With the craft secure, they draped it in camo netting, then Holt set to cutting branches while Nomad focused on loosely weaving them into place on top of the boat. By the time they were finished, both were sweating and tired; the sun was sinking low over the river; and the beer was long gone. But as long as no one looked too closely, the boat seemed like nothing more than another collection of waterside shrubs and detritus.

Work complete, they shouldered their packs and headed inland. For a while they traveled in silence, and then Holt couldn't contain himself.

"Major, gotta tell you, this is bad business."

Nomad looked at him. "Going on foot?"

Holt shook his head. "Naah. This whole thing with the locals. I mean, yeah, it was the right thing to do in the moment, but I'm not seeing a good ending here."

"Do tell."

"For one, we're slowed down, and that puts the hostages at risk. For another, we just—hang on." He darted off the path. When he came back, he was holding the weapons that had belonged to the runner. "These might be useful."

"Good call. We should send someone back for the others."

"Anyway." Holt wiped his forehead with his sleeve. "We've potentially put the mission at risk. When those guys don't report in, Urbina or whoever's working for him is gonna know something's up."

"Granted. But we were committed."

Holt shook his head. "Fine. Then how 'bout this? When Urbina realizes his boys haven't come back, he's going to want payback. Which means he'll be headed for that village loaded for bear, and we can't stick around to help them. We stay to protect Erubiel, we blow the mission and the hostages die. We move on to our objective, and . . . ."

"What are you saying, Holt?" Nomad's voice was quiet, his expression grim.

Holt spoke in a rush. "I'm saying maybe we shouldn't have helped. That we're going to end up doing more harm than good."

There was silence for a moment, and then they were through the last belt of trees and into the village. "Like I said," Nomad told him, "we're committed. Though I've got a couple of thoughts on how we can turn things a little bit around. Maybe." He dropped his gear on the ground. "Midas! Need you over here!" He turned back to Holt. "Go give those to the headman. He'll know which of his people can shoot. Then we'll talk."

The road the soldiers had tried to flee down barely deserved the name. It was a muddy rut cut into the jungle, kept clear by traffic and semi-regular applications of fire and machete. Nomad could see tire marks running deep into its surface. When it rained, odds were it was impassible for anything not powered by four-wheel drive and particularly fervent prayers.

About a hundred yards out of the village and well after the makeshift wooden bridge, the road abruptly cut right. The turn was almost blind, a sharp bend necessitated by some combination of boggy ground and massive root systems punching up from the jungle floor.

Beyond the bend, the road zig-zagged off into the jungle, the terrain dictating a series of twists and turns that no sane planner would have ever dared try to implement.

"This'll work," Nomad said to himself, then toggled the comms on. "Midas. Status?"

There was a pause. "Managed to save two who were shot. One in the leg, one in the shoulder. Lost one other, and there were three dead before we got here. There was nothing we could do. A few others were beaten. There were some concussions, some broken bones. I set them as best I could."

"Roger that. Good work. Any idea what went down here?"

"Yes, sir. Apparently the Amazonas patrols had been coming through regularly. Sometimes they'd trade, sometimes they'd just help themselves to some of the villagers' stuff, and the locals figured a little payoff was better than fighting. But the take kept on getting bigger, and when the latest patrol came through, Erubiel told them that it was done. Push came to shove, it got nasty, and shoving turned into shooting." There was a pause.

"The soldiers, they went crazy. I talked to Erubiel's son. He made his run for it to try to draw them away from the village after they started shooting. I guess it worked. But now—now they're sure the soldiers will come back, and come back in force. They'd pack up and leave, but the wounded can't really move."

"Where the hell would they go to?"

"No idea, sir. Right now, it's a mess. Their boats are sunk. They can't cross the river; we can't give them a ride downstream . . . ." Midas's voice trailed off. "Orders, sir?"

"Tell them—" Nomad thought for a second. "Wait. They traded with the soldiers before things went to hell?"

"Yessir."

"Did the villagers go there, or did they wait for the soldiers to show up?"

"I don't know."

"Find out. If they've got a good route to the camp, I want to know about it. And ask them to stay put. The soldiers are at least partially our problem. Weaver, you on the channel?"

"Affirmative. What have you got?"

Nomad took a deep breath. "The truck. See if you can get it rolling. Midas, get him some help from the villagers if you can."

"It's not drivable," Weaver cut in.

"I know. But if it's pushable, I want it here."

"And where's here?"

"Right where the next truck's gonna come screaming around the bend."

Weaver chuckled. "I like the way you think. On it."

"Holt?"

"Yeah?"

"The runners come back with the hostiles' guns?"

"Yeah, but there's not a ton of ammo."

"Move past it. Get with the headman, get those guns in the hands of the people who'll use them, then give them whatever training you can."

Holt sounded surprised. "All due respect, I'm an engineer, not a range instructor."

"You're a Ghost, so stop trying to bullshit me. If you can't teach point and shoot, you wouldn't be in this unit. Get help from Weaver if you really need it for the finer points."

"Roger that." It came out as a sigh.

"All right, people. We're almost out of light. Let's do this."

Fifteen minutes later, the shriek of bending metal told Nomad that Weaver and the truck were coming.

He stood up from where he'd been rigging grenades with improvised tripwires across the road, then started waving in Weaver and the villagers pushing the truck. When they were ten feet from the bend, Nomad signaled them to halt.

"Whoa, whoa, whoa. Far enough."

The truck squelched to a stop, and the man who'd been sitting at the steering wheel hopped out. Weaver patted him on the back, then walked over to Nomad. "One truck, signed, sealed, and delivered."

"Great." Nomad stared at it. "Okay. Knock off the mirrors, bust out whatever glass is left, and then cover it with leaves and crap. I don't want a reflection through the trees giving it away."

Weaver nodded. "After that?"

"Get Midas to make it clear that everyone stays off this road. I'm setting up a couple more surprises and don't want any of our friends setting them off."

"Then we move on to the research camp?"

"Then we move. Oh, and see if you can—"

"Pick out some good firing points and maybe work up some cover back in the village for whoever gets past this? Way ahead of you." He shook his head in mock sadness. "Tell me, my friend. Seeing as I keep anticipating what your orders are gonna be, they gonna give me my own team based on my clear insight into the intricacies of command?"

Nomad laughed. "God save us from the day. Besides, I need you keeping me honest."

"Ain't that the truth?"

The men were mostly finished with the truck when Midas came trotting up the road, Erubiel keeping pace with him stride for stride. Nomad stood and walked over to meet them, paying his respects to the village chief.

"Major." Midas clearly had something on his mind. "The chief would like to tell you about—" Before he could finish, the headman started talking, gesturing toward the jungle.

"What's he saying?"

Midas held up one warning finger, then waited until

the man wound down before responding. "He says the soldiers were lazy. The route they took to the village, the one you see here, it's easy, but it's slow and crooked. It's not the fastest way. He knows a quicker way to their camp. It's through the jungle, but we can be on top of them in maybe two hours if we move out now."

"That's appreciated, Midas, but we're not headed to their camp, remember? We've got some scientists to rescue."

"Major." Weaver paused. "He also told me that when his people checked out the camp the other day, they saw some people who weren't soldiers."

"Weren't soldiers?"

Midas tapped his wrist console. "I showed him the pictures of Professor Crotty and her team. He called his people in and they identified the three as the strangers they'd seen in camp."

"You're telling me you believe the hostages have been moved, based on secondhand intel you just picked up?"

"Yes I do, sir." He glanced at Erubiel. "He's got no reason to lie on this."

"Except maybe wanting us to go finish off the guys who have been bothering him," Weaver cut in, edging into the conversation. "You might want to consider that."

"In which case we'll still likely find useful intel." Midas's voice was steady. "Major, I believe him. It's more recent than the last intel Wizard had, and it makes sense for them to consolidate."

Nomad held his gaze. "You realize, if we're wrong on this, we're potentially walking into a buzz saw."

"Yessir."

"And you're still willing to go with it?"

Midas nodded, twice. "Yessir."

"All right, then." Nomad turned to Weaver. "Change of plans. We're going to go hit them where they live." He looked around. "No more delays. Midas, get Erubiel to show you that path, and thank him for us."

"Yessir. He, uh, also says not to worry. With the guns his people took from the dead soldiers and the help we've given them, they can defend themselves. We don't have to stay." He sounded embarrassed by the end of it.

Weaver frowned. "Major, you know even with everything we've given them, there's no way they can hold off professionals if the pros are serious."

"Belay that talk, Weaver," Nomad said quietly. Then, louder, "You've got your orders, Midas. Weaver, go tell Holt playtime's over. Sun's almost down. We're back on the clock."

INTERLUDE - WEAVER AND NOMAD

The op was simple, to the point where Joker was grumbling about why they'd even called for the Ghosts. An experimental UAV had gone down in contested territory in Peru, and Uncle Sam— and the DIA—didn't want anyone else getting their hands on it. "Anyone else" in this case meant drug cartels, FARC rebels, government troops looking to make a quick buck, or anyone else who wasn't on the US government payroll.

"Tell me again why we're here?"

That was the new guy, the sniper called Weaver. Nomad had trained with him a bit—in the GST, you trained with everyone—but he, and Joker and Sage, had never worked with him before. Nomad knew he was an ex-SEAL and that he didn't talk about how he'd gotten the prominent scar on his face, but beyond that he was a closed book.

The whup-whup-whup of the helo's blades nearly drowned out Sage's patient explanation. "DIA was testing an experimental UAV by scanning for coca fields in what was supposed to be clear airspace. Dry run for the real hot zones. Something happened, and it went down in no-man's land instead. We get to bring it home, or, failing that, destroy it."

"Hell, I can just shoot it from up here," Weaver said. Despite himself, Nomad found himself chuckling. Joker shot him a dirty look. Nobody was allowed to be funny on Joker's squad. That's how he'd earned the name.

Sage continued as if he hadn't been interrupted. "We've got a good sense of the area it went down in, but not the exact location. Joker and I will rappel down at one end of the search zone. Weaver, you're with Nomad at the other end. We'll sweep and meet in the middle. Radio silence unless you make contact or you find it. Understood?"

"Yessir." Nomad looked over at Weaver, who seemed deeply unconcerned by what was about to happen. After a long moment, Weaver nodded. "I hear you."

"Good." Sage stood, his compact form silhouetted against the open doors of their Bell 205. The Ghosts' regular transports made for a smoother ride, but it was easier to blend in with the older helo. Plenty of close-mouthed men with guns rented those, and nobody asked too many questions.

As the pilot barked a warning that they were a minute out, Joker rose and moved opposite him. "We're out first. See you at the LZ."

The helo slowed, hovered, and eased down toward the ground. Joker and Sage clipped on, tested the connections on their ropes, then tossed them out the side. The ropes snaked down, and then the two men put on heavy gloves. Another second, and they were out and over the side, braking three times on their way down the line.

The helo held position for a moment longer, waiting for the two men on the ground to clear the space. When they were clear, the crew chief pulled the pin on the ropes. They dropped to the ground, and the unencumbered helo headed west over a sharp, lightly forested ridge.

"I can see why they're not setting down," Weaver said. "No place flat enough for this thing to land."

Nomad nodded. "Going to make getting back onboard a pain in the ass."

"You said it."

"One minute," came the voice of the pilot.

"You heard the man," Nomad said, and did one last patdown of his gear before shrugging into his heavy gloves. Weaver, he noticed, didn't do the patdown.

He caught him staring. "I checked before. Gotta have faith in your work, right?"

"Right, I guess." Nomad moved to the door and tied

on, as the pilot called, "Thirty seconds!" Weaver slipped his gloves on and did the same, then they moved out onto the skid and turned to face the interior, brake hands on the rope. The helo slowed; their deployment bags went over the side; and the pilot's voice came over the comms loud and clear. "Ropes! Ropes! Ropes!"

Nomad leapt over the side, rope in hand, and started his descent. On the other side, Weaver did the same. Then he was down on the ground and moving. After a second, the ropes came coiling down, and the helo was pulling away into the distance.

Nomad dusted himself off and started coiling up his rope to hide it. Weaver, he saw, was already doing the same. "So where do we go from here?"

Weaver tapped his wrist comms. "Map shows our search area." He looked around at the wooded, steep-sided hills. Wisps of cloud snaked around the highest points, promising rain later and wind sooner than that. "Kind of wish they'd splurged for the topographic option, though."

He tapped the map, and it zoomed in on what looked like their current location. "LZ is about ten klicks west-northwest, over some nasty terrain. We're not doing this as the crow flies, that's for damn sure."

"We get to the top of that ridge there," Nomad suggested, "and we can scan the whole valley here. No need to walk it inch by inch. That drone had a thirty-foot wingspan. We'll see the reflection."

"We'll be exposed," Weaver countered.

"You see anybody else out here?"

"Not yet." But he stashed the rope under some leaves and started walking. After a moment, he turned to Nomad. "You coming?"

"I'm coming."

They crested the deceptively green ridge nearly an hour later, slogging up the knife-edged sides at a painfully slow rate. At the top, they were almost immediately enveloped in fog, which Weaver declared wasn't going anywhere, and so they moved along the ridge to a lower vantage point.

What they saw was stunning.

Spread out below them was a green, relatively flat valley. Small farms here and there had been carved out of the forest, and a simple rutted dirt road ran down the middle of it. In a field to the west of the road the shine of broken glass and metal was obvious, as was the gash the UAV had made in the earth going down.

Surrounding it were what looked like a half-dozen farmers, one of whom was leaning against a pickup truck.

"Down!" Weaver dropped, then inched back below the top of the ridge line. Nomad followed his example.

"What the hell are those farmers going to do with a UAV?" Nomad asked.

"What the hell do you think they're farming?" Weaver handed Nomad a pair of binoculars. A quick scan of the fields showed coca, coca, and more coca. "No wonder it went down here. This place was probably off the map."

"Until the drone showed up. Someone panicked and shot it down." Nomad finished the thought. "Well, we can't take them from here."

"Possibly." Weaver thought for a minute. "The real issue is that the LZ's on the other side of this valley. We go down there, we're walking into a fight."

"And if we don't go down there . . . ." He focused the binos on the farmers. They all wore blue jeans and checked plaid shirts, and most of them had various models of assault rifles slung across their backs. "Welp. Looks like they're farming lead." He handed the binos back to Weaver. "I'll bet they heard the helo and panicked. That's why they're grabbing the drone now." He groaned. "They know we're here."

"They know somebody's here," Weaver corrected him. "If they knew it was us, they'd be headed this way. Instead . . . ." He pointed down into the valley, toward the largest of the farmhouses. It was a rambling affair, painted a dark green, and it had a long, low barn next to it. "They'll be headed for that with the drone."

"Which means they're going to come right past our position." Below, the men were grunting and heaving as they lifted the wreckage of the drone into the pickup truck. One of the men went down, clutching his back. The others ignored him and kept on working.

"You want to call this in?"

Weaver shook his head. "Not yet. Let's see if I'm right. If I am, then the objective's a sitting duck. And if I'm not, it's going to come right past us anyway, and there's no way Joker and Sage can get here in time to help."

Nomad looked at him suspiciously. "Why exactly are you on this op?"

"Why do you think?"

"I thought it was because this was going to be a milk run and you're FNG. Now, however, how many ops did you do up here with the SEALs?"

"Enough." Weaver absently traced the line of his scar. "Enough. So, you trust I know what I'm talking about?"

"For this, anyway." He shifted position, sidling left. "If we head down there, we're trapped with them. If we stay here, they're out of range."

"Uh-uh." Weaver shook his head. "Out of your range. Not mine." He took a deep breath. "Here's what we're going to do. They come across, and I'm going to take the shot and nail the sweet spot on the UAV. Your job is to keep them off me once they realize they're getting shot at and start coming up that hill. At that point, we either make it out of here as heroes or we get our asses chased all the way to Lima by angry men with guns. You up to it?"

"You still think it's a good idea not to call for backup?"

"You still think it would make any difference?"

Nomad smirked. "You're crazy."

"I'm practical," Weaver replied. "They're headed our way. Let's do this."

Nomad nodded. "Let's do this."

CHAPTER 8

The trail Erubiel showed Midas was invisible until they were on top of it. A thin strip of packed earth literally stomped out of the jungle by the passage of feet both human and otherwise, it seemed about as inviting as a boomslang. Throw in the lengthening shadows from the encroaching dusk, and it looked like a door into nothing.

"This is it?" Nomad asked.

Midas nodded. "Erubiel says that they deliberately keep it overgrown so the soldiers don't stumble onto it."

The village headman had gone back home to see to the wounded and comfort the grieving among his people, but not before taking Midas to the trailhead and loading him up with all sorts of useful tidbits about how to handle the jungle.

"Do you think we can trust him?"

Midas unsheathed his machete and spun it experimentally a couple of times. "I'm sure we can. He's clearly got no love for the Amazonas Free Staters, not after what they did to his people and his son. And he—"

"He seems to like you," Weaver finished. "Don't rely too much on that. But I think you're right. He'd love us to put a dull stick in those soldiers' eyes."

"Look." Midas sounded faintly exasperated. "The thing you have to understand is that this is not a movie. Erubiel and his people are not going to be our friends forever because I, or we, did something for them. They appreciate it, and right now our interests line up. But they have their own business to take care of, and they've been doing just fine out here for a long, long time."

"I didn't mean—"

Midas cut him off. "I just think it's important to make this clear. I think we can trust them, but we shouldn't rely on them. We're not their concern. In a week, we'll be gone, and they'll still be living here dealing with whatever comes down. On their terms."

Holt coughed softly and peered down the trail. "It bothers me that none of what we're seeing—the village, the road, any of this—showed up on satellite. Intel doesn't match the terrain. I don't like it."

Weaver wasn't having any of it. "The way stuff grows down here, it doesn't surprise me satellite didn't see it. It's like an entire jungle made of kudzu. Blink twice, and that crap swallows your house."

"That's not your call to make," Holt replied, then turned to Nomad. "Boss? What do we do?"

Nomad gestured down the trail. "Midas, you've got a point."

"He's got a machete."

"Quiet, Holt. You've got our six. Do not engage without permission, and keep an eye out for the wildlife. Anyone gets poisoned by a frog, we're leaving you here. Midas? Let's go."

The sun had gone down by the time they started, draping the jungle in heavy, smothering darkness. Here and there a small break in the canopy offered a glimpse of the sky, but those were few and far between. The rest of the time was seemingly endless plodding along the seemingly endless path, one tree looking very much like the next. They'd switched to NVG when it had gone full dark, but even so, the jungle made for slow going. Erubiel's path was clear enough, but he hadn't been joking when he talked about how the soldiers' road was an easier way.

Around them, the night muttered and growled its disapproval of their presence. The steady chop and swish of Midas's machete served as counterpoint, a rhythm against which the shrieks of monkeys and birds fell short.

"The old man did say two hours, right?" Holt asked three hours into the trek. "Because if he did, I want his running shoes."

"I think he knows the trail a little better than we do," Weaver retorted.

"Keep it down, both of you," Nomad added. "I think we've got something. Holt?"

"I'll check it out." He edged cautiously ahead a dozen yards, the machete sliding cleanly back into its sheath. Up ahead, through the trees, he could see the faint glow of what looked to be halogen lights, and if he listened carefully, he could hear the grumble of an overworked generator. Any closer, and the lights would bloom out the view on his night vision painfully; any closer, and he probably wouldn't need them.

He patched into the comms link. "It looks like there's an encampment up ahead. It's well lit, and it's big. I think we've found it."

"Roger that. GPS confirms we're in Wizard's best guess. Holt, can you get a little closer? I need more to go on than bright lights, big jungle."

"Roger that."

"We'll be coming up behind you."

"Uh-uh, hold position."

"What have you got?"

"I'm picking up multiple IR sources that aren't moving, most of them eye height."

"Animals?"

"Negative. Single sources, but bright. I'm guessing IR cameras. Let me take a closer look." There was a pause.

"Yup. Repurposed trail cameras. Probably stolen from the geeks."

"Are they sending feedback to the camp?"

Holt thought about it for a second. "Gotta assume so. So taking them out isn't an option."

"Can we go around?"

"Negative. The whole damn camp is ringed with them. Overlapping fields, too—someone's a little paranoid."

"They've got good reason to be." Nomad considered. "Okay, we can't go through and we can't go around. Which means over."

"Major, hate to break it to you, but there's not enough tree cover here for us to play Tarzan."

Nomad was all business. "Not us. Get that UAV flying. I want a good look at how the camp's laid out and where they're likely keeping the hostages."

"Roger that."

"And see if you can ID the control center for those cameras."

"I'll put it on the list."

"Midas, go cover him. I don't want Holt needing to watch his back when he should be watching the feed."

"Copy that. I'm on my way." And with that, he slithered forward, a gray shape blending into the black of the night.

"That dude is uncanny," said Weaver, echoing what Nomad was thinking. "We don't get him killed, he's gonna be one of the ones that gets talked about for a long time."

"I'll try to keep him alive. As for you, I want you back

here when the shit hits the fan. We go in, we're going to have ten, fifteen seconds tops before whatever alarms they've got rigged to those cameras go off. Soon as they do, I want you dropping targets in the center of the compound. You keep their focus there. We're going in through the back of the tent where they're keeping the hostages, a clean snatch and grab. Your job is to keep them from noticing that's what's really going on."

Imperceptibly in the dark, Weaver nodded. "Beats driving the damn boat."

"You get to do that later. We're going to fall back toward the village along the road. Priority one is getting those civilians out of here."

Weaver coughed. "We're going to be taking civilians who don't have the goggles down the road you rigged in the dark?"

"Traps are marked, we'll get them off the train before anyone steps in it."

"That's reassuring." Weaver took a long look through his scope. "Mmm. Gonna want to get about thirty yards thataway for a better solution. Too much garbage in the way here."

"I thought you loved nature."

"I do. On my television, where it belongs." He rose into a half-crouch. "Let me know when it's go time."

Nomad flashed him a quick smile. "Wouldn't dream of leaving you out. Check in when you're in position."

"Roger that." And then he, too, was gone.

Holt cut in. "Bird is airborne. I'm taking her in."

"Roger that. Good luck."

Holt didn't answer. Instead, he carefully guided the drone to a height just below the canopy, then flicked it into FLIR mode. The inky blob from the feed transformed into a sharp black-and-white image showing the jungle, the cameras, and the camp beyond them, and Midas.

Frowning, Holt eased the drone over the line of cameras and into the camp. It was bigger than he'd expected, laid out along a long central clearing that doubled as a road. The structures in the center were buildings: a barracks, a couple of small huts that looked like officers' quarters, and two offset buildings that he guessed were the HQ and the armory. Lights were rigged on stands or attached to trees, all pointing down to avoid any leakage through the canopy for spying eyes above. A sprinkling of tent surrounded them, including one with multiple faint heat signatures inside and two brighter ones out front. A particularly bright heat source toward the far end of the camp caught his attention. He pulled the drone in closer and realized it was a truck, the same make and model he'd seen at the village earlier. As he watched, a handful of soldiers started loading up the back.

"Nomad, we've got a problem."

"Go ahead."

"Looks like the hostiles are packing up for a little payback at the village." He paused. "There's no way to warn them, is there?"

"You know the answer to that, Holt."

"Roger." He thought for a minute. "Orders?"

"You find me the hostages?"

"Affirmative. Got a line on the HQ, too, and a head

count on hostiles. I'm seeing twenty plus our hostages. Two outside the tent where they're being held, can't tell if there's anyone in there with them."

"Understood. Got anything else for me?"

"Yeah. I think I can take out the control board for the cameras."

"How?"

"Wizard and I modded the drone's weapons loadout. It now comes with a single use directional EMP burst. I get close enough, it'll fry everything in that building that's unshielded. And I don't think they're bringing cybersecurity consultants out here to harden things."

"All right. Anything else?"

"Just a minute." He guided the drone farther into the camp, praying the night noises covered the thin whine of the rotors. "Down there? That's the generator. Next to it? Looks like six barrels of fuel."

Nomad considered for a moment. "I'm sensing an opportunity here. Your bird going to be able to fly after you set off the pulse?"

Holt shrugged, mainly for his own benefit. "In theory, the EMP's directional and she's shielded. In practice?" He let his voice trail off.

"Okay, feed me the location of the tent with the packages and the guards outside. Then when I give the go, you hit the cameras with the EMP. If the bird's still flying after that, hit the generator and then the fuel. Midas, you're with me. We're cutting the back of that tent open and pulling the hostages out. Weaver, you've got your orders."

"That I do," came the steadying, comforting drawl. "What's the plan for exfil?"

"Run like hell. Head for the village."

"I guess that'll do. Road or path?"

"They've got trucks. We're staying the hell off that road. They can't drive back down that trail. Midas, you'll take point. Whatever it takes, get the hostages back to the boat. Weaver, you'll be with him. Holt, you and me, we get to cover their asses should it become necessary."

Holt laughed. "I'll take that action." There were some clicking noises as he directed the drone to a new location. "Bird is in position. Awaiting your go."

"Weaver?"

"Ready."

"Midas?"

"On my way."

Nomad picked his way around the perimeter of the camp, careful to stay out of range of the cameras. Occasional footfalls told him Midas was moving in the same direction.

Eventually he spotted it: the square, blocky shape silhouetted against the camp's light. A quick check with the NVG showed a few more of the telltale cameras, cunningly placed in the trees with overlapping fields of view. Someone had been thinking about keeping this place secure, that much was clear, though the disconnect between the sloppy behavior Nomad had seen at the village and the sharp planning here was puzzling. Best to just assume the enemy was as capable and smart as possible, and take anything less than that as a gift.

He settled down into position, outside the camera range, then checked his comms. "Midas?"

"Fifteen meters from you and closing."

"I copy. Weaver, do you have a shot?"

"Do I ever. Everything's green."

"That's just the NVG. Stand by, then." A rustle in the undergrowth told him without turning that Midas had dropped into position next to him. "Holt?"

"Bird is in position. Payload is primed. Just say the word."

Nomad took a deep breath. "Go."

"Roger that," Holt answered, his voice calm. "Triggering directional EMP now."

There was a crackle of feedback on the commlink, and then some of the lights in the camp went dark. Around the perimeter, so did the eyes on the cameras, while panicked voices could be heard for the first time over the jungle sounds.

"Weaver? Weapons free. Midas, let's go."

Before Nomad finished the first sentence, a shot rang out, matched by a strangled yell inside the camp. Two more followed in rapid succession, and now the hubbub exploded. Bursts of fire could be heard spraying wildly into the night as the soldiers shot at an invisible enemy or dove for cover.

Nomad processed all of this peripherally. "Sensor out!" he called, and tossed one that landed next to the tent. Four figures inside flared into view—the three hostages and one soldier, looming over them as chaos erupted outside. "I've got one hostile in the tent!" he yelled, as he sprinted for the tent, knife in hand. Without looking, he could tell Midas was in position beside him. They broke through the tree line and slammed up against the back of the tent, the canvas bulging inward as they hit. "Cover me," Nomad ordered, then drove his knife into the tent wall. He ripped across and then down, then pulled back and out of the way as Midas stepped into the breach.

Inside, Midas could see the four figures the sensor had called out. Three were handcuffed to cots, two women and a man. Their captor was already firing into the gap in the canvas as Midas's face appeared. The bullets whizzed past as Midas ducked out of the way. "No good!" he yelled.

"Hostages still alive?" Nomad pulled a flashbang off his belt.

"Affirmative!" More bullets stitched through the fabric, narrowly missing Nomad.

"Banger!" With his left hand, Nomad pulled back the torn tent wall. With his right, he tossed the grenade, praying he still had his fastball. Bullets exploded around him as the soldier switched to the new, suddenly visible target, and then the world went white. There was a cacophony of voices from inside the tent, audible through the Peltor ear protectors they all wore, and then a hand on his back was pushing him down to the ground. Looking up, he saw a rough outline that looked a lot like Midas speaking urgently about the hostages.

"I'm okay!" he said. "Get the hostages!"

Midas stepped into the tent. There was a single shot, and then the louder sounds of battle from farther in the camp took precedence. Nomad shook his head, then barked into his mic. "Holt! Is your bird still in the air?"

"Yeah, she's still flying."

Nomad grunted his satisfaction. "Good. Go to target Bravo and light it up."

"Roger that, she's on her way!" The long, rolling boom of Weaver's rifle cut through the night, with machine guns chattering in response. *So far,* Nomad thought, *so good,* and he stepped into the tent.

The scene on the ground was chaos. That much, Holt could see from the drone's camera. The makeshift shielding he'd rigged up had done its job, as had the directional pulse, and half the electronics in the camp were fried. The response on the ground, particularly with Weaver adding to the confusion, was everything he could have hoped for. Men were throwing themselves down behind any cover they could find, while others were spraying the jungle wildly. An officer emerged from the headquarters building and started bellowing orders. He got out maybe a half dozen words before he was dropped, a bullet from Weaver throwing the men around him into more confusion.

A series of rounds slammed into a nearby tree, sending splintered bark everywhere. Holt froze and then scurried back and to his right. No sense helping the opposition get lucky. There was a dip in the jungle floor, hidden behind some thick, low greenery, and he ducked behind it.

More bullets flew past. "Ah, hell," he said, and risked a quick look.

They were coming. Three soldiers had surged out from the camp, and they were headed his way. One stopped and fired a burst of suppressive fire, the bullets scything off the top few inches of his cover. Tattered leaves rained down, their edges smelling faintly of gunpowder and smoke.

"Shit!" He rolled left. He could see the men moving quickly, spreading out and calling back and forth to one another as they advanced.

Too late to run, he decided. If he stood, they'd nail him. If he waited, they'd probably nail him by accident or stumble right across him.

So it was going to be fight, while his drone hung in midair like a big, fat target, instead of delivering the distraction that Nomad had wanted.

Frowning, he drew his sidearm. Long gun would get caught too easily in the undergrowth. The last thing he needed was some hanging vine snagging his muzzle at a critical moment. No, this was knife and pistol work.

The soldiers were close now, the nearest almost on top of him. Carefully, he knelt, aimed, and fired at the one farthest away.

The shot caught the man in the belly, and he yelled in pain as it hit. Involuntarily, he squeezed the trigger on his AK, and sent a wave of fire into the night. The unexpected sound was enough to make the other two turn, and that gave Holt the opening he was looking for.

He popped up out of cover and squeezed off a couple of rounds at the soldier closest to him. One took him in the shoulder, the other in the throat, and he dropped with a gurgle.

The last man was no fool. He made a good guess where the fire was coming from and strafed the jungle near Holt's position. Holt hustled backwards, hugging the ground as the bullets flew overhead. When he looked up, the man was gone.

Holt rolled to his feet and slid behind a tree, listening. By all rights, the guy should have showed up like a Roman candle on NVG, but with the explosive shenanigans back at the camp, the NVG was half-useless.

Fortunately, that wasn't his only option. "Sensor out," he muttered into the comm channel, and tossed a sensor grenade in what he hoped was the right direction.

The sensor hit with a soft thud. On his HUD, Holt could see a soft blue pulse spread out rapidly, hugging the ground, moving over the trees, and—

There! Outlined in yellow, the figure of a man way too close, moving stealthily through the brush. Another minute, and he would have been right on top of Holt.

But that was a minute he didn't have.

Holt carefully drew a bead, then fired. The bullet was off the mark, and he could see the yellow figure dive out of the way. He cursed and ducked, just as a series of bullets smacked into the tree he'd been hiding behind. He returned fire, then ducked down, repeating the process until he heard the distinctive single click that announced to the world he was dry.

The other guy, he was sure, had heard it too. He took off, zig-zagging through the trees, deliberately making noise as he went.

The trap was baited. Behind him, he could hear

the soldier following, sprinting through the darkened jungle.

Good enough, Holt decided when he was sure the pursuit was on. He slammed up against a tree, then slithered around it and willed himself into immobility and silence. Barely breathing, he waited.

They were out of range of the sensor now, and Holt didn't dare use another. Instead, he listened. The soldier coming closer now, his pace slowing as the edge of the pursuit's adrenaline rush wore off. Carefully scanning left and right, he kept walking, boots whisper-loud with each step. Holt could hear his breathing now, realized the man was on top of his position. If he hadn't hidden himself quite right, if the man took one step in the wrong direction . . . .

He walked past.

And Holt stepped out from behind the tree and put his pistol to the man's neck. "Drop it," he said.

"You're out," the soldier replied, and twisted in Holt's grasp.

Holt pulled the trigger.

"I reloaded," he told the dead man, then pulled the drone control protocol back up on his wrist console. "Baby better still be flying."

Midas looked over his shoulder as Nomad walked in. "Major. We've got a problem. I searched the guard. No keys." He pointed to the handcuffs holding the three prisoners to their bedframes.

"We've got the tools we need. Dr. Kathleen Crotty?" The woman in the middle, the shorter and older of the two, raised her unbound hand. She looked tired but alert, and the determination was plainly written on her face.

"I assume you're our way out of here?" she said.

"Yes ma'am." Nomad looked at the tent door, then back at Midas. "We're here to get you and your people home safely. But to do that, you all are going to have to do exactly what I say. If you don't, we will still get you out of here, but you'll enjoy it a lot less."

"I don't care, just help us!" said the younger woman. She pulled frantically on the handcuff holding her to the bed, rattling it helplessly when it refused to give.

"Easy, Melanie," Dr. Crotty said. "I'm sure these gentlemen have a plan for getting us out safely." She turned to face Nomad. "You do have a plan, I trust?"

Nomad nodded. "Midas, tool kit. Dr. Crotty, if you would be so kind as to lay your hand flat on the bedframe and pull that handcuff as tight as it can go? Holt, what's taking you so long?"

"You're gonna chop her hand off? No way! I'll stay here!" The second research assistant scrambled back as far as the restraint would let him.

"Mr. Stanton!" Crotty's words were as sharp-edged as Midas's weapon. "Get a hold of yourself." She pulled her arm back, stretching the handcuffs to their maximum length. "If you miss, miss clean," she said, and closed her eyes.

"We plan for this sort of thing, ma'am," Midas said, and pulled a small pair of bolt cutters out of his kit. "I've had to improvise with a machete. It's not always pretty." He set the bolt cutters against the chain, then squeezed. There was a brief screech of metal, then soft jingling as broken links went everywhere. Midas immediately approached her side and helped her up. "Can you stand?" he asked. She nodded. "Can you run?"

"I'm going to have to," she replied, and turned to her assistants, who stared in slack-jawed shock. "Melanie, Gilbert, get yourselves together." Midas handed her his canteen even as the other two pulled their cuffs tight, and she took a long draught. "Thank you, Mr. . . ."

"We don't have names, ma'am," Midas replied. "Just the job."

"Of course," she snorted. "You two ready?"

"Yes, Dr. Crotty," they recited in unison. Midas gave Crotty a brief nod, then walked over to where Stanton sat, trying hard to control his shaking. "You're not even going to notice . . ." Midas said, and cut the links. The handcuffs broke, and Stanton tumbled back from the sudden slack.

". . . a thing," Midas finished. He turned to Carpenter, who was watching the whole thing, shocked. "Miss?"

"Yeah?" she answered weakly.

"Hold still."

As he raised the bolt cutters, a soldier came through the front flap of the tent, shouting for the guard inside. His face registered surprise for the half-second it took for Nomad to take him down, and then he collapsed on the floor. "Holt! I need that distraction, like, *now!*"

"Sorry." Holt's voice was strained. "Was trying to get

us a prisoner for insurance. Didn't quite work out. Time to target is three . . . two . . . one."

There was an explosion outside, and then another one, and then another.

"Target spiked! Drone's offline, got caught in the shockwave. Falling back to rendezvous point!" There was a pause, and then Holt added a solitary "Whoohoo!" for good measure.

"Midas? Any time now."

Midas went to work again, and the last of the handcuffs shattered. Carpenter reeled back and Midas caught her, then helped her to her feet. She stared at him, then took a deep breath. "I'm okay," she said. "Let's go."

"But the laptops, they've got all our work," Stanton interjected softly. "We can't leave them."

"Can and will," his boss replied. "I love and value our work. But I am not getting shot for it, not today." She gestured to the back of the tent. "Gentlemen, what do we do?"

Nomad pointed to the opening. "This gentleman's going to lead the way. You're going to follow him to a trail that we hope the people who took you hostage don't know about, and we're going to run as fast and as long as we can. Follow him; stay in single file. I'll be right behind you."

Crotty nodded. "Then let's go."

Midas stepped through the tent flap, back into the night. His arm was visible through the partial tear, making a "come on" gesture. Crotty followed, then Carpenter, then Stanton. Nomad quickly grabbed the guns from the two dead men and then followed them out into the night.

Aim. Wait. Shoot. Move.

The pattern was easy enough in concept. It was the execution that some people found hard.

Weaver's first shot had taken out a swaggering bully whose body language and general unpleasantness to his fellow soldiers had annoyed him. He'd watched the man through his scope waiting for Nomad to give the go code, and had decided that if he had to pick a target, this guy had volunteered for the job. And when the call came, he got dropped. Weaver squeezed off a couple of additional shots, just to add to the initial chaos, then quickly humped it to a new position and let the cycle take hold. He could hear Nomad barking orders over the comms, could hear Holt occasionally answering, but he kept radio silence.

An officer stepped out of one of the buildings, shouting and rallying the men. Some of the random fire stopped. Soldiers shook themselves out of pure reaction mode and started remembering their training.

"We can't have that sort of thing," Weaver whispered softly, and squeezed the trigger. Through the scope, he saw the man go down. There was faint, distant shouting, and then he picked up and was on the move again.

The jungle was no longer dark, thanks to the pillars of orange fire gusting up into the night and threatening to turn half the trees in the neighborhood into living torches. The shouting from the camp had taken on a different tenor now, with men panicking about the fire more than they were the mysterious adversary in the woods. Gunfire still barked out occasionally, but it sounded like half the men in the camp were rushing to try to do something about the fire.

With luck, between that and Weaver's efforts, they'd be too distracted to check on the hostages immediately. But even in the best case imaginable, someone would come looking, and soon.

Midas was moving steadily through the underbrush, acutely aware of how exposed the firelight made them. Crotty was right behind him, with the other two supporting each other and stumbling onward. In the distance, he could see Holt, already at the rally point and in position to lay down cover fire if there was pursuit.

"Weaver? Time to go."

"I hear you." The sniper sounded mildly irritated. "The ant hill down there is well and truly kicked over. Give me one minute—" The sound of a shot being fired echoed loudly through the commlink. "—and I'm on my way."

"Roger that. We'll wait for you."

"You go. I'll catch up. Weaver out."

Midas paused, looking back at Nomad for direction.

"We keep going," Nomad said. "Without the packages, he'll be moving faster than we are. And so will they." He jerked a thumb over his shoulder, back at the burning camp. "Let's keep moving."

"Yessir."

Holt was up and ready when they reached his position,

and he quickly fell in next to Nomad. "Hostages don't look too good," he said by way of a greeting. "They gonna make it back?"

"The other option is asking for a ride in one of their pickups. Too bad we couldn't disable the motor pool."

"We were a little busy. That one truck tore out as soon as the fun started. Headed the other way."

"Crap." Nomad exhaled. "Worst case scenario, they've gone for help and they'll be coming back after us. Which means we move now. We'll push the hostages as hard as we can as long as we can, and then push a little farther."

"I love the way you plan," Holt cracked, and then his smile faded to a more serious expression. "How do you want to handle this?"

Nomad didn't look up. "They catch up with us, you and I turn around and hold them. Good thing is this path is so narrow any pursuit's going to be a turkey shoot."

"What about the fight we might be walking into back at the village?"

Nomad was somber. "We'll handle that when we get there. Maybe we'll get lucky for a change. Let's worry about the immediate threat for now."

Twenty minutes on, Weaver caught up to them. He'd maintained radio silence, but there was no mistaking the lean figure loping down the trail after them. Nomad had Midas slow the pace slightly, and Weaver was with them in a matter of moments.

"What's it looking like back there?" Nomad asked.

"The camp's a hot mess."

"Any pursuit?"

Weaver shook his head. "Not for a little while, at least. They're still putting out the fire and getting close-in patrols going. Gonna take them a while to find this route, take them longer to organize to go down it. Assuming they even do."

"I'll take that action," said Holt, and Nomad shot him a look. "What?"

Just then, Stanton stumbled and fell. Midas halted, and turned back to give him a hand up. "I'm fine, I'm fine," the research assistant said. "Just a little . . . you know . . . ."

"Can we stop here and rest for a moment?" Crotty's voice was concerned. "If there's no pursuit—"

"A little farther," Nomad said. "If they're not pursuing us now, we need to take advantage of that time. The farther we get before they start hunting, the better the chance they'll give up or head in the wrong direction."

"My people can't go any farther. They're dead on their feet," Crotty protested.

"Beats just dead," Holt said, without smiling.

Nomad smiled tightly. "Professor, apologies for his bluntness, but we've got to keep moving. We'll give your people as much rest as we can, but right now, we've got to go." He nodded to Holt. "Give Mr. Stanton a hand. And let's keep moving."

CHAPTER 9

They made it another thirty minutes before Nomad called a halt. Carpenter and Stanton were both visibly flagging, stumbling to put one foot in front of the other in the dark. Crotty was holding up better, but she clearly looked relieved when the column eased to a stop.

"Five minutes," Nomad decided. "Midas, Holt, give 'em a quick medical once-over. Make sure no one's in shock or bleeding." He unclipped his canteen and handed it to Stanton, who took a deep swig, then wiped his mouth with the back of his hand. "Thank you," he said, and passed it to Carpenter.

"Here." Weaver had pulled a couple of protein bars out of his kit and handed them around. "Don't know what they were feeding you back there, but I'm guessing it wasn't escape fuel."

Crotty took one of the bars and nodded her thanks. "It was more neglect than mistreatment," she said, "but things were getting, I don't know, maybe the right word is 'anxious,' the last few days. I think we were becoming a problem, and I don't know how much longer they would have kept us." She bit into the bar and chewed ravenously.

"Last few days?" Nomad leaned in, curious. "What happened to change things?"

She thought for a minute. "There was a visitor at the camp. The soldiers there called him 'Colonel,' showed him a lot of respect. He was there for a couple of hours, and then after that, everything changed. Got harder-edged, if you know what I mean."

Weaver and Nomad exchanged a look.

"Urbina?"

"Urbina."

Nomad turned back to the professor. "Did you meet him?"

"Briefly." She took the last bites of the protein bar, chewed and swallowed. Weaver passed her a canteen and she drank, then handed it back. "They brought him in to see us. He didn't actually say anything to us. Just sort of . . . assessed things. He spoke to the local officers in Spanish, though. He said that our presence there was an unfortunate distraction from the real business at hand, and that he didn't much like distractions." She shuddered. "I've been working down here on and off for the better part of fifteen years. I've seen a lot of things without blinking. But that man, he was cold. Frightening."

"You speak Spanish?"

Crotty gave a short, bitter laugh. "Of course I do, and so does my team. This isn't Ohio. You come into a country that isn't yours, you act with respect. For the little things, and for the big ones." She stood. "Do we need to get moving again?"

Nomad nodded. "Yeah, we do." He offered Carpenter a hand up, which she took. Stanton refused assistance, but he leaned heavily on a tree when he made it to his feet. Midas looked to Nomad, who glanced down the trail ahead. Nodding, Midas took off again, though at a slower pace than he had set before. The scientists fell in behind him, as did Weaver. Holt started to follow, but Nomad held up a cautioning hand.

"How far do you think we've gotten, Holt?"

Holt pursed his lips as he thought for a second. "Not real far?"

Nomad's grimace showed just how accurate that answer was. "You know it took us three hours to get out here? At this pace, it's going to take us six to get back, and that's if we don't run into any trouble."

"Or take any extra breaks. Not good."

Nomad took a few steps back along the path. "Which means that if they try to pursue, they'll catch us. Unless we can slow them down."

Holt grinned, a ghastly sight in the glare of the NVG.

"So what's the plan?"

"The plan is we leave a couple of surprises. Make them cautious. And if we find a good spot, you and me, we dig in and wait."

Holt gave a low whistle. "You and me against how many? There were twenty at the camp, and then if they got reinforcements, well, that's some pretty steep odds."

"I'm not saying we pull a last stand. They get close, we bloody their noses, then fall back to the next good spot while they're still trying to figure out what hit them."

"That could work."

Nomad snorted. "It had better. The alternative's a running firefight with our passengers in the middle of it." He hunkered down in the middle of the path. "Got any thoughts?"

Holt nodded slowly. "Could do a couple more trip-wires, maybe. Could string some stuff at neckheight, that'll slow down anyone in too much of a hurry."

"All right then. Get on this." He tapped open his comms. "Weaver, Midas. You copy?"

"We hear you," Weaver answered. "You want us to wait for you?"

"Negative. Holt and I are going to cover our tracks a little bit. You keep the train moving. We'll be in touch."

"What I wouldn't give for one helicopter," Weaver said by way of an answer. "Weaver out."

The first distant explosion went off an hour later. Holt and Nomad, crouched behind a makeshift barricade of fallen branches they'd hauled across the path, looked at each other as the blast faded in the distance.

"One of yours?" Nomad asked,

"Nah. Grenade tripwire. Yours. But who's keeping score?"

"Major, you two all right?" Weaver' voice cut in.

"Everything's frosty, Weaver," Nomad replied. "Looks like the bad guys finally got their pursuit untracked, that's all. How are the packages doing?"

"They're zombified. God's honest truth, I'm this close to carrying them, because they've got nothing left."

"Acknowledged. Just keep going somehow, you hear me? Piggyback rides are on the table."

"You only say that because you're not here to give one. Weaver out."

Holt smirked. "Man, he loves shit-talking you. How far you two go back?"

"A couple of years," Nomad conceded. "I made GST four years ago. He was a couple years after. Been squaddies ever since, though the whole me-giving-him-orders thing is new."

"I can see that. You two got good function together. And if I haven't said it yet, that plan back at the camp wasn't too bad."

"Not good enough. I should have prioritized the truck."

"Live and learn," Holt said. "Ideally, anyway."

There was another distant bang, followed by some faint shouting.

"They should be at the first barricade by now," Nomad observed.

"The one with the ants?"

Nomad nodded.

"Thank God for whoever invented gloves. Let's hope they're a little underdressed."

Some of the wood they'd pulled to lay across the path had sat on top of some kind of ant colony, and the little bastards had swarmed out to defend it. Only their combat gear had saved them from being chewed on like a cheap steak.

"Got a confession to make," Holt continued. "Bee stings, yellow jackets, all that stuff—I'm allergic as hell. So if any of those ants had gotten a piece of me . . . ."

Nomad stared at him incredulously. "You're kidding. And you're out here?"

Holt patted his chest. "I always pack a couple of Epipens. Really ought to buy stock in the company that makes them, cause I do so damn much for their bottom line."

They shared a brief laugh, one that quickly faded to a sober silence. "How long before they're in range?"

Nomad thought about it for a minute. "Ten minutes, maybe, before things get hot. We just hit 'em once and then fall back. We get pulled into anything bigger, we're dead."

"Not my first rodeo, chief," Holt responded. "Shit. I think they're spreading out off the path."

"Took them long enough," Nomad said. "They're not going to go too far. As long as we keep them in front of us."

They watched in silence for another few minutes, then Holt nudged Nomad. "Over there. Ten o'clock. You see?"

At the far edge of their field of vision, a pale figure was visible picking its way quietly through the jungle.

"I see him," Nomad answered. "Looks like he brought friends." More shapes were visible now, a half dozen in the first rank, spread out in a loose line centered on the path. Behind them came more men, moving in tighter formation along the path.

"You know, they're going to a hell of a lot of effort to bring back hostages they were going to get rid of anyway."

"I don't think it's about that any more, Holt." He scanned the first row of hostiles. "Okay, the two widest flankers. I've got left, you've got right?"

"Roger that. Lining up my shot."

Nomad peered through his sight at his target. The man was moving cautiously, limping a little bit as he went. He stopped, bent down and examined something on the ground, and then picked up and kept moving, an indistinct blob coming into focus as a man and an enemy. "Target acquired," he said softly. "Holt?"

"Shot's lined up and good to go. Waiting on your call."

"Fire."

Two shots rang out simultaneously. Nomad saw his target spin and fall. A quick scan to the right showed Holt's target down as well. The rest of the men immediately hit the dirt, shouting about shooters and commands to get to cover.

Nomad gestured to Holt, then to the trail at their backs. Holt nodded. The two of them picked up and ran for the next ambush point while the shouts faded behind them.

Up ahead, the sound of the synced shot was faint, but enough to silence the jungle's usual night noises.

"Was that us or them?" Stanton asked. "Are they coming?"

"That was us," Weaver told him. "Yeah, they're coming, but they've got a ways to go to catch us. And they've got to get through Nomad and Holt. That's what you heard."

"Do we?" Stanton took a deep breath to steady himself. "Do we need to go back and help them?"

Weaver laughed. "That is the funniest damn thing I've heard all year." Then, more softly, "Good on you to offer, but they're back there so you don't have to try to pull a trigger against guys who've maybe been doing this their whole lives. Best thing you and I can do to help those two out is keep moving, and take advantage of the time they're buying us."

"I understand." Stanton shuddered. "Not what I imagined when I signed on with Professor Crotty, you know? I mean, you tell your parents you're going somewhere for a project, they get a head full of bad movies about what it's going to be like, when usually the worst things you've got to fight are lousy food and going stir-crazy out there. You never expect, well, you never expect this. You never expect the action movie to happen to you."

"We'll get you to the end credits, don't you worry about that. Now keep moving." He looked around, eyes narrowed in suspicion. "Would hate for us to end up part of a surprise second-act plot twist."

By the third ambush, the pursuers had gotten smart. Rather than simply advancing along the axis of the path, they now moved cover to cover, leapfrogging each other as they moved forward. Every so often, one would stop and examine the path, looking for signs of Nomad and Holt's passage, and issue orders based on what he'd seen.

"Can we drop the hostile on the path?" Holt asked. "He looks like the brains of the outfit. We hit him, it's gonna shake them all up. Could buy a bunch of time that way."

"Agreed." Nomad settled in, targeting the soldier. "Let's double up. Don't want to risk missing this one."

"Roger that. Lining him up now."

The two men were set up on the back side of a small, steep hill that rose from the jungle floor like a breaching whale. Here and there, rocks jutted up from the dirt, too low to make good cover, but better than nothing.

Down on the trail, the crouching man traced something, possibly a footprint, in the dirt. He pointed, and a couple of the other soldiers trotted off into the jungle. Then, slowly, he scanned the area, his eyes coming to rest on the crest of the hill up ahead.

"Ah, crap. We're made."

"Fire." Nomad squeezed the trigger. Holt did the same.

And the man on the trail threw himself back and out of the line of fire as if he'd known it was coming. One soldier rushed to cover him. Others opened fire on the hill, the sound ripping through the night air like a swarm of angry hornets.

"Fall back," Nomad ordered. "We can't win this."

"Let me take a second crack at him," Holt demanded. "I've got the shot!"

"Negative! We get out of here, now!"

"But—"

"Now!"

Nomad ran. Holt followed, chancing one last look over his shoulder, just in time to see one of the pursuers rear back to throw a grenade. "Grenade!" he shouted. He threw himself behind the largest trunk he could find, hoping Nomad had done the same. An instant later, the blast ripped through the jungle, shredding leaf and branch and slamming shrapnel into wood.

"You okay?" Nomad called.

"Yeah. You?"

"Got a splinter." He leaned out from behind the tree now liberally pockmarked by shrapnel. "Shhh."

For a moment, neither of them spoke. Faintly but distinctly, they could hear footsteps coming up the hill, and coming fast.

"Got any frags left?" Nomad asked.

"One," Holt answered. "Was saving it for an emergency."

"I think this counts."

Holt had already pulled the pin. "You would," he said,

and tossed it into the still-dissipating cloud of smoke from the previous blast. "Frag out."

The grenade vanished into the night, hitting the ground with an audible clink. The stealthy sounds of pursuit dissolved into panic and chaos, and then the blast hit.

The shouting stopped immediately after that.

"You hear anyone still coming?" Nomad edged around the tree for a look.

"Negative. You?" Holt's ears were ringing and his eyes were watering. *That last one was too close,* he thought, a theory that got reinforced when he saw that a flying piece of fragmentation grenade had cut a neat slice through the sleeve of an arm he'd been unable to quite get behind cover.

"Nada. Cover me. I'm going to check it out."

"Will do."

Nomad ducked out from behind what was left of the tree he'd been using for cover. The zone between where he'd been hiding and where the two grenades had gone off had been thoroughly blasted, leaving little cover. Nomad made the best of what he could, moving back toward the crest of the hill. When he finally reached it, he paused, then peeked out over the edge.

Only silence met him. A quick scan to the left and the right confirmed it—apart from a series of rapidly cooling bodies, there were no soldiers in sight. They'd melted back into the jungle.

"Holt, I'm not seeing anyone. I think they fell back. Sensor?"

"Yeah." There was a soft thump as the device hit the jungle floor, but the only hostiles the sweep showed were down and rapidly cooling.

Holt emerged from cover. "If they were behind us we'd be dead already. You think they just gave up?"

Nomad thought for a minute. "Looks like. They'd taken a lot of casualties, and the officer leading them at the end there was on the stick. I'm guessing he didn't want to lose any more men."

"Yeah, or he's got something else up his sleeve. Speaking of which . . . ." Holt picked at the neat slice in his sleeve. "That was a little close."

"That'll teach you to pick a thicker tree. Come on, Nomad and Weaver have a hell of a head start on us."

"Pretty much," Holt agreed. "Hey, Major, one thing that's bothering me. Back at the camp, one of the fighters who came at me spoke English."

"So? A lot of people down here speak English."

"No, he spoke American English. Like, middle class grew up in the suburbs English. What the hell is a guy like that doing fighting for the Amazonas Free State, when nobody outside here knows what the hell Amazonas Free State is?"

"That's a good question. Right now, I've no answers." Nomad pointed to the trail. "Let's move."

CHAPTER 10

They caught up with Midas, Weaver, and the hostages just before dawn outside the village. Weaver called another halt when he saw them, and the four Ghosts convened just out of earshot.

"Took you long enough to catch up," Weaver offered. Midas simply nodded.

"Thanks." Nomad rubbed his eyes. "Hell of a night. How are our guests doing?" He looked over and saw that the scientists had taken advantage of the stop to slump to the ground. Carpenter and Stanton's heads bobbed low as they fought off the edge of sleep. Crotty was more alert, but even she looked utterly drained.

"I think they're about done, Major." Midas's assessment was to the point. "If we press on to the boat, I don't know if they'll make it. Here, on the other hand, maybe Erubiel will let us stay for a couple of hours."

"You did save his kid," Holt pointed out.

"It's more than that," Midas responded quietly. "But that's my suggestion. It's your call."

"They did pull back," Weaver rumbled. "Maybe we don't need to push quite so hard for a little bit. Besides, you walk any of those hostages to death, the Old Man's going to be pissed."

"All right," Nomad said. "We hoof it into the village and hunker down for a couple of hours. Then we move again, make the final push. You got that?"

Midas, he noticed wasn't paying attention. Instead, he was looking out into the jungle, off in the direction of the road the soldiers had preferred.

"What have you got, Midas?" Nomad followed Midas's eyes but saw nothing.

"Not sure," he said. "But something doesn't feel right. I thought I—" He trailed off, shaking his head. "We'd better move. I'll get them up." He walked back to where the three scientists were sitting and helped them to their feet. Just ahead, the buildings of the village were visible through the last curtains of undergrowth.

"What do you think?" Nomad asked Weaver.

"I trust the kid's instincts," Weaver responded. "But I

don't want to sit here and wait to see what he was right about. C'mon."

They heard the sound before they saw anything.

Trucks.

Midas smacked himself on the side of the head in frustration. "Now we know why they broke off pursuit. They knew where we were going. They just doubled back and loaded up."

"We've got basically zero time. Holt, take the hostages. Get them under cover." Nomad pulled out the pistols he'd taken off the dead men in the tent at the camp. "And give them these."

He tossed Holt the guns. "Why me?" Holt asked plaintively as he caught them.

"Because the locals like you. And because you're out of frags. Now go!"

Holt opened his mouth to respond, realized he had nothing, and instead turned to the hostages. "Okay, people, you're gonna come with me." Wearily, Crotty got to her feet, her assistants following, even as the sound of truck engines got louder. "And you're gonna do it fast." He started hustling them off to the far side of the compound, holding up Stanton as he nearly slipped and fell.

"All right. Midas, get Erubiel and his people up. They can fight or they can run, I don't care which. I just don't want them caught in their beds when those assholes arrive."

Midas turned to run, stopped and looked back. "What are we doing?"

Nomad stared at him. "We could maybe make it to the river, maybe not. Even if we did, we'd be sitting ducks out on the water. And that's assuming we'd get Crotty and her people that far. No, only once choice. We fight."

"All right." Midas sprinted towards the headman's house, his body language indecipherable.

Weaver watched him run, then cocked his head. "You sure this isn't just an excuse to watch those assholes come round the bend and get a face full of truck? Cause don't think I forgot about that."

Nomad gave a tired laugh. "I confess, I wouldn't mind seeing that up close." He started moving toward where the road vanished under the trees. Weaver followed him at speed.

They got there just ahead of the enemy convoy, which consisted of two pickups loaded with fighters barreling down the road at unsafe speeds. Without speaking, Weaver vanished into the brush on the right side of the road, while Nomad went left. The trucks were picking up speed in the home stretch, horns blaring as they roared in for the kill. Some of the soldiers were already firing into the air or taking long-range potshots toward the village. The loud SPANG of bullets hitting corrugated metal echoed back under the trees.

"Major. Hostages are secured in the jungle out the other side of the village. Request permission to get my ass back over there and join in the ruckus?"

"Negative. Stay with the civilians. Will revise if—"

"Here they come," interrupted Weaver, and things got loud in a hurry.

The first truck came screeching around the turn, tires barely gripping, and then slammed full force into the damaged truck placed across the road. There was a sickening crunch and the sound of shattering glass, and soldiers crying out as they were thrown out of the back of the truck. The driver didn't hear them; he and the soldier riding shotgun were dead already, chests crushed by the impact.

The second vehicle didn't have time to slow down before it plowed into the back of the first one right at the bend of the curve. Instead of flattening out into the obstruction, the second truck slewed right, its back end sliding off the road. It kept skidding until it found a tree to broadside, at which point the chassis bent like a pretzel. More soldiers went flying. Others ducked down into the truck bed and held on, taking the brunt of the shock when the truck hit the tree.

And then, their tripwires thoroughly pulled by the trucks, the grenades Nomad had so carefully placed went off.

The soldiers from the second truck didn't stand a chance. Shrapnel ripped through them, punching through the truck's side panel and wreaking carnage on the men still within. The men in the first truck who'd been thrown sufficiently wide caught some of the blasts as well, going down like wheat in a hailstorm. The cab of the second truck shielded a few of the men still groggily trying to crawl out of the bed of the first, but most of their comrades were already down. To make matters worse, a hole had been punched in the second truck's fuel tank, and was now leaking diesel all over the road.

"Weaver!" Nomad barked. "Before they pull it together!"

Weaver was already firing, dropping the survivors where they stood. One managed to get a couple of rounds off before Nomad dropped him, and then it was suddenly quiet. Nomad carefully stepped through the carnage, Weaver covering him as he looked for survivors playing possum.

None of them were.

"Shit," Weaver said, "this cannot possibly be it."

"Looks like it is, though. This is going to be one for the record books." He opened the cab of the second truck long enough to make sure the two men in there were both definitely dead, and then backed away. Only the slow gurgle of fuel leaking onto the road disturbed the sudden stillness.

"Where the hell is Midas," Nomad asked, not particularly anticipating an answer. "Midas, this is Nomad. Give me a sitrep, over?"

There was nothing. Nomad turned to Weaver. "That's not good."

Weaver nodded in agreement. "Not good at all. And—oh, damn."

Another sound was tearing through the early morning quiet, the roar of another engine revved and coming hell for leather.

"I knew that wasn't it," Weaver said quietly, and then the truck swerved into view. Like the others, it was a modified Toyota pickup, packed with armed men. Unlike the others, it had a man standing in the back, the distinctive shape of an RPG-7 clearly visible at his shoulder.

Nomad was suddenly, acutely aware of the diesel puddling around his boots. "RPG! Take cover!" he said, and dove into the brush just as the soldier in the pickup fired.

The projectile corkscrewed in, slamming into the back of the second truck where it lay pinned against the tree. A vicious explosion split the air, with the shriek of torn metal singing counterpoint. Then the fuel caught, and a pillar of flame shot upward with a deafening roar. Suddenly detached doors and tires went flying, carving swaths of destruction as they plowed through the jungle.

Nomad hugged the ground as a sheet of flaming hot metal flew overhead, burying itself six inches deep in the tree trunk behind him. He'd dodged the first explosion, but the second had picked him up and slammed him into the dirt with feeling.

Groggily, he struggled to get up. "Weaver? Can you hear me?" he whispered, and got only silence back. He went to tap his mic and realized it was gone. The blast had torn the helmet right off his head, and his earpiece and mic with it.

Already, the third truck was pulling up and disgorging soldiers. They moved quickly and professionally, fanning out into the jungle in twos. Far too many to take on solo. Far too many even with Weaver's help. But with his comms gone, Weaver might as well have been on the moon, to say nothing of Midas and Holt.

Nomad crawled back towards the village. There was a shout of triumph behind him, and then a rap of metal on hard ceramic that told him someone had found his headgear. No way could that be allowed to stay in enemy hands, Nomad told himself. Had to get it back, assuming he survived.

And then there was Holt, with the hostages. Falling too far back would potentially lead the fight right to them. Pulling the enemy's attention away from the village, however—and it was strange how quiet the village was, he realized—might buy enough time for Holt to get the hostages down to the boat and back into friendly territory.

There was a burst of fire from the other side of the road, then some shouted discussion and a wet thump. Nomad edged right, slowly easing to his feet behind the cover of a thick, vine-covered tree trunk. A line of enemy soldiers was moving toward him, weapons ready.

He leaned out from behind the tree and opened fire.

Weaver was already running before Nomad said a word. The blast from the rocket launcher staggered him; the one from the fuel tank going up flung him ten feet along the jungle floor. He skidded to a stop. "Nomad? Do you copy?"

There was no answer.

"Shit." He pulled himself up off the ground, keeping low, and ducked behind a fallen log half-absorbed by an ornate collection of shelf fungi. Through the trees, he could see enemy soldiers moving purposefully off the road. They were in no hurry; they had numbers on their side, and they had a good read on what they were up against.

As Weaver watched, a soldier stooped, disarmed one of Nomad's remaining booby traps and kept moving with his sweep. If they kept moving, sooner or later they'd flush him out from under cover or out of the jungle into the village, at which point he'd get lit up. So the only option was go wide.

Staying low, he sidestepped left, following the log as long as he could. From its jagged base he crawled over behind another tree, then another. A quick look up told him that the searchers were advancing. There was a rustle in the leaves back toward the road, and three of the soldiers opened fire. Something shrieked, and then the soldier who'd disarmed the trap stepped forward to poke at the target. He came away a minute later with a mass of bloody fur in his hand, some sort of rodent caught in the wrong place at the wrong time, but evidence that the soldiers had hair triggers and very good aim.

The soldiers kept walking, and Weaver kept sidling left. They were close now, moving almost parallel to him. He edged farther back, pressing himself into the dirt. Something crawled onto his face and up his cheek. He held still, praying it wasn't poisonous, that it wouldn't bite, that it didn't have friends.

It paused, just below his left eye, and then started moving again.

Nomad held still. He'd been trained for moments like this. No movement, no reaction, no giving in to the urge to just quickly reach up and swipe the damn thing off his face. Nothing that could spoil the shot.

Except this time, he'd be on the receiving end.

Weaver could hear the soldiers' voices now, chattering back and forth. He'd picked up enough Spanish to know what they were talking about, chatter about finding and killing whoever had hit the camp, and then taking any remaining frustration out on the village. They weren't in a hurry, either. They had enough time to do the job right.

The insect moved again. Weaver thought about all the crap he'd been giving Holt about the local wildlife and silently told himself that this was karma, and the best way to pay it off was to just sit there and take it as the soldiers walked past.

They walked past, and they kept walking

Weaver let out a tiny sigh of relief. He let them get ten yards past him, then began sliding parallel to the road, away from the village. The enemy kept moving, a row of backs fading into the jungle as he made his way behind them. A little more time, and he could set up in a good spot, either to start picking off hostiles and turning their fire inward on their own position, or, if there was no hope for it and the rest of the squad were dead, to prep for a run down to the river and the boat.

Suddenly, there was a sound of gunfire from the other side of the road. He knew that sound, he'd heard it in Donetsk and a dozen other places. Nomad's weapon.

There was shouting and the sound of returning fire.

"I do not approve of any of this," Weaver said for emphasis, and flicked the ant off his face. And then he started firing.

"What's going on?" Crotty asked as the sounds of metal meeting metal at too high a rate of speed cut through the morning quiet. Holt held up a hand for silence as gunfire and a series of explosions followed.

"That's the Major taking care of business. We're gonna stay right here and keep our heads down until the bullets stop flying. You got that?" Holt's head was on a swivel, constantly looking from the jungle to the civilians in his care to the impenetrable jungle on the other side of the village where something was going down.

She nodded. "Are you sure this spot's safe?"

Holt had taken them clear through the village and out the other side, into the jungle he'd cut through earlier. There was a hollow he'd seen on his way in, and he'd tucked them down in it before pulling down some branches to provide additional visual cover. Not for the first time, he wished he had the experimental reactive camo he'd heard DARPA was working on. He'd read about it, but the tech was years away. At the moment, the effect faded if you moved too fast, and the power unit on the gear tended to overheat and catch fire at inopportune moments.

But right now, if he could get his hands on one and drape it over his little cadre, he'd gladly take the risk.

There was more gunfire, the big boom of Weaver's gun mixing with the anxious chatter of Russian-made automatic weaponry. Then everything fell silent.

"You think it's over?" Stanton asked. "Are we safe?"

Holt didn't answer, making a shushing gesture with his hand instead. No way the fight was over that fast, his gut told him. Something wasn't sitting right. He could hear Weaver and Midas chatting over the comms, commenting on what had just gone down.

Then, suddenly, two words: "Take cover!"

He reached out and grabbed the civilians, then pulled them down as he hugged the dirt. "Down!" he shouted, even as a massive explosion rocked the clearing. An instant later, a second one followed as a pillar of fire blasted its way up through the trees. Weaver was shouting something on the comms and Nomad wasn't answering, and suddenly the sound of gunfire was everywhere again.

Crotty peeked up from the dirt. "What's happening?"

Holt made a decision.

"Here," he said, handing her the pistols Nomad had given him. "Do you know how to use one of these?"

She took the guns, examined them, and then nodded. "You don't last long out here if you don't know how to shoot."

"Good. Anyone wearing a uniform who's not me or one of my buddies comes near you, you shoot. Don't shoot unless you have to. Hiding's still your best bet." Holt looked toward the fire, where the sounds of shooting had intensified.

"You're leaving us here." It wasn't a question.

"Briefly," he said, and then he was up and over and moving toward the fight.

Nomad dropped two men before the enemy could

return fire, then ran in a zigzag away from the road and the village. The soldiers' reactions were efficient; they dropped to cover and returned fire. Bullets slammed into trees and punched holes in leaves.

Nomad took cover behind a tree trunk not really big enough for the job, then leaned out and fired toward the road. Heads that had popped up ducked back down, but not for long, and a withering hail of fire slammed Nomad's position as a handful of the enemy soldiers advanced.

He felt at his belt for his last grenade; smoke, not frag. Under the circumstances, it would do. Pulling the pin, he tossed it into the undergrowth ahead of the leading enemy elements. It immediately started spewing a cloud of thick white haze. More firing came through the cloud, but it was wild now, and coughing and shouting were mixed in with the reports.

Nomad crouched and ran, targeting a collapsed tangle of trees that had fallen onto one another. Vines had snaked up around the entire edifice, giving it the look of a vague, shambling human shape. He'd almost reached it when the first of the enemy soldiers emerged from the smoke. Nomad stopped, turned, and fired, dropping the man as more of his allies emerged, stumbling into the clean air. More movement on the right told him that they were moving to flank the smoke as well, converging on his location. Bullets ripped through the vines as he ducked behind them, then more nearly took his ear off as he leaned out to spray at the flankers on his right.

More gunfire broke out on the other side of the road. A couple of the soldiers on Nomad's left paused to look back for a second, which gave him an opening. One went down, another took a bullet in the arm, and then Nomad was off again, sprinting through the trees in a long circle.

"What's going on?" Stanton asked. "Why did he leave us here?"

"Hush," Crotty said, and tossed Carpenter one of the pistols. She caught it expertly, pulled back the slide, and popped the clip.

"Eight shots left," she said. "If something happens, it's going to be a short fight."

"I'm praying for no fight," Crotty said, and peered over the top of the hollow. She could see Holt sprinting from building to building, working his way toward the confused sounds of combat. "But if something goes down, fire them all."

Carpenter nodded. Stanton froze, then turned toward the deeper jungle. "What was that?"

"What was what?" Carpenter popped the clip back in. "I didn't hear anything."

"I swear, I heard something moving." He paused. "There it is again! Over there!"

He pointed. Crotty strained to look but saw nothing. "I'm sorry," she said. "I don't see any—"

At which point someone pressed the muzzle of a gun into the back of her neck.

She raised her hands slowly, nodding at Carpenter to do the same. A soft prod from the gun, and she dropped the pistol on the ground.

Figures were coming out of the green now, men and women with a motley assortment of firearms and machetes. And in the middle of them, the soldier she'd heard called Midas, standing next to an older man she assumed was the chief of the village. Midas pointed to her, then turned to the chief and said something softly. The chief nodded, and then the pressure at the back of her neck was gone.

"I'm sorry about that," Midas said, as he moved over to the hollow. "These people are not inclined to take chances with strangers right now."

"I can see that," Crotty said dryly, and rubbed the spot where the gun had been pressed against her. "This is their village?"

Midas nodded. "They knew the soldiers were coming, so they fell back to the jungle, hoping to avoid a fight." He cocked his head towards the sounds of gunfire. "I don't think they're going to avoid it anymore."

"Your man with the sunglasses, he went running into that."

"Then I think the Major will have a talk with him about following orders. Now stay down and keep quiet; for your sake." Then he was gone, along with the villagers, moving in a silent wave toward the fight.

The soldier Weaver had targeted fell, arms spasming. It took a second for his partner to register what had happened, and that was long enough for another round to catch him center mass. He went over, the reflexive squeeze of the trigger as he died sending his allies ducking for cover. Weaver shifted back and left, closer to the road, then turned his aim on the road. The flames had died down somewhat on the second truck, but it was still burning merrily. Next to it, the one it had crashed into was torn up and burning as well.

But the vehicle they'd dragged across the road, while partially obstructed, was still in one piece. Weaver mentally estimated where the fuel tank might be on a truck like that, adjusted his aim, and made sure he had a tracer round in the chamber. Then, he fired.

The round punched into the side of the truck and burrowed deep into its guts. An instant later, a flame licked up underneath the chassis, and the entire vehicle was suddenly wreathed in flames. The soldiers nearest the road stumbled back. The ones farther into the jungle kept coming. Weaver squeezed off another round, then fell back. They were concentrating fire on him now, closing in. More fire came from the road, as the soldiers stationed there opened up, catching him in a crossfire. Bullets stitched a line in a tree next to him, spraying him with sawdust and splinters. There were too many. Options were closing down. In desperation, he cut toward the road. The fire from the jungle trailed off, the soldiers afraid of hitting their own, but now the soldiers in the muddy track had a bead on him, as more bullets spat through the trees. Then he was out of the woods and onto the road, firing as he moved. He could hear hostiles moving around both sides of the truck, so he threw himself up over the side and into the bed. The move caught one of the soldiers coming around the other way by surprise, and Weaver slammed the butt of his rifle into the side of the man's head. He went over, and Weaver went out the other side of the truck and kept running.

The soldiers from his side of the road, illuminated by new flames, followed.

By the time Holt reached the tree line, the sounds of the fight had moved deeper into the jungle. The flames of the burning truck silhouetted soldiers running and firing, with only occasional sounds of return fire to provide counterpoint. "Weaver! Nomad! Do you copy?"

"Running like hell," Weaver answered. "Nomad's alive but incommunicado, over! Where the hell are you?"

"Inbound!"

He sprinted into the jungle.

Nomad could hear the firing moving toward him, even as he moved away. His pursuers were more cautious now but just as dogged, and the last time he'd stopped to fire he'd nearly had his head taken off. But at least they were following him, away from the village and the hostages. And they hadn't caught him yet.

More gunfire sounded to the rear of the pursuit, followed by heavy return fire. What it meant, he had no idea, but it bought him another couple seconds of distraction to put more distance between himself and the nearest hostile. The ground sloped upward here, slowing him slightly, and then more rounds slammed into the dirt near his feet. He slipped, stumbled, kept going.

Ahead of him, a figure loomed out of the foliage. The man raised his weapon, a battle-scarred AK, and fired.

The best thing he could do, Holt decided, was listen to the sound of pursuit and then follow it. Now that he was under the canopy, the jungle muted some of the sounds of gunfire, but there was too much of it for even the densest foliage to diffuse. Having a cloud of what was obviously popped smoke drifting slowly toward him didn't hurt, either. He put his head down and ran.

There was movement ahead, soldiers popping briefly into view as they fell back from the smoke. Good enough, Holt decided, and opened fire.

From a distance, Holt saw Nomad go down.

"Weaver! Midas! Nomad's hit! Moving to assist!"

"I see you, Holt," Weaver chimed in. "Headed the same way! Midas, where are you?"

Midas's answer was lost to Holt as a wave of blistering fire rolled downhill from the soldiers who'd closed on Nomad. He threw himself down as the bullets scythed through where he'd been standing a second before. Rolling to his right, he tossed out a sensor with his off hand. It bounced twice on the hill, hesitated, and then flared to life.

What it showed wasn't pretty. The soldiers were coming back downhill, and they'd gotten reinforcements. Two of them were crouched over the crumpled blue figure of Nomad, doing what, it wasn't clear. On the far left, he could see Weaver, moving at a dead run. But the real issue was the wall of yellow headed his way. A track of bullets pocked the ground to his left, and Holt scrambled back. From his knees, he squeezed off a few rounds, then flung himself behind a tree as the ground exploded from well-placed fire. One of the yellow figures dropped as Weaver yelled "Target down!" But the rest kept coming. He peeked around the tree and nearly got his head taken off by a burst of enemy fire for his trouble.

"Weaver! What are they doing with Nomad?"

"Looks like they're picking him up. I'm guessing he's alive!"

"We've got to get him back!"

"I'm open to suggestions!"

A grenade hit the ground ahead of Holt's position and bounced downhill toward him.

"Grenade!" He dropped and rolled downhill away from it, hoping he'd angled right and that shrapnel would pass over him. Otherwise, it was too close and he was going to get turned into human linguini.

The blast went off, sending Holt sprawling. A glance behind him told him that the tree he'd used for cover had nearly been severed at the base, but on the bright side, the hostiles had temporarily paused their advance, ducking down behind cover as they let the grenade do their dirty work for them. But even as he watched, they rose and started sweeping methodically toward him.

"Weaver? You okay?"

"Yeah, out of blast range. They're definitely moving Nomad. I'm hearing another truck engine—shit, we've got to end this fast!"

"I'm trying, I'm trying." He turned, popped up, and fired toward the enemy. One of the yellow shapes on his HUD folded up and went down, but the others closed rank and poured fire on his position. "They're extending their flank, trying to cut me off from the village." He could see enemy soldiers now moving to his right, spreading out and then disappearing as they moved out of sensor range. "They're in the weeds."

"Fall back toward the road. I'm going to try to— sonofabitch!" The sounds of heavy fire came through, in real life and echoing over Weaver's comms. "I'm pinned down. Can't get to Nomad! Midas, wherever the hell you are, now would be a good time!"

In response, there was a series of gunshots from Holt's right. Enemy soldiers went down in a wave as Midas burst into view. With him was Erubiel, grim-faced and firing a captured AK expertly. As the soldiers turned to face the new threat, Holt saw his opportunity, rising and pouring fire on them.

Caught in the crossfire, the soldiers fell back or simply fell. Midas and the villagers swept forward as Holt pivoted and headed for Weaver. Already he could see the soldiers who'd been pinning the sniper down falling back, abandoning the fight in favor of retreating into the jungle and self-preservation.

"You good, Weaver?"

"Couple close calls, but yeah. Truck engine's fading. They've already pulled out with Nomad. Midas, don't over-extend!"

"These people know what they're doing, Weaver," came the reply. "Going to push them back, but nobody's running into an ambush."

"Roger that." Weaver sounded tired, the adrenaline of the fight already starting to fade. "Holt, form up on me. We'll link up and put a bow on this?"

"Roger that. On my way."

CHAPTER 11

The fire had mostly sputtered out by the time the last shots were fired, the sheer dampness of the forest keeping it from spreading. Bodies of the dead were neatly laid out, the soldiers stripped of anything useful by villagers already thinking ahead to the next possible confrontation. Holt had vanished briefly to check on the hostages, who were shaken but determined. With Midas's help, he'd gotten them a place to lie down and rest in one of the remaining houses, while he and the remaining Ghosts gathered to pick through the wreckage and plan their next move.

"So do we go after him?" Holt asked, peering toward the trucks in hopes of seeing something intact in one of the cabs. All that met his gaze was blackened metal and melted plastic. Nothing had survived.

"Negative. We get the packages out of here and into Protasio's hands. Then we go after him."

"That's cold, Weaver." Holt's tone stopped somewhere just short of disapproving. "I thought you and he were tight."

"We were. We are. And he'd do the same thing if it were me, and you would, too, if you thought about it. We have a job to do and we do it. Period."

Midas looked up from picking through the brush on the side of the road. "Should we call OVERLORD? See if we can get some backup?"

"We'll call him," Weaver answered. "But we're not getting backup. Not while there's a job to do."

Midas didn't answer, instead stooping to the ground and picking something up. He turned and the other two saw immediately what it was: Nomad's helmet. "Holt, do you think you can do something with this?"

"Yeah." He walked over and took it from Midas's hands. "Looks like it took a direct punch to some of the more sensitive systems. I'll see what I can salvage. When it's time," he added defiantly.

"When it's time," Weaver echoed. "Hell, I don't like this any better than you two do. But what we've got to do, that's clear."

"Yeah." Holt sounded deflated. He stooped to pick

up a half-melted blob of plastic, then tossed it aside. "So what's the plan?"

"Stay here till nightfall, if Erubiel will let us. Rest up, reload, then get the hostages downriver and into good hands. Nomad didn't like being on the river during the day, and he wasn't wrong. I'm guessing they've got heavier craft on the water than our little old thing."

"Do we really want to wait that long?"

"No, Holt, we don't. But I'm not seeing a better option." Weaver stopped and looked around. For an instant, he wondered how long it would take for the jungle to forget what had happened there today. How long for the vines to crawl over and pull apart the wreckage, for the scavengers to devour the bodies, and the green to cover up the blast scars and burned patches. Not long at all, he decided, which was the best news he'd heard all damn day.

"Right. All of Nomad's booby traps are disarmed. Nothing left out here to surprise Erubiel's people. Let's head in."

"Yeah." They turned and started the walk back to the village. As they crossed the bridge, Holt nudged Midas. "Hey, was it just me or did these guys fight a lot smarter here than they did at the camp? Much more organized than the jamokes down on the river, too."

Midas nodded. "It's something to think about when we go back for the second package."

"You don't think they're coming back here?" Weaver interjected.

Midas shook his head. "They've got Nomad. That's

going to take some of their attention. Besides, I think we hurt them badly enough that it would take awhile to pull together another op."

"Not to mention the fact that nothing's getting through that road without help from God almighty or a bunch of HE," Holt added. "Midas's right. Nobody's coming back for awhile."

Weaver stooped and picked a metal shard off the ground. It was still warm, and he tossed it backhand into the woods. "Hello. How'd you get this far." He shook his head. "So much for go in, get out, keep it quiet."

"I think that plan was dead in the water the moment the Old Man told us there were two exfils," Midas said, his tone serious.

Then they were out from under the trees and walking into the village. He turned to the other two. "I'm going to ask Erubiel if there's a place we can get some food and some sleep for a couple of hours. Then we'll be on our way and he won't have to worry about us anymore." He looked around. "They've got funeral business to attend to in any case, and we should probably let them take care of their own without us in the way."

"Could have said that a long time ago," Holt answered, but it was under his breath and looking away. Then, louder, "I gotta say, Master Sergeant, you're taking this awful well." Holt's words were light but his expression was sour.

"How do you mean?" Weaver's tone was guarded.

"I mean Nomad's in enemy hands, and I know the two of you are tight, but you're talking like nothing happened." Midas tried to step in, but Holt waved him off and kept going. "That's either cool or cold, and for the life of me I can't figure out which."

Weaver stopped and turned. "Listen very carefully, because I will say this once and once only. Nomad and I go way, way back. We've pulled each other's asses out of the fire more times than I can count. You don't know the shit we've been through together, and you do not want to know. And right now, my first instinct is to go right after the sons of bitches who have him and bring him back, just like I know that would be his first instinct if it was me that got grabbed.

"But my first thought is that we do the mission, because that is who we are and what we do. We are Ghosts, and that means something. We drop the mission, even to get one of our own back, we lose what makes us special. And if it were Nomad standing here now, he'd be telling you the exact same thing.

"So here's the news: we are going to finish the mission. We are going to get those other civilians back. And then, with or without the Old Man's blessing, we going to get in the saddle, go back in-country, and pull our man—my friend—out. And God help anyone who gets in our way. But only after we finish the mission. Am I understood?"

Holt blinked, twice, and said nothing. Midas interrupted the silence, assuring Weaver that he and Holt did indeed understand and that the mission of course came first.

"Good," Weaver growled. "We'll get him back, trust me on this one. It's just not the time right now."

He looked around. "And the sooner we take care of

the mission, the sooner we get to bring Nomad home."

And with that Weaver stalked away, leaving Holt shaking his head in the sniper's wake.

Midas and Weaver walked into the longhouse in the center of the village, which had clearly been made up for impromptu company. Holt was already inside, with the three former hostages sacked out on thin mattresses at his feet. A couple more lay empty, waiting for occupants.

Holt held Nomad's helmet and was tsk-tsking over it as he assessed the damage. "Don't know what exactly he did to this, but it's going to be a bitch to fix," he said as he looked up. "I don't suppose anyone brought a spare?"

"Negative. I'm just glad that when that thing popped loose, it didn't take his head with it." The edge to Weaver's voice belied the light words, as he dropped down onto one of the empty mattresses and stretched out. "Wake me up in a couple of hours so I can call the Old Man and you can get some shut-eye, too."

"Will do." He examined the helmet again, lips pursed. "I don't suppose you've got a soldering iron, pliers, and some industrial grade epoxy on you?" But Weaver was already out. Holt grinned. "Didn't think so."

A soft buzzing woke Weaver. He checked his wrist readout. 1200 hours. Half an hour till the communications bird was overhead.

He sat up. Holt was gently snoring in his chair, the guts of Nomad's helmet spilled out in his lap. Crotty and her people were dead to the world, curled up on their mattresses. Midas stood by the door, relaxed but ready. When he saw Weaver move, he nodded.

Weaver yawned. "I need to go put that call into the Old Man. When I get back, your turn to check for light leaks." He glanced at Holt. "Don't wake him up. He's had a rough day."

Midas nodded again, smiling faintly, and then stepped aside to let Weaver out.

He headed down to the river, moving carefully. Just his luck, he thought, to find the one hostile who'd zagged instead of zigged and ended up on the wrong side of the village.

But nothing crossed his path, and he reached the boat in plenty of time. Cautiously, he pulled the branches aside, keeping an eye out for snakes, but anything that had moved decided he wasn't worth the bother, and he was able to pull the Harris rig out without too much trouble.

At 1230, his earpiece buzzed again. Showtime.

"OVERLORD, this is BLUECAT. Do you copy?"

For a moment, there was nothing but silence. Then Mitchell's voice came through, loud and clear. "BLUECAT, this is OVERLORD. I hear you loud and clear. What's your status?" And then a moment later. "Weaver? Where's Nomad?"

"Status is shitty. Made our first three catches, but we've got a man overboard." He thought for a second. "We've got the packages in a secure location. All three are a little the worse for wear, but healthy. Going to be taking them down river tonight. If you can warn PESCADOR we're coming, that'll be a big help, because I've got no idea what the hell is waiting for us at the border."

"Copy that. What's Nomad's status?"

"In enemy hands, presumably wounded." Quickly, Weaver filled Mitchell in on the fight at the village. "He was pulling the pursuit away from the civilians when he got taken down." He hesitated. "I am assuming that we are greenlit to continue the mission and to attempt an extraction?"

Mitchell's voice was full of frustration. "Weaver, mission first."

"We don't leave our own behind, sir."

"We're not going to. But unless a miracle falls in your lap, you have no idea where the hell they've taken him. They've got at least half a day's head start, they've got vehicles, and you're going to lose at least another twelve hours delivering Crotty and her crew. On the other hand, we have solid intel on Kwan and Messina, and they will remain your priority."

"Understood, Colonel." Something splashed out in the river. He turned to look and was rewarded with a glimpse of a huge arapaima sinking back into the depths. "Well, I'll be," he muttered.

"Weaver?"

"Sorry, sir. Thought I saw something." He coughed once and asked, delicately, "I know we can't scrub the mission, even down a man, but I don't suppose there's any chance of backup? Hell, at this point, I'd even take Stone."

"Stone's spoken for. That's part of the equation that landed the team in this mess, Weaver. I wish I could give you all the help in the world, but my pockets are empty." His frustration was increasingly palpable. "At least I have a little good news for you. Sage and Joker are both recovering nicely. I'll send them your best."

"Thank you, sir."

"Anything else?" Already the transmission was sounding fried around the edges, the signal failing as the satellite continued on its path.

"No, sir. Letting the team get some shut-eye, and then we'll be moving by last light. Will check in tomorrow to confirm handoff."

"Roger that. Good luck, Weaver. OVERLORD out."

Weaver sat on the riverbank for another few minutes, watching the waters roll by. No more fish broke the surface. The one he'd seen had been a real monster, about six feet long and thick as a tree trunk. Ones that big were rare as hell, he knew; overfishing by sport anglers looking to mount the most impressive trophy they could find had scrubbed the big ones out. But he'd seen one, one that maybe wasn't even supposed to be here, and it had shown itself to him and gone on its way.

"Maybe it's a sign," he said to himself, as he got up and headed back in. "Or maybe you're big enough to just not give a damn."

CHAPTER 12

Nomad awoke in the back of a truck, his shoulder throbbing and sticky with blood. He was on the floor of the bed, surrounded by unhappy-looking soldiers of the Amazonas Free State, and they were making good time in what he suspected was the wrong direction.

A quick check of his person told him what he already presumed. No gun, no gear, no nothing. They hadn't tied him up, possibly because they didn't think he'd wake up and possibly because they figured they had enough

numbers to keep him in line. Either seemed like a reasonable assumption. The wound in his shoulder throbbed.
The round clearly hadn't hit anything major, or he'd have
bled out, but the field dressing was sloppy. Blood was still
leaking out, and he was pretty sure that if he lasted long
enough, there'd be some kind of infection to manage.

One of the soldiers saw him move and, without getting up, kicked him in the ribs. Nomad inhaled sharply,
which alerted others to his new status. There was a soft
click, and he opened his eyes to see a Browning HP in
his face. The man holding it was older, thin, wiry, and
bald, and he said something very softly to the other men
in the truck bed. One of them responded with something
Nomad was pretty sure translated to "No, we need him
alive."

The older man hesitated a minute, then drew back the
pistol. "*Con vida,*" he said. "*Pero nadie dijo 'sano y salvo.'*"

The men in the back of the truck nodded. Nomad
tried to throw himself over the side, but strong hands
restrained him, and then they went to work.

Night had crept most of the way in by the time the team
made its way down to the river.

Weaver had gone well ahead of the other two, both to
prep their transportation and, as he put it, to get the hell
away from everyone else. He'd finished clearing out foliage covering the boat, not to mention the wildlife he'd
missed previously, and had the engine quietly rumbling
when the rest of the squad arrived, along with Crotty and

her team. She stepped onboard with aplomb, leaving her assistants to scramble after.

"Erubiel knows we're not coming back?" Holt asked Midas, as the two pushed the boat away from shore and then leaped in.

"As much as he thinks you're the funniest thing ever, I think he's happier that way," Midas said. "I don't disagree with him. You can try and step lightly, but you always leave a bigger footprint than you imagined."

Holt looked back toward the village, hidden behind walls of thick green, thinking about flames and bodies on the ground. "I think I know what you mean."

The boat shook as he leapt in, causing the researchers to grab wildly for handholds. "Easy, folks," Weaver told them. "Just relax, she's not tipping over. We're going to try to get downriver so we can hand you off to the Brazilian authorities, and they'll get you home. If we're lucky, it'll be a quick trip. If we're not, we're gonna tell you to get down, at which point you duck under the benches and do not get up or make a sound until we tell you to." He throttled the engine, and the boat swung away from the bank and into the current. "Oh, and please keep your hands and feet inside the damn boat at all times, because I would hate like hell to have to explain to the State Department that we rescued you, but then you got yourself eaten."

"I think we can handle that," Crotty said, amused. "Anything else, or are we set?"

"Food and water's in the locker over there, if you want anything. You need to hit the can, you're on your own."

With that, the boat fully joined the main current and started picking up speed.

The river was still high, thick with the detritus of the storm on the way in, but moving downstream instead of up removed some of the danger of careening flotsam. Low clouds scudded across the sky, reducing the moon to a faint blob. The trees rose on either side, an impenetrable wall of darker black against the night, more than sufficient incentive for Weaver to keep to the center of the channel. Bats dipped and darted and shrieked, feeding off the clouds of insects that swarmed over the water's surface.

Weaver joined Midas at the back of the boat, while Holt carved out a little space to continue working on the broken helmet. "No light," Weaver cautioned him.

"You really think this is my first rodeo?" Holt shot back, and buried himself in his work.

"The way he talks, I would kill to see that man in an actual rodeo," Weaver noted. "We've got a good few hours before we approach the border."

Midas moved to the waterproof locker that held the comms gear and pulled it out. "He might surprise you. In the meantime, I'd better call our contacts and let them know we're coming," he said as he was setting it up. It powered on with a reassuring hum. "I think we are good to go."

"Then go," said Holt. "A little help wouldn't hurt, if you take my meaning."

"I generally do." Midas leaned in to the radio and picked up the mic.

"PESCADOR, this is BLUECAT. Do you copy?"

There was a hiss of static, and then Lt. Correa's voice crackled over the line. "BLUECAT, this is PESCADOR. We read you. How was the fishing?"

"Mixed day on the river. We caught three. Can't wait to get them up on the wall at home."

"Sounds like a good catch. Run into any problems?"

Holt coughed delicately. Midas raised a cautioning finger at him, then responded. "Nothing we couldn't handle. We're headed in on the down low. Might need an assist hauling the catch in. Got a couple caiman in the river to worry about, could maybe use a bigger net."

Correa paused before answering, and her voice had a weary edge to it. "Once you're in our pond, we'll be happy to help you land the catch. We're not allowed to go fishing at the neighbors'."

"And if we're caught fishing in the wrong pond?" The question hung there for a moment.

"You'll probably wash downstream. If there's anything I can do when you get back to our pond, let me know. I'll have my ears on. PESCADOR out."

"Well, that was helpful," Weaver offered.

"Captain Protasio is a cautious man. I don't think he wants 'started an international incident' in his jacket," Midas said. "He's not going to start a shootout with the Venezuelans over us."

"Those aren't Venezuelan regulars we tangled with," Weaver retorted pointedly. "He could blow those assholes clear off the riverbank and Caracas would probably send him a thank-you note. He's just putting our nuts in a vise over Holt. And that's on him, not our guy."

A loud splash from the far bank caught both of their attention. "What's that?" Holt asked.

"Caimans," Crotty answered. "They're nocturnal feeders, mostly. I know the river looks calm, but underneath, there's a million life-or-death struggles going on every minute." She shrugged. "Part of why I got into botany, honestly. I got tired of watching animals eat one another."

"What are you doing out here, Professor?" Weaver asked. "You and your team, you're a long way from home."

"Home doesn't offer a lot of chances at finding new anticancer drugs. Out in the field, there are a million undiscovered plant species, and all it takes is finding the right one to alleviate a lot of human misery. And the other side of it is, rain forests are disappearing fast, everywhere you look. God alone knows how many cures have been clear-cut or burned right out of existence. If people like me don't come out here, we risk losing so much that we never even knew was there."

"And if you find something?" Weaver sounded unconvinced.

Crotty gave a low laugh. "If we find something, then there's cycles of research and testing and—trust me, gentlemen, you may think you had a hard fight today, but that's because you've never tangled with the FDA's approval process. Let's just say that I am unlikely to get rich or famous from anything I discover. But if my team and I do locate something promising, then maybe down the road it does some good. And in the meantime, it buys a little protection for the patch of jungle where it was found."

Midas shifted in his seat to face Crotty. "How did you get captured? Your dossier said that your team's been out there awhile with no problems."

"Of course I have a dossier," Crotty noted. "This was my fifth year coming out to this camp, my first year with a new sponsor for the expedition. Small team, because the sponsor wasn't exactly generous. They wanted Champagne on a beer budget and their name on all the equipment. It's standard operating procedure when you're dealing with first-timers, but finding funding these days is so hard, you grin and bear it. I had fifty grad students apply to come along, because the opportunities just aren't there anymore. Those two," and she jerked a thumb at Stanton and Carpenter, both of whom were fast asleep, "were the best. They did solid work in the field, and they didn't get on each others' nerves, or mine, too much."

"I think the Major would have been jealous," Midas said, and Weaver gave him an elbow in the ribs. "So, your team was fine, and you'd been out here before. This should have been, well, not routine, but at least not a problem. Any issues with the locals before things went down? With soldiers?"

Crotty shook her head. "Never. We traded with some of the indigenous villages and got along fine. Worked with some of them, too. They'd bring in specimens, or guide us to new collecting sites. The one where we stopped, I think we traded with them once. But there was never any friction. And the soldiers, once we crossed the border, that was always the last we saw of them." She shuddered. "Until this year."

"What happened?"

"Our camp was pretty far out in the bush. Like I said, we never saw soldiers. And then one day, a patrol came out of the trees and the officer in charge announced that we were now under the protection of the Amazonas Free State. Then they turned around and marched back into the jungle. I wanted to leave immediately, but Stanton talked me into staying. They hadn't threatened us, he said. We should continue the work, especially since some of the preliminary results looked very interesting." She rolled her eyes. "If we get back home, I'm going to fail him, just for that."

"Yeah, that seemed like a bad call," Weaver volunteered. "How long before they came back?"

"A week. Long enough for the little voice in the back of my head to get lulled back to sleep. They came into the camp in the middle of the night. Held us at gunpoint and marched us out of there and into that camp. They were in a hurry. They grabbed the computers and some of the other electronics, but left the samples. The generator's failed by now, so anything we were trying to preserve's probably been eaten by ants." She looked up. "Don't worry, I'm not going to ask you to go back there to rescue my precious work. The jungle will keep it until this gets straightened out and I go back. Or someone else does." She slumped where she sat. "Lord knows, right now I just want to go home."

She said nothing after that, just curled up and went to sleep as the Ghosts watched the shadows of the jungle roll by.

CHAPTER 13

It was the throbbing in his shoulder that woke Nomad up, though that was far from the only place that hurt. Urbina's men had really laid into him, and from the rasping pain in his chest, it seemed likely that they'd broken a couple of ribs. But it was the shoulder that really hurt, even if, as he now saw, the dressing had been changed and the bleeding largely stopped. Even the slightest shift in position was a reminder that his anatomy was not functioning as intended.

Apart from the medical attention, the amenities were slight. They'd ziptied him to a chair and left him in the middle of what looked like the interior of a prefab building. There was a bucket in the corner and not much else. A lean soldier in his mid-twenties stood guard, a shiny new AK-103 in his hands. His face was scarred from acne and he was going prematurely bald, and his expression suggested he was hoping Nomad would try to escape so he could shoot him.

Instead, Nomad coughed. "Could I have a drink of water?"

The guard said nothing.

"Please. I'm not asking you to untie me. I just need,"— he coughed again—"some water."

The guard fidgeted and looked away.

"Come on, just one sip. I'm begging you."

"I have my orders," the guard replied in a surprisingly deep bass. "You will be given water on the schedule that the Colonel has arranged. You will be fed the same way. Otherwise, you are to receive nothing. It is worth my life to give you that drink of water, not that I would in any case." He spat on the ground at Nomad's feet for emphasis. "And how arrogant to assume I would speak English."

"You're not afraid of me, are you?" Nomad felt like he was laying it on a little too thick. "Seriously, I don't care where it comes from."

"I should get you water straight from the river and let you shit yourself to death," the man replied. "No water. No food. Not until Colonel Urbina gives the word. And no more talking."

"If you get me that drink of water, I swear I'll shut up. Just, please."

By means of response, the guard dug into his shirt pocket and pulled out a sweat-stained handkerchief. He shoved it into Nomad's mouth as a makeshift gag.

"I said no more talking."

The front door opened, and Urbina stepped inside. "Corporal Abreu," he said to the guard. "You're dismissed."

"Yes Colonel." He started to leave, then stopped and looked back over his shoulder. "*El pidió agua. Yo no le daría a él.*"

"Good work, soldier," Urbina said. "Not everyone can follow orders."

Beaming, the guard left the building. Urbina waited for him to go, then stepped forward and pulled the handkerchief out of Nomad's mouth.

Gasping for air, Nomad went into a coughing jag, bending nearly in two as he hacked and wheezed. Urbina looked on with polite disinterest, until the hacking stopped and Nomad could look up once again. "Is this where you apologize for the behavior of your subordinates and try to convince me to switch sides?"

Urbina gave a puzzled frown. "No. Hernán followed orders. I see no need to apologize. Unlike you, who's trespassing in a country where he's not wanted."

"Most of Venezuela didn't want you around either, as I recall," was Nomad's response, and Urbina's expression told him that he'd scored a hit.

"Venezuela is yesterday's news," he snapped. "I have

other concerns now. Like, my own country here, and what to do with you."

Nomad laughed. "Torture me? Isn't that the usual answer?"

"Torture you?" Urbina stopped and turned. "Why torture you?"

"Intel about my mission?"

"Your mission, obviously, has failed. Besides, torture is crude and the information it yields is always . . . uncertain. Trust me. I know from experience." The ghost of the secret policeman he'd once been was plain to see on his face. "The worst thing I could do to you, honestly, is nothing."

"Nothing?"

"Nothing. You're in the jungle, yes? The Amazon rain forest. The wildest place on earth. If I simply leave you tied to that chair, helpless, and open the door, what do you think is going to happen? How long before the insects come? The scorpions? And after them, the birds who realize you can't defend your eyes and tongue?"

"In the middle of your camp?" Nomad was incredulous. "I think not."

Urbina shrugged. "Men like you constantly forget, this is not your place. You can train all you want on whatever obstacle courses they build for you, but there is nothing like the jungle. You understand it or you don't, and if you don't, you end up feeding it." He shook his head. "You come blundering in here, thinking this is going to be the same as any other operation, and of course you fail. You make yourself," and he paused, "my problem."

"Sorry to inconvenience you," Nomad replied. "You could just let me go."

"I think that would be a very bad idea," said Urbina. "Like I said, you are my problem. But I have a solution. There are people, many people, who would pay very good money to get their hands on an elite American soldier like yourself." He began ticking them off on his fingers. "The Russians, of course. I am told soldiers like you have many, many fans in Moscow. My new friends in Bolivia, who've just moved down from Mexico, had some stories to tell about things that happened in Mexico City, and they might be interested in getting a small chance at payback. At last resort, your own government, of course, though they tend to be on the cheap side. The list goes on."

"Very few of those sound like good options," Nomad said.

"They are the only ones you have, soldier." Urbina leaned in close. "You'll get your water, eventually. But as soon as I can, I'm loading you up and shipping you out. You're safer in transit than you are here."

With that, Urbina walked away. The guard, Hernán, poked his lean face in to satisfy himself that Nomad was still there. Then the door closed, and he was alone with his thoughts and the sounds of the camp and the jungle.

CHAPTER 14

It was nearly 0300 hours when they hit final approach
to the border.

Weaver killed the boat's motor, leaving nothing but
night noises and the slow gurgle of the river. "Okay,
here's the situation. Nomad's dead or in enemy hands;
we've got our three new friends in the boat; there's hostiles between us and the border; and the Brazilians ain't
going to do shit to help us until we get on the right side

of the line. We need options, and we need to know what's ahead of us. Holt?"

"Way ahead of you." Holt had his NVG flipped down and active. "Two boats on the river between us and the border. They're doing patrols with their lights out—looking to intercept and surprise, not interdict. Someone must have gotten on the horn in a hurry."

"Can we cut west and use the island for cover again?"

"No can do. I'm seeing a couple of unfriendlies on the sandbar. Besides, don't like our odds if we've got to sneak civilians through there."

"Now just a minute—" Stanton interjected, but Weaver cut him off. "That's exactly what the man's talking about. Now get low, stay low, and if we're lucky in a couple of hours you're going to be drinking a cold caipirinha at the bar. You got it?"

Stanton nodded. "Good," Weaver growled. "Now, like I said. Get. Down."

Stanton's silhouette sank out of sight.

Weaver turned back to the other Ghosts. "We need a plan. We can't sneak past them and we can't go upriver. So we've got to go through. But if we do that, then there's no way we can get back across and the second half of the op's blown."

"We could tie up on the western bank and hoof it over the border." Even Midas sounded dubious, and it was his idea. "Call for pickup for them on the other side."

Weaver shook his head, "Bank's too steep. We'd have to backtrack a hell of way upriver to get to a workable landing. Besides, we've got no idea if they're patrolling that side of the river. If they are and we walk into them with the packages, well, forget it."

Holt coughed theatrically. Weaver and Midas turned to look at him. "I think," he said, "I have a fix. The sandbar extends across the border,"

"Barely," said Weaver.

"It's enough. I'll deal with the men on the island. Weaver, cover me on the way in. Once I give the all clear, drift down and offload the hostages. I'll walk them to the other side, and you can call for pickup."

Weaver frowned. "Two questions. One, how are you getting to the island? Two, what happens if one of those guys sounds the alarm?"

"Second one's easy. Midas's got an M-203. I'm guessing he knows how to use it."

Weaver snorted. "And the first question?"

"Like this." Without another word, he slid over the side.

"Get back in the boat! The river's full of . . . of . . . blast." Midas's voice was a frantic whisper. Only the ripples of the river answered, but through the IR he could clearly see Holt drifting downstream, intent on the deeper patch of darkness rising out of the water. "Well," he finally said. "Now what?"

"We hold position," Weaver said, and unlimbered his weapon. "I cover his ass, you make sure we don't get spotted, and if we do? You blow them out of the water, and to hell with the consequences. We'll find another way to get back in-country for Nomad."

"Roger that." Midas stared downriver for another long minute. "He left his helmet. So, no sensors. No

VENEZUELA

⚠️ SANDBANK

BORDER CHECKPOINT

BRAZIL

RIO NEGRO

 REVOLUTIONARY FREE STATE OF AMAZONAS
CONTROLLED AREA

↑ N

night vision. What was he thinking?"

Weaver shook his head. "In my professional opinion, he's thinking he screwed up somehow to get Nomad captured, and this is what's going to fix it." He paused reflectively. "Of course, getting himself killed isn't going to even things up. Bit late to tell him that now."

The island was easy to see even in the darkness, the trees so dense they rose from the water like a sheer cliff face. Here and there, smaller patches of shadow shifted, men waiting impatiently for someone to try to pass. Now and then lights flared and then subsided to pinpoints of reddish glow; lighters fading to cigarettes, the bored sentry's most dangerous temptation.

There were four now, he could see. They gathered and broke apart at irregular intervals, more concerned with defeating their own restlessness than with doing their job. If they'd been disciplined, Holt wouldn't have liked his odds. Like this, however, there was a chance.

He let the current carry him downstream, feet barely kicking to correct course when an eddy pulled him toward the center of the river. Something brushed against his leg, slimy and cold, and then it was gone. The night hunters were out, he knew. And he was one of them.

Coming up on the island, he let his feet drag bottom. His progress slowed and then stopped, and carefully, he emerged from the water. One man stood near the northern tip of the island, the dim glow from his dying cigarette marking his position and direction. He was looking east, out over the river, a rifle in his hands.

Slowly, Holt edged toward the island. His right hand went to his belt, reaching for his knife. It came free soundlessly as he slipped closer. The sentry took a last pull from his cigarette, then let the gun drop as he tossed the butt into the river. Holt took another slow step, then another. His feet hit the shoreline, water ebbing silently out of his boots.

And then gunshot split the night.

The sound echoed from farther down the island, rolling across the river and onward. The sentry jumped, his gun instantly in his hand as he turned to his right. "What the hell?" he barked in Spanish. "You see something?"

The shouted reply was punctuated by laughter and the sound of frenzied splashing down-island. "Caiman," came the reply. "Big-ass son of a bitch. Was headed right for us. Had to pull the trigger or we would have been lunch."

"Idiot! They could hear that shot for miles!"

"Like they can't hear us talking now!" Some indistinct yelling from the river boats cut in, and whoever was talking downstream shifted to answer them, saying everything was all right and not to worry.

"Fucking imbeciles," the sentry muttered, and reached in his pocket for his cigarettes. Sighing, he pulled one out of the crumpled pack, then put it to his lips. The gun he let dangle by its strap as he went for a lighter, still fuming about his idiot companions. Down island, it sounded like they were trying to haul the dying caiman out of the river. More loud splashing suggested they weren't being entirely successful.

The sentry shook his head and bent his head, cupping one hand around the cigarette as the lighter flared to life. He lit the cigarette and smoked it contentedly.

Holt stepped up behind him, wrapping one hand around his face to cover his mouth and nose and jamming the blade of his knife into the man's kidney with the other. The sentry gasped and sagged, the lit cigarette falling from his lips to land on the wet mulch of the forest floor.

Holt let the man sag forward, easing his weight toward the ground. He was dead before he hit.

Wiping the bloody knife clean, Holt paused, listening for an alarm. There was none. He took the sentry's rifle and slung it over his back. Then he picked up the still-burning cigarette and wedged it into a forked tree branch at about head height. Let anyone still looking this way be fooled, at least for a minute, he thought. Then he quietly rolled the body into the water and headed south.

The gunshot rang out across the river.

"Can you see him? Can you see him!"

"Negative," Weaver growled. "We're not going in, not before the signal." He paused. "I think I see him on the riverbank. Got someone near him. Shit. Now you're making me jumpy."

"If we hear more shots?" Midas asked.

"That's a pretty good signal."

"And if we don't?"

"We trust him."

Down near the dead caiman, the party was winding down. One of the sentries was still fiddling with the corpse, using a belt knife to try to dig out teeth to take as souvenirs. The other two had had enough, however, and had faded back into the trees. One walked up the north-south spine of the island slowly, scanning from side to side as he went. The other, much to Holt's dismay, he couldn't see. He froze in the underbrush, breathing shallow. The crunch of footsteps on leaf and sand got steadily louder as the first sentry walked closer. Holt considered his options. Taking the man out was a calculated risk as long as he didn't know where the other sentry was. On the other hand, if the soldier made it to the north end of the island and found the cigarette, or spotted Weaver and company on the river, the game was up anyway.

It was time to fight smart.

Holt reached for his belt and grabbed a sensor. It wouldn't do him any good, but if it lit up the hostiles, then Midas and Weaver at least would be able to see when he'd cleared the island and be able to move in safely. He primed it and gave it a gentle roll toward the center of the island. It came to a stop, but instead of offering the usual gentle ping that indicated it was active, it did nothing, just sitting there inert instead.

"Son of a—" Holt swore under his breath. *Last time I go into the field with some POS experimental gear. Damn thing's probably not waterproof, and they gave them to us for this op? Effing brilliant.* Mentally making a note to come back for the dud later, he took a deep breath. Weaver and Midas could just freaking guess when he was done; he was going to do it the old fashioned way.

Slowly, carefully, he shifted his weight. The soldier loomed out of the darkness, bobbing cigarette glow a dead giveaway as to his position as he got closer. The soldier inhaled and the orange-red ember flared up, briefly illuminating his face, and then he threw it aside and kept walking. The still-glowing butt cartwheeled over Holt's shoulder and landed somewhere on the ground behind him. He found himself praying he hadn't been lit up, that the butt hadn't landed on something particularly flammable, that this guy was going to just keep on walking . . .

. . . and he did, eyes briefly sweeping over where Holt was waiting, not registering what he'd seen until a split second later.

That was all the time Holt needed. He exploded out of the underbrush, wrapping one arm around the man's throat and half-turning him. The sentry's hands scrabbled for his gun but it was too late; Holt reached across with his other hand and snapped the man's neck. With a wheeze, he collapsed in Holt's arms, and the Ghost hauled him into the underbrush before he hit ground. Then he waited, listening. If the second sentry had seen him, he would have been dead already, or at least in a hell of a bad spot. But there was no sign of him, just the grumbling curses of the last sentry down at the other end of the sandbar.

Two down, two to go, and he knew where one was. That made the choice of targets easier. The trick would be getting him away from the waterline, where the men on the river could see him.

Something tickled his nostrils and he sniffed.

Smoke.

He finished the body and looked for the faint glow of the smoldering cigarette, finding it as much by smell as by sight. The leaf it was on was just starting to smolder, so he picked it up and then ground the mulch quietly under his heel. Then, moving silently, he edged south, toward where the fourth sentry was still on what passed for a beach.

Holt stopped maybe fifteen feet back from the edge of the trees, his fingers getting uncomfortably warm. "This has to be the dumbest thing I've ever tried," he muttered, and tossed the cigarette butt toward the man at the water's edge.

It flared up briefly as it flew, tumbling end over end, and then somehow, miraculously, it hit its target on the shoulder.

"What the?" the man said, and turned around. A half-second's inspection revealed the smoldering butt at his feet. He picked it up, squinted at it suspiciously, and then threw it into the river. "Come on, man. What are you messing with me for?"

There was no answer.

"Lieutenant? Paco? Come on guys, not funny. Why'd you throw that at me, huh? You could have got me in the eye!"

Holt held his breath and so, too, did the jungle. He risked a glance behind him. No sign of that other sentry, the one who'd vanished. All he needed now was for that guy to come blundering in.

"This is bullshit!" The sentry he'd tagged was getting angry now, starting to yell. "You think this is funny, huh? Hide in the woods and throw shit at me? You'd better come out!" He waited three seconds, possibly as long as five, and then declared, "All right, better remember you started this, assholes!" Without drawing his gun, the man stalked into the trees.

Holt let him get far enough in that the jungle would hide him from the view of the boats, and then took him down. It took the man a moment to realize that he wasn't facing one of his friends, but that was all it took for Holt to crush his larynx and drop him permanently.

He hit the leaves with a soft thud.

"One to go," Holt reminded himself, and moved off into the darkness.

If the man hadn't come up the middle and wasn't close enough to hear and respond to his buddy's angry shouts, then he had to be at the far end of the island. And if the soldier was at the far end and hadn't come past Holt, that put him on the western side.

It was time to move.

"Got any movement on the river?"

Midas eased his head up over the gunwale and did a slow scan. Curls of mist were rising from the water, dancing above the current. By morning, they'd be full-blown fog, but for now, they just fuzzed everything the night vision goggles showed.

"Still two unfriendlies, still holding position."

"What about on the island?"

Midas shifted position. "I'm seeing one figure along the waterline." Midas squinted. "Little to the west, maybe fifteen meters down."

"Is that our guy?"

Midas shook his head, leaving all sorts of interesting afterimages in his goggles' screen. "Don't think so. No reason for Holt just to be standing there, right?"

Weaver nodded "Right. So where is he? They haven't caught him, or we would have heard. Which means—"

"There he is." Midas pointed. Weaver followed his gaze. A second figure was emerging from the trees, catching the first rough shape completely by surprise. There was a brief struggle, and then only one man was standing. He looked in their rough direction and made a sweeping gesture: Bring it in.

"You think that's him?" Weaver asked.

"Could be a trap," Midas said cautiously.

"Well then, that would make today just perfect." He turned and addressed the hostages, still curled up in the bottom of the boat. "You hear me tell you go, you go. One of our people is on the island. He'll guide you down across the border. You keep low, you move fast, you don't talk. You got me?"

"But what if—"

"I said, don't talk." Weaver pushed off from the shore, letting the current pull the boat lazily downriver. He'd used the time while they were waiting to cut a rough pole from some fallen wood along the riverbank. With that, he poled the craft along the shallow, silty bottom, taking care not to get pulled into the main channel. Midas sat at the prow of the boat, weapon ready, perched motionless like a gargoyle.

Finally, the prow scraped soft mud and the boat ground to a halt. Holt stepped out into the water, helping to pull it in the last few feet while Midas hopped out and began helping the hostages up.

"This is it, people. Time to move. Just keep it fast and keep it quiet, and these nice men will get you where you're going." Weaver's voice was barely a whisper.

Crotty was the last one out. "Thank you," she said, as Midas helped her over the side.

"Don't thank any of us till we get you home," Weaver replied. He turned to Midas. "You and Holt, get them down to the south end of the island. Those boats get frisky, you are weapons free. Keep the civilians' heads down, and don't start anything if you can help it. I'll call our friends and tell them they need to arrange pickup."

"Understood."

"And Midas? Keep these people safe."

Midas nodded, then turned and helped the hostages climb onshore. Holt paused for a moment to retrieve his gear from the boat, then followed him.

Weaver watched them go, then fired up the radio. "PESCADOR, this is BLUECAT, do you copy?"

It wasn't Correa's voice this time, but Protasio's. "Reading you loud and clear, BLUECAT. What's your status?"

"I've got three fish I want to give you, but the local rangers want to make me throw them back. Can you come upriver for a handoff?"

"How far upriver?"

"Your side. We'll be delivering them to you south of the border and trying to keep the eyes on the river off them. All you need to do is reel them in, take them home, and not wake the neighbors."

"And will you be with them?" Protasio's voice had an edge.

"Negative. Still got a day of fishing left to do. Just treat them gentle. They bruise easy."

"Understood." Protasio was all business again. "We'll signal you when we're approaching your coordinates. PESCADOR out."

"Roger that, PESCADOR. BLUECAT out."

He cut the connection. "That went well," he said to himself, then went rummaging in the gear locker for a particular bulky package. It took him a minute to find, and then he tucked it under his arm and loped off after the rest of the team.

He caught up with them at the edge of the trees. "PESCADOR's inbound. ETA two minutes."

"Roger that." Holt looked at him for a minute, then at the package. "You've got to be kidding. Emergency raft?"

Weaver nodded. "Protasio's not going to be able to bring whatever he's piloting in too close. Which means we need to get these people out to him. We can't use the boat, and your little stunt aside, they can't swim. So what does that leave us?"

"You are out of your mind," Holt answered, shaking his head.

"That's my business," said Weaver, and triggered the raft's inflation mechanism. The hiss of the inflation mechanism blended with the sounds of the river. Gently, he and Holt eased it into the water, and then he motioned back to Midas.

"Time to go," Midas said, and gestured toward the raft. The researchers moved wearily, their energy swallowed by too much tension.

"Get in," Weaver said. "You're going to take this downriver to where a representative of the Brazilian government is going to pick you up and bring you in. Stay low, do not try to paddle, and do not talk."

Crotty stared at him. "You're just putting us out there?"

"Yes. Because we can't go with you." He jerked a thumb toward the river, where the enemy boats sat, waiting. "But we'll be watching them for you. It's going to be perfectly safe."

"So many people have told me that on this trip," Crotty said, but she eased herself into the raft. Carpenter and Stanton followed.

Downriver, there was the sound of engines.

"Time go to." Weaver gave the raft a gentle shove. It drifted silently down the side channel, the black rubber nearly invisible against the black water it rode on. Then it was out into open water, moving slowly and hugging the bank. Crotty looked back, once, then vanished as she crouched down.

"Midas, Holt." Weaver gestured to the waterline on the east side of the island. "Eyes on our friends. They get frisky, blow them out of the water."

"Roger that." The pair moved silently together, then vanished from sight.

Weaver could hear the boat coming upstream now, its engine roaring. A searchlight stabbed out from the prow, and he suddenly had ice crawl through his veins at the thought of the raft accidentally getting lit up. But the searchlight stayed pointed ahead, and then the boat hove into view.

"Where the hell was Protasio keeping that?" Weaver gave a low whistle. The boat, a CB90H riverine patrol vessel, was fully visible now, running lights illuminating it for maximum effect and to pull the eyes of any observers away from anything else that might be on the river. Weaver could see the soldier manning the spotlight; he could also see others manning the Browning M2HBs, casually pointed upriver.

As the CB90H approached the border, it slowed until it was just holding position. The searchlight picked over the boats, then froze on the one farther from the station, blinding everyone on board. One man with lieutenant's bars on his sleeve stood up, hand shading his eyes, and addressed the launch in Spanish. "Whoever you are, state your name and hold your position. You are about to violate a sovereign border and if you do, you will be fired on."

A bullhorn from the deck of the launch answered: Protasio, speaking in Portuguese-accented Spanish. "Captain Protasio sends his respects. Whom do we have the pleasure of addressing?" The spotlight stayed on the lieutenant doing the talking; the second boat started inching toward the east bank. One of the machine gunners on the patrol boat angled his weapon in parallel with their movements.

The lieutenant looked at his allies, then at the Brazilians. His voice took on a frantic edge. "Never mind that. What are you doing here?"

Protasio was all sweetness and light as he answered, honey on a knife blade. "We heard you were looking to secure the border. It is our pleasure to help our friends from Venezuela in such an important task."

There was some hurried discussion in the two smaller boats. "You have no right to cross our border."

"We would not dream of doing so. We'll just sit here on our side and wait with you. Surely, you can accept this in the spirit of international cooperation."

The raft was drifting farther now, moving out into the main current and picking up speed. Another minute, and it would be past Protasio's position and headed downriver, out of control.

There was more discussion on the northern side of the border, and then, "We've been told the criminals we were looking for have been apprehended. There is no longer any need for the border to be secured." The man paused and waited for some kind of acknowledgment from the Brazilians. He got none, tried to stare the unblinking searchlight down for another instant, and then peeled in toward shore. The second boat followed.

The standoff over, the Brazilian boat waited until they

reached land, then turned ponderously and headed back downriver. Within moments, it vanished into the darkness that had swallowed the raft.

"Think it worked?" Holt asked.

Weaver shrugged. "Looks like. I expect Captain Protasio will be letting us know if he lost them. We'd better get back." The three men jogged back north, then climbed into their boat.

After a moment, the radio buzzed. "PESCADOR to BLUECAT. Do you copy?"

"Yes we do, Captain," he answered. "How's your fishing going?"

"Mostly small-fry tonight. But we did reel in three exotic specimens. They're safe and sound on board."

"Thanks for the pickup, PESCADOR. Take good care of them. I promised one a caipirinha."

Protasio seemed unamused. "He will probably have to wait until morning. The bars, they are all closed. May I speak with your friend?"

Weaver shot Midas and Holt a look. Holt shrugged, Midas nodded, and Weaver turned back to the radio.

"He liked the fishing upstream so much he decided to stay. We're going to go pick him up."

There was silence on the other end. "Ah. That is . . . unfortunate. I wish you happy hunting."

"We're going fishing," Weaver corrected him.

"No, BLUECAT. No you're not. PESCADOR out."

"Well, damn." Weaver moved to the back and started up the engine. It idled lightly. "Think it was a mistake to tell him?"

Midas answered, "It might make him more inclined to help."

Holt agreed. "Especially if he thinks he's saving Nomad's ass."

"Truth. Let's get him back, and then we can worry about it. Right now, I'm just glad the Amazonas types stood down."

"I don't think they're interested in things getting hot, either." Midas crawled to his usual position at the prow.

"Would have made our lives easier," Holt groused as Weaver started backing them away from the island and off into the night.

It was several hours later when Urbina ducked back into the building, carrying a smartphone and looking pleased with himself. Hernán and another guard Perryman didn't recognize followed. "Good news, Major," Urbina said as Nomad blearily watched him approach. "There's considerable interest in you on the market. There was some initial disbelief, but with the help of some of your equipment, I was able to convince them that you were in fact genuine." He walked around behind the chair Nomad was tied to, stooping low to inspect the zipties.

"Hmm," he said. "A little tight, perhaps, but I clearly specified to my buyers that you were up for auction 'as is.'" As he walked around, he took pictures with the cell phone. "Proof of life," he said. "It's okay. You don't have to smile."

Nomad just clenched his jaw and looked straight ahead, saying nothing. "Always the good soldier?" Urbina taunted him as he took one last shot, a close-up of Perryman's bruised and battered face. "There's no need. You're not going home. I'm not asking you to betray anything. I honestly don't care about your secrets. What's going to happen here will happen without you. So relax."

He studied Nomad's face for a minute. "Oh. I see. You are trained to resist. You need something to overcome, to fight against. And I'm not giving you that, am I? No torture, no interrogation—and you don't know what to do." He walked to the entrance of the tent. "It's sad, really. I should have left that rag in. It would have made you feel much better." And then he and his guards were gone.

INTERLUDE - HOLT

"Now, Sergeant Moretta, would you like to explain to me what exactly happened last night?" The officer sitting behind the desk had introduced himself as Lt. Colonel Mitchell. Moretta had never met him or heard of him; he just knew that the presence of a full-bird colonel asking him very pointed questions was a very bad sign.

A pair of burly, uncommunicative MPs had escorted Moretta here, some sort of conference room that had been emptied of everything except a single desk and two chairs. One of the chairs was already occupied by Lt. Col. Mitchell, and he had spent several minutes looking through a folder on that desk before he'd deigned to glance up and acknowledge Moretta's presence.

It had taken several more minutes after that before Mitchell ordered him to sit down, something for which he and his various aches and contusions were privately grateful. Mitchell looked like he was ready for the parade ground; Moretta looked like he'd just been tossed in a cement mixer that had been rolled downhill.

Which, in a sense, he had.

"Sir." Moretta sat up straight in his chair and ignored the stabbing pain behind his left eye. "There was a fight, sir."

"I know there was a fight." Mitchell leaned forward. "I have it on very good authority that you were in the middle of that fight. There are even some very fine soldiers saying that you started the fight, and that there were, shall we say, interesting circumstances surrounding it. Now, you can stop trying to cover your ass and tell me what went down, or I can go get my fancy hat and a couple of friends and we can turn this into a full court martial." Moretta opened his mouth to speak, but Mitchell waved him to silence. "Think very carefully before you answer."

Moretta drew a deep breath, and then very carefully answered. "Sir. Yes, there was a fight. Yes, I was involved. No, I did not instigate the fight, and my participation was to protect a fellow service member from what seemed to be unfair odds. Sir."

Mitchell ignored him for a moment, instead picking up a folder from the desk and flipping it open. "I see. And that is why we have multiple witnesses on the record as hearing you say, and this is a quote, *Been waiting all god-damn night for this*." He looked up. "Would you care to revise your statement?"

"Do you want the whole story, sir?"

"I did ask for it, didn't I?"

"Yessir." Moretta swallowed, which caused a brief moment of stabbing pain in the back of his neck, where someone had nailed him with a still-full Budweiser tall-boy from halfway across the room. "I went into the bar to grab a beer."

"Were you there to meet anyone?"

He shook his head. "No, sir. Just wanted a quiet beer and some room to think about something I was working on."

Mitchell raised an eyebrow. "And what would that be?"

"Working on modifying drone weapon payloads, sir."

"You are aware that we have some very highly trained people whose job it is to do that, soldier?"

"Yessir. But they haven't been out in the field, most of them, and I'm pretty good with code and electronics, so I figured I could maybe draw up some schematics and, I don' know, maybe get a prototype put together." He could feel his accent creeping back in around the edges, a sign of stress, which naturally stressed him out even more. "But I was stuck and wanted to take a break, and just think about things. Y'know, get 'lil bit of distance from the problem."

"And how did you meet Sergeant Graham?"

Moretta blinked. "Sir. You know about—never mind. Right. Sergeant Graham. Well, I walked up to the bar to get that beer, and I saw he was reading AiMT on his MRT, which you don't see often. So I introduced myself and asked him if he'd read the piece on neural network routing in sensor arrays, which I hadn't found a lot of people on base to talk to about. He said he had and we started talking—okay, we started arguing, but good arguing. I excused myself for a moment, got my beer, then came back and sat down and we started talking again."

"And what did you think of Sergeant Graham?"

Moretta scratched his chin. "I liked him. He was smart, but not a jerk about it. I mean, he was wrong about a bunch of things—no way his take on augmenting armor's power trains with photovoltaics is gonna be feasible for, like, fifteen years, but smart. Even if he was from New York."

"How many beers did you have with Sergeant Graham?"

"Three, I think. Maybe four. You know how it is, sir. You start talking to someone and time just flies, and then you look up, and it's midnight, and you've got a dozen empties on the table in front of you." He coughed once. "Not that we each had a dozen empties, sir."

"I'm sure you didn't," Mitchell said wryly. There was no air conditioning in the room, and the air was getting uncomfortably warm and close. Moretta could feel sweat starting to bead up on his forehead. Mitchell, on the other hand, looked perfectly composed. Had to be some kind of officer thing, he decided. You make the grade, you get the skills.

"Let's say for a moment that I accept your story so far. That I find your initiative, on some level, admirable. You still haven't explained how exactly you started a fight that has landed . . ." He picked up the folder again and flipped through a couple of pages. ". . . has landed five soldiers in sick bay with various ailments up to and including concussions, lost teeth, and at least one compound fracture." He stared at Moretta. Moretta stared back.

"As I told you, sir, I did not instigate the fight."

"Then who did?"

He took a deep breath, then a second one. "Do you know Sergeant Graham, sir?" Mitchell nodded. "Then you know he can come across as, well, kind of nerdy. And when he gets into it, he talks over people and tells them when they're wrong, and, well, yeah."

"And he was so thrilled with your conversation that he got excited and started correcting everyone within earshot?"

"That and the beer, sir. But yes, he was sounding a little, well—actually, if you take my meaning."

"I do."

"Well, sir, there were some guys at the next table who were pounding beers faster than we were, and I guess a couple of them had dealt with some kind of tech failure in the field, and they didn't really like anyone on that side of things. They, uh, had some names for Graham."

"I take it these names were not flattering?"

"No, sir, they were not."

"And were these men also soldiers?"

Moretta nodded twice. "Yessir."

"And do you remember which unit they were from?"

"No, sir. And even if I did, I'd have made myself forget before you asked me, if you take my meaning."

"Interesting." The side of Mitchell's mouth curled in the faintest hint of a smile. "What did these men do to start the fight?"

"At first, sir, if I can speak plainly, they were just assholes. Talkin' loud about how they didn't want to drink with brainiac none. Graham, he ignored them, and that just got them mad. So they started insulting him. He kept ignoring them, and the bartender told them to cut it out, but they didn't, and he didn't do nothing. I guess they were regulars or something. But it bothered me, so I told them to knock it off. Instead, they came over to the table—there were four of them—and they started giving me crap as well as Graham. Now Graham, he was cool, but them yelling at me kind of got my blood up, so I yelled back, and then one of them took a swing."

"At you?"

"No, sir. At Graham. And I don't know how he did it, but he dodged the punch. Didn't hit back, either. But that just got them really mad, and one of them knocked his MRT off the table. It hit the floor, and the screen cracked, and they started laughing, and I didn't think that was right. Then they dared Graham to do something about it, all four of them, and I sure as hell didn't think that was a fair fight."

"So you joined in?"

"So I hit one of them before they could take another swing at Sergeant Graham, yes."

Moretta paused for a moment, thinking back to the evening in the bar. It had gone down pretty much exactly as he'd described, give or take a few details, such as the fact that he'd judged the tactical situation and then hit the soldier with a chair, and, well, details were details.

"I see. What did you do next?"

"Well, sir, the bar kind of went up after that. Felt like there were some unresolved tensions getting worked out. Me, I tried to stay on just those four who'd been hassling Graham, but things got a little confused."

"And did you shout that you'd been waiting for the fight all night?"

Moretta hung his head in what might have been embarrassment. "Yessir."

"Had you been?"

Even with his head down, Moretta couldn't resist a small grin. "No, sir. Just wanted them to think I was crazier than they were. The other guy thinks you're crazy, that adds a little fear to his thought process. It slows him down."

"I see." Mitchell rubbed the bridge of his nose. "Sergeant Moretta, you are here for some very specific, very selective training, are you not?"

"I am, sir."

"And the normal course of that training does not include, among other things, bar brawls, disabling fellow soldiers, or conveniently leaving out details when asked a direct question by a senior officer. Are you aware of *that*, soldier?"

Moretta met his gaze. "Yes, sir. I am."

"Then let me make things perfectly clear for you: This will not happen again. If I receive any further word of you causing the slightest hint of a ruckus, I will have your head on a stick. Oh, and you're banned from any establishment serving alcohol for the next two weeks." He stood up. "Dismissed."

"Sir." Moretta saluted, then turned and walked out at speed. Mitchell watched him go, shaking his head. He waited until Moretta had left the room, then turned and exited by the rear door.

Graham was waiting for him, there, reading something on what looked to be a brand new MRT. When he saw Mitchell emerge, he tucked it away. "How did it go, sir?"

Mitchell snorted. "He's a smartass. Which, under these circumstances, makes him a dumbass. Thinks on his feet well enough, and he was very intent on letting me know that the fight wasn't your fault. Which can be construed, in certain circles, as admitting it was his."

"He was more an . . . accelerant, sir. The men from the 10th—"

Mitchell cut him off. "I know, I know. But he sang your praises, and he left out the part where he whacked at least one of those men across the back of the head with a chair. It's a miracle Moretta still has any teeth."

"If I'd unloaded on him, he wouldn't," Graham said mildly. "You understand why I recommended Moretta as a possible recruit?"

"I understand you want another geek to talk shop

with, yes." Mitchell thought for a minute. "I'll be making my recommendation later today. I think we're going to be watching Sergeant Moretta very closely. It's one thing to know how he handles himself in a bar fight, but I'd like a little more data from the field."

"You've got his jacket. His service record should speak for itself. He's been around the block a few times."

"I prefer seeing things with my own eyes. Oh, and if you see him again, give him these." Mitchell reached into a pocket and pulled out a beaten-up pair of Oakleys. "Bartender pulled these off one of the ceiling fans. Tried telling me how they got up there, and I told them that I did not want to know. But they're Moretta's. Considering the size of the shiner he had, I'm thinking he missed them."

Graham laughed. "I won't let him know where they came from, sir. And thank you."

"If he works out, I'll thank you."

"And if he doesn't?"

"You need to find a new drinking buddy."

CHAPTER 15

They'd tied up for the night a slow hour's travel north of the border when another brief rainstorm came through. It guttered out, but Weaver called a halt to further travel in the darkness.

They made a small fire, far enough from the river that the trees would block out any light, and slung up hammocks in the trees. "You do not want to sleep on the ground here," Weaver said as he set his up. "Ants."

"What, not the bright orange spiders? Or the jaguars? Or the land-walking piranhas?" Holt was brusque, preoccupied.

"Trust me, you do not want to mess with the ants," Weaver answered. "There's one down here, they call it a bullet ant. You know why?"

"They're shaped like bullets?"

"Because when they bite you, it feels like you've been shot. Now, you want to imagine what happens when you roll over on one of those and he calls his buddies for help?"

Holt snorted disbelief. "Ants don't talk."

"It's chemical. Pheromones. They let off the one that says, 'I've been squished, go get him,' and you are in a world of hurt. Literally."

"Shit." Holt finished with the hammock and stashed his gear in it. "I'm going to go catch us some dinner. And you're going to owe me twenty bucks."

"Just make sure you watch out for the candiru. You know, the little—"

"Enough!" Holt stomped off, managing to simultaneously convey his irritation and move silently toward the water. Weaver watched him go, bemused.

"You ride him pretty hard." Midas had long since finished setting up his hammock and had shed most of his gear. Stripped down to a t-shirt, he looked like he was on a weekend camping trip. Only the shotgun at his hip gave him away.

Weaver gave a nonchalant gesture. "He's a guy who likes riding everyone else hard. Does him some good to receive instead of give every now and then. It'll help him work on his delivery."

"You're not worried it'll make him bitter?"

"Naah. We're all past that. Bitter's maybe what gets you here, but it's not something you stay with." He gave Midas a once-over. "Now you, for example. I've read your file. I know where you came from and where you've been, but I still can't figure out why. You want to enlighten me?"

Midas turned to look at the fire. "It's all there."

"No it isn't. Trust me, I'm a careful reader."

"You really want to know?"

"Hell yeah."

"It's because I would have made a terrible priest." He threw a small stick on the fire. It caught, flared up, and almost instantly burned down to embers.

Weaver moved over and squatted down next to him. "Come again?"

"I realized in seminary that I have a certain . . . lack of faith." Weaver opened his mouth to comment, and Midas waved him off. "Not in God. In people. I'd seen things. Gotten to a point where I didn't trust people to be good any more. And you can't be that way and be a priest, not a good one."

"So you decided to do this instead," Weaver said. It wasn't a question, just a statement of fact.

Midas nodded. "Eventually. I like to think that this work that we do, it will help me prove myself wrong. That even in the worst places we might go, we'll find good in people."

"And if not?"

For a moment, there was just the pop and crackle of the fire.

"And if not," Midas said softly, "then I'm in a place where I can do something about it."

They sat in silence for a long moment after that, until loud splashing and cursing from the river brought them to their feet. Weaver reached for his sidearm, Midas his Super-Shorty. "Holt, you okay?" Weaver asked cautiously.

"Just get down here," Holt bellowed. Midas and Weaver sprang forward, sprinting through the trees.

On the muddy riverbank, they found Holt struggling with a massive fish on the end of his line. He'd clearly tried to reel it in already, as there were muddy wet patches all over his clothes and his face. The fish was at least four feet long, bright red and thrashing around in the shallows. Holt's rod was bent nearly double as the fish pulled at it, and his boots had left deep furrows in the muddy riverbank as he'd been hauled relentlessly forward.

"What can we do?" Weaver called.

"In the boat . . . net . . . need to land this sucker!" Holt spoke through gritted teeth. Another splash from the river, and he slid two inches closer to the water.

"Got it!" Midas leaped into the boat and began looking for the net. After a minute, he gave a shout of triumph and held it up.

"Get down here!"

But before Midas could leap back out of the boat, the line caught on an underwater root, snagged, and snapped. Holt stumbled back and would have fallen if

Weaver hadn't caught him. The fish rolled over once, then vanished into the stream.

"Shit," Holt said, followed by, "You can let go of me now."

"You're welcome."

"Damn it. Almost had it. Should have had it." Holt made as if to throw the rod down in disgust, then thought better of it and laid it gently in the boat. "Screw it. Protein bars for me." He marched off the beach and into the jungle.

As he passed Weaver, he muttered, "Still don't owe you twenty."

At dawn, they rolled out again.

Holt had spent half the night tinkering with Nomad's helmet, and once they pushed off, he went at it again. Meanwhile, slow, seamless greenery rolled by as they headed north toward the coordinates Wizard had given them for the Kwan-Messina camp.

Midas sat in the prow, fidgeting far more than was normal for him. He'd made a couple of comments about enjoying the view, but since then, his discussion had largely been limited to calling out pieces of flotsam Weaver might want to avoid. Holt had stayed hunkered down with his work, ignoring the other two and the scenery.

As for Weaver, he was equal parts worried and bored.

"What the hell are you doing up there?"

Holt looked up and blinked. "Trying to get something, anything, out of Nomad's dome," he answered. "Doesn't help that you're driving this thing like a bootlegger headed for the county line. Hard to do precision work when we keep bouncing off the water like that."

"You find a better ride, you take it."

"If I could, I would."

Weaver snorted. "How's that coming, anyway?"

"I give it fifty-fifty odds I can rig a little something. But if I can," he squinted and wiped a little spray off his face, "then we are in business."

"Do tell?"

"If we get really lucky, I should be able to bounce a systems check pulse through the helmet and get the rest of his gear, which I am assuming they kept instead of dumping roadside, to give an answering ping. We get that, we've got his coordinates."

"We've got his pants' coordinates." Weaver shook his head. "But, that's a hell of a thing. Keep working on it. Let me know if you get lucky."

"I thought that was what Nomad was mad at me about back at the hotel." Holt grinned. "I kid, I kid. But really, if you could slow it down just a little bit."

"Negative on that. We are running out of time."

And he opened the throttle a little wider.

They fed Nomad eventually, mouthful by mouthful, with his hands still ziptied to the chair. Later, they released him long enough to use the bucket in the corner, two armed guards watching him at all times and his feet hobbled by zipties at the ankle as he did so. When he was finished, they strapped him back in.

Later, Urbina returned, in good spirits. He'd brought with him a small stool, which he placed down in front of where Nomad was held, and sat himself down on it.

"How's your Russian, my friend?" He leaned forward. "There is a very good chance that's where you'll be going."

"It's got to be better than here," Nomad replied, keeping his eyes on the wall behind Urbina.

Urbina gave him a conspiratorial grin. "For a while, I might have agreed."

"But not anymore?"

"You have to understand, soldier, that while I viewed my being sent here as a punishment, I was comfortable with that. I had done . . . things that I was not necessarily proud of, but that I thought were necessary for the good of the state. At least that is what I told myself. One's moral struggles always become nobler in hindsight."

"Why are you telling me this?" Nomad asked, his head lolling. "You said you weren't going to torture me."

The colonel reached out and patted Nomad on the cheek, then stood and started pacing.

"It's because you don't matter that I can tell you this. Confession is good for the soul. That's what the padres always say. Well, who here do you think I can talk to? Safely, and as an equal? Not to my men, of course. Not to the men I have made my bargain with. They can't be shown any sign of weakness, or they will pounce, and I'll have to deal with them. No, you're the perfect listener because you are a leader, an officer, and yet at the same time you are nothing. You understand what I say on a gut level, but your opinions are worthless because at any moment, I could have you shot. It's a wonderful thing, don't you think?"

"I'd feel better about it if you got me some water." Nomad could feel his lips beginning to crack. His own voice sounded hoarse in his ears. "Or is that part of the experience for you?"

"In time, in time," Urbina dismissed him. "The thing you have to understand is that I belong here. It took me a while to understand. At first, I thought that yes, this posting was punishment for what I had done. I hated it here. And then I started to see the beauty in this place, and eventually, the opportunity."

"Opportunity?"

"Major, we were, for all intents and purposes, abandoned here. Caracas stopped sending us money. Then they stopped sending us equipment. And then, finally, they stopped sending us medicine and food. We had to fend for ourselves or die. And so we did. We found ways. People who were interested in the possibilities of the jungle. People who were looking for partners. And I realized, I had been sent here for a reason."

"To set up a tin-pot dictatorship?"

Urbina shook his head. "To attract investors. Those who could see the potential in this place. A place where the government doesn't pretend to care about drugs. Or the environment." He paused for a moment. "The tax haven business is going to take a little while to attract, I think. But that's all right."

"You're out of your mind," Nomad said.

"No, I'm out of Venezuela." He got up to go. "It's

a shame you won't be around to see all this come to fruition."

"I really don't need to experience your messiah complex first-hand."

Urbina shook his head. "A savior complex means you want to save something. I want to *build* something, and with my partners, build is exactly what we will do."

"You're nuts. You've got no infrastructure, you've got no population, you've got no partners—"

"I have all the partners I need. And what they have, Major, is money. That will give us everything we need, or are going to need, down the line. Everything else is negotiable. Details," he said, picking up the stool and walking out without looking back.

It was just after noon, and the insects had come out to play. They swarmed the Ghosts, searching for exposed flesh to land on and sample. The repellent they'd been provided proved only marginally useful, and things were so bad that Holt was wondering out loud about a dip in the river to try to shake some of the bugs off.

"How's the helmet looking, Holt?" Weaver asked as he brought the boat in to shore.

"We'll know in a little bit," Holt answered. "Why the stop? Lunch break?"

"Got to check in with the Old Man. Also, my arms are tired."

"You could let me steer?"

"Not on your life." The boat hummed to a stop amidst

a tangle of exposed roots and wet dirt. The familiar buzz in his ear let Weaver know the commsat was passing directly overhead. He pulled out the comms rig and set up the collapsible antenna for signal boost. "Hope the tree cover doesn't bust up the channel."

"Unlikely," Holt replied. "What's actually going to happen is—" He looked around, caught himself, and dropped to silence.

"I swear, Holt, I'll be interested later. Right now, got a call to make." Weaver activated the rig and started the call.

"OVERLORD, this is BLUECAT. Do you copy?"

"Reading you loud and clear." Mitchell's voice echoed back through the headset. "Status?"

"Catch number one has been delivered to the fisherman. We are currently inbound on our second fishing grounds. Hoping for an easier catch this time."

"Roger that. You got enough bait?"

He looked over at where Midas was swapping out spent magazines. "Should be enough as long as this doesn't turn into an extended expedition."

"Roger that. We've got a better fix on where the fish are biting. Going to upload those coordinates to you now. Latest IMINT shows they've hacked an airstrip and what looks like a helo pad out of the jungle at the site. I'm guessing pretty soon, everyone's going to know about your new fishing hole, unless you do something to keep it on the down low."

"Just interested in two particular fish, sir. And avoiding the piranha. BLUECAT out."

"Copy that, BLUECAT. Happy fishing. This is OVERLORD out."

"So what does this mean for us?" Midas asked. "The airstrip? Are they bringing in reinforcements?"

"Could be," Nomad acknowledged. "Or they could have found some friends who wanted to stop by. We won't know until we get there."

"Bigger question is, are we going to have to worry about air cover?" Holt was, as usual, more direct. "Cause I left my LAW in my other pants."

"We'll be fine without your little rocket launcher. They're not going to be carving a runway long enough for anything serious out here. I'm more worried about helos. But either way, we know about it now, so the list of possible unpleasant surprises gets a lot smaller."

"From your mouth to God's ears," Holt answered.

An electronic chirp indicated the uploaded coordinates had arrived, and Weaver punched them up on his HUD. The target location was just at the edge of their cruising range if they hoped to make it back downriver under their own power, just off the Rio Negro itself. Cruising directly up to it wasn't an option, which meant finding another approach that would work for getting the hostages out quickly without exposing the boat to enemy eyes.

Fortunately, as Midas pointed out, there was a small tributary of the main river trunk that snaked north and east into the wilderness downriver from the site. Heading up that channel, then humping it across the jungle to the site, made the most sense.

It wasn't a good plan, Weaver admitted, but it had potential. And so he turned the boat up the tributary, its waters a slightly muddier variant of the impenetrable black of the Rio Negro. With Weaver steering and Midas at the prow calling out obstacles, they'd slowly motored their way upstream, seeing no one and hearing nothing but the local wildlife and the gurgle of the rushing water.

The tributary took a sharp bend north, leading closer to the target site. Weaver navigated the boat as best he could until the waterway became almost too narrow to turn around in. "End of the line," he said. "Any farther, I'm going to have to back us out of here."

"Yeah." Holt took a critical look around. "We might have to leave in a hurry."

cxfHe leaped onshore with a rope and tied the boat to a particularly sturdy tree. Weaver followed him. "Midas, you got us an optimum route to the site?"

Midas tapped his wrist control and sent the image of a map to the other two.

"Roger that. Here's our best route to the location where Kwan and Messina were being held. The terrain looks flat, and I'm not seeing any significant obstacles. East of here, it starts to get a lot more mountainous, but we're at the edge of the forest plain. As long as the foliage doesn't slow us down too much, we should make good time. The same goes for the way back, obviously, even with the packages."

Weaver started pulling gear out of the boat and putting it on the shore. "Midas, I do believe that is the longest thing I've ever heard you say."

Midas gave a grin. "It's the longest thing that needed saying." He turned to Holt. "Any luck with the helmet?"

"I thought you'd never ask." He looked from Weaver to Midas and back again. "I think I can get that pulse out. But before I do it, what's the plan if I get a response, and Nomad's a hundred miles in the wrong direction? We've barely got enough kit to make this work for one more stop. We try two, and . . . ." His voice trailed off, leaving no doubt as to what he thought would happen.

Weaver and Midas looked at each other. "We do the mission," Weaver finally said, through gritted teeth. "It has always been this: We do the mission. Midas?"

Tight-lipped, he agreed. "Mission first. Then we go back and do what we have to do."

"As long as we're clear." Holt brought up the helmet and made a few adjustments, then tapped a couple of commands into his wrist console. "Here goes nothing."

The eyepiece on Nomad's helmet flared to life, a brilliant blue in the gloom under the trees. A brief flurry of diagnostics flew across the HUD, and then suddenly there was a loud crackling sound as the smell of burned rubber filled the air. The eyepiece flickered and flared, and then went dark as a small jet of flame burst out of the side of the helmet's processor unit. "Shit, shit, shit," Holt said, and dropped it. It hit the ground, rolled, and went into the water with an angry hiss.

The Ghosts looked at each other for a moment. "That's coming out of my paycheck, isn't it," Holt said sadly.

"Well, I'm not going in after it," Weaver said. "You

learn free-diving on the bayou? Cause that could help right about now."

Midas ignored their banter. "The coordinates? Did you get the ping?"

"Give me one minute and I'll find out." Holt typed in a series of commands on the forearm console, then waited.

A minute later, there was an electronic chirp, and Holt said, "Oh, you have *got* to be kidding me!"

"Holt?"

"I'm going to send through the location," Holt said. "Hang on."

The image of the map blinked onto the other men's HUDs. "This looks familiar—" Midas began.

"Let me send you the map for the Kwan-Messina site." Holt said. There was another chirp.

"I don't freaking believe it," Weaver said. "They took him to the same site. He's got to be in with the other hostages."

"It's too easy," Hold said. "It's got to be a trap."

"How many detention facilities you think they've got down here?" Weaver demanded.

"Look, man, just because you want it to be this simple—"

"It's not about what I want, it's about the job. And this says the job just got a whole hell of a lot easier."

"Both of you, knock it off." Weaver and Holt turned to look at Midas. "We can only move based on the intel we have. This is what we got. If it's a trap, we go in with our eyes open. If it's just their logistics working in our favor, even better. But this is where we have to go." He shot Holt a glance. "Unless you'd rather comb all of Amazonas on foot?"

Holt shook his head. "It's not that, it's just . . . got a bad feeling, that's all. I don't trust good news in the field."

"Trust your own work, then," Weaver said. "And we're Ghosts. We don't get luck. We make luck."

CHAPTER 16

Another humiliating feeding, another visit from Urbina.

"We're getting close," he announced as he sat down. "Normally, I'd have one of my lieutenants bring you the news, but I do enjoy watching you try not to react. Your training is quite good."

"And your English is excellent."

"Thank you. Your government paid for my lessons."

Nomad tried to keep the surprise off his face and

failed. "I was recruited as a double agent. Your CIA was very eager to get people inside Chavez's government and military. It was easy to convince them that I was looking to sell out. My handlers heard what they wanted to hear, and as a result, they were very generous with knowledge, with money, with equipment. And then, I turned them in, because I was many things, but not a traitor."

"You are one now. Or does declaring yourself independent somehow fall out of that category?"

Urbina picked his words carefully. "The government I gave my oath to no longer exists. You cannot betray what you were never a part of. The idiots in Caracas, they may claim to be Chavezistas, but they are the real betrayers."

"Why do I have trouble believing your story? There was nothing in your jacket about you having been recruited as a US asset."

"Because," Urbina grinned humorlessly, "the CIA does not like to advertise its failures. Especially not to the Pentagon. I learned a lot, you see, when those handlers were taken. I got to practice on them. Much of what they said was nonsense, of course, but sometimes you can tease out little bits of truth. And that is what I got. Little bits of truth about them, about the CIA, about your country—all very useful in my career."

"And what is that career? What's it come to? Kidnapping scientists by accident in the middle of nowhere?"

"The scientists were an accident. If it hadn't cost me so many men, I would almost thank you for solving that problem for me. Live and learn, yes?"

"And the other two?"

Urbina looked genuinely puzzled. "What other two? I've taken no more hostages, and my men haven't done so, either."

"You know exactly who I'm talking about. Messina and Kwan. The archaeologists."

"The archaeologists?" Urbina tilted his head back and laughed. "Oh, no. I think someone fed you some bad intel. Those two aren't being held hostage here at all. The only person being kept here against his will is you, and we'll clear that up soon enough."

He rose from his stool. "I'll let you think on that. In the meantime, my imaginary partners in Bolivia are expecting a phone call about where to put a refinery site. Good day."

The ground was drier on this march, though not by much, and the ground slightly rockier. There was no path to follow, no game trail headed their way, just endless jungle. Initially Midas took point, but all three took turns swinging the machete as needed.

Early on, Holt started grousing about all the warnings he'd gotten about wildlife without having actually seen any. Midas offered to find a fer-de-lance for him to take home as a pet, which ended that conversation quickly. Beyond that, they moved in silence.

When they closed on the coordinates Nomad's gear had given them, Weaver called a halt. "We should be hitting some sort of surveillance perimeter soon. Maybe scouts, maybe cameras, maybe God-knows-what. Holt, you want to take point? You're better at sniffing out the gear than the rest of us."

"I've been keeping a close eye for the last two hours. Didn't want to run into any surprises."

"Did you find any?"

"The only surprise would be if I didn't find any." Holt's tone was uncharacteristically grim. "What's our ROE if we do see a sentry?"

Midas answered, "Sneak around if we can, quiet kill if we can't. We can't allow them to get word back."

"We drop a sentry, and the clock starts ticking anyway," Holt pointed out.

"We don't, and the alarm goes off." Weaver cocked his head and looked at Holt. "Man, Nomad's not here. You don't have to play the loyal opposition."

"Someone's got to," Holt shot back. "Nomad's your buddy. Your judgment's compromised. Midas, you're smart as hell but you're green, doing the go-along-get-along thing. Someone's got to call out the bear traps before we walk into them."

"We walk into this as a team," Weaver insisted.

"I want the team to walk out again. Look, we've gotta think about this before we go in."

"Maybe we've all already thought about it, Holt."

Holt turned to Midas, surprised.

Midas continued, "We're all professionals. Calling out the basics—you're second-guessing yourself. Second-guessing all of us. You're better than that. None of us have anything to prove. We've just got a job to do."

"Well, damn," Holt said finally. "My mouth has been well and truly shut. Let us go do this thing."

Weaver quirked an eyebrow. "You serious?"

"As death. Midas don't talk much, but when he does, you better listen." He put his hand out, and Midas handed him the machete. "Let's go see what's waiting for us."

They heard the camp before they saw it. It was big and loud, and the sounds of human activity punched into the jungle in a way that drowned everything else out. The Ghosts had bypassed one sentry on the way in, noting the man's position for future reference on the exfil. But there were no cameras, no tripwires or mines or booby traps. The size and remoteness of the camp made those who ran it confident that no intruder would find it and that no one would attack in force.

They'd dropped behind a small rise that gave a good view of the camp. Midas had moved ahead slightly to a rock outcropping, getting to get a sense of the layout, while Weaver and Holt hung back.

They could see that the main camp was laid out efficiently, and with the intent to make something permanent. It had been set up close to the river, with a small boathouse and a dock sitting on the water. A series of armed riverine craft bobbed in the current. Most were converted commercial boats with mounted weapons. Mixed in were a pair of new-looking G-25 Guardians, riverine hunter-killer boats whose production had been licensed out to UNOCAR and which had been tweaked for these river conditions. Sentries stood guard at the waterside. As they watched, a second G-25 came in and disgorged a quartet of soldiers. Others immediately leapt in and began refueling the vessel and reloading its three mounted guns for its next run out.

As for the camp proper, it had been laid out with forethought and intelligence. There was one road in, one road out, and an orderly set of small, prefab buildings was set up on a grid. Surrounding them was a ring of tents, and the jungle had been cleared to a distance of twenty meters on all sides to prevent anyone from getting too close while still under cover. Light poles jutted up here and there, promising islands of illumination in the ocean of rain forest darkness. Razor wire at the edge of the green served to discourage animals and other unwanted visitors from wandering into camp. Patrols swept the space, while tree-mounted cameras scanned the jungle. Soldiers wearing a hodgepodge of uniforms and insignia moved through the camp with discipline and purpose. Most carried AK-103s as well as sidearms, and they looked lean and tested by the elements. On the side away from the river was a motor pool housing several jeeps. Instead of the ubiquitous pickups, there was also a series of blocky M35 Fenix cargo trucks that looked shockingly new as well as a sizable contingent of construction equipment two-thirds covered in jungle mud. A fuel tanker sat off to the side of the road, well back from the main camp, to mitigate the possible damage from a fire. The airstrip lay beyond it.

Weaver had seen jungle airstrips before. Most seemed like they'd been hacked out of the foliage with minimum effort, just wide and long enough to allow something to take off and smoothed just enough to keep axles from snapping on landing.

This one, on the other hand, looked like professional work. The airstrip was eight meters wide and more than 200 long, meticulously carved from the jungle. It sat maybe fifty meters away from the camp proper, running northeast-southwest in a way that led it past the encampment instead of riding right up to it. The strip itself had been clear-cut and hammered flat, the hard-packed dirt seeming more like reddish concrete than soil. A lone windsock flew on one side, flapping languidly in the occasional breeze, and a massive berm had been built up at one end. Next to the airstrip, attached by a short path, was a moderately sized clearing pressed into use as a helipad. It, too, had been carved out and maintained with an attention to detail; a small shed at the near side housed what looked to be barrels of fuel. A hulking Sikorsky S-61 sat square in the middle of the pad, its aging fuselage painstakingly painted in jungle camo. The view was obscured by the camo netting thrown over the bird; more attempts had been made to disguise the runway and the helipad proper.

"Are you all seeing what I'm seeing?"

"Roger that, Weaver. A Sea King. I didn't know any of those were still flying." Holt sounded impressed despite himself. "The question is, what's it doing here?"

"Bolivarian Defense Force was still running a couple

last time I checked. I'm guessing the Amazonas types nationalized it."

"They also strapped a couple of guns to it," Midas added. "Still, it feels like a weak excuse for an air force."

"Better than anything else around here," Holt retorted. "I'm thinking we can't just go in, guns blazing. We don't know where the hostages are; we don't know where Nomad is; we don't know how many they've got; and we don't have the numbers for a stand-up fight. So, we watch?"

Weaver answered. "We watch. Wish we still had your drone, but as long as we're wishing for things, might as well wish for the 25th Infantry to show up with bells on."

There was silence for a moment. "That would be pretty sweet," Holt said finally. Weaver and Midas laughed. "Gonna swing right, try to get a different angle. Check-in at 1600?"

"Roger that," Weaver replied. "Midas, you want to swing toward the river, see what you can see from there?"

"Copy that." The two men moved, while Nomad crouched down and watched.

They observed the camp in silence, Holt and Midas sliding to their respective positions quickly and without complication. All three concurred; the camp was a model of efficiency. Sentries held their posts without fidgeting or smoking, blending into the forest so well that Weaver had to switch to NVG in the gathering twilight to find them. There was no bravado here, no squabbling or messing around. The buildings were cleared of vines and creepers; the paths between them and the tents were clear and solid; and the movements of the men stationed here were clean and purposeful.

"It occurs to me," said Weaver after a few more minutes of observation, "that the guys we're seeing here don't even seem like they're part of the same outfit as the guys down at the border. And I think I know why."

"Do tell." Holt watched a pair of soldiers exit a large tent near the center of the encampment, then head out into the jungle at a brisk trot.

"All these guys got sent down here and forgotten, right? They got put on a helo and sent to the ass end of the Amazon. Now who do you send off like that?"

"Fuck-ups. Guys you don't want around in case the shit hits the fan."

Weaver nodded. "Right. And those, I think, were the guys we saw down on the water. Maybe even the ones who were hassling the village. But who else do you send?"

Holt thought for a minute. "The guys who really, really like it out here?"

"Yup." Weaver's face was stony. "The badasses. I knew this was going to get worse."

"Doesn't matter if we're up against minor leaguers or the all-star team. Like you said, we're here to do a job. And we do it. Everything else is details."

"Yeah, but these are some details. You see the unit insignia on those two? Same one as Urbina."

Holt continued to peer down at the camp. "Then we'd best not get captured, too, cause I hear those guys know how to work a body. Which brings us back to the hostages."

Midas was pessimistic. "Depending on how they've been treated, they might not be in any shape to walk. We can't carry them and fight at the same time."

Weaver's expression was dark. "We'll assess the situation when we see them. If they can't run, then we need to make sure there's no pursuit."

"That sounds like it would be a good idea if we were extracting Usain goddamned Bolt. You saw how messy it was last time. And now we're up against guys who are better-prepped and just plain better. Plus, there's the airstrip, whatever that means."

Weaver pointed up. "I think we're about to find out."

Nomad heard it then, the low drone of a small plane engine, getting louder. "Recognize that?" Weaver asked. "Cessna Denali. What the hell is one of them doing out here?"

"Maybe we should go ask them."

"That would be a spectacularly bad idea. Holt, you're closest. What have we got?"

"She's coming in . . . I wouldn't think this runway would be long enough, but they've got a good pilot, maybe. Hey, there's a logo on the tail. Corporate. Small, but I think I can make it out. Trying to zoom in . . . holy crap. Oil company. What the hell?"

"There aren't supposed to be any oil deposits here," Midas chimed in. "What could they be interested in?"

"Dunno." Holt was back on the case as the propeller's whine got louder. "Here she comes, and . . . she's down."

And indeed, the plane dropped expertly onto the runway and cruised to a halt well short of the berm. As it eased to a stop, soldiers rushed out to help the passenger off the plane. The first was a man in a dark blue bespoke suit, silver-haired and red-faced, looking like someone had poured a drill rig wildcatter into a dark-blue Brooks Brothers three-piece. Behind him, keeping an ostentatious difference, was a small, slightly potbellied man with dark hair and an olive complexion. He was dressed in a button-down short-sleeve shirt and khakis, and he looked like he'd just been viciously awakened from a nap. The first man chatted briefly with one of the soldiers greeting them, slapped the soldier on the back, and then turned to face a small party that was approaching on foot from the center of camp. The second merely stood back, arms folded across his chest, and watched.

"Oh, shit. Are you two seeing what I'm seeing?" Holt asked.

"That's Urbina heading over there!" Even Midas sounded surprised. "None of this adds up. What's he doing here? Why is he talking to these people? Where are the hostages—"

"And what the hell is Nomad doing in the middle of all this?"

"Couple of bodyguards are getting off the plane too, now," Holt added. "I'm surprised they didn't go first. Oil guy and his buddy have gotta feel pretty comfortable. Now why would that be?"

"I don't know," Weaver said. "But I've got a bad feeling about it. Get pictures, Holt. Get lots of pictures."

CHAPTER 17

Instead of a meal, Nomad got visitors, and a gag. The latter was supplied by Hernán, who had been assigned regular guard duty by the colonel for some imagined infraction, and who resented Nomad more every hour as a result.

"Don't even try to talk," he warned Nomad, then snapped to attention as the door opened and a pair of burly PMC types entered. The pair were 'roided up and dressed to impress, showing off how badass and ostentatiously armed and earpieced they were. The one on the left nodded and murmured something into his mic, and then the door opened again. The two bodyguards flanked the doorway as three more men came through: a red-faced businessman in a suit that screamed Wall Street, not Amazon jungle; a shorter man dressed like he'd made a wrong turn at an accountants' convention; and behind him, Col. Urbina.

"What the hell are we looking at, Urbina?" asked the accountant, pulling his sunglasses off his face in annoyance. Nomad immediately revised his assessment of the man; the package said pencil-pusher, but the eyes were those of a stone killer.

"Gotta agree with El Pulpo here," added the American. White-haired and muscular, he had hands that had obviously seen hard labor in their time, and his accent was straight out of a Texas oil field. "I thought that whole hostage business was over and done with."

"You were worried about security, Mr. Briggs. Allow me to show you proof of what our border security can do. You are looking at one of the American government's most expensive soldiers, who attempted to disrupt a field operation of ours. He failed."

The man's face got impressively red as Urbina spoke. "Let me get this straight, Colonel. You've got a US Army Special Forces guy tied to a chair, and this is supposed to reassure me? What this means is that not only does that pack of jackasses in Washington know what we're up to, but they're moving to stop it."

"He has no idea what's actually going on, and neither do his superiors. His unit had been sent in to rescue some kidnapped *archaeologists*." He said the last word with particular emphasis, and it had the desired effect as Briggs burst into laughter.

"Oh did he? Good luck finding those, son." He chuckled.

"Cut the crap, Urbina," the man called El Pulpo— the octopus—said. "My people want nothing to do with people like him. You draw attention from the American government, you lose our interest."

"Relax," Urbina said, gesturing expansively. "He won't be here long enough to be a problem."

Briggs frowned and turned to Urbina. "Seeing as the man was on a wild goose chase and you can't keep him here or old Pulpo there is gonna crap bricks, what exactly were you planning to do with him? I mean, we can't have him going back to the States, but just killing him don't sit quite right."

"I can promise you, he is not going back to the United States. Currently our friend is the subject of a bidding war between certain elements in the Russian government, two theoretically allied governments, and a representative of a certain non-state actor. Each of them have a use for him and none would send him home when they were finished. The Russians even paid extra to keep the US out of the bidding. And in the meantime, it is, as you say, cash on the barrelhead."

"Huh." Briggs rubbed his chin with thick, calloused fingers. "Sorry about this, son," he said. "Hate to see this happen to a good man. But business is business, and somebody's got to be the price of doing it."

"Bullshit." El Pulpo stalked over to Nomad. "Selling him off is an idiot plan. Too many ways for it to go wrong, too many possible leaks. Kill him, Urbina. Kill him and dump the body in the river, and do it quick. The last thing you want is to attract attention from US Special Forces."

Urbina waved him off. "They won't come after him. Not here. It's too risky. And he'll be gone before the Americans even know I had him."

"They don't need to come after him. If he's got a GPS implant, they can just send an airstrike."

"They're not going to violate international airspace. They still pretend that matters, as long as they can sneak men like this—" he gestured at Nomad "—over the border to do their dirty work instead. He's a prize of war and I'm treating him like one. And when he doesn't come back, maybe they'll be a little less interested in sending another one like him."

"Santa Blanca is going to be very wary of doing business in a place that has a bull's-eye painted on it by Uncle Sam."

"Tell your backers they have nothing to worry about. This one—" he jerked a thumb at Nomad again "—is going to be just one more man eaten by the jungle."

"You'd better pray you're right," Pulpo growled.

Looking uncomfortable, Briggs took a step back. "I think we're done here, don't you?"

Urbina nodded. "As you wish. We don't need to discuss business in front of him, I'm sure." The odd procession filed out in reverse order, the bodyguards moving so quickly Hernán was nearly trampled.

Urbina went last. As he was leaving, he looked back over his shoulder at Nomad. "I told you I had partners. Mr. Briggs, the cartel—the money will flow. And you will see what I build here. Or perhaps you won't. Hernán?"

"Yes, Colonel?"

"Wait a couple of minutes, and then take off the gag."

"Yes, Colonel." He snapped off a salute, which Urbina returned before walking out into the jungle twilight.

"I think I've ID'ed the building that Nomad's in." Midas's voice broke hours of silent observation.

"How you figure, Midas?" Holt sounded more curious than challenging.

"Third building in on the left. Prefab. Guard out front. I've seen them bring a meal in a couple of times. Just saw the guard go in and grab a bucket."

"Could be Nomad, could be the hostages," said Weaver. "Why you figure it's our guy?"

"One meal, not two." Midas paused for a moment. "Actually, that's odd. I haven't seen meals taken anywhere else in this place. Just to that one building."

"So either the hostages are being kept in the mess hall or things just got even more interesting." Weaver chewed on that for a minute. "Which means the hostages are dead, moved, or being punished. Two cases out of three means Nomad's the only objective here."

"You sure you're not seeing what you want to see?" Holt asked. "I get the logic, but it's awful convenient."

"You keep watching the HQ. What's the latest?"

"The traveling party went into the hut Midas ID'ed a couple of hours ago. Since then, they've been holed up in HQ. The jet's being refueled as we speak and they're moving lights onto the runway—I'm guessing they're prepping for a night takeoff."

"Got a match on the visitor?"

"And the muscle. The guy from the plane is Jerry Briggs, from Oklahoma. Big shot with Caton Oil. Heads their new projects division."

"You pull that from the satellite link?"

"Nope. Remembered him from when his company put a couple of platforms just off the Louisiana coast and one of them burped a few thousand gallons of crude oil all over my favorite beach. He showed up in the aftermath to kiss some hands and shake some babies and wrote a couple of what were probably bad checks to the cleanup effort. If he's here, that company's not messing around."

"Roger that. And the bodyguards?"

"Insignia on their shirts gave them away. They work for a PMC called Watchgate. Big in the oil business. They get a lot of contracts for protecting wells and refineries in rough country."

"It doesn't get much rougher than this. And I think we just figured out why that mook you dropped at the compound spoke English. Midas, what's your take?"

"The guard just went back into the building. I can confirm the visit earlier. It lasted about ten minutes. Guard shifts run four hours. This one has about an hour to go."

"That gives us our window. Okay. We can't take on

the whole camp. So we need most of the camp doing something else. Like putting out a big-ass fire. Midas, time for you and Holt to switch posts. Then I want you to figure out a targeting solution on anything that looks flammable. Start with the fuel truck and work up a list from there. If you can ID an ammo dump, prioritize it."

"Won't they be expecting something like that after the raid where we rescued Crotty?"

"If they think we're going to repeat that, they'll be watching for drones and EMPs first. I wanna get straight to the good stuff."

"If you say so," Midas answered doubtfully.

"Their own damn fault for putting the good stuff out where we could see it."

Despite himself, Midas grinned. "On the move."

"Holt, you and I are going to get Nomad. We've got the pattern on the patrols, just need to get through the wire. Once we're in, Midas lights things up. We pull Nomad out and fall back into the jungle, lay low until we can get back to the boat."

"You realize, if this goes sideways, we're fucked." Holt's tone was light but strained.

"I am aware of that," Weaver replied. "But you can say that about every damn op."

"Yeah, but the odds are a little longer on this one than most ops. No backup, no helo for exfil, numbers on their side, they've got air cover and we're down a man going in. This is not a recipe for success."

"Neither is bitching about how bad the odds are, Holt. Try to figure out a way to even those odds a little more, but if you can't do that, at least you can stop making them worse by pissing me off."

"I'm just saying," Holt grumbled. "Sorry."

"It's cool. You're blowing off steam. Just don't need to be dealing with that right now, you understand?"

"Yeah." Holt paused. "But we're still fucked."

"Fucked is as fucked does," Weaver said calmly. "Now, do you have any actual suggestions, or do we roll?"

"I like it up to the 'getting out of here' part," Holt said. "Any chance we could work on—holy crap, you're not going to believe this."

"I'm seeing it, too," Midas added. "I'd say that's visual confirmation."

"Confirmation of what?"

"Nomad just exited the building where he was being held. And he looks pissed."

The first duty of the prisoner is to escape.

Nomad knew the mantra as well as anyone, though he'd never had to put it into practice. But he'd heard enough from Urbina, and it was time to break out. The trick being, he still wasn't sure quite how to go about it.

Hernán had long since retreated to his post outside to glower in silence, leaving Nomad to his own devices, which were few. The bucket he was allowed to use for his necessaries was in the back right corner, thankfully empty. Besides that there was, of course, the chair, a clunky metal thing in late-sixties institutional style that had been bolted to the floor, which had been his prison and was his best hope for a weapon.

If, of course, he could get out of it.

If they'd left him his boots, he reflected, it would have been no problem, as it was easy enough to rig up a quick friction saw with the laces. But they'd stripped him barefoot, the better to hinder any sort of escape attempt. And without them, he was going to have to do this the hard way.

His hands were ziptied to the back of the chair, instead of the arms, making it harder for him to escape. They'd pulled the ties painfully tight, which was both good and bad. Bad in that he was already starting to lose feeling in his fingers; good in that a tight ziptie was a ziptie under strain and therefore easier to rupture.

He tried pulling on the tie, flexing his shoulders in hopes of snapping the bond. It didn't work; the angle was too tight, and the wound in his shoulder robbed him of the strength that might have gotten the job done. Next up was seeing if he could saw through the ties on the surface of the chair, but here, too, he was defeated. The range of motion he had simply wasn't wide enough to build up sufficient friction.

Which left one option, and that was going to be painful.

Briefly, he wondered how the others were doing. They'd be coming back for him, that much he knew. But that wasn't going to do a lot of good if he was already bundled onto a plane to a GRU gulag or some terrorist compound. And the way Urbina had been talking, whichever option it was would be decided soon.

Taking a deep breath, he tucked his right leg in

onto the seat of the chair, under his body. He followed with the left, leaving him effectively crouching on the chair. Slowly, carefully, he stood, his shoulder agonizingly painful as the pull on his arms increased. The chair groaned and he crouched and waited for it to steady; too much noise would attract Hernán's attention, and then he'd be screwed.

The noises subsided, and he took a series of deep breaths.

If he couldn't move his arms to build up the energy to pop the ties, then he'd have to move the rest of himself, letting his body generate the force his arms couldn't. He'd done this once before, in Germany, to win a bar bet with a couple of MPs, but he'd had two working shoulders then, and wasn't feeling a whole lot of pain in any case.

He'd won the bet. This time, the stakes were higher.

He let himself drop. And at the last second, he wrenched his hands apart, as hard as he could.

The ziptie snapped, plastic scattering everywhere. He came down hard, slamming off the seat and onto the floor. The chair wobbled once, then settled back onto its legs. And Nomad crouched, motionless, waiting for the noise to attract the guard.

The guard didn't come.

He stood slowly, careful to not make any noise, trying not to press his luck. Still, there was nothing from outside the tent.

Nomad flexed his arms experimentally. The feeling was flooding back into his swollen and numb fingers; the pain in his shoulder had subsided a bit. And he was free.

Nomad took another look at the chair, the only other thing in the room. It really was old-school military issue, designed to be as durable and uncomfortable as possible. He'd spent years sitting in similar chairs in briefing rooms around the world. The whole thing was painted a flat gray, scratched and nicked here and there to show gray metal underneath.

An experimental shove told him that the bolts to the floor weren't going to give. But if the bolts were strong, closer examination showed that the welds and joins on the various pieces were unwieldy and poorly done. A couple of solid hits, and the whole thing would likely break into its component parts. But that would mean noise, which would mean alerting Hernán.

Which left the bucket.

INTERLUDE - NOMAD

One of the two men was Salvatore, the other one was Hume, and Nomad swore to himself that if they got out of this alive, he was going to remember which one was which.

The three of them were pinned down in what had apparently once been a convenience store, before things had gotten hot in downtown Mexico City. Rebels had mounted a coup attempt and fighting had broken out all over the country, but the heat was highest here, in the capital. And caught in the middle were the US troops that had only been allowed on Mexican soil by special dispensation in the first place.

The more immediate concern, however, was the squad of Mexican soldiers spraying the store with automatic weapons fire while Nomad and his new companions ducked for cover as best they could.

"What the hell unit are you from, anyway?" Nomad yelled over the sound of the gunfire. "And is there any chance your friends are coming for you?"

"Group for Specialized Tactics," came the reply from Salvatore, or maybe Hume.

"What the hell? I thought you were a training unit." The man closer to the front of the store—Nomad was pretty sure it was Hume—reached up and blind-fired at the encroaching enemies. There was a grunt of pain, and then the suppressive fire stopped for a minute while someone shouted urgently in Spanish for a medic. Then they opened up again, the thunder of the guns punctuated with the occasional cymbal crash of shattered glass as a bullet found an unbroken bottle.

"A lot of folks think that," said the soldier crouching behind the counter—almost certainly Salvatore—as he pulled a grenade from his belt. "You're gonna wanna get ready in about five seconds."

"Are you crazy? We don't have enough—"

Salvatore rose up and slung the grenade sidearm out the ruined front window. It hit off broken asphalt and concrete once with a sharp, metallic ping, then rolled to a stop. The gunfire abruptly cut off as the men outside threw themselves to the ground or scrambled for cover, shouting in panic. As one, Salvatore and Hume rose and sprayed the area in front of the store with precise shots, dropping enemy soldiers with mechanical precision.

"Get down!" Nomad yelled.

"It's a dud," Salvatore replied cheerfully. "Always carry one with me. Now let's get out of here before the survivors figure it out. Hume?"

"Back door. Follow me. Move!"

Nomad moved, Salvatore following close behind. Hume hit the back door of the shop, a sturdy-looking metal slab, with his shoulder, and it popped open. He dove through, the other two firing, just as one of the rebel soldiers out front figured out he'd been duped and opened fire. A hail of bullets chased them out the back door into an alley half-blocked with broken masonry and abandoned trash bins.

"Keep running!" Salvatore shouted, cutting left. Hume paused, turned, and fired a burst back into the store before following, flanking Nomad as they ran.

"I thought you said that grenade was a dud!"

"The one I threw out front was. The one I left in the shop—"

The sound of the detonation cut him off. A jet of debris blasted out the open back door, and then there was silence.

"That one was real," Hume finished. "Now, soldier, what the hell are we going to do with you?"

"I'm hoping you won't shoot me." Hume and Salvatore exchanged glances. Salvatore smirked.

"Screw it, we've worked with worse. And this is looking a little familiar."

"Lightning strikes twice." Salvatore turned back to Nomad. "Separated from your unit?"

"Yeah. We were supposed to be helping secure the area around the Zócalo when a column of Panhards rolled up flying the national colors. We let our guard down, and they pulled down the flags and opened up. We scattered, those of us who could. Can't raise anyone else."

"Damn, that's cold." Salvatore chewed on his lower lip for a minute. "Okay, you're with us until we hook up with another friendly unit you can slide over to. Until then, you follow orders, you keep your mouth shut, and you don't ask what we're doing or why we're doing it. Cause if I told you, Hume here would have to shoot you, and he hates doing that."

"It's true," Hume said, solemnly nodding. "Now, are we going to stand here and get ourselves killed, or are we going to move?"

As if in emphasis, a series of explosions erupted a few blocks south of where they stood. Pillars of smoke and debris rose up, one after another, and the sound of rifle fire and the thump of heavier weapons filled the air. A squadron of jets screamed overhead, low enough that Nomad could see the gold-and-black coiled hawk insignia on their tails. They dumped their payloads on the source of the explosions, then banked west and flew off at speed.

The shockwave that hit an instant later threw Nomad to the ground. As he picked himself up, he noticed that Hume and Salvatore had both braced themselves for the impact and were already on the move. "Crenshaw's boys don't fuck around," Salvatore said, offering Nomad a hand up. "Time to motivate."

They jogged up the street, away from the site the jets had just bombed. Firing could still be heard in the distance, but it was sporadic; whoever had been dug in on that block was likely now buried or pulverized.

"What's the mission?" Nomad asked.

"Extraction," Hume answered. "Mexican officer who assisted us got pulled off the street, and he's in 'special holding.' Which means they're going to shoot his ass. And we're going to keep that from happening."

"We can't get you on our channel." Salvatore sounded exasperated. "So here's what you need to know: The rebels are going to off him publicly as an example, and he's being held in a scrapyard because we've apparently blown the shit out of all the prisons. We're going to go in and get him. If you're still with us when we get there, then we will go in and get him, and you will provide suppression. Are we good?"

Nomad nodded. "We're good."

"Whoa, whoa, whoa, hold up." Hume edged to a stop as they neared a corner. "GPS says go left. Cross-com says they've got sentries on the cross street."

"Drone?"

"Looking at the feed now." Nomad could see images flickering across the man's eyepiece, one more advantage they had that he'd only seen in prototype, if at all. "Okay. Two behind a barricade at the next intersection. Full squad at the entrance to the salvage yard. Got a fix on the building they're keeping him in." He peered around the corner. "Sync the shot?"

"Roger that." Salvatore moved behind a parked, miraculously undamaged car, and edged toward the intersection. Nomad held back, watching. Then Salvatore said "Go," and they fired simultaneously.

"Tangos down?"

"Confirmed. We're clear. Let's go."

They moved up the street, Salvatore and Hume in the lead, Nomad trailing. They moved cover to cover, methodically, but not slowly. Finally, Hume dropped behind a Mercedes that had seen better days; flying debris had done a number on the paint job, and all the driver-side windows had been smashed. A single massive bullet hole in the hood announced that this car wouldn't be going anywhere under its own power.

"Damn." Hume turned to Salvatore. "Someone knocked the drone down. HQ is trying to get another UAV in position, but the airspace over Mexico City looks like someone threw up a plate of spaghetti."

"Got it." Salvatore looked around. "You hear that?"

Nomad strained to listen. There was a faint, angry rumble, but mixed with the explosions and distant rat-a-tats of gunfire. "There's . . . something? I dunno. Maybe the Metro?"

Salvatore looked unconvinced. "They're still running trains in this? Then they're tougher than New Yorkers, and nobody's that tough." Hume rolled his eyes, but Salvatore held up a hand to stop any further ribbing. "The objective's over there. Guards are dug in behind sand-bags, and the drone showed me at least one mounted .50 cal. I say we give the UAV operators a couple of minutes.

Dig in here. If they can get us some eyes, good. In the meantime, we're not getting chewed up advancing over open ground."

Hume scowled. "We can engage from here. Drop two before they know what hit them. Not like we've got the time to wait."

Nomad held up his hand. "Wait. It's getting louder." He looked down. "Ground's shaking, too."

Hume and Salvatore looked at each other. "Oh, shit."

The vehicle powered out of the alley in front of them, knocking over stray bits of wall and rubble as it roared toward them. Masonry groaned and collapsed as Nomad flung himself clear. Salvatore and Hume were lost in a cloud of smoke, one lit up from the inside by intense machine gun fire.

Nomad hit the ground and rolled. He could see the vehicle; it was an ERC-90 tank destroyer that had taken some fire. The vehicle's armor was blackened and crumpled in places, the main gun knocked off true. But the engine was clearly intact, and riding up top was a machine gunner seemingly intent on blasting his targets into paste. A hail of bullets slammed out toward Salvatore's last known position. Return fire slackened and cut off, and when the dust cloud cleared, Salvatore was nowhere to be seen.

Hume, on the other hand, was visibly down and under a pile of rubble. A wall had collapsed on him. He was moving, but pinned.

The gunner and Nomad saw Hume at the same. He shouted something, and the tank killer pivoted ponderously. It surged forward, wheels spitting up broken brick and concrete as it headed for where Hume lay trapped.

Without thinking, Nomad moved. His first burst of fire spattered off the side of the vehicle as the gunner spun to face the sudden new threat. The second took the man in the chest. He squeezed off one final burst that carved a vicious semicircle in the pavement and then slumped down.

But it was still moving, and so was Nomad. Sprinting, he reached the ERC-90 and leaped up onto it. The gaps torn in its armor gave him the handholds he needed, and he scurried up to where the dead gunner lolled in the open hatch. He could hear shouting down below. Desperately trying to move the body out of the way, he was dropped a frag down inside and threw himself off toward the ground.

He landed hard, the wind knocked out of him. A jet of material, some of it red, blasted out the top of the hatch, and then the tank killer lurched to a halt bare inches away from where Hume was still pinned.

Wincing, Nomad picked himself up and stumbled to Hume. Salvatore was already there, moving aside piles of brick. He looked up as Nomad reached them. "Nice shooting."

"I thought they got you," Nomad replied, as he dropped down and joined in Salvatore's efforts. "It looked like—"

"It looked like it was too goddamned close. But what you did, that took guts. Don't think we're going to forget it."

"It was just instinct, I swear," Nomad answered. "Didn't even think about it."

"Yeah, well, that kind of reaction is exactly what we're looking for in—"

"Can you two stop giving each other a tongue bath for one minute?" Hume struggled to a sitting position. He was covered in dust, and there was a nasty cut on his forehead, but he seemed otherwise unharmed. "Because I think the guys at the scrapyard just might have heard us?"

Nomad looked up. A squad of rebel soldiers was advancing on their position, an officer shouting orders.

Hume looked at him and then gestured to the incoming hostiles. "Buy us enough time for him to dig me out? Then we got this."

Salvatore nodded. "We got this. You game?"

Nomad said nothing, just lined up his shot and fired at the leading hostile. And then the enemy was firing back, and in the back of his mind, he heard a small voice saying, *Nice to be part of a team, isn't it?*

CHAPTER 18

The problem was that Hernán was good. Disciplined and professional, he wasn't likely to be taken in by cheap stunts or suddenly convenient cries for help.

Nomad adjusted his stance and a wave of agony emanated from his shoulder. He touched the skin around the wound, and it felt warm. Probably infected and a definite vulnerability in a fight.

He walked over to the corner to get the bucket. It was faintly redolent, clearly repurposed from an industrial paint job of some sort. The handle was metal, but the body was rigid plastic. It was heavy enough to hurt, not heavy enough to do real damage. It was all he had.

Quietly, he picked it up and brought it over to the chair. He sat down, took a few deep breaths to center himself, and started dragging the bucket back and forth on the concrete floor. It was loud enough to make a racket and different-sounding enough to attract attention. At least, that was the plan.

He dragged it back and forth a few more times. There was no response, no sign Hernán had even heard. Grimacing, he banged it against the chair a few times for emphasis, then dragged it even more loudly on the floor.

After a moment, the door cracked open. Nomad stopped instantly, tucking the bucket under the chair and his hands behind him.

"What the hell?" Hernán's voice was full of irritation. "What's going on in there?"

"Some kind of animal got in," Nomad answered. "You want to come in here and take care of it before it spills the pee bucket all over the floor?"

"Hah. Would serve you right to sit in that."

"You'd be the one cleaning it up, not me," Nomad pointed out.

"Bastard." Slowly, the door opened. Hernán walked in, rifle trained on Nomad. He relaxed a little when he saw Nomad still in the chair, hands still behind his back. "So what kind of animal—" he started to ask.

Nomad rose from his chair, grabbing the bucket by the handle and swinging it out from beneath the chair.

The makeshift weapon came across his body and slapped the rifle barrel out of the way as Hernán took a reflexive step back, then Nomad reversed his swing and brought it up under the man's jaw.

He staggered, one hand flying off the gun, and Nomad saw his opportunity. Dropping the bucket, he slammed down onto the gun itself with his elbow. It wrenched free from Hernán's grip and clattered to the floor.

Rather than go for the gun, Hernán went for the body. He threw a series of quick jabs at Nomad, looking for the vulnerable shoulder. The first two, Nomad blocked. The third one got through, staggering him.

Hernán pressed his advantage, driving Nomad back with a flurry of punches. "Finally," he said. "You gave me an excuse. Killed trying to escape. I should thank you!"

He let loose with a roundhouse right, and Nomad stepped inside the punch. Shifting, he grabbed Hernán's arm and turned the wayward punch into a throw. The guard went flying, and Nomad dove for the rifle. He got his hands on it just as Hernán rolled to his feet and pulled his sidearm. The two circled each other warily, weapons raised.

"Stalemate," Nomad said, and gestured at the door. "You want to live, you let me walk out of here. You pull the trigger, we both die."

"I don't think so," Hernán replied, and threw the gun at Nomad's head. He almost managed to duck out of the way, but it grazed him on the right temple. It was a light blow, but one that bought just enough time for Hernán to reach him on a bull rush.

Nomad got the rifle between himself and his charging

opponent barely in time, and then the two of them went over. Nomad's head hit the concrete with a painful shock, dazing him, and Hernán took advantage, leaning in and dropping a forearm across Nomad's throat. Gasping, Nomad wrenched the rifle left, bringing the stock up into Hernán's ribs once, twice, and then on a third time it was enough to roll them over so that Nomad was on top.

Hernán let go of Nomad's throat and instead dug an elbow into his shoulder. Nomad could feel something rip—maybe the bandage, maybe something underneath—and a trickle of hot blood bloomed through his shirt. Already, he could feel his grip with that arm slipping, the strength draining out of his fingers. If he was going to win this, he'd have to end it quickly.

He grunted with pain, then brought the rifle up with two hands and all the strength he could muster. Hernán tried to bring his hands down to block, but it was too late, and the center of the rifle caught him squarely on the chin. His head flew back and bounced off the floor, and then Hernán went limp.

Quickly, Nomad checked to make sure Hernán was truly out. He was.

With a sigh of relief, Nomad eased himself up. He could feel the blood leaking from his shoulder now, a slow stream of warmth that he was probably going to have to do something about soon, but at least he didn't seem to be at risk of bleeding out. Hobbling slightly, he locked the door of the hut to make sure what he had to do next wouldn't be disturbed.

And then he went to work.

The first thing Nomad did was secure Hernán's weapons, a by-now familiar AK-103 and a shiny new Glock 17. The second thing he did was check the size of Hernán's boots, which were close enough for jazz. Nomad appropriated his footgear and shirt as well, then tied the unconscious guard to the chair using his belt in place of the ziptie. It wasn't perfect, but it would hold for long enough.

Then he woke Hernán up.

"Come on, Hernán. I've got a couple of questions for you." Nomad walked around behind the man, then eased the pistol into position at the back of his neck.

"I . . . What? I'm not telling you a damn thing. Go ahead and shoot me."

"You're loyal. I respect that. And you could have treated me a lot worse, which is why you're still alive. But you really should answer my questions before I decide I don't have any more time to waste and pull the trigger."

"And you should shoot me before I start yelling for help, and you die in here," Hernán responded. "I'm not afraid."

"Look, I'll make this easy. I'm not going to ask you to sell out your colonel. All I'm asking is where they're keeping the hostages."

Hernán sounded genuinely puzzled. "Hostages? You rescued them already. That is when we caught you. You have a concussion, I think."

Nomad tapped him lightly on the back of the head. "Wrong answer. There are two archaeologists, Messina and Kwan. A couple of their people came running out of the jungle claiming they'd been kidnapped. You tell me where they are, and then I'll go away."

"Kidnapped? You think they were kidnapped?" Hernán laughed heartily. "This, this is the best part of things. You are an idiot, and they weren't kidnapped. And because I want to see you humiliated before you are caught and killed, I will tell you where to go. Three buildings down, toward the water. That's where your 'hostages' are. I hope you choke on what you find." Before Nomad could answer, he started straining against his bonds, grunting with the effort.

Nomad watched for a second to make sure he wouldn't be getting loose quite yet, then grabbed the kerchief that had given him so much trouble and tied it in place as a gag. "Kind of gross, I know. But consider the alternative."

He waited a moment to make sure the man could breathe, then stalked out into the night in his ill-fitting boots.

The foot traffic in the camp had slowed after the sun had gone down. No one stopped or approached Nomad as he forced himself to walk calmly up to the building Hernán had indicated. Light shone out from under the door and from the windows, but there was no guard in evidence.

He tried the door. It was unlocked. Looking around to make sure he was unobserved, he stepped inside and locked the door behind him.

What he saw did not look like a holding cell. On a long table down the left side of the hut were dozens of pottery sherds laid out in some esoteric order and neatly labeled. A pair of beds, one messily unmade, were to the right, with a walled-off area he could only assume was a small toilet bulging out from the corner. There were foot lockers, one closed and one open and stuffed with clothes. Packs and field gear were in evidence everywhere, stowed in whatever space was available. Fluorescent lights provided the harsh glow Nomad had seen under the door, though in here it was more mixed with the faint blue coming off multiple monitors. Those were attached to a whole series of computers, desktops and laptops, on a pair of desks parked side by side at the end of the room, a snake's nest of cable at their feet.

And at one of those desks, looking very surprised, was Dr. Andrew Messina.

"You're supposed to knock before you—" he said as he turned around. The shock of white hair in the picture Wizard had provided had long since been tamed by a more jungle-friendly buzz cut, but the lean, tanned face matched.

What was new was the expression of terrified surprise. "Who the hell are you?"

Nomad walked over to his workstation. "Dr. Messina, I'm from the United States government, and until about fifteen seconds ago I was here to bring you home. It looks like I was misinformed."

Messina stared at the battered, bloody figure in front of him and made a quick calculation. Instead of running, he turned and immediately started shutting down every computer he could get his hands on. "You don't understand," he wailed. "You have to leave, right now! This is . . . it's not safe!"

He'd shut down two of the systems before Nomad grabbed the back of the desk chair and yanked. Messina flailed as he was pulled back away from the computers, then Nomad spun him around and said, "Where's Kwan? What's going on here? Talk."

In response, Messina threw himself out of the chair and tried to scramble away. Nomad let him get halfway up before shoving him back down and grabbing a fistful of shirt. "I said, talk. What the hell is going on here? Why aren't you locked up? And where's Kwan?"

"Herbert's out in the field, okay? He's not here! He's not getting back for a week. Why do you want to know?"

"The field?" Nomad blinked. "He's working? Of course he's working. And you're working. Which means you're not hostages at all. You never were. So what's going on, Dr. Messina? What the hell are you doing out here in the middle of a rebel army?"

"I'm just a scientist. I'm doing research out here and those men are here to provide protection."

"Bull. Shit." Nomad hauled Messina upright. "I know who you are, Dr. Messina. I know where you live, we know where you work, and I know that archaeologists don't get a goddamn private army to watch them dig. You're lucky if you can get a couple of grad students who aren't gonna pee in your canteen once they get out of cell phone range. Now I ask you again, what is going on down here?"

"Nothing, I swear! They just showed up one day and stayed, and we didn't want to make any trouble."

"Let me explain this to you. I'm not really all that invested in you right now, if you take my meaning. You can change that by coming clean, and I will do my best to get you out of this jungle and back home to the States in one piece without being brought up on charges. Or you can keep trying to snow me, in which case I'll make sure your friends outside know you told me everything. I don't think they'll be forgiving."

"I haven't told you a damn thing! Let me go! I said let me—"

Nomad shoved his borrowed pistol was into Messina's face, and he quickly stopped talking.

"Dr. Messina, I am going to ask you one last time. I have been shot, beaten, kidnapped, and mocked on your behalf, only to find it was all unnecessary. You are sawing on my last nerve, and if it snaps, neither of us is going to like what happens next. So tell me, what the *hell* is going on here?"

Messina stared at the gun and swallowed hard. He gazed over Nomad's shoulder at the door and could see that help wasn't coming. Nomad's foreboding expression told him that yelling for help was a bad idea. All the fight went out of him in an instant, and he slid down in his chair.

"Okay, you want to know what the deal is? It's very simple. Caton came to me and Herbert independently with an offer we couldn't refuse. They'd bankroll our work in perpetuity, in exchange for us working in certain areas that interested them. Since I'd been wanting to get in-country for ages, it was a no-brainer. The Venezuelan government wasn't being very generous with permissions to come out here. And if I was going, Herbert wanted to go. Jealous little twerp. Always riding my coattails."

"Dr. Crotty didn't seem to have any trouble getting permission."

"Plant lady?" His voice was bitter. "Take a look at the sort of money Brazil's raking in on all the magic herbs and superfoods people found in the jungle down there. Of course they let *her* in. Old pots aren't as sexy for the bottom line."

Nomad shook his head. "Whatever. So you were down here to dig up cookware? Then where did all this come from?"

"What we're out here looking for, it's a certain type of pottery. The decoration on the pottery uses a particular kind of clay, and that clay's a good indicator for certain mineral deposits."

"Mineral deposits?"

"How thick are you? Oil. Natural gas. Kwan and I were here to tell them where to dig. But they didn't want anyone to know *how* they were looking, so we had to make it seem like any other expedition. We figured we'd run it like your average dig, do some work while we were searching for the pieces they wanted, and get paid enough to fund the rest of our careers. Only we didn't know they'd cut a deal with Colonel Urbina and his people."

"What kind of deal?"

"Look, if Plant Lady finds something, the government gets cut in on it. Probably nationalizes it, even. My new friends at Caton, they want the oil, but if word gets out that it's here, the government's just going to nationalize it. So they're bankrolling Urbina to let him carve out a little petro-state of his own while the central government's not really in shape to do anything about it. He gets a country and all the big guns they can buy him to play with, and in exchange, he gives them unhindered access to the oil deposits we—me and Kwan—locate."

"That's nuts. How are they going to get drilling equipment out here?"

Messina threw up his hands. "I'm pretty sure Brazil won't mind a buffer state between them and whatever the hell is going down in Caracas these days. There's always someone who'll play ball, you see. Everyone's got a price. People. Universities. Countries. It's all the same."

"So that's what happened to you? You got bought?"

"I got bought, Kwan got bought, and then we found out that they owned us. We set up camp and started work. A week on, Urbina arrived and took over. Some of this—" He waved at the camp as a whole. "—was set up and waiting for us. The rest got set up after his people arrived. We didn't have an airstrip. We didn't need one. But it wasn't really about us anymore."

"What happened to your people?"

"Some of them went along once it became clear what was going on. Some didn't. They're gone now." He made a throat-slashing gesture. "The colonel's very efficient."

"And the ones who ran?"

"They were in the field when Urbina rolled in. They came back to camp, saw the soldiers, and panicked. I'm not surprised the story they got out was garbled."

"You piece of crap. Those were your people."

Messina looked up at him. "But it wasn't me. Not everybody's born to be the hero. Some of us are just wired for self-preservation."

Nomad stared down. "I can see that. One last question. Did you find what you were looking for?"

His shoulders slumped. "Yeah. Yeah, we did."

"Thank you, professor. You've been very helpful." Nomad walked over to the desk and pulled a thumb drive out of a laptop. "I assume I'll find something useful on this?"

"No! Wait! You can't!" Messina sputtered. "That's my research!"

"I'm sure you've got it backed up." Nomad grabbed and pocketed a pair of other thumb drives, as well as a phablet and a couple of notepads, shoving them into his pockets. "Right. Be taking these with me. Keep working that self-preservation angle, professor. Try not to get yourself shot when they find out I was here and you're still breathing."

Messina half-rose out of his chair. "Wait. You're leaving? You're leaving me here? Can you do that?"

"You're not a hostage. I have no authority to bring you back." He walked to the door and unlocked it. "And I can't guarantee your safety if you come with me. It's going to be a long walk through some rough terrain. But if you choose to come with me and request my assistance,

I'll try to get you home so you can stand trial for what happened to your assistants. It's your call."

Messina's face blanched. He sank down into his chair, rocking back and forth, head in his hands. "I can't! I just . . . I can't."

"I didn't think you could," said Nomad, and stepped out.

Ten seconds later, the night exploded.

CHAPTER 19

"Does anyone have the slightest idea what Nomad is doing down there?"

"Negative, Weaver." Holt sounded as puzzled as Weaver felt. "Going for the hostages, maybe?"

"But Midas called it. There's no guard on that building, and no food going in or out. So no hostages. Keep an eye on it, Holt. Midas, you have a targeting solution on something flammable?"

"Roger that. Lined up on the tanker; ammo dump looks like it's hardened. I'll say this: the nice thing about doing this from under tree cover is that there's no wind."

"I copy. What are you packing?"

"M433. Standard round. It should get the job done. Got six rounds of that, one white star cluster, a couple of double HE, and some buckshot. Twelve total."

"Just remember to pace yourself." Weaver shifted position slightly and looked down on the camp. "Targets, in order, are the tanker, the plane, and the docks. Motor pool, I'm not worrying about. We exfil through the jungle, those trucks won't be able to follow."

"I hear you. What do we go on?"

"If Nomad needs help. If we see the hostages. Or if someone walks into the hut where Nomad was being held. If he can get his ass out of there without needing fireworks, I am A-OK with that. But this thing's got too many moving parts."

"Tell me about it," Holt chimed in. "No movement on Nomad, but Urbina and his guests just walked out of the HQ building. They're headed back towards the plane. Do you want me to take the shot?"

"Negative. Briggs isn't worth it."

"I meant Urbina." Holt paused. "Okay, yeah, definitely headed toward the airstrip. Midas, are you picking them up?"

"I see them now," Midas confirmed. "This could get tricky."

"They're shaking hands," Holt reported. "I can see the runway lights coming on from here. Looks like their business is done and, oh crap. We've got a situation."

"Details?"

"Relief detail's early at the prison hut. He's looking around for the other guard."

Weaver sounded grim. "He goes in, we go live. What about Nomad?"

"Weaver, they're spinning up on the runway. The tanker's pulling back."

"The tanker's still your target. Holt, what about Nomad?"

"There's nothing. Wait, he's coming out. He's walking out solo, and, wait, the guard just went into the other hut. It's showtime."

"Weaver?"

Weaver could see Nomad now, moving purposefully through the camp. There was no way to get a message to him, no way to warn him that all hell was about to break loose.

"Take the shot," he said, and waited for hell to rain on down.

Midas squeezed the trigger and was rewarded with the soft "whump" of a 40mm grenade leaving the premises at high velocity. Before the first one hit, he'd already reloaded, pulling the next shell from his belt.

There was a roar from the airfield and he looked down at his handiwork. The first grenade had hit the tanker and bounced off before detonating, sending men flying and tearing a rip in the side of the truck. Briggs was staggering for the plane, his bodyguards practically hauling him along as they raced for safety. The other man dropped, rolled, and then headed for the tree line.

"Sorry," Midas said. He dropped his aim a fraction of an inch and fired again.

The round impacted directly underneath the tanker. The first explosion tore the guts out of it; the second blew its midsection sky-high on a pillar of orange and red.

"Tanker down. Switching to secondary target."

"Roger that," Weaver replied. "Holt and I are inbound on Nomad. Keep it hot."

"Copy that." He could see the fire spreading across the field. Flaming debris had hit a couple of tents, and one of them had caught. Men were rushing in from all sides. In the middle of the chaos, Urbina was directing traffic, yelling orders and controlling the panic. Briggs had been pulled up and into the plane, which was turning around for an escape run even as one of the bodyguards pulled the door shut. Of the other man, there was no sign. Best guess was that he was already dead; a close second was that he'd gone under the trees. Either way, he was out of the fight.

Midas pulled a double HE round from his belt and slammed it home, adjusted his aim, and waited.

The plane finished its turn and started down the runway, slowly at first, then picking up speed. One of the lights went up in a spectacular blast as the plane went past it, but the blast went up, not out, and the Cessna kept rolling.

Midas swiveled right, estimated the plane's

acceleration, and fired ahead of it.

The round sailed in a long, graceful arc and hit just in front of the landing gear. The resulting explosion peeled away the front tires and punched the landing gear proper out of true. The plane continued forward, the shriek of damaged metal rising up over the shouting and the flames as its momentum tore the strut loose. It bent itself in half, and the plane's nose dug into the dirt, the propeller blades slamming into the ground and chewing themselves to ribbons. The plane slewed right, shuddering into another mobile lighting unit and toppling it, and then slammed up against the trees at the end of the runway. Flames started to lick at the side of the fuselage.

He didn't wait to see if anyone got out. Already, bullets were zipping overhead as a few soldiers traced the shots back to his position. Staying low, he reloaded and ran.

"Weaver, secondary target is down. Moving to firing position Bravo, targeting tertiary objective."

"Roger that, Midas," Weaver answered. "Nice shooting."

Weaver pivoted his attention to the camp, where rather than chase the fire, the sentries walking the cleared strip inside the wire had knelt and brought their guns up in case it was a diversion.

"Smart boys," Weaver said, "Holt, you reading the sentries?"

"Copy. I've targeted the one on the left."

"I've got the right. On my mark, fire."

The two men never knew what hit them, pitching forward simultaneously.

"Clean kills," Holt announced.

"Copy that. Meet me at the wire closest to where we dropped them."

"Copy that."

Weaver rose and started sprinting for the rendezvous point. Secondary explosions at the airstrip shed lurid light on the fight, bathing everything in fiery orange. He could hear shouted orders, and then the whup-whup-whup of the helo's blades spinning up.

"Midas! They're putting the helo in the air. Can you target it?"

"Negative, Weaver. Not from current position. Lining up tertiary target now."

"Right. But you get a shot on that bird, you take it!"

"Roger that."

Up ahead, the perimeter fence stood out in stark silhouette, the light from the burning airfield throwing it into relief. Holt got there a second before he did. "Standard setup," he said. "Two rolls on the bottom, one on the top. No problem."

Weaver nodded, then knelt and cupped his hands into a step. Holt placed one foot in the makeshift support, then Weaver lifted and Holt jumped, and he was over and rolling on the other side. Holt dropped to a guard position while Weaver retreated into the jungle and grabbed a heavy fallen branch. He slid it under the wire to Holt, who used it to lift up the coils of wire high enough for Weaver to slither underneath.

Weaver pulled himself to his feet, and the pair quickly

moved to take cover behind the tents at the edge of the cleared perimeter. "Nomad's last known position was by that building. Let's walk it so he won't try to drop one of us by mistake."

"I hear you." Holt pulled a sensor grenade from his belt. "Let's see what we're walking into. Sensor out." The readout crackled with static for a minute, and then flared into life. "Remember, one of these guys is Nomad. He's not gonna register as friendly."

"Copy that. We're looking for a solo ping who's moving to cover instead."

"Right. I think I've got a hit. Three o'clock."

Weaver worked his way around the corner of the tent, then motioned Holt to follow. Holt moved to the next tent while Weaver scanned the area. A parade of yellow figures trotted past a few rows down, moving at double-time and weapons ready. Another figure stood at the front of the hut Nomad had been held in; they could hear him yelling. Others patrolled in pairs, stalking down the rows looking for the escaped prisoner. And over where Holt had indicated, a lone shape crouched behind cover, waiting for a patrol to pass.

"Got him." Weaver breathed. "Heads up, two coming our way." Weaver and Holt froze as the pair approached, anxiously searching.

Weaver rose as the second guard passed him, grabbing him from behind and, in one well-practiced move, snapping the man's neck. The sound alerted the first guard, who turned, saw Weaver, and then died as Holt emerged from the shadows to take him down.

"Bodies in the tent?" Holt suggested, and Weaver nodded, pointing to the one he'd been sheltering behind. They dropped both bodies inside and out of view.

"Nice thing about the sensors, they warn you if you're gonna walk in on someone."

"When they work." Weaver set his victim's feet down. "Where's Nomad?"

Holt was already outside the tent. "On the move, but not in a good spot. Patrol's headed back his way."

"We'd better get there before they do." Weaver stepped back into the firelit night. Sirens were blaring now, adding to the overall chaos. Overhead, the steady whup of the helicopter added to the mix, and searchlight beams stabbed down into the trees, looking for targets. Out at the road, soldiers were slamming a gate shut and stacking up behind it, ready to defend the camp against external threats.

Nomad, he saw, had moved closer to the river, putting one of the prefabs between him and the band of a half-dozen soldiers spilling his way. Another pair of soldiers patrolled the space between them, cautiously checking down every intersection and inside every tent.

"They think they're hunting one," he said. "They don't know we're inside the wire. They chase Nomad, we pick 'em off at the fringes."

"Roger that. Gotta keep them off balance."

"Divide and conquer?"

"Let's go."

Weaver glided off to the left, Holt to the right.

The last sputtering light of the sensor told Weaver the tent on his left was unoccupied. He slid in, then set up, his muzzle facing the tent flap. The two closest guards were approaching; he could hear them arguing. One didn't want to check the tents, saying it was a waste of time. The other, who clearly ranked him, insisted on thoroughness.

"You tell him," Weaver muttered.

They were at the next tent over now, and the junior was irate. "You see? He's not here! Why aren't we looking in the jungle?"

"The helicopter is searching the jungle," the other man replied. "Check the next tent."

"There's no one in there. Why would he hide when he could run because everyone's fighting the fire? He could just—"

The tent flap pulled open. Weaver fired twice, in quick succession. The two men hit the ground, and Weaver proceeded to pull them inside. Satisfied they couldn't be seen, he ducked out of the tent. "Holt? Two hostiles down. You?"

"Working on it."

Holt cut the call and focused on the men in front of him. The sensor had gone out, but he didn't need it now. He'd come up behind the patrol, and the hardest part wasn't seeing them; it was keeping up without being seen.

The men were ruthless in their efficiency, clearing each tent and building in textbook fashion. Each one was empty; each search brought them closer to Nomad, who, when Holt last saw him, had been zig-zagging from building to building, heading toward the center of camp. "Why's he doing that?" Holt wondered, then focused his attention back on the patrol.

They were checking one of the huts now, a squat building with a door in the front and the back. Four of the men were stacked up at the back door, while the other two had gone around the front to prevent anyone from escaping that way. A perfect opportunity, Holt decided. He shifted just behind the next building.

Quietly, he risked another sensor, dropping it to the ground at his feet. He could see the two silhouetted against the side of the building already, but moments like this called for precision and avoiding any surprises. The soldiers' shape flared into yellow wireframe, bright even against the reflected firelight. Holt leaned around the side of the building, letting his HUD show a target lock indicator on the nearer of the two, and waited. They stood, stock-still, weapons trained on the doorway, waiting for the same thing. For the millionth time, he thought about a system of multiple target locks for a single weapon, something he'd heard some spook lab around the Beltway was working on. It would have been nice if they could hurry up and get it in the right hands already.

From the other side of the hut, Holt heard a door being kicked in, the shouts of the men moving in. He squeezed the trigger.

The first man never had a chance. Holt neatly headshot

him, and he staggered back two steps before collapsing. The other involuntarily shied back as the spray of blood washed across his face. He raised his arm reflexively to protect his eyes, and Holt caught him with three in the chest. The man went down, gurgling blood and falling in the middle of the doorway. Someone inside attempted to shove it open and ran up against the mass of the fallen man, which told Holt it was time to leave. He drifted across the way to the shadow of another building, and asked himself, *If I were Nomad, where would I be going?*

The dock was a trickier shot than the airstrip, Midas learned. While the M203 had the range to drop a round in the middle of it, being under canopy instead of out in the open meant the cartridge would have to go in on a relatively flat arc, high enough to go over the pieces of the encampment but low enough not to get caught on any overhanging branches.

And then there was the helicopter, which was hovering uncomfortably close to his position and trying to punch through the leaves with spotlights so the onboard gunners could light him up.

The jungle canopy was thick enough to give him cover, but here and there daggers of spotlight slipped through gaps in the leaves, passing dangerously close to his position. If he could get a shot off, the odds were good he could park a round someplace where it could do a great deal of damage. But just as they couldn't hit him with the spotlights through the trees, he couldn't get the shot up through the ceiling of greenery. And stepping out into the open to fire was suicide.

Which left one option.

One of the gunners in the helo let loose with an experimental burst, ripping through the leaves and carving a line in the jungle floor. More light poured through the gap, and, encouraged, the gunner tried again. Torn leaves and branches fluttered down in all directions as the men in the helo fired randomly, hoping for a lucky hit or maybe just to tear a big enough hole that he'd have nowhere to run.

If he was going to do it, he was going to have to do it now.

Midas crossed himself and said a quick prayer, then grabbed the tree trunk in front of him. With a grunt, he started climbing.

The rough bark, mixed with knots and gnarls and the stumps of broken-off branches, made the first twenty feet an easy climb. Above that, limbs thick enough to support his weight—or at least part of it—spread out in all directions, providing a ladder to the top of the canopy proper.

The helo circled around again, a flurry of rounds cutting another swath through the leaves. Midas pressed himself against the trunk as a burst sawed through the canopy a dozen feet from where he stood, chewing through leaves and branches alike. The air filled with sawdust and smoke as the savaged branches fell to the jungle floor.

Midas kept climbing. The wind from the rotors tore

through the trees, making the branches shake. Midas's boot slipped as the branch he was standing on whipped back and forth. Only a sudden, desperate grab saved him. He hung on for dear life as the Sikorsky hovered overhead, buffeted by rotor wash. The gunners continued to pour down fire on the trees, opening huge gaps in the leaf cover.

The branches above him danced. This was as high as he could go. He hooked his legs around the biggest limb he could find, and waited for an opening. As the boughs above him whipped back and forth, he could see the helicopter, its painted belly almost directly overhead.

He looked down. Sixty feet to the ground. Jumping out of the way was not an option.

Carefully, he reached down to his belt for the white star cluster round. Useless as a weapon, it was exactly what he needed. He loaded the cartridge, aimed at a spot past the helo and over the camp, and fired.

The round arced out over the compound and burst into shards of brilliant white light. For a brief instant, everything was illuminated in the harsh glare.

The helo turned ponderously, rushing to gain altitude as the crew searched for the flare's target. Facing the river, it rose into the night.

Midas reloaded with a standard HE round and fired again. The cartridge hit the helo high on the fuselage, just below the main rotor, and exploded.

The rotor didn't tear itself off, not at first. The

explosion disconnected two of the blades, sending them scything into the camp down below. The lopsided remnant of the rotor was insufficient to the task of keeping the helo in the air and it wobbled, listing to starboard. A gunner fell out, screaming, as the Sea King began its flailing descent. It spun twice more, then the rest of the main rotor disintegrated and it plummeted into the compound. It crushed one building, then spun, so the tail rotor cut through a second. Soldiers unlucky enough to be close went down like wheat. As Midas watched, fire broke out at a couple of points on the wrecked helo, further illuminating the glare from the still-blazing plane on the airstrip.

"Midas, this is Weaver. Did you just do what I think you did?"

"Affirmative."

"Let's just hope you didn't just drop that bird on Nomad. His last known vector was toward the center of camp."

Midas felt his guts turn to ice. "What? I didn't see him."

"If we're lucky, it's cause he wasn't there to see. What's your progress on tertiary objective?"

"It's still standing. I don't think I can hit it from here. Need a new firing position."

"Well, get on it." Weaver cursed, and the sound of gunfire came over the link. "And for the record, hell of a shot."

CHAPTER 20

The most important thing to do when a helo falls from the sky in your direction is to get the hell out of the way.

From the second he'd seen the fireball at the airstrip, Nomad had known that the rest of the team was here. What he didn't know was where they were or how to get in touch with them without his gear.

He'd considered heading for the wire, but decided against it. Even with the men rushing to the airstrip, Urbina's men would be looking to the perimeter now to defend against the expected attack. And if they were moving men to the edges of the camp, that meant they were moving them out of the middle. And if he got really lucky, he'd get a shot at Urbina.

The plan had been working reasonably well until the Sea King came crashing down. One of the shattered blades knifed through the roof of the building Nomad was hiding behind, punching straight through the wall and out the other side. He looked up, saw the bird wobbling its way downward at speed, and ran.

He threw himself behind another building as the helo dove in, getting as much distance as he could. A soldier was already there, ducking and covering against the impact, when Nomad slid to a stop next to him. The two men stared at each other, then the soldier went for his pistol, and Nomad threw a haymaker. Fist connected with chin before the gun came up all the way, and the man slumped back against the wall.

Then the helo hit, and the ground shook, and shrapnel tore through the air in all directions. It hit the far side of Nomad's cover with a repeated SPANG, the sound of metal on metal at too-high velocity, while the crunch of aluminum and steel and bone echoed off the trees.

Nomad waited until the dust settled and picked himself up. He kicked the unconscious soldier's pistol away, then edged around the corner to survey the situation.

The damage was immense. Two buildings were flattened, a dozen men or more dead in the wreckage. One of the buildings was simply crushed, with the weight of the Sikorsky sitting squarely on it. The other had been peeled open by the tail like a can of tuna. Past that, severe damage had been done to the front of the HQ. Soldiers were flocking to the scene, some helping the wounded, some picking through the wreckage, some looking for someone to extract payback from.

Urbina stood in front of the headquarters building. The left side of his face was bloody, but he ignored it as he directed his men.

The lights of the compound flickered and went out. Several of the light poles arced and showered sparks onto the ground below, and the smell of ozone filled the air. One of the poles toppled onto the downed helicopter, adding to the chaos.

Nomad raised the AK and stared down the sights at Urbina. One burst would do it, chopping the head off the opposition and increasing the chaos on site, giving him that much of a better chance to somehow get away. He leaned out and steadied his breath, silently commanding Urbina to hold still for just one moment.

Behind him, there was a shout.

Nomad turned. The soldier he'd knocked out was awake and staggering forward, intent on tackling Nomad before he could get the shot off. He tried to sidestep, but the man caught his arm and spun him around. Nomad brought up the butt of the AK in a defensive maneuver as the soldier swung wildly, giving ground as he attempted to keep the bulk of the building between himself and the buzzing mayhem around the helo.

Another swing, another step back, and Nomad shoved the rifle stock into the soldier's stomach. He

folded. Nomad dropped a full-force elbow on the back of
his head, and he crumpled to the ground again. A quick
check told him the man was well and truly out this time.
Sliding into the long shadow cast by the burning helicopter, he looked for Urbina, who was nowhere to be found.
And with the crash, soldiers were starting to flood back
into the center of camp. It was time to go.

The last of the four remaining guards dropped at
Weaver's feet. Two of the others lay nearby, while
the fourth was half a row down, where Holt had dis-
patched him. Both men had switched to NVG. As
long as they didn't look directly at any of the fires
devouring the camp, it gave them a decided advantage
in the smoky night.

"What have we got?" Holt asked.

"We've got to get in there and see if we can locate
Nomad. Then we've got to hook up with Midas and get
the hell out of here."

Holt nodded. "First priority is Nomad. Midas can
take care of himself."

"I wanted him to help take care of us." Weaver
reloaded, thinking out loud. "Where'd you last see
Nomad?"

"Other side of that structure, inbound." He pointed,
and then blinked. "Oh, shit. You see what I see?"

"I think I do."

In unison, they opened fire.

One of the side effects of the camp's tidy, disciplined layout was that it offered long and clear sightlines. Even at night, even in a camp wracked by destruction, this was the case.

Which was why Nomad found himself retreating backwards, firing repeatedly at the squad of soldiers pursuing him. They'd come round the corner looking for God-knows-what before he'd made thirty yards, and had instead found the soldier Nomad had knocked out. Bad luck and a piece of burning debris wafting on the night air had revealed him at the worst possible moment, and now the chase was on.

He fired again, causing his pursuers to dive out of the way, and cut left between a building that was mostly still standing and a tent that had taken a direct hit from a large piece of debris. One of the soldiers tore around the corner after him and opened fire. Nomad zig-zagged as bullets kicked up dust at his heels. One last burst behind him as he ran, and then he heard the too-familiar cough and rattle of an empty magazine. He threw the AK aside and ran. Behind him, more soldiers poured into the gap, pausing in their pursuit only to throw lead in his direction.

He still had Hernán's pistol, he remembered. That could buy him a few more seconds. He reached into his belt to pull it out, and suddenly there was thunder in front of him.

Two shots rang out and the lead pursuers stumbled and

fell into the dust. "Down!" Weaver shouted, and as Nomad kissed dirt, Holt opened up over his head. Two more of the soldiers went down. The rest dove for cover. As Holt squeezed off bursts of suppressive fire, Weaver darted out and helped Nomad crawl out of the alley and behind a tent.

"Good timing," Nomad wheezed.

"You looked like you were handling it up till then—Jesus, your shoulder. Can you fight?"

Nomad tapped the still-bleeding wound with the pistol. "Yeah. Not my throwing arm. I can fight. By the way, those hostages? Not hostages. It's a con."

Weaver nodded. "We've got a lot of pieces to put together when we get out of here, but right now, we need to be thinking exfil. Our best shot," and he pointed toward the river, "is to steal a boat. Get downriver, hold them off until we hit the border."

"And if they're waiting for us there?"

"Beats dying here." Weaver leaned out and fired, silencing a steady gunfire crackle that had sent Holt sprawling. "You ready to move?"

Nomad dusted himself off and stood. "One question. Where's Midas?"

"Out there, trying to get off one last shot." He tapped his mic on. "Midas, change of plans. We've acquired Nomad and are heading for the docks. They are no longer a target. Meet up with us there."

"Roger that. If unable, what's rendezvous Bravo?"

"Regroup on the boat. Do you copy?"

"I copy," Midas acknowledged. "Midas out."

"Let's get us a ride."

CHAPTER 21

The guard was still at his post at the dock, scanning for approaching hostiles from within a wooden guard-house. "You see him?" Nomad asked.

"One in the box, Roger that." Weaver circled left. "Lining up the shot."

"Take it fast." The hubbub of the approaching soldiers was getting louder.

"Got him." Weaver fired. The bullet punched through the wood of the hut at chest height and dropped the sentry before he knew what hit him.

"All right, let's move." Nomad started sprinting for the docks, Holt and Weaver right behind him.

A shout and a rapid burst of fire told them they'd been spotted. A quick look behind told Holt that most of the remaining camp seemed to be in pursuit, some sprinting flat out, others dripping and laying down fire in advance of their comrades.

Holt tugged a frag out of a pouch, pulled the pin, and tossed it over his shoulder. "Frag out!" he yelled, putting his head down and sprinting. Behind him, the pursuers scattered, ducking behind whatever cover they could find before the thump of the blast and the jangle of shrapnel punching holes in things briefly overwhelmed the other sounds of the fight.

"Go, go, go!" Nomad was shouting as they pounded up onto the dock. It was heavy, made of local timber freshly sawed and set, and it extended well out from shore. At the end, closest to the current, were the two G-25s, the twin prides of Urbina's fleet.

"At the end, on the left," Weaver shouted. He ran, firing down at the tied-up boats as he went. Most of his shots went into the water. A few punched through the bottoms of the craft, which immediately started filling with water.

The pursuit had regained its feet, the flankers once again opening fire. Pieces of the dock splintered up into the air as near misses slammed into it. Holt turned and started firing, walking himself back as he laid down bursts of suppressive fire. "You got us a boat?" he yelled over his shoulder. "Can't hold them much longer!" He ducked behind the surviving bulk of the guardhouse as more rounds flew his way. Someone was concentrating fire on his position, and massive holes tore open in the wood of his cover.

"Working on it!" Weaver yelled back. He leaped down into the Guardian they'd previously seen. "Son of a bitch, they left the keys in it. Full tank, full ammo for the guns, we are in business. What the hell, the goddamn gauges are even in English. Nomad! Untie us."

"Got it!"

"Holt! Get back here!"

Heavier gunners were coming up, and the cover of the guardhouse had started to disintegrate under the pressure. Holt leaned out and fired, then pulled back immediately when the response nearly took his head off. "Cover me!"

Nomad looked at his pistol, then jumped into the boat. It was a small vessel with little cover. A canopy shielded the pilot from the elements but offered nothing else in the way of protection. A heavy machine gun was mounted up front, with two smaller ones on the sides.

He slotted himself in behind one of the guns and checked to make sure it was loaded. It was.

"Holt, now!" he yelled, and let it rip.

Holt rose to his feet and sprinted toward the end of the dock. Nomad deliberately shot high, pouring lead over Holt's head as he ran. Some of the pursuers scattered, others realized the fire was over their heads and rushed the dock.

Urbina led the charge.

A quick survey of the camp told Midas everything he needed to know about his chances of meeting up with the others. The fire on the airstrip was finally coming under control, but the one from the downed helo was spreading. There were still numerous soldiers moving through the compound, and the ring of razor wire remained unbroken. The odds of him making it in one piece were slim.

His best move would be to head for the boat, getting ahead of any pursuit the camp was likely to muster after things were under control.

But there was one thing to do first.

Carefully, he made his way back down the tree, the process going considerably quicker than the climb. Working his way around the perimeter of the camp, he could see fights breaking out near the docks as he descended, Holt and Weaver clearing the way.

"Weaver, this is Midas. There's no way I can get to you. I'll meet you at Bravo."

"Copy that, Midas. Stay safe."

"You too. Midas out."

He could see one of the boats pulling out into the river, the other Ghosts on board. Already, soldiers were swarming onto the dock to follow, piling into the remaining boats.

Quickly, he checked his remaining ammo for the M203. Mostly buckshot remained, but there were a couple of HE cartridges left. He started loading and firing.

The first round hadn't hit by the time he launched the second; the second hadn't hit before he started running. Behind him, he could hear the distant thump of the grenades going off, and then he was deep in the trees and moving fast.

The engines thundered on as Nomad released the hawser holding the boat to the dock, and Holt leapt onboard. He came down almost on top of Nomad, who neatly stepped out of the way and back behind the machine gun. Holt gave the weapon an admiring look. "How big's the play on the guns?"

"Hundred and twenty degrees. We won't be able to shoot behind us."

"But they'll have us in their sights the whole time. Great!"

"Hang on!" Weaver slammed the throttle wide open and the boat curled away from the dock at speed. Holt crouched while Nomad positioned himself behind the starboard gun. At a nod from Nomad, Holt opened up on the dock, spraying it and the boats equally with fire. Advancing soldiers flung themselves down. One soldier was caught in the burst and staggered into the river with a splash. Next to him, a boat Holt had holed started taking on water and listing.

"Last mag," Holt announced as he reloaded. "Gotta make this count."

"You'd better," said Nomad. "They're forming up to pursue." He could see soldiers leaping into the boats Holt hadn't managed to sink, including the other G-25.

"And there's Urbina," said Holt, opening fire. The bullets flew harmlessly over the man's head as he leapt into the patrol boat, followed by a trio of soldiers. Already, the first of the pursuers was casting off and pulling out into the river, roaring ahead full steam.

The second Guardian pulled out as well as Holt fired another burst, but the movement of the boat sent his shots wide. "Urbina's on the river!" he yelled. "Got maybe five boats in pursuit. Six more getting ready to—"

The first of Midas's shells hit the remains of the unfortunate guard post, flattening it and sending wooden shrapnel everywhere. The second landed in the middle of the dock. The resulting blast tore it in half, upending boats and throwing soldiers into the water. Some came spluttering up for air, some didn't.

"Scratch that secondary pursuit," Nomad called to Weaver. "Can we outrun them?"

"Don't know!" Weaver yelled over the engines' roar. "We're in the fastest thing on the river, but Urbina's saying the same thing. I'll do what I can; just keep them off us!"

"You heard the man, Holt."

"Oh yeah, I did." Holt knelt next to the port motor, weapon ready. Behind him, the pursuers fanned out across the river. A soldier was visible behind the gun in the prow of Urbina's boat. Others didn't have mounted weapons, but soldiers were lined up in their prows, the pop-pop-pop of single-shot fire carrying over the roar on the engines.

"Holt! Can you keep their heads down?"

"Negative! Not at this range!"

A bullet smacked into the back of the boat, just below the rail. It punched through the hull and fell, spent, at Holt's feet.

"Or maybe not."

Midas ran, shedding unnecessary gear as he went. He had a sense of the terrain now from the traverse in. As a result, he could fly over it, NVG making up for the dark beneath the trees.

The trek in had taken hours. It had been slow and cautious, which was the exact opposite of what Midas needed now. He took it on faith that the enemy had not found their route since they'd come this way earlier; that they hadn't rigged traps or an ambush.

That he could just run.

The way in had taken hours. The way back had to take minutes.

In the distance, he could hear gunfire. The river curved around in a long bend, one that he was cutting across the base of. If it took long enough for the rest of the team to navigate that curve, if they managed to stay ahead of their pursuers at the same time, and if he could keep pushing, then maybe he wasn't out of the fight yet.

Up ahead now, he could see the dark gash in the night that was the narrow tributary channel they'd come up. The boat had to be nearby, and if he could find the boat, then things might get interesting.

He offered up a prayer and ran faster.

Holt set and fired at the nearest boat, a converted fishing vessel overloaded with soldiers. One pitched forward into the water and vanished. Another howled and
grabbed his arm. The man next to him shoved him out
of the way. The others leaned in and returned fire.

Holt ducked. Most of the enemy fire went high. The
rest went wide, close enough that the individual whine of
each round going past could be heard.

"You gonna give me some help?" Holt yelled at
Nomad.

"Don't have the angle!" Nomad swung the gun back
as far as he could. None of the pursuing boats were even
close to being in the line of fire. "Weaver! Can you slew
us left?"

"It's gonna let them get closer!" More bullets tore past
the boat, some ripping through the canopy near Weaver's
head. "Then again . . . ."

He spun the wheel left, the boat nearly heeling over
at the sharp turn. Nomad waited until the Guardian
righted itself, then adjusted his aim low and opened fire.
The pass brought them broadside to three of the boats
chasing them. The pilot of the boat farthest on the right
cut the rudder hard right to try to avoid Nomad's fire.
The edge of the prow caught a protruding tree root at
full speed. Aluminum crumpled as the boat spun and
flipped, dumping its occupants into the water. It spun
twice in midair and then came down on its damaged
side, half on the bank and half in the river.

The other boats sped on, closer now. A rain of fire spattered on the shield covering the gunner on the other Guardian, and Weaver responded with a burst of his own that chewed up the water five feet short.

Nomad swapped sides as Weaver cut back right, moving in front of the remaining pursuers. He poured fire across their bows. One dropped back as a lucky shot found the pilot and sent him over the side. The other leapt forward on an intercept course. "Weaver! Starboard side! Closing fast!"

"I see them!" Weaver cut the strafing run and turned the boat downriver, but the pursuing boat was close now. Nomad ripped off another burst, but the pilot skillfully evaded it and pulled in close. The men on board opened up. The first volley was wild, but they were close enough the second one wouldn't be.

"Holt?"

"Got it." He pulled a frag out of a pouch at his hip, the last one he had left. A quick pull, and then he skyhooked it into the approaching boat.

It landed with a loud "tink," followed by a series of splashes as the soldiers threw themselves overboard. Bereft of its pilot, the boat slewed right, plowing over an unfortunate soldier and diving straight for the bank before the grenade exploded, punching a hole in the bottom. It began sinking.

"Two down," Holt called out.

"Three left," Weaver answered.

Urbina's Guardian moved up on the left. The starboard side gunner opened up, throwing up a curtain of spray as the bullets stitched close. Weaver heeled the boat hard right, allowing one of the other pursuing boats to close. It pulled in between the Guardians, accidentally shielding the Ghosts from the machine-gun fire, but its soldiers opened up instead, aiming not at Holt or Nomad, but at the boat's engines. A series of shots hammered the starboard engine. Nomad expertly dropped three of the soldiers with the pistol and the boat fell back, but the damage was done. Smoke rose from the wrecked engine, while a vicious grinding sound overcame the usual throaty hum.

"Take the wheel." Weaver swapped positions with Nomad. "What have we got?"

"We've got one functioning engine, multiple holes in the hull, water pouring in, and Urbina coming up fast." Holt crouched low, pistol in his hand. "No way we can outrun them."

Already, the other surviving patrol boat had pulled up alongside the laboring Guardian, soldiers clustered along its side laying down fire. Bullets punched holes in the canopy screen, in the lockers on deck, in the hull just above the water line. Holt moved behind the starboard machine gun and returned a long, rattling burst. The boat peeled away, but in the meantime, the other Guardian had pulled closer, its forward .50 cal spitting a steady stream of fire. More rounds slammed into the already smoldering portside engine, causing it to cut out entirely. Weaver crouched and fired. The round impacted against the edge of the eyeslit on the defensive shield, sending the gunner ducking out of the way.

"Holt! Get to the prow! Now!" Nomad yelled. "Get

that gun up and ready."

"Roger that. But what are we—"

"Weaver! Down!"

Weaver dropped out of sight as Nomad threw the engine into reverse. Only one propeller's screw bit water, swinging the boat around as it jerked and shuddered. Weaver slammed up against the inside of the hull, river water sloshing against him.

"This isn't a car, Nomad!" he shouted, just as Holt opened fire.

The rounds jackhammered the front of Urbina's craft, pounding through the windshield behind them. The pilot fell backwards, arms flailing, and Urbina had to leap out of the way to avoid getting tagged. Then he was firing, single pistol shots that could be heard over the roar of Holt's MG. The two boats swept past each other, Urbina and Nomad exchanging fire from nearly point-blank range. The colonel's Guardian, sans pilot, roared forward while the Ghosts' vessel wallowed back, and black water separated them once again.

Nomad threw the remaining engine into forward gear. It leaped upstream, even as the other two boats saw their chance and closed.

Holt saw his chance, too. He opened fire, aiming low and sweeping across. The two boats surged forward, then hit the wake from Urbina's maneuver and rose up, prows in the air, for a long second.

Holt swung the gun left to right, stitching rounds across the bottom of each boat's hull. A line of holes appeared on each, so thick it nearly tore them in half.

And then they crashed back down on the other side of the wake, and the water started rushing in. The one on the right made a desperate run for shore while the other, trapped by the pilot's indecision, veered off and sank.

Which left just Urbina, who was coming around wide for another run.

"I'm dry," Holt announced. "That took everything I had up here."

"Port's dry, too," Weaver echoed.

"Can you drop him?" Slowly, Nomad was turning the boat back downstream, but the lopsided thrust and heavy current made it tricky. Low on power and taking the current broadside, the boat struggled to make the adjustment. All the while, Urbina's new pilot was bringing him around warily in a wide circle, keeping out of range of the forward gun and looping around in hopes of getting another run at the surviving engine.

Up ahead, a gap showed deeper black on the east bank of the river. "Tributary," Weaver pointed out. "We get in there, he can't outmaneuver us."

"I'll try. Keep him honest?"

"Will do."

Weaver fired, waited, and fired again as the other Guardian looped closer. The remaining glass of the pilot's windshield shattered, rounds slammed against the shield on the forward .50 cal, but nobody went down. At the back of the boat stood Urbina, coolly confident, waiting for the end of the chase.

The boat struggled toward the mouth of the tributary. The remaining engine was sputtering now. Forced to do too much, it was struggling to do anything. The crawl toward shelter became agonizingly slow.

Urbina was upriver now, his vessel swinging in for the kill. It surged forward, and then changed course, cutting closer to shore.

"Shit. He's onto us." Weaver kept firing, almost mechanically. "He's going to get in between and cut us off, force us back into deeper water."

Even as Weaver called it, Urbina pulled past. The starboard-side gun barked, tearing holes in the hull and shredding the remains of the pilot's canopy. Nomad threw himself to the deck as bullets pounded the console and tore through the spot where he'd been standing an instant before. A rising gurgling sound told Weaver the boat was sinking; a look down confirmed it.

"You've almost ruined everything," Urbina shouted, as his boat slowed to hover in front of the mouth of the tributary, now impossibly far away. "But there will be another American greedy enough to give me what I need." He held up a waterproof document pouch he'd slung over his shoulder. "They'll rebuild the camp. I'll find more men. Everything I need is here. And you? You die here. The Russians, they'll be disappointed. I'll have to give them back their money. But it's a small price to pay."

Inside the crippled Guardian, the water was rising. "You got anything?" Weaver asked.

"We try to jump to his boat and maybe we'll get lucky?" Holt slithered over to where they were crouched down.

"We'd get chewed up in the water."

"You got a better idea?" The gunner let his weapon play across the side of the boat again, and more debris crashed down. The Guardian was listing now, taking on water more and more rapidly.

"Okay, it's dark." Nomad thought furiously. "I'm betting their NVG doesn't work too well on water. We go down with the boat, use the wreck for cover, swim around underwater, and get to shore."

"If we don't get eaten," said Weaver.

"Do *you* have a better plan?"

"Right, we do this." The water rose.

"Ready?"

There was a sudden roar in the darkness, a familiar one.

"That sounds like—" Weaver began, and then the team's boat came surging out of the tributary, Midas at the helm.

It caught Urbina's Guardian broadside, crumpling the side of the boat and knocking the unprepared gunner into the water. The pilot fell and Urbina staggered, even as Midas sprinted along the length of the converted fishing boat, pistol in hand. He leaped onto the mortally wounded G-25, putting a round into the struggling pilot as he landed.

Off balance, Urbina raised his pistol and fired. Midas ducked under the shot and closed. Urbina shifted his aim, ready to fire again, this time at point blank range.

Two shots from Nomad took him in the back of the head. The pistol fell from his fingers and slid down the deck, an instant before he collapsed and followed.

"Major," Midas said.

"Midas," Nomad acknowledged him. "Interesting approach. Why the hell didn't you just shoot him from over there?"

"Had to knock the gunner off or he could have chewed me up." Midas sounded faintly pleased with himself, which from anyone else would have been chest-thumping bragging. "And I knew you'd have my six."

"Don't ever fucking do that again," Nomad said. "But I'm glad as hell you did."

"Yes, Major. Thank you." He looked around. "It looks like this boat's still functional. Let me come to you and we can get out of here. Right now, you don't want to be in the water." As if on cue, something big lurched off the bank and into the water nearby.

"You do that, Midas," Nomad said. "And if you don't mind, you do that fast."

CHAPTER 22

They limped downriver, licking their wounds.

The impact with Urbina's Guardian had crumpled the front end of DeScalso's boat. The compartment where Midas had stashed the comms rig had been smashed as well, and water was slowly seeping in through stressed seams. They'd reloaded from diminished ammo supplies in damaged lockers; to conserve what was left of their fuel, they coasted with the current where they could.

Midas had rebandaged Nomad's shoulder. Now he had the wheel as Holt stood lookout, and Weaver and Nomad leafed through the papers they'd taken off Urbina.

"This is some serious shit," said Weaver with a low whistle. "Glad he brought it with him, or no one was ever going to believe us."

"I'm guessing he didn't want to leave papers in a camp that was actively on fire." Nomad held up a thumb drive he'd pulled from the pouch. "I'm betting these are backups, but there's something nice about having the original."

"You can't dust a file for prints," Weaver said matter-of-factly. "And hell yeah, this is original. In exchange for those oil rights, Briggs was buying Urbina his whole Christmas list. Explains the English-language G-25s, too—they weren't handed off by the Venezuelan army when these guys were still an official border force; they were part of the first delivery."

"Yeah. Huh. The deal included Services contract with Watchgate, too, to boost his numbers while they got drilling up and running and built a couple company towns. Then they were going to stick around to protect the operations." Nomad frowned. "You're right, this stuff is way out there. And—hey, look at this, a timetable for taking over Puerto Ayacucho—they almost pulled it off."

"Might do it yet," Weaver flipped through a few more pages. "I know we got Urbina. Pretty sure we got Briggs, or if we didn't, he's got a long walk home. But somebody's going to rise up and start calling himself colonel. And ·

Caton's just going to send someone else. You think Uncle Sam's going to tell Caracas about the oil field? Cause I sure don't. No, it's just going to keep going. Like it always does. All we did up there was add to the body count."

"You got me out. Got Crotty and her people. And considering Urbina's track record, taking him out of commission's not a bad thing. Maybe another one of his people will rise up. Maybe the next guy's a little different. Maybe without Urbina, they take the stuff Briggs had already brought them and head home. We did the job."

"Yeah, about that. How are you going to explain to the Old Man that Wizard got snowed on the second batch of hostages? It's gonna shake his faith in the universe."

"I'll think of something." Nomad yawned. "Wake me up when we get close to the border. The shoulder's killing me." He closed his eyes and lay down, out before Weaver could answer.

"How close are we, Midas?" Weaver asked. "I can take over if you need."

"I'm fine, thank you," Midas answered. "If I need a hand, I'll tell you before Holt volunteers."

"I heard that!" Holt called from the prow. "I can handle one of these things better than either of you."

"Take a knee, gator chow," Weaver called back, shaking his head. "This op cannot be over soon enough."

"I hear you," Midas said softly. "Though it has been . . . exciting." He checked his wrist comm. "If we continue to let the current drive us, it's four hours to the border."

"And if we use the engines, we cut that time in less than half, but we've got basically zero maneuverability when we get close. I can just see Protasio letting us drift right on past town if we don't have enough fuel to turn in."

"I am sure he'd throw us a paddle." Weaver couldn't tell if Midas was smiling. Probably was, he decided. Good enough.

"Open it up to quarter throttle," he decided. "We can afford that much, and the sooner we're out of range of Radio Free Amazonas, the happier we're all going to be."

"Copy that." Weaver tapped the throttle ever so gently, and they eased away toward the border.

Above the island, they were waiting.

Holt spotted them first, before the Ghosts drifted into range. "We've got contact. Two boats in the river and filled with hostiles, two more on shore and prepped at the border station."

Nomad borrowed the glasses. "The way they're set up, we'd have to go right down the middle. We'd take fire from both sides."

"We can try to run the gauntlet," Weaver said doubtfully. "If we're going to fight, I'd rather try to pick them off from here. Make them come upriver at us."

Nomad turned to Midas. "Got anything left for the underbarrel?"

"Buckshot only. If we get close, I can do some damage."

"All right." Nomad took another look downriver. "Holt, you said you can handle this thing?"

"Yep."

"Take the wheel and hold us steady. Weaver, pick your targets. You are weapons free. Midas, give him cover. I'll spot. Let's go."

"You sure about this?" Weaver asked as Nomad settled in next to him.

"I trust the team," Nomad answered. "We got this."

"I hope you're right." Weaver propped his rifle on the edge of the gunwale and stared into the scope. "Tell Holt to hold her steadier. I'm getting too much vertical play."

"Roger that. Holt, can you do anything?"

"On this river? Only if I run us aground, which is its own special kind of problem. It's hard enough holding position without blowing our fuel or our cover."

"Right. Stop talking. Lining up my shot." Weaver peered down the scope. He zeroed in on one of the men in the closer of the two vessels in the river. It was, he realized, the guard who'd taken the fishing rod before.

A sudden rumbling noise distracted him. "Holt? What the hell are you doing back there?"

"It's not me. Look."

Downriver, on the Brazilian side of the border, the CB 90H was moving north fast and with intent.

Weaver looked up. "What the hell. Protasio?"

Nomad scanned the deck with the binos. "I'm not seeing him. It's . . . it's Correa. And she's loaded for bear."

Holt blinked in surprise. "Shit. She's coming right up to the border. Spoiling for a fight." He turned to Midas. "You got anything to do with this?"

Midas nodded. "I may have let her know we were

coming downriver before the radio was trashed. She relayed the message to Captain Protasio and was unimpressed with his response."

"Well, I'm impressed with hers." Nomad nudged Weaver. "If she's serious, you take the shot and she'll back our play." Faintly, they could hear Correa and one of the officers on shore having a heated exchange.

Weaver didn't look up. "That sounds a hell of a lot better than us going into it alone."

"It sounds a hell of a lot like an international incident, which is what we were down here trying to avoid. There's got to be another way."

"If you think so, you'd better find it quick. Because this is like tap dancing in a minefield right here."

"Dance like no one's watching, right?" Nomad glanced around at the team. They were battered and bloodied. Midas looked like he'd been in a car accident; the impact with Urbina's boat had left him bruised and aching from head to toe. All of them were exhausted, worn down and worn out.

These were the men he'd been to war with, and who would go to war with him instantly if he just gave the word.

"All right. You got anything better, you've got thirty seconds to let me know. Otherwise, Weaver, line up your shot on whichever one of them's talking to Correa. Holt, stay on the helm. Hold her steady. Midas, you've got buckshot? I want you to hold one round back. Otherwise, weapons free. On my mark, we fire, and then Holt, you bring us in close. We do that, Midas, you strafe to keep their heads down. That should buy enough time for us to make the run for the border before the smoke clears. Got it?"

"Got it." Weaver was already looking through the scope on his rifle, working through firing solutions.

"Got it." Holt's firearm was carefully placed in reach.

"Got it," Midas said, grimly counting out shells and loading the M203.

"Last chance to come up with something better. If not—"

"Sir?" It was Midas. "I might have something."

"What have you got?"

Midas pointed to the western riverbank. "We go around."

Holt shook his head, remembering. "Yeah. We thought about that with the hostages, but we couldn't get them up the bank, and we weren't sure about moving them through the jungle in case there were hostiles."

"But we aren't transporting civilians now," Nomad said. "So we ditch the boat, hoof it over the border, and rendezvous with Correa downstream. Is that what you're suggesting?"

Midas grinned. "That is exactly what I'm suggesting."

"What do we do with the boat?" Weaver asked.

"Sink it."

Holt smirked. "DeScalso's going to be pissed."

"With all due respect, right now, fuck DeScalso."

Nomad looked around at the team. There was a new energy to them. They'd been ready to fight, waiting on his command. But there was more to leadership than combat. There was more to a team than just the fight. He could lead them into battle one more time, though they'd had the living hell beaten out of them. Low on ammo, low on everything, just enough left for one more good fight.

Or he could lead them home.

"All right." The squad leaned in. One by one he met their eyes, saw the energy there. "We could take them. We know we could take them. But we don't have to. So let's do this smart. Holt, bring us in to shore. Weaver, make sure nobody downstream suddenly looks our way and gets ideas. And Midas?"

"Yessir?"

"You get to explain this to Correa when we make it out the other side."

"We've got a perfectly good fight staring us in the face and you want to sneak around it instead?" Weaver was disbelieving, but there was a sly humor in his tone. "It's like I don't even know you people anymore." He sat up and pulled his rifle back.

"For fuck's sake," Nomad said, "there's a goddamn good reason they call us Ghosts."

EPILOGUE

"The Old Man wants to see you," was the message waiting for Nomad when he woke up. There wasn't a time attached to the note, which meant "immediately" and "no matter what else you're doing." Nomad grimaced as his shoulder twinged, then got dressed in a hurry. You didn't keep the Old Man waiting, ever. Particularly not after a mission like that.

The walk to Mitchell's office felt twice as long as it actually took, which gave Nomad more time to mull over why he'd been summoned. Very few of the answers he came up with were good enough for him. Questions over the mission, over the interaction with the civilians, over the freshly strained relationship with the Brazilians—the hits just kept on coming. There was only one constant in all of them: He'd been given command of a Ghost squad, and after the way he'd screwed it up, they'd never let him get near command again.

Mitchell's door was closed. Nomad knocked on it, twice. "Come in," came the familiar voice from the other side of the door, and Nomad did so.

Mitchell's office was smaller than Nomad had imagined it would be. The heavy wooden desk was the biggest thing in the room by far. A couple of bookshelves looked like afterthoughts, and the walls were bare except for a series of whiteboards and one framed photograph of a waterfall. Mitchell, seated behind the desk, noticed Nomad looking at it. "Hocking Hills, back in Ohio. My dad used to take me there when I was a kid. All the places I've been, and that's still the first place I'd go back to if I had my druthers." He gestured to the empty chair on the visitor's side. "Sit down." Nomad sat. Mitchell looked as exhausted as Nomad felt. There were deep bags under his eyes, and his face was locked into a tight frown. For a long moment, he said nothing, focusing instead on something on one of the monitors sitting on his desk. Then he looked up.

"Major, how would you rate your performance on this mission?"

Nomad exhaled, slowly. "Sir. Honestly? I'm not real high on myself right now."

"Really." The response was cold and flat. "Why not?"

"Sir. Number one, I got my sorry ass captured. That should be enough right there."

Mitchell was relentless. "The way you're talking, it isn't. Keep going."

Nomad ticked them off on his fingers. In the back of his head, he could hear the voice of self-preservation telling him he was an idiot for laying all this out there, for giving them ammunition to use against him when he didn't have to, but it was too late to stop, even if he wanted to. "Two, didn't back up my team. Not with the Brazilians, not when Midas wanted to help the locals. Was too damn worried about not fucking up the mission that I screwed up the squad from the get-go. Three, I underestimated the number of possible ways things could go bad once we got in-country." He took a deep breath. "Should I go on?"

Mitchell shook his head. "Major, did I ever tell you how my first op as Ghost Lead went down?"

"No, sir. That was Korea, right? Operation Broken Wings?"

Mitchell laughed ruefully. "Officially, yes. Unofficially, there was one before that. We linked up with the White Skull Brigade, an elite SK unit. We were supposed to go in and bottle up a tank column as they headed to the DMZ. Piece of cake, right?"

"I never heard about this, sir."

"That's because it's been scrubbed from the files. And you know why? Because it all went sideways. We stopped the T-83s, but we got spotted, and since we were in

DPRK territory, that was a no-no. So we had to go clean things up. Make the North Koreans think that it had just been the White Skulls."

"I don't see where you're going with this, sir."

"Bullshit you don't. I'm saying, on my first op as Ghost Lead, things didn't exactly go smoothly either, and a lot of that came out of decisions I made in the field. But I kept my head in the game, and after a while I stopped trying to win the war in one battle. I let my people do what they did best, and we got out of there in one piece. And when we got back to the FOB, Buzz Gordon chewed my ass out six ways from Sunday, and then he turned us around and sent my team right back out." He leaned forward. "*My* team. Because nobody gets this thing perfect the first time, or the tenth time. What you did wasn't by the playbook, but you brought those hostages out, and you brought all your people home in better shape than you were. I'll take that."

"Sir." Nomad shut his eyes for a second and took a calming breath. "But my—but the team?"

"Holt has informed me personally that you have, and I quote, stones the size of boulders, and that he's looking forward to driving you up the wall again on your next op."

"You're not serious."

"Dead serious. High praise from Midas, too. And I know better than to ask Weaver. So you're stuck with the gig, is what I'm saying, though six months from now you probably won't be thanking me for it."

"I'll thank you now, sir."

"Good. Now that we've got that out of the way, let's take a closer look at the shit sandwich you accidentally served up with what you found. Half of DC is trying to jump down my throat over this. E-Ring is going absolutely bananas over the out-of-the-box failed petro-state they're trying to build down there, and there's a half dozen agencies that want a piece of Caton over this. Oh, and State's going to want to debrief you as soon as I decide you're healthy enough to talk to them."

"When will that be?"

"When you convince me you're not likely to strangle any of them when they ask you the same damn question for the fifteenth time. In any case, you may have kept it out of the papers, but that doesn't mean you didn't shake up the ant farm. My gut tells me wherever this is going, it's nowhere good."

"Your gut or Wizard's?"

"They're pretty much the same thing at this point. But that is tomorrow's problem. And probably the day after's, and the day after that's, too. You go on and get out of here. Your team's waiting for you at the Liberator. I suggest you join them. I'll worry about this for now. Got a meeting with some CIA puke, for starters, and that's the last thing you need."

"Sir?"

Mitchell stood. "You heard me, Major. Dismissed."

Nomad stood and saluted. "Sir. Thank you."

"You earned it, Major Perryman. The hard way. Now follow orders and get the hell out of here." He checked his watch. "If I survive this CIA dog and pony show, maybe I'll join you over there."

"I'd like that, sir." Nomad turned and walked out. He waited until he was in the hallway to let his face break into a wide grin. He took a moment to gather himself, then headed out, double quick, towards the Liberator Bar and Grill.

Because that's where the team—his team—was waiting for him.

CIA Case Officer Karen Bowman wasn't bad as far as spooks went. That was Mitchell's initial impression of her, but if she kept talking, he was willing to change his mind.

The meeting had started off pleasantly enough. She'd been on time—none of the usual spy bullshit where they made you wait to demonstrate how important they were—and offered to skip the usual PowerPoint nonsense to get straight to the point. She was young, which meant she had to be good if the senior ghouls at Langley were letting her walk into the lion's den solo. Then again, Mitchell decided, any woman making any kind of headway up there was, by definition, very, *very* good.

If she was doing this, she had to want it. Which explained why she'd hopped a flight down to Bragg to talk to him about what his people had seen and how it tied in to the very delicate matter she'd been working on.

She wanted to make sure Nomad hadn't messed anything up.

"Lieutenant Colonel."

He snapped his attention back to her. "Agent. Run me through this again, to make sure I haven't missed anything."

She gave a curt nod. "You know already that Colonel Urbina's operation was being funded by various external organizations who wanted to create what was in essence a failed state they could exert control over. This would enable them to run whatever operations they wanted— drilling, growing narcotics, you name it—without fear of legal oversight or government interference." She let her face curve into a tight, humorless smile. "Easy enough, when you own the government. Anyway, based on what your man Perryman said in his debrief, we've been able to ID one of the men he saw when he was a prisoner. He's known as El Pulpo, and he's a logistics maven for the Santa Blanca cartel. The cartel's been shoved out of Mexico by the competition, and while they're flush with cash, they need a new base of operations so they've got irons in a couple of different fires. Which is another way of saying we'd suspected they had a presence in the region, and El Pulpo's presence confirmed it."

Mitchell leaned forward and practically growled. "Correct me if I'm wrong, but did you just tell me that you were aware of the Santa Blanca cartel presence in my team's AO and you did not think this was worth sharing?"

"We didn't exactly know you had a team going in, Colonel. You JSOC guys aren't big on sharing, either." She adjusted her glasses. "God forbid we all realize we're on the same side one of these days. We might actually accomplish something."

"What, and put all the middlemen out of jobs?"

She laughed. "You got me there. But my point stands. With the FARC surrender accords turning things on their ear, we *anticipated* that Santa Blanca was making inroads into South America. We suspected that the Free State of Amazonas was a possible point of entry for them, but we weren't sure. And until we were sure, we weren't going to say anything, because we're already involved, and the last thing we need *right now* is complications."

Mitchell cocked his head. "Right now. You're very careful with your words, agent. Which leads me to believe that when you say 'right now,' you actually mean 'down the line we're going to be giving you a call.' Am I correct?"

"We don't know what's coming down the line," she said, impassive. "What we do know, and I'm going way out on a limb here trusting you with this, is that with Urbina out of the way, we have a good idea of where Santa Blanca is going to stake their claim, and we've got someone in place waiting for them to scoop him up because he has a very useful set of skills. We're talking years of deep cover work that I'm not inclined to piss away. But, if everything goes as planned, then eventually, yes, we will have a line on key cartel targets, and we will need people in the field who can do something about them." She stared at him. "When I talked to Delta, they recommended your outfit. The same with DEVGRU. Daniel Sykes practically climbed over my desk to sing your praises. Hell, I've got an ex-Vympel defector chilling in a safe house in Maine who still has nightmares about your team. And so I am asking you, when the time comes, will your people be ready for the call? Because if this thing goes where I think it will—if down the line we're looking at the creation of a full-blown narco-state under Santa Blanca discipline —then we're going to need more than strong language to prevent that."

"My people," Mitchell retorted, "are always ready. But if you want to set up a joint GST-CIA op, that's going to require some handshakes way above either of our pay grades."

"You leave that to me. I've gotten very good at that."

Mitchell nodded. "I'll bet you have. All right, then. You get your asset in there. I'll keep my teams out of your way until you ask for them. And when you ask, you'd damn well better make a case for them that I can't refuse. Because if I find out you're asking because you don't want to get your hands dirty, then there will be consequences."

Bowman stared at him, then stood. "Colonel, if the day comes when I'm asking, it'll be because I have no other choice." She extended her hand. After a moment, he took it. "I'll be in touch," she said, grabbed her brief-case, and walked out.

Mitchell watched her go. "I bet you will," he said softly. "I just bet you will."

Holt said something to the bartender, who shook his head but then pulled four dark glass bottles out from under the bar. Holt took them, two in each hand, and brought them back to the table where Midas, Weaver, and Nomad were sitting. Holt put a bottle down in front of each of them, then dropped into an empty chair and pulled off his omnipresent sunglasses.

"What's this?" Weaver asked, staring at the drink in front of him suspiciously.

"Regional special. Correa's recommendation. I brought a case back with me for a special occasion." He lifted his bottle. "You think this counts?"

"According to the Old Man, it does," Nomad said, and took a long pull from his beer. "Damn, not bad at all."

Weaver pursed his lips and shook his head sagely. "I believe that, if only because Mr. Moretta here said it was Correa's call. If he'd picked it out, it probably would have tasted like caiman piss."

Midas stifled a laugh just before he took a swig from his bottle and took a moment to compose himself. "Don't do that," he said. "Another second and I would have wasted half the bottle."

"And cleaned out your sinuses in the process, no doubt." Nomad raised his drink toward the center of the table. "Gentlemen, to a job well done."

"Agreed." "Roger that." "Amen." They clinked their bottles together, and each took a pull.

"So what's next?" Weaver asked when they came up for air. He gave Nomad an expectant look.

"You damn well know what's up, Coray." Nomad snorted in disbelief. "Downtime. And then, when that's over . . ."

"Yes?" Midas leaned in.

"When that's over this team gets back together and train like bastards to make sure the next op is a little less exciting." Nomad sat back in his chair, a little gingerly. "If we can run one of these without anyone getting captured or nearly getting a boat shot out from under us—"

"Or caimans," Weaver interjected.

"What is it with you and the damn caimans?" Holt demanded.

Weaver grinned. "I respect their honest professionalism. Also, gator boy, it drives you nuts."

Holt opened his mouth to respond, then noticed Midas was once again stifling laughter. "Something funny?" he asked.

"No," Midas replied. "Just a couple of guys trying to be."

That broke the entire table. As the laughter died down, Weaver slapped Midas on the back. "I didn't know you had that in you."

"I always carry two jokes," Midas replied, deadpan, and that set Weaver off again.

Nomad took a deep breath and looked around the table, feeling the same sense of camaraderie he'd felt on the river. "So in any case, there it is. You want out, now's the time to say so. You want in, I think we can do something pretty special." He turned. "Assuming Midas doesn't crack us all up while we're in the field and get our asses shot."

"No worries," Midas said with a small smile. "I pick my moments carefully."

Nomad nodded. "Right. Anyone got any—"

"Well, lookie here." Weaver extended one long arm to point at the television over the bar, where in the absence of sports, some financial program with three ticker lines scrolling across the bottom of the screen was blathering on. Up above, a talking head was making sad faces next to a picture of the Caton oil executive who'd visited Urbina at his camp. The caption underneath said it all: "Killed in Light Aircraft Crash."

"Technically, I suppose that's accurate," Holt said, and tipped his bottle in Midas's direction as a sign of respect. "But I'm guessing they're not saying he went down where it all went down."

"Gulf of Mexico is what they're reporting," Midas replied. Holt looked at him, and Midas shrugged. "Got a cousin who's deaf. I learned to lip read as a kid. Got some ASL, too."

"You're just full of surprises, aren't you?" Weaver mock-groused, then grinned. "Nobody's ever going to know that story, but that's how it goes. Good thing I sold my Caton stock before the news broke."

"You didn't!" Midas was aghast. "That's insider trading!"

"It doesn't get too much more inside than being neck deep in the shit," Weaver responded blandly.

Midas opened his mouth to respond, but Nomad shut him down. "Relax. He didn't have any Caton stock." He turned to look at his friend. "Did you?"

"Question's moot now," said Weaver, and grinned wickedly. Midas continued to stare until Weaver had to look away. "I'm just messing with you. I try to stay out of energy stocks." He leaned forward and stage-whispered, "Too unstable."

"I'll bet," Nomad said, and finished his beer. He waved the empty at Holt. "How many more of these you got back there?"

"A few. Had to swap a couple for the cooler space here."

"What if I ordered you to bring another round?"

"I'd tell you to fuck off, Major."

Nomad grinned. "Good man. Next round's on me." He rose to head to the bar, and looked around the table.

Weaver was already launching into a story about how DeScalso had thrown a fit over the boat. It had apparently come downriver the next day, complete with a pair of defectors from Urbina's army. One of them had been carrying a fishing rod.

Midas sat and listened, saying little, but nodding, grinning and pushing things along with just the right interjection here and there. Holt was already calling bullshit on the whole story, challenging Weaver on every point, all of it flowing so smoothly it looked like they'd rehearsed it.

The same pride he'd felt on the river welled up in him—this team, his team, was a team. Rough around the edges, maybe, and not exactly by the book, but by the book wouldn't have gotten the job done down on the river. He'd be proud to go into the field with them again, that much he knew, and he was humbled by the fact they wanted him to lead them.

Smiling to himself, he headed for the bar.

Acknowledgements

I'd like to thank Sam Strachman for giving me the opportunity to write a book I've wanted to for a very long time. Thanks also to Jay Posey, whose friendship, encouragement, and love of the Ghosts were the rock I leaned on for this. Huge thanks go to Brian Upton, Steve Reid, Gary Stelmack and everyone at Red Storm who helped create the Ghosts and to all the devs in all the studios over the years who've kept the legend alive and well. Thanks also to Olivier Henriot, Anne Reid, and Ian Mayor for being my Ubi writer sanity check. A tip of the cap to my agent, Robert Fleck, for navigating the dark waters of getting this off the ground, and to Holly Rawlinson, Caroline Lamache, Romain Foucher De Brandois, Alexis Kosciuszko, and Anthony Marcantonio at Ubisoft for making it happen. Huge thanks to Raven and Pilot Jack for their time, technical expertise, and kind words and to Travis Getz for making that connection. Oh, and to Tom Clancy, for starting the ball rolling many years ago.

And of course, to friends and family for their support and occasional willingness to leave me in my writing troll cave for extended periods of time. Thank you all.

About the author

The central Clancy writer for Ubisoft/Red Storm, Richard Dansky has written for and designed games in the Tom Clancy's series since 1999. The lead writer on *Tom Clancy's The Division*, his credits also include *Tom Clancy's Splinter Cell Blacklist*, *Tom Clancy's Rainbow Six Raven Shield*, *Tom Clancy's H.A.W.X*, and *Tom Clancy's Ghost Recon Future Soldier*. Author of six other novels, he is also the designer of the 20th anniversary edition of legendary roleplaying game *Wraith: The Oblivion*. He lives in North Carolina, with an ever-changing number of cats and bottles of single malt scotch.

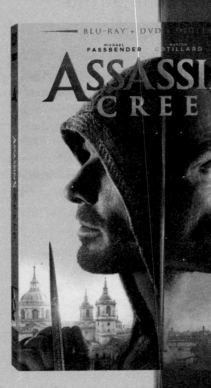

ACHIEVE 100% SYNCHRONIZATION
WHEN YOU BRING HOME

BLU-RAY™ + DVD + DIGITAL HD

MICHAEL FASSBENDER · MARION COTILLARD · JEREMY IRONS

ASSASSIN'S CREED

INCLUDES
OVER 90 MINUTES
OF **EXTRAS**

ON DIGITAL HD MARCH 10
ON BLU-RAY™ & DVD MARCH 28

 INTENSE SEQUENCES OF VIOLENCE AND ACTION, THEMATIC ELEMENTS AND BRIEF STRONG LANGUAGE

Special Features May Not Be Rated. Closed Captioned Or In High Definition.

Explore the wild Bolivian landscape and take on the vicious Santa Blanca cartel with this official Prima Games Guide!

❯ COMPLETE EVERY MISSION
Contains all the information you need to succeed at every task the Ghosts take on, in solo or co-op.

❯ DETAILED MAPS
Navigate the lush and dangerous world of *Wildlands* with critical locations revealed for every main and side mission.

❯ COMPREHENSIVE PROVINCE INFO
Find every weapon case, Kingslayer file, bonus medal, skill point, and more for each and every province.

❯ AND MUCH MORE!
Strategies and Loadouts for each Ghost archetype

Achievements and Trophies

Tips for Co-op teams

www.primagames.com   www.ubisoft.com